The HUMAN PSYCHE

in

Love, War and Enlightenment

by

P. J. Snow

First published 2009

National Library of Australia Cataloguing-in-Publication entry:

Author:	Snow, Peter.
Title:	The human psyche / Peter Snow.
ISBN:	9781921555428 (hbk.)
Subjects:	Mind and body.
	Philosophy of mind.
Dewey Number:	128.2

Boolarong Press
Publishing your dream

Published by Boolarong Press, Salisbury, Brisbane, Australia.

Printed and bound by Watson Ferguson & Company, Salisbury, Brisbane, Australia.

Dedication

I dedicate this book to my Mother, Jessie Elizabeth Snow (nee Stevens), who first taught me the art of wondering, and to my Father, Major Herbert Arthur Snow, Royal Signals, whom I remember as the gentlest of gentlemen.

Acknowledgements

Over the ten years spent writing this book, it seems that I have received assistance and encouragement from a very large number of people. Listed below are those whose council most indelibly engraved itself upon my memory. If I have failed to mention anyone who feels they deserved acknowledgement, then let me assure them that the omission of their name has not been deliberate.

In relation to the creation of this book, I am particularly indebted to my colleague and friend, Dr. John David Leah. Many of the fundamental concepts and associated factual frameworks presented herein emerged from shared conversations and adventures that have spanned the last 30 years. I would also like to specifically acknowledge the generous assistance of Dr. Arthur Prochazka who was instrumental in my receiving an Alberta Heritage Foundation for Medical Research that enabled me to complete much of the ground work in the scholarly environment of the University of Alberta, Edmonton, Alberta, Canada.

The following people gave generously of their time and patience to read the entirety of the manuscript prior to its publication; Mss. Lesley Finlayson, Carol Ford, Wendy Kelly, Cate Mitchell, Tammy Nulty and Robyn Rigby and Drs. Kerry Heckenberg, Norman Heckenberg, Peter Kitchener, Denis Lynn, Donald Meyers, Mark Plenderleith and Ian Ross. In addition, many people assisted with editing smaller sections of the text, commenting on the figures, tracking down information or advising in areas of their expertise. These individuals are Mss. Sanam Arthur, Frances Atkinson, Marisa Giorgi, Ann Jessey, Paula Lampe, Cheryl Routley, Cheryl Smith, Dianne Trussel and Joanne Whiteside and Messrs. Tony Cordeaux, David Giorgi, John Spady and Craig Staude and Drs. Molly Ahlgren (the late), Steve Arnold, Alan Boyne, Johnny Buckland-Nicks, William Calvin, Fu-Shiang Chia, Harry Garfinkle, Piero Giorgi, Stuart Glover, Adam Hamlin, John Heningham, Michael Honey, Kimora, Todd Paton, Kier Pearson, Charles Smith, Benjamin Snow, Douglas Stuart, Tatyana Tsyrlina and Peter Wilson.

For their generous supply of specific information, figures or research documents I am indebted to Drs. A. D. (Bud) Craig, Richard Bandler, Hanna Damasio, Dianne Kornberg, Rolf Kötter, Patricia Goldman-Rakic (the late), Grazyna Rajkowska, Edmund Rolls, Katerina Semendeferi and Harry Uylings.

The mask of disgust, kindly photographed by staff at the Burke Museum, University of Washington, Seattle, Washington, appears in the frontpiece of Section 4 with the generous permission of its owner, Martha Avery and its creator, the Mongolian artist, Tengisbold. The painting of the dream ship appears as the frontpiece of Section 7 with the kind permission of its creator, the Tasmanian artist, Colin Abel. Dan Kelly, CEO, Boolarong Press has been incredibly helpful with regard to the preparation of this book for printing and publishing. The original figures were designed by me and were professionally redrafted by Matt Bird, Zae.ya Designs.

This work could never have been successfully completed had I not had access to the facilities and the scholarly milieu and first class facilities of the Helen Riaboff Whiteley Center, Friday Harbor Laboratories, University of Washington, Washington, USA.

Finally, for their personal and, at times, practical support, I am indebted to my children, Katherine, Lesley and Ben, their partners, Peter Hubczenko and Belinda Giersch and their mother Jennifer Wilson. Lastly, I would like to give special recognition to my partner, Carol Ford, for her undying support, her skilled contributions and her love that has allowed me some sense of accomplishment amid the traumatic process of publication.

PREFACE

The human psyche is a subject of such vast proportions that it can seem beyond the grasp of any individual. Yet unraveling its labyrinths will reveal the true essence of our species and, at last, enable us to make sense of our history, our every day behavior and our dreams. It is the human psyche that reveals our affinities with the animal world while at the same time conferring upon us a diverse spectrum of intellectual abilities that enable us to transcend the forces of nature that hold captive the destiny of all other species.

Upon reading an early draft of this work, a colleague commented that he had difficulty identifying the persona of the author, pointing out that many readers feel uneasy about anonymity. Yet the subject matter is such that one is driven to write from a global rather than an individual perspective, often moving significantly away from the modes of expression most favored by one's own personality. With this in mind it seemed wise to reveal a little of my own path to this task – a path that, from within, seems not to have begun but to have been my companion for as long as I can remember.

As a young boy I was totally immersed in the natural world. Without any formal biological education I divided my time between hunting and fishing and the unguided collection, keeping and observation of animals. A young boy does not think like a man but the serendipity of life can sow the seeds of wonderment long before the intellect has the capacity to truly address significant issues. One day in a family heirloom called the "Miracle of Life", my search for the mysteries of the body was diverted by a picture showing the workings of a man's brain as a series of offices and work rooms. It was not too grandly entitled "The Workshop of the Head". I have used it as the first plate in this book because, it was my first inkling that within our brain there is a subdivision of labor that, despite the caption, resembles not a workshop but an institution wherein there is a clear separation between the executive offices and the factory floor. Many a wisdom is gained in the pursuit of hedonism.

Still it was not until I became a neuroscientist, that my obsession with ideas emerged. I soon became committed to a life of theorizing while being obliged to perform the same daily toil of those not so afflicted. It was long after that before I realized that my fellowship was in distinct minority, a realization that resolved me to seek out a globally relevant realm of human endeavor upon which to focus my imagination. What this realm might be was never in doubt for I was already deeply involved in research on the brain and had begun a series of journeys to India which would be interwoven with trips to many different cultures East and West. Inadvertently it seemed, I would return to India again and again, perhaps because I was born in Jubbulpore or perhaps because I perceived in the Indian psyche that enlightened balance between East and West, indicative of the geographic location of the sub-continent. It was over this period of travel and exploration that I became increasingly fascinated with mysticism as a direct portrayal of human nature.

Psychology had sought out the persona delving into the spiritual and extracting a few insights before jumping back to rigid experimentation that endeavored to enshrine learning as key to human understanding. Mythology had analyzed the esoteric creations of humanity, interpreting them as iconic reflections of actual components of the psyche and so divining within myth the fundamental forces that constitute human nature and emerge in all human dramas. Philosopher-scientists like C. P. Snow began to recognize that artists and scientists thought in radically different ways, often about very different subjects. Psychiatry had explored the malfunctioning of higher consciousness and neurology had demonstrated many astounding links between parts of the brain and each and every element of experience. Psychotrophic and hedonic drugs revealed to a whole generation, all manner of unimaginable things about consciousness and motivation. As the areas of the brain they affected became known, it became possible to see the origin of fundamental states of consciousness that were clearly extremes of experiences that color everyday life. The psyche was unfolding. With a power characteristic of great subtlety, meditation enabled me, as many before me, to see the nature of the mind as distinct from emotions and moods. Finally, with the development of brain scanners we could at last map the patterns of activity within the living brain that accompanied the separate experiences of thought and emotion. These observations confirmed the insights of the Indian mystics that both the mind and our emotional centers are anatomically separate organs of the brain which give rise, respectively, to the experiences of thought and emotion. At last the inner world of humans could be wrenched from the grasp of religion and philosophy. The systematic exploration of the human psyche had truly begun.

Alongside the advances of neuroscience, the new field of neurogenetics began to show the powerful influence of genes on the size of those parts of the brain that enable us to experience life. If, because of one's genes, a particular part of one's brain was unusually large, then clearly the function(s) served by that part would be more powerfully expressed than it would be in individuals with different genes. If these parts also have a role in consciousness, then the experiences of the individual would naturally reflect this aspect of their genetical makeup. Are people very similar or very different in how they experience and perform in the world? Could it be that some people have stronger emotions and others more powerful thoughts, simply because of genes? Aside from intelligence, do all people think in the same way? Is another person's experience of thought qualitatively identical to ours? Are any such differences more apparent between different communities, populations, societies, groups, cultures or races? Where do cultures really come from? If one accepts that facial shape, skin color and body form are inherited, then what is the basis, scientific and moral, of the politically correct view that all humans have identical brains and that all behavioral and cultural diversity is learned? Where do those oceanic moments come from and what brings us into the oblivion of darkness? If spiritual experience is the same in all human beings, then why is there such a diversity of religions across the world? Who is God and where is the human soul? Do animals, and particularly the apes, have brains capable of similar experiences? Why, unlike any animal, do we kill and maim so many of our own species? What is enlightenment?

Still I did not begin for years. Indeed the impetus to begin only came in late 1998 when, without the slightest regard for the time honored principles of Higher Education, the Australian Government employed a legion of highly paid, profit motivated, non-specific managers to convert Australian Universities into educational supermarkets for wealthy Asians. Saddened by the demise of basic research, it was nevertheless with some relish, that I deposited the flotsam and jetsam of 25 years of research and teaching into the trash and left for the holy city of Rishikesh which sits north of Delhi where the Ganges emerges from the Himalayan foothills. There I began drafting a series of chapters that became questions and theoretical challenges. My next bout of writing was during the monsoons in Darjeeling, India, after which I had the opportunity to work in the University of Alberta, Canada, the Whiteley Center, Friday Harbor Laboratories, University of Washington, USA and the Gulf Islands, British Columbia. Parts of this book were also written during expeditions to Guatemala, Peru and Sikkim and the task completed in Australia.

The scientific mind always asks; how is it so? For scientists, having hypotheses is an essential part of existence. However, scientists are a minority. Those people more taken with the dharma of life seek not a question or a theory but a story with which they may empathize. They are not concerned with the ensemble of ideas which clutter the scientific mind, but with the very "isness" of things and, in particular, the "isness of being" that, for them, is the essence of human nature. My challenge has been to construct a story that encompasses not only my own vantage point but also that of others – a task that ideally requires a number of quite different literary styles.

In psychology (the science of man) it is said a theory gains much credulity if many people empathize with it. In creating this work I have been guided by the same principle. In addition, however, I have endeavored to integrate the many insights gained from the dysfunctional psyche, the constructs of philosophy, the dynamics of all mythologies, the fundamental truths of all religions, all forms of spiritual practice, the wisdom of the mystics and intellectuals, the voice of common sense and most importantly, the, sometimes shadowy, sometimes pristine, inner realms of human experience.

I have tried to keep names to a minimum. Those I do mention are certainly not the only people to have made a significant contribution. I did not wish to fill the text with references. All I provide is recommended reading. Having been an academic and a professional scientist I have great regard for detail and documentation. However, in the present case I would suggest that the free referencing services of the World Wide Web can enable anyone to track down reliable information. To the skeptics I would say that before they take intellectual umbrage they should read on and if they are still dissatisfied then they should channel their angst into revising those areas where they consider I have erred. I would hope that the neuroscientists among them will see that my efforts give a voice to their discipline in matters that in the past have been surrendered to the emotive, exploitative and manipulative ways of politicians and shysters of all sorts – an error of judgment that humanity can no longer afford to ignore.

When we begin to use names to refer to things, stages in our evolutionary history, religions, forms of realization and even areas of the brain, we begin to live an entirely different truth – the truth of the academic and of the intellectual. Much of my purpose here is to utilize Ocham's razor to cut away the fat and speak directly of that which can only be addressed in such a manner. The mystical vision is not one of mystery but one of direct truth. We speak here not of the sun's gold but of the gold that is the sun. Contrary to what most believe, it is the focus and form of our thoughts and not their contents that engage our life and fashion both our destiny and our culture.

If you find, in the reading of this work, a growing desire to liberate yourself from at least some of your long-held beliefs and attitudes, then my primary intention will have been achieved. It was never my intention to write a heavily documented, impenetrable, scholarly work, but instead, upon establishing the truth, to write an account of the human psyche as a journey – a journey that I would ask you to embark upon without attachment. Do not read this book as a Christian, a Hindu, a Moslem, a Jain or a Jew. Just for a while step outside the box and put away the apparent "truths" of your social and professional conditioning. Do not read as a scientist, a politician, a doctor or a businessman. Set aside for the moment your parenthood, your adolescence, your brotherhood and sisterhood. Be not a wife, a husband or a lover. Be instead that most intricate of creations, that miracle of life that is the alert, awake and receptive human being. Fly with me above the clouds where knowledge and understanding become one. Leave behind your beliefs and join me on this journey of journeys, this journey to into the very heart of human nature.

Peter J. Snow, B.Sc (1st Hons), Ph.D.
September, 2009

KAMALA SUTRA

"Do not believe in anything because you have heard it;
Do not believe in traditions, because they have been handed down for many generations;
Do not believe in anything, because it is spoken and rumoured by many;
Do not believe in anything, simply because it is found written in your religious books;
Do not believe in anything, merely on the authority of your teachers and elders;
But after observation and analysis, when you find that anything agrees with reason and is conducive to the good and benefit of one and all, then accept it and live up to it."

LORD BUDDHA

CONTENTS

List of Figures

The HUMAN PSYCHE

in

Love, War and Enlightenment

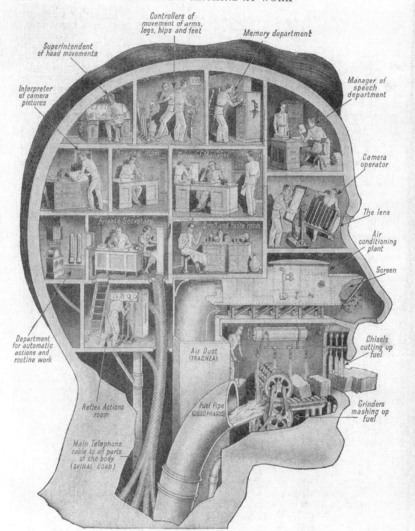

Controllers of movement of arms, legs, hips and feet

Memory department

Superintendent of head movements

Manager of speech department

Interpreter of camera pictures

Camera operator

The lens

Air conditioning plant

Screen

Private Secretary

Smell and taste room

Department for automatic actions and routine work

Chisels cutting up fuel

Reflex Actions room

Air Duct (TRACHEA)

Grinders mashing up fuel

Fuel Pipe (OESOPHAGUS)

Main Telephone cable to all parts of the body (SPINAL CORD)

THE WORKSHOP OF THE HEAD

In this picture the various parts of the head are illustrated in a technical instead of a physiological way. It should be compared with the diagrams on pages 356 and 357, where the various parts of the brain are illustrated in detail and the scientific names of the various centres are given. The brain does the work of a great central telephone exchange; while in the spinal cord are groups of nerve cells acting as local exchanges.

Section 1

The Human Psyche - the Duality of Being

"In a period of human history when all available energy is spent in the investigation of nature, very little attention is paid to the essence of man, which is his psyche…."

Carl Gustav Jung (1875-1961). Swiss Psychiatrist/Psychologist, Founder of Analytical Psychology.

Chapter 1 – In the Beginning

"There is a dream dreaming us." A Kalahari Bushman.

Existence is divided between two worlds: the *outer world* and the *inner world*. When, as little children, we close our eyes and snuggle under the covers, we are intentionally seeking our inner world, often as a first step towards the panacea of sleep. The division of human consciousness into inner and outer realms is so fundamental to all human experience that as adults we are often challenged to say whether our thoughts, emotions, moods, perceptions and actions are derived from events within us or around us. This book is an attempt to resolve this state of affairs, by looking at humanity from the perspective of how human consciousness generates the various archetypal experiences from which we must chart a path through life. Such experiences are archetypal because they are largely the product of the three essential components of our inner world, *thought*, *emotion* and *mood*. It is these experiential components of inner consciousness, together with the parts of the brain that create them, that are here defined as the *psyche* (Figure 1.1). At this point in the history of human knowledge, this endeavor is an acute divergence from the systematic dissection of behavior and the plethora of theories through which an army of psychologists, mystics, priests and philosophers have sought to understand human nature.

Our journey begins with an exposé of how our every human experience, be it a simple touch, an abstract thought or a transcendental moment, reflects activity in discrete parts of the brain (Section 2: The Nature of Consciousness). If one of those parts is damaged then, the related experience is forever lost and its past existence usually forgotten. In comprehending the nature of human consciousness, we cannot help but see that, as individuals, we are not really exploring the world at large but only those parts of the physical, social and ideational world which gain access to the neural circuits that compose our mind. Practically speaking, establishing the physical identity of, and the interactions between, those brain areas that enable us to experience particular thoughts, emotions, moods and perceptions, gives us the opportunity to begin to understand how the psyche generates not only archetypal experiences of thought, emotion and mood but also the archetypal patterns of behavior that characterize both the life of individuals and the essentially episodic history of humanity.

Throughout childhood the brain grows and the psyche becomes progressively and conspicuously more complicated. What begins as sensations from the viscera soon develops into a system capable of generating emotion and mood – the elements of the psyche responsible for those basic urges that drive all instinctual behaviors. Much infant and child behavior contains this spontaneity of action that characterizes our instinctual urges. Only the maturation of the mind throughout childhood and adolescence ensures that, from an early age, deliberation, intention and planning progressively replace instinct. As the mind matures, our inner world becomes an arena wherein thought increasingly engages emotion and mood in a ceaseless battle for supremacy over our behavior.

The most definitive aspect of humanity is its ability to use intelligence to solve the challenges of survival - an ability dependent upon a discrete part of the human brain called the mind. In Section 3 we begin by examining the place of the mind in eastern and western philosophy, in religious and spiritual doctrines and clinical neuropsychology. Often referred to in spiritual literature as an "organ of the brain", the neural tissue composing the human mind is without question the most complicated piece of biological engineering yet to evolve on Earth. While our instincts manifest themselves through our emotional centers, as the agent of the mind, thought retains a considerable level of independence in the structuring of our behavior. As we shall see, the parts of the brain that form the mind become operational between the first and the fifteenth year of life – a period over which there is the sequential elaboration of emotional intelligence, temporal intelligence, practical intelligence and finally, in the adolescent teenager, the most defining aspect of humanity, abstract intelligence.

Humans, and particularly westerners, struggle to mentally resolve the issues of life. Yet, from the beginning all such efforts are disrupted by the constant tumult of our organic being. Behind our cognitively contrived scenarios, our emotions bubble and boil pulling our thoughts this way and that, occasionally flying to one extreme there to conjure either the darkness or the euphoria of mood. While we are dependent upon our thoughts, their seemingly rational and reasoned protocols are little more than vehicles for the actualization of our social and visceral needs. In Section 4 we look at how our psyche integrates the emotions of other people with our own emotions in the construction of emotional intelligence. In Section 5 we explore the relationship of both thought and emotion to mood. It is from a deeper appreciation of the experience of mood that we see how its extremes represent the experiential origins of the religious icons, Heaven and Hell. A consequence of this is that when the parts of the brain that elaborate mood are damaged, the psyche looses its regulatory constraints, without which, the previously normal individual may newly suffer from depression or mania or begin to behave in a psychopathic manner.

The inner realms of consciousness that constitute the human psyche are entirely the product of the anterior $1/3^{rd}$ of the human brain, known as the *prefrontal lobes*. In contrast, sensations and perceptions of external origin manifest themselves via the posterior 2/3rds of the brain. With the exception of the apes, the prefrontal lobes of other mammals compose a far smaller proportion of the brain. Such differences in the size of the prefrontal lobes are reflected in the behavior of each species such that the greater the size of the prefrontal lobes, the more complex are the behavioral repertoires of that species. Living mammals can be arranged in a series that reflects both the proportion of their brain composing the prefrontal lobes and the complexity of their behavior. This series extends from the small rodents, whose prefrontal lobes compose only a few percent of the brain, through the cats, dogs, monkeys and finally, apes and humans, whose prefrontal lobes compose approximately 30% of the brain (Figure 1.2). It must, however, be kept in mind that although humans evolved from apes and apes from monkeys, monkeys did not evolve from dogs, nor did dogs from cats, nor cats from rats.

5

Large prefrontal lobes translate into a complex and powerful psyche which enables the use of thought in generating the strategies of complex behavior. In accord with this, many scholars have inferred that humans are at the top of a behavioral hierarchy formed by the evolution of successively more intelligent species. This fact has been widely exploited by philosophers and the scribes of various religions, as contributing to the view that, as the most intelligent species, we are closer to God than other living things.

The true story begins about 65 million years ago (mya) when a meteor, estimated to be 15 km in diameter, hit the Earth, causing conditions that are believed to have (a) precipitated the extinction of the dinosaurs and (b) generated a very large number of mutations amongst the primitive mammals. The natural selection of those mutants that had advantageous physical or behavioral characteristics, provided the source of a large number of new species in what is called, the *adaptive radiation of the mammals*. Like their living descendants, the members of each new species had brains and bodies that were essentially variations on a generalized mammalian theme. Today the living descendants of each of these species have brains that fill part of a continuum of form, complexity and sophistication – a continuum that remains superficially suggestive of an evolutionary progression. Thus as we move from the rodent to the human, there is gradual increase in the proportion of the brain allocated to the prefrontal lobes – cortex that in humans represents our inner realms of consciousness.

Most mutations are lethal. This is particularly true when it comes to mutations that affect the almost infinite complexities of the brain. At the time of the adaptive radiation, each new species had a brain built on the basic mammalian plan. The brain of each species was also specialized to enable it to generate the unique behavior patterns necessary for exploiting a particular niche and competing successfully with other species for the resources offered by that niche. In nature, the instincts of rats ensure that they are perfectly adapted to their niche. Rats learn by the same processes through which we establish emotional memories. Contrary to common belief, this form of learning is not indicative of what most humans would consider to be intelligence. Over the tens of millions years since their evolution, there may well have been numerous mutations that produced a cognitively competent, calculating rat but if so, then these "intelligent" mutants clearly had less survival potential than ordinary rats empowered solely by their instincts. As it stands, the behavior of some mammals (eg. rodents) is totally instinctual while that of others (eg. apes) is conspicuously cognitive in origin. Only the graded increases in brain size that is apparent when we move from the monkey to the ape and, via our, extinct, bipedal hominid ancestors, to the human, are truly indicative of thee evolution of our astounding cerebral attributes (Section 6: The Origins of Thought and the Diversity of Culture).

Life would be simple if within human consciousness there was such a thing as reality. Alas, though the great majority of people believe this to be so, there is an abundance of evidence to show that the only "reality" available to humans is that which is created within their own brain. For example, many human experiences, such as those resulting from imagination, attention and dreams, are characterized by the generation of internal imagery – imagery that is only tenuously related to the reality of the moment (Section 7: Reality and the Control of Consciousness).

The concept of reality as an identifiable entity that may be shared with others is further challenged by the existence of brain systems that continuously control our state of consciousness. It is through the influence of these systems that most psychoactive and hedonic drugs, including alcohol and tobacco, assert their effects. Virtually all people use some form of chemical to satiate what appears to be an inherent human desire to alter the state of their consciousness. The complex issues surrounding the legality and management of recreational drugs and the related health issues desperately need to be removed from the political and legal arena and to be revisited with some sensitivity to the human condition and the rationality of a completely open, educated mind. Until the smokescreen of misinformation is replaced with factual education, societies will continue to suffer (a) from a volatile, criminal and highly profitable black market and (b) unlimited public access to legal, highly addictive substances that kill and maim millions of human beings each and every year (*The Legality of Drugs*: Chapter 3: Section 7).

In our short history, the attention of many creative minds has revealed the principles underlying heredity, the nature of matter, the extent and age of the universe and the origins of sensation, perception and movement. We are now on the threshold of yet another fundamental revelation, the comprehension of the human psyche – that enigmatic source of creative energy that, as the balance of nature is progressively lost, will soon become the sole guardian of the human species and the biology of the Earth.

Love, war, wisdom, spiritual experience, cruelty, politics and economics are all products of the human psyche that impact upon all humans. They should not be confused with specific gifts such as intelligence, empathy, the acuity of sensation, motor aptitude or musical ability that are inherent properties of the brain. As with all parts of the body, genes play a crucial role in determining the properties of the brain. Consequently, genes also influence the complex products of the human psyche, thereby having a subtle yet profound influence over the lives of individuals and the culture in which they participate.

Sadly, human history is a history of war, cruelty and coercion. It is only recently that neuroscience has at last begun to address human behavior at a level that enables the integration of its findings with preexisting spiritual insights and philosophical perspectives. This emergent synthesis is one that enables us to (a) take an objective look at our identity and (b) to realize that there is no one but ourselves to save us from our greed (Section 8: The Nature, Intellect and Future of Humanity). Given our nature, there is no way back from our present situation. There is only the road ahead, a one way street to a new epoch of human life and hopefully a new deal for the plants and animals that sustain our bodies and, through the nurture of our instincts, reinforce our sense of being part of a greater whole.

Chapter 2 – Inheritance and the Human Brain

Size and the Animal Kingdom

"But for that stupendous hominid eventuality, Planet Earth would have continued indefinitely with its biological 'infestation'......deemed to be forever conceptually dead, a continuing darkness without glimmer of the transcendent illumination and meaning that has been given by...*Homo sapiens sapiens*." John Carew Eccles (1903-1997). Australian Neurophysiologist and Nobel Laureate.

The complexity of human behavior far outflanks that of any animal. Yet, at the heart of human behavior are many of the same forces that drive animal life. A study of the brains of animals soon reveals components that form the core of the human brain. It is therefore not surprising to find that the motivational forces underlying the behavior of animals are important within our own psyche. It follows that by bridging the gap between the neurobiology and behavior of animals we gain unprecedented insights into which elements of our behavior are instinctual in origin and which are the product of our thoughts.

The sophistication of an animal's behavior is conspicuously related to its position on the evolutionary tree. The fish, which evolved more than 500 mya, utilize a set of simple, fixed behavioral routines, while the apes which evolved 25 to 30 mya, manifest a level of behavioral complexity that, socially and politically, approaches that of humans. Throughout the primates there is a correlation between the size of the brain and both the preferred size of the social group and the level of behavioral innovation. Generally speaking, the brain increases in size from the behaviorally simple fish, through the amphibia, reptiles and early mammals to the behaviorally complex human. However, even this is not always true, the human brain being smaller than the brain of the horse. Not only does the mammalian brain vary enormously in size but between different species there is a crude relationship between body size and brain size. Thus, the marsupial mouse has a brain that is less than one centimeter across, while the elephant has a brain that is around 20 centimeters across.

Consider first the issue of body size. All vertebrates are essentially constructed around a common body plan. All have sensory organs (including the skin), muscle and viscera that must be monitored and controlled by the central nervous system. Moreover, there is little essential difference in the behavioral complexity of a large, compared to that of a small, shark and the same can be said of a large and a small mammal. Thus, such differences in brain size must arise because any animal with a large body will require many replicates of the control and sensory systems found in a small animal. For example, the tiny limb muscles of the marsupial mouse require relatively few motoneurons while the human thigh muscle requires over 1,000 motoneurons. Similarly, the smaller skin of the mouse can be effectively innervated by relatively few sensory neurons and the relatively small amount of information they pick up, processed in an appropriately small area of the mouse's brain. In contrast, many more sensory neurons are required to innervate the skin of the elephant and these in turn demand a much larger area of the brain for making sense of information from the elephant's larger body surface. The same is true of even complex perceptions such as those that enable the evaluation of space around an animal. Operating at the microscale of life, a tiny animal need only monitor a smaller volume of what we would call extrapersonal space, negating the need for the large area of the brain that would be required to represent the extrapersonal space around a large animal. Thus, one reason that a larger animal needs a larger brain is because the various sensory, perceptual and motor control systems of the smaller species have to be replicated many, many times to accommodate its large body and larger presence within the outside world. Quite simply, a large mammal and a big fish both need many replicas of the component neural control systems that make up small varieties of these lifeforms. This principle also applies to the invertebrates. The tiniest ant and the giant cockroach are, like the mouse and the elephant, both built on design principles that are qualitatively similar yet quantitatively distinct.

Brain size is also strongly related to the level of behavioral sophistication of the host species. Thus, when different species are matched for body weight, the brain of any mammalian species tends to exceed the size of the brain of any reptile, fish or amphibian. Monkeys and apes have brains that are approximately twice the size of similarly sized non-primate mammals. This approach has, however, led lay people to some spurious conclusions about animal intelligence. For example, because the brain of aquatic mammals such as whale and the dolphin exceed in size the brain of the human, it has been fashionable to marvel at the potential intelligence of the cetaceans. To detect the fallacy here one need only consider that a fish is only capable of very primitive, mechanistic behaviors and yet may have a brain that is far larger than the brain of many smaller, behaviorally complex mammals. Body size is a confounding issue that essentially negates any attempts to relate brain size to performance. Only when we look carefully within a particular group of animals, such as the primates, do we find a clear relationship between sophistication of behavior and brain size.

Brain Size and Intelligence
"Cognitive, psychometric, genetic and neuroimaging studies are converging and the emergence of mechanistic models of intelligence is inevitable." Gray, J. R. and Thompson, P. M. (2004). Neurobiology of Intelligence: Science and Ethics. *Nature Neuroscience Reviews* 5, 471-482.

To understand the nature and origins of intelligence it is critical to appreciate how the brain enables us to experiences the world around us as distinct from the world within us. By far the most difficult and yet most important thing to accept is that *all* possible experiences available to any individual, are a consequence of neural activity in particular parts of their cerebral cortex - a 2 to 4 mm layer of grey matter that on average is about 2.5 mm thick and that cloaks each hemisphere of the brain (*The Dissection of Consciousness*: Chapter 2: Section 2). Because the cortex is a laminar structure that lies just beneath the skull, it is relatively easy to record the brainwaves it generates, from the surface of the head and to use brain scanners to map cortical activity while people perform various tasks (eg. reading) or have particular experiences (eg. orgasm).

The cortex covering the back 2/3rds of each hemisphere is responsive to the outside world and so is called the *sensorium* of the brain. Within the cortex of the sensorium are the *primary cortical receiving areas* or the *primary sensory representations* – areas of cortex that respond to virtually raw sensory information. For example, nerve cells in the primary visual representation (BA17) respond to simple components of the visual world such as the orientation of edges, while nerve cells in the primary somatosensory representation (BA3b) respond to simple touch. All our senses, inner and outer, are allocated a primary sensory representation.

Also within the sensorium are a number of *perceptual representations* that integrate information they receive from the primary sensory representations into familiar, meaningful constructs of the world that can be internally aroused during the processes of dreaming and imagination. It is within the perceptual representations that the cortex first reassembles the outer world into recognizable objects and/or happenings and the inner world into recognizable emotions and moods.

In humans the frontal $1/3^{rd}$ of each hemisphere is called the prefrontal lobe. It is the cortex covering our prefrontal lobes that enables us to experience (be aware of) our thoughts, emotions and moods. As we will see it is the physical size of various parts of the prefrontal cortex that determines the power of our emotions, the predictive capacity of mood and the complexity of our mental processes that, in turn, impact directly upon the level and nature of our intelligence.

Everyone accepts that longer legs result in a greater locomotive capacity, just as shorter more compact bodies help to preserve heat in a cold environment. It has therefore often been assumed that a larger brain must be related to an enhancement of that most revered of human attributes, intelligence. Many theoreticians have suggested that our *general intelligence* influences our performance in a wide spectrum of activities, some of which we can now say, dependent on parts of the cerebral cortex that do not support cognition. Only in recent times has it become clear that our thought processes *are* elaborated by a circumscribed area of our cerebral cortex the size and complexity of which might be the most critical factor in determining the intelligence of an individual. Again, dolphins and whales display empathetic social interactions, engage in play and mimicry and even respond to the complex spoken commands of a human trainer. These abilities and the fact that they have a larger brain than humans have led more impressionable people to suggest that they might have an intelligence approaching that of humans. This is, however, very unlikely because the prefrontal cortex, which is recognized as the seat of intelligence, constitutes only a very small part of the cetacean cortex. If indeed they are intelligent, then one must assume that the cetacean equivalent of thought must be quite unlike that found in humans and other higher primates.

Until the advent of brain scanners, measuring the brain required removing it from the skull. This alone severely limited early investigations as the subjects had to be dead and any statement about their intelligence made from posthumous reports of colleagues, friends and relatives. To overcome this problem, scientists argued that as the brain got bigger the skull should also enlarge. Therefore measuring the skull could be a reliable way of measuring the size of the brain contained within it. Such a procedure could be easily applied not only to living people but also to the remains of extinct prehumans. In one of the first recorded studies using this approach, the skull size of all men in a regiment was measured and correlated with an estimate of their intelligence arrived at by consulting the commanding officers. While the frailties of this study are obvious, there has, over time, emerged data that shows a correlation between head size and cognitive function as assessed by standardized intelligence tests.

Brain scanners now enable very accurate measurements of the size, shape and activity of the living brain. Such studies confirm that brain size is related to mental aptitude and that the correlation is far better than the relationship between general intelligence and skull size. More importantly they have enabled individual gifts to be related directly to the size of particular parts of the human cortex – the size of the prefrontal lobes being directly related to the score achieved in a variety of intelligence tests. Lay people have always assumed that brain size is intimately linked to performance. Modern research has given substance to this belief and we can anticipate that as it is moved from domain of politically dangerous theory to simple fact, its potential to arouse emotion and outrage will at last be replaced by a desire to understand and work productively with each other independent of the inherent differences in the structuring of our intelligence.

Brain Size in Human Evolution
"Nobody comes without a gift; everybody brings a certain potential. But the idea of equality is dangerous, because the rose has to be the rose and the marigold has to be the marigold and the lotus has to be the lotus. If you start trying to make them equal then you will destroy them all; the roses, the lotuses, the marigolds, all will be destroyed. You can succeed in creating plastic flowers which will be equal to each other, but they will be dead." Sri Sri Bhagwan Rajneesh (Osho), (1931-1990). Indian Mystic and Professor of Philosophy and Psychology.

Our hominid relatives were creatures with an upright posture and bipedal locomotion. They include the now extinct prehumans, which together with modern man form the family Hominidae (order Primates). The family most closely related to the Hominidae today is the Pongidae, the anthropoid apes including the gorilla, the chimpanzee, the bonobo and the orangutan. So close are we to chimps that if one were a chimp or a bonobo then looking across the animal kingdom one's closest relative would be a human. Indeed, the similarity is such that long before Darwin's publication of the theory of evolution, the great Swedish taxonomist, Carl Linnaeus gave the name *Homo sapiens* (man the knower) to living humans and *Homo troglodytes* (man the cave dweller) to the common chimpanzee which earlier explorers considered to be a "caveman".

The evolutionionary increase in brain size throughout the hominids and the postulated, concurrent increases in the complexity of intelligence based behavior has always been the central theme of anthropology. While the comprehension of many complex biological systems requires a statistical approach, the progressive evolution of the human brain is characterized by what appear to be almost quantal jumps in size along the lineage of our hominid relatives. These are detailed in the following paragraphs but the reader who is not drawn to quantification need only take "ball park" estimation of the actual numbers to appreciate the origins of our unmatched mental abilities.

The earliest contender for hominid status is the man-ape, *Sahelanthropus tchadensis* which lived in Africa 7 mya. At 365 cc, its brain was similar in size to the brain of living chimpanzees. Over the next 3 million years at least three other hominid species (*Orrorin tugenensis, Ardipithecus ramidus* and *A. kadabba*) evolved and then became extinct, making way for the first of several species of australopithecines, *Australopithecus anamensis* which evolved about 4.2 mya. Most workers agree that the last of the true, gracile australopithecines, *A. africanus*, evolved around 3.5 mya and survived to about 1.0 mya.

The male australopithecines stood only 1.5 meters tall while the females were around 1 meter, the smallest species being not much taller than a chimpanzee. The brain volume of the australopithecines has been conservatively estimated to be between 390 and 550 cc. In comparison the brain of the chimp is around 390 cc while that of the orangutan and gorilla is around 440 and 650 cc, respectively. On size alone, it seems that the earliest hominids were no more intellectually advanced than today's living apes.

The earliest member of the genus *Homo* is believed to have evolved from the australopithecines. In terms of the evolution of intelligence, the appearance of *Homo habilis* (man the able) was highly significant. This hominid appeared in East Africa between 2.5 and 1.8 mya and became extinct while still in Africa about 1.5 mya. Its large teeth and skeletal structure have led some workers to conclude that it is an advanced australopithecine that should actually be referred to it as *Australopithecus habilis*.

At 590 to 690 cc the estimated brain volume of *H. habilis* is significantly larger than the brains of either the earlier australopithecines or any ape, whether living or extinct. It is generally believed that this hominid had the mental capacity necessary to "invent" the first crude stone tools and to communicate through a rudimentary form of language. There is, however, no evidence that this creature was able to use fire - a level of sophistication not seen until the evolution of the first hominid to venture out of Africa, *Homo erectus*.

There is some debate about whether *H. erectus* evolved directly from *H. habilis* or whether it evolved 1.9 mya from a different species, *Homo ergaster*. The most recent specimen of *H. erectus* was found in Java and is dated at a mere 27 thousand years ago (kya), indicating that it was still inhabiting the world long after the evolution of modern humans and may have interbred with them, on rare occasions.

A typical male *H. erectus* stood about 1.8 meters and weighted about 68kg making it not unlike modern humans in stature. However, over the 1.9 million years of *H. erectus's* existence, natural selection seems to have favored a variety of anatomical forms which no doubt tailored the species to more successfully inhabit the wide diversity of environments it would have encountered in its journeys across Eurasia.

This variation has resulted in much debate as to whether all such remains should be classified as *H. erectus* or a variety of related but separate species. For present purposes we will adopt the former interpretation. Thus, it follows that the brain of individuals living more than 700 kya were between about 830 to 1,300 cc while those that lived less than 100 kya had brain volumes of 1,060 to 1,300 cc. It is significant that across the entire sample, the most striking anatomical variations are those that determine mental, perceptual and motor capabilities and are, therefore critical to the hominid's ability to adapt to the different habitats. In the global wanderings of *H. erectus*, nature was experimenting with intelligence as the principal means of adapting to a vast diversity of environments - an experiment that would be repeated when an even more cerebrally advanced hominid migrated out of Africa to assert its dominance over the entire world.

When it comes to humans and prehumans it seems that favorable mutations most often happened in Africa. It was there, just under 1 mya, that *Homo heidelbergensis* is thought to have evolved from *H. erectus* or, as some may have it, the intermediary and exclusively African form, *Homo ergaster*. The brain of *H. heidelbergensis* was between 900 and 1,200 cc placing it in the upper range of its ancestor, *H. erectus. H. heidelbergensis* soon migrated into Europe where it gave rise to *Homo neanderthalensis* about 300 to 400 kya. As early as 270 kya in Africa, *H. heidelbergensis* is considered to have evolved into forms closely resembling *Homo sapiens*. The oldest remains of anatomically modern humans were found in Ethiopia and are 160,000 years old. Approximately 45 kya, *H. sapiens* was in southern Europe where anthropologists at first referred to them as Cro-Magnons, after the site in southern France, where their remains were first discovered. Until their disappearance of from Europe 10,000 years later, *H. neanderthalensis* coexisted and, it seems, occasionally cohabitated with, Paleolithic humans, resulting in the *introgression* of Neanderthal genes into the human genome. Because of their deleterious effects, natural selection would have rapidly eliminated many introgressed Neanderthal genes. Only some would bestow advantage on our species. Today it is estimated that 5% of our genes have been survived from our indiscretions with the genome of extinct hominid species. One such introgressed Neanderthal gene is microcephalin (MCPH1) – a gene known to be advantageous because it is involved in the up regulation of brain size.

Ultimately the physiological requirements of the body exert a limit on the potential size of the human brain. Because the brain and particularly the cerebral cortex require so much oxygen, mutations that cause very large increases in brain size would be lethal unless they were accompanied by mutations that markedly increased the brain's blood supply. The brain volume of modern humans ranges from 1,050 cc to around 1,700 cc. This extraordinarily large variation is associated with a distinct geographic distribution arrived at largely through the prehistorical migratory patterns of humans since they left Africa between 70 and 100 kya. Many studies confirm that on average the Far East Asians (Chinese, Japanese and Koreans) have larger brains than the Caucasians (Europe, Britain, the Middle East, much of supra-Saharan Africa and India) who have larger brains than the hunter-gatherers of Africa and Australia – the

Akka pygmies of Africa, at 1,085 cc, having the smallest mean cranial volume of all modern humans. Clearly the genetical control of brain size is such that natural selection has had sufficient time to effectively alter the mean brain size of isolated human populations. As we shall see the most significant changes were those affecting the allocation of cortex to the four different domains of human thought. In this process not only was it possible to increase overall intelligence but it was also possible to selectively enhance particular domains of intelligence in response to the specific cognitive challenges of any circumscribed habitat.

Humans are watchers of the past, striving ever for insights into the essence of their origins that might explain the vast diversity of their cultures. It is in the service of this quest that the discoveries of anthropology and archeology again and again reveal a time upon the Earth when the hominid spirit was not so shrouded by the preoccupations of a highly complex mind - a time when long, long ago, creatures not unlike us, sat by their fires and watched in simple awe the passing of the moon.

Genes and the Determination of Brain Size
"It is the large brain capacity which allows man to live as a human being, enjoying tastes, canned salmon, television, and the atomic bomb." Gustav H. R. von Koenigswald (1902-1982). German/Dutch Paleontologist.

Imagine the dire consequences of simply being born as a fully-grown, mature adult with an essentially empty yet operational mind. Without the grace of childhood, one would have to spend many years coming to grips with a completely foreign postpartum world. Lacking any prior knowledge, it would be almost impossible not to injure one's self or others, or to avoid transgressing hallowed societal rules. Fortunately we are saved from this fate because throughout the primates, and indeed our extinct hominid ancestors, there is a clear and important relationship between the size of the brain and the amount of brain growth that occurs after birth. Thus, we find that the brain of a newborn macaque monkey is 70% of the adult size while that of the chimp is 40% rising to 80% only at the age of one year. Estimates of the prehuman hominids indicate that at birth the australopithecine brain was about 60% adult size while the newborn *H. habilis* brain was 46% adult size. The brain of newborn, small-brained *H. erectus* (or *H. ergaster*) was 35% adult size, while the brain of the large-brained *H. erectus* was 29% adult size. Like the apes and monkeys the brains of the extinct hominids grew very rapidly over the first year, small-brained *H. erectus* reaching 70% of the adult size and large-brained *H. erectus* reaching 90%. In comparison, the human brain is only 25% adult size at birth and increases to only 50% over the first year and reaching only 95% by the age of ten. Compared with the brains of our extinct hominid ancestors and the living apes, our brain undergoes 75% of its growth while it is steering us through the turbulence of life after birth. Consequently, the potential of environmental influences on brain development and behavior is greater in humans than in any other primate, living or extinct.

Postnatal brain growth and the duration of postnatal immaturity are paralleled by the percentage of life spent playing. Each of these variables, reach their zenith in the human. In particular, much human brain development takes place during many years of postnatal life. On this basis alone there can be little doubt that the basic conditioning required for a human to be a functional member of society is markedly more than that required by our hominid ancestors.

Studies of identical twins have proven beyond any doubt that genes determine brain size. Thus, although the brain size of primates is correlated with the duration of postnatal maturation, there are genes that have an exclusive influence. The clue to finding the first of these genes resulted from investigations into the origin of a disease called microencephaly. People with microencephaly have smaller heads and brains. The structure of their brain is normal but its surface areas and hence the area of their cerebral cortex is reduced to about 50 to 60% of its normal size. As a consequence they suffer moderate to severe mental retardation but do not have significant motor deficits such as cerebral palsy. Their condition appears to be partially related to mutations of a gene called *ASPM* for *abnormal spindle-like microencephaly*.

In the very early embryonic stages the brain is simply a mass of dividing cells called stem cells. Some of these are stimulated to become neural stem cells that, in turn, are destined to become neurons by the actions of the protein made by the ASPM gene. The more neural stem cells that are available, the bigger will be the mature brain. Unfavorable mutations of the human ASPM gene decrease the number of neural stems cells causing a concurrent decrease in the size of the brain.

Regulating the production of neurons is such a basic function that the ASPM gene can be traced back through the animal kingdom to a truncated version in the DNA of the fly. From its origins in tiniest invertebrates it seems that the ASPM gene has been under strong selective pressure, continuing to exert its effects even after that great metamorphosis of nature that marked the evolution of the first vertebrates. This is particularly so over the 7 million year lineage that separates us from our common ancestor with the chimpanzees. Over this period the hominid brain has increased in volume by a factor of 2.7 to 3.8, from 365 cc in the man-ape, *Sahelanthropus tchadensis* to between the 1,000 to 1,400 cc in modern humans. Despite the fact that the ASPM gene has also been associated with regulation of non-neural tissues, it powerful selection possibly account for at least some of this almost exponential increase in brain size that has so characterized hominid evolution.

The ASPM gene is only one of a number of genes that have shown an accelerated rate of mutational change along the human lineage. It is also only one of a number of genes controlling brain size. What is particularly fascinating is that most of the genes that show an accelerated rate of change are also the genes that either control brain size or directly influence behavior. As long as increases in brain size continue to be advantageous to human survival, we can expect that natural selection will continue to favor genes that increase the size of the brain.

Manipulating the genes that influence brain growth has the potential to produce humans with enormous brains. Already manipulating a gene that produces a protein called beta-catenin has enabled the production of mice with brains and heads so large that they could not survive to adulthood. While the cortex of normal mice is not large enough to require the folding that produces the sulci and gyri of the human cortex,

15

these *transgenic mice* produced so much beta-catenin that their cortex could only fit inside their enlarged cranium by developing folds. Transferring this technology to the human species will inevitably give us the opportunity to genetically engineer humans with a level of intelligence so high that we cannot with our present mental abilities, imagine (*The Mental Limitations of Humanity*: Chapter 3: Section 8).

Clearly the increase in brain size that has accompanied our evolution is the result of many mutations in a large but as yet undetermined number of genes that influence brain size and behavior. Attempts to correlate IQ with the variants of the ASPM gene have so far failed. In the unlikely event that we should survive for any significant evolutionary period, the extreme selective pressure on cerebralization, behavioral strategy and intelligence that are each so critical to the survival in the modern world, will ensure that the size of the human brain will continue to increase at an exponential rate.

Population as a Consequence of the Human Intelligence
"Population, when unchecked, increases in a geometrical ratio." Thomas Malthus (1766-1834). English Economist and Demographer.

The evolution of the human mind has given humans the intellectual ability to dominate and exploit all other forms of life. Some experts postulate that not only are we the most prolific mammalian species on Earth, outnumbering even rats, but that there is now more human flesh on the Earth than any other species. Certainly, the escalation of the world's population over the last 100 years is an irrefutable indicator of an impending global catastrophe of unprecedented levels (Figure 1.3).

At the time of writing there are close to 6,800,000,000 (or 6.8 billion) people. Early population estimates are naturally capricious. Nevertheless around 30 kya, in the late or upper Paleolithic, it is thought that the number of people in Europe was in the tens of thousands. In 10,000 BC the global population was estimated to be around 4,000,000. Human numbers began to increase significantly after the last ice age left conditions that were favorable to the annual cultivation of seed plants and tubers. Improved agricultural conditions were not the only benefit left by the retreating ice. As temperatures rose, the people of Europe, who by virtue of their inventiveness had survived 30,000 years of climatic extremes, now had opportunity to redirect their ingenuity towards newly imagined goals that ultimately would increase their survival potential to unprecedented levels. The inventiveness of these early Europeans would be the cardinal factor in the extraordinary proliferation of the human species.

By 8000 BC agriculture was being practiced in the *fertile crescent of Mesopotamia* (modern Iraq, Turkey, Syria and Jordan). As a direct consequence of agriculture the world population had risen to around 50,000,000 by 1000 BC. By 1 AD, the population had increased 4 times to 200,000,000. By 1000 AD it was 310,000,000, by 1500 it was 425,000,000 and by 1750 it had reached 791,000,000. In 1802 the human population reached 1 billion, in 1928, 2 billion, in 1961, 3 billion, in 1974, 4 billion, in 1987, 5 billion and in 1999, 6 billion. These figures show that for most of the 19th and 20th century there was a rapid decrease in the number of years required to add another billion people to the world. Thus, while the increase from 1 billion in 1802 to 2 billion in 1928 required about 126 years, the number of years required to add each additional billion is 33, from 2 to 3 billion, 13 from 3 to 4 billion, 13 from 4 to 5 billion and 12 from 5 to 6 billion. In terms of the doubling of population, it took 126 years to double from 1 to 2 billion, 46 years to double from 2 to 4 billion and 38 years to double from 3 to 6 billion. Experts put 7.5 billion as a reasonable target for the middle of the 21st century but estimates from the United Nations suggest that there will be 7.6 by 2020, 8.2 by 2030, 8.7 by 2040 and 8.9 by 2050. Currently our population is increasing by over 100 million with each passing year and although birth rates are falling, the advances of medicine are continuing to increase human longevity. The bottom line is that these increases are of such magnitude that humans are at real risk of being propelled into massive resource-related wars.

Brain Size and Racism
"The scientific theory that there are genetically conditioned mental or behavioral differences between races cannot be called racist. It would be just as illogical to condemn the recognition of physical differences between races as racist". Arthur Jensen (born: 1923). American Educational Psychologist.

Humans have always insisted upon placing a barrier between themselves and the animal world. Science, philosophy and most religions have played their part in edifying our species, purposely severing our ties with nature, placing us midway between animal life and the unattainable perfection of a hypothetical deity. Unfortunately, this encouragement to reflect upon our collective superiority has provided an intellectual construct that readily accommodates our psyche's instinctual inclination towards *xenophobia* - the intense, yet irrational fear of people who are not like us (*The Nature and Nurture of Racism*: Chapter 2: Section 1). Despite the somewhat forlorn attempts of well-meaning anthropologists and geneticists to use the politically correct "royal we" when referring to human characteristics, nobody, least of all the modern descendants of the world's so-called preliterate peoples, is blind to the cognitive, emotional, thymic and physical diversity of humankind. Understanding and adjusting to the innate diversity of people is particularly important to the preservation and welfare of less dominant, minority cultures. In the real world, this is rare and minorities are more often relegated to a subordinate class.

The activities of racist groups such as the Nazis have caused many people to consider studies on the relationship between brain size and intellectual capabilities as serving ideologies of racial supremacy. Nothing could be further from the truth. Mutual understanding can only bring harmony to the peoples of the world and mutual understanding cannot arise from lies, whether or not they are concocted for virtuous or, alas, political reasons. Unfortunately, the atmosphere of political sensitivity that has surrounded all issues relating to race has enabled the publication of misinformation by people working at the highest levels of investigation – a strategy that ironically characterizes the techniques of propaganda traditionally used by all governments that have promoted racist ideologies. Moreover, to the inevitable detriment of all parties, the results of several carefully conducted studies have been essentially hidden from public scrutiny. In other cases research teams have made conspicuously strained efforts to interpret their data supporting the relationship between human brain size and mental aptitude in an almost exclusively, politically correct manner. For example, studies revealing that the brain size of men between the ages of 50 and 80 is related to the level of global cognitive functioning and speed of information processing, were interpreted by the investigating scientists as indicating that a large head or brain might protect the elderly against the cognitive deterioration which often accompanies aging.

People are simply different from one another, mentally and physically, the more so if they come from different genetical stock or, to put it in politically incorrect form, different racial origins. Of course, such differences do not need to be labeled as inferior or superior. No judgment need be made. Within any population, the cognitive abilities of its members are contained within an envelope that before the mass migrations of modern times had been sculptured by natural selection to best accommodate them to the nuances of their circumscribed habitat. The existence of this envelope even within relatively small populations indicates that a variation in cognitive ability is healthy. Indeed, although human IQ is said to range from around 50 to 200, in an operational sense, this range represents an enormous variation in abilities – a variation that has always existed even within relatively small human populations.

Despite racist ideologies about ethnic purity, there has never been and there never will be, such thing as a *pure race* wherein everyone has the same level of intelligence. The very idea of a pure race is a misnomer because, in truth, it is simply impossible to create. The health of any population depends on genetic variation because this ensures that there will always be people whose genetical constitution enables them to survive should the environmental change. In the realm of cognition and intelligence, genetic variation provides a population a variety of cognitive styles that enable it to generate a host of different strategies in meeting the challenges of survival.

In a pure race, all people would have exactly the same genetical composition. It follows that all members of a pure race would have the same form and level of intelligence and therefore the same basic personality. In practice the only way to approach this situation would be to repeatedly mate sisters with brothers or parents with children for about 20 generations – a practice rarely attempted in human history. Even if this could be achieved the pure race resulting from this process, would lack the genetic variation that enables normal populations to adapt to the inevitable environmental changes and to maintain individuals with particular gifts that are critical to the survival of the whole community. In such circumstances, many progeny would die because of the increased probability of a child receiving two deleterious genes from its closely related and genetically similar parents. In contrast, the progeny of mixed race marriages can express intellectual and physical promise beyond those of unmixed marriages - a principle known in genetics as *hybrid vigor*. Perhaps it is significant that in current international affairs, many place hope in what appears to be the multiple talents of US President and Nobel Laureate, Barack Obama, a highly intelligent man whose mother was primarily of English descent whose father was a native of Kenya. In a pure race everyone would be the same and all possibilities of hybrid vigor would be lost forever. While the capacity of the mind is reflected in intelligence, the composition of the mind, in terms of the different domains of intelligence, is indicative of personality. Normally, the marked tendency of complementary personalities to mate ensures the preservation of a diversity of mental functioning both in terms of overall aptitude and the prevailing cognitive style. There is good reason for the oft-observed phenomena that opposites attract. Without a store of genetic diversity, every member of a pure race would have the same personality and the same mental aptitude.

Whether it exploits differences in physical appearance or cognitive style, racism has its biological origins in the intrinsic fear all humans have of the unknown. Such a response to the unknown is an important survival mechanism, there being a good possibility that many animals, people and physical objects that are unfamiliar to the developing child are also dangerous. As we shall see later (*The Tyranny of Fear in Childhood:* Chapter 4: Section 4) the association of fear with an animal, person or object is powerfully reinforced when a child witnesses its parents responding fearfully to the trigger. Once such conditioning has taken place deprogramming is difficult. Consequently, even charitable people who have been taught racial biases find themselves unintentionally confronted with negative stereotypes when they encounter someone of a different race. Such experiences can be so powerful that individuals are temporarily impaired in their performance of cognitive tasks. Furthermore, when subjects who harbor racial biases were presented with unfamiliar faces of different race, brain scans showed that their emotional centers and the part of their right prefrontal cortex involved in evaluating and inhibiting imitative behavior, were both activated. Taken collectively, what these observations mean is that even in societies where racism is outlawed and declared as politically incorrect, people still respond inwardly to a person of different race.

Although racism is a stain upon any society or country, there is also great danger of misrepresenting biological truths about the diversity of humans, truths which humanity has striven so hard to elucidate and frequently purports to cherish. Repeatedly throughout history racial biases have been exploited for the attainment of wealth, power and sex. Yet, as science is showing, the arguments and principles upon which racism is based are both logically and morally bankrupt. Nevertheless, if lies are used to cover up and explain away human diversity, then all opportunity to use our new insights into human nature to our collective advantage will be lost in a political inspired morass.

Ultimately the facts of human biology show that any ideas of racial supremacy have about as much validity as arguing that red flowers are better than blue flowers. The essence of racism is subjective judgment. In its very nature science is neither judgmental nor subjective. Certainly a smaller or larger brain or this or that cognitive style have no relationship to that most precious of life's commodities, happiness. In this as in virtually all things, people are simply different from one another at the level of their genetical makeup.

The Nature and Nurture of Racism:
"And have you not noticed that opinions not based on knowledge are ugly things?"
Plato (428-348 BC). Greek Philosopher.

Issues of equality, diversity, race and intelligence form a political minefield. Even with the most altruistic intentions, simply writing about such things is to invite censure. In this book I will touch upon many aspects of human diversity and in so doing run the gauntlet of being labeled a racist by those who consider that humanitarian ideals can only emerge in a world organized in accord with their personal attitudes and not, the admittedly, cold and politically incorrect realities of nature.

So how can we distinguish racism from the simple identification and documentation of the vast physical, intellectual, emotional and cultural variety of humankind? Many well meaning scientists, anthropologists and social psychologists have suffered accusations of racism simply because their work has brought to light, significant and important differences between different groups of humans. In such matters there is endless opportunity for grandstanding by well meaning, yet poorly informed do-gooders. In reality, however, the recognition of differences can only bring understanding and enhanced communication between, otherwise potentially hostile peoples. Only when we are not bound by the illusion of sameness can we begin to accept the fundamental differences between races, populations, cultures, groups and tribes, amongst which the most important and conspicuous relate to the part of the brain that conducts the processes of thought. Some human populations are tall, some are short, some are white some are black. As we shall see, when left to their natural state, some populations are capable of complex inventions that physically change the world, others, are focused on people, their emotional life and nature (*Creativity, Modal Personality and the Mind*: Chapter 2: Section 8). The fact is that over the last 10,000 to 40,000 years the exponential increases in population has resulted in a 10 to 100 fold increase in human mutation rates. Despite the mixing of races afforded by modern intercontinental travel, the human species is diversifying at an accelerated rate, providing a wealth of hominid forms amongst which natural selection will favor only those best equipped to survive the new world.

Racism is not about differences but purposeful misinterpretation of differences usually for political and economic ends. Peck orders are common in the largely instinctual world of animals. Racism is not, however, about the instinctual urge to dominate but about judgment and belief. Racists use cognitively hatched strategies to assert power over others who are inherently different, physically, culturally and, as we shall see, mentally (*The Origins of Culture*: Chapter 2: Section 8). Racism is about persuading a majority of the populace that an alien group coexisting within their culture is both hostile and parasitic. The racist's perception is that because these people contribute neither warmth nor competence, they qualify as an extreme out-group, worthy only of exploitation and deserving only of eradication.

In psychology appreciating the inherent strategy with which an individual approaches his or her life is a major step in understanding that person at the level of personality. The same holds in regard to our appreciation of the cultural differences that characterize different world populations. Whether we call them races, countries, populations, cultures or societies, until modern times the world was composed of relatively isolated cultures that each seem to have a distinct collective identity or "personality" (*The Diversity of Intelligence*: Chapter 2: Section 8). Certainly, differences in physical or sensory prowess of different populations are easily observed. The inveterate traveler is an explorer of human cultures who, often unknowlingly, is seeking an internally consistent picture of a diverse humanity. Given the plenipotentiary powers of thought in directing the behavior of humans, the traveler's quest will inevitably reveal the influence of heredity on the psyche of each and every society. It is painfully obvious from birth that we are not identical brains in different bodies. As ancient wisdom becomes interwoven with the new findings of human neurogenetics one might hope that new perspectives will provide a holistic understanding of the human nature, wherein the cognitive diversity across the world is seen as a valuable resource rather than an opportunity for domination and exploitation

More than anywhere, it is in designing our educational systems that we most urgently need to address issues arising from the diversity of cognitive styles. For example, people who are dominated by emotional intelligence will have intellectual abilities and educational needs that relate to an entirely different domain of existence from those of people whose intellect is dominated by practicality. One of the most fundamental issues of education is deciding to what degree we promote the natural gifts of a child and to what degree we attempt to enhance those inevitable areas of deficit. This is an issue within any society but becomes more acute when a fusion of cultures precipitates the coalescence of inherently diverse cognitive styles (*The Diversity of Intelligence*: Chapter 2: Section 8). Of all parts of the human brain, the mind is the organ that contributes most to our individuality – a contribution that is powerfully influenced by inheritance. Particularly in societies where there is a mix of radically different racial backgrounds, there is a pressing, humanitarian need to set aside the politically correct fantasy that all individuals have the same intellectual potential and to address the realities concerning genes and the nature of intelligence. In truth, the only people who share an essentially identical mind are identical twins who typically follow exactly the same educational path. For the rest of humanity, the genetic specification of our mentality determines our individuality while ensuring that we are inherently adapted to serve the more or less archetypal roles that manifest in all human societies.

In times of Empire, the British occupied half the world. The sun, it was said, never set on the British Empire. The lands not occupied by the British, were mostly occupied by other European countries. Even up to the second half of the 20th century, it was generally held that the "savages" occupying countries outside of the European enclave, could be saved from their degenerate ways and helped towards material success by the indomitable combination of western education and Christianity. Europeans envisaged most other cultures as conspicuously inferior because, for unknown reasons, they had failed to develop science, writing, complex art and mathematics or to use these insights to invent guns, televisions and motorcars. Many races were considered particularly backward because they appeared not to realize the immediate survival advantage of irreversibly converting forests into farms. The superiority of the Europeans over all other populations or races was so firmly held that it was taught in European schools as a simple fact of nature. Under the sway of economically inspired propaganda, even highly intelligent Europeans were adamant that to allow the other peoples of the world to remain as they were, would be morally wrong. The Europeans of the 18th and 19th century successfully promoted the idea that a European education would benefit all cultures and all races even if it was largely composed of culturally irrelevant material. Few questioned the validity of this principle for it served as a believable excuse for the colonization of much of the non-Caucasian world. For at least 200 years, every educated European was subjected to this essentially racist conditioning which fostered a permissive view towards atrocities committed over many decades by the colonial oppressors.

The essence of politics is the retention of power through the manipulation of the societal sentiments (*The Evolution of Politics and Economics*: Chapter 3: Section 8). Though some scholars argued that non-Europeans were inherently different, others promoted the idea that any differences were only skin deep and could be at least partially overcome by the imposition of western culture and education. The tacit assumption was that even these peoples would be better off with a European education but that even then they would still be inferior because, despite being lifted out of the mire of ignorance and barbarism, they were still not European. Without our modern comprehension of the global diversity of cognitive styles, no efforts were made to adapt education so that it extended and affirmed, rather than negated, the cultures of the occupied countries. Instead the view taken was that if education and the products of western industry could "civilize" these "primitive" cultures, then there was surely justification enough for their invasion, "liberation", repressive occupation, mechanization, religious conversion, re-education and more than a little exploitation, to cover the costs of western investments. In recent times, similar arguments have been used to justify the invasion of the oil rich Iraq and the murder of around 50,000 people by the USA, Britain, Australia and a consortium of other countries, infamously referred to as the "coalition of the willing". Having all but decimated the natural resources of India and the non-Caucasian world, this group of economically powerful, resource hungry Caucasian countries are today still seeking to temporarily meet their unsustainable needs simply by pillaging the less powerful Caucasian countries.

The great irony is that these endeavors find an intellectual foundation in those well meaning, though misguided scholars, who, in the face of all evidence to the contrary, continue to claim that all human populations are cognitively identical and so can only benefit from the imposition of western education, culture and religion. This is, of course, utterly false and misleading. One can only hope that their emphatic denial of the extent of the inherent intellectual diversity of human populations, cultures or races, causes them to suffer the same obscurity that awaited the antievolutionist intellectuals of 19th century Britain, who chose the irrational dogma of the church over Charles Darwin's carefully argued theory of evolution. So often in history, what was at first dressed up as humanitarian assistance of a technologically weaker culture, soon revealed itself as a subtle yet unstoppable exercise in cultural devastation.

Ultimately, the forced imposition of a radically different culture upon a society is often paramount to genocide. Speaking of the death of a child, many years after British colonization, the elders of an Andaman Islander tribe are quoted as saying, "What does it matter? Our god has died." The resignation in these words highlights the effects of denying human diversity and forcibly imposing the ways of a totally alien culture upon another. While it is true that cultures reflect the products of beliefs, skills and ideas passed on from generation to generation, behind these cognitive constructs, a culture is very much the product of genes – genes that influence our emotions, moods and thoughts by determining the internal structure and physiology of the psyche of each and every human and each and every population or race. Be they in the mold of the hunter-gatherer, the native Indian or the urban man, the great cultures of the world owe their magnificence to the diversity of cognitive style that, as we shall see, is heavily influenced by the genetic variation upon which the tree of man is fashioned.

With few exceptions, both history and the modern world provide numerous examples of the catastrophic results of mixing different cultures or races. From the standpoint of modern biology this is not in the least surprising. Xenophobia is an innate property of the human psyche. In the brain, the same systems that represent and distinguish between familiar and unfamiliar inanimate objects are also used to represent and distinguish between familiar and unfamiliar people. In this way xenophobia is essentially a form of *neophobia*, the instinctual, cautionary fear all mammals have for anything unfamiliar – be it a snake or a monolith from outer space. In the wild, it is easy to see how neophobia is crucial to survival. Experiments show that if it is negated by either brain surgery or the use of drugs, the individual is immediately at risk (*The Social Arm of Fear and Apprehension*: Chapter 4: Section 4). In a world inhabited by human populations which look, sound, feel, smell and probably taste different, xenophobia must have always been critical to survival. Only when ensconced in a secure, safe environment, are humans drawn to espousing good intentions towards all humanity and weaving these intentions into laws, attitudes and morally founded definitions of politically correct behavior. On other occasions, under threat of injury, death or even simply destitution, they quickly become natural born killers, primed to strike down the alien without a moment's deliberation. Beyond the protective veneer of modern civilization, an immediate, aggressive response to individuals of an alien culture can mean the difference between life and death. The tribal lives of native peoples are always interwoven with the dangers of nature and the inevitable tribal warfare. The individual would soon be killed or captured, if he or she did not have an inherent, automatic, fight or flight reaction to the unfamiliar, be it an inanimate object, an animal or another human being.

What then are the essential differences, if any, between racism and xenophobia? With modern brain scanners it is possible to probe the human psyche in search of the origins of inter-racial hostility. The first of such studies focused on xenophobia and was aimed at determining the manner in which the brain differentiates between same-

23

race and other-race faces. When black and white Americans viewed photos of white Caucasian-Americans and black African-Americans, it became clear that Caucasian-Americans are better at remembering the faces of other Caucasian-Americans, while African-Americans were best at remembering African-American faces. In this facial memory task a part of the brain called the *fusiform face area* or *fusiform gyrus* (BA37) was more strongly activated by pictures of same-race faces (*The Art of Children*: Chapter 2: Section 3). The selective activation of the fusiform area to same-race faces is a critical step in our brain's capacity to attend to and register a potential friend versus a potential foe.

This is, however, far from the whole story. Many people can recognize pictures of close friends, even when those friends are from quite different racial or ethnic backgrounds. To reveal the effects of race on the brain's responses to the familiarity, or otherwise, of another person's face, brain imaging was performed on a group of Oriental-Koreans who were asked to judge the familiarity of both Oriental-Korean and Caucasian-American faces. The photos of both races contained some individuals who were known to the subjects. In these studies, powerful activation of the fusiform area followed the presentation of both familiar and unfamiliar same-race, as well as familiar other-race, pictures. Only pictures of unfamiliar, other-race individuals failed to strongly activate the face representation. It seems that the fusiform area acts as an attentional filter, responding preferentially to familiar faces of any race but to unfamiliar faces only if they belong to people of the same race as the observer.

While the fusiform area of our brain is crucial to the visual identification of people, who are either known to us, or belonging to our group, tribe, race or nation, our actual responses to unfamiliar aliens are mediated by quite different parts of the brain. Thus, the presentation of an unfamiliar foreign face evokes activity in the part of the brain's emotional centers that is involved in fear, anxiety and aggression, called the *amygdala* (Section 4: Chapter 4: The First Emotions - Anger, Fear and Lust). This response is large even if the picture of the foreign face is flashed on a screen for only $1/30^{th}$ of a second. If, however, the image is maintained for half a second, the mind is activated and the amygdala response is repressed. Therefore, initially the presentation of an unfamiliar foreign face seems to directly activate the brains center for negative emotions, in what could be referred to as *automatic, negative empathy* (*The Nature of Empathy*: Chapter 2: Section 4).

When white Americans view unfamiliar faces, whether black or white, the level of amygdala activation was correlated with the subjects score on a test especially designed to give an indirectly, clandestine measure of racism. Results showed that people who harbor racist beliefs suffer disruption of their thoughts when then interact with other-race individuals. It seems that, in those harboring racial sentiments, this mental interference of other-race encounters frees the amygdala even more from any inadvertent (in the case of racists) repression from the mind. In contrast, under the antiracist policies of most modern societies, the mind will be conditioned to assert a repressive influence over the amygdala's automatic response to other-race images.

The disruptive effect of other-race images on the ongoing thoughts of the racist, persist, even in racist people who have completely lost their amygdala. It follows that the harboring of mentally formed concepts of racial inferiority - what we commonly refer to as *racism* - is not the product of the automatic other-race responses of the amygdala. In fact, as outlined above, the responsiveness of the amygdala is itself regulated by our social conditioned beliefs about racial diversity. Many people are concerned that research highlighting racial diversity will be used by racists as evidence of superiority or inferiority. However, the facts show that racists have no need of the findings of neurogenetics or any other rational endeavor. Like the deeply religious, racists are simply steeped in a set of beliefs that they adhere to irrespective of new insights into the human condition. The religious bigot believes in the superiority of his religion, the moral bigot believes in the righteousness of his attitude and the racial bigot believes in the superiority of his race.

Superficially, most people would think that in a racially homogeneous society the absence of foreigners might result in the absence of discrimination. Unfortunately, all who seek power intuitively appreciate that instilling and maintaining fear in a society is the most effective means of persuading people to surrender their independence and ultimately their money to the will of the state and its leaders. Power seekers are intuitively aware that the brain systems that generate the attitudes and sentiments underlying racism can be activated by an encounter with any specified out-group. Politicians, dictators and governments are always eager to demonize an appropriate out-group and then to canvass votes by committing themselves to the arrest, punishment and ultimate destruction of the members of that group. Given the impropriety of attacking particular ethnic groups, the modern politician or dictator is obliged to seek out vulnerable, same-race, minority out-groups. In Nazi Germany, the Jews were targeted as public enemies that had to be murdered for the benefit of the Gentiles. In modern society the homeless, the user of drugs (alcohol and tobacco, excepted), the unemployed, the criminal and more recently, the Moslem terrorist, make attractive, and most importantly, indefensible targets for the politically ambitious and the morally empowered. Any who support the philosophies of these groups are discriminated against much as were the friends of Germany's Jews. The process is one where the powerful solicit the Government to establish a propaganda war against an out-group making any defense from other factions of the society, as tantamount to supporting anarchy or, in some cases, treason.

In orchestrating these scenarios, governments and dictators make every effort to ensure that their society's condemnation of an out-group, is unanimous, emphatic and, most importantly, permanent. When those that rule adopt this time-honored strategy, they are tapping into the same archaic brain mechanisms that, in the past, have caused many societies to trespass against minority groups of different creed, color, habit or belief, or to attack neighboring tribes or countries. Humans are highly social beings and as such are cognitively, as well as emotionally, inclined towards the exclusion and destruction of out-groups, if for no other reason than that they take a share of available resources. The brain mechanisms underlying these sentiments were revealed when brain imaging was performed on subjects viewing photos of various social out-groups.

Amongst these groups were two extreme out-groups, who like the homeless and the user of illegal drugs, are stereotypically presented as being both hostile and incompetent and thus lacking in both warmth and ability. Whereas photos of societal groups typically activate the mind, no mental activity accompanied the presentation of photos of the two most extreme out-groups. Instead, pictures of these extreme out-groups automatically activated not only the amygdala but also another emotional center, the *insula*, known to mediate disgust (*Disgust and the Windows of the Id*: Chapter 6: Section 4). These automatic responses to extreme out-groups reflect our automatic responses to unfamiliar, other-race faces. Both are indicative of discriminatory societal conditioning and both can be modified by social reform.

Chapter 3 – The Nature of Higher Consciousness

Language, Lobotomy and the Mind

"You raise the blade, you make the change,
 you rearrange me 'til I'm sane.
 You lock the door and throw away the key,
 there's someone in my head but it's not me."

Roger Waters, English Singer, Songwriter and Musician. From: *Brain Damage.* In: *The Darkside of the Moon*. Pink Floyd Music Publishers, London, 1973.

Language has great significance to understanding the origins of human thought, for language survives even after loss of those parts of the cortex which are necessary for the processes of reason. Indeed it is commonly assumed that our ability to speak is the basis of our complex social organization. This, however, is a fallacy as careful studies of human communication show that up to 90% of human communication is non-verbal. Moreover, in the living non-human primates, as in our long extinct hominid relatives, the australopithecines, complex social organization exists in the absence of spoken language. We cannot converse with our pet dog, but it is easy to see that like other higher mammals it can read us as well as a close friend. Watch a group of monkeys and they too will be watching you. You will be surprised at how easily you can understand their ways by simply reading their body language and even more surprised when, comprehending your preoccupation, they steal the bananas from your grocery bag. Long before the hominids, through eons of pre-linguistic time the hunter and the hunted have enjoyed the silent communication of the body.

It is most likely that human language is of primary importance, not to the psychosocial realm of our existence, but to meeting the purely practical challenges of survival. Indeed *Homo habilis*, the first of our hominid ancestors, is commonly believed to have had basic speech and to be the first hominid capable of inventing and fashioning very basic stone tools (*Brain Size in Human Evolution*: Chapter 2: Section 1). Perhaps the importance of communication to methodology explains why the ability to invent useful objects and the ability to speak seem to have appeared coincidently along our ancestral lineage. In support of this is the fascinating observation that the language areas in the cortex of modern humans respond when they are shown a tool - an observation that testifies to the survival of a neural network that essentially unites the utilitarian potential of objects to the generation of speech.

Introspectively, it seems that our speech is inseparable from our faculties of complex reasoning. Indeed when the neuroscientists focus their fantastic machines upon the brain of a talking human, they can detect involvement of parts of the prefrontal cortex that are known to contain our faculties of complex reasoning and creativity. Yet if we look a little deeper we can see that in the absence of thought we may have little to say even though we certainly retain the ability to speak. In fact, the dissociation between complex reasoning and language is a common experience of everyday life. For example, we may find ourselves saying, "I spoke before I thought" or "When I was speaking I was thinking of something else" or "I have to pay attention to - keep my thoughts focused upon - what I am saying". Who we may ask is the thinker and who is speaker?

Language it would seem is run by a simplistic mind of its own that has contact with the world outside and that sometimes goes on organizing speech even when our complex thoughts are far, far away. The neurological literature tells of a girl, severely impaired intellectually, who spoke perfect English that was without significant content. Linguists believe that this simple *language mind* is programmed to support a universal grammar called *mentalese* that is fundamental to all human languages. It would seem that this mentalese may be used for other things, for when cognitively challenged it is not uncommon for humans to use verbalization drawing upon their language mind to support their faculties of complex reasoning. Within each person, the cooperative between the speaker and the thinker has potential beyond the scope of either party.

That language does not require the intellect is revealed by its survival after the loss of both prefrontal lobes (Figure 1.4). In the dark ages of psychiatry, when the surgeon's knife not infrequently swept away the inner realms of reason, mood and emotion, language, together with the cerebral organ of speech, was often spared. In those times prefrontal lobotomies were carried out under local anesthetic which meant that the awake patient could be closely observed while his frontal lobes were being "disconnected". Accounts of this gruesome procedure make clear reference to the progressive onset of barren speech followed by silence as the last connections between the prefrontal cortex and the rest of the brain, were severed. Usually the procedure did not permanently abolish speech even though it destroyed the conceptual representations of existence that give life and significance to language. Once recovered, the lobotomized individual no longer retained the capacity to entertain ideas and frames of reason. For them the significance of time, intentions and ideas were forever gone, leaving behind the "nowness" of an eternal moment, a consciousness purged of the iconic representation of future yet pervaded by the bones of language wherein are contained the virtually meaningless memories of an now incomprehensible past. The mind of the lobotomized person is the simple mind of human speech.

The simple mind of speech is part of what is known as our *cerebral organ of speech*. This organ is made up of an area in the posterior parts of the cortex that deciphers spoken and written words (*Wernicke's area*, BA22) and a more anterior part of the cortex that constructs the complex set of oral movements which form our words and sentences (*Broca's Motor Speech area*, BA44/45). Naturally the sounds of speech are brought to Wernicke's area from the auditory receiving areas of the cortex (BA41/42). In contrast, information about writing is brought to Wernicke's area from a visual area (fusiform gyrus, BA37) specialized, in literate people, for the recognition of letters. In non-human primates and presumably in preliterate people this area is responsive to faces, hands and animal forms – elements that emerge in the *hieroglyphics* of a number of ancient cultures. Clearly, even our perceptions are very much the subject of the imagery we are exposed to during our maturation, reading being a tangible expression of the astounding adaptability of the cortical areas that nevertheless continue to be devoted to a particular domain of existence.

As well as generating the movements of human speech, in both humans and non-human primates, Broca's area is also involved in gesturing – an activity of such importance that it survives in neurological patients who have lost the ability to perform other movements. The involvement of Broca's area in gesturing is even more important in monkeys because, outside having specific calls for different predators, they appear to lack a structured language. In keeping with its role in both verbal language and gesturing, Broca's area contains specialized cortical neurons called *mirror neurons* – neurons that in motor areas are specialized for registering the movements of other agents but that also have the capacity to drive the same movements in the observer (*Mimicry, Movement Primitives and the Mind*: Chapter 3: Section 6).

Broca's area lies just behind the plane of section that was typically used for disconnecting prefrontal lobes. It is composed of two structurally distinct, neighboring cortical areas (BA44 and BA45). It seems that in the learning of language, Broca's area essentially categorizes objects within our immediate surroundings in a manner which best serves the nominative processes basic to speech. For the production of coherent, grammatically meaningful sentences to survive prefrontal lobotomy, both components of Broca's area, must be left intact. However, without the parts of the prefrontal lobes responsible for thought and emotional stability, the speech of the lobotomized patient lacks both the logical structure of reason and the prosody of speech – elements that ensure that the language of normal people is both meaningful and emotionally expressive.

Broca's area embodies our immediate surroundings into a very simple, descriptive model of reality. It cannot substitute for the interpretative elements of conceptual consciousness that are the foundations of true mentation - elements that commandeer the cerebral organ of speech for the purpose of conceptualizing emotions, the properties of objects and abstract problems. The simplistic, practical thoughts of Broca's area may have enabled the production of crude stone tools by our first verbally empowered ancestor, *H. habilis*. It is, however, only the sophistication and size of the human mind, and not so much our highly developed language areas that truly distinguishes us from our predecessors.

Elements of the Psyche
"...myth is not manufactured; rather, it is a spontaneous production of the living psyche; it bears within it, undamaged, the germ power of its source." Joseph Campbell (1904-1987). American Mythologist.

Some might argue that language, particularly the repetitive babbling of children, is very much the product of the inner world. Certainly the mind inserts content into language but it is the emotions that are the source of its melodies. Thus, it seems that Broca's area must divide its energies between the emotions and the mind, acting as a vehicle for the expression of these two elements of the psyche, rather than as an independent component of the psyche. Anatomically, the cortex of the psyche lies in front of Broca's area, wrapping around the three-sided pyramid that forms the prefrontal lobe of each hemisphere (Figure 1.5). If we could travel back in time and examine the brains of all those animal forms that preceded us, we would see that the cortex covering the undersurface (orbital surface) of our prefrontal lobe was the first part of prefrontal cortex to evolve; cortex that would account for the predictive or psychological aspect of mood. The next part was the cortex covering the middle surface of the prefrontal lobes, cortex that, in our brain, enables us to experience our emotions. The cortex that covers the outer surface of the prefrontal lobes evolved next; cortex within which would be assembled the still-hidden algorithms of human thought.

Thought, mood and emotion compose three experientially unique elements of the inner world (Figure 1.6). In essence, our emotions are the expression of our *needs*, while our thoughts provide the *means* by which we may actualize those needs and our moods enable us to *predict* the likelihood of our success in such a mission (Figure 1.7). The cortex of the mind supports the conceptual frameworks relevant to both the inner and outer realms of our existence. Whether a thought be within the psychosocial realm or the practical, its experience is evidence of what can be referred to as *conceptual consciousness*. Most thoughts are transient events highly responsive to our distance senses, vision and hearing, in the process of establishing our behavioral strategies, yet also sensitive to the equally transient perturbations of our emotions that reflect our innate urges, to, for example, feed, have sex or seek safety. The cortex serving our emotions is very responsive to our most ancient senses, smell, taste and touch. In contrast, mood is less localizable to one particular area of the cortex. Mood traps us at one emotional extreme, simultaneously generating an anticipatory aura that powerfully influences the mind in its endeavor to create a protocol for effective action. Whereas our emotions are a consequence of transient perturbations of the viscera, our moods reflect our long-term circumstances, our hormones and the general physiological condition of our body – factors central to our correctly evaluating the likelihood our success or failure.

Authority and Complementation in Consciousness
"Think left and think right and think low and think high.
Oh, the thinks you can think up if only you try."
Theodor Seuss Geisel (Dr. Seuss), (1904-1991). American Children's Author and Cartoonist.

There exists a virtual cult whose new-age edicts and books are hijacked from careful scientific studies of patients who had, for clinical reasons, suffered the surgical disconnection of the two hemispheres of their brain. These studies give fascinating insights into how natural selection has modified the utility of structurally identical areas of cortex on each hemisphere so that they serve different aspects of human existence. Only the advent of brain imaging has enabled the analyses of the, often subtle, differences in the function between discrete cortical areas on the left versus the right hemisphere. For example, in the left hemisphere the part of the cortex dedicated to practical thought is concerned only with the physical properties of things while the equivalent area in the right hemisphere represents things in relation to their symbolic identity (Section 3: Chapter 3: The Origins of Practicality – The Material Mind).

Although the behavioral studies of hemispheric specialization revealed fascinating, holistic differences between the left and right hemispheres, they were also necessarily vague. Some examples of properties attributed to the left versus right hemisphere are as follows: sequential versus simultaneous; analytical versus holistic; verbal versus nonverbal; temporal versus spatial; logical versus intuitive; past versus future; deliberate versus impulsive; objective versus subjective. There are many more that often do not seem to be strictly opposites in an antonymous sense. Unfortunately, these, admittedly tantalizing, left-right differences have fallen prey to human imagination. So it is we find claims that the left brain supports the masculine psyche while the right supports the feminine, or, even more outrageous, the idea that the left brain is responsible for western philosophy while the right is responsible for eastern philosophy.

Not all animals appear to always require both hemispheres in order to function. Marine mammals show what is known as *unihemispheric sleep* – a condition wherein one hemisphere sleeps while the other remains fully functional (*Sleep and Dreams in Animals*: Chapter 2: Section 7). As either side may sleep while the other is awake, it seems there is no evidence in these animals for any serious lateralization of brain function. This does not, however, contradict the observations on hemispheric specialization in the human brain because most of the left-right differences in humans involve cognition and emotion – elements conjured by the prefrontal lobes which, in marine mammals, are very small and probably entirely devoted to emotions and instinct.

Amongst humans there are at least two examples of children who have been born with only a single hemisphere. What is extraordinary is that although these individuals may suffer difficulties with movement on one side, they lead intellectual and social lives that are relatively normal. Again it seems that the hemispheric differences in normal people are of primary importance, not to the sensory-motor aspects of existence but to subtle differences in the focus of thought, emotion and mood - those realms of consciousness that relate to our inner life and so constitute the psyche. These observations support the original indications that patients with split brains appear to have distinct left and right personas. It seems that if we place aside the subtle and complementary differences between the higher functions of the left and right hemispheres then each side of the human brain does have the neural ensemble that would enable it to manifest itself as a complete person. Loss of one hemisphere in an adult would almost certainly be fatal. This is, however, not always the case when there is a congenital absence of one hemisphere. Exposed to all the environmental influences of a normal childhood, the single developmentally-immature hemisphere of the unihemispheric infant presumably has the potential to take on all additional roles that might otherwise be foisted on the other, non-existent hemisphere. The survival of a child with only one hemisphere is indicative of the adaptability of the brain and bears testimony to the sensitivity of the developing brain to nurture and abuse. As far as the human psyche goes, it seems that at birth each side of the brain has the potential to be a complete human being.

Further research will continue to reveal the generalities regarding the developmental origins of asymmetry in hemispheric function. Even in the embryonic stages the nervous control of the viscera is a necessary condition for maintaining life. One fascinating idea is that the autonomic nervous system – the special part of the nervous system that controls our vital functions – is from its embryonic stages, asymmetrical and so, even before birth, would have an asymmetrical influence over the still developing central nervous system. The outcome of this would almost certainly be specializations in the representation of the inner world within the left and right sides of the brain.

In life, the complementary roles of the left and right hemispheres represent a cooperative policy of brain organization. This view is strengthened by the precise reciprocal nature of the so-called *commissural* connections between the two hemispheres – precise in that each small area of the cortex of one hemisphere is interconnected to, and interacts with, the same small area within the cortex of the opposite hemisphere. The interactions between left and right sides thus preserve an intimacy characteristic of their close cooperation in representing very discrete aspects of existence. By comparison the functional organization of the cortex within one hemisphere is strikingly competitive and hierarchical. Particularly between the different components of the psyche, there is, within a single hemisphere, a constant vying for position, emotion being one moment in charge, only to be, in the next moment, subjugated to the power of mind or obscured by the persistence of mood. This explains why observations on split-brain patients demonstrate that each hemisphere has the capacity to engage those elements of higher consciousness that are the foundations of our inner life and that form the psyche of every normal human being. Of course, in normal people both sides contribute to the individual. Nevertheless, it is in the rivalry between elements of the psyche within each hemisphere and not the essentially complementary interactions between the hemispheres, that is to be found the most fundamental and irrefutable insights into the behavioral identity of the human being.

Faith, Hope and Belief
"Give us this day our daily faith, but deliver us, dear God, from belief." Aldous Huxley (1894-1963). English Author.

When he wrote these words in Island, Aldous Huxley was warning us of the illusory nature of the human mind and the reliance of all creative thought upon mentally elaborated substrates which so easily become our beliefs. When we use our mind to hatch a scheme for resolving a problem we do so on the basis of our beliefs. Throughout this process we are pervaded with a seemingly well founded sense of *hope*, hope that we have thought everything through, that our beliefs match the realities of the situation, that we will achieve our objective and so be released from further concern. Finally, we believe that we will feel good, not only at the moment we achieve the desired outcome, but also (and this is tricky part) in the future when we expect to reap the fruits of our carefully devised plan.

Faith is what we harbor when we move beyond the realms of control. Faith is the gambler's trump card. Faith is our blind trust that because we are alive, happy and well today, we will be alive, well and happy tomorrow. Both faith and hope are empowered by the optimism of euphoric mood and disempowered by the pessimism of dark mood.

It is very unlikely that any animal below the highest non-human primates has the mental capacity to entertain either faith or hope. Without any mental faculties, belief plays no part in the existence of the lower mammals and their behavior is consequently motivated entirely by instinctual urges. Hope, faith and the attendant beliefs, are not the products of instinct but products of our mind. Within us hope and faith are the cognitive elaborated representatives of our life force. Both are necessary elements within the healthy human psyche and both are usefully touted in the doctrines of all religions. The problem is that like all things within our mind, faith, hope and belief have lives of their own. For this reason, faith and hope can be easily manipulated by others for ends that perhaps we might never have foreseen. We can, for instance, be drawn to a religion because of a need to share and explore our spiritual being with others, only to find ourselves involved in hostilities towards others whose beliefs conflict with those of our new found friends. Faith, hope and belief are the con men of our psyche. Advertisers stop at nothing to get us to link our faith to the products of their clients. In the personal realm too, it is easy to see how we can project our hope and faith upon other people, the government, a deity, a perceived savior, a wife, husband, child or parent. In its very nature, our mind has the intrinsic capacity to adopt any belief system, religious or political. Yet, being entirely the products of thought, faith, hope and belief do not exist outside the psyche. You cannot sell a rat a vacuum cleaner. He has nothing in his brain with which to make a belief. In humans, severing the prefrontal lobes from the brain effectively destroys the psyche. As we have seen, language may survive as long as Broca's area is spared. So it is that the more intuitive lobotomized patients can enunciate that they have lost themselves and lost also their place in time. In such a being the issues of faith, hope and belief are virtually nonexistent. The neural machinery for ideating and achieving goals has essentially been deleted from consciousness and with them have departed those sirens of the never-never, faith, hope and belief.

Section 1: Recommended Reading

Armstrong, K. *A History of God: The 4000-Year Quest of Judaism, Christianity and Islam.* Alfred A. Knopf, New York, 1994.

Blakemore, C. *Mechanics of the Mind.* Cambridge University Press, London, 1977.

Boring, E. G. *A History of Experimental Psychology.* Appleton, Century, Crofts Inc., 1957.

Eccles, J. C. *Evolution of the Brain: Creation of the Self.* Routledge, London and New York, 1989.

Gray, J. R. and Thompson, P. M. (2004). Neurobiology of Intelligence: Science and Ethics. *Nature Neuroscience Reviews* **5**, 471-482.

Jobling, M. A., Hurles, M. E. and Tyler-Smith, C. *Human Evolutionary Genetics: Origins, Peoples and Disease.* Garland Publishing, New York, 2004.

Joseph, R. *The Right Brain and the Unconscious: Discovering the Stranger Within.* Plenum Press, New York and London, 1992.

Mukerjee, M. *The Land of the Naked People: Encounters with Stone Age Islanders.* Houghton Nifflin and Co., Boston, New York, 2003.

Newberg, A. and D'Aquili, E. *Why God Won't Go Away: Brain Science and the Biology of Belief.* Ballantine Book, New York, 2001.

Sawyer, G. J. and Deak, V. *The Last Human: A Guide to Twenty-Two Species of Extinct Humans.* Nevraumont Publishing Company, New York City, 2007.

Snow, C. P. *Two Cultures and the Scientific Revolution.* Cambridge University Press, Cambridge, New York, 1964.

Springer, S. P. and Deutsch, G. *Left Brain, Right Brain.* 3rd Edition, W.H. Freeman and Co, New York, 2000.

Whyte, L. L. *The Unconscious Before Freud.* Social Science Paperbacks, Tavistock Publications Copyright Basic Books, 1960.

Section 2

The Nature of Consciousness

"It is both near and far, both within and without every creature; it moves and is unmoving. It is subtlety, it is beyond comprehension. It is indivisible, yet appears divided in separate creatures. Know it to be the creator, the preserver, and the destroyer. Dwelling in every heart, it is beyond darkness. It is called the light of lights, the object and goal of knowledge, and knowledge itself."

The Bhagavad-Gita (Hindu Scriptures). Written between 5th and 2nd Century BC.

Chapter 1 - The Origins, Mythology and Organization of Consciousness

The Gift of Awareness

"The mystical is not *how* the world is but *that* it is." Ludwig Wittgenstein (1889-1951). Austrian/British Philosopher.

The phenomenon of consciousness is the greatest mystery of existence. Consciousness flows like a river, threading together each moment into an experience we call life. Indeed, our very awareness of "being" exists only because we may access this cosmic medium that conjures dream from sleep as it does the knowing of each wakeful moment. Only through consciousness can we know sensation, perception, thought, emotion and mood. Without the faculty of consciousness we would not see, hear, touch, smell, taste, sense the stirrings of our urges, know the pinnacles of euphoria and the crippling angst of darkness, experience thought and feel anger, hope, despair, compassion, love and hatred. The child matures into consciousness the being lives within consciousness and, with the death of the brain, the aged pass from consciousness, leaving only their body and their fading footsteps within the memories of their descendants.

In the unification of the peoples of this world, nothing is of more significance than understanding the inherent nature and diversity of human consciousness. History may tell us the story of our ways over the last 5,000 years, but understanding consciousness enables us to know ourselves across the diversity of all humanity, for the life of every human is inevitably mapped upon the broad slate of human consciousness. It is through comprehending consciousness that we may glimpse the stillness of the aged and yet it is through consciousness that the little child remains always within us. The witch doctor, the medicine man, the eastern sage, the great thinker of the western tradition and every ordinary and extraordinary person, all have emerged from this greater whole which encompasses the length and breadth of human experience. Never can we seek to understand humanity without knowingly, or unknowingly, embarking upon a journey into human consciousness.

The word consciousness comes from the Latin roots *con* ("with" or to "see above") and *scire* ("to know"). In keeping with this definition consciousness is a property of the highest level of the nervous system, the *cerebral cortex*. Consciousness begins when the parts of the cortex that first receive information from our sensory organs begin to mature. Even in the embryo each of our senses is claiming a piece of cortex in order to ensure it has a representation in consciousness. Shortly after birth our eyes, ears, skin, muscle, joints, our organs of smell and taste and the component organs of our viscera, send sensory information to the cortex where each input lays claim to the related *primary sensory area of the cortex*. These primary sensations are then relayed to other cortical areas where they are reconstructed into perceptions - meaningful constructs of our outer and inner worlds that are familiar components of our every day experiences, our dreams and our imaginings. Each type of perception is represented separately such that we may speak of the *perceptual areas of the cortex*. In constructing our perceptions the perceptual areas do not necessarily draw equally on all primary sensory areas. Thus, the representation of color is constructed from the primary visual areas while the representation of object identity draws upon primary representations of vision, audition, touch, smell and probably taste. What is most important, is that in contrast to the perceptual areas, the primary sensory areas of the cortex do not participate in dreams and imaginings but instead give our normal experiences a distinct aura of being truly grounded in real sensations (*The Manipulation of Mental Imagery*: Chapter 1: Section 7).

When the child first emerges from the womb, only the areas of cortex serving the primary representation of touch, movement, olfaction and taste are operative. The newborn infant is therefore said to be in the sensorimotor stage of development. Not only is there an absence of thought but there is probably little involvement of the largely immature cerebral cortex in infant behavior. Over the first year of life there is maturation of those areas of cortex destined to serve perception. As these become operative consciousness literally expands and the child becomes availed of an entirely new set of experiences wherein meaningful perceptions are reconstructed from the representation of the raw elements of sensory information available from the, already operative, primary sensory areas. Over the same period, areas of the cortex responsive to the organs of the body mature and there arises a specialized set of perceptions that are the essence of our urges and emotions. So it is that by the end of the first year of life our perceptions of the outside world, along with feelings arising from the visceral body, combine within the cortex to produce the experiences of infanthood - experiences that remain transient until maturation of the brain's long-term memory systems banish the amnesia of early infancy.

Throughout childhood and even adolescence, consciousness continues to expand as new areas of cortex mature. Some of these areas serve aspects of thought and so constitute the highest realms of human consciousness - realms that dominate human life but are difficult to detect even in the behavior the most cerebrally advanced non-human primates. In the human child, one domain after another is added until upon the threshold of adulthood the highest level of human thought emerges to take command over all. Nevertheless, thought only becomes an entity in behavior when, towards the end of the first year of life, the first cortical area to serve cognition begins to mature. From that time until puberty the perceptual areas continue to feed information to those slowly maturing areas of cortex that are to become the adult mind. The singular purpose of this is the establishment of neuronal networks capable of amassing all significant perceptions of day-to-day existence into conceptual frameworks that preserve the ideas, concepts and beliefs that are the very substance of thought. So it is that "with" (*con*) our human variety of consciousness, we may "know" (*scire*) but at the same time "see above", all purely factual knowledge.

Defining Consciousness
"The brain is wider than the sky,
for to put them side by side,
the one the other will contain,
with ease and you beside."
Emily Dickinson (1830-1886). American Poet.

Many mysterious elements have been proposed in attempts to define and explain consciousness. Sub-atomic particles, quantum physics, the organelles of nerve cells, complex mathematical algorithms and arduous philosophical arguments have all been invoked. The new age cults talk of "energies" they have "felt" and discovered names for in ancient scriptures. These things have become the tales of contemporary western mythology, but in truth their relationship to consciousness is no less allegorical than the folktale or religious parable. Meanwhile consciousness goes on happening, subject only to the environment, genetics and the biology of the individual.

The antithesis of consciousness is unconsciousness. When we are unconscious we essentially lack awareness. In its broadest sense, the word consciousness means simply a state of awareness. However, its usage by many pundits, eastern and western, does not always comply with this definition. For example, Indian mystics commonly refer to consciousness as being the state achieved when we are experiencing the inner or all-pervading self. All other experiences, sensory, perceptual or mental are regarded as superfluous to this realm of pure and self-defining awareness. However, in the West and, in particular, America, another often-touted view is that consciousness is equivalent to thought. "I think and therefore I am" is the catch cry. In this view, the cognitive elaboration of self-identity (the *ego*) is taken as the critical sign of consciousness and animals that cannot be shown to have a cognitive representation of themselves are considered to completely lack awareness. Therefore the East and the West typically have diametrically opposite ideas about consciousness, the former often equating it with the soul or inner-self and the latter equating it with the mind (Figure 2.1). Both visions are misleading and both are quite wrong. The eastern view of consciousness is incorrect because it does not emphasize thought and perception as important elements of consciousness, while the western view overlooks the critical message of introspective practice that acknowledges the survival of consciousness even in the complete absence of thought - an insight supported by the retention of consciousness after the cognitive centers have completely destroyed by prefrontal lobotomy (Section 3: Chapter 1: The Nature of the Mind). In truth consciousness is a phenomenon that arises from cortical activity, whether this be within the cortex's representations of thought, emotion, perception or simple sensation. All areas of the cortex contribute to consciousness because all have the inherent capacity to generate experience.

Ultimately it is just not possible to define consciousness. Consciousness is too much part of the process of definition. Imagine that I ask you to define the sky. You will speak of its color, of the clouds and the horizon. You will tell me of the light of the sun and the moon and of their celestial passage across the great dome of space. You will explain about the stars and how in the darkest nights they give us a sense of place. You will tell me of the clouds, the chariots of the gods, painting faces of old men whose beards twist across the blue to disappear like wisps of mist in the warmth of the morning sun. All these aspects can be brought together and yet still you have not captured for me, the sky. There are no words for such a purpose. Description is a poor substitute for experience. Behold the sky, allow it to be only the sky and within you some indefinable energy will awaken. The firmament has slipped past your senses and past your mind to work its magic in those realms of emotion that so challenge verbal definition. The Germans talk of a hunted sky when the dark and threatening clouds warn us of a great storm - a sky that fills the heart with fear. Look at the sky and let it conjure within you what it will. Let it play tag with your inner realms. Allow it past the smoke screen of your thoughts to where it may become part of your inner being. What this sky is, still no person can say. So it is also for this thing we call consciousness. Like the sky we may dissect consciousness into its component parts, we may caste it in our great mythologies, embody it in our most powerful Gods and yet still never arrive at an apt expression for the whole. Consciousness is, like the sky, a phenomenon. There is no all-encompassing definition for such things; they are, in the most absolute sense, of themselves. In the opening words of the *Tao Te Ching*, "The tao that can be spoken about is not the Absolute Tao". So it is with consciousness, for he who watches it, is himself part thereof. How can we know such a thing?

Life, Death and Consciousness
"Partly from the observation of such animals as rabbits, apes and dogs, and partly from cases of injury to man's brain, it has been found that the cerebrum is the seat of sensation, intelligence and the will." Philipp, U. and Mercer, S. "The Human Machine at Work." In: *The Miracle of Life*. H. Wheeler (Editor), Odham's Press, London, c. 1935, p. 355.

To many people, life and consciousness are synonymous. Some believe that plants are conscious. Others assign consciousness to inanimate objects, give their cars names and interpret their erratic behavior as a feature of their personality and mood. Little children believe their teddy bears are conscious and even as adults we feel the allure of attribution in the facial expressions of stuffed toys. Centuries after the industrial revolution we are still equate the operations performed by a machine with consciousness. Without a second thought we automatically interpret biological imagery or the automicity of movement as indicative of the capacity of the object to experience. Such observations are sufficient to persuade us that here is something that is not only alive, but also conscious. As we shall see much later, this drive to identify life and to attribute to it intention, is not just a product of delusional thinking but emanates from a set of inherited brain circuits that automatically focus even the virtually unconscious newborn, on its social milieu (Section 6: Chapter 2: The Origins of Social Learning).

Yet we can err in the opposite direction. The spontaneous reaction of people to the condition known as *locked-in syndrome* is the perfect example. Resulting from a brainstem lesion, the patient is unable to move anything but the eyes. No output is possible. Both verbal language and the language of the body are completely lost. Until recently all who observed such individuals considered them to be alive but essentially unconscious. Inside, however, their cortex is completely operational, sensitive to a world it cannot influence, observant of the life of others through a screen of almost total paralysis. From the outside there is no sign of awareness, but behind the mask of immobility, consciousness flows by without so much as a whisper.

41

We know that we are alive only because we are conscious. Yet life can exist without consciousness. In the depths of coma we are totally unconscious. Similarly, under general anesthesia and in deep sleep, consciousness ceases to exist. Though much of the brain may be operating more or less normally, the cerebral cortex has closed down. If it remains closed down then we erroneously refer to the patient as being *brain dead*. In truth, however, little of their brain may be dead. Only those parts critically necessary for the person to experience life have died. Brain death is a condition that results from the death of many, or even all, brain cells in the cerebral cortex. The heart is still beating and the blood still circulates through the body. Inside, an incomplete, though functional nervous system continues carrying out its regulatory functions. Only the thin layer of nerve cells that form the surface of the cerebral hemispheres of the brain has passed away, only consciousness and the functions dependent upon the cerebral cortex are no more.

With the death of cortex, consciousness departs. Before us lies the heartbreaking spectacle of a familiar human form from which the person we once knew has gone forever. Though still alive, this being shows not the slightest sign of perception. There is no awareness of the moment, no memory of yesterday and no thoughts of tomorrow. There is no presence. All that survives is a living body and the neural control systems that have survived 550 million years of vertebrate evolution to maintain the purely vegetative domain of human existence. What was once our comrade, our lover or our parent is now only a biological object. Stripped of its most powerful yet mysterious property, this humanoid lifeform will never again generate meaningful behavior. The spirit of consciousness has left the body. The machine is still running but the ghost within has long since fled.

In their faces and their bodies, in their gesticulations and their forms, humans are more animated than any animal. This is because the sophistication and size of the human cerebral cortex far exceeds that of even our closest living relatives, the chimpanzees. Consequently, in the human, both the cortex and consciousness seem to be more important to the formulation of behavior than they are in any animal. Indeed, we are so dependent upon the cortex and the conscious state, that when consciousness is lost or the cortex dies, not even the most rudimentary components of behavior survive.

Looking at the brains of the living representatives of progressively more primitive vertebrates shows that the further we go back in evolution, the greater is the role of the sub-cortical centers in the generation of behavior. Fish, for example, successfully negotiate life virtually without a true cerebral cortex. This trend continues even throughout the mammals such that the cortex of the lower, behaviorally simple species (eg. rodents) has far weaker connections to the lower echelons of the nervous system than are found in the human. It is reasonable to assume, that as a consequence of the pressures of natural selection, biological systems such as the brain are optimized in both their economy and efficiency. In terms of efficient organization and the control of complex behavior, the mammalian brain follows a progression of increasing cortical control wherein the executive suite has progressively more direct access to the factory floor, with a concomitant reduction in the powers of middle management.

In the process of our evolution, natural selection has favored directly linking the seat of consciousness to the lowest parts of the nervous system. In humans the vast array of information, available almost instantly at the level of the cerebral cortex, has clearly augured for the direct connection of this highest of stations to lower centers. The reliance of human movement on the integrity of the cortex is just one consequence of this evolutionary progression that has seen an increasingly powerful link between consciousness and behavior.

The Compartmentalization of Consciousness

"The specific histological differentiation of the cortical areas proves irrefutably their specific functional differentiation.....the large number of specially built structural regions points to a spatial separation of many functions and.....the sharply delimited localization of the physiological processes which correspond to it." Korbinian Brodmann (1868-1918). German Neurologist and Neuroanatomist.

Human consciousness is the stage upon which each and every aspect of awareness plays a part. Upon this stage vision and hearing powerfully influence thought, while taste, smell and touch impact upon emotion and mood. Physically speaking this stage is the thin (mean 2.5mm) sheet of gray matter covering the hemispheres of our brain called the cerebral cortex. In 1908 the great German neuroanatomist Korbinian Brodmann (1868-1918) showed that this sheet could be divided into 44 structurally discrete areas. Using modern methods other workers have detected 4 new areas. The different areas of cortex are based on the size, density and distribution of the component nerve cells. They are therefore referred to as the *cytoarchitectonic areas of Brodmann* or simply *Brodmann's areas* (Figure 2.2)

In 1909 much of the central nervous system lay shrouded in mystery awaiting the advances in science and technolology that would enable neuroscientist to unlock its secrets. Nevertheless, as the above quotation shows, Brodmann knew exactly what he had elucidated within the highest realm of the human brain. Thus, although he did not speak of consciousness *per se*, Brodmann's map of the cerebral cortex was to become the most significant tool for the exploration of human consciousness. Throughout the 20th century it was repeatedly found that Brodmann's areas not only served different functions but that they were also individually responsible for each specific element of human experience. Even though subsequent anatomical studies prompted the subdivision of some areas, the sub- areas so formed, typically processed related information and so contributed to closely related aspects of a given experience. What this means is that all experience is fashioned from a finite and relatively small number of areas that make up the cerebral cortex of the human. Each area (or sub-area) is the anatomical substrate for a particular aspect of human experience. If we could recreate normal patterns of activity in these areas, either individually or in combinations, it would be theoretically possible to recreate all the experiences available to a normal human being. As each area doubtless exists to some degree in the cortex of every normal human, we can also view Brodmann's areas as defining, what are essentially archetypal elements of human experience, elements that are identical in all humans and that form the core of all human communication. At any moment, whatever areas of our cortex are active determines, *what is so* in that moment.

Observing Consciousness

"If we could look through the skull into the brain of a consciously thinking person, and if the place of optimal excitability were luminous, then we should see playing over the cerebral surface a bright spot with fantastic, waving borders, constantly fluctuating in size and form, and surrounded by a darkness, more or less deep, covering the rest of the hemisphere." Ivan Pavlov (1839-1946). Russian Physiological Psychologist, Physician and Nobel Laureate.

Every time we are puzzled at the behavior of another person or an event that involves people, we are pondering the ways of human consciousness. We revel in drama, in prediction of what others might do, embarking upon lengthy analyses of the past in our never-ending quest for comprehension. We are the most creative and complex creatures on Earth and yet we are also more war-like and cruel than any beast, imagined or real. Consequently, so much of our conversation centers on this seemingly imponderable mystery of why human life is so. In this search for understanding, psychologists have written whole books on a single sentence uttered by a client in a counseling session. Philosophers have argued endlessly about the nature of being. Behavioral scientists spend their entire lives trying to completely describe the origins of our simplest activities. In desolate mountain caves, mystics sit for decades entranced by glimpses of what lies behind the cacophony of day-to-day life. In art and music we seek to express what is beyond our words. Our enormous capacity for thought persuades us that we are logical beings and that argument will inevitably bring solutions. Yet to most people, facts are of little interest. Responsive to this desire for the speculative, the media is filled with idle stories about what well-known people might do in the future and why they did this or that in the past. On average 60% of our conversations are spent gossiping about relationships and personal experiences. It seems we are eternally bound to what has been called our *social brain* and are, as a species, challenged to rise above the sociopolitical concerns that, as we shall see, so dominate the thoughts and behavior of our closest relatives, the apes. It is the arousal of our emotions and our fascination with possibility that sells our newspapers and kindles our love of theater, where, through dynamic caricature and myth, we reinforce our sense of identity by watching and rewatching the most common scenarios of human life. The importance of our social world ensures that our abilities at abstract thought are often orientated towards an endless quest for self-understanding. Yet though we crave self-knowledge, when we strive to see our reflection in the endless sea of faces, we often find the stranger looking back at the estranged. Ultimately, it is the power and diversity of the human mind, which not only distinguishes us behaviorally from the apes but also makes us so potentially dangerous to one another.

In what has been considered a western koan, Mark Twain once wrote that, "There ain't no way to find out why a snorer can't hear himself". At the time Twain was writing, this was true, and together with other imponderables, such as why are we unable to tickle ourselves, it was accepted as simply part of human nature. Since then science has broken down many imponderables, revealing the methods and mechanisms underlying phenomena that previously seemed to be manifestations of magic. The invention of brain scanners has enabled just such a process in relation to human experience. At last it is possible to observe activity in particular parts of the living cortex and to associate this with what a person is experiencing. Now we can take snapshots of the brain of a snoring person or simply look at what really happens when we tickle ourselves and are tickled by others.

With our vast knowledge of when and how different parts of the brain become active we will soon be able dissect the sequential elaboration of every form of human experience. Already brain scanners have helped us to understand the origin of fundamental experiences such as bliss, darkness, pleasure and pain. As technology advances we may expect to be able to watch the moment-to-moment processes of consciousness and so potentially be able to "see" and perhaps even decode the thoughts and feelings of others just by "looking" into their brains.

The essence of wisdom is the complete understanding of human nature, an achievement that can only emerge directly from an insight into all domains of human consciousness and how they interact within the cerebral cortex. Such an understanding reveals the human being in his or her most intimate and immutable form. In this context, the analysis and comprehension of the nature of human consciousness provides a vivid and objective insight into the ways of humanity and the association of those ways with our animal ancestors.

The Awareness of Time
"Man's short-term subjective time scale may depend upon the constancy of his internal temperature. For so-called cold-blooded animals this would not hold. For them time would presumably pass slowly on warm days and rapidly on cold days....time would not appear to flow steadily in the linear sort of way familiar to us mammals." Hudson Hoagland (1899-1982). American Physiologist and Humanitarian.

Our awareness of the passage of time remains a particularly mysterious aspect of human consciousness. In certain scenarios humans appear to be capable of very precise estimations of time. Asked to press a key, at intervals of 0.7 seconds to tens of seconds after a trigger, most subjects soon become adept at estimating the passage of time to within a few percent. Obviously resolving time in this manner does not necessarily implicate consciousness beyond the awareness of the intention to do so. An awareness of time is perhaps more evident in situations where the passage of time is an essential part of an ongoing experience. In such circumstances, any awareness of time is necessarily influenced by situational and physiological factors. In a socially rewarding situation, time passes more quickly, whereas in isolation or in negative social interaction, it passes more slowly. Time drags when we are bored and races when we are entranced by our surroundings.

In the 1930's, while caring for his sick wife, the physiologist-humanitarian Hudson Hoagland noted that when her temperature was high she consistently overestimated time. This observation led subsequent researchers to conclude that raising the brain's temperature alters a person's time perception by 20%. Other experiments have shown that amphetamine (speed), which increases the excitability of the brain also speeds up the brain's internal clock with the result that subjects have a distorted appreciation of how much time that has passed in the outside world.

Mountaineers often report extreme distortions of time at very high altitudes, when the brain, and particularly the energy dependent cortex, is critically deprived of oxygen. Under these conditions simple thoughts that once seemed instantaneous become prolonged feats of concentration. Such responses indicate that our assessment of the passage of time also depends on the global functioning of the cortex. This essentially means that our awareness of time differs radically from our awareness of, for example, touch, vision or thought, which are each a product of a particular area of cortex. it seems that the passage of time is dependent on the global functioning of the cerebral cortex - a view supported by experiments that show that estimates of real time in the order of minutes are disrupted by rotating a strong magnetic field counterclockwise around the head. The absence of a distinct area of cortex devoted to the representation of time means that we can know time only as a phenomenon that accompanies the majority of our experiences.

The cortex has long been known to produce regular electrical oscillations or brain waves. The frequency and magnitude of our brainwaves reflect the state of our cerebral cortex, enabling us to differentiate between death, deep sleep, dream sleep and various levels of wakefulness (*The Cortex in Sleep and Dreams*: Chapter 2: Section 7). During sleep, sensory information is less able to influence the cortex and so does not penetrate consciousness. This alone may well account for the loss of time perception because our cognitive registration of chronological time seems to depend upon timing cues derived from the senses, amongst which the cortex's auditory representations are most influential. As we will see later, these timing cues are delivered from the auditory cortex to a particular part of the human mind by a special brain pathway called the dorsal stream (*The Origins of Hypothesis – The Abstract* Mind: Chapter 3: Section 3). This probably accounts for why, in sensory deprivation, there is often a complete loss of our cognitive ability to estimate the passage of time. In the absolute silence of the isolation tank, in the emptiness of meditation or in the depths of night, the passage of time becomes less and less discernable. In such circumstances significant blocks of time simply disappear as though they never existed.

Continuity and the Moment in Consciousness
"An instant realization sees endless time.
Endless time is as one moment.
When one comprehends the endless moment,
He realizes the person who is seeing it."
Zen Koan No 47, Three Gates of Tosotsu, complied by Wumen Hui-K'ai (1183-1260). Chinese Zen Master.

Consciousness seems like a continuous process. Time appears to pass smoothly. Only the clock divides it into seconds, minutes and hours. Yet everywhere in our speech and mythologies we find evidence for the momentary nature of experience.

Momentary perhaps, but when we ask how long these moments last, mythology reminds us of the importance of circumstance. Thus, in his description of Hell, Dante tells us how the suffering of its denizens is so intense that each moment stretches into eternity. The Buddha used the word *vinnanasota* to refer to the streaming of consciousness, though he too was aware of the momentary nature of experience. In fact, it has been said of Buddha that he could detect 28,000 events in what, to a normal person, is but a single moment. Thus, even in the ancient mythologies of Buddhism the moment was seen to be of such significance that its fine resolution was thought to be indicative of the enlightened state.

What is at issue here is not the validity of the Perfect One's ability to resolve time but the embodiment, into metaphorical form, of the realization that human consciousness is not a continuous process. Human consciousness is made up of moments. In the same way that a motion picture is really a series of individual pictures, research has shown that consciousness is actually made up of distinct, measurable fragments of time. The very word, *moment*, exists only to enable us to better describe to others the essentially digital nature of our experiences.

Human consciousness moves from one instant to the next. At any instant, all those parts of the cortex that are active contribute to our momentary experience. Yet so familiar are we with the momentary nature of consciousness that we rarely notice it. To realize it we have to watch very carefully. When we do, sooner or later something, only transiently perceived, fills a moment of our awareness and then is gone. Given the momentary nature of consciousness it is not surprising that the footsteps of so many ghosts are fleeting.

Competition and Attention in Consciousness
"The function of consciousness is to preserve the organism, and it succeeds because it is an organ of attention and intention. ….. The conscious organism tends towards apprehension of the external world in attention and of the future world in intention." Edwin G. Boring (1886-1968). American Psychologist and Historian of Experimental Psychology.

Within the brain consciousness is in great demand. Within our brain different lines of information engage in a never-ending competition for access to the neural circuitry of our cortex from whence awareness is possible. It matters not whether something is in the mental, emotional or physical realm, its embodiment into cortical activity, and so its admittance to consciousness, is not a *fait accompli*. Whether signals arise from the organs of our viscera, or whether they arise from our external sense organs, there is only a small chance that they will reach consciousness. Indeed, this explains why we are astoundingly unaware of the details of most of our movements and even many of our more prolonged behavioral repertoires. Beneath consciousness our brain automatically accomplishes many things that we take for granted, so much so that, as we shall see, some have questioned whether consciousness is essential for human behavior.

Our thoughts, emotions and moods are responsible for our *intention* but what enters our awareness is ultimately what commands our *attention*. In very young children, as in the lower mammals, attention is largely driven by the cortex's visceroemotional centers, whereas in adult humans attention is powerfully controlled by the machinations of mind. We call the latter *directed attention* because, being directed by our thoughts, it carries a strong sense of intention. In contrast, we might refer to the form of attention driven by our visceroemotional centers, as *instinctual attention* (*Instinct and the Imagery of Dreams*: Chapter 2: Section 7).

By definition attentional systems focus on some things and omit others. However, even without its attentional systems the cortex has its own intrinsic mechanisms that limit the entry of new information. For example, when one part is highly active, the surrounding areas are inhibited – a phenomenon known as *surround inhibition*. Only during a *grand mal* epileptic seizure does this system break down. Normally the whole of cortex can never be synchronously active. Activity is always localized and consequently what enters our awareness is whatever experience arises from these islands of active cortex.

The surround inhibition that stops the whole cortex from lighting up at once, ensures that during normalcy, cortical activity is always patchy, the position of the patches being determined by our circumstances and our attentional focus. In any instant we have a "vision" (or Gestalt) of all these things that *synchronously* excite the cortex (*Constructing the Gestalt*: Chapter 4: Section 2). However, not only is it unnecessary to experience everything that is around us but to do so would be incompatible with the selectivity required for goal-orientated behavior. For example, it does not help to be distracted by a beautiful sunset when one is being stalked by a tiger. At least in normal states of consciousness, what enters our awareness is only a small part of what is actually available. In this, volition may or may not play a role as the things that do penetrate consciousness typically represent a circumstantially and historically determined selection from a vast and largely unseen whole. What gets in is only a small portion of what *is* - a portion defined entirely by the prevailing circumstances, our visceroemotional needs, our inherent personality and the life-long conditioning of our mind. In plotting our path in life, the allocation of cortex to different areas of Brodmann, especially those that support thought, determines very much what we will observe and what we will miss along the way.

Drugs and the Control of Consciousness

"Just a little pin prick….. There is no pain you are receding,
A distant ship smoke on the horizon,
You are only coming through in waves,
Your lips move but I can't hear what you're saying…."
David Gilmour and Roger Waters, English Singers, Songwriters and Muscians. From: *Comfortably Numb.* In: *The Wall.* Pink Floyd Music Publishers, London, 1979.

The most telling indicator of the biological origins of consciousness is the very clear and almost instantaneous effect of neuroactive drugs. A drug is simply a chemical molecule that affects living tissue in some way. Virtually all drugs are compounds or molecules. Drug molecules are usually composed of stereotyped aggregates of many atoms of elements such as carbon, hydrogen, nitrogen and oxygen.

Each molecule of any particular drug has a certain characteristic 3-dimensional structure or shape. If it affects the nervous system then we call it a neuroactive drug. If the drug affects our moods, emotions or thoughts we call it a psychoactive, or psychotrophic, drug.

The introduction of neuroactive drugs into the brain interferes with the communication between the nerve cells of our cortex and in so doing alters our consciousness. Drugs can change our sensations, emotions, moods, perceptions, thoughts and patterns of movement. Some drugs inhibit cortical nerve cells and completely abolish consciousness. If such effects are reversible, these drugs can be useful as general anesthetics.

If particle physics, mathematics, magic or mysticism holds the key to the mystery of consciousness, then how is it that drugs which affect the communication between cortical nerve cells over periods of seconds, minutes and even hours, also affect consciousness over the same time periods? A physicist friend of mine once remarked that it is one thing to use physics to analyze apparently mystical phenomena, but quite another to take a mystical view of physics. The same can be said for the science of life. Consciousness is its own mystery - a mystery that seems to be squarely placed in the biological world. That other mysteries exist does not invite us to seek relationship between apparently unconnected domains of human wonderment.

The Content and Phenomenon of Consciousness
"Existence precedes essence." Jean-Paul Sartre (1905–1980). French Existentialist Philosopher and Author.

The distinction between the *phenomenon of consciousness* and the *contents of consciousness* was one of the earliest and most profound insights of the ancient Hindu sages. It was they who chose to see in Lord Shiva (or Siva), the symbolic representation of *unmanifest consciousness*. In so doing they established a distinction between consciousness, as an intrinsic property of the quiescent cerebral cortex, and the contents of consciousness that arise from cortical activity. When Shiva dances he takes on the form of Nataraja, the Cosmic Dancer. In Hindu mythology, Nataraja represents the endless re-incarnation of the cosmic energy that revitalizes consciousness (Figure 2.3). In the science of consciousness, Nataraja represents the oxygenated blood, which is drawn to active areas of the cortex there to provide metabolic energy to this biological substrate of human experience. It is said that when Shiva dances the Universe sings. Translated from metaphor to reality this essentially means that when the cortex is active, consciousness happens and the processes of life and experience are again one.

The silhouette of Nataraja is said to be identical in form to the sign for Aum or Om. Om is also the beginning of the Buddhist incantation *Om mani padme hum*, "The jewel is in the lotus" that adorns the prayer wheels and temple gongs throughout Tibet, Nepal, Bhutan, Burma, northern India and much of the free East. As a word, Om is perhaps the most significant term in eastern mysticism. Through its presence in the image of Nataraja, Om symbolizes the apparent vastness of human consciousness, manifesting as the universal mantra, the mystical Sanskrit symbol for the

"Inexpressible Absolute", the last word to be uttered after which there can be only silence, the path through which the individual self (the ego) surrenders to the all-pervading self (*Atman*) and the creative sound that if properly intonated is said to contain all sounds.

Shiva is the most powerful God in the Hindu trinity of Brahma, Shiva and Vishnu. In associating the universal gift of consciousness with Shiva the sages of old expressed their vision of consciousness as the greatest gift of humankind. There can be little doubt that they came to this conclusion through long years of meditation wherein the experience of empty, yet awake, consciousness enabled them to see the tremendous significance of simple awareness to human life. The aspiration to know empty consciousness was born in India and today it remains, as ever it will, India's greatest contribution to human understanding.

Chapter 2 - The Dissection of Consciousness

The Composition of the Cerebral Cortex

"The brain is a monstrous, beautiful mess. Its billions of nerve cells-called neurons-lie in a tangled web that displays cognitive powers far exceeding any of the silicon machines we have built to mimic it". William F. Allman, American Author. From: *Apprentices of Wonder. Inside the Neural Network Revolution.* Bantam Books, New York, 1989.

The human cerebral cortex forms a thin mantle of gray matter that completely covers the two cerebral hemispheres. Putting aside the very large variation in the size of the human brain, the surface area of one hemisphere is typically about 900 to 1200 sq cm. This means that flattened out, the cortex of one hemisphere would cover a square with sides of between 30 and 45cm. To accommodate this large sheet of tissue inside the skull, the surfaces of the hemispheres are convoluted. Each outward convolution is called a *gyrus* and each inward one, a *sulcus*.

Even ignoring individual differences in brain size, it is as difficult to accurately count the total number of nerve cells in the human cortex as it is to estimate the number of stars in our galaxy. In the cortex everything is so incredibly tiny while in the galaxy everything is so far away. Various methods suggest that the number of nerve cells in the cortex of one hemisphere is somewhere between 16,000,000,000 and 32,000,000,000. It is far easier to accurately estimate the number nerve cells in a very small volume, say one cubic millimeter, of cortex. However, again, when this is done different results are obtained from different areas of cortex. Thus, in humans we can only say that each cubic millimeter of cortex contains between 30,000 and 60,000 nerve cells, each of which make an average of 10,000 connections, or *synapses*, to other nerve cells.

It has been shown that while the volume of cortex in women and men is, on average, identical, men have 13% more nerve cells than women. Another way of saying this is that in women, a greater volume of cortex is allocated to the processes of nerve cells that form the interconnections between cortical neurons. This politically inappropriate data underscores fundamental differences between the cortices of men and women and researchers were quick to point out that even though the male cortex has more functional units (nerve cells), the female cortex contains more complex interconnections.

Magnified, the cortex is like a huge city wherein all the individuals are highly dependent upon one another. Yet at any moment, each citizen may have a significant role to play. Each neurotransmitter, each part of each nerve cell, the molecular and the microscopic, all make contributions to this realm of knowing. There are so many dynamic elements contributing to the whole that the state of the cerebral cortex is never static. In fact, at any instant the state of your cerebral cortex is never absolutely identical to its state in any other instant. That we can recognize particular states of consciousness (eg. fear, fatigue, attentiveness etc.), even in different individuals, is a strong testimony to the existence of tight organizational constraints within this vast and potentially chaotic network of nerve cells.

The Mapping of Consciousness

"The brain is a tissue. It is a complicated, intricately woven tissue, like nothing else we know of in the universe, but it is composed of cells, as any tissue is. They are, to be sure, highly specialized cells, but they function according to the laws that govern any other cells. Their electrical and chemical signals can be detected, recorded and interpreted and their chemicals can be identified; the connections that constitute the brain's woven feltwork can be mapped. In short, the brain can be studied, just as the kidney can." David H. Hubel (born: 1926). American Neurophysiologist and Nobel Laureate.

Even on the surface two human cortices never look exactly the same. The position and size of most gyri and sulci vary too much between individuals to enable them to be used to accurately localize functionally specific areas of the cortex in different people. Brodmann's maps were therefore an important step in reliably linking function to a particular area of the cortex. The only drawback was that in order to define the boundaries of his areas the subject's brain had to be sliced up and the slices studied under the microscope. Improvements in brain imaging may mean that one may soon be able to have one's cortex mapped without first being dead.

Since the identification of Brodmann's areas, he and others have described the cytoarchitecture of the cortex of the great apes, monkeys and a variety of non-primate mammals such as the dog, cat and rat. Of most significance is that no mammals so far examined have areas not found in the human cortex. However, although each of these animals has many of the areas of Brodmann that are found in humans, only the apes and the more behaviorally advanced monkeys have virtually all. The primordia of each domain of human consciousness are therefore clearly present within the cortex of at least some of these higher primates. It is of course important to remember that even the brain of the apes is less than half the average size of the human brain. All of Brodmann's areas are therefore much smaller in the most behaviorally advanced, nonhuman primates.

At the time when Brodmann published his work, little was known about the functions of different parts of the cerebral cortex. Nevertheless systematic analyses of the effects of injury to different parts of the human cortex slowly led to hypotheses on the function of some of Brodmann's areas. Moreover, the identification of Brodmann's areas in animals has enabled them to be studied experimentally, providing information and insights critical to the interpretation of data on human brain injuries. In this way the maps of Brodmann's areas have become charts of cortical specialization that can be used by brain scientists and neurologists to voyage within what was once the no-mans land of human consciousness.

For most of the first half of the 20th century the world was torn apart by global war. By the time the Second World War began there had already been some significant advances in the brain sciences. The ravages of war provided neurologists of the time with tens of thousands of young and otherwise healthy patients from whose shattered brains they could begin to deduce much about the organization of human consciousness. The Russian neurologist, Aleksandr Romanovich Luria was ideally situated to study the never-ending stream of Russian soldiers with traumatic head injuries. Inevitably he would encounter patients with very confined brain damage and from their symptoms be able to gain a relatively clear appreciation of what the damaged area might have done within the healthy intact brain. Often such patients seemed superficially normal, sometimes barely aware of their own deficits, which were only revealed by very specific tests. There were no brain scanners in those days. For the damaged area to be accurately defined, the patient had first to die and be available for autopsy. Only after death could the extent of damage be assessed but ironically if damage to the cortex was confined to a small region, the patient generally lived. Nevertheless, Luria was able to relate the often-enigmatic constellations of deficits to damage located in specific areas of the cortex, interpreting his findings by consulting the substantial body of published work on the cerebral cortex of animals. The publication in 1962 of his life's work, *Higher Cortical Functions in Man* marked the beginning of a new chapter of human understanding wherein the most subtle of human experiences would become accessible to research through the then still fledgling science of consciousness. What could previously be divined only by prolonged introspection, portrayed in the plastic arts or alluded to in the nuances of poetry and elegant prose, would soon be revealed by the dissection of the organizational principles of higher consciousness.

The Micro-organization of Consciousness
"Swiftly the brain becomes an enchanted loom, where millions of flashing shuttles weave a dissolving pattern - always a meaningful pattern - though never an abiding one." Charles S. Sherrington (1857-1952). Pioneer of Neurophysiology and Nobel Laureate.

Philosophers and mystics have always been permitted to talk about consciousness. Not so the scientist. The topic seemed too esoteric to approach rationally, too all pervading to access through experimentation and too indefinable to warrant research funding. In both their nature and training, scientists are given to systematically and precisely analyzing confined problems. The larger issues of life typically have too many indefinite aspects to be entertained by the scientific mind. Wherever subjective or even human experience is involved, the scientist is both naturally inclined and trained to be deeply skeptical. Thus, although subjective experience has almost certainly provided the kernel of inspiration to almost every neuroscientist, as a group they remained, until quite recently, tediously unwilling to relate their results to the comprehension of human awareness. Nevertheless in the postwar years the grandparents of today's neuroscientists continued to accumulate information on the localization across the cortex of what they were obliged to call "function". This only changed when, inspired by new technologies, a new generation of brain scientists was at last able to directly relate activity in the human brain to even sedentary activities such as thought. Today our newfound ability to study the seat of consciousness challenges neuroscientists to unite their unique visions of the brain's most enigmatic functions with the passionate and almost ethereal life of a large proportion of the rest of humanity.

As well as providing a very large database for the study of neurological deficits, the Second World War brought quantum leaps in electronics and information technology, fields that are critical to research on the brain. The most significant technological advance was the computer. Out of World War II were born the first attempts to construct an "intelligent" machine, a computer specifically designed to decode the messages from the German Enigma machines. Six such machines were reserved for encoding the most secret orders of the German High Command. The allies captured one machine, taking care to replace it with a replica, before spiriting the original back to England. Only through the efforts of the brilliant mathematician Alan Turing in creating the predecessor of the first true computer, could Enigma's millions of combinations have been deciphered. Awarded the OBE in 1954, Turing chose suicide as an escape from a court directive that forced him to submit to hormone injections as a "cure" for his homosexuality. But what he set in place was to revolutionize our understanding of consciousness. The theoretical frameworks surrounding his vision have been critical to comprehending the modular nature of cortex, while technically computers would eventually control and run the intricate machines, which today enable us to see into the living brain. Turing's lectures on machine intelligence would provide great impetus for the new field of *artificial intelligence*. The conspicuous gulf that still exists between machine "intelligence" and human intelligence has done much to focus attention upon the nature and origin of consciousness.

The war also facilitated the development of electronic amplifiers, oscilloscopes and all manner of measuring and recording devices that could be easily adapted to the study of the brain. It was this emergent technology, which in the early 1950s enabled an American scientist, Vernon Mountcastle, to begin studying the responses of small groups of cortical nerve cells by inserting very thin, insulated needle electrodes into the cerebral cortex of the monkey. Through the tiny (around 1/1000 mm), exposed tips of these microelectrodes, Mountcastle was able to record the minute (typically 1/2000 volt) electrical impulses of single cortical nerve cells. He chose to study an area of Brodmann known as area 3b, an area that runs in a transverse strip across the middle of each hemisphere and elaborates the experience of simple touch.

At that time area 3b was one of several of Brodmann's areas that seemed to have a definite "function". Before Mountcastle, others had shown that touching the head or face activated nerve cells in the lateral part of area 3b, while touching the feet and legs affected the part of area 3b closest to the midline of the brain. Touching the hands activated parts of area 3b that are between the representation of the arms and the face. Thus, information from the skin activates a transverse strip of cortex such that the body surface is represented as a small figurine with the head positioned laterally and the toes medially. In the human cortex this topographical representation of the human body surface in neuronal activity is called the *homunculus*. Because the skin is "projected" upon area 3b in a precise point-to-point manner it is said to be *somatotopically represented* (*The Origin of Animal Powers*: Chapter 2: Section 2).

To Mountcastle, the somatotopic organization of Brodmann's area 3b was simply background information. As he began his experiment his mind was focused on an entirely different level of understanding. What he was seeking was knowledge of *how* this sheet of nervous tissue that so conspicuously held, and still holds, the secret of consciousness, actually works. If he could extract some principles of cortical circuitry for something as simple as touch, perhaps he or those that would follow him could come to understand the operational principles underlying all aspects of consciousness. Using a specially constructed microdrive, Mountcastle inserted his microelectrode perpendicular to the surface of the cortex. It being impossible to do such experiments on humans, he made his observations on the cortex of anesthetized monkeys, choosing to work in the part of area 3b that responds to touching the hand.

As the tip of the microelectrode was driven through the cortex, it would pass within 1/10 of a millimeter (100 microns) of roughly 2,000 nerve cells. Brushing the skin of the monkey's hand, Mountcastle sought a point in the microelectrode's path where the impulses of one nerve cell were much larger than the impulses of all others, indicating the proximity of this neuron to the electrode tip. At that point he stopped advancing the microelectrode and proceeded to lightly tap or brush the skin of the monkey's hand, seeking out the exact area that activated the nerve cell - an area known as the *receptive field* of the neuron. The receptive field of the neuron would be carefully plotted on a drawing of the monkey's hand along with the depth of the microelectrode tip below the surface of the cortex. The microelectrode was then driven further into the cortex in search of another responsive and isolatable nerve cell, which would be mapped and documented in the same way.

Almost immediately there emerged a great truth about the biology of consciousness. In a single vertical track through the cortex it was usually possible to map the responses of about 5 or 6 different nerve cells. Each cell was recorded at a different depth from the cortical surface. What was extraordinary was that, in any single penetration all responsive cells were excited by roughly the same small area of skin. When Mountcastle withdrew the microelectrode and moved it to a point a few millimeters away from the first track, he found that all the nerve cells he encountered again had concentric receptive fields, although at this new recording location, their receptive fields were focused on a different part of the hand. Instantly it became apparent that one small patch of skin had exclusive access to all the nerve cells within a very tiny volume of the cerebral cortex with a surface area roughly the diameter of the ball in a ballpoint pen. Many careful experiments showed that this volume of cortex had the form of a hexagon-shaped column about 0.5 mm across that extended throughout the depth of the cortex. These functional units became known as the *cortical columns* or *modules*.

As a theory, the columnar organization of the cortex met with great resistance. In Mountcastle's words, "When the general hypothesis of columnar organization was first presented....it was met with disbelief by almost all neuroscientists.... The classical idea of laminar organization of the cortex was dominant, and suggestions for functional specificity for each of the cellular layers [of the cortex] were frequently made, eg. that the supragranular [upper] layers are specialized for 'psychic' functions" (Mountcastle, 1997). Before long, however, the modular organization of the cerebral cortex began to be elucidated within the visual, auditory, motor and prefrontal regions. Although, in these different locations, the cortical modules are not all exactly the same size and shape, modular organization is now accepted as a fundamental principle of the cortex's functional and structural architecture.

The information that arrives at a module determines its contribution to consciousness. Because modules receiving similar information are located in the same area of Brodmann, the function of any module, in both consciousness and cortical mechanism, is determined by where it is situated across the cortex. Modules in area 3b respond to the skin, modules in the visual cortex respond to visual stimuli. But no matter where a module is it clearly makes a unitary contribution to consciousness.

To look in more detail at what a module must do let us use the modules of area 3b as a simple example. In a human such a module might contain around 45,000 nerve cells. Obviously, these neurons do not all do exactly the same thing. For example, not all respond in the same way to touching the appropriate area of skin. This has led theoreticians to suggest that the nerve cells in a single module are grouped into discrete, though interactive, networks called subsets. These subsets form minicolumns within physical confines of the main module. Some estimate that the number of neurons in a subset may be as small as 100, although given the number of nerve cells in a module, this estimate seems to be rather low, particularly as some neurons in each module are almost certainly interconnected with neurons in different minicolumns. Nevertheless, within a single module, each subset, network, or minicolumn is considered to serve a particular task such as retaining a simple record (or memory trace) of past inputs to, or outputs from, the module, connecting the module to either lower parts of the brain or other parts of the cortex, the subconscious or mechanistic processing of information and, of course, the elaboration of awareness. This last, and for present purposes, most significant minicolumn, has been called the *subset for consciousness*.

The idea that each module contains one neural network that is the subset for consciousness, gains some support from studies of the responses of single cortical nerve cells. In all such studies, some cells, and only some cells, show activity patterns that crudely mimic what we actually feel under similar stimulus conditions. Thus it seems likely that only when certain nerve cells, that are presumably part of the subset for consciousness, are activated, do we have the experience that reflects the information flowing into the host module.

Alongside the idea of a discrete subset for consciousness, it is necessary to consider another aspect of conscious experience. This arises from the demonstration that we only have an experience if the part of cortex contributing to it is sufficiently active. In mechanistic terms there are two alternative ways by which an experience may be evoked. In the first, the activity in all the neurons composing a particular subset for consciousness merely increases as the stimulus (eg. touch) intensity increases. Only when some *threshold activity level* is reached does the original stimulus become an experience. In the second, any single neuron either responds or remains silent and with increasing stimulus intensity all that changes is the number of responsive neurons. In this schema the original stimulus only reaches awareness when a *threshold number of neurons* become active. Either way increments in neural activity, in some mysterious manner, progressively approach a threshold level at which consciousness happens.

Modularity is found everywhere in the biological and physical world. The Earth is composed of particles, molecules are made up of atoms and atoms are composed of recognizable subatomic particles. In the living world trees are covered with identical leaves, the cochlea of our ear is formed from identical units that each code a different frequency of sound, our kidneys are made up of many filtration units called nephrons, and, of course, all living tissue is composed of cells. People are grouped into families, families into communities and communities into populations. The computer is based on modularity as is virtually every sophisticated electronic device. The cortex is a piece of biological engineering and as such it is perhaps not too surprising to find that its basic structure is also modular. The question is what does the activation of a single module elaborate within the void of otherwise empty consciousness?

When we talk of our experiences we usually refer to the complex scenarios of life. Such experiences reflect synchronous patterns of activity across many areas of our cerebral cortex. These patterns are momentary, ever changing and almost infinite in number. Thus, in any moment the experience one is having derives from a composite of many patches of above-threshold cortical activity. Usually many adjacent modules within an active patch of cortex contribute to an experience. Theoretically, however, the smallest patch of cortex capable of elaborating an experience must be the size of the surface area of a single module (about 0.2 mm^2 in area 3b). As the smallest neuronal aggregate that can elaborate an experience, the module can be regarded as the *elementary particle of consciousness*.

Under the conditions of sensory deprivation or deep meditation, a simple touch on the hand will do little more than excite a module or two within area 3b. In that moment we will experience a touch upon our hand, nothing more than this particle of consciousness, borne past us on the winds of time - an event that arouses a tiny spot on our vast cortex and in so doing brings the feeling of touch. A sensation has come from nowhere and departed to oblivion, leaving only a tiny footprint on the sands of consciousness. Other things may follow but in that moment there is only this single touch; a *unitary experience*, immune from any significance that might normally be imparted by association, interpretation and identification. Something indefinable stirs and calls to us from across the void of unmanifested consciousness. Yet when witnessed in dispassionate isolation, are not all elements of our knowing, be they images, interpretations, thoughts, emotions or ideas, like this simple touch? Realization of the intrinsic insignificance of all elements of consciousness is not only a truism born of the modular organization of the cortex but also one of the great lessons of meditative practice. No matter where it is in the cortex, a single active module can be regarded as giving rise to a unitary experience - an experience that is of itself, unreferenced to all others, and yet in the very nature of its insignificance, critically instructive about the nature of awareness.

The Allocation of Consciousness

"An expert is a man who has stopped thinking - he knows." Frank Lloyd Wright. (1867-1959). American Architect and Author.

It seems that human experience knows no bounds, that it is infinitely large. Through language, art and music we attempt both to form bonds with others and to observe and understand ourselves. By recognizing uniformity in experience we reinforce our allegiance with other human beings and the higher non-human primates. In so doing we are intuitively postulating that the repertoire of experiences we have is common to all other human beings and that we are, by heritage, part of an experiential whole, wherein, above the day-to-day matters of survival, we may know the ultimate panacea of belonging. This intuition of commonality is absolutely correct, in so far as irrespective of the size of the brain and its cortex, every healthy human has the same areas of Brodmann. To some degree all healthy humans have available to them all realms of consciousness elaborated by the archetypal human cortex. This does not mean that the prominence of any domain of experience is even remotely the same in different people. Indeed, because the size of individual areas of Brodmann varies enormously between individuals quite the opposite appears to be the case. Moreover, like the size of the brain, the size of Brodmann's areas is under the control of genes. Consequently, the politically correct, humanistically persuasive view that all humans are the same, is again, conspicuously incorrect. Unless they are identical twins that share the same genes, even members of the same family differ widely in their aptitudes, perceptions, emotions, moods and their dominant form of intelligence. Inherent diversity and not uniformity is the key to understanding the human psyche in relation to the astounding variety of human behavior. During the 200,000 years since the evolution of anatomically modern humans, the cortex must have been subject to intense selective modification in the endless tailoring of the behavior of migrating waves of humans to the nuances of a wide variety of ever-changing physical, biological and climatic circumstances.

The bigger a given area of Brodmann, the larger the number of modules it will contain. Just for argument's sake let us pretend that all modules are like those identified by Mountcastle in area 3b, where each module occupies an area of cortex of about 0.2 mm^2. If we accept that the surface area of one hemisphere is between 90,000 and 120,000 mm^2 then we can calculate that there is space for between 450,000 and 600,000 such modules. On this basis we can say that there is between 450,000 and 600,000 elementary particles of consciousness in each hemisphere that are grouped into 48 areas of Brodmann. If the cortex was divvied up equally among all the domains of consciousness, each of Brodmann's areas could contain between 9,375 and 12,500 of these modules. Under these circumstances each area of Brodmann would have an equal voice in consciousness. However, one has only to glance at any diagram of the brain showing Brodmann's areas to realize that very different amounts of cortex are allocated to different areas. Similarly, one has only to observe human talents and human awareness to see that ability and consciousness follow suit. In the genetically controlled process of allocating modules to particular areas of Brodmann, we are all given certain gifts and yet denied significant ability in other realms. For example, in different individuals the area of cortex allocated to vision can vary by a factor of three and the same principle holds true for other functions such as touch or the generation of movements, emotions or thoughts. Most importantly, as this process is under the control of genes, it will clearly be powerfully influenced by inheritance.

This is not to say that training has no effect on how well we do something. Training can increase the complexity of a cortical area, presumably by tuning the neuronal circuits within the relevant modules. Training can thus enable a particular area of Brodmann or part thereof, to operate at a more sophisticated level. There is, however, little evidence that training can radically increase the number of modules available for a particular function. Compared to the genetic specification of the size and shape of Brodmann's areas in our cortex, training has little effect upon our destiny. Where social insects like ants and bees manifest a variety of behavioral and physical forms, the better to achieve specific tasks for the benefit of all, the human species (and possibly all mammals) meets the challenge of the subdivision of labor by an inherent variation in the size of Brodmann's areas. You can learn to play a musical instrument but you cannot learn to be a Chopin or a McCartney. The physically gifted sportswoman, the emotionally intelligent psychologist, the teacher and the masterful theoretician all arise from this source that is the origin of the special gifts of the individual. There are visual people, haptic (touch) people, auditory people, olfactory people, sporty people, thoughtful people and emotional people, just to name a few. The overwhelming evidence is that all of these individuals are the way they are largely because of the genetically controlled allocation of modules to specific areas of their cerebral cortex.

The Origin of Animal Powers
"The Gods of the Ethiopians are dark-skinned and snub-nosed; the Gods of the Thracians are fair and blue-eyed; if oxen could paint, their Gods would be oxen." Xenophanes of Colophon (c. 570-480 BC). Greek Philosopher and Religious Critic.

Wherever an area of Brodmann has expanded it has been accompanied by an increase in the number of modules rather than a change in the size of individual modules. Again, in the words of Mountcastle (1997), "It is remarkable that the size of columns is preserved in evolution: primitive primates like the tree shrew, with a small prefrontal cortex, have callosal columns that are the same width as….[those] of macaque monkeys with a 10 times larger prefrontal surface area. This is compatible with the idea that [in the process of evolution] the cortex expands with the addition of new functional columns of the same size." Through the expansion of individual areas the computing power of that particular domain of consciousness is increased (*The Construction of Mind*: Chapter 3: Section 8). Clearly, in the evolution of the cerebral cortex, natural selection has operated on genes that control the size of particular areas of Brodmann, rather than the size of the modules within any area.

The behavior of all animals is necessarily tailored to the niche they have evolved to occupy. It follows that some areas of Brodmann must be of greater significance to some species than to others. Moreover, not all mammals have all the areas of Brodmann found in humans. When an area is completely absent, it is reasonable to conclude that the species in question lacks both the ability and the expression in consciousness, of whatever is handled by that area in the cortex of other mammals. We may thus speak of the *modular power* of a particular area of Brodmann - a factor dependent on the size of that area in a species compared to its size in others.

It is not unusual for certain animal species to be regarded as spiritually significant because they have unique abilities that enable them to outperform all other species in a particular domain of existence. In native societies these animals are chosen as totems while in western nations they appear as national emblems. In religious mythology, these animals are often called upon to manifest their totem powers. The massive strength of the now extinct cave bears is considered by some to be part of the idolatry of the powerfully built Neanderthals. The sure sightedness of the eagle appears repeatedly in the legends of the North America Indians. In Hindu myth the intelligence of the monkey is embodied in Hanuman the great Monkey General of the Upanishads. In the mythologizing of extremes of performance manifested in the animal world, the seers of many cultures were unwittingly acknowledging the specialized expansion of the areas of the cortex that serve those aspects of behavior. At the highest level of the vertebrate brain, the cortex has undergone continuous modification by natural selection of behavior patterns that enable a species to survive in a given environment. If we posit that in higher mammals, high levels of cortical activity are accompanied by an experience of the information flowing into the active areas, then we might also posit that animal powers, embodied into the spirit world of hunter-gatherer and of native peoples, are an obtuse means of referring to the experiential world of each species.

A comparison of the cortex of the cat and the raccoon provide a comparative example of modular power. Even though the cortex of the cat is approximately the same size as the cortex of the raccoon, the area of cortex excited by touch in the raccoon is 5 times the size of the touch representation in the cat. Consequently, the modular power of the raccoon's somatosensory cortex far exceeds the modular power of the cats.

The raccoon often works at night, searching for its food by pushing its forepaws under fallen leaves and litter. In contrast, the cat uses its whiskers and not its forepaw to explore the world. The skin of the raccoon forepaw monopolizes more of the raccoon's cortex than any other input and so may be considered as a dominant element of raccoon consciousness. The sensitivity of the forepaw to touch is of far more significance to the raccoon than it is to the cat and the relative modular power of touch in both species follows suit. In the court of consciousness the skin of the forepaw and indeed the overall sense of touch will speak with more voices in the raccoon than it does in the cat.

Because of the large amount of cortex allocated to representing the skin on the raccoon's paw, it is very likely that the sensitivity of the skin on its paw exceeds that of any other patch of skin anywhere in the animal kingdom. Other animals show radically different somatosensory specializations that again are specifically tailored to the niche they occupy. For example, like the raccoon, the star-nose mole also eats grubs and insects burrowing through the earth with its strong claws. Unlike the raccoon, it feels for these tiny wriggling forms, not with its paws, which are specialized for digging, but with its bizarre, radially segmented, stellate nose. In this animal a very large area of cortex is dedicated to representing tactile information from the skin of the nose. The rat is different again. Even more than the cat, the rat uses its exquisitely sensitive whiskers, the so-called mystacial vibrissae, to guide its every movement. So important are the whiskers to the rat that approximately half its somatosensory cortex is allocated to their representation whereas the skin of its forepaws, like that of its nose, activates only a very small area of cortex.

It is possible to draw a picture of these three mammals according to the way their body surface is represented in the cortex. The resultant drawings are gross distortions of their true body form but accurate representations of the sensitivity of their skin. The *ratunculus, molunculus* and *raccoonunculus* are essentially iconic representations of how these animals would sense the size of different parts of their body on the basis of their cutaneous sensation. Thus, in the rat, the whiskers would dominate cutaneous sensibility, while in the star-nose mole and the raccoon the skin of the nose and the forepaw would dominate, respectively.

It is important to recognize that even with something as simple as the awareness of touch, neither the cortex nor consciousness accurately portrays physical reality. Instead what is represented in consciousness is related to the biological significance of any particular part of the body surface. Whether within the domain of touch, vision, hearing, olfaction, taste or movement or, as we shall see, thought, mood and emotion, the cortical representations are distorted in a manner that produces the special behavioral adaptations necessary for a species to compete successfully for a particular niche. The recognition of totem powers is essentially a means of symbolizing prominent aspects of animal and human behavior that have their origin in the increased allocation of cortex to areas of Brodmann that serve particular functions.

The Hand in Human Consciousness
"When I was a child I had a fever.
My hands felt just like two balloons."
David Gilmour and Roger Water, English Singers, Songwriters and Muscians.
From: *Comfortably Numb*. In: *The Wall*. Pink Floyd Music Publishers, London, 1979.

In the ascendancy of the primates it is the skin of the hand that enables the exploration and manipulation the immediate surroundings. This trend reached its zenith in modern humans who have a higher manual ability than any other species of mammal. Although not as sensitive as the raccoon's paw, the very high tactile sensitivity of the human hand is achieved by the allocation of a disproportionately large amount of the somatosensory cortex to the small areas of skin covering the fingers and thumb. Similarly, our incredible manual abilities are likewise achieved by the allocation of a disproportionately large amount of motor cortex (Brodmann's area 4) to the control of hand movements. Only the lips, tongue and genitals have a tactile sensitivity and somatosensory representation approaching those of the hand. However, the prominence of the hand in human consciousness is not confined to the sense of

61

touch. The hand is also powerfully represented in several areas of the cortex devoted to visual perception. Thus, it is rare that an hour passes during which our hands are not part of our visual field. Across the human brain only the face is more widely represented than the hand. As an icon of human dexterity the hand finds a place within our visual system from whence it gains access to the mind where it enjoys a symbolic and functional significance of a magnitude challenged only by the importance of the human face.

The hand is everywhere in the affairs of humans. We shake hands as a sign of trust. In some religions, the laying on of hands is a common way of expressing religious unity. In the Indian tradition of *suttee* (from Sanskrit *satW* meaning 'faithful wife'), a wife who survived her husband was obliged to throw herself upon his funeral pyre, leaving only her handprints as a testimony to her existence. Many fundamentalist Muslim societies still cut off the hand of convicted thieves, a practice made all the more barbaric by the participation of doctors who have presumably sworn to devote their training to the service of healing. Handprints are found amidst the earliest surviving art, the cave paintings of the Paleolithic peoples of Europe. In numerous cultures the hand is used to execute significant elements of ritual dance. When spoken language fails, the hand is the basis of sign language. The hand abounds in mythology and religious iconography. The hands of the Buddha signify various aspects of his teachings. Deities in both Hinduism and in Buddhism are often shown as possessing a multitude of hands. The extreme sensitivity of the hand is realized in the image of Christ, nailed through his hands to the cross. Finally, second only to the face, the apparition of the hand is a common entity in altered states of consciousness. Though constituting only a small part of our body, the hand is of paramount significance in our day-to-day life, in our explorations of extrapersonal space and thus, in our consciousness.

The prominence of the hand in art and religious iconography results from its prominence in somatosensory, motor and visual areas of the cortex. It is probable that if our skin was represented in the cortex in the same way as the rat or the star-nose mole, we might find our religious iconography and mythology filled with pictures of our whiskers or our noses, respectively. Nor would this seem in the least strange to us for it would emerge naturally as a consequence of the enhanced cortical representation of these parts of the body surface over all others.

Chapter 3 - The Dawn of Consciousness

A New Energy

"…our brains are built to deal with events on radically different *timescales* from those that characterize evolutionary change. We are equipped to appreciate processes that take seconds, minutes, years or, at most, decades to complete. Darwinism is a theory of cumulative processes so slow that they take between thousands and millions of decades to complete." Richard Dawkins, English Evolutionary Biologist and Author. From: *The Blind Watchmaker,* Norton and Co., United Kingdom, 1986.

Consciousness is arguably the most astounding phenomenon of nature. To appreciate how something so enigmatic and yet so central to our existence came to be, requires some comprehension of the infinitely slow process through which natural selection fashioned the massive neuronal labyrinths of the human cortex from the first living cells.

Long ago there was a time when there was no life on the planet Earth. The world still boiled and froze, disturbed only by the forces of geology and the occasional intrusions of matter from outer space. The earliest undisputed fossil records indicate that bacteria and cyanobacteria came into existence between 4,000 and 3,500 mya. Before this, the Earth was a desolate planet spinning on its axis, its surfaces alternatively warmed by the furnaces of the sun and cooled under the pale reflected light of its single moon, biding its time until by some serendipity of molecular arrangement, there appeared a microscopic, replicating, membrane-bound form that was to be the predecessor of the living, replicating cell. To appreciate how long ago this happened, imagine that you are among the 0.003% of humans who currently live to be 100 years old. If you were to live one million years, you would have to live 10,000, one hundred-year, life times. To be born at the time when the first living cells appeared, you would have had to live 35 million (35,000,000), one hundred-year life times.

When people are unable to comprehend the evolution of life on Earth, it usually reflects their difficulty in envisaging time on a scale of tens of millions of human lifetimes. We are not equipped with a clock that works on such a time scale. Human consciousness is naturally attuned to birth, life and death. The infinity that precedes and follows our brief period of awareness can never be known directly. That great majority of people believe in the myth of divine creation reflects the difficulty the human mind has in comprehending time on a scale of hundreds of millions of years. Rather than struggle trying to comprehend such vast timescales many people choose to understand our existence in terms of tales that are so simplistic that they resemble the preoperational thoughts of little children. To grasp the void of cosmic time that separates the "now" from the origins of life, demands that we accept a level of personal and collective insignificance that is incompatible with most people's ego. Yet who could be so arrogant as to believe that they are more than dust passing on the winds of time? Is not each person just another struggling organism to be consumed by a few decades of life in the ceaseless battle for survival? Nothing can enable us to know, experientially, the passage of even one million years. When we journey beyond our origins, the timelessness of eternity and the timelessness of the moment are equally incomprehensible. By endowing us with the capacity to think, the human mind gives us the ability to identify abstract problems (eg. where do we come from?) and to propose potential solutions (eg. something called God made us). When confronted with time spans of many million years the human mind naturally grabs the nearest straw and in the absence of any insight or relevant knowledge, the nearest straw is usually a simplistic story that will not evoke social disharmony. Beginning in this way myths and legends give us psychological solace for our conspicuous mortality, yet in so doing dull the wonderment and independence that awaits he or she whose alert intellect cannot so easily turn away from the mysteries of life. As history repeatedly shows, blind faith in any story, ideology or person, ultimately translates into war and genocide. Myth can help us understand our relationships with each other and with nature, but to grasp what came before human consciousness requires us to exercise our intelligence.

Not until 1,500 mya did the first multicellular animals - the sponges, sea anemones and jellyfish – would make their appearance. Of these, even the most primitive "animals", the sponges, seem to have some semblance of a nervous system, responding over minutes to an electrical stimulus by altering the direction of the flow of the water current they generate for catching food. Rapidly conducting nerves and a nervous system capable of driving muscle contraction first arose in the sea anemones. The exploitation of bioelectrically-controlled coordination had begun. It would, however, take 1,500 million years for natural selection to transform the sponge's primitive neural networks into a vastly complex central nervous system under the command of the human cerebral cortex.

Life before Consciousness
[Animals] "are repetitious to the point of insanity." Edward O. Wilson (born: 1929). American Biologist and Author.

Animals without a cerebral cortex are everywhere. Flying, crawling, swimming, burrowing, stuck onto rocks, or spending their parasitic lives lolling about in the intestinal soup of a million hosts; the invertebrates, the animals without backbones, are a biological miracle of diversity. Each species of insect, worm or snail has its own special little niche within the universe of the gigantic. Yet, academic arguments aside, the invertebrates completely lack what we intuitively recognize as intelligence.

Invertebrates have even been referred to as "silicon chips with legs". Their seething communities are the products of a level of microengineering still unequalled in the great laboratories of the world. Observe the smallest ant you can find. It is almost invisible to the human eye. A tiny dot, borne along by 3 pairs of microscopic legs, each no thicker than a whisker, each containing a complete set of muscles that contract and relax in the coordinated cycle of steps generated and regulated by intricate assemblages of nerve cells housed in the protective walls of its minute articulated body. Those so inclined to speak of magic should think again, for were such "miracles" of nature not here for us to observe, they would certainly evade the imagination of even the most outrageous storyteller.

The invertebrate animals, the insects, spiders, crabs, snails, squid, sea anemones, jellyfish, worms, starfish and sponges do not have a cerebral cortex. In fact, they do not have a nervous system anything like that found in the vertebrate animals. In the most primitive invertebrates, the sea anemones and the jellyfish, the nervous system consists of small aggregates of nerve cells (ganglia) connected by a network of minute nerves. In segmented invertebrates such as the worms, insects, crustaceans and spiders, the ganglia are arranged in a line through the body cavity and are connected to one another by two nerve trunks. In the basic plan one ganglion is allocated to each segment, so that in the insects, there is one ganglion to control each of the three pairs of legs. At the front end is an especially complicated ganglion that constitutes a brain. Although the tiny brains of the invertebrates are completely unlike the brain of any vertebrate, they do indeed do some of the very basic things we might expect from a brain. Thus the invertebrate receives information from eyes (when present), the antenna and the sense organs of body and it "decides" whether to send out the commands that can switch the animal from one centrally generated stereotyped behavior (say walking) to another (say flight).

Not only do the invertebrates have a brain but they can also, in a sense, "learn". With prolonged training they will change their behavior in response to a stimulus. Yet this learning does not indicate consciousness, it indicates that the connections in their nervous system can be altered according to circumstances. The most advanced invertebrate is the octopus. With their sophisticated visual systems octopi can be trained to discriminate different visual symbols. Their behavior involves a set of complicated repertoires. The relationship between the stimulus and the animal's response can be modified but even in the octopus the basic patterns of movement that form the core of any response are always an automated selection of one of a fixed number of behavioral routines. Only in the fish, where the rudimentary precursor of the cortex, the pallium, holds the highest office, does the fixedness of behavior approach that of the invertebrates. Only with the evolution of the cortex of higher vertebrates did behavior become finely tuned to the nuances of present circumstances and the experiences of the distant past.

To fit inside the smallest ant, the invertebrate nervous system needed to be very small yet capable of generating quite complicated behavioral routines. From the operational standpoint, the number of nerve cells needed to produce a behavior had to be minimized. Whereas we humans have between 16 and 32 billion nerve cells just in our cortex, the invertebrates had to make do with a nervous system made up of only a few thousand. To achieve this each invertebrate nerve cell had to act much like an integrated circuit, performing a number of complex computational functions that in the vertebrate nervous system would utilize an entire network of nerve cells. In the invertebrates, single nerve cells are easily identifiable in different individuals of a species and play an exclusive and precise role in behavior. The computational functions of a nerve cell depend much upon the complexity of the branching of its dendrites and axon. Therefore in the invertebrates, a particular nerve cell must have the same branching structure in every member of the species. And indeed this is so, for in any species of invertebrate, individual nerve cells that serve a particular function have a characteristic structure that makes them recognizable in every other member of that species and even, to a lesser extent, in members of closely related species. Nerve cell X that innervates muscle Y will look the same and do the same thing in every individual American cockroach and we may find in both the grasshopper and the locust nerve cells that serve an almost identical function and look almost the same as their homologues in the cockroach.

It is not easy to teach new tricks to an invertebrate. When you become familiar with an invertebrate, there is nothing surprising. It is easy to outsmart a cockroach, because by our standards cockroaches are predictable. Few people would derive much interest from a pet cockroach or a pet worm. To humans, the antics of an invertebrate animal soon become repetitive and boring. Yet it is true that invertebrates can perform the most amazingly complex, though stereotyped, tasks; spiders build fantastic webs and honeybees use a complicated "dance" to convey to their companions the distance and direction of the flowers. But each component of these behavioral routines is preprogrammed; each is made up of what neurobiologists call a *fixed-action pattern*. The invertebrates seem to operate as incredibly contrived neural machines, which have been tailored and retailored over hundreds of millions of years to the requirements of very specific niches. For these very good reasons, few people believe that the invertebrates possess the gift of consciousness and most who have worked with them regard them as being run by genetically specified neural machinery.

The Birth of the Cerebral Cortex

"Even those who take consciousness seriously are often drawn to the idea of an evolutionary explanation of consciousness. After all, consciousness is such a ubiquitous and central feature that if seems that it must have arisen during the evolutionary process for a *reason*." David Chalmers, Australian Philosopher and Author. From: *The Conscious Mind – in Search of a Fundamental Theory*. Oxford University Press, New Yord, Oxford, 1996.

Amphioxus is a slimy fish-like creature up to 8 cm in length, commonly known as the *lancelet*. It has a mouth but no jaws and no eyes, living exclusively on microscopic organisms it filters from the water. Neither a true vertebrate nor a true invertebrate, *Amphioxus* is believed to be the transitional stage in evolution between these two great divisions of the animal kingdom. While it lacks the spinal column characteristic of the true vertebrates, its body is structured around a stout central rod or notochord. It is the notochord that defines *Amphioxus* as a member of the *Chordata*, a group containing all vertebrate animals. Chordates are found as fossils that are up to 590 million years old but estimates based on mutation rates indicate that they may have evolved almost 1,000 mya. The notochord of *Amphioxus* functions like the vertebrate spine, enabling the body to bend along a stiff yet pliable axis rather than collapse when the muscles of either side contract. In *Amphioxus* nature was experimenting with a new body plan, a plan that, for the first time, involved a rigid internal skeleton, a plan that was a forerunner of the first true vertebrates, the primitive fish.

The central nervous system of *Amphioxus* is a hollow cylinder of nervous tissue, closed at both ends. This *neural tube* runs the length of the animal and innervates the muscles of the body. During early embryonic growth, the nervous system of every species of vertebrate passes through all the stages of evolutionary development that are reached by those vertebrate species which are of more primitive form than itself. In the very early embryonic stages all vertebrates, including humans, have both a notocord and a neural tube. Thus, at the very earliest stage, the embryonic nervous system of all vertebrates, including humans, resemble the nervous system of *Amphioxus*. Nevertheless, in true vertebrates, early fetal development is accompanied by an expansion of the anterior end of the neural tube that slowly grows into a brain. This does not happen in *Amphioxus*. In *Amphioxus*, where the brain should be, all we can see is a slight swelling of the neural tube. *Amphioxus* virtually lacks a brain. Clearly the cerebral cortex did not exist at the very beginning of the vertebrate epoch. Like the invertebrates, *Amphioxus* does not have even the primordia of those neural tissues that we know are required for consciousness.

The first true vertebrates are thought to have arisen from a mutation of the genome of *Amphioxus*. Their fossilized remains tell us they were here in the Ordovician (505-438 mya) or even the Cambrian (543-505 mya) period. Unlike *Amphioxus* they had a primordial skull sufficiently large to house a tiny brain. Unfortunately, we know little of their habits for their brains are turned to dust while the niches they once inhabited have long since disappeared or become someone else's home. We can only deduce their behavior from living vertebrates that resemble them in their body plan.

The most primitive vertebrates still living on the Earth are the cyclostomes and the hagfish. Like *Amphioxus* these similarly slimy creatures lack jaws. Unlike *Amphioxus* they have a vertebral column, a skull and a small, structurally simple brain on one end of their spinal cords. In these ways the early fish were a great advance over *Amphioxus*. Yet still, in the cyclostomes there is no mantle of gray matter resembling even a primitive version of the cerebral cortex. The anterior end of the cyclostome brain is covered in white matter. Only beneath this sheet of nervous processes (axons) is there a thin sheet of gray matter called the *pallium*, a word meaning "cloak". This pallium is the highest level of the cyclostomes brain. If we look at a series of brains from the fish, *Amphibia*, reptiles and mammals, we can see that over the last 500 million years of vertebrate existence, it is this pallium that slowly moves to the outer surface of the brain, increasing in size and complexity until it takes on the internal architecture of the cerebral cortex. Over the hundreds of millions of years since the age when *Amphioxus* was the most sophisticated organism on Earth, mutations created a progression of lifeforms with a larger and more sophisticated pallium or cerebral cortex, fostering in each new species, an ever-increasing flexibility of behavior that enabled adaptation to the ever changing environment. Over this vast period of time, some mutations must have spawned new lifeforms that lacked a pallium. Today, however, none of these survive and we must presume that deprived of the adaptive advantages of cerebralization they and their progeny were doomed. With the cyclostomes, the chain of cerebral development had been set in motion. With the pallium, a new mysterious element entered the behavior of animals. In a few tens of millions of years, new species of fish with increasingly sophisticated pallia evolved. Along the chain of evolution, the pallium was slowly relocated, forming a rind or cortex over the surface of the cerebral hemispheres. With the evolution of the cerebral cortex the biological substrate for consciousness had at last arrived.

A Gene for Consciousness
"There once was a man who said, 'God,
Must think it exceedingly odd,
If he finds that this tree,
Continues to be,
When there's no one about in the Quad.'"
Ronald Knox (1888-1957). English Author, Theologian and Dignitary of the Roman Catholic Church.

Every one of our organs, our appendages, expressions and postures, each control system and even the myriad of biochemical cycles so critical to the correct functioning of our cells, can be traced back through the succession of animals that have led to our evolution. For each feature there is a gene or a set of genes. That this is also the case with the cerebral cortex is not in the least surprising. That there may be genes for consciousness might seem to be an extraordinary hypothesis, yet clearly the progressive increase in the complexity of the cerebral cortex reveals the progressive addition or restructuring of genes necessary for one to experience life. Unfortunately, the link between the small pallium of the fish, the most primitive vertebrates and the massive human cortex does not help to establish when, along the evolutionary tree, consciousness first appeared.

In its more primordial form the cerebral cortex does not necessarily fulfill the same functions as it does in humans. We can show that our cerebral cortex is essential for consciousness, but this does not mean that because fish are equipped with a pallium, they have awareness. Nor can we say that consciousness arose with the evolution of the advanced reptiles by which time a neopallium (later to become the neocortex) had developed on the surface of the brain. In all mammals, including the human, the cortex can be traced back to three types of pallia: the primitive pallium or *paleopallium* of fish, the *archipallium*, which first appeared in the *Amphibia*, and the *neopallium* that accompanied the evolution of the advanced reptiles. In the mammals these three types of pallia were replaced by *paleocortex, archicortex* and *neocortex*, each retaining the general functions served by homonymous type of pallium. Because many researchers now refer to the archipallium of the amphibians and the neopallium of reptiles as simply the cortex, we will continue to use the term pallium only when referring to the true primordial origin of the cerebral cortex - the paleopallium of the fish.

It is as yet impossible to say at what stage of the vertebrate evolutionary tree animals became conscious. As we move from the human back through the mammals to the reptiles and on to the pallia of the fish, the internal microscopic structure of cortex becomes increasingly simple. Even the branching of the processes of cortical (or pallial) neurons becomes less profuse the further back we go, suggesting that as well as adding more nerve cells to the cortex, natural selection has favored an increase in the processing power of individual cortical neurons. There can be no doubt that somewhere along this cline in neuronal architecture, a level of complexity was achieved that first enabled awareness. It is, however, debatable whether the emergence of consciousness served to improve the functioning of the organism, or whether consciousness simply happened at a point in evolution when cortical circuitry reached a certain level of sophistication. The biological origin of consciousness may be more completely understood when scientists are better funded to analyze the workings of the cortex, or pallium, of species that represent each significant stage along the chain of vertebrate evolution. It is not beyond the bounds of possibility that one day we may discover a gene, or set of genes, critical to the phenomenon of consciousness and those aspects of cortical circuitry that underlie it.

Chapter 4 - The Purpose, Unification and Disintegration of Consciousness

The Recognition and Subtraction of Consciousness

"The patient [a newborn baby] startled in the presence of loud noises.... If we handled the patient roughly he cried weakly, but otherwise like any other infant, and when we cuddled him he showed contentment and settled down in our arms. When a finger was placed into his mouth he sucked vigorously.... He would sleep after feeding and awaken when hungry, expressing his hunger by crying." Nielsen J. M. and Sedgwick, R. P. (1949). Instincts and emotions in an anencephalic monster. *Journal of Nervous and Mental Diseases* 110, 387-394.

When autopsied after a survival period of 85 days, this child had no neural tissue above the middle of the brainstem. Not only was there no cortex, but most of the areas that feed information up to the cortex were also missing. That its behavior was almost identical to a normal child is a testimony to the primeval origin of the behavior of the newborn infant. These observations raise the question of what a mammal or a human being can do without a cortex or, presumably, any vestige of consciousness.

It is a truism that you do not really know if anyone else but yourself is conscious. We have only the words of others to reassure us that they experience things and are not just biological automatons that only appear to be normal conscious humans. Indeed, it may be that all things, animate and inanimate are conscious, but are simply unable to reveal this to us. Do not people muse that "if only these stones would talk what a story they would tell?" Since the beginning of recorded time humans have consulted the sun and the moon about all manner of complicated social issues. Some years ago, in an inadvertent return to animism, many Americans were drawn into a fad of buying a rock and affording it the same social status as an animate pet. This activity was an interesting exercise because it forced rock owners to imagine the essential things that distinguish the animate objects from inanimate objects. The fantasy was that rocks, or at least pet rocks, do have the ability to experience their surroundings and have thoughts, moods and emotions. More globally, the cosmically inspired have often been reticent to acknowledge the distinctive contrasts between animal matter and physical matter. Just as little children think that the trees make the wind, so too do these people believe that consciousness is a property of all matter rather than exclusively the product of the living cortex. There is surely no better way of creating a mystery or a myth than to present the poorly tutored, impressionable mind with an indefinable phenomenon.

Ultimately, we can only know consciousness from within and we can never be sure that any other thing, or even any other person, is conscious. Such philosophical arguments go on and on despite thousands of observations and experiments which show consciousness to be the product of a piece of living cortex. In the animal world, the presence and level of cerebral sophistication remains the most powerful indicator of the capacity for consciousness. In fact, biologists inadvertently use the level of cortical development when they intuitively categorize all vertebrates into a hierarchy that matches the complexity of their behavior. We sit at the top of the evolutionary tree and we have by far the most sophisticated and multifunctional cerebral cortex of all species. The exponential increase in the number of extinct species over the last one hundred years is a tragic, yet pertinent, testimony to the power of our cerebral complexity in the decimation of the physical environment alongside the ruthless, unchecked exploitation of all living things.

What then, does consciousness bestow upon an otherwise unconscious agent? Marsupial mammals are very immature at birth. The newborn kangaroo is less than one centimeter long and has hardly any brain. Yet, totally dependent upon the neural circuitry of its barely operational spinal cord and lower brainstem, it crawls from the birth canal to the pouch where it attaches to the nipple. What are even more astounding are the results of a series of experiments where scientists removed all accessible cortex from brains of young rats and raised them to adulthood. The reasonable consensus is that these animals are totally unconscious. Unconscious they may be, but much of their behavior is typical of normal, corticated rats. Rats prepared in this way can walk and even appear to "explore" their box. When the bending of their whiskers signals an opening such as the experimenter's sleeve, the rat pushes forward, driven by primitive motor centers in the brainstem and spinal cord, to seek the safety of shelter. Similarly, if their mouths contact pellets of food, they begin to bite and chew. What is, however, most astonishing is that these completely unconscious mammals engage in sex, give birth and, in captivity, succeed in raising 60% of their young.

Shelter, food and sex are things we struggle most of our life to attain. Yet the decorticated rat is also driven to attain these things in the complete absence of consciousness. Why do we not simply shut down our mind and ceasing all cognitive concern, sniff and grope our way through day and night, moving endlessly from feast to fornication? Why not indeed? After all the very kernel of wisdom is adherence to the fundamental laws of nature, laws that are encoded in the ancient core of the nervous system, still intact in our decorticated rats. Without consciousness, this core instigates those behavioral routines that are instinctual, and, as such, the very essence of an organism's survival. The anencephalic child, the newborn marsupial and the decorticated rat are not unlike the normal newborn infant in that they too exploit neuronal networks that lie far below consciousness. It was the primordia of these same networks, which 550 mya enabled the first vertebrates to survive and reproduce successfully, establishing a lineage of lifeforms wherein existed the germ of both consciousness and the human mind.

In an absolutely predictable environment, the ancient set of subroutines available to our unconscious, "cortexless" rat, is sufficient to enable both survival and reproduction. Exposed to the dangers and diversity of a natural environment, our rat would not survive a single day. Even if the ancient core of their nervous system could detect a natural predator (eg. a snake), the best it could do would be to evoke a primitive, stereotyped escape response. Without either long-term memory or an awareness of the moment-by-moment changes of circumstance, even the most basic maneuvers are impossible. The decorticated rat is essentially a sophisticated neural robot, hardwired to slavishly follow a handful of stereotyped subroutines, many of which are inherited from its reptilian ancestors. Even in a community of normal, conscious rats, a decorticated rat would very soon become someone's dinner.

Given these insights, it is not surprising that in the convent, monastery or ashram, life facilitates the witnessing of empty consciousness. In the following of simplistic routines within the confines of a safe environment, consciousness need hardly be aroused. Indeed, in modern civilization many westerners live in highly protected, artificial environments that are insulated from either biological or physical threat. Because of our extraordinary powers of creative thought, our efforts to tame nature have gone far beyond the requirements of survival and reproduction. We have built our defenses against nature, enshrined ourselves within roof and walls, devised temperature controlled, motorized compartments to carry us through the outside world and assembled a vast array of medicines to protect us against the inner threat of disease. In our individual houses most of us live a life of routines not vastly different from the decorticated rats. It is therefore arguable that, in the modern lifestyle, the integrative functions of the cortex are of little significance to survival. Certainly the most important aspects of human life are those indelibly written in the most ancient parts of our brain that provide the inherent drive to seek out food, shelter and sex. Yet in reality, we no longer hunt to survive but instead repress our natural inclinations in favor of performing repetitive tasks for which, like the laboratory rat, we are provided with food and shelter. Our talent for manipulating the environment has freed us from the yoke of substantial physical and mental labor and thereby enabled us to conjure the great mischiefs that modern humans have perpetrated upon the Earth, nature and each other.

The Experience of Mechanism
"The biological function of awareness is still uncertain, but appears to be narrower than has often been thought." Lancelot L. Whyte (1896-1972). Scottish Financier, Industrial Engineer, Intellectual and Author.

There is a principle derived from physical chemistry that states that a large aggregation of molecules will have properties that cannot be predicted from the properties of the individual molecule. These properties are called *emergent properties*. Any highly complex system has the potential to generate unpredicted behavior - to have emergent properties. Computers are particularly renowned for producing unanticipated outcomes. Clearly the cerebral cortex with its tens of billions of neurons and trillions of connections, together with a massive array of neurotransmitter systems, is a prime candidate for emergent properties. Anyone who has looked upon its complexities can only wonder that human behavior is in any way predictable. It is this complexity which has led some theoreticians to suggest that consciousness is not a goal of evolution but simply an emergent property of the cortex – a property that has serendipitously appeared as a consequence of the natural selection of other entirely mechanistic properties. Perhaps the cortex evolved because it performed the intricate and extremely rapid operations that underlie much of our behavior, and only as a spurious, serendipitous aside, did it simultaneously elaborate experience. That is to say, it may be that any experience arising from the cortex's involvement in a process is irrelevant to the actualization of that process, which simply goes on of its own accord.

The view here is that everything our cortex does could be as easily achieved without the elaboration of awareness. We might say that when the cortex is sleeping we do nothing and when it awakens we do something and serendipitously experience the process and outcome of its actions.

The evidence for this bizarre idea is that action-related activity can be recorded in the cortex up to 0.5 of a second (500 milliseconds) prior to our having the experience of taking that action. To appreciate what this might mean, it helps to ask yourself whether you would really know if the cerebral initiation of your actions always preceded your awareness of your decision to perform them by 0.5 of a second. There is certainly an abundance of evidence that, in some states (eg. deep sleep), cortical circuitry can be activated to a certain level without the elaboration of an experience. So much can be achieved through reflexes and automated patterns and habits that perhaps the machine is doing all the work and our experiences are always simply a little behind. Nor does the possession of a mind with its premeditation of action, contradict this idea, because it is equally possible that our experiences of our thoughts also lag behind the cortical activity that creates them. If indeed mechanism does precede experience, then whether it be thought, emotion or perception, we inadvertently pass through life always slightly behind the moment.

Constructing the Gestalt

"We conclude that we only then become conscious of objects when we distinguish them for one another; when we do not notice the difference of things which are presented to us, then we are not aware of what enters our senses." Christian Baron von Wolff (1679-1754). German Mathematician, Philosopher and Scientist.

Even if consciousness is of no consequence to action, it is clear that the cerebral cortex is a unique part of the brain in that it deals with information in a global manner. Before reaching the cortex, all the various lines of sensory information are kept separate. Information concerning vision, audition, touch, smell, taste and a plethora of visceral sensations arrive at their respective primary sensory receiving areas. Only in the perceptual areas of the cortex and those areas devoted to thought, emotion and mood do these simple sensory representations become woven into the instantaneous, multimodal, emotionally rendered, ideational picture of life that constitutes the *Gestalt*.

No other part of the brain has the connections or 2-dimensional laminar structure that enables the cortex to function as the projection screen of life. In humans and the other higher primates this screen enables the experience of all sensations, perceptions, thoughts and emotions. At the other extreme the pallia of the most primitive vertebrates, the fish, essentially contain a representation of memories - memories related to the fish's location in one part and memories of reward or punishment in another part. So it is that the primordium of the cerebral cortex is partly devoted to what we would call in a human, spatial versus emotional memory. It therefore seems that long before sensation or perception became cortical functions, these two fundamental domains of memory were of paramount importance to the behavior of the first vertebrates. Only over the subsequent 550 million years of evolution has the cortex become progressively involved in the processes of sensation, perception and finally thought. In the human cortex these elements of past and present are bound together in time as a single experience - an experience that is normally *holistic* in nature, in that the whole has a distinctive quality that cannot be imagined from an experience of the individual components. Mechanistically speaking, our cortex provides an immediate, multifaceted association, interpretation and response to a vast diversity of circumstances.

Most of our experiences are composed of many elements of consciousness. For example, a touch, an odor, a sound and a vision might all come together with an assemblage of emotions and thoughts, to create within us the experience of, for example, meeting a particular person. When that person becomes very familiar to us, only one of these experiential elements can be enough to provoke within us a brief, yet seemingly holistic, glimpse of their presence – a common experience of those who have lost a loved one. A familiar voice may conjure an emotion, a thought and an internal image related to that person, even though these elements of experience are represented far from the cortex's primary auditory areas.

This linking of particular parts of the cortex is achieved by special cortical association neurons that make connections across the cortex, essentially *binding* one part to another. The strength of these transcortical or association pathways varies between different parts of the cortex. Some links, such as those between areas involved in thought and visual imagery, depend upon many association neurons and are part of the inherent structure of the cortex. Other areas are linked up by relatively few association neurons. The strength of these transcortical pathways changes with experience. This happens because the potential of each association neuron to excite the piece of cortex to which it projects, is highly malleable. By increasing the strength of these transcortical linkages, activity at one point in the cortex will evoke almost synchronous activity at another. Whatever aspects of perception are normally represented at each of these two areas, for example, form and color, are therefore always associated with one another. Within the cortex, the form of a banana, represented in one area of cortex, is linked through transcortical connections with the color yellow, represented in another area of cortex, to create the single cohesive perception (experience) of a yellow banana.

It is important to appreciate that this form of associative learning is not just restricted to the perceptual areas but can involve cortical areas devoted to emotion and cognition. Thus, a series of emotionally blissful encounters may, in addition to evoking joy, cause the mind to create an icon for love that is always associated with the smell, taste, appearance and sound of the object of our love. When the cortical areas responsible for these aspects of our blissful experiences become bound together, then activating any one of them might readily evoke the joyfulness that characterized our original oceanic experience.

That it takes so long to lose such associations reflects the slow weakening of transcortical connections that have, in our distant past, been repeatedly reinforced by circumstances now long since changed. The strengthening and weakening of transcortical pathways are critical steps in the processes of associative learning and forgetting that are so conspicuously part of long-term memory. They also, however, represent processes by which our cerebral cortex and indeed our consciousness remain delicately attuned to the ever-changing circumstances of existence.

While the transcortical pathways stitch together related aspects of consciousness, they cannot account for the myriad of novel, multifaceted experiences that are also part of every moment of existence. For example, when we look at a banana our cortex registers its shape, size and color in quite separate areas of cortex and yet we see the holistic vision of a banana. This holistic image is possible because, when we are alert, those pieces of our cortex that are relevant to our perception of a banana only accept information in short intervals that recur at about 40 times per second – a periodicity that matches a particular type of brainwave known as the gamma wave (*The Cortex in Sleep and Dreams*: Chapter 2: Section 7). Information about the banana arrives at the relevant areas of cortex but is only "allowed in" or sampled during these short periods of admittance. Between these sampling periods, the cortex essentially sleeps in that it is relatively unresponsive to input. Each sample therefore constitutes a moment when all those related elements of consciousness are being synchronously activated such that they contribute to a single momentary, yet multifaceted, experience. If this process did not exist, then each individual piece of information (eg. the banana's color, shape or size) would enter our awareness at different times and would thus fail to gain expression as associated aspects of a *single unified experience* or Gestalt. By synchronizing the admittance to cortex, the component experiences conjured by the activation of different cortical areas, are only allowed to occur within a single moment. This process therefore ensures that a diversity of synchronous inputs can only be expressed as integrated components of a single, holistic experience.

The Disintegration of Consciousness

"I became less and less able to see and feel. Presently I was going down a long black tunnel with a tremendous alive sort of light bursting in at the far end. I shot out of the tunnel into this light. I was the light, I was part of it, and I knew everything!" Drab, K. J. (1981). The Tunnel Experience - Reality or Hallucination? *The Journal of Near-Death Studies*. 1, 126-152.

Wherever geography and geology have provided opportunity, humans have always believed that their Gods inhabit the peaks of high mountains. Mountains are naturally mysterious places where splendid vistas play tag with the hallucinatory aura of being high above the Earth's surface. In 1978 Peter Habler and Rhinhold Messner became the first mountaineers to climb Everest without the aid of oxygen. At 8,848 meters the oxygen level at the summit is about 33% that at sea level. Thus, while at sea level the air contains only 21% of oxygen, on the summit of Everest it contains only 7% of oxygen. Concerned that his brain cells might actually die, Habler made an extremely rapid descent reaching the South Col in just one hour. His concern was justified in that nerve cells that continue to be highly active under conditions of low oxygen do die. Given the cortex's high oxygen requirements, cortical cells are prime candidates for microasphyxiation. In those days, Habler could not have known that the cortex has a built-in mechanism for protecting its delicate networks from hypoxia - a mechanism that maintains, to the last, a modicum of consciousness, preserving function in those parts of cortical circuitry that relate input to output while shutting down the transcortical associational pathways. In fact, this exact same mechanism is the basis of the so-called "partner syndrome" reported by high altitude mountaineers as a feeling of being accompanied by another, usually older person. The domains of consciousness that are the mind and the sensations of an exhausted body have separated and as separate elements of reality, these two beings wander together far above the smell of earth.

Up to 8 million Americans are said to have had near-death or out-of-body experiences. As in the case of mountaineers, these experiences were almost always associated with hypoxia. Perhaps consciousness remained when the heart stopped briefly, perhaps a patient woke while in a coma or under a general anesthetic, or perhaps, deprived of oxygen, a meditator began to witness two or more quite separate realms of awareness where only one had previously existed. There is no doubt that hypoxia contributes to some degree to the disintegration of consciousness that occurs under prolonged meditation. Certainly, for the psychically inquisitive, the witnessing of such states can provide a rare and unique insight into the elements of experience that characterize our every day existence.

The dissociation of consciousness can be produced in two ways. The first is via the administration of the dissociative anesthetic, Ketamine. The second is by reducing the level of available oxygen. In the human brain most oxygenated blood is supplied to the cerebral cortex. Fish have only the primordia of the cortex (pallium) and compared to the vascularization of the mammalian brain, very little blood is allocated to the brain of the fish. The basal metabolic rate is a measure of the energy used when we are at rest. The adult human brain consumes 20% of this energy while the brain of the child uses 50%.

Most of the energy used by the human brain is burned up by the cerebral cortex. It seems that the complexity and cellular density of the human cerebral cortex simply demands a very large amount of well-oxygenated blood without which both cortical function and human consciousness are severely compromised. It is highly likely that the dissociation of consciousness induced by Ketamine and by low levels of oxygen is caused by the shutting down of those transcortical pathways that spread excitation across the cortex. In the event of hypoxia, this process would reduce the activity of cortical neurons that, in the absence of enough oxygen, might otherwise excite themselves to death - a process known as *excitotoxicity*. Clinically, these ideas have led to the use of dissociative drugs to artificially switch off the associational, transcortical pathways thereby reversibly decreasing cortical excitability and enabling cortical neurons to survive a period of low blood pressure and low oxygen.

In normal everyday life, messages are flashed across the cortical acreage as a normal part of the dance of consciousness. Dissociation breaks down these pathways and fragments consciousness, separating not only sensation from thought but also thought from emotion. It is this separation of the head and the heart together with the erection enhancing effects of hypoxia that are the basis for the dangerous use of partial asphyxiation as a tool to enhance the pleasure and intrigue of sexual intercourse. A tragic and perverse aspect of this phenomenon is said to have arisen in the days of slavery when the erection producing effects of hypoxia provided an additional attraction to the public hangings of Negroes, giving birth to the expression, "well hung".

In modern times, the experience of dissociated consciousness has been called the *tunnel experience*. With higher levels of asphyxiation or under high doses of dissociative anesthetics, consciousness recedes to a point where it is dominated by this very basic visual hallucination. The postulated origin of the tunnel experience is as follows. In a dissociated state the retina of the eye still activates the primary sensory areas of the visual cortex. However, these areas become progressively less able to communicate with the higher visual areas that give rise to meaningful visual perceptions. Consequently, it is postulated that vision will be experienced simply as the light falling upon the retina. The retina is not a homogeneous sheet of light receptors, there being more receptor cells in the middle than at the edges. As the cortex dissociates, the imprint of the retina on the cortical receiving areas will produce an experience of a bright spot in the center of the visual field. As dissociation increases, computer simulations suggest that this bright spot (arising from the area of highly active primary visual cortex) increases in size giving the subjective experience of entering a tunnel of light, eventually to become enveloped in the same.

Those who have almost drowned speak of a period of unexpected peace that precedes the complete loss of consciousness. When hypoxia reaches a certain level, consciousness fragments, concerns disappear and there ensues a blissful state. There can be little doubt that the dissociation of the cortex underlies many experiences that have been widely interpreted as having great spiritual significance. Not only is the experience of dissociated consciousness blissful, but it is also highly instructive. The witnessing of the heart and the head, the ability to confine and so focus thought without the intrusion of emotions and the recognition of the sensory experiences as passing icons of existence, all testify to the independence of the fundamental components that make up the experiential life of humans. The lesson of fragmented consciousness is an insight into the journey of human life, revealing to us the eternal cycle of birth and death, and ultimately transporting us to the very foundations of the psyche. It is to be found in the Tibetan's description of the slow, natural progression of death wherein the viscerally responsive emotional centers survive to the last, rendering in the final hours of life a vivid sense of the Buddha within. There are profound similarities between accounts of dissociated and transcendental experiences. In the words of Joseph Campbell (1974), "If we remove that glasslike barrier of which Ramakrishna spoke, both our God and ourselves will explode then into light, sheer light, one light, beyond names and forms, beyond thought and experience, beyond even the concepts 'being' and 'non-being'." In the knowing of such states begins the quest for wisdom, a quest that inevitably leads to an experiential comprehension of the domains of human consciousness and the supreme understanding of human existence.

Section 2: Recommended Reading

Allman, W. F. *Apprentices of Wonder. Inside the Neural Network Revolution.* Bantam Books, New York, 1989

Blakemore, S. *Dying to Live – Near Death Experiences.* Prometheus Books, New York, 1992.

Butler, A. B. and Hodos W. *Comparative Vertebrate Neuroanatomy: Evolution and Adaptation.* 2nd Edition, Wiley-Liss, New York, 2005.

Campbell, J. *The Mythic Image.* Bollingen Series, Princeton University Press, Princeton, Oxford, 1974.

Chalmers, D. J. *The Conscious Mind – in Search of a Fundamental Theory.* Oxford University Press, New Yord, Oxford, 1996.

Dawkins, R. *The Blind Watchmaker,* Norton and Co., New York, 1986.

Dawkins, R. *The Ancestor's Tale: A Pilgrimage to the Dawn of Life.* Weidenfeld and Nicoloson, London, 2004.

Dehaene, S. *The Number Sense: How the Mind Creates Mathematics.* Oxford University Press, Oxford, 1999.

Fuster, J. M. *Memory in the Cerebral Cortex.* Bradford, MIT Press, Masschusetts, London, 1999.

Fuster, J. M. *The Prefrontal Cortex Anatomy, Physiology and Neurophysiology of the Frontal Lobe.* 2nd Edition, Raven Press, New York, 1989.

Gard, R. A. (Editor). *Buddhism.* Washington Square Press, New York, 1963.

Harvey, A. and Matousek, M. *Dialogues with a Modern Mystic.* Quest Books, London, 1994.

Humphreys, N. *Seeing Red: A Study in Consciousness.* Belknap Press, 2008.

Jansen, K. L. R. *Ketamine, Dreams and Realities.* MAPS, New York, 2004.

Libet, B. "Neurophysiology of Consciousness – Selected Papers and New Essays of Benjamin Libet." In: *Contemporary Neuroscientists Selected Papers of Leaders in Brain Research Series*, Birkhauser, Boston, Basel and Berlin, 1993, pp. 1-402.

Luria, A. M. *Higher Cortical Functions in Man*, 2nd Edition, Basic Books, Inc., Publishers, New York, 1962.

Metzinger, T. (Editor). *Conscious Experience.* Imprint Academic, Schoningh, 1995.

Mountcastle, V. B. *The Sensory Hand Neural Mechanisms of Somatic Sensation.* Harvard University Press, Harvard, 2005.

Karten, H. J. *Evolutionary Developmental Biology of the Cerebral Cortex.* No. 228 (Novartis Foundation Symposia), Wiley and Son, Chichester, 2000.

Philipp, U. and Mercer, S. "The Human Machine at Work." In: *The Miracle of Life.* H. Wheeler (Editor), Odham's Press, London, c. 1935.

Searle, J. R. *The Rediscovery of the Mind.* Bradford Books, MIT Press, Massachusetts, 1994.

Sen, K. M. *Hinduism: The World's Oldest Faith.* Penguin Books, Baltimore, Maryland, 1967.

Squire, L. R. *Memory and the Brain.* 1st Edition, Oxford University Press, 1987.

Unsworth, W. *Everest: The Ultimate Book of the Ultimate Mountain.* Grafton Books, 1989.

20

Section 3:
The Human Mind in Creation, Illusion and Society

"At Babylon there was a great resort of people of various nations, who inhabited Chaldaea, and lived in a lawless manner like the beasts of the field. In the first year there appeared, from that part of the Erythraean sea.... an animal .....by name Oannes, whose whole body was that of a fish.... This Being was accustomed to pass the day among men.....and he gave them an insight into letters and sciences, and arts of every kind. He taught them to construct cities, to found temples, to compile laws, and explained to them the principles of geometrical knowledge. He made them distinguish the seeds of the Earth, and showed them how to collect the fruits; in short, he instructed them in everything which could tend to soften manners and humanize their lives. From that time, nothing material has been added by way of improvement to his instructions. And when the sun had set, this Being, Oannes, retired again into the sea...."

Inscribed by the Babylonian priest Berossus in relation to the first true civilization, the Sumerians of Mesopotamia, 3rd century BC.

Chapter 1. The Nature of the Mind

"I want to know how God created this world.… I want to know His thoughts; the rest are details." Albert Einstein (1879-1955). Theoretical Physicist and Nobel Laureate.

To the ancient peoples of the Earth, the seeds of civilization were the gifts of *culture-bringers*, strange beings that appeared suddenly and upon imparting their knowledge disappeared into the ether from whence they had come. In southern Iraq the Babylonians paid homage to Oannes while the Mexicans worshipped a godlike being called Quetzalcoatl. Quetzalcoatl came from across the sea in a boat that moved without paddles and taught people how to build houses, make fire and live in peace. The figure of Quetzalcoatl seems to recur under different aliases throughout Central and South America. The Mayans call him Kulkulkan, the great organizer and founder of cities who taught them the laws and how to make calendars for measuring the passage of time. To the Incas of Peru he was known as Virococha who is said to have first appeared at Tiahuanaco in Boliva where he delivered the gifts of reason and order to a previously chaotic world. His work done Viracocha took his leave, sailing away with his followers, the Viracochas, across the Pacific Ocean, towards the setting sun and the edge of the world, which lay, in those times of magic, beyond the consciousness of man.

So powerful is human mentation that all ancient civilizations believed their inventions to be gifts of an entirely alien consciousness. In accord with this belief many established deities that embodied the powers of the human intellect. Thus, to the Romans the goddess Mens unified mind and consciousness, while in Central America the Mayan god Nuam was the creator of mind and thought. To the ancient Egyptians the mind was represented by the goddess Sia, who was said, in deference to the animistic beliefs of prehistoric ages, to have emerged from the penis of Re the Sun God. Within the identity of these divine beings, the ancients preserved their insights into the creative powers of the human psyche, laying the foundations of psychology alongside the need for a higher source of wisdom that transcends the individual.

Steeped in superstition and living before the global knowledge base of modern times, the ancients could not conceive that our incredible creative powers could arise from within. So it was, and has forever been, that in all places where humans gathered in substantial numbers, the mysterious yet highly inventive power of human thought could only be comprehended as a gift from our celestial masters. This, no doubt, suited the power hungry, who clearly grasped the psychological advantage of linking humanity's greatest gift to the divine. As William Blake perceived, "God is an allegory of kings". The common person's need to recognize and revere a higher force is easily transformed into a need for a human leader, be he king, chieftain or political dictator. While humans have always recognized their ability to teach and learn, only in the last few centuries have they begun to appreciate the vast creative potential inherent in our capacity for abstract thought.

Significant change began with the birth of the Buddha (literally "the awakened one") in the village of Lumbini near the border of India and Nepal. Gotama Siddhārtha

(560-477 BC) was a Kshatriya (upper caste) Hindu and the son of the chief of the Śākya clan, which caused him to be referred to as Śākyamuni or "Sage of the Śākyas". Upon his birth a seer is said to have predicted that he would either become a great king or that he would save the world. At 29 years of age he renounced all earthly attachments to practice the most severe austerities in the quest for enlightenment. Nevertheless, it is said that enlightenment eluded him until the idle words of a passing musician transported him to the realization of "The Middle Way" - a path that seeks always a balance between the renunciations of the ascetic and the consuming, hedonically-orientated agendas of everyday life. Central to this theme was the realization, arrived at through introspective practice, that consciousness is retained even when the mind is completely silent and that in this state of "no mind", the "isness" of the World reveals the illusory nature of thought. Through prolonged meditation the seeker could develop the ability to drop thought and so free the mind for the performance of tasks that were either essential to life or generous in intent.

For many decades Buddha wandered through the Ganges valley followed by a small band of yellow-robed followers who called themselves *bhikkus* or "disciples". Even 200 years after his death Buddhism remained an insignificant religion lost amongst the infinite variety of Hindu sects. Nor did things change until, in the third century BC, the great Mauryan emperor, Ashoka (304-232 BC) converted to Buddhism. Ashoka came to power through a bloody family struggle and in 260 BC proceeded to expand the already huge Mauryan empire by attacking Kalinga (now Orissa). Though successful, the horrific civilian and military losses so moved Ashoka that he renounced war forever. Filled with a first hand knowledge of the destructive potential of human thought, he adopted the teachings of the Buddha and launched a campaign to bring about a spiritual, moral and social reform that established his empire as a model for a tolerant humane style of government throughout Asia.

It is impossible to over emphasize the significance of this single realization to human understanding. Buddhism remained the most influential religion in India for the next 1,000 years. Indian Monks carried the Buddha's teachings throughout the East and thousands came to India to study in its great monastic universities. Eventually, in the minds of millions of people, compassion and caring replaced greed and desire as slowly the human energy once expended upon war and domination was harnessed to the service of the heart. Buddhism would fade and rise anew but through the teachings of the Buddha ordinary people would arrive at an entirely new awareness of mind. No longer were their thoughts the gifts of some imaginary deity. At last humanity could claim its inventions as its own and take responsibility for its deeds, ill or good. Within the realizations of the Buddha, the power of being and the power of thought were seen as omnipotent, though independent, elements of human consciousness.

In his Colombo Lectures of 1897 the Indian mystic Swami Vivekananda commented, "the first proposition the Hindu boy learns is that the mind is matter." Today it is still India that reminds us that the *mind is the organ of thought*, the organ that through its conceptual prowess gives life to the abstract, and through planning, a foundation to the future. Within human consciousness, it is the mind, which elaborates the *unmistakable experience of thought*. In the Indo-eastern vision, the human mind is the creative yet capricious master, lying awake within us, ever ready to absorb us into the follies of unwarranted anticipation of an essentially indeterminate future.

The mystics emphasize that when the mind is active, one is not just preoccupied with one's thoughts, one actually becomes those thoughts. Even the Christian savior, awaiting crucifixion, is reputed to have said, "I would be thought, being wholly thought". In such times we might say that we are *of* the mind. In those seconds, minutes, hours and days when we are lost in our mind, the information and issues that fill our thoughts easily become the totality of our experiential life. Insulated from our sensations, emotions and, even our moods, our powerful mental processes entrap us in a space where concepts, challenges, problems and relevance are compared and modified in a ceaseless endeavor to produce plans and strategies; theoretical devices with which we hope to negotiate our largely imaginary world. It is ironic that while westerners motivate their children by indoctrinating them to respond to all challenges of life with cognitively derived strategies - a process called worry - the other peoples of the world traditionally see significant value in training the mind to rest.

Belief is the villain here, for belief is the child of argument and argument is the fundamental process of deductive thought. We might say that if God had any purpose in giving a mind to humankind, it was surely that it enabled humans to believe in him. The mind is the organ of belief. There is an Australian children's story about a young bunyip, a mythological Australian animal that lives in a small lake called a billabong. It goes something like this. The bunyip emerges from the billabong and addressing a passing kangaroo, says "Who am I?" "You're a bunyip", says the kangaroo."What is a bunyip?", says the bunyip. But it's too late, the kangaroo is gone. Other encounters are similarly uninformative. Finally, the bunyip comes to an impressive looking building. Cameras scan the bush, alarms bristle and signs stop the bunyip in his tracks. Inside sits a scientist writing in a huge book. Around him screens show images of the bunyip from every possible angle. Staring into the nearest camera the bunyip asks, "Am I a bunyip?" Without looking up from his book, the scientist mutters, "No", then, as if as an after thought, he mutters, "Bunyips simply don't exist!"

Less than a century after the Buddha's death, the Greek philosopher, Plato (428-348 BC) began addressing the relationship of human thought processes to wisdom. A consummate philosopher with a fascination for mathematics, Plato was clearly enamored of the human intellect. "Man" he pronounced, is "a being in search of meaning" and Plato left no doubt that man's search was conducted within the processes of thought. To Plato the more sophisticated were a man's powers of reasoning, the higher he was on a ladder that reached from the imbecile to the divine. Himself driven by the ravages of unstable mood, Plato nevertheless was obsessed with the power of thought and knowledge over the behavior and destiny of the human being.

For all that, it is a simple matter to witness the nature of our most basic thought processes. Imagine that it is morning and you are waking from your slumbers. Reluctant to leave the land of nod, you send an arm out to silence the alarm clock. Deep inside you strive to hold those fleeting moments of dream, shielding the now restless beast of consciousness from the tyranny of wishes and needs. Closing your eyes you linger a little longer, half way between sleep and wakefulness, watching your mind as it replays its recollections of your real identity, reminding you of your relationship to the world of things, ideas and people. To the last you shy away from the concerns that will steal the hours of yet another day. You stumble from bed, brush your teeth, put on the coffee and shower. And then, and only then, do you realize it is Saturday morning.

In those fleeting moments when sleep first leaves our eyes, we are conscious of only the most elementary aspects of our immediate circumstances. Even as we wake there forms, from unitary elements of consciousness, an increasingly complete rendition of our surroundings. Slowly the new day seeps into our awareness, bringing to life an ever more complex series of realizations. The veil of sleep is cast aside as the cortex awakens and the network of principles, concerns and beliefs that compose the stuff of mind lays claim to each and every waking moment. In the same way as our sensations (eg. our sense of light) awaken our perceptions (eg. that it is morning in my room), our perceptions arouse our powers of reasoning (eg. in the morning I have to go to work) that, in turn, remind us of important conceptual frameworks (eg. I live in a world of time, dates and deadlines) and eventually situationally-relevant information and novel ideas (eg. it is actually Saturday and I can return to bed).

Both Plato and his student Aristotle understood that thought can occupy several levels of complexity. The Greek word *dianoia* actually stands for both "thought" and "understanding", indicating that, in their view, the level of a person's intellect (their "power" or "faculty of knowing") was tightly equated with the predominant level of that person's thoughts. Plato and Aristotle envisaged the progression of the intellect much as ascending steps along a hierarchical ladder. As we shall see, modern research has shown that the rungs of this ladder are roughly equivalent to distinct domains of thought, which, in turn, are the products of activity in anatomically distinct parts of the prefrontal cortex.

The first rung on Plato's ladder is embodied in the word *eikasia*, meaning "conjecture" or "likelihood". This level requires little strategic thought other than perceiving a potential for reward in a given scenario. The recognition of such likelihood reflects experience gained in the trial and error processes of day-to-day life. It is likelihood that leads people back to the most encouraging path. In eikasia, there is little in the way of cerebrally derived solutions. No radical or immediate change of strategy is required. There is not even evidence for the "aha experience" so indicative of quiet deliberation (*Searching for Solutions*: Chapter 5: Section 6). Without even knowing it, the heroin addict becomes increasingly adept at injecting himself, retaining deep within his motor centers the habitual impetus to inject, long after withdrawal from the drug. As part of what we now call *operant conditioning*, our brain's ancient reward systems can reinforce the neural circuitry involved in certain motor skills so as to produce a progressively increased likelihood of success upon repeated attempts. Little intellect is required. Through the plasticity of connections in subconscious centers of the brain (eg. the basal ganglia and cerebellum) the correct sequence of movements "automatically" gets easier and easier and the desired outcome is thus increasingly attainable. All we have to do at this level is to recognize from past experience the indicators of success.

The second rung is *techne*, a Greek term referring to the application of well established principles involved in the construction of objects or the accomplishment of specific goals. Today techne is most often expressed as teachable technology that utilizes the known in the process of material productivity. At a basic level techne employs a form reasoning that we often call common sense, while in its highest echelons it is practical creativity.

The third rung is *episteme*, a Greek term for "science". There exists some important hair splitting here between Aristotle and Plato. To Plato, episteme was knowledge and he distinguished it from *doxa* or "opinion". To Aristotle, episteme carried the implication of a "disinterested knowledge of principles", meaning knowledge at an abstract level that was not bound to the practical and physical realities of techne. Philosophy and science both contain much knowledge that one cannot directly touch, see or hear in the world around us. Theories such as the particulate theory of matter, which propose that everything is made of atoms and molecules, appear to be correct and therefore are, in a sense, facts that we may teach as elements of knowledge. However, they are still theories created within a realm of cognition that is specifically tailored to comprehension of phenomena. To better distinguish between the practical and abstract levels of thought, new terms were needed which reflected the quite different cognitive processes underlying episteme and techne. The answer was provided when Aristotle coined the terms, *intellectus practicus*, the realm of the practical that is more or less equivalent to techne, and *intellectus speculativeus*, the realm of the abstract and the equivalent of episteme.

Philosophers are fond of reminding us that philosophy is derived from the Greek *philos*, meaning "love of", and *sophia* meaning "wisdom". A man who calls himself a philosopher is essentially claiming to be wise. Yet philosophers are, in the structure of their personality, people naturally gifted in logical thought and abstract argument. It is to Plato's credit that in his hierarchical view of humanity he identified, like many others, the existence of a realm of true wisdom through which he believed humankind was linked to the divine. Plato called this fourth rung of his ladder, *sophia*. From it grew the classical Greek concept of *sophrosyne*, the bringing together (*syne*) of wisdom (*sophia*) within a single individual. Excellence of character, soundness of mind, seeing how all could be turned to the common good and a host of lesser virtues were required to attain sophrosyne. In the 11th century, the combination of compassion and moral perfection implicit in the idea of sophrosyne so moved St. Augustine that he assigned the order of sophia to the God of Christianity.

The definition of sophia recognizes within the realms of human thought a domain of psychosocial comprehension that is distinct from techne, episteme or eikasia. The ability to draw upon factual knowledge and indulge in intellectual speculation is important, but sophia can only be achieved when these abilities are combined with a high level of emotional intelligence. In this way, Plato's sophia and the concept of sophrosyne resemble the coalescence of the "intuitive mind" with the "logical mind" –

a concept embodied in the Hindu yogi's description of the third eye. From the Hindu perspective, *sophia* is the contemplative level that is reached only when the serpent goddess Kundalini has risen from the base of the spine to the level of the sixth, or second highest, Chakra (*Ajna*). For the Jews this level of awareness is described by two sefirots, reached in the ascension of the tree of life. One of these is *binah* - the understanding and the intelligence of God - and other is *hokhmah* - the contact point of the divine mind with human thought. For the Christian this level is attained with the sacrament of *ordination* - the achievement of priesthood, which formally or informally occurs when our personal growth qualifies us to give effective council in the traumas of life that arise from the inevitable conflicts between the head and the heart. Thus, Hinduism, Christianity and Judaism recognize a state of cognitive responsiveness that characterizes a person whose mind has achieved a delicate balance between the practical, abstract and psychosocial domains of cognition. In western psychological vernacular, such a person is said to be *actualized*.

If Buddha and Plato could have lived in the 20th century they would have been fascinated by the case of an enigmatic child, which appeared and reappeared in neurological literature spanning several decades. Surviving a difficult labor, JP was born in December 1912. Although he began to walk and talk at 1 year of age, throughout childhood and adolescence JP's behavior was always abnormal. In particular he was given to wandering. This habit began at the age of 2 years and persisted into adult life. His reading skills and language skills were always good but he did badly when a challenge involved mathematics, abstract reasoning or planning. When one would have expected learning, his memory failed and as a result he was never able to hold a job. Socially he was full of contradictions. On one hand he had beautiful manners being totally attentive to his audience, his neurologist commenting that, "He gives everything he has to the moment when he is talking to one". Against this, however, he seemed to lack social awareness, thrusting himself into the center of attention and being excessively boastful so that he became extremely unpopular with his schoolmates. On his first day at school, his teacher was in the process of writing a note to his parents telling them what a well-mannered son they had, when, looking up, she found him masturbating in front of the class.

Emotionally JP seemed to lack anxiety, insight and depth. Throughout his life he failed to form emotional attachments to either his parents or other human beings male or female. Neither happy nor sad, his pain and his pleasure were always short lived. He also seemed to lack the natural impulses of sexuality, aggression and self-preservation. When it was opportune to do so, he lied, cheated and stole, on one occasion borrowing a glove and defecating in it before returning it to its owner, to enjoy no doubt the spectacle of emotional arousal. Though brutally punished by his unrelenting father, he never seemed to either learn from his punishment or to bear any grudge in relation to his mistreatment. The immediacy of his behavior suggested strongly that, when things were out of his sight, they were out of his "mind". His neurologists summarized his condition as reflecting "an unawareness of his total life situation involving todays and tomorrows". Thirty years later they described him as "the same uncomplicated, straightforward, outrageously boastful little boy he was at

20", concluding that he had essentially "been a stranger in this world without knowing it".

In 1933 following a series of X-rays, an exploratory operation was performed to assess the neurological basis of JP's deficits. The operating neurosurgeon reported that while "the [left] frontal lobe was reduced in size to 50% its normal contour. Much to my surprise the right frontal fossa was entirely devoid of cortical tissue." JP's prefrontal cortex was composed of a small percentage of what was probably the posterior part of his left prefrontal lobe. Put simply, he literally lacked the cortical tissue that in a normal human enables the powers of reason. In this way his brain can be compared to that of a lower mammal, except that he was endowed with the areas that support human language and the associated capacity for a very basic level of thought. This accounts for his neurologist's final assessment that JP was "a very simplified human organism with only rudimentary mechanisms for social adjustment".

Incapable of complex reasoning, insight, foresight, empathy and judgment, JP clearly lacked the domains of conceptual consciousness that elaborate our emotional and "intellectual" realms of intelligence. Yet he clearly did have the capacity for a simplistic level of thought. Thus, although his comprehension of human society was flawed, he demonstrated a modicum of practicality and common sense. That JP lacked most of his prefrontal lobes tells us that his simplistic thoughts, like those that fill the first and last moments of our day, were insufficiently complicated to mediate the complexities of normal human behavior. In normalcy the prefrontal cortex enables the comprehension of ideas and concepts and the fashioning of long-term, behavioral strategies. Without it only simple thoughts of the type required to structure language and deal effectively with familiar objects, are possible. Many lower mammals have very little prefrontal cortex. Perhaps their consciousness is a little like JPs, a simple reflection of present circumstances without significant reference to past or future experiences.

Plato recognized that at a conceptual level, the mind is a platform upon which the processes of a wholly acquired system of logic can be inscribed. It follows that our carefully thought out principles are not necessarily linked to any significant truth about life or the world. As the Hindus recognized when they coined the word *maya*, such a level of mentation can easily become the source of ideational illusion. Still, most of us believe that our principles are sacrosanct. They are the products of our lifelong concerns and so we are not easily persuaded that they are simply creations of a neural machine called the mind. In reality, however, our complex thoughts are simply a composite of our conditioning against the background of our moods and emotions. The mystics' truth is not about intelligence. Their truth is a knowing of what Buddha has called the "isness" of our existence. In the struggle for survival, the ability to engage in complex reasoning has been relentlessly favored by natural selection because it gave the first humans the competence to invent the solutions to otherwise insurmountable threats. Indeed, within our brain the powerful link between our cognitive centers and our reward systems provides the irrepressible impetus to apply our thought processes to the task of invention. Technology and its roots in science are the most obvious products of this faculty. The ideational capacity of the human mind is not, however, confined to technology. Thus throughout human history our mental creativity has slowly become focused upon elucidating the governing principles central not only to life itself but also to that most complex of all biological systems, the human psyche.

The Buddha was an Indian and the Indians are closely related to the Europeans. The so-called, eastern vision of the human mind actually belongs to India. For the Europeans, unable to see beyond the impracticalities of Indian thought, it is both ironic and instructive that the Indian vision of the mind is compatible with all modern, western-based studies of the cognitive functions of the brain. Mind is indeed a logic machine given to the production of conceptual frameworks that become our beliefs. As part of our conditioning, the mind is most powerfully programmed during childhood and adolescence. However, unlike a real computer the mind is not so easily reprogrammed, for the software of this biological machine is physically constructed within the neuronal circuitry responsible for our thoughts. Many like to debate whether we really do have freedom of thought but in truth, few people realize the persistent yet subtle influence of our early experiences over our subsequent behavior. From early childhood to adolescence, layer after layer of conditioning is laid down and reinforced by our parents, teachers, priests and politicians. Through meditative practice it is easy to see how our life long strategies inadvertently arise from our conditioning and persist, largely incognito, long after the circumstances that molded them have disappeared.

Left to its own devices the human mind will inevitably become the autocratic master of the psyche, enslaving us to the service of principles, rules and beliefs that may have long since, lost their vitality. The life of people with a closed mind inevitably stagnates. Today at the beginning of the 3rd millennium, it is still the living sages of the East who beseech us to recognize, within introspective practice, the difference between the "isness" of our true identity, and our ego (our cognitively elaborated identity). Only they seek to turn us ever inwards, there to experience directly the innate laws of nature, so easily hidden from the thinking brain.

The intensive neuroscientific and psychological studies of the last century have opened us to the realizations that (a) the human mind is actually made up of a small number of discrete elements and that (b) even in the nature of our thoughts we are not identical to one another. Thus, while it is true that the specific content of our thoughts is determined by our life experiences, each person and potentially each circumscribed population is genetically predisposed to particular domains of thought. Although the brains of all humans are based on the same archetypal plan, each of us has a unique cerebral identity, the witnessing of which is a basic step in the path to self-knowledge and the acquisition of wisdom. When we have looked into ourselves and into the depths of humanity, we can see that some individuals understand the ways of people yet are bewildered and bemused by the ability and inclination of others to exploit deductive logic. Others have the gift of practicality yet lack emotional intelligence. Some ruminate about great theories, yet remain forever impractical. Some are brilliant planners others shine only in the moment. The combinations are diverse yet sufficiently finite in number to account for the archetypes of personality that pervade the myths, art and theatre of each and every culture.

The mystics and the established spiritual icons of all religions are, or were, people with great insight into human nature. However, even with their awareness of the innate, they had difficulty accommodating the power of thought, which with its ethereal quality seemed to emanate from something beyond biology. Certainly something in their message is missing, for their words have not saved us from horrendous conflicts. In knowing ourselves we have to go beyond the heart for our bad deeds are inevitably a consequence of our rampant mentality. In this deeply spiritual matter, science has finally come of age. The *modern mystic* can no longer turn away from science for, in this new age, its discoveries are at last revealing the hidden origins of our thoughts, a revelation that must ultimately embody the operational principles of the human mind.

Chapter 2. The Journey of the Mind

The Thoughts of Children

"..modern psychology begins.....at the very moment when humankind said, give me a feral mind, for from this mind I can ascertain what is given and what is acquired from the environment." Douglas Candland, Psychologist. From: *Feral Children and Clever Animals: Reflections on Human Nature.* Oxford University Press, New York, Oxford, 1993.

At some time or other we all wonder where our thoughts have come from. Who or what caused us to think the way we do? Who would we be if we grew to adulthood without any human contact? Undoubtedly the greatest insights into these questions came early in the 20th century when the great Swiss psychologist Jean Piaget (1896-1980) presented evidence that the thought processes in children of European descent pass through distinctive stages. Although these emerge sequentially between infancy and puberty, subsequent research shows that there is some overlap between the finalization of one stage and the beginning of the next. The exact time of onset, the duration and level of expression of any particular stage can vary somewhat between different individuals and indeed different human populations. Nurture too can have an influence here, for exposing a child to intense training in a particular domain of cognition can advance the onset of that particular stage. Nevertheless the order of cognitive development outlined by Piaget has stood the test of time. Today it is found within virtually every child psychology textbook and forms the cornerstone of the system of education employed throughout the western world as well as those hunter-gatherer, native and Asian cultures that have so tragically fallen under western domination.

The mind controls our behavior at the level of strategy. Piaget's findings showed that at different stages of postnatal development, the behavior of a child reflects radically different domains of thought. Only upon attaining adulthood can a person comprehend and manipulate the psychosocial, physical, abstract and temporal domains of their existence and, even then, not all individuals are equally gifted in each domain, the emergent differences in personality being very much the product of inheritance.

For the first few months after birth only the sensorimotor cortex is mature. Indeed, in what is probably an overestimate, Piaget regarded the first two years of infant behavior as the *sensorimotor stage*. Thus, although the young infant is seductively responsive to our overtures, it is very unlikely that it actually experiences emotions or entertains thoughts. The anencephalic child referred to earlier is good evidence of the level of behavioral complexity possible without any cerebral cortex (*The Recognition and Subtraction of Consciousness*: Chapter 4: Section 2). Certainly for at least the first 6 months, the behavior of the normal child appears to be determined by inherited, mostly subcortical, neural networks that produce movements towards any immediate source of warmth and nutrition. It is in this period that the infant's emotional centers finally mature and begin to respond to the body language of its careers while eliciting the melodic babbling that is the origin of prosody in adult speech. Six months also marks the earliest efforts at spoken language indicating the early yet postnatal maturation of the language areas, Broca's motor speech area (BA44 and BA45) and Wernicke's area (BA22).

Only at the age of 12 months is there common agreement that the child is able to mentally represent the actions of others. Only then does the behavior of the child reveal the existence of an internal representation of its social surroundings - an internal representation that becomes the foundations of its emotional intelligence. Piaget provided evidence that once started, this *preoperational stage* dominated the child's cognitive strategies between the ages of 3 and 7. Unfortunately, preoperational is a misnomer because during this stage, the mind is clearly beginning to become operational as indicated by the child's ability to comprehend or "mentalize" the behavioral inclinations of other people. In this stage it is therefore said that the child has acquired a *Theory of Mind* (also known as *Mental State Attribution*). From that point it slowly establishes a set of psychosocial concepts that account for the behavior of other people - concepts which embody the moral codes of the host society. The infant therefore enters its second year with a modicum of *emotional intelligence* enabling it to operate effectively in its very simple relationships with others.

In Piagetian theory the next domain of thought appears between the ages of 7 to 11 years and lies within the domain of practicality. In this phase of cognitive development the child becomes capable of performing what Piaget called *concrete operations*, a stage heralding a newfound awareness of the technically correct interrelationships between tangible, physical parameters, such as length, area, shape, weight, volume and form. In terms of the brain, this faculty reflects the maturation of a neural system capable of elaborating a conceptual awareness of real, concrete entities within the child's surroundings. In attaining the ability to perform concrete operations the child is newly availed of a practical, objective, common sense logic.

The last element of thought develops between the ages of 11 and 15 years and is known as the stage of *formal operations*. In this stage the child becomes capable of conceptualizing abstractions, enabling it to consider possibility, erect hypotheses and comprehend principles, ultimately establishing an entirely abstract model of its existence. This element of thought is fundamental to the scientific process because through it, wholly intangible entities of the physical world such as time and space become represented as identifiable, though ethereal, elements of knowledge.

Piaget did not define planning as a separate domain of thought. However, many of our thoughts lie within the domain of planning. Particularly in western society planning is a dominant and conspicuous element in behavior, which is first detectable between the ages of 3 and 6 years. Modern brain scanning techniques have enabled researchers to define a distinct area of the human prefrontal cortex that participates in the cognitive elaboration of plans and their retention in what has become known as *prospective memory*, the memory of our wholly anticipated future.

There are only two simple ways by which the brain could produce Piaget's sequence of cognitive development. In the first, we might posit that there exists a single area of cortex that constitutes the human mind. Throughout childhood this area would need to be continuously modified to accommodate concepts that embody ever more diverse aspects of human life. Thus, during the preoperational phase of childhood, the foundations of our emotional intelligence would be constructed within the neural primordia of the mind. Next, a network would be needed to represent future plans as subroutines marked upon some conceptual registration of hours, days, weeks, months and even years. To represent the wholly practical or objective elements of intelligence, a third network would have to be established within the same cortical tissue. Finally, with the onset of puberty, a fourth network would have to be added to enable the neural representation and manipulation of entirely abstract entities that serve the processes of complex reasoning. Though interactive, these four interdigitated, neural networks would have to function with relative independence in the solution of challenges derived from vastly different aspects of life. Suffice it to say, that there is no single cortical or brain area wherein, over the span of 15 years, there are such radical changes in either the manner in which it processes information or in the information it processes. This method of representing the four domains of cognition from within a single piece of neural tissue, would be rather like trying to run a mental hospital, a government department, a furniture factory and a high school in the same suite of rooms.

In the second model, we might posit the allocation of a different area of the prefrontal cortex to each element of thought, envisaging thus that each area matures over the period of childhood where its cognitive properties best serve survival. In this model, the cortical substrate for the psychosocial, temporal, practical and abstract domains of human thought develops during distinct phases of childhood (Figure 3.1). Common sense and what information we presently have about the progressive maturation of specific areas of the human brain between infancy and puberty provide strong support for this second model. In the following sections we will see that the human mind is actually composed of four structurally distinct areas of the prefrontal cortex that deal somewhat independently with psychosocial, temporal, practical and abstract issues. Within every normal human being each area elaborates an experientially distinct domain of thought, giving rise to a unique element of human intelligence. I will therefore refer to these parts of the human brain as the *social mind, temporal mind, material mind* and *abstract mind*.

The Art of Children
"one of the strongest and widely held assumptions about children's drawings is that there is a sequential development which reflects general intellectual and conceptual development. A broad parallelism is seen to exist between the child's drawing development and the development of his speech, his formation of concepts and, indeed, his thinking." Lorna Selfe, Child Psychologist and Author. From: *Normal and anomalous Representational Drawing Ability in Children*. Academic Press, New York, London, 1983.

Humans live differently to apes for a singular reason; they possess a vastly enhanced capacity for thought. Because the human mind utilizes such a large area of cortex, thought, quite naturally, dominates our consciousness. Our thoughts crowd our waking moments so much so that we are often driven to express them in the hopes of quelling our restless mind. When circumstances prevent us from expressing our thoughts we look for other ways of quieting their clamor. Some do this by focusing the mind on entertainment or work. Others resort to sport to draw consciousness away from the mind and into the kinaesthetic centers where the movements of the body become the focus of experience. Many silence thought with dangerous legal and illegal drugs. A few train their mind to switch off through meditation. Given the opportunity, children, in their moments of confinement, more often than not draw pictures.

Psychologists have long recognized that the art of both children and adults provides an insight into the nature of their thought processes. This insight comes not from the content of children's pictures but the way the young artist chooses to represent his subjects. It is the style of children's drawings that is significant. The style of our art captures not only what we perceive in our "mind's eye" but also the operational principles of our cognitive processes that create those images (*Defining Attention and Imagination*: Chapter 1: Section 7). So it is that through the art of children we may discern the paradigms of the mind as they exist throughout the stages of cognitive development that so define the path of childhood.

What actually happens within is as follows. After birth a human infant soon begins to "recognize" certain objects. Neurologically this is surprising as the part of the temporal lobe that enables us as adults to identify and imagine objects and people (the so-called "object area" or BA20), only matures much later. The young child's ability to see objects probably arises as a function of two other pieces of cortex that mature long before the object area. The first of these is the fusiform gyrus (BA37) that in adults is preferentially activated by familiar human faces, same-race human faces, the faces of animals and, finally, the bodily forms of any species (*The Nature and Nurture of Racism*: Chapter 2: Section 1). The second piece of cortex, the *superior temporal sulcus*, responds to biodynamic imagery composed of socially meaningful movements, postures and, in particular, facial expressions and conveys this information to the developing social mind (*The Origins of Emotional Intelligence*: Chapter 3: Section 3). Both these areas presumably play a critical role in the conceptualization of imagery that underlies the art of the preoperational child - an endeavor that, like the areas that serve visual perception, is dominated by the face, less concerned with body parts and little affected by the physical elements of the world that might otherwise bestow a sense of reality upon their highly primal, animistic offerings.

By the age of 3 to 4 years the social mind is mature and the drawings of child are focused on the things that satiate its viscerally inspired needs, amongst which nothing is of more significance than the human face. The face dominates the child's earliest artistic efforts but it is also critical to the child's reading of the intentions and emotions of others. Via the cortex's emotional centers and the superior temporal sulcus, facial expressions and particularly the orientation and direction of gaze, so critical to assessing intention, have profound influence on the newly mature social mind. In the same way, the representation of faces, body parts and bodily form in the fusiform gyrus, finds its way to the developing language areas, first Wernicke's area and then Broca's area where verbal communication is commenced under the supervision of the social mind's inductively orientated learning strategies.

The drawings of the preoperational child show people as nothing but large faces, supported by thin lines representing the legs. To the adult, the mechanical impracticality of these "tadpole" forms or "encephalopods" is striking. With increasing age, a torso is added and with time the size of the torso as compared to the size of the face approaches the correct proportion. The addition of arms, hands, fingers, legs and even feet and toes accompany this process. Animals appear quite early but like humans they are at first mostly faces. Before all else the child's art, like its language, reflects its immersion in the psychosocial domain of existence.

Slowly more and more objects enter the child's drawings. Initially all things are about humans but as time passes their pictures betray a growing interest in those loyal and friendly inanimate objects that fill their every day life. People now inhabit a world containing items of furniture, houses, animals, trees and that ancient icon of animism, the sun. Typically all objects have a face and so qualify as part of an extended family. At 6 all things are still drawn in only two dimensions, a characteristic that persists such that even by 10, not all children are able to incorporate depth into their drawings. This inability to conceptualize the third dimension also expresses itself in the relative scale of the objects in their drawings. Thus, whereas an adult artist uses size to convey a sense of the distance between the observer and any object, the size of things in the drawings of the preoperational child do not reflect this relationship. The family dog may be shown as being the same size and at the same distance from the observer, as the family car. Similarly, the relative position of items is of little concern. Thus, one may find the family house floating in space in a manner that indicates the child's satisfaction with representing "home" in an iconic manner entirely compatible with its innate bond with domesticity.

The preoperational child's distorted representation of reality testifies to the absence of thought processes concerned with the details of its physical surroundings. In the years that follow, the progressive maturation and programming of the material mind enable a more accurate reproduction of size and form. During this concrete operational phase (7-11 years), the child increasingly incorporates the details of reality into its drawings. Bodily proportions of people are less biased to the face and the body and limbs are often clothed particular preference being shown to uniforms that identify individuals with specific roles. In this way the art of middle childhood becomes newly focused upon the parametric properties (size, shape etc.) of objects and people as well as the symbolic aspects of their appearance.

By puberty the drawings of most children indicate a capacity to conceptualize the third dimension and, for the first time, objects are appropriately scaled in relation to their distance from the observer. The more gifted child may show an appreciation of the dynamic attributes of living things over physical objects. Thus, as the child enters the last Piagetian stage of formal operations, it expresses in its art a conceptual appreciation of space and, through the rendering of movement, time - the two intangible phenomena that are critical to the development of the abstract mind. As we shall see, these are also the salient features of the 38,000 year-old cave paintings of Paleolithic Europe, considered by many to be indicative of the leap in cognitive ability that inspired the European-based technological revolution and ultimately, the creation of the modern world.

The development of art in childhood seems to be associated with the development of the brain's cognitive centers. However, even in normal children there is considerable variation in the age at which a child progresses from one style to the next. Thus, about 25% of children begin to introduce the third dimension as early as 7 years of age whereas others have not, even at the age of 10. With the exception of a very few autistic savants, who, while still within the preoperational age bracket, manifest an outstanding ability to render the third dimension, this rarely happens spontaneously before the age of 7 (*The Mechanistic World of Autism:* Chapter 4: Section 3).

It has been said, that children who draw well are invariably bright. Indeed, it is generally assumed that drawing ability crudely reflects the general mental age of the child as assessed by conventional western tests of intelligence. Mentally retarded children are, indeed, relatively more deficient in the correct rendition of proportion and dimension, though relatively less handicapped on the inclusion of specific body parts. Such difficulties point to deficits of the abstract mind while the ability to accurately reproduce images of the body speaks to the presence of an operative social mind even in the intellectually disabled (*The Little People*: Chapter 4: Section 3). In the words of Lorna Selfe (1983) "The child draws what he knows, not what he sees." Art and language are undoubtedly manifestations of the cognitive processes that inspire them. In the following sections we will see that when we observe humans at large, these inherited abilities, while indicative of an individual's inventive potential, can be to some degree be influenced by learning and opportunity.

The Neuropsychology of Art

"I have sometimes heard painters say that they paint 'for themselves': but I think they would soon have painted their fill if they lived on a desert island. The primary purpose of all art forms, whether it's music, literature, or the visual arts, is to say something to the outside world; in other words, to make a personal thought, a striking idea, an inner emotion perceptible to other people's senses in such a way that there is no uncertainty about the maker's intentions." Maurits C. Escher (1898-1972). Dutch Graphic Artist.

Over the last fifty years there has been an exponential increase in our understanding of how the brain processes images and how, as part of the process of imagination, it can also generate internal imagery (*Defining Attention and Imagination*: Chapter 1: Section 7). This research began with the unraveling of the mechanisms underlying simple sensations, such as touch, sound or light before addressing how the cortex uses this sensory information to reconstruct and represent real objects and events such as a violin, a pineapple or, in the realm of sound, a familiar voice. With respect to vision, the properties of any object – its size, color, motility, form and even its expression of recognizable body language – are separately represented within a small, dedicated area the cortex. To art psychologists this provided a long awaited opportunity to relate the production of art to parts of the brain that were clearly dedicated to the perception of visual images – an endeavor that marked the beginning of a new sub-discipline known as the *neuropsychology of art*.

Unfortunately, the cortex's perceptual centers have nothing to do with ideation, intention or motivation: factors that are essential to the generation of imagination and creativity. People who have suffered prefrontal lobotomy do not generate art, even though the cortex subserving visual perception is intact. Similarly, the art of those who suffer aberrations of the mind, such as is seen in autism or William's syndrome, generate particular forms of art that reflect their special cognitive skills and deficits (*The Little People* and *The Mechanistic World of Autism*: Chapter 5: Section 3). Just as we have seen in children, the deterministic, driving force behind the production of art by adults, is a reflection of mental activity, activating the perceptual centers as part of the process of imagination (*The Exploration of Attention and Mental Imagery*: Chapter 1: Section 7). It follows that attempts to relate art to the brain mechanisms underlying visual perception has helped us to comprehend how we "see" images but it has yet to address the most important aspect of imagination, namely the influence of the mind.

Because art has its origins in the human mind, it is to be expected that the art of any circumscribed, isolated population will be strongly influenced by those genes which control the development and structural balance of the mind (*Genes and the Creation of Personality*: Chapter 2: Section 3). For example, a particular population may be perceptually equipped to "see" depth and movement but it might still lack the cognitive predisposition to spontaneously make these perceptual elements part of their attempts to draw. Just as children of a certain age draw pictures reflective of their stage of cognitive development, an undisturbed, isolated, human population will only spontaneously produce art that is reflective of its genetically determined mental set. Nevertheless, to some degree history shows us that radically different styles of art can be learned, even by people whose minds that have no predisposition towards a given style (*The Mind in the Wild*: Chapter 6: Section 6). At a cross-cultural level, the neuropsychology of art begins, not with understanding how the cortex's perceptual areas influence art but how the minds of individuals with a radically different mental set, conjure visual imaginings – an endeavor that is fundamental to understanding not only the relationship between personality, imagination and artistic style but more broadly, the diversity of art across all cultures of the modern world.

Genes and the Creation of Personality
"We don't see things as they are, we see them as we are." Anais Nin (1903-1977). Cuban/Spanish/French Author and Diarist.

Like all aspects of development, the behavioral changes that characterize childhood are orchestrated by genes. When we encounter a person with consistently abnormal behavior it is often because their genome is not like everyone else's. The structure of genes can be randomly altered by influence of radiation on DNA. When this happens, the result is called a mutation. Passed on in the sperm or egg to the next generation, a mutated gene may produce a different outcome in the body or the brain of the progeny. If expressed, the mutation will produce some significant aberration of normalcy that will be passed to subsequent generations. This is as true for parts of the cortex as it is for the color of our eyes. As the physical substrate for the different components of the mind are specialized areas of the cerebral cortex, it is not surprising that there are mutations that selectively alter the prominence of our emotional, practical, temporal or abstract domains of intelligence (Section 3: Chapter 3: Aberrations of the Mind). It is through just this process that natural selection has, over the last 200,000 years, enabled relatively isolated human populations to adapt their behavioral strategies to the unique conditions of vastly different geographic locations.

The journey of adult life is very much the journey of the mind. By comparison, the journey of childhood is a transformational process wherein we witness a slow progression from an obsession with the interpersonal to the entertainment of the abstract. The developmental changes that accompany this process are themselves inscribed in our genetic makeup. Geneticists call such a sequence of change an *epigenetic series* because one set of genes is required to orchestrate one stage of development and another to orchestrate the next. As the body and the brain move through different developmental phases, different sets of genes switch on and off. In this way our physical and mental growth into adulthood, and even our descent into senescence, are controlled by numerous epigenetic series. Nature plays a powerful role in determining our cerebral potentialities. What we might be is inherited from our parents, but how we develop our cerebral gifts is highly dependent on their mentoring skills.

As the little child grows, genes that have been inactive, or repressed, switch on and manifest their effects on development. Some of these genes code for the maturation of new areas of the brain, such as a piece of cortex that enables us to think about our emotions in relation to the behavior of other human beings. Other genes code for maturation of parts of the cortex that are related to mood and others to parts that are related to our perceptions and so on. Because different domains of the mind mature at different points throughout childhood, we can even say that the sort of thoughts children have at a particular stage of childhood reflect very much which sets of genes are being read and which are still turned off.

These principles are beautifully illustrated by careful comparisons of the cognitive preferences of adopted children with those of their natural and adoptive parents. For instance, in their verbal and spatial abilities, the resemblance of adopted children to their natural parents increases up to the age of 16 - a period that spans both the Piagetian stages of thought development and the post-natal maturation of those areas of cortex which constitute the human mind. There is even a hiatus of change in the seventh year of life - a time when the emotionally cognizant child is newly inspired to respond to the objective and practical challenges that underpin concrete operations. Thus, it seems that contrary to the popular and politically correct opinion, a common family environment contributes little to similarities between the cognitive and behavioral strategy of family members. Instead these features seem to depend almost entirely upon genetics and inheritance. There seems little doubt that this progression towards cognitive similarity with the natural parents reflects the importance of genes in the specification and serial maturation of each of the four elements of the human mind.

When the fertilized egg divides into two separate cells there is potential for two genetically identical people to enter the world. In identical twins we have the opportunity to witness directly the power of inheritance in the structuring of human behavior. Personality is most universally defined as an enduring core that determines the ways of the individual. Tested on the Myers-Briggs personality indicator, identical twins demonstrate very close correspondence on the Extraversion-Introversion, Thinking-Feeling, Sensing-Intuition and Judgment-Perception dipoles. This test is derived from Jungian personality theory born of Carl Jung's elucidation of recognizable archetypal characters within the mythologies of human populations that had been geographically isolated for many millennia. Jung argued persuasively that these archetypes are projections into legend of the stereotyped roles that repeatedly emerge in every society. What else can man do but draw upon what he knows? In the embodiment of timeless wisdom into story, the sages of all ages and cultures have been obliged to draw upon the only data available - that vast, though not incomprehensible, theatre of human life. That identical twins share the same Jungian archetype confirms that Jung's definitions have substance in human genetics. In the modern vision of human nature, the archetypes of mythology are actually behavioral phenotypes that most likely reflect the genetically specified areal size of the four operationally distinct components of the human mind.

The western preoccupation with learning and formal education has done much to hide the significance of genetics to human behavior. There is, of course, no doubt that beyond the mere acquisition of knowledge, mental exercise can improve one's ability. Given a powerful exposure to psychosocial matters we can improve the emotional intelligence of the most withdrawn child. Such malleability of personality in response to the environment is more apparent before the age of 20 and declines over the next 20 years, such that personalities of older people are typically less likely to adapt to changes in their social or physical environment. However, even in childhood and adolescence environmental changes within the spectrum of normalcy, do not result in any truly dramatic and permanent alterations of personality. We can no more make a scientifically inclined child into a top psychologist than we can create a musical genius from someone whose natural talents lie within the visual arts. Cortex is cortex, the elements of conceptual consciousness are, in their biological origin and plasticity, no different to those areas of the cortex that control our sensations, perceptions and movements. We are individuals first and although education can improve our abilities it is foolish and cruel to try to force a person or a race to excel in a domain that is outside their genetically ascribed mental set.

Our genes make us who we are mentally, physically and emotionally. This needs to be known and accepted, because whether or not it is politically correct, it is definitely a fundamental truth of nature. As far as the mind goes, each circumscribed population of humans must preserve a diversity of personality types, for without this variation the multidimensional needs of any society could not be adequately serviced. One need only imagine a society composed exclusively of the scientifically or administratively inclined, to see that natural selection will act to preserve, at all costs, a diversity of behavioral strategies. The very gap between the scientific, bureaucratic and humanistic approaches to life has its origin, not in the differences of educational or cultural background, but simply in the inherent diversity of the human mind. Again it is through modern science, against a backdrop of ancient wisdom that we come to a more accurate and pervasive understanding of ourselves, there the more clearly to see that amazing diversity of humankind which gives rise to that global pantomime the Hindus so aptly call, the *dance of life*.

Chapter 3. The Components of the Human Mind

"In the remote past, so Frobenius thinks, man first assimilated the phenomena of vegetation and animal life and then conceived an idea of time and space, of months and seasons, of the course of the sun and moon." John Huizinga (1872-1945). Dutch Cultural Historian, commenting on the writings of Leo Frobenius.

The human mind is composed of four discrete components, the social, temporal, material and abstract mind (Figure 3.2). With a little introspection, it is easy to see how any one of these components elaborates within us a discrete domain of thought. Indeed, if a matter is persistently difficult to resolve, we can often observe how we eventually entertain it within one realm of contemplation after another. Many conversations and debates occur only because people of different personalities have different preferred perspectives upon a common subject. For instance, in discussing an issue about their son, one parent might spontaneously look at the problem from the practical point of view while the other might spontaneously evaluate it in the context of the child's social and emotional life. Each parent automatically selects a different domain of thought, so bringing a different aspect of intelligence to bear upon the matter. In order to understand the raw nature of our emotional, temporal, practical and abstract intelligence it is important to look beyond the subject matter of our thoughts and passively witness the mind as four radically different theatres of deliberation. Technically the adult mind can be likened to four computers programmed quite differently in order to select, dissect, reorganize and integrate four radically different types of information in order to prepare a strategy of action. When all are consulted about a particular matter, our little network has within it a conceptual image of human life and thus the cognitive foundations of wisdom. In this chapter we will look at the origins of each of domain of thought and explore how they influence our behavior at the strategic level.

The Origins of Emotional Intelligence - The Social Mind
"A man is always a teller of tales, he lives surrounded by his stories and the stories of others, he sees everything that happens to him through them; and he tries to live his life as if he were recounting it." Jean-Paul Sartre (1905-1980). French Existential Philosopher and Author.

There exists within the cortex an area of conceptual consciousness that is conditioned by the social milieu of childhood, a system that malfunctions in those psychiatric conditions that compromise social bonding. This area is the social mind.

It was Piaget's theories on the sequential development of different forms of thought that provided the insights needed to localize the social mind. The key lay in his definition of the earliest or preoperational phase of cognitive development, a period when the young child is completely absorbed in developing an understanding of people and indeed sees personal identity even in conspicuously inanimate objects (*The Thoughts of Children*: Chapter 2: Section 3). Operationally, the purpose of this phase is the development of a conceptual construct that enables an understanding of the dynamics of social interaction. In early development the social mind thus establishes the fundamental concepts wherein are preserved the consistent patterns of communication between the child and the parents that are so critical to physical and psychological development.

Naturally the preoperational child finds particular delight in animals, especially those higher mammals that manifest facial expressions and body postures closely resembling the non-verbal language of humans. However, in the absence of any other domain of cognition the preoperational child cannot help projecting human socioemotional traits, even upon inanimate objects - a process Piaget called *preoperational egocentrism*. The animated objects that inhabit children's stories are, in fact, designed to appeal to this aspect of early mental development. As adults these early cognitive interpretations continue to manifest as a subliminal inclination to interpret the behavior of animals in human terms (*anthropomorphism*). Indeed, there can be little doubt that the retention of aspects of preoperational thought accounts for the essentially animistic beliefs of a significant proportion of humanity and, in particular, the hunter-gatherers.

In modern neuropsychological terms, the preoperational child can comprehend or "mentalize" the intentions of other people and thus is said to have acquired the conceptual ability known as Theory of Mind. By exploiting this paradigm scientists have been able to use brain imaging to confirm that understanding how others think is the task of the social mind. The test they use asks subjects to say how a person might think given certain information about their life. In one such test subjects were asked to examine a set of objects before choosing which would belong to a certain well-known person. For instance, presented with a kettle, a compass, a key, a violin and a telescope the subjects might be asked to choose which ones would be likely to belong to the famous nautical explorer Christopher Columbus. In order to choose the correct items (compass and telescope) the subjects have to use their emotional intelligence to envisage the mental set of the famous person. To do this they have to have within their mind an internal blueprint of human nature that enables them to correctly identify what objects a person of a particular personality or mental set, might possess. That all normal people can do this indicates that they have a mental construct that essentially categorizes people in relation to a wholly derived and often invisible theory of personality – a construct that is highly compromised or even completely absent in the autistic (*The Mechanistic World of Autism*: Chapter 4: Section 3).

When given this Theory of Mind test, brain images of subjects show increases in activity in an anatomically distinct part of the prefrontal cortex called Brodmann's area 9 (BA9). When similar tests are given to subjects suffering from socially debilitating conditions of autism or Asperger's syndrome, they performed poorly and brain imaging revealed only very weak activation of BA9 (Section 3: Chapter 4: Aberrations of the Mind). This area of prefrontal cortex therefore fulfills the criteria of the social mind.

Brain imaging also shows that the social mind participates in a host of people-related situations. For example, familiar odors, tickling, pain, reporting on the pleasantness versus unpleasantness of words, rhyming, naming of letters, the reading of words, swallowing, judging the recency of conversation, remembering and recalling the names of objects, recalling life events (*autobiographical episodic memories*), implementing an action, the semantic content of sentences, stories that touch upon the relationships between people and the experience of happiness, sadness or disgust, induced by film clips or simple recall, are all associated with activity in the social mind. The social mind is also aroused by pictures of unpleasant themes, such as frightened animals, mutilated bodies or human violence, or pictures of pleasant themes such as erotica, babies or sports events. However, emotionally neutral pictures showing inanimate objects, people with neutral facial expressions or complex scenes or patterns, fail to excite the social mind. The participation of the social mind in all these scenarios testifies to its containing what is essentially a conceptual framework of the social and emotional aspects of life. Armed with this framework the social mind can focus attention on matters specifically relevant to our relationships and, more broadly, on our emotional responses to the behavior and body language of all lifeforms. Ultimately the social mind is the source of our cognitive links with the animate world.

About one year after birth billions of interconnected nerve cells that compose BA9 begin to function as the social mind, becoming responsive to two subtly related inputs; one representing the emotions of the infant and the other the emotions and related intentions of its mother. The emotions of the infant are represented in the specialized area of cortex - the *anterior cingulate gyrus* - which acts as the executor of its emotions (*The Triad of Emotion*: Chapter 3: Section 4). The emotions of its mother are represented in cortical areas that respond to biodynamic imagery including vocalizations, body language and facial expressions. In the adult brain, the mind has considerable influence over the emotional centers. This is not so, however, for in the first 9 months of life when the cortex of the mind is still immature and inoperative. Without the regulatory influence of the social mind, the infant's emotional centers are largely at the disposal of sensory information from the viscera - sensory information that signals biological needs such as hunger, thirst and discomfort. In its instinctually driven search for satiation, the infant uses touch, smell, taste, hearing and vision to seek out sustenance within its largely social environment. Let us consider then, exactly how these different channels of sensation - visceral and environmental – interact in the early conditioning of the maturing social mind. Although, the infant receives important information about its surroundings from all domains of sensation, we will, for simplicity, focus only on socially relevant information arriving through the visual system.

Imagine the very common scenario wherein a mother smiles and immediately begins to nurse her baby. When the infant is presented with a smiling face, specialized areas of its cortex that register biodynamic imagery will generate a unique pattern of nerve impulses and send this "representation" of the smile to the still maturing circuitry of the social mind. Almost simultaneously the viscera responds to the ingestion of the mother's milk and sensory signals registering the satiation of hunger are sent to the infant's emotional centers. This "representation" of the satiation of hunger is also sent to the infant's as yet immature social mind. Every time the mother smiles and feeds her child the newly formed and highly malleable circuitry of the infant's social mind is activated by incoming information registering these two completely different but highly inter-related events - one involving the facial expressions and body language of the mother and the other the response of the infant's visceral body to the ingestion of her milk. It is inevitable that when such a sensitive, plastic and complex system is repeatedly activated by two, essentially synchronous, yet separate sources, that the nuances of their interactions will be indelibly inscribed into its circuitry. In this manner, the social mind stitches together these two events by archiving the interactions between the mother's smile and the infant's satiation as specific spatiotemporal patterns of neuronal activity that represent these intimate and life-sustaining interactions between mother and child. This synthesis that embodies the relationship between two vastly dissimilar events (sucking and satiation) into a primordial, yet wholly cerebral, representation is arguable the first and most fundamental element of human culture to crystallize within the developing human mind (*The Origins of Culture*: Chapter 2: Section 8).

The social mind is the first area of conceptual consciousness to mature and become functional. At this critical time a human being starts to become a social being. With the maturation of the social mind, there emerges the first evidence that there is a conceptual process underlying the child's behavior. However, exactly when this begins to happen is difficult to ascertain and remains controversial. Indeed, comparing the criteria used by psychologists for demonstrating the onset of cognition in early infancy with the criteria used by animal behaviorists for demonstrating cognition in non-human primates, reveals a strong and persistent inclination of the human researchers to describe the early onset of thought in humans and yet to stringently question its existence in adult, non-human primates. The result is that our estimates of when infant cognition begins are probably too early, while our estimates of when thought first occurred amongst our animal relatives is probably too far up the evolutionary tree. Nevertheless, some evidence suggests that infants show a cognitive awareness of the intentions of others as early as 9 months of age. By 12 months they have composed a working model of their life in which attachment to their caregivers is characterized by the child's obvious anticipation of particular forms of interaction. By 18 months they have an understanding of pretence, indicating that in their day-to-day interactions they comprehend the regular behavior patterns of their carers. Finally, by 4 years of age deliberate deception is commonplace, indicating that the child has developed a level of emotional intelligence that enables it to predict and manipulate the urges, motivations, moods and emotions of other people. Where once loud noises, hunger, thirst or discomfort caused the infant to cry and struggle, now a newly appointed executor is master of all, revealing its presence as a deliberate and divisive force in the determination of behavior. The child's search for satiation once driven by instinct is at last under the direction of a programmable neural machine capable of creating and instigating strategies that, with increasing age, represent an ever greater portion of the individual's emotional and social life.

In the young child three aspects of life are critical to the programming of the social mind. The first relates to the child's direct experience of pleasure, pain and fear. The second is an ability to register the facial expressions and body language of other people. The third is the anticipatory registration of whether an action or a situation will bring reward or punishment. These three sources of information are available from cortical areas that all mature prior to the biological maturation of the social mind. Our visceral perturbations, in the form of fear and pleasure, influence the social mind via our emotional centers (*The Triad of Emotion*: Chapter 3: Section 4). The emotional disposition that forecasts the intentions of other agents, people or even animals, is sent to the social mind from an area of the post-prefrontal cortex, known to respond to biodynamic imagery. Finally a specialized part of the prefrontal cortex called the orbital cortex provides predictions of the outcome of any proposed sequence of behavior – a role that, in adults, is particular relevant to social behavior in that it has great influence over our reasoning about moral issues (*The Relationship between Mood and Anticipation*: Chapter 3: Section 5). Given these connections, the newly mature social mind cannot but progressively elaborate conceptual representations in which emotion, the behavior of others and the prediction of outcome are integrated into an operationally derived construct of the child's psychosocial milieu.

In order to comprehend the intentions of others, the young child is highly dependent upon identifying people and reading their facial expressions and body language. In this process information on biodynamic imagery and facial identity is fed directly to the social mind from the cortex of the superior temporal sulcus and a specialized part of the object area (BA20) (*The Art of Children*: Chapter 2: Section 3), respectively. In addition, a third area, the fusiform gyrus (BA37), assembles information about the familiarity of the facial and bodily forms of both humans and animals and passes it on to the emotional centers from whence it can directly influence the machinations of the social mind.

The social mind brings to cognition the very essence of our psychobiological nature, forming its primordial conceptual representations exclusively from our emotional centers and our reading of the behavior of others agents, human or animal. In this way the machinations of the social mind are little concerned with conventional "knowledge", be it practical, biological or, in the context of it being the "science" of man, psychological. The social mind is programmed to integrate feelings - feelings conjured by the visceral manifestations of basic urges like sex, hunger and thirst with the bodily and facial gesticulations and sounds of others. To the newborn infant, none of these things has significance. In the absence of an operative social mind, these elements cannot be more than raw perceptual experiences. The first domain of conceptualization, the social mind is born into a consciousness that does not yet contain any significant constructs of life. At least in the early preoperational period, the programming of the social mind must synthesize its blueprints of existence entirely from experience, both inner and outer. The nature of its learning, as reflected in the learning strategies of infants, is therefore almost entirely inductive.

The Origins of the Future - The Temporal Mind
"It's a poor sort of memory that only works backward." Lewis Carroll (pseudonym of Charles Lutwidge Dodgson) (1832-1898). English Logician, Mathematician, Photographer, and Author of *Alice in Wonderland*.

One of the most conspicuous outcomes of prefrontal lobotomy is a loss of the ability to plan and a profound indifference to the future. After a prefrontal lobotomy, future survives only in the definition of the word and ceases to exist as an intrinsically meaningful icon of cerebral life. Most humans are prone to believe that their ability to think is a sufficient indication that the subject of their thoughts has a place in reality. Our innately acquired ability to mentally represent the future naturally inclines us towards a spurious belief in permanency, from which the equally spurious concepts of immortality and reincarnation inevitably arise. In terms of survival, however, planning is an entirely practical endeavor. In the creation and maintenance of what is known as modern civilization, our ability to plan and to remember those plans is of secondary importance only to our ability for abstract creativity.

When we cannot attain a complex goal by a single action, we are obliged to subdivide our project into a series of smaller tasks. As planning is so fundamental to all human populations there must be a cortical area dedicated to that process. Such an area would be responsible for breaking up major objectives into a sequence of executable sub-goals, creating a memory trace of these sub-goals, checking that each one is achieved at the correct point in the sequence and consulting memories of relevant past experiences. The cortical area that fulfils these requirements is the frontopolar part of the prefrontal cortex, or BA10 - a region that constitutes the temporal mind.

When the human brain is scanned during tasks that involve planning BA10 is activated. In this process BA10 creates a map of past, drawing upon episodic memories and integrating these with our mind's imaginings of what might be possible – a process we might called *temporal imagination* (*The Exploration of Attention and Mental Imagery*: Chapter 1: Section 7). Thus, BA10 manages and monitors each sub-goal while retaining the overall plan(s) in a special form of working memory that has been referred to as a *memory of the future* or *prospective memory*.

Clearly the radically different goals that may be conjured within the social, material or abstract mind (or any combination of the three) require quite radically different planning strategies. We might therefore expect that different parts of the temporal mind (BA10) must be allocated to each type of planning. This indeed seems to be the case, for regions of BA10 that participate in emotionally charged plans are spatially separate from regions participating in non-emotional plans. Such a spatial representation of plans according to the domain of existence they serve has great advantage as it provides separate cortical substrates for each type of plan which, in turn, enables selective access to the unique insights, memories and sensitivities germane to each plan.

Children do not show the preoccupation with long segments of the future so characteristic of the western adult. In fact, young children cannot make a long and involved plan. Therefore to assess their planning abilities a test must be both short and simple and fall within their limited concentration span. Traditionally the so-called Tower of London test has been used, a task requiring the performance of a set of operations in the correct sequence. Children of 3 to 6 years of age are able to succeed at this test. However, in the social domain children as young as 18 months are able to anticipate the actions of others and by 4 years they have the ability to make short but temporally-organized attempts to deceive their carers. Thus, planning within the bounds of emotional intelligence seems possible at least by the late preoperational phase of cognitive development. As they progress through childhood children become increasingly able to plan over more extended periods of the future, a process which doubtless relates to their progression through the different Piagetian stages of cognitive development.

The old saying, "The best made plans of mice and men are bound to fall asunder", underscores the intrinsic danger of putting too much store in one's future aspirations. In truth, just as our theories, beliefs and social attitudes are often non-existent in the real world, so too does the temporal mind's propensity to plan and organize draw us ever into the illusion (*maya*) of a tomorrow that may never come. Often, however, our plans do come to fruition, their successful maturation marking achievements that could never be attained without a significant level of temporal intelligence.

The Origins of Practicality - The Material Mind
"A Thneed's a Fine Something-That-All-People-Need!
It's a shirt. It's a sock. It's a glove. It's a hat.
But it has other uses. Yes far beyond that.
You can use it for carpets. For pillows! For sheets!
Or curtains! Or covers for bicycle seats!"
Theodor Seuss Geisel (Dr. Seuss), (1904-1991). American Children's Author and Cartoonist.

Our dominance over all other animals is a direct result of our ability to modify our surroundings by cerebral, rather than purely physical, effort. This capacity of ours to construct new objects has moved some to suggest that *Homo faber*, man the maker, more adequately captures our essence, than *Homo sapiens*, man the knower. In the ascendancy of the hominids, the first species to make stone tools and, perhaps not coincidentally, to have spoken "language", was called *Homo habilis*, man the able, in recognition of its possession of manual skill, backed up by a cerebral capacity for *practical creativity*.

Changing the world around us requires the ability to select particular objects within our surroundings (eg. sticks and bark) and to use them in the construction of entirely new objects (eg. a hut), which we anticipate will satisfy a pressing need. If we have never encountered the object we need, we will have to create it in our mind in the process we call imagination. Although this seems like a simple process it is very rare that any physical creation is completely the product of one individual's imagination. For one thing it is almost impossible to conceive of a practical challenge that would not be served by past experience. However, when humans attempt to create a prototypical object it becomes essential to hold its schematic form in the mind - a process known as *schematic anticipation*.

To indulge in schematic anticipation one needs mental access to the characteristics of all familiar objects so that their usefulness to the practical challenge at hand can be assessed. For instance, if we want to make a tool for killing an animal, it helps to know that stone is hard, brittle and can support a sharp edge. If we want to make a symbol like a cross, it is helpful to know that wood can be cut into lengths that can be easily pinned or glued together - not all practical creativity necessarily serves an exclusively practical need. The more things we can retain the properties of, the more sophisticated will be our creations and the more efficient the creative process. How often do we find ourselves, pondering a practical problem and muttering, "I am just looking for something heavy to hold this in place until I can find what is causing the...." and so on? At such times our ruminations are concerned with known properties of an, as yet unidentified object for which we have a practical need. This domain of thought is conducted within the *material mind*.

On the basis of size and shape alone the world is composed of a bewildering array of things. Just the array of objects made by human beings boggle the mind and beyond the man-made, nature presents us with everything from the formless amoeba to the precisely bioengineered shell. Fortunately the material mind does not have to store information about every object. Just as a champion chess player does not have to play out the almost infinite number of games that might follow each possible move, so too our thinker does not have to go through every object known to him before taking effective action. From the time of its maturation, the challenge to the material mind is to group certain objects in accord with those specific properties that render them of potential use to the problem in hand and to ignore others that are essentially useless. The efficiency with which it does this depends upon two things (a) its computational power and (b) whether it has been educated in the technical nuances of the specific challenge. Never could the material mind contain a representation of even the tiniest fraction of what really is. Instead we find therein a process that highlights certain items in accord with their usefulness and, as a consequence, dismisses many things which have no relevance to the task in hand. This process is practical thought.

The material mind elaborates a functionally useful representation of the physical world, utilizing that most cerebral of tools, conceptualization. Essentially one cup is much like another. All have similar properties. Each is a container, each has a handle, and each sits upright upon a flat surface and so on. All cups are simply variations on a theme. If you have seen one, you have seen them all. Form, size, structure, texture, color, sound, odor, taste, density, composition and surface area are all important but ultimately the material mind establishes a conceptual framework that embodies only the significant properties of all cups. It is not concerned with the specific features of particular cups. As a *modus operandi* within the physical world, conceptualization has great potential. Using this approach we soon notice that jars, buckets, water tanks, bowls and even plates all have some functional affinity with cups. All these things can be admitted to the more universal order of container. Nor are the symbolic properties of objects denied, as, for example, in Freudian psychosexual theory the cup is seen as a symbol of the vagina. As we shall see, the material mind also groups objects in accord with their symbolic relevance. Ultimately, the material mind's concern with the interrelatedness of real things is the essential key to practicality.

To better understand the process of practical creativity let us consider the simple need to build a shelter on a beach. It is a moot point as to whether we have previous experience of building or even encountering a shelter. Perhaps we have taken shelter in a cave and so we are already aware of the advantage of putting a protective barrier between the elements and ourselves. On this beach, however, all we have available is a pile of rocks, some palm leaves, water, shells, rotting seaweed, an empty beer bottle, the half-dried corpse of a bird, various types of plants, some mushrooms and one hundred, smelly, dead fish. Amongst this motley collection of things, some element of our mind need only recognize the outstanding potential of the rocks and the palm leaves to the creation walls and a roof, and we are home. Everything else is just flotsam and jetsam. We need not even waste a moment's thought upon the other objects. If we had no faculty to represent objects at a conceptual level we would simply try to utilize each object irrespective of its usefulness - an approach would almost certainly result in some unpleasant experiences.

In perusing the options, the most important thing for the material mind to detect is familiarity - familiarity not only with things *per se* but also with their attributes. For example, even a cursory knowledge of the properties of rotting flesh will persuade us to omit the dead fish from our building plans. The result of our efforts is not just something called a shelter, but a new object, which itself has emergent properties that endow it with a usefulness beyond that of its component parts. As more shelters are devised, shelters themselves become the objects or building blocks of creativity and their properties in turn become significant in the construction of towns and cities.

The transition from creating a shelter to creating a city does not necessarily indicate an increase in practical ability. Only the capacity of the material mind can influence this. The greater the capacity of our material mind, the greater our *practical intelligence* and the more attributes we will be able to consider when working in the world of things. In postulating the identity of an object, the material mind need take account only of the significant features from a potentially endless list. Thus, for one object, color, shape and smell may determine its associations while another may be conceptualized in accord with sound, taste, and weight. How often do we say, "I never thought of using that in this way"? Within each person whatever properties of an object are regarded as relevant will become the personalized currency of all future creative processes involving that object. To a plumber a pipe is for transporting fluids, to a mechanic it is an object for applying more torque to a wrench.

Up to now we have considered practicality as that which serves a physical need. A shelter protects us from the rain, a cup holds water and pipes convey fluids or serve as levers. However, there are many examples of physical creativity that do not serve practical needs. In religion and the arts, technical creativity is often taken to its zenith in the fashioning of psychologically transporting objects that have great symbolic significance. Only the material mind has the capacity to meet this creative challenge by its independent registration of the *iconic significance* versus the *parametric properties* of objects. In keeping with hemispheric specialization, the conceptualization of objects in accordance with their symbolic significance is the business of the material mind of the right hemisphere while the parametric properties of objects falls to the material mind in the left hemisphere. The product of the material mind therefore always represents a balance achieved within the individual of these two elements of practicality.

As adults we hardly notice how we are continuously testing the reality of our perceptions. If we hear a baby cry in a nearby room we investigate whether it is a real baby that we can see, touch and smell, or whether the sound we heard comes from something else like a radio or an animal. What we are essentially doing is verifying the presence of a real baby using all of our senses. In nature the need to verify first observations is all the more important because mimicry is so widespread in the animal kingdom. As the human child passes through the stages of cognitive development, this process of verification is important to the psychosocial, material and abstract domains of thought. In the emotional realm, we may wish to verify our initial divination of the emotions underlying the intentions of others. In the abstract realm, verification might concern comprehending the arguments behind the ideas or beliefs of another. However, the psychosocial and the abstract domain have in common that the entities they deal with have no manifestations in the real world. Both emotion and ideas are nervous constructs. Things are totally different in the material realm. The material mind thinks about real things. Such things have properties, like weight, area and volume. For these reasons we can say that the business of the material mind is the verification and subsequent manipulation of reality.

Very young children can clearly perceive most things in their surroundings. As we have seen, however, perception is not a substitute for thought. The capacity to understand physical reality arises in the middle years of childhood and corresponds with the child's ability to perform concrete operations. Following this period the now pubescent adolescent (ages 11-15) is typically obsessed with his newfound ability to explore ideas and possibilities and, often to the dismay of parents, apportions little time to practical matters. In the preoperational stage (ages 2-7), the thoughts of children are largely confined to the emotional realm such that in the physical domain of life, they are easily deceived. Three year-olds are, for instance, readily tricked by physical appearances. Even though they may watch a piece of white paper being placed behind a blue filter, they express the belief that the paper is truly blue. By 6 years of age they still make blatant errors in discerning between appearance and reality. Not until the material mind is sufficiently matured do children show the ability to cognitively manipulate the physical parameters of objects. Until that time their physical reality has little influence over their cognitive processes.

As any practically gifted person will tell you, there is an acute difference between recognizing an object and being able to see its usefulness. To recognize it we need only to identify it, a process requiring no more insight than locating its name within our language areas. To assess its usefulness we must be cognizant of its properties. Most people who have survived prefrontal lobotomy can still perceive and identify objects as a consequence of their language areas remaining operative. However, the lobotomized patient is characteristically unable to interpret novel objects or scenarios.

It is very hard to seek within the brain a site for practicality. The objects around us naturally permeate many domains of consciousness. Any smelly, colored, noisy form has the potential to excite many of the cortex's perceptual areas. To pinpoint the material mind has required a combination of insight and clever experimental design.

Inspecting and identifying objects or judging their familiarity requires thought. Presented with a familiar shape, color, sound or smell, we are naturally reminded of certain objects or people. The more difficult the task the more deeply we will have to think about it to come up with an answer. Scanning the brains of people while they are engaging in such tasks enables scientists to work out which areas of cortex are involved in thinking about practical challenges. When this is done BA47 and BA45 are activated.

The response of BA45 to tasks involving the presentation of objects was not surprising because, as part of Broca's motor speech area, BA45 has long been known to be important in the *naming of objects*. However, the involvement of the more anterior BA47 was puzzling, especially because considerable evidence indicated that our perceptual awareness of objects is conjured within post-prefrontal parts of the cortex. These object-sensitive, post-prefrontal representations send the information they collect to BA47 and BA45 via a very important neural highway called the *ventral stream*. With its arrival at BA45 a name could be attached. At this stage, the representation of an object across cortical space may seem to be complete. The question was, however, what function could the activation of BA47 be serving? An important clue was that, BA47 responded to familiar objects and not to unfamiliar objects. Familiar objects are distinguishable from unfamiliar ones in one very important way, namely their usefulness. To successfully utilize an object in a task we must appreciate its usefulness. In operational terms, there is only one task left for BA47 to perform that has not already been achieved in downstream cortical areas. That task is the elaboration of first order concepts that embody the practical and symbolic properties of a vast array of objects enabling us to immediately assess their usefulness.

In the concrete operational phase the child develops a comprehension of linear dimensions, the numbers of items in an array (irrespective of how they are arranged) and the amount of material in an object (irrespective of its shape). Modern studies in child psychology emphasize that there is variation in the exact age children attain each Piagetian level and that intensive education can be used to force an earlier development of competence. However, what concerns us here, are the operational principles that are significant to the development of practicality in a typical child. The ages typically cited are averages determined from observations made mostly on children of European descent. Between the sixth and seventh years there develops the ability to judge that the amount of liquid in a glass is not indicated only by the height of the column of fluid but also by its diameter. Between the 8th and 11th years, the child can estimate the equivalence of the area of two differently shaped outlines. Also at this stage comes the ability to appreciate that the weight of a clay ball is the same even if the clay is subsequently reformed into a different shape. For the first time volume and form are understood as separate parameters providing a crude comprehension of the third dimension, depth. By the 10th to 12th years shape and volume are clearly assessed as independent quantities.

For any individual child the level of performance on these tasks is situationally dependent. For instance, the young child may fail to correctly judge the relative size of differently shaped lumps of clay but is surprisingly successful in this task if differently shaped cookies are presented as the subject material. Just as many of the first words learnt by infants are related to their visceral needs, so too do children entering the phase of concrete operations do better on practical tasks if the props are composed of objects related to those needs. Similarly, older children when asked to describe the view of a doll placed upon the other side of a scale model do better if the doll and the objects are regularly used in their make believe games. Familiarity and reward clearly assert a critical influence over the arousal of the material mind.

As part of our cerebral organ of speech BA45 is always activated in language tasks. However, brain scans taken during certain linguistic challenges reveal that BA47 is often seconded to the task. The manner in which BA47 and BA45 participate in language, exemplifies the rational-emotive dichotomy between the left and right hemispheres of the brain. Thus, on the right side these areas combine to meet the subjective challenges of language, participating in the generation of emotional tone (prosody), retrieving the "correct" words and even halting speech. In contrast, within the rational left hemisphere, these areas are responsible for the more technical aspects of speech including semantic and syntactic processing, word encoding and, to rub salt in the wound, registering the success of word retrieval by that ever troublesome, overly sensitive right hemisphere.

The theoretical relevance of speech to a highly communal, practically able species is obvious. Evidence is emerging to show that Broca's motor speech area not only drives language but has some potential to organize and respond to body movements in the process of motor learning and communication. There is little doubt that the evolutionary expansion of the material mind through the prehumans has nurtured the seed of language which probably began with the evolution of *Homo habilis* and is apparent even in the primordia of Broca's area found in living non-human primates. As well as being part of the material mind the anterior part of Broca's area (BA45) orchestrates the movements of speech and the nominative (naming) process that necessarily involves the descriptive identification of real things. In this process BA45 is highly interactive with the more anterior BA47 wherein there is a representation of the symbolic significance and parametric properties of both inanimate and animate (including people) objects. Given the strong interactions between BA47 and the anterior part of Broca's area, BA45, one can easily imagine how the material mind can generate the inspiration to communicate with other agents about a particular practical challenge. The involvement of the material mind with language indicates that its influences are not confined to the identification and manipulation of things but also play a vital role in human communication.

The Origin of Hypothesis - The Abstract Mind
"Picture a massless particle." Koan of Modern Physics.

A strong impact to the side of the forehead and slightly above most people's hairline, has the potential to damage the cortex covering the convex, upper surface of the prefrontal lobe. Damage to this part of the cortex produces what is known as apathetic syndrome, a condition characterized by a lack of awareness and initiative, reduced levels of cognitively derived motivation and the loss of both attentional focus and motility (hypokinesis). The ability to rotate mental images of objects, manipulate ideas and to plan is also severely compromised. Because of these observations this part of the prefrontal cortex has long been suspected of being the biological substrate of our powers of reason. The center of this region is occupied by BA46, an area of cortex that only matures around the 15th year of life when, as Piaget observed, an adolescent is newly able to contemplate hypotheses and possibilities.

In 1781 at the age of 57, the German philosopher, Immanuel Kant (1724-1804), published his *Critique of Pure Reason* wherein he sought to define the origins of abstract thought. The only tools available to him were argument, introspection and half a century of existence. Armed thus, Kant proposed that our complex reasoning stemmed from two elements: an *a priori* or preexisting element and an *a posteriori* or acquired element. He envisaged his *a priori* element as the very structural foundation of our capacity to think at the level of ideas and theories. He further postulated that this *a priori* element did not arise from our worldly experiences, but that it was fashioned instead, by our inevitable encounter with the intangible phenomena of space and time. In contrast, he saw his *a posteriori* element as being created by the day-to-day experiences of life. In Kant's proposal, space and time are recognized as phenomena, which because they cannot be appreciated directly are essentially intangible. Kant asserted that these particular intangible phenomena are essential to establishing the substrate upon which all abstract thought is dependent - a postulate in which Kant was inadvertently elucidating a great truth about the biological substrate underlying our powers of complex reasoning.

As Kant followed his suggestion with a lengthy consideration of what is meant by *phenomena*, it is perhaps useful to clarify what is meant here by *intangible phenomena*. Let us take the most conspicuous intangible phenomena, space and time, as examples. Even though we know both exist in the world around us, we cannot observe either directly. In comparison, color, size, form, sound, odor, taste and texture are phenomena that characterize discrete elements of our surroundings and as such can be directly sensed and instantly evaluated. All penetrate our consciousness through specific sensory pathways. All contribute to the identification, organization and conceptualization of the psychosocial and material domains of our existence. In contrast, we cannot see, hear, smell, taste or touch either space or time. Space and time are ethereal elements of the universe that pervade even the most esoteric domains of art and literature. The mere mention of them can transport us into an almost transcendent state of cerebral wonderment. Space and time can only be arbitrarily quantified. Both are cerebrally knowable but neither can be directly perceived.

Initially the location of objects in space enters our consciousness through visual, auditory and somaesthetic information that is brought together in part of the parietal cortex – a region located posterior to the prefrontal areas. This spatial information is sent forward through each hemisphere to BA46 via a second neural highway called the *dorsal stream*. As well as information about space, the dorsal stream also carries time related information extracted from the auditory system's processing of sound. In the same way as the ventral stream delivers information to BA47 (the material mind) about the identity of familiar objects, so the dorsal stream delivers information about space and time to BA46 (the abstract mind). The question is what does BA46 do with this information?

When an adult human suffers a prefrontal lobotomy the parietal cortex is left intact and as we would expect the patient retains his ability to perceive the spatial location of objects. Even years before the maturation of BA46, children are clearly aware of where things are in their surroundings. Only the fact that space is poorly represented in their drawings indicates that this aspect of existence has yet to be represented in thought (*The Art of Children*: Chapter 2: Section 3). As to what BA46 does with the information relayed to it from the parietal cortex, there can be only one answer. The spatial and temporal information received by BA46 has already generated an awareness of space by activating the (post-prefrontal) parietal cortex. By the process of elimination the only thing left to be extracted from the spatiotemporal information arriving at BA46, must be a set of conceptual constructs fashioned to embrace the properties of space and time. As space and time cannot be directly sensed, these constructs are not the product of sensory realities. Instead, they constitute second or higher order concepts that register space and time as ideational icons that are at least one step removed from reality. It is presumably through this process that BA46 becomes tuned to the creation of hypotheses and beliefs that, in turn, can be manipulated entirely within the matrices of abstract thought.

The reason a piece of cortex can be constructed and tuned to serve such an abstract and even esoteric function, stems from a simple developmental principle of cortical circuitry. This states that, as a piece of cortex matures, the architecture of its neural networks is potently influenced by the inputs it receives from other areas of the cortex or elsewhere in the brain. The "purpose", as such, is the tuning of the neural networks in a manner that serves the survival of the animal or person. While the gross internal structure of the cerebral cortex, including the regional specializations in structure which define Brodmann's areas, is determined by genes, the fine tuning of cerebral circuitry is determined by the nature of the information it receives from elsewhere. In the immediately pre-pubescent years of a human life, space and time arrive at the door of the still immature abstract mind. Challenged with these inputs, the living neural circuitry of BA46 will configure itself, possibly by establishing circuitry that minimizes its own response to incoming information and so reduces the unnecessary expenditure of metabolic energy. As predicted by Kant more than two hundred years ago, the abstract mind is structurally configured around space and time and so developmentally tailored, to the ideational manipulation of all intangible phenomena such as atomic structure or the nature of consciousness.

Ockham's Razor is a metaphor for the *Principle of Parsimony*, the cutting away of useless or gratuitous ideas in the explanation and acceptance of the simplest hypothesis that is in accord with our observations. Ockhamism was the product of

William of Ockham (14th Century) whom in wielding his razor declared that contrary to previous opinion, our "intellect" is not necessarily distinct from our "will". It turns out that he was correct because the cerebral energy devoted to working out a final strategy is both the process of intellect (understanding) and will (motivation). Thus, although all motivation has its origin in the cortex's emotional centers, the importance of the abstract mind in fashioning behavior means that it is critical to both these functions.

When we are challenged with a difficult theoretical problem we hold our head as though we would like to massage those overworked prefrontal areas that in such moments seem to contain our entire being. Brain scans show that in such moments the abstract mind is highly active. For example, the enigmatic task of attending to the color of the word "blue" written in red ink causes activation of BA46; the degree of activation being proportional to the *mental effort* required to meet the challenge. It is activity in the abstract mind that we seem to monitor in assessing our usage of *cerebral energy*. If the abstract mind is damaged, the intellect is diminished such that we are unable to understand and therefore solve new problems.

Like the material mind, the abstract mind of each hemisphere is specialized. Thus, BA46 in the left hemisphere is directly related to effort or "willed action", while in the right hemisphere BA46 responds according to the logistical complexity of the task in hand. The abstract mind almost simultaneously addresses cognitive challenge in two ways; on the left BA46 produces an idea, pronouncing that "it might work", and on the right BA46 throws up its metaphorical hands and complains that "it looks very difficult". The left elaborates an idea and the right checks its plausibility.

The capacity for entertaining the possible only begins around eleventh year. By 15 it is complete and in Piagetian terms, the teenager is now fully capable of performing formal operations. In this last phase of childhood, reasoning increasingly utilizes hypothesis as part of an analytical process that crudely resembles the scientific method. With the maturation of the abstract mind there is established an entirely personal set of constructs (beliefs), amongst which the transitory self-orientated concepts that characterize teenage egocentrism constitute one of the most prominent illusions (*maya*) of the pubescent teenager. To the chagrin of every parent, there emerges in the teenager the ultimate tool for the creation of idealistic attitudes and opinions. Neither the empathetic ruminations of social mind nor the stabilizing influences of the material mind can compete with the novelty of a wholly new dimension of wonderment. In consequence of this the teenager is highly receptive to religious doctrines, political theories, nationalistic fervor and a host of other ideational obsessions. Things that were once only facts and stories become pregnant with possibilities. Principles become the focus mental life as deductive logic interacts with life experiences in the generation of conceptual beliefs that will dominate behavior for many a year to come.

The ability to make complex hypotheses on a firm platform is the distinguishing feature of humanity and yet the cognitive capacity to do so is, in itself, a highly dangerous characteristic of the human psyche. So powerfully does the possible dominate the newly matured psyche that the suicide notes of young teenagers sometimes indicate that they have the completely unfounded, hypothetical belief that taking their own life will not end their existence – a belief shared by 67% of Americans. This tragic scenario underscores the extreme danger of indoctrinating children and teenagers into the completely hypothetical beliefs such as, for example, that there is an afterlife - a belief common to all religions and deeply woven into new age dogmas of reincarnation. In a world where many people do not have to concern themselves with practicalities in order to survive, we are at risk of surrendering ourselves completely to the penchant of the abstract mind to create ideologies, which, in reality, often have disastrous outcomes.

Science and philosophy owe their existence to thoughts that involve the manipulation of possibilities and hypothetical ideas. The abstract mind does not indulge in the "what" of things, it is wired up to resolve the "hows" and alas, to contemplate the "whys" that so easily trap the unwary into a lifetime of fruitless navel gazing. In the final selection of behavioral strategy the abstract mind has plenipotentiary power over all other domains of thought. When subjects are presented with the cognitive challenges utilized in IQ tests, the abstract mind (BA46) is always activated often in concert with the practical (BA47), social (BA9) or even temporal (BA10) mind. These findings show that, for all its diversity of function, general intelligence, or the so-called Spearman's G-factor (*The Measurement of Intelligence*: Chapter 2: Section 8), is primarily dependent upon our abilities in the realm of the hypothetical. Humans dominated by the abstract mind, most of whom are of European origin, operate as totally cerebral animals, experiencing life as a ideational journey in which people and things are integrated and understood through an internally framework of theories and principles.

Thought processes within the social, material and temporal domains of mind are orientated towards the integration of information from the cortex's perceptual representations into meaningful, first-order concepts such as friend, foe, length, form and color. In contrast, thought processes within the mature abstract mind utilize the first-order concepts elaborated by the social, material and temporal domains of mind to create second- or higher-order concepts that do not necessarily exist outside of theory. This process, by which the abstract mind reflects upon the conceptual products of the other domains of the mind, constitutes what is known in psychology as *metacognition* – the ability to think about our thoughts.

The functions of the abstract mind are what most distinguish human beings from our closest primate relatives. But is the abstract mind really the highest level of the human brain? In fashioning our strategy of behavior are we truly responsive to a center that derives so much from the conceptualization of the intangible? To complete its candidacy for this position we need to establish the existence of channels that bring to its door all things conceptual and give it command over our actions. Both the position of BA46 in the cortex and its interconnections with the rest of the brain, do fulfill these criteria. Thus, BA47 (the material mind) is powerfully interconnected with BA46 (the abstract mind), enabling our conceptualization of abstract phenomena to be addressed by, and in return to address, the world of real things. On the opposite (medial) side the abstract mind is also strongly interconnected with the psychosocially orientated, social mind (BA9), enabling the application of hypothetical thought to the psychosocial domain of life - a process to which much psychological theory owes its origins. Along the anterior border of BA46, the abstract mind is in direct communication with BA10 (the temporal mind), enabling it to play a critical role in the development, reconstruction and execution of plans stored within our prospective memory banks by BA10 (*The Origins of the Future - the Temporal Mind*: Chapter 3: Section 3). Finally, neuroanatomical studies show that BA46 is powerfully connected to the cortex's principle motor and premotor areas (BAs 8, 6 and 4), from whence the movement of the eyes and the component movements implicit in all behavior, arise. In this way the abstract mind holds the executive power of both creation and veto over all demands for physical action that arise from other domains of the psyche. Viewed within the living, behaving brain, the abstract mind sits at the hub of the cerebral cortex from where it can exert these plenipotentiary powers over all that we are and all that we do. However, this does not mean that all people or even all human races or populations are dominated by abstract thought. Although a power in its own right, the abstract mind must act in accordance with the demands of other cognitive domains. For example, the behavioral strategies, attention and imagination of a person with a large social mind will be dominated by their emotional intelligence even though their actions, like all actions, will be mediated through, in their case, a less powerful abstract mind. What is important to appreciate is that, whether dominant or not, the abstract mind is always the last link in the chain of command. After the abstract mind there is nowhere else to go. Once there we have arrived at the highest level of human consciousness. To use the words that once adorned the desk of the one-time President of the United States, Harry S. Truman, "The buck stops here!"

The Origins of Understanding - The Third Eye
"Einstein repeatedly expressed suspicion of the restrictions of linear [logical] thought, concluding that propositions arrived at by purely logical means, were completely empty of reality even if one could properly explain what "reality" means; it was intuition he declared, that had been crucial to his thinking." Peter Matthiessen, American Author. From: *The Snow Leopard*. Viking Press, New York, 1978.

The Hindu yogis recognize seven Chakras that constitute discrete, hierarchically-organized experiences of the inner world or psyche. That the Chakras are recognizable experiences, means that each must arise from activity in a particular part of the cerebral cortex. The 6th Chakra is the second highest. From the 6th Chakra the world is "seen" through the *Third Eye*. In this state of elevated awareness there is said to be fusion between the "intuitive" and "logical" aspects of mind. Thus, either several areas of mind always contribute the experience of the 6th Chakra or a special area exists which is able to provide a simultaneous experience of logical and intuitive thought. Such an experience would naturally appear to have transcendental properties, for although it still involves thought processes so conspicuously absent during the "no mind" experience of the 7th and highest Chakra, the 6th Chakra embodies a balance between the often contradictory energies of the heart and the head.

117

The use of the word intuition in the definition of the 6th Chakra and elsewhere, requires some clarification. From the Latin *in* ("in") and *tueri* ("to look at"), intuition means the power to know how something happens, or will happen, without depending on the power of reasoning. Such knowing is most conspicuous in the inductive processes that characterize the psychosocial domain of thought. Indeed, our emotional intelligence arises from an integration of our raw emotions with the body language of others. Emotional intelligence is essentially a comprehension of the fundamental laws that govern the life of all mammals and more broadly, the entirety of the natural world. It cannot, therefore, have a basis in deductive logic. For these reasons emotional intelligence is often confused with intuition. Indeed, it is often said that women are "more intuitive" than men, whereas in truth they are generally "more emotionally intelligent" that men. Intuition is not the same thing as emotional intelligence. Highly intuitive men with little emotional intelligence are astoundingly common. Intuition is a knowing, a direct seeing of the truth. It can, for instance, involve a "knowing" or a hunch that relates specifically to either practical or hypothetical ideation. Like Plato's Sophia, the 6th Chakra is arrived at when there is a coalescence of the abstract and the social mind. In the awakened quiescence of this state, the augmentation of intuition and insight are inevitable.

Recent studies of the structure of the prefrontal lobes of humans and the higher non-human primates have revealed the existence of an area which resembles in cellular structure both BA9, the social mind, and BA46, the abstract mind. Neurobiologists refer to this area as Brodmann's area 9/46 (BA9/46) and it has even been identified in the relatively small prefrontal lobes of the macaque monkeys. Although it clearly involved in cognition, little is yet known about how its role differs from those of BA46 and BA9. Perhaps here is a region of cortex with a neural architecture capable of accomodating both realms of thought. Within such a network the psychosocial aspects of life might be interwoven with the purely hypothetical to generate conceptual frameworks that are the product of both emotional and abstract intelligence – concepts that manifests in our thoughts as that inexplicable knowing we call intuition.

Woven into the fabric of many religions is the expectation that soon upon the Earth there will be born a new human being, one who will bring humanity the insights necessary to transcend all suffering. One day a savior will come to us and we will be forever changed. One day there will be a new incarnation of Vishnu. One day Christ will be reborn amongst us. One day, somewhere in our midst, a mutation of the human genome will see the progenitor of a new humanity, a humanity that may even take responsibility for our languishing Earth and not just say its God's work. Although they do not speak of genes, the mystics have long foreseen the need for such a transformation. The "Perfect One" will come and make us whole. The vision of this destiny is the vision of the third eye - that realized level in human consciousness, where the two great tributaries of human thought are at last united.

Chapter 4. Aberrations of the Mind

When the genes that are responsible for the normal development of a particular part of the brain are mutated, we have an opportunity to observe human behavior under conditions where there is malformation and malfunction of the affected part. Thus, certain psychiatric conditions provide significant insights into how the thoughts and behavior of normal people are subdivided between the structurally independent parts of the human mind. The following sections focus on several of these conditions that arise from improper development of specific components of the mind.

The Little People
"The childhood shows the man,
As morning shows the day."
John Milton (1608-1674). English Poet, Polemicist and Author.

Our mythologies are filled with the stories of the elves and leprechauns. Romantic and expressive in their ways, the little people can be seen dancing in forest glades or singing the night away, surrounded always by friends, whose love is pure, boundless and eternal. Myth is often allegorical and so never entirely fictional. These elfin people exist, even today. They suffer, if suffering it can be called, from a genetical abnormality called Williams-Beuren or simply Williams Syndrome that occurs in one of every 7,500 babies. They are small in stature, elf-like in features and easily frightened by certain classes of sounds (hyperacusis). In many ways the Williams people resemble young children. They are, for instance, relatively indifferent to the passage of time. Also like children they are predominantly orientated towards the interpersonal rather than the practical or material aspects of life. Because of their gentle, pervasive and often ethereal ways, some say of the Williams people that they have been "touched by God". However, on conventional IQ tests which evaluate our abilities of complex reasoning, the Williams people perform poorly, achieving scores of around 60, the average in the general population being, by definition, 100. On the basis of IQ measurement alone the Williams people therefore resemble people with Down's syndrome who clearly suffer from mental retardation. Like those with Down's syndrome, abstract concepts and long-term planning gain little expression within the consciousness of the Williams people. However, unlike those with Down's syndrome, the Williams people are powerfully orientated towards, and even insightful within, the psychosocial arena of life.

As a phenomenon of the mind, Williams Syndrome beautifully illustrates the fundamental dichotomy between emotional and intellectual intelligence. Nowhere is this more apparent than in the spoken language of the Williams people. Whereas most mentally retarded individuals (including Down's people) have poor language skills, the Williams people are masters of the metaphor, utilizing in their almost poetic prose, vocabularies that are far larger than would be expected on the basis of their psychologically-assessed, mental age. Asked to describe an elephant one Williams child said, "It has long, gray ears, fan ears, ears that can blow in the wind". Despite this, when presented with a technically complex scenario the Williams people have difficulty comprehending it in a systematic, analytical manner. Presented with a bowl of fruit they clearly recognize and can verbally identify the fruit and the bowl. However, when asked to draw what they see they fail to illustrate the special functional and spatial relationship between these two items, instead drawing the fruit and the bowl separate from one another. Their difficulty is in attaching relevance to the spatial relationships of things. Within their thoughts the fruit and the bowl both have an independent existence. Yet the Williams people are outstandingly good at remembering people's faces and have a good comprehension of the identity of objects that clearly includes their iconographic significance. Indeed, whether animate or inanimate, it seems each object in their world has a separate and often a personal significance in the scheme of things. We cannot communicate what does not enter our awareness. A person who cannot comprehend the significance of spatial relationships will not represent them in their artistic renditions of things. The Williams people are indifferent to the important logical concept that the bowl holds the fruit together and so stops it rolling off the table. A person who thinks like the Williams people would speak preferentially of images and forms using a vernacular that is rich in emotional tone.

Many of the Williams people are drawn to music. Despite their cognitive difficulties they have, like Tolkien's elves, an outstanding memory for complex passages of music and the words of lengthy songs. In addition, they have a near perfect perception of pitch, as well as a very precise sense of rhythm. One individual is recorded as saying, "Music is my favorite way of thinking". Modern studies of professional musicians show that in their right hemisphere, the part of cortex that is involved in the perception of sound, is larger than normal. An enlarged planum temporale (part of BA42) provides a person with more cortical space and so more cortical modules with which to distinguish between and remember patterns of musical notes. The planum temporale is often larger in Williams people explaining their penchant for music.

Like ordinary people, the topics that catch the imagination of the Williams people and find their way into their language, accurately reflect the operational principles of their mind. Loving, trusting, caring and always sensitive to the needs of others, the Williams people clearly have a high level of emotional intelligence. Within them the heart gains easy mastery over the head. Indeed, the parts of the cortex known to represent emotions and biodynamic imagery, as well as the social mind (BA9) are disproportionately large. In addition, their gifts of verbal and symbolic expression, perception of detail and face recognition indicate that Broca's motor speech area and the material mind (BA47) are fully functional. Against this, their difficulties with spatial relationships and their low IQ scores are correlated with a reduced allocation of cortex to the spatiotemporal representations that are critical to the normal development of the abstract mind (BA46). It is within the citadel of deductive logic (the abstract mind) and possibly also within the center of planning (the temporal mind, BA10) that the cognitive capacities of the Williams people fall short of those of ordinary humans.

It is in the nature of consciousness that when there are deficits in one arena, other arenas become more significant. If you had an operation that removed all your cerebral cortex except the visual areas, you would quite naturally spend the rest of your conscious life absorbed in the visual world. Conversely, if we are deprived of sight we would naturally become more preoccupied smell, taste, touch and hearing. So it is that the malfunctioning of their abstract mind ensures that the behavior of the Williams people is always dominated by cortex serving their emotional intelligence. Elves do not build skyscrapers or design rockets to the moon. Instead they court us with their unbridled celebration of life. Like the elves, the Williams people symbolize a purely romantic existence. Centered in the psychosocial domain of life their vision is truly the consciousness of the metaphor. They may not comprehend the complex logic behind writing a check, but presented with a wordless picture book they will immediately create a dramatic story that would challenge the imagination and sensitivities of most that sit upon our stock exchanges. Like the young child and like the "little people" of our mythologies, the Williams people personify that domain of wisdom that flows from a spontaneous comprehension of human and animal nature. Spared from reasoned judgments and their attendant moral beliefs, they are free to reflect upon the loveliness of being. "Everyone in the world is my friend" one girl was quoted as saying. The Williams people confront us with the unbridled innocence of childhood framed as an open invitation to be within this moment and therefore all moments that are to follow.

Yet for all their virtues, it can be a great embarrassment to have elves at the table. They are always singing, talking to the trees and telling silly stories. They just do not seem to have grown up. How could they be trusted to take care of business? So it is that historically we have not wholly embraced the Williams people. How could we when so much of our survival depends on our acting upon a comprehensive understanding of complex principles? So it is that some believe that in centuries past the Williams people formed little enclaves outside the villages of ordinary people; small almost invisible communities, where they lived precariously as furtive, inquisitive and innocent representatives of the golden age of childhood.

The Mechanistic World of Autism
"The machine unmakes the man. Now that the machine is so perfect, the engineer is nobody." Ralph Waldo Emerson (1803-1882). American Essayist, Philosopher and Poet.

Better to be always a child than never to know the magic of childhood. Whereas the Williams people are forever trapped in childhood, other people are born into a consciousness that never knows the playfulness of social contact. Their vision is a mechanistic realm of social sterility. So practically orientated are they that even close family members can be almost indistinguishable from inanimate objects. While they may enjoy rough and tumble play, display temper tantrums and giggle, these elements of behavior are expressed as raw emotions that persist when ordinary children have begun establishing workable social strategies through make-believe games. Such a person is said to be *autistic*.

Autism affects 1 or 2 children in every thousand, being 3 to 4 times more common in boys than girls. Autism and related conditions are found twice as often amongst the children of engineers – a profession that requires a very high level of mechanistic thinking. Nevertheless, up to 37% of autistic children suffer perinatal trauma that could potentially threaten the early maturation of the developing social mind, which typically becomes operational between 9 to 12 months of age. More than 60% continue to need care throughout their lives.

The deeply autistic person lives in a world that, if we were to enter as adults, we would experience as an unbearable sojourn within the depths of solitary confinement. Within the consciousness of an autistic person there seems to be little space in which to envisage human nature. Unable to understand what can and cannot be surmised about the intentions of others, the autistic person appears to be remote and indifferent. Their poor level of emotional intelligence indicates a severe deficit in the operation of the social mind. In this respect autism is the antithesis of Williams syndrome. Unable to bond with others, deeply autistic persons are socially isolated, being sometimes given to repetitive, self-stimulatory activities like rocking or banging their heads. Their everyday behavior may involve slavishly following rigid, almost mechanical routines, while with little awareness of human interaction, they commonly believe that their thoughts are placed in their heads by telepathy.

Between 1 to 4 years of age, normal children progressively develop the ability to comprehend the intentions of other people, acquiring thus what is called a Theory of Mind. In the deeply autistic child this phase is simply missed. Sometimes there are hints of future problems in the early postnatal months. However, usually autism becomes conspicuous between 18 and 36 months. While the normal child is becoming highly social and interacting personally, even with inanimate objects, the autistic child usually withdraws socially, rejecting its carers and neglecting whatever communicative skills it had previously acquired. For a parent there is perhaps no more painful experience than encountering autism in one's child. For at a time when the ordinary child awakens to celebrate life in the company of its family, the autistic child withdraws into a world of silent, cold observation. As one mother remarked, "We would find our son staring at the dust particles as they floated in the sunlight, oblivious to our presence, seemingly unable to sense or respond to us".

Growing up completely absorbed in the material world, the deeply autistic child lacks an inner blueprint of humanity. Indeed, the nuances of the living world that are our principal connection with our biological origins find no place within the consciousness of the deeply autistic. Cognitively remote, even from their own emotions and moods, often hypersensitive to touch, sound, sight and even smell, the deeply autistic can only express their feelings directly as irrepressible vocalizations such as are known to arise when the emotional centers of the brain are electrically stimulated. In normal infant development, the moods and emotions of others are read from their body language and incorporated into the conceptual frameworks of the social mind. Like normal infants, autistic children can attribute goals to animated shapes (eg. moving circles and triangles) and show autonomic arousal when they are confronted with another person in distress. They also do badly when asked to perform the mental task of matching the emotions portrayed in 4 stereotyped facial expressions with those expressed in 4 different vocalizations and they are particularly impaired in responding to complex, socially-related, emotional responses like embarrassment.

The source of their difficulties is revealed by brain scans. These indicate that in autism there is always dysfunction in that part of the cortex (the fusiform gyrus, BA37) that responds to the familiarity of facial and bodily form and that normally relays this information to the emotional centers which, in turn, influence the social mind. In extreme cases, dysfunction extends to the cortical representation of biodynamic imagery (superior temporal sulcus) that is directly interconnected with the social mind and also plays an important role in social imagination. The consequence of these deficits is that the deeply autistic, preoperational child is compromised in its ability to build up a cognitive construct of its psychosocial world. Like normal children the autistic child may spontaneously coo and babble for the first 6 months of its life. However, just when the normal child begins to attempt interaction through language, the autistic child falls silent. Unable to interpret the nuances of its psychosocial milieu that normally provide the incentive to experiment with speech, it simply retreats into an asocial world from whence (in stark contrast to the Williams people) 50% of autistic children are totally unable to learn language. The emergent adult suffers a permanent and probably structural deficit of the social mind and is consequently obliged to deal with life by applying the mechanistic strategies that characterize the behavioral repertoires of the autistic.

Speech is learned inductively as part of social experience. A fully operational social mind is necessary for normal levels of human interaction and human interaction is essential for the inductive learning process that underlies our initial acquisition of language. Trial and error and not grammatical comprehension are critical. What cannot be framed cannot be said or otherwise expressed. Robbed of the seat of emotional intelligence a deeply autistic child simply lacks the cognitive machinery that enables it to implement anything other than the most rudimentary communication with parents and siblings. Instead of finding their way into strategic action, their biological urges and desires can only be expressed directly from the emotional centers from whence they burst forth as uncontrolled vocal and physical displays of raw emotion. The social arm of the ego is greatly compromised, the concept of self being almost entirely fashioned within the realms of practical and abstract thought, where it often finds an identity in terms of the technical and operational principles of machinery. By default, in its purest form the autistic mind is a mind isolated from the living world and thus entirely preoccupied with objects, plans and ideas related to the phenomena and components of wholly physical and abstract realms of cognition.

In milder cases of autism, language does develop but its onset is delayed until as late as 5 to 8 years of age. The usage of language in autism is illuminating with respect to the autistic mind. While a few autistic speakers use only single words, others often repeat the same phrase irrespective of the social setting. Some parrot what other people say to them, a condition linguists call *echolalia* and one that possibly indicates the emergence of primitive brain circuitry that enables vocal mimicry (*Mimicry, Movement Primitives and the Mind*: Chapter 2: Section 6). While some learn to read, they have difficulty in guessing missing words or in recognizing silly or inappropriate words in sentences such as "There is an electric apple". Most telling of their cognitive difficulties within the interpersonal is their tendency to confuse pronouns, failing to grasp that words like "my", "I" and "you" must be selected on the basis of who is speaking. For example, when Bill's teacher asks, "What is my name?" Bill will answer, "My name is Bill". This difficulty in the identification of self as a social entity versus the identity of others again reflects deficits in the social mind.

Given their difficulties with learning language, one might expect the autistic person to utilize, more than others, the language of the body. After all, non-verbal communication accounts for 90% of our communication. However, the facial expressions and gestures of the deeply autistic rarely match their attempts at verbalization. When present, speech tends to be high-pitched, singsong or robot-like. Because they have trouble reading the body language of others, their own attempts at non-verbal communication are often reliant on what have been called *instrumental gestures*, such as pointing or physically pushing someone towards a door. In contrast, they lack or avoid *expressive gestures*, such as hugging or offering consolation. The same tendency also pervades autistic speech. Thus, the melody of words that so color the speech of the Williams people is completely missing from the speech of the autistic.

Much is written about the special gifts of the autistic that are commonly known as *savant skills*, or the misnomer, *islets of intelligence*. While one in ten autistic people have notable talents there have been only about 100 people described as savants. Of these only 25 are presently living. Savant skills include exceptional abilities to memorize entire television shows, pages in a phone book or the results of every significant football game for the last 20 years. Other autistic toddlers as young as 3 years are able to draw very detailed, realistic 3-dimensional pictures at an age when their ordinary counterparts are learning to draw straight lines and are locked into 2-dimensional, highly animated representations. Some possess such a high level of spatial comprehension that they can easily put together complex jigsaw puzzles while others are able to comprehend writing and so are able to read even before they have attempted to speak. A few autistic children can play a song after hearing it once or name any note that they hear while others can learn the words to many languages but remain fixated upon the grammatical rules of their native tongue.

The special gifts of the *autistic savants* are again very instructive regarding the composite nature and serial development of the human mind. The disruption of the social mind as a result of malfunction of the facial and body language representations means that the autistic child is highly dependent on the temporal, practical and abstract domains of cognition. Different areas of the cerebral cortex mature at different post-natal ages. If some of the pathways that feed into a piece of cortex are missing at the time it matures, then it can become utilized by inputs that are normally confined to a neighboring piece of cortex. The cortex of the social mind is mature by early infancy, while the cortex of the temporal, material and abstract mind matures later in childhood. Therefore, should the normal inputs to BA9 (the social mind) be missing, it may become dominated by inputs that normally go only to BA10 (the temporal mind), BA47 (the material mind) or BA46 (the abstract mind). Consequently, the cortex that would have become the social mind will fail to develop the appropriate circuitry but instead evolve circuitry related to one or more of the other three domains of cognition.

It is easy to see how in an autistic child, a premature ability for 3-dimensional representation could arise by those inputs that normally underlie the establishment of the abstract mind (BA46) taking over the underutilized, though newly mature cortex of BA9 that would have otherwise been configured to conceptualize the psychosocial domain of existence. Similarly, a vast multilingual store of synonyms or the ability to simply "see" the day of a future or past date are savant gifts that might reflect the utilization of the cortex of BA9 for the conceptualization of information that is normally fed exclusively to either BA47 or BA10, respectively.

Whereas the Williams people live life as a story, nothing identifies the autistic mind as clearly as a miscomprehension of theatre. It is after all the social mind that draws people to the theatre, usually in the hopes of better understanding their emotional responses to their social milieu. Lacking an internal model for psychosocial interactions the autistic person has no basis for comprehending the theatrical. When, at a traditional Punch and Judy show Punch disappears from the stage, ordinary children become restless in anticipation of his inevitable return. Not so the autistic child. Unable to fathom Punch's intentions it simply watches without the anticipation born of psychosocial comprehension. The normal child easily grasps the social dynamic. They know that at any moment Punch will pounce back upon the stage and frighten Judy. The autistic child sees only that Punch has gone. What is to come, he or she cannot imagine. To the deeply autistic, life is an abstract representation of the interactions of physical entities, of which some have an unexplainable capacity to speak, touch and move.

Asperger's Syndrome - Living Through the Intellect
"One soul that lives and breathes with love and spontaneity,
One that calculates and orders, hides, fears and rage,
No effort on my part can change his state of mind,
My love doesn't warm him,
My care doesn't reach him,
My personality doesn't win him,
My feelings and opinions don't sway him." Extract from the poem: *"My Asperger Marriage"* by Carol, December 2002:
http://www.autismnsw.com.au/publications/KeynotesWinter04/Winter4.pdf

We all know people who have limited social skills but who are certainly not autistic. Nor can they be regarded as social phobics, for they do not have an aversion to people but simply an imponderable indifference to the society of others. Even amongst normal people social ability is highly variable. Through personality structure alone, some people revel in the diversity of human nature, while others find more joy in meeting practical challenges. Some know of the heavens and some know of the Earth. Most societies tolerate a wide range of social behavior, such that even the socially inept are still within the boundaries of "normalcy". There are, however, people whom although not autistic, are dramatically insensitive to the emotions of others and who have as a consequence, great difficult comprehending the dynamics of any social setting. These people suffer from what is known as Asperger's syndrome.

Many neurological and psychiatric conditions are part of a continuum. So it is that the characteristics of autism lie at one end of a behavioral spectrum. Whereas the deeply autistic person is totally cut off from the world of people, the person with Asperger's syndrome usually develops a quasi-normal existence within society. Impoverished in their vision of the human nature, their ability to develop a theory about the mind of another person lies somewhere between that of that of the normal and the autistic psyche. Moving one step further from the autistic condition, there emerges a special set of children whose mental characteristics fulfill the criteria for what has become known as the *Einstein Syndrome*. The name of the syndrome derives from the life history of Albert Einstein. Like this group of children his speech development lagged behind that of other children while his intellectual development surged ahead. Approximately 87% of these children are boys. As toddlers they excel at puzzles, have excellent memories and are intellectually precocious. Their difficulties in psychosocial matters are not restricted to language but also manifest in a delayed mastery of the toilet, intense reactions to noise, pain and frustration and a preference for solitary play. Somewhat isolated from people they form a subpopulation of intellectually gifted people in whom eccentricity and genius are common bedfellows.

Individuals with Asperger's syndrome typically fail to develop peer relationships and lack the motivation to share enjoyment, achievements or interests with others. Like autism, Asperger's syndrome seems to involve an early malfunctioning of the cortical sites that give normal people an awareness of the non-verbal signals of others. Consequently, the aspergic individual does not seek eye contact or reciprocation in relation to facial expressions or body posture. Also as in autism, people with Asperger's syndrome can be inflexibly bound to pointless routines and rituals, often showing a preoccupation with the parts of objects. Unlike the autistic person, their use of verbal language is not delayed but is somewhat abnormal in that despite an excellent vocabulary they are typically limited in their ability to verbally communicate intimacy.

As in Einstein's syndrome, children with Asperger's syndrome can maintain focus on a circumscribed subject and often show a high level of intellectual achievement. Thus, although socially compromised, the Asperger's person may appear as a brilliant, though absent-minded eccentric. As in autism, an explanation for this may be that the material and abstract mind develop earlier by utilizing still immature cortical tissue that, in the normal individual, might have been used for the social mind.

Aspergic people find it difficult to read other people or to answer questions about how they themselves feel. Not infrequently, they attempt to compensate for their low emotional intelligence by formally studying psychological theory. If they are intelligent they may be drawn, at an early age, into reading philosophy and religion in a quest to establish a blueprint of the ways of other humans, a schema arrived at in normal children automatically through inductive learning. Despite these efforts they are likely to remain forever misfits, lacking the spontaneity of response that so often guides appropriate behavior in the ongoing dynamic of social life. Understanding facts and rational logic is, by default, the *forte* of the Aspergic person. With only a sketchy comprehension of human nature they often make socially outrageous propositions or ask astonishingly silly questions about people, being afterwards quite unable to understand the negative reactions of others.

With little insight into the psychosocial domain and unable to guide their social interactions by relating personal interactions to their gut feelings, Aspergic people naturally have great difficulty in seeing where others are "coming from". Privately they are inclined to be dismissive of others, extending their indifference to animals that for ordinary people provide a comforting and responsive reassurance of the biological foundations of human existence. Inevitably most Aspergic people end up living alone where, faced by a relentless, psychologically imposed, isolation, they are at high risk of suicide.

The Freewheeling Mind of Schizophrenia

"A crazy syrup at the synapse,
festering like a witches brew,
can it be so? this sauce the source
of all the nightmares in my brain,
can chemistry account for pain?"
Emma's Poem. Emma suffered from schizophrenia, a disease of the mind. Emma was 19 when she took her own life.

Approximately 10% of people with schizophrenia commit suicide. "Schizophrenia", wrote the psychologist R. D. Laing in, The Divided-Self, "cannot be understood without understanding despair." In the East when a person dies it is said that they have left their body. When a person suffering from schizophrenia takes their own life they are seeking to escape their mind.

Schizophrenia literally means the *splitting of the mind*. In the general population schizophrenia affects approximately 1 in every 100 individuals. Roughly 25 to 30% of modern America's homeless population suffers from schizophrenia. Members of certain families are more at risk than others indicating a strong genetical basis. However, identical twins do not always share this disease showing that the environment also has some influence. Schizophrenia manifests itself between the ages of 17 and 25 years, approximately 2 to 10 years after the maturation of the abstract mind (BA46). Schizophrenia typically afflicts men at a somewhat younger age than women. Very rarely schizoid symptoms are apparent in children as young as 5 years, a time when the social mind (BA9) has only recently matured.

The experience of a schizophrenic episode is best described as a chaotic flow of thoughts that is accompanied by hallucinations in the form of voices or visions. The hearing of voices is the most common form of hallucination being experienced by about 65% of sufferers. To the schizophrenic these voices appear to have a life of their own. The voices of schizophrenia are not simply sounds or phrases but fully formed verbal communications, which seem to come from one or more, usually hostile, agents that are both omniscient and omnipresent. One man, who had been pursued for several days by these specters, wrote, "As before, I could catch part of their talk, but, in the theatre crowds, I could see them nowhere. I heard one of them, a woman, say: 'You can't get away from us; we'll lay for you and get you after a while!'…. I tried to escape from them by means of subway trains, darting up and down subway exits and entrances, jumping on and off trains, until after midnight. But, at every station where I got off the train, I heard the voices of these pursuers as close as ever" (L. Percy King Letter, c. 1940).

We are all capable of using our "mind's eye" to imagine voices and create visual imagery (*Subjectivity of Mental* Imagery: Chapter 1: Section 6). However, when we listen closely to our internal dialogue, it is very clear that the participating voices do not arise from our surroundings. Like our dreams, our imaginings have a surrealistic quality that dissociates them from reality, even though within them, we may recognize metaphors that represent the familiar constructs of our mind (*The Content of Dreams*: Chapter 2: Section 7). What is it that is different in schizophrenic consciousness that allows the conjured to take wing within the ether of reality?

The answer lies in a fundamental truth regarding the conscious perception of sensation. Put very simply, although each of our five senses involves the activation of a number of different areas of the cortex, it is the activity in the very earliest or *primary cortical receiving area* of each sense that makes us feel that a *sensation is grounded in reality*. When we use our imagination to conjure a visual image or an inner dialogue, brain scans show that the primary cortical receiving areas of our visual or auditory systems, respectively, remain silent (*The Exploration of Attention and Mental Imagery*: Chapter 1: Section 7). Experientially too, things created within our "mind's eye" simply "feel" different from normal sensory experience. Normally when information from our senses activates the primary sensory receiving areas of our cortex, the experience we have has a quality that causes us to naturally accept that it is from the outside world. In normal people the cortex's primary sensory areas are activated only by incoming sensory information but are inaccessible to the imaginings of the mind. In schizophrenia, however, brain scans tell us that the alien voices are associated with activity within the primary auditory cortex – activity that is clearly not the result of auditory stimulation. It is the unique grounding quality, conferred by the cortex's primary sensory representations, that cause the schizophrenic to emphatically believe that the alien voices accompanying their chaotic thoughts are located in the outside world where lives that elusive butterfly, we call *reality*.

At times we all experience a flow of thought. During this process it is easy to observe how, unless we are confused, the flow is typically orientated towards the solution of a particular problem or issue. Such thoughts may relate to a social dilemma, a practical problem or an abstract conundrum, but always they remain focused and relevant. Not so in schizophrenia. The delinquent thoughts of the schizophrenic readily transgress tried and true thematic boundaries. In schizophrenia, the normal progressive flow of thought resembles the bursting of a dam wherein diverse, and often unrelated, sensations, interpretations, plans and concepts join in the production of a cacophony of ideas and strategies. To observe the breaking of this dam we need only examine the speech of schizophrenics. Therein one may find almost simultaneous references to social mores, religious beliefs, various concepts of self-identity, attitudes, feelings, unfettered urges and practical rules mixed with a selection of the physical and psychological principles that the individual uses to conceptualize an often disturbingly aberrant vision of his social, physical and intellectual circumstances. Things take on an ever-changing identity, both of themselves and in relation to other objects. Gut feelings play tag with unwanted and sometimes terrifying ideas. A simple object such as a cup may in one moment be envisaged as a container, while in the next as an object of art, the next the Freudian symbol for a vagina and the next as a sign of an evil presence that is trying to trick one into drinking poison. The human mind is empowered with the ability to create mental imagery within a fraction of a second. So it is that during a schizophrenic episode chaos rules outside as well as inside the brain's executive office.

Amongst the relatives of schizophrenics it is not uncommon to find what have been called *schizotypal personalities*. These people, who appear to share some of the genetical constitution that underlies schizophrenia, manifest a propensity towards *magical thinking*. The new age preoccupation with previous lives, unexplainable "happenings" and divining the future probably draws heavily upon this subgroup. Their burden of irrationality is light compared to the mischief wrought by schizophrenia where thought easily becomes a fragmented, confusing and ultimately frightening experience.

Brain scans and neuroanatomical studies of schizophrenic patients reveal abnormalities in the social and abstract mind (BA9 and BA46). This perhaps explains why schizophrenia does not fully manifest until the developing child has reached puberty and begins to rely upon the recently mature abstract mind. As early as 5 years schizophrenia may manifest as delusional ideas about the intentions of others, reminiscent of the Theory of Mind difficulties experienced by people with Asperger's syndrome, but only after puberty when this is coupled with confusion at a level of hypothetical thought, do the fully blown symptoms of schizophrenia appear.

To the listener there often seems to be an important thread running through the schizophrenic's pronouncements. So strong and universal has been this sense of significance, that it has often been suggested that in hunter-gatherer and native tribes, schizophrenics made ideal candidates for witchdoctors, shamans and mystics. Although this particularly western viewpoint is no more likely to be true than the proposition that most priests, rabbis and ministers are also in touch with "God" through the ravages of a mental illness, the dialogue of schizophrenic conversation may still transport and intrigue the naive listener. In truth, however, there is nothing here of any tangible significance. So from where does the feeling come that within the pronouncements of the schizophrenic there are to be found profound insights? It arises it seems, from the sheer poetry of the schizophrenic's prose. Stripped of the confinements of goal orientation, devoid of any practical, social or theoretical relevance, the ever-cycling dialogue of the schizophrenic lays bare the basic components of reason that largely determine the behavioral strategies and personality structure of all humanity. Unadulterated by any useful content, released from the confines of logic and human understanding, the words of the schizophrenic often reveal the elemental foundations of human thought. It is small wonder that as witnesses of their pronouncements, we cannot help but be intrigued by this exposé of these omnipotent components of human comprehension.

One persistent theory of schizophrenia involves the neural systems within our brain that make us feel good, our so-called reward systems. There are many things, such as sex, eating, successfully solving a problem and all hedonic, recreational drugs, including nicotine and alcohol, that make us feel good. No matter what makes us feel good, the feeling is always the result of an increased release of a chemical called *dopamine* onto the nerve cells of our prefrontal cortex. When dopamine is released in the prefrontal cortex its predominant effect is to inhibit nervous activity, thereby silencing our thoughts by shutting down the mind. Even a small thing like someone smiling at us, releases a little dopamine, transiently quieting the mind to bring us a moment of cerebral peace. Many studies have shown that in the brain of schizophrenics there is an abnormally high level of dopamine (*The Controllers of State*: Chapter 3: Section 7). Of course, a high level of dopamine may itself be a symptom of a broad spectrum of neurological abnormalities. However, the amount of dopamine produced in the brain decreases throughout adult life and alongside this schizophrenia is seen to abate with the onset of old age.

Normally if we think about one subject, we cannot, without timesharing our mind, really think about anything else. We often say that we cannot think of two things at once. The mind only becomes available for new thoughts when the old train of thought is completed and for the tiniest fraction of a second the mind is both quiet and receptive. Typically this only happens when we have been able to drop our thoughts or when we have resolved an issue. Theory has it that if there were an excess of inhibitory dopamine in the prefrontal cortex, our thoughts would be turned off before they come to fruition, wiping clean the cerebral blackboard to enable new thoughts to arise that in turn will be prematurely stifled by the excess of dopamine. With an excess of dopamine, thought after thought could start only to be immediately switched off before completion and consummation, in order to make way for an entirely new thought that, in turn, will be prematurely terminated. This process could account for the unwanted cacophony of incomplete and diverse mental representations that characterize a schizophrenic episode.

The dopamine theory of schizophrenia also derives some support from a serious mental illness that results from a chronic loss of those nerve cells in the brain that make dopamine. This mental illness is called sleeping sickness or *encephalitis lethargica*. While schizophrenics have too much dopamine, sleeping sickness patients suffer from a loss of dopamine that literally paralyses the body and freezes thought for decades. When transiently awakened by the use of drugs, such patients reported that they were not actually unconscious but instead trapped within a *frozen consciousness* that was composed of a thought that persisted for eternity. One woman described her experience of frozen consciousness as living in a still pond forever reflecting itself, empty of all possibilities. The antithetical relationship with the freewheeling mind of the dopamine-rich schizophrenic is obvious.

Of all mental illnesses schizophrenia is most difficult to understand. The mystics say that you may comprehend the moods and urges that drive people and you may become familiar with their individual personalities but you can know only a tiny percentage of their thoughts. Understanding schizophrenia provides a key to a deeper understanding of the mechanisms of thought in ordinary humans. The key is that the comprehension of humanity does not lie in the analysis of the contents of thought but in the understanding of the nature of the processes involved in fashioning our thoughts. Mental illness isolates as nothing else can. Pursued by the voices and shadows of unwanted ghosts, yet treated to the occasional glimpses of focused thought, the schizophrenic is obliged to live in a fragmented consciousness as the victim of a malfunctioning human mind.

Section 3: Recommended Reading

Barlow, H., Blakemore, C. and Weston-Smith, M. (Editors). *Images and Understanding: Thoughts about Images Ideas about Understanding.* Cambridge University Press, Cambridge, 1991.

Baron-Cohen, S. *Mindblindness: An Essay on Autism and Theory of Mind.* Bradford Books, MIT Press, Masschusetts, London, 1995.

Berk, L. E. *Child Development.* 8th Edition, Allyn and Bacon, London, 2008.

Calvin, W. H. *A Brief History of the Mind: From Apes to Intellect and Beyond.* Oxford University Press, USA, 2005.

Candland, D. K. *Feral Children and Clever Animals: Reflections on Human Nature.* Oxford University Press, New York, Oxford, 1993.

Frith, U. *Autism: Explaining the Enigma.* 2nd Edition, Wiley-Blackwell, Oxford, 2003.

Gombrich, E. H. *Art and Illusion: A Study of the Psychology of Pictorial Representation.* Phaidon Press, Oxford, 1988

Goleman, D. *Emotional Intelligence: Why It Can Matter More Than IQ.* 10th Edition, Bantam Books, New York, 2001.

Goleman, D. *Social Intelligence: The New Science of Human Relationships.* Hutchinson, London, 1998.

Hermelin, B. *Bright Splinters of the Mind.* Jessica Kingsley Publishers, London, 2001.

Kant, I. *Critique of Pure Reason.* First published, 1781.

Huizinga, J. *Homo Ludens - a study of the play element in culture.* Beacon Free, Boston, 1955 (first published in German in 1944).

Kellog, S. and O'Dell, R. *The Psychology of Children's Art.* Random House, New York, 1967.

Laing, R. D. *The Divided Self: An Existential Study of Sanity and Madness.* Penguin, USA, 1965.

Levick, M. F. *They Could Not Talk and So They Drew: Children's Styles of Coping and Thinking.* Charles C. Thomas, Springfield, Illinois, USA, 1983.

Mithen, S. *The Prehistory of the Mind: The Cognitive Origins of Art, Religion and Science.* Thames and Hudson, London, 1999.

Marchant, L. (author), Boesch, C. (Editor) and Hohmann, G. (Editor). *Behavioral Diversity in Chimpanzees and Bonobos.* Cambridge University Press, Cambridge, 2002.

Myss, C. *Anatomy of the Spirit –The Seven Stages of Power and Healing.* Bantam Books, Sydney, New York, London, 1996.

Reat, N. R. *Buddhism: A History.* Jain Publishing Company, Freemont, California, 1994.

Segal, N. L. *Indivisible by Two: Lives of Extraordinary Twins.* Harvard University Press, Harvard, 2007.

Piaget, J. *Language and Thought of the Child.* 1st Edition, Routledge, London, New York, 2001.

Piaget, J. *Psychology of Intelligence.* 1st Edition, Routledge, London, New York, 2001.

Plotkin, H. *Evolution in Mind: An Introduction to Evolutionary Psychology.* Harvard University Press, Harvard, 1998.

Pinker, S. *How the Mind Works.* W. W. Norton and Co., London, 1999.

Selfe, L. *Normal and anomalous Representational Drawing Ability in Children.* Academic Press, New York, London, 1983.

Selfe, L. *Nadia: A Case of Extraordinary Drawing Ability in an Autistic Child.* Harcourt, San Diego, New York, 1979.

Smith, A. C. *Schizophrenia and Madness.* George Allen and Unwin, London, 1982.

Snow, P. J. (2003). Charting the Domains of Human Thought – A new theory on the operational basis of the mind. *J. Consciousness Studies* **10,** 3-17.

Sowell T. *The Einstein Syndrome: Bright Children Who Talk Late.* Basic Books, New York, 2002.

Zaidel, D. *Neuropsychology of Art: Neurological, Cognitive and Evolutionary Perspectives (Brain Damage, Behavior, and Cognition).* Psychology Press, New York, Sussex, 2005.

Section 4

Emotion - the Nature of Being

"Our Birth....is but a sleep and a forgetting:
The Soul that rises with us, our life's Star,
Hath had elsewhere its setting,
And cometh from afar,
Not in entire nakedness,
But trailing clouds of glory do we come,
From God, who is our home:
Heaven lies about us in our infancy!"

William Wordsworth (1770-1850). English Poet.

Chapter 1 - The Identity of Emotion

Emotion and the Dance of Life

"The hearts know in silence the secrets of the days and the nights. But your ears thirst for the sound of your heart's knowledge." Kahlil Gibran (1883-1931). Lebanese American Poet, Author and Mystic.

Passing in and out of awareness like butterflies fluttering across the sill of an open window, emotions give color to the canvas of human consciousness. Indifferent to our cognitively fashioned wishes, irreverent towards our goals and commitments, our emotions are the experiential manifestations of archaic instinctual urges, within us solely to represent our basic biological needs in consciousness. It is our emotions that propel us into the dance of life, a dance that continues while we are busy making what seem to be sensible plans. If we were to say that the body is our temple wherein the High Priest or Priestess of Mind can safely contrive his or her plans and beliefs, then we might also say that our emotions are the lamentations and exultations of the congregation.

Emotions are transient elements of consciousness, lasting only seconds or minutes before they evaporate into the cosmos. Like the shadow on the staircase or the moment of fragrance borne on the summer breeze, our emotions are no sooner upon us than they are gone. One moment we may be consumed by anger or fear while in the next we may be filled with the *joie de vivre*. In contrast, thought is always vitally concerned with the past and future while mood provides a basis for predicting success or failure (*The Relationship between Mood and Anticipation*: Chapter 3: Section 5). Thus, whereas emotional experience is always confined to the moment both mood and thought have a pervasive and persistent quality. Indeed, one reason emotions have remained so poorly understood is because, outside of meditative practice, there is rarely a time when they are not overshadowed by the machinations of the mind. Yet when we are swept away by our emotions, good or bad, all vestiges of future or past simply disappear. To be completely within the realm of emotion is be completely in the now.

Emotions are the representation in consciousness of the part of the human psyche that we share with all mammals. As human beings, however, we are obliged to operate through a vast network of cognitive processes. The result is that our emotions are an eternal source of inner conflict. How often do we extol the virtues of discipline and deliberation, while in the next moment find ourselves envying those who freely indulge their animal propensities? Again and again in each and every human life, as in generation after generation, the battle between the mind and the emotions, between our learned moral principles and our instincts, is reenacted. In our hearts we covet the impulsive freedom of the wild, but in our minds we are uneasy with the unknowns of the wilderness. Always, we are divided between the contradictory forces of thought and emotion. For this reason, it is said that the longest road is that which joins the heart and the head.

Even in apes, the highest non-human primates, instinct plays a prominent role in fashioning behavior. In humans, however, the mind has become so powerful that our mental conditioning is critical to determining how we act. Indeed, the conditioning of the mind plays a central role in determining the social behavior of all human societies. It is through such conditioning that the flagrant expressions of our urges and emotions are kept within societal norms - a clear indication that the human mind has the power to suppress our biological impulses. This does not, however, mean that our emotions are always subordinate to our thoughts. The human mind has, after all, evolved as a neural organ specifically designed to better serve the needs of our visceral body. Ultimately, it is our emotions, which drive back the boundaries of rational judgment, turning our mind to their causes and usurping its creative powers to the service of an insatiable and entirely instinctual appetite for consumption and sex.

Emotion and Spiritual Experience

"There is an important distinction within the ambiguous word *feeling* which means both emotions and sensations. Emotion refers to a state of the self, whilst sensation refers to elements of perception. Andrew Sims, Psychiatrist. From: *Symptoms in the Mind - An Introduction to Descriptive Psychopathology.* W.B. Saunders, London, Sydney, Toronto, Philadelphia and Tokyo, 1995.

When we peel away the omnipotence of human thought, we experience directly the pulsations and secretions of our visceral body, elements of the psyche that inevitably remind us of our ancestry within the vast Kingdom of *Animalia*. Only when all thought ceases do we literally become the organic forces that fuel all vertebrate life - forces that normally inhabit the very boundaries of human consciousness from whence they give us a sense of unity with all things natural. As turbulent yet transient elements of existence, it is these visceral energies that are responsible for those enigmatic experiences we call emotions. It is the seeking of a direct understanding of such experiences that reveals the all-pervading or inner self - a realm of experience known by a multitude of synonyms and embodied in the personas of numerous deities that populate the mythologies of all religions.

To avoid the connotations of religious dogma, our most ecstatic experiences are often called "God experiences". These emerge naturally from emotional centers that promote bonding and love. They are distinct from the more primitive and highly negative experiences of anger and fear that are often called "Hell experiences". Both extremes exist independently of thought. Both are, in this sense, parts of our inner being and both are thus, by definition, part of spiritual experience. When we seek a direct understanding of emotion, we inevitably join the mystic on his tortuous journey to the very foundations of the human soul.

Emotion and Visceral Control

"These changes—the more rapid pulse, the deeper breathing, the increase of sugar in the blood, the secretion from the adrenal glands—were very diverse and seemed unrelated. Then, one wakeful night, after a considerable collection of these changes had been disclosed, the idea flashed through my mind that they could be nicely integrated if conceived as bodily preparations for supreme effort in flight or in fighting." Walter Bradford Cannon (1871-1945). American Physiologist.

The sensory information from the organs of our body is assembled in our emotional centers to provide us with a snapshot of our physiological condition. Neurobiologists refer to this process as *interoception*. It is this *barometric reading of our inner milieu* that is used by a special part of our nervous system called the *autonomic nervous system* to automatically regulate our physiology. The autonomic nervous system is a motor system specialized for controlling our body's vital organs. In this it resembles our skeletal motor system through which we initiate and control movements of our face, head, limbs and trunk. The only difference is that we have such limited voluntary control over our autonomic nervous system that we cannot, through conscious effort, regulate our viscera in the same way as we can evoke and control movements of our skeletal body.

The autonomic nervous system has two divisions, the *parasympathetic* and *sympathetic*. In the control of most, though not all, of our organs these two divisions oppose one another. For example, the sympathetic division increases heart rate while the parasympathetic division decreases heart rate. The job of each division of the autonomic nervous system is to assess our physiological status by reading the sensory information coming back from all our organs and to restore our inner milieu to the state of perfect balance called *homeostasis*. When through illness or circumstances our viscera are in turmoil, we easily become emotionally distraught. Only when homeostasis has been achieved do our emotions fall into perfect harmony.

The autonomic nervous system differs from the somatic nervous system in one other very important way. Whereas the left and right sides of the somatic nervous system are structurally identical, the human autonomic nervous system is grossly asymmetrical. Thus, sensory information arising from each organ tends to affect one side of the brain more than the other. As our visceral senses develop very early in life, this asymmetry of emotionally relevant, visceral sensory information is thought to result in the different responses of emotional centers on the left and right hemispheres of the brain. Such differences may well account for the asymmetry of the human face. More broadly, however, they would inevitably establish left right differences in other elements of the psyche, especially those that mature after the emotional centers (*Authority and Complementation in Consciousness*: Chapter 3: Section 1).

For many years the pundits of western medicine believed that the highest level of the autonomic nervous system was a sub-cortical and therefore subconscious brain center called the *hypothalamus*. The hypothalamus controls our viscera and the release of hormones into the blood stream. However, the cortex's centers of mood and emotion are both highly interactive with the hypothalamus. Our viscera are actually at the bottom end of a number of sensory-to-motor loops, each of which passes through successively higher levels of the brain. At the top end of the longest loop are the parts of our cerebral cortex that enable us to experience emotion. Beneath this the next longest loop involves the hypothalamus while still shorter loops channel visceral information from the viscera into increasingly simple autonomic centers located at still lower levels of the brain. The emergent system is one where there is opportunity for the cerebral cortex to participate in influencing our physiological state, against a background of subcortical control loops that "automatically" regulate our bodily functions. The participation of the cortex in this process enables us to experience a range of our visceral functions – experiences we refer to as emotions.

Emotions and Inner Health

"See that every emotion has a corresponding sensation in the body, and the sensation in turn creates that same emotion." Sri Sri Ravi Shankar. Contemporary Indian Mystic and Humanitarian.

Before humans knew anything about the viscera, the association of symptoms with particular organs was simply impossible. Indeed, primitive societies often saw their aches, pains and psychiatric abnormalities as direct evidence of possession by demons or evil spirits. Even in western medicine the doctor's most challenging task is often identifying the source of those unpleasant and unwanted feelings of illness.

One of the best ways of seeing the relationship between our emotions and our visceral sensations is through the practice of meditation. Meditation is no more and no less than the process of silencing thought, the better to focus consciousness on the remainder of the inner world. In its origins, meditation probably extends back at least 200,000 years to times when the first humans whiled away long nights in the shadowy darkness of their caves and shelters. Nor would it be in the least surprising if our hominid predecessors used introspection to better monitor their internal health. The virtue of silent and thoughtless introspection is that, in the absence of cognitive distraction, there arises naturally an enhanced sensitivity to the condition of the inner body. When in the stillness of meditation all thoughts cease, when functionally speaking the mind disappears, we cannot but experience a heightened sensitivity to the rhythms of our viscera, thereby becoming sensitized to any prevailing pathologies that might otherwise fester beneath the mental furor of everyday life. Thus, to become progressively more aware of the inner world is *ipso facto* to increase our comprehension of the many voices of our own emotions. When in meditation we peer into inner consciousness we do not see the solid forms of the outside world or even the conceptual frameworks of thought but instead we literally become the visceral energies of an insatiable host around which evolution has created a vast and complicated brain.

Until recently, such insights had been lost from logic-based schools of western medicine. In the West our emotions have been regarded as indicative of the state of our mental, rather than our physiological, health. Only now with the great advances of neuroscience are we beginning to comprehend the powerful interrelatedness of these two components. In contrast, the traditional eastern civilizations and the world's native and hunter-gatherer peoples accept insight as a valid, if capricious, tool of medical diagnosis.

The area of our cortex involved in the perception of our emotions, the anterior cingulate gyrus, is strongly connected to our social mind, which in turn is responsible for integrating our inner feelings with the body language of other people in the formation of meaningful psychosocial concepts. The larger the area of cortex devoted to the social mind (BA 9), the higher must be an individual's capacity to do this and the greater their emotional intelligence. At least some individuals with a very high emotional intelligence appear to have the capacity to deduce, from the nuances of body language, the visceral malfunction that accompanies illness. Indeed, it has been demonstrated that in people of high emotional intelligence, the anterior cingulate gyrus, is more responsive to the emotional perturbations of others. Such individuals are presumably so adept at empathizing that they can simply read the visceral health of other people. Today it seems that the puzzling diagnostic successes of a gifted few almost certainly reflect the link between our viscera, our emotions and our high level of non-verbal signaling - a link conspicuous only to a highly developed social mind. In each and every moment, our emotions subtly, and often subliminally, influence our body language. Those who can decipher these messages in terms of the viscera are, in effect, the shamans and witch doctors of the West, to whom we give the name *medical intuitives*.

The Companionship of Emotions

"A Sheikh was asked: 'What is Sufism?' He said: "To feel joy in the heart when sorrow appears." Jaläl ad-Din Muhammad Rumi (1207-1273). Persian Sufi Mystic and Poet.

These words embrace a common theme touched upon by many mystics and writers. It recognizes that even antithetical states like joy and sadness are actually *companion emotions* that experientially have much in common. They are two sides of the same coin. Who has not cried for joy and yet, as the tears begin to flow, seen at once all the desperate sorrows of life? And of love, of course, we may say the same, for in the depths of loneliness, when timeless despair paints gray our every wall, there echoes within the gentle caress of love such that we are momentarily restored to that intimacy wherein we were once so completely described.

The companion emotions are inexorably bound together in art, poetry, literature and theatre because they are truly antithetical states. Without a thesis there can be no antithesis. Anger and fear, joy and sadness are arguably recognizable states only because they exist as a pair of experiential extremes. Just as there can be no pleasure without pain, there can be no anger without fear and no joy without sadness. The only condition is that companion emotions must be pertinent to the same domain of existence and the same *genre* of behavior. Thus, fear and aggression are essentially antisocial emotions of reptilian origin, while joy and sadness are social emotions reflecting the nurturing process that is the essence of all mammalian life. In this way each pair of companion emotions has a common evolutionary origin; the evolution of each pair being linked to the evolution of a particular part of the emotional centers that are found in our human brain. Our companion emotions are not only companions in the dance of life but also neuroanatomical and physiological bedfellows. To eradicate fear from the human experience you must eradicate anger, to eradicate sadness you must eradicate joy.

Emotion and Religion

"Surely men as inspirators, known and unknown to the world, have shared a common, uncommon discovery. The Tao of Lao-tse, Nirvana of Buddha, Jehovah of Moses, The Father of Jesus, the Allah of Mohammed - all point to the experience. No-thing-ness, spirit - once touched, the whole life clears." Attributed to Lord Shiva.

The Christian scriptures warn us about conceptualizing God in our own image. Taken superficially we may interpret this as meaning we should refrain from making idols. There is, however, a deeper significance that relates our extraordinary ability to generate internal imagery as part of the process of imagination (*The Cultural Exploitation of Mental* Imagery: Chapter 1: Section 7). Although this system is often referred to as the "mind's eye" it is also capable of creating imagery within the auditory, olfactory, gustatory, tactile, motor and even emotional domains of experience. All that is required is the thought of something and the mind's capacity to activate the cortex's perceptual representations will do the rest.

Mohandas Gandhi has said that, "God is not a person, he is an eternal principle." But in truth God is not even a principle but an experience, which like our ordinary emotional experiences, has no physical identity. However, the human mind is such that it is never satisfied with such things. Instead it seeks always to identify, to conceptualize and as part of imagination to manifest its concepts as internal images. Thus, in the matter of intangibles, be they emotional or spiritual, the mind will not be satisfied until it has symbolized them in both iconic and verbal form. This is what the human mind does. It cannot do anything else. In truth, however, no more can we image our God from our transcendental experiences, than we can image space, time or the daily life of our unseen viscera.

There are many religions but the domains of consciousness within all humans are more or less the same. Religions are the creation of the mind. With the possible exception of the Neanderthals there is little evidence that our hominid ancestors had the mental abilities to create complex and abstract mythologies. Spirituality is the seeking of our biological center, a knowing of our inherent and universal nature. If we imagine that all the religions of the world are arranged around the circumference of a circle, then the center is spirituality. In this sense the animistic religions with their reverence for nature are closer to this center than the complex theoretical frameworks of Judaism, Islam and Christianity. Certainly no mentally elaborated framework, religious or otherwise, can create those moments of blissful awareness when we are one with the universe. Indeed, the experiencing of such moments is entirely reliant on the silencing of all thought. Only with the cessation of thought and reason are humans able to know directly the experience of what many call God. In the words of Vivekananda, "The end of all religions is the realization of God". People squabble about religion, not about the nature of spiritual experience. The eternal acrimony between the Hindus and the Moslems is not over the matter of their personal experience of God. No one argues that his or her experience of God is better than that of another. The conflicts between all religions are simply disagreements about religious rituals, themselves created entirely by human beings. All so-called religious conflicts are the same, and behind most are the even baser motives of power, sex and profit.

All experiences must have behind them some area of cortex. What cannot be invoked by cortical activity cannot be invoked at all. The Buddha himself would let us have no foolish talk of magic. So the question is what parts of the cortex elaborate our moments of divine association? We seek a place where there are no thoughts, no sense of time, no past or future - a place which is free from care that is pervaded with an aura of inactive playfulness, where unconditional love abounds and where we are cradled in the natural, seemingly eternal, rhythms of our organic center. The first thing to realize is that, in life, such a state of consciousness happens only rarely. The Tibetans recognize this for they say that when the body is sick, when inside there is only pain, then the *self is lost*. The Buddha within is no longer at home. *Atman*, the all-pervading self, the experiential equivalent of those transcendental moments when we are one with God, is simply inaccessible. Our organic body is the temple wherein we meet directly with God. When our body is healthy and free from pain, when our viscera are replete, when our urges are laid to rest and when our mind is quiet, then and only then may the door to Nirvana open. The entirely subjective lessons to be learned in that place concern the essence of human nature and are, by definition, the foundations of all mystical wisdom.

There is only one place within the cortex, which can deliver the elementary components of a God experience. That place is quite naturally the center of mammalian bonding, the executive station of our inner realms, the center of love and the origin of our innate vitality that inspires all action. This domain of consciousness is the product of a part of the cortex of the anterior cingulate gyrus, an area which, as we shall see, acts as the executor of all emotion. Like Hell experiences, God experiences must be common to all humans simply because they reflect the internal milieu which, given the constancy in structure and function of our internal organs, must be relatively invariant throughout all of humanity. By connecting us directly to the very essence of nature such experiences not only link us globally but they also reveal the forces and rhythms that drive all vertebrate lifeforms. In the course of our life, our emotions constitute the first elements of inner consciousness, elements that normally disappear only when in death our viscera cease to function. Because our emotions span the entirety of our conscious life, they lend themselves to the fanciful ideas of religion that posit that we existed before we were born and that we will continue to exist after consciousness has been extinguished by death.

Only the human mind is large enough to harbor beliefs for which the soul has no need. The warning about making images of God is a warning not to indulge our mind. It cautions us that the practice of imagining the divine essentially siphons consciousness into the process of thought, guaranteeing that we shall miss those moments of inner audience wherein transcendence may arise. In the evolution of mammals, the mind and thus imagination are relatively recent gifts of natural selection. By comparison, the all-pervading, or inner, self is a heritage that began to take shape more than 260 mya when the first mammals evolved and the newly formed cingulate gyrus brought joy, disgust and sadness to a previously reptilian world dominated by fear and aggression. Within the ether of human consciousness, God and nature are identical forces. When we abuse nature, irrespective of our religious beliefs, we abuse our God.

So what are humans looking for when they establish and practice a religion? The answer is surely a system to bring a unity to the inevitable conflict between human emotions and the human mind. Yet many religions have shied away from addressing the matter of emotion, reluctant to accept the animalistic realm of human behavior, their scholarly clergy seemingly oblivious to the fact that all religions have their origins in the ancient ideas of animism. That we are dependent upon nature, that we have arisen from animal ancestors, seems to them incompatible with our purer, theoretical aspirations towards godliness. Plato, for example, believed that humanity moved closer to godliness with the progressive development of the intellect. Yet despite the fact that all beliefs are the product of thought, the so-called God experience emerges only when the mind is quiescent. Mental effort cannot bring one closer to the divine. It is ironical that the pundits of most religions see the animal centers that compose the core of our brain as unsavory, though unfortunately persistent, components of the human being. Virtually all major religions foster a singular arrogance about the superiority of man that, given our origins and our dependence on biology, is frighteningly anti-nature. Fundamentalists even go so far as to suggest that the evolutionary tree which links us to the animal realms, and even the homologies between our DNA and that of animals, are either bogus or part of a divine plot to test our faith in almighty creation. Ultimately human emotion continues to confront the doyens of many religions and this doubtless underlies their most conspicuous failure – their inability to guide humanity towards peace and happiness.

Religious belief begins because humans are unable to accept that bliss, euphoria, pain and darkness are a biologically normal part of consciousness. Just as they were once in doubt that their inventions could arise from the creative processes of human thought, they continue to doubt that their emotions and moods are part of human inheritance. Thus, to explain their peak experiences, low and high, humans are always ready to invoke their inventive prowess. Indeed, the typical human is so dominated by thought, that few are able to take any other course. For example, the European mind, in particular, has great difficulty in countenancing the emptiness of Zen with its focus on the void wherein all things are of themselves. The massive human propensity to think must be indulged and the result is the foolish postulation that greater, unseen powers are responsible for all things good and bad. It is curious that the same humans are conspicuously sensible about other matters such that none would think of constructing a roof, before they had observed the walls.

Where religion once offered human understanding, modern societies must look towards expensive psychology and psychiatry. Modern religions continue to offer edicts and little else. Few of their usually well-meaning officials have the insight, experience or education to teach in any fullness those matters that so divide the heart from the head. With our burgeoning population and accompanying stresses, the human psyche is increasingly in chaos. Today only the mystics instruct us to look beyond the confines of religious belief, opening for us a greater vista that inevitably will be as unpopular with the labor and profit orientated state as it is with power-based orthodox religions and those many individuals for whom life and belief are synonymous.

It is perhaps unfair to single out one religion from the others for none is significantly free from the intrinsic evils of belief. However, it is instructive to give an example of a religion that is, despite the complexities of its mythologies, serendipitously in tune with our emergent comprehension of the psychobiology of humans. The one I have been moved to select is Hinduism. Hinduism has survived for millennia in a continent often dominated by callously indifferent or hostile invaders. Of Hinduism it is said that it is more a way of life than a religion that one cannot become a Hindu and that one must be born to that life. In its essence Hinduism strives to encompass and not encroach upon human nature. The commonly perceived evils of the caste system aside, Hinduism reflects and accommodates the lifestyle of its practitioners rather than foisting upon them "mind-made" rules and beliefs that can never encompass human nature. Hinduism is a vibrant yet intricate pantomime of life. Certainly the Hindu Gods and Goddesses are completely unlike those untarnished deities of the Christian pantheon. The Gods of the Hindus are not reformed beings. On the contrary, they seem to revel in their copious human frailties. They are scheming, mischievous, seductive and charged with emotion. It is said that even Vishnu, Brahma and Shiva have been known to argue over who has the biggest penis! Their wisdom is not to be found in edicts but in the raw expression of the forces of life. No doleful icons for the Hindus; for them, Shiva dances and the Universe sings. Krishna plays his flute and the cowgirls are brought to ecstasy by the passion of his notes. Humanity is of nature and it is from realizing the origins of our psyche within nature that all religions have an opportunity to begin moving towards a new harmony of appreciative acceptance of the true origins and diversity of the human being.

Chapter 2 - The Communication of Emotions

The Language of Emotion

"If one should seek to name each particular one of them [emotion] of which the human heart is the seat, each race of men….[would find]….names for some shade of feeling which other races have left undiscriminated…." William James (1842-1910). American Psychologist and Philosopher.

There are many truths not found in words and most of them are emotional truths. Like art, language is not the product of emotions but of the human mind (*Emotions and the Development of Language*: Chapter 5: Section 4). Language is essentially a vehicle of logic. Even though it is said that the ancient tongue of Sanskrit enables one to speak directly about experiences of the inner realms, it is difficult to see how individual words could ever capture the indistinct apparitions of the visceroemotional world. Nevertheless, most languages have become heavily seeded with words describing the nuances of emotional experience, words for which there are often no equivalent in other tongues. Emotion remains the most challenging arena of linguistics, such that only in its most inspired and poetic cadences, can language portray the ebb and flow of the heart.

In the mind, emotions can only ever be concepts that are represented in essentially iconic form. The more common a visceral state, the more likely we are to create for it, a cerebral identity. Armed with an iconic representation of an emotion it is a simple matter for us to invent for it, a name - a word that enables us to describe our inner state to others. The result is that there are literally hundreds of words that attempt to catch the nuances of those fleeting feelings of the inner realm. For example, the emotion of joy may be referred to as ecstasy, elation, delight, gaiety, rapture and so on. The vocabulary of emotion is clearly the most labile, expansive and inadequate domain of language. More than any other factor, the chaotic language of emotion has contributed to the confusion over the analysis and subsequent comprehension of our inner world.

Where words fail, body language and facial expression remain as the most fundamental channels of emotional communication. Indeed, facial expressions and body language are for no other purpose than the communication of our emotions. For example, people do not make intense facial expressions when they are alone even though they may be experiencing strong emotions. Even infants of 10 months usually only smile when the caregiver is present. As any pet owner with sufficient social confidence to befriend a warm-blooded animal will tell you, mammals can accurately read and respond to the feelings of their human carers. Especially the higher mammals, dogs, monkeys, apes and probably dolphins, appear to have the ability to empathize - to recreate our emotional state within their own emotional centers. Without the influence of our powerful cognitive abilities, these animals are obliged to rely upon accurately reproducing within their own emotional centers the instinctual drives that they perceive within the emotional centers of humans and other animals. They achieve this by being highly tuned-in to the body language and the facial expressions of other agents. If we accept that they can indeed empathize with humans and even foreign animal species and that they have the same emotional centers as we do, then it is entirely reasonably to believe that they do experience emotion and that, in their raw form, those experiences are much the same as our own.

The first of our ancestors to be included in the genus Homo, *Homo habilis*, appeared 2.5 mya - about the time the pigmy chimps or bonobos (*Pan paniscus*) and the chimpanzees (*Pan troglodytes*) evolved from a common ancestor. Most believe that the *H. habilis* was the first of our ancestors to fashion stone tools and the first to communicate linguistically (*The Origins of Practicality - The Material Mind*: Chapter 3: Section 3). It is, however, unlikely that language evolved to serve the expression of emotion. The grunts, groans, moans, shrieks and squeals of the animal world could have evolved for no other reason than the direct communication of urges and there is reason to believe that they serve us equally as well. Human words are the children of scholarship and the servants of practicality. Before the arrival of *H. habilis*, the upright walking australopithecines were presumably voicing their emotions through decipherable vocalizations, much like modern day chimpanzees that utter recognizable, structured calls to convey simple messages to their fellow chimps. It is probable that the ability to create tools and to use a simple language evolved synchronously because the principal importance of human speech was, and still is, the conveyance of life-saving practical knowledge - knowledge that formed the kernel of creative thought that would ultimately consume the Earth.

Since the beginning of recorded history the theatrical arts have used body language and facial expressions to evoke specific emotions in their audience. Through theatre we have opportunity to indulge in the extremes of emotional life, without serious consequence. Psychologists call this practice *pantomime recognition*. By watching professional actors we can hone our skills of reading and mimicking body language. Theatre enables us to enter the world of great lovers or pathological killers without risk to our emotions or our body. The *Natya Sastra* is the world's oldest surviving text on stagecraft. Written in India between 200 BC and 200 AD, it describes how to use the face, body and hands to portray emotion. To test the cross-cultural constancy and historical longevity of body language and facial expressions, Indian and American college students were exposed to enactments of a number of emotions using instructions from the Natya Sastra. The actors played roles that portrayed anger, disgust, fear, heroism, humor, amusement, love, peace, sadness, embarrassment and wonder. Both groups of students were highly successful in identifying the emotions that were being enacted, indicating again that the emotional significance of body language and facial expression extends across cultural and racial boundaries.

In day-to-day life, the sensitive person is always inadvertently comparing the content of speech with an assessment of the ongoing emotions of the other party. Our awareness of the emotions of another depends heavily upon specialized areas of our visual cortex that specifically register the expressions, postures and movements of other beings. This information is sent to the brain's emotional centers where, as part of the process of empathy it elaborates a rendition of the raw emotions of the other. This having been achieved, these raw emotions become accessible to the social mind that is simultaneously receiving information directly from perceptual areas of the cortex that are specialized for reading body language and biodynamic imagery. The result is a detailed representation of the emotions, and thus the immediate needs of the other which can be measured against their spoken words. Only when these two assessments match, do we say that the other is, "speaking their truth".

Facial Expressions and the Primary Emotions

"Just as water mirrors your face, so your face mirrors your heart." Proverbs 27:19 (*The Message*), Bible.

In the communication of emotions, not even body language is as significant as facial expressions. This is particularly so of the primates. In the malleability of its form, the primate face is markedly different from the faces of fish, frogs, lizards, snakes and most other mammals. The face of the higher primates and, in particular, the apes, is a fantastically elastic instrument. Like humans, the chimps, bonobos, gorillas and orangutans have the capacity to use the face to convey all the subtleties of emotion. The higher we go on the hierarchy of behavioral complexity, the less hair hides the face and the more complex is the facial musculature. Such a marvel is the biomechanical engineering of the human face that it has been said that humans can make up to 7,000 facial expressions.

The presentation of a face activates more parts of the cortex than any other stimulus. In adults the social, material and abstract mind are all responsive to images of the face. We can easily envisage faces in the flames of the campfire or the clouds scudding across the night sky. Any object even crudely reminiscent of this omnipotent element of psychobiology is enough to evoke in the "mind's eye" a simulation of an archetypal face. Even the faces of animals penetrate our higher centers more readily than most other objects. Indeed, it is because the brain is so sensitive to the face that plants and invertebrate animals have evolved face-like patterns to frighten off potential predators.

The primate brain is so responsive to the face that some have suggested that parts of the visual system are hardwired for its perception so that the image of the face in human consciousness is essentially inherited as part of the legacy of simply being human. In a highly social species, facial recognition is critical to discriminating friend from foe – be they of a different race or even a different species. For example, chimps that are in close contact with humans recognize the faces of other chimps far better than human faces. In general, a familiar face elicits positive emotions while an alien face arouses the negative. But the question is, whether this responsiveness to particular faces is inherited or acquired?

Children first show sensitivity to the facial expressions of their carers between 7 and 12 months. At 12 months the child takes no interest in inanimate, non-interactive objects unless they are adorned with a rudimentary face. It therefore seems that the fundamentals of facial recognition are present by the end of the first year of life and that the neural circuits that respond to faces are slowly tuned to those that are consistently present. This process has been studied in adult monkeys where it has been shown that single cortical neurons in the face representations, slowly tune-in to the nuances of a particular face, eventually responding to it irrespective of its orientation to the line of sight.

The founder of evolutionary theory, Charles Darwin, first postulated the importance of the face in the communication of emotion. From his epic journey he provided evidence that people in literate and preliterate cultures have an innate capacity to identify the expressions of joy, surprise, sadness, anger, disgust, contempt, and fear. To confirm this, modern scientists traveled the world armed with pictures of people making faces that portrayed to westerners, particular emotions. Five distinctive universal or archetypal expressions emerged as being recognizable to all human populations, including the Fore tribe, who live in an isolated stone-age culture deep in the highlands of Papua New Guinea. These archetypal expressions were of *anger, fear, disgust, sadness* and *joy*. The emotional states behind these universal expressions have become known as the *primary emotions*.

The existence of obvious similarities in facial expressions between humans, apes, monkeys and even dogs indicates the powerful involvement of genes in the determination of archetypal facial expressions. This led Darwin to propose, more than a century ago, the existence of what are today are called *motor primitives* - inherited neural circuits that drive basic, recognizable sequences of movements and postures observable in humans and more primitive vertebrate species (*Mimicry, Movement Primitives and the Mind*: Chapter 2: Section 6). Today we know that each stereotyped movement we make, be it scratching or smiling, is actually supported by a specific neural circuit that functions as a motor program sequencing the precisely timed contractions of relevant muscles. Some motor primitives like the rhythmical locomotory movements of fins, legs, arms and body are clearly a reflection of our genetical links to animals that evolved long before our primate relatives. Other motor primitives like facial expressions are reflective of our primate origins and typically involve brain circuitry not found in lower mammals. Thus, Darwin argued that our facial expressions must also be inherited and not acquired by early experience - a proposal supported by the finding that children who are deaf and blind since birth develop the entire gamut of facial expressions.

It was not long, however, before careful examination of human expressions indicated that there is not a single face for each emotion but a range of related variations on a theme. Just as our emotions and the words we use to describe them seem to be continuously variable around a small number of themes, so too do our facial expressions. Detailed studies soon revealed that although a particular configuration of the human face could be universally identified as anger, it was possible to define up to 60 variations on this archetypal theme. The same is true of fear, disgust, sadness and joy. Just as our emotional centers respond in a graded manner so too can the human face represent the nuances of emotions that temper each archetypal state.

Essentially each primary emotion forms the basic template for a family of related emotional states and an accompanying family of words and facial expressions. In words, the anger family follows a progression through annoyance, resentment, indignation, outrage, vengeance and finally rage. We may think of such families of words as constellations constructed around an icon that represents a particular primary emotion. This does not, however, explain how our emotional centers can, in the first place, produce such widely varying responses upon a relatively small number of primary themes. To understand this we need to recall that our emotions arise from a vastly complex assemblage of visceral organs operating against a background of ever-changing hormone levels. If this were not the case then our emotional experiences would comprise a very small number of states each representing the all-or-none experience of one primary emotion. Thus, while each of the five primary emotions arise from activity in particular parts of our emotional centers, the level of activation of each part is presumably modulated by information arising from a large array of complex organs. Ultimately human emotions are composed of variations upon, and combinations of a small number of themes each of which is the product of specific sets of genes that can be traced at least as far back as our reptilian ancestors. Because our emotions seem to form a virtual continuum of experience, our vocabulary of emotion is, similarly, both large and cross culturally variable.

The Masked Face of Emotion

"Involuntary suggestions, not to be confused with involuntary impressions, which often arise suddenly in the soul." Friedrich Eduard Beneke (1798-1854). German Psychologist and Philosopher.

As language is a poor way of expressing or arousing emotions, it is not surprising to find that emotions can be aroused without any cognitive knowledge of the causative factors. When an odor, taste, sound, touch or image is too weak to enter our awareness and yet can be shown to evoke emotional arousal, we say that the stimulus has entered our brain *subliminally*. Through activating our emotional centers such a stimulus will necessarily have an indirect effect upon our thoughts. A subliminal stimulus is therefore, as the dictionary says, a stimulus that influences the mind without our being aware of it. Every day we are exposed to many subliminal stimuli. For instance, sexually attractant pheromones and the many subtleties of voice, body language and particularly facial expression, affect us without themselves coming to our awareness.

The practice of using emotionally evocative subliminal imagery or sound to manipulate our mind is known as *subliminal suggestion*. Though it is now illegal to use subliminal suggestion in the media, it is important to recognize its propaganda potential. For instance, subliminal suggestion could easily move a populace to inadvertently discriminate against any targeted group or even make war upon another country. It may be that we are very principled and intellectually clever, but since our infancy it is our raw emotions and not the mind that have been the pied piper of our psyche. The way to a man's heart may be through his stomach, but the way to everyone's head is through their gut feelings and these are the targets of all effective subliminal stimuli.

As facial expressions are so important in assessing the emotions of others, the finding that very brief presentations of particular facial expressions subliminally activate our centers of emotion and mood was to be expected. What this means, however, is that our brain subconsciously registers the emotions of other people without the need for mental effort. In order to demonstrate our subliminal sensitivity to facial expressions people were asked to watch a screen on which was flashed an angry face, followed immediately by an emotionally neutral face. When presented with an angry face for a very short time (1/30th second) and a neutral face for a significantly longer time (1/5th second), subjects reported that they simply did not "see" the angry face. Although the angry face would certainly have activated the nerve cells in their retina and possibly the visual representations in the cortex, the image did not persist for long enough to reach awareness. It did, however, elicit in the subjects a pulse of fear which could be detected physiologically as a change in electrical resistance of the skin, indicating a modicum of sweating. Somehow the threatening countenance sneaks past consciousness to evoke within us a bodily reaction that is experienced as fear.

The Nature of Empathy

"Anyone who has had a physical misfortune knows that many acquaintances who would feel for him in no other circumstances genuinely feel for him in this one. The sympathy is visceral: it is a sign that we cannot deny our common humanity." Charles Percy Snow (1905-1980). English Physicist, Author and Government Advisor.

It was only in 1909 that the word empathy was translated from the German word *Einfühlung*, meaning "feeling into". Empathy is a process by which our brain conjures, within its own visceroemotional centers, the feelings being experienced by another person. Because the neural substrates for empathy are the emotional centers of the vertebrate brain, empathy is not an exclusively human process. The emotional centers of all mammals, and probably all vertebrates, have evolved in a manner that enables them to be attuned to the emotional centers of other individuals of the same species.

Human infants will often cry in response to the distress in another infant. As the mind does not begin to become operational until around the twelfth postnatal month, this empathic response appears to be entirely the result of the direct transference of emotions between the emotional centers of the two infants. Not until the child is a little over 1 year old and its social mind has begun to mature, does it try to comfort a family member in distress. Unlike the direct transference of emotions between younger infants, this circumstantial expression of empathy reflects the child's newly formed ability to conceptualize its social milieu – a process entirely mediated by its newfound emotional intelligence. Adult females are typically more emotionally intelligent and are therefore more empathetic than adult males, just as both girl children and female apes are more empathetic that their male counterparts.

Most people tend to think of empathy as a phenomenon that specifically drives altruistic behaviors. More often, however, the process of empathy has to do with survival of the empathizing individual. For example, a flock of birds might all show fright in response to the cry of a frightened individual that has suddenly become aware of impending danger. The emotional perturbations of the individual are mirrored in the emotional centers of its cohorts. This form of empathy is particularly prominent in the behavior of the lower vertebrates, the reptiles, amphibians and fish because it enables transference of one individual's instinctual reactions of fear and aggression, to its unwary conspecifics.

Empathy often extends across the boundaries of speciation. Well-documented instances include one case in which a female bonobo cared for a stunned bird until it could fly and another where a female gorilla rescued and comforted a 3 year-old boy who had fallen 18 feet into its enclosure. Again, the process of empathy is more commonly linked to survival than to altruism. Just as the cry of a frightened bird arouses similar emotional responses in its conspecifics, so too can the same cry elicit fear in a nearby human hunter-gatherer. The attunement of the emotional perturbations of the individual to those of other agents, is such a fundamental feature of animal and human behavior that it is conspicuous to even the casual observer.

Before the strict controls over animal experimentation, many studies were made of the effects upon animals of witnessing suffering or discomfort in another individual. One such experiment showed that a rat encountering another rat suspended in a harness will press a bar that lowers the animal to the ground. Once on the ground the rescuer rat stayed close to the harnessed rat, orienting towards it as if to reassure it of its safety. In another more traumatic scenario, a rat seeing another rat receiving an electric shock showed distress that was greater if the witnessing rat had previously experienced shock – a methodology often used in the torture of humans. In a similar experiment, monkeys were trained to pull two chains that delivered different amounts of food. They were then placed in a situation where pulling the chain that delivered the largest reward administered a shock to another monkey. Upon witnessing this, four out of six monkeys chose the chain that did not administer the shock even though it provided only half the amount of food. The remaining two monkeys were so traumatized that they refused to pull either chain for 5 and 12 days after witnessing the effects of shock, literally starving themselves to avoid hurting another individual. These effects were augmented if the witnessing monkeys were part of the social milieu of the shocked individual – an observation implicating emotional intelligence in the creation of their response.

Unlike monkeys, humans have a very powerful mind. So the question is do humans respond like monkeys and rats and automatically empathize with the suffering of other humans or can they be persuaded otherwise by appealing to their mentally-concocted, belief systems. In 1963 Yale psychologist Stanley Milgram conducted what was essentially a classic study on human empathy. Known as Milgram's obedience experiment, the protocol aimed to test whether ordinary people would administer increasingly strong shocks to another restrained human, when instructed to do so by an authority figure. Subjects were told they were participating in a learning experiment. What they did not know was that the restrained person was an actor who was informed of the strength of the would-be shock and would act accordingly. Before the experiment subjects were given a sample shock of 45 volts, a level that was about 1/10th of the maximum. As the experiment proceeded, subjects initially behaved in much the same way as the monkeys, expressing some reticence to obey orders to increase the voltage. In so doing, subjects were clearly empathizing with the apparent pain of the restrained victim. Ultimately, however, 65% of human subjects were prepared to increase the shock to the maximum level of 450 volts while the remaining 35% were persuaded to administer shocks of up to 300 volts. Whereas empathy is a commanding factor in monkey behavior, the human mind clearly has the power to negate its influences in preference to a cognitively inspired agenda provided by a figure of authority. It is this power of the human mind over emotion that surely lies at the center of the great majority of state-orchestrated, human atrocities. Ironically, however, it is also the power of the human mind that enables the cognitive evocation of empathy.

In the higher mammals and particularly the primates, facial expressions are powerful cues for eliciting empathy. Indeed, it is almost impossible to watch a slide show of facial expressions portraying different emotions and, with each new image, not feel within the body an involuntary stirring of the appropriate emotion. In this scenario, the emotions portrayed by each image activate those perceptual areas (superior temporal sulcus and gyrus) that respond specifically to socially relevant biodynamic imagery. These areas, in turn, activate our emotional centers. It is through the specialized perceptual areas that the emotional disposition of other agents, whether animal or human, gains direct access to the viewer's emotional centers. In humans, however, the importance of the mind in creating behavioral strategy means that in many situations it is essential that empathy be contingent upon our ongoing thoughts. If it were not, then upon entering a room of smiling people we would be unable to maintain any cognitive purpose but instead, like the proverbial fool of the Tarot, be swept along by the propensity of our emotional centers to automatically tune-in to the prevailing emotional state of our cohorts, irrespective of any more critical cognitive objective. Within our psyche, only the power of the human mind ensures that our plans and objectives are maintained irrespective of our brain's instinctual inclination to automatically empathize.

This influence of the mind over empathetic behavior is seen in the progressive stages of human infanthood. From infancy to around 14 months, infants orient to the distress of others, often responding vocally by uttering their own distress cries while imitating the distressed behaviors and facial expressions of the other. Only during the second year of life, when the social mind is beginning to mature and assert a cognitive influence over the infant's behavior do helping behaviors begin to appear. With increasing age the continuing maturation of the mind results in a decreasing expression of the raw emotional reactions to distress and a concomitant increase in cognitively contrived helping behaviors. The degree to which this happens within any individual is dependent on both their gender and their personality.

So it is that the human brain achieves empathy in two quite different ways. The first involves the immediate and direct activation of our emotional centers in response to the emotions of other people. This form of empathy does not involve the mind but depends instead upon the activation of our emotional centers by those perceptual centers that exist within the cortex specifically to register the emotional displays of other people. This form of empathy has been called *automatic* or *proximate empathy*. The second form of empathy is dependent upon the mind and its capacity to influence our emotional centers. This form of empathy is called upon when someone beseeches us to "put ourselves in the other person's shoes". To do this, we have to use our mind to imagine the feelings of the other person and, as in all tasks of imagination, to activate our emotional centers in a manner that evokes the same feelings in us as we *believe* they are experiencing (*The Manipulation of Mental Imagery*: Chapter 2: Section 7). This form of empathy has been called *controlled* or *ultimate empathy*. Throughout the remainder of this book we will use the term *automatic empathy* to refer to that form of empathy that arises when the emotional displays of another directly activate our emotional centers, and *controlled empathy* to refer to the form of empathy which is dependent upon a prior cognitive assessment of another's feelings. As controlled empathy is a purposeful act, it constitutes what has been called *inner imitation* (*Tuning-In to Others*: Chapter 2: Section 6). Using the same line of argument, automatic empathy, as a non-cognitive process, can be regarded as an act of *inner mimi*cry – a phenomenon also called the *chameleon effect*. The term *contact high* refers to this inherent inclination of our emotional centers to elaborate the positive emotional states of those around us, in much the same way as these centers conjure negative feelings or a *contact low*, when we are in the company of depressed, anxious or frightened individuals.

As an instinctive response, automatic empathy is rarely incorrect, whereas being dependent upon our beliefs, controlled empathy can often be wide of the mark. Only mammals endowed with a mind can generate both controlled and automatic empathy while those lower mammals that lack the cortex of the mind confined to expressing automatic empathy. Automatic empathy is therefore the most archaic form of empathy that probably stretches back through the reptiles, amphibia and fish, species wherein the an accurate registration of the body language of conspecifics, and even other species, might be crucial to survival.

It is a common observation that mimicking an emotionally charged expression can involuntarily generate a subjective experience of that emotion. Just feeling our face taking on the same expression as another seems to cause our emotions to fall into line with theirs. We can feel the expression we are making only because our face is heavily supplied with sensory nerves. These sensory nerves activate our somatosensory cortex that enables us to experience the expressions we are making. Thanks to our somatosensory cortex, smiling and frowning feel very different. Patients who have suffered damage to their somatosensory cortex are unable to sense their own facial expressions. What is even more fascinating is that, as a corollary of this deficit, they are also unable to sense the emotions portrayed in the facial expressions of others. In order to empathize with the facial expressions of others, our cortex must recreate within itself the sensations of those expressions. When the neural substrate that enables us to do this is damaged, then we are permanently deprived of this means of empathizing.

Humans appear to have an intuitive awareness of this process for it is commonplace for us to force a particular facial expression in an attempt to bring our own emotions in synch with those being expressed by the people around us. For example, when we try to imagine the emotions associated with a kiss, we almost involuntarily pucker up our lips and perform the component movements, in much the same way as we sniff, when asked to imagine a smell (*The Manipulation of Mental Imagery*: Chapter 1: Section 7). Even love songs often tell us that smiling will help mend a broken heart, the antithesis of this being the old saying that if you frown too much you may get stuck with that face, and the related feelings, forever.

Deprived of human company, we rarely make the facial expressions. The recent use, by the USA, of long-term solitary confinement of "terrorists" exploits this human need to empathize as a punitive tool. Ordinary criminals are not spared this form of psychological torture. At the time of writing, there are, across the world, tens of thousands of prisoners who spend their lives entombed in small, often windowless rooms, deprived not only of any form of mental stimulation but also of the need for company so fundamental to the psyche of any social animal. It is impossible to estimate the deep and permanent psychological damage, caused when the human psyche is prevented from empathizing with other humans for very long periods of time. To the innately social human being, nothing, save physical torture or the murder of close relatives, is more destructive to the psyche that the deprivation of empathic communication.

Emotion in Deception and Truth
"It seems to me that there are two kinds of trickery: the 'fronts' people assume before one another's eyes, and the 'front' a writer puts on the face of reality." Francoise Sagan (1935-2004). French Playwright.

In most cultures it is considered proper to cognitively control one's facial expressions. For many decades, keeping a stiff upper lip was an instruction given to many a British schoolboy. The expression of grief or despair was thought to only worsen the experience of an already bad situation. Always some emotions are simply contraindicated for certain scenarios. For instance, we would not wish to offend others by smiling at a funeral or looking miserable at a wedding (some religious traditions excepted).

All humans practice emotional deception. This behavior begins in childhood and is easily identified in non-human primates. When modern anthropologists carefully restudied so-called innocent, equatorial societies, they have found social deception to be as prominent as in the western cultures. The face has from time immemorial been as much a trickster as a teller of truths. If a person does not speak when approached, we have only their body language and their face from which to assess their predisposition. Yet we can never be sure of what, or whom, lies behind those smiling eyes. The face is so often "used" to give the impression of concern where none exists. The iconic smile of the apparently, ever cheerful, supermarket checkout person is a prime example. Only when we are at ease and present in the moment do our facial expressions arise automatically enabling those around us to simply see how we are feeling.

In the contrived, advertisement orientated world of modern times, we are continually subjected to people who attempt to deceive by appearances. It is hard to imagine what distorted perceptions of social reality emerge as a consequence of this repetitious undermining of emotional communication. Yet when we accuse someone of lying we are rarely referring to emotional deception. Usually we mean that they have told us, in words, either a fact or a story that is not true. If it is something we don't care about, we regard the lie as insignificant; but if it is important to us, we regard the lie as a serious transgression of our trust. The irony is that most of us have been instructed by our parents, priests and teachers to hide our emotions and urges but at the same time speak the truth at all costs. Perhaps it is because human language evolved for practical purposes that we take such umbrage at the practical lie while, like the cognitively empowered non-human primates, we continually practice emotional deceits.

When it comes to emotional deception our politicians, real estate agents and used car salesmen bear the brunt of our indictments. Almost by definition their jobs require a high level of emotional pretense. Yet they are no different from others, except that they intuitively know that all motivation begins within the realm of emotion. Globally it is clear that all wars and rebellions are started and maintained by arousing the emotions of people. There can be no doubt that government-inspired, emotionally-charged media releases will be registered in the emotional centers of the populace which, in turn, will propel each individual into situations he or she would otherwise never entertain. Only behind the façade of these carefully orchestrated scenarios do we inevitably find the rational interests of a circumscribed, powerful and essentially psychopathic minority. The fieldmarshall revered for his battle strategies is only a pawn beside those who can turn our hearts by filling us with fear and anger. Be they mystic, dictator or democratically elected politician, all who achieve and maintain power over others do so from an inherent, deep appreciation of our sensitivities to theatre.

Chapter 3: The Creation of Emotion

The Nature of the Id

"With his victim momentarily paralyzed, by fright and pain, Tennine [a Kamodo Dragon] lunges at its soft under belly. Grabbing hold of the erupted intestines, he quickly eviscerates the deer with side-to-side lashing of his powerful jaws. He flails the intestines from side to side to free the contents and quickly gulps them down. As the deer goes into shock, the dragon's jaws plunge like a scooping digger into the thoracic cavity for the heart and lungs. The hunt is over." Paul D. MacLean (1913-2007). Pioneer, Neuroscience of Emotion.

The id is a term employed by Sigmund Freud in his psychoanalytical model of the human psyche. In its inception the id was seen to lie within the subconscious and yet to have the constant inclination to weave its spells within the human mind. Id is a Latin word that translates to "it", a word that, as a noun, is frequently used to convey the ominous and foreboding quality of the unknown. While many contemporary psychologists consider the id an overly simple concept, it is still a useful one, for it highlights the constellation of instinctive, animalistic urges that drive what we irrationally believe to be our independent minds. In its original definition the id was regarded as a wholly subconscious reservoir of instinctive drives that vie with one another for immediate satiation, without regard to global issues governing survival. However, if this were strictly true humans would never have experiences related to their innate urges and consequently would be unable to introspectively define the existence of their visceroemotional, animal centers.

To be recognizable the id needs some living cortex through which its emissaries can enter human awareness. This means that there must be areas of cortex that are exclusively devoted to representing our animal propensities - areas that conjure those inner stirrings we call emotion. In such a vision, the id does not lie within the subconscious, but enters the game of life from those subtle realms of consciousness that linger beneath the cognitive traffic that so dominates human consciousness. Indeed, an experiential appreciation of the id can only be gained when we take leave of the realms of thought and embark upon the inner journey. Deeply committed to the practice of educated thought, westerners could rarely see what their meditative eastern counterparts had been observing for millennia. Only through the insights of Freud into the nature of dreams did the id become a recognizable force in the western vision of the human psyche.

The Focus of Our Visceral Life

"Man is an intelligence in servitude to his organs." Aldous Huxley (1894-1963). English Author.

It is as well that Sigmund Freud and his rebellious protégé Carl Jung had such gifts as could inspire wonder about the place of our emotional life within the human psyche, for as Freud's emphasis upon our anal and oral fixations preempted, the task of plumbing the origins of emotion has been, from the beginning, a grisly one. In the challenge of deciphering human emotion, theories of a collective unconscious, filled with the mentally significant but emotionally barren paraphernalia of mythology, proved to be only another playground for the faint hearted. The true understanding of emotion was to come from the blood and guts of the physiology laboratory. There, for more than a century, an army of stalwart souls sought the nervous system's involvement in such earthy matters as the production of sweat, urine and feces. Today things are only a little easier. The humors of the body must still be invoked but now a whole human can often be substituted for the surgically prepared laboratory animal. Using sophisticated electronic recording techniques and brain scanners, it is now possible to observe in the awake human brain, the spatiotemporal patterns of cortical activity evoked by the perturbation of particular organs.

People will do anything for money. Some sell their souls to the devil, others fight wars for the government and still others readily submit to the systematic manipulation of their viscera while men and women in white coats scrutinize their brains through hugely expensive machines. Anal retentives need not apply. Being nearest to the orifices of the body, the first organs targeted by these seekers of the id were the rectum and the esophagus. For controlled stimulation of the same, the inflatable balloon has been the tool of choice. On the end of a catheter (tube), the balloon can be inserted a measured distance into the anus or the mouth and then blown up to exert measurable pressures upon the surrounding tissues. To rhythmically distend and relax target structures, it may be pulsed with air once ever second or two. With the oral approach, the upper (3 cm from the top) and the lower (5 cm from the bottom) ends of the esophagus are typically selected. With the anal approach, the rectum approximately 10 cm beyond the anus was targeted. The spiritually inspired may anticipate that in this way we will eventually learn how the organs of the body are represented within human consciousness and so comprehend the biological origin of those mysterious experiences of the bodies "sacred centers" known as the lower, or animal, Chakras.

Because the inner lining of the digestive track is actually continuous with our skin, zoologists commonly regard our gut contents as being essentially outside the body. This notion was beautifully captured by a colleague who while stricken in foreign parts wrote, "We are running through India and India is running through us." Nevertheless, from the perspective of sensation the outside and inside surfaces are not remotely similar. Compared to localizing a stimulus on the skin, the localization of stimulation points within our visceral organs, is notoriously capricious. In the case of the esophagus, it seems the deeper one inserts the balloon, the more difficulty the subject has in saying where exactly it is located. When the upper part of the esophagus is stretched, subjects feel a localizable sensation in their upper chest while the same stimulus at the deeper level evokes a diffuse sensation across the lower chest. The same story holds true when the rectum and the anus are similarly explored. As far as our ordinary tactile sensations are concerned, both our esophagus and our rear passage seem to make an, albeit small, contribution to our somatosensory sensations. However, the experience of having these regions stimulated differs markedly from the stimulation of our skin because the sensory nerves from our viscera primarily activate parts of our cortex responsible for emotional experiences.

157

Life on the Edge - The Limbic System

"The concepts of the closed circuit, of the balanced functions, and of the hierarchical processing are prominent. The corresponding symbols of the circle, the balance and the ladder have served for a long time in explaining the unexplained. It is no accident that the greatest mysteries in our understanding of the brain remain with the limbic system; questions concerning the integration of all brain functions, the generation of consciousness or psyche, and finally the seat of the soul." Kotter, R. and Meyer, N. (1992). The limbic system: a review of its empirical foundation. *Behavioral Brain Research*, 52, 105-127.

Most human beings naturally consider the mind to be the ultimate executor of all behavior, dominant over, though responsive to, the solicitous demands of our visceroemotional centers. However, when we project our knowledge of the behavior and brain structure of living mammals back through the 230 million years of mammalian evolution, it is clear that the essentially "mindless" early mammals must have been wholly controlled by an integrated, dictatorial system dedicated to their instinctual urges and visceral needs. Working under the auspices of the church, ever anxious to delineate our animal propensities from the more illustrious, god-like qualities of an idealized humanity, the western scientists of the 19th century were keen to identify just such a system. In their piety they imagined a virtually independent network, singularly devoted to the service and expression of those unsavory bodily functions and animalistic behaviors amongst which sex was the most infamous. Naturally they sought to locate this network below the highest echelons of the brain, leaving the mind to more civilized functions. In 1878 the eminent neurologist and anthropologist Paul Broca (1824-1880) christened this system the "great limbic lobe" or as it has since been rephrased, the *limbic system*.

Fortunately nature does not necessarily respect boundaries that emerge from man-made classifications. Almost from the beginning the strict delineation of instinct from thought caused problems. Nevertheless, there remained a critical need to identify a circumscribed system that controlled organic life. The concept of the limbic system was supposed to achieve this by delineating the parts of the brain responsible for our baser urges. As this system was seen as being beyond volition it has been referred to in modern times as the "central autonomic network". Although a complexity in its own right, Broca's definition of the limbic system fulfilled the need of the newly established discipline of neuropsychology to provide a touchstone for such profound philosophical and spiritual issues as the relationship between brain activity and the soul, the inner being, the id and transcendental experience. Over the next century the growing popularity of eastern spirituality brought home the realization that our visceral world was not just the seat of emotion but also the source of all mystical, spiritual and mythological insight.

The term limbic is derived from the Latin word *limbus*, meaning edge or boundary. Paul Broca adopted this word to highlight the fact that the areas of cortex believed to be responsible for our emotions and the control of our organs were located around the edge of the cortex of each cerebral hemisphere. Since they first evolved, these areas had been pushed to the edges of the cortex by the progressive evolution of new cortical areas during the 230 million year ascendancy of the mammals.

Given that the limbic system has often been seen as encompassing the soul, Broca's choice of name has an astounding, though serendipitous, link to Christian mythology wherein the word *limbus* has potent associations with our inner being. In times when the world was thought to be flat, Christian scholars saw the *limbus* (or the concept of limbo) as a place beyond the physical and material realms where certain classes of souls awaited judgment. With some theological refinement there arose the *limbus patrum* (father's limbo), where were collected the souls of Old Testament saints who, being unfortunate enough to have lived before Christ, had to await liberation by the Savior. To this was added the *limbus infantium* (children's limbo), a similar holding ground for the souls of infants who had the misfortune to die before being cleansed of the original sin by baptism. And finally in the service of popular morality there was the *limbus fatuorum*, a fool's paradise where moldered away the souls of those guilty of the less than admirable evocations of our basic urges. That the souls of all these unfortunates are compelled to reside at the edge of the universe is in a curious way quite apt, for the anterior cingulate gyrus elaborates our awareness of our inner being, is composed of a primitive, transitional form of neocortex (*proisocortex*) and is located along the edge of our vast, perceptually and cognitively disposed neocortex. It seems that our spirit does indeed rest within the *limbus of consciousness*, where our viscera play the ancient tunes of our biological heritage, ushering us into our earliest moments of postnatal consciousness, as in the gentle arms of death they will serenade us into eternal sleep.

The Triad of Emotion
"There can be no knowledge without emotion. We may be aware of a truth, yet until we have felt its force, it is not ours. To the cognition of the brain must be added the experience of the soul." Arnold Bennett, (1867-1931). British Novelist and Playwright.

Our emotions arise from activity in three strongly interconnected centers. Two of these, the aforementioned, *anterior cingulate gyrus* (BAs 24, 25 and 32) and the *insula*, are parts of the cerebral cortex and therefore have the potential to elaborate directly those enigmatic feelings we call emotions. The other, the *amygdala*, is an archaic brain structure that in the reptiles, amphibians and fish is a part of the cerebral cortex and that therefore exerts a powerful influence over their behavior (Figure 4.1). However, the evolution of the mammals has seen the amygdala secede from the cortex to form an almond shaped, sub-cortical structure within the front end of each temporal lobe. In this position it is very close to parts of the cortex that enable us to consolidate memories, to recognize people and objects and to judge the familiarity in our surroundings. From here it is generally believed that the amygdala affects our emotions via both its direct connections to the anterior cingulate gyrus and by exerting a powerful descending influence over our visceral and hormonal status which enables it to generate visceral sensations that are an integral part of our experiences of anger, fear and lust.

159

Together these denizens of our inner world form the *triad of emotion*. The triad of emotion can be thought of as a committee charged with the responsibility of meeting the immediate needs of our body by representing them as our instinctual urges. An idea of the political leanings of its members can be gleaned from an appreciation of their connections to two specialized cortical areas on the underside of the prefrontal lobes (the *medial* and *lateral orbital cortex*) that enable our *immediate* assessment of the imminence of reward or punishment - areas that are critical to the phenomenon of mood (*The Relationship between Mood and Anticipation*: Chapter 3: Section 5). Thus, the amygdala interacts powerfully with the area that predicts punishment, while the anterior cingulate speaks preferentially to the area that predicts reward and the insula supplies emotionally significant information to these two opposing forces.

Beyond the internal politics of the triad, it is vital to appreciate, which of the three members is ultimately in charge. In the reptiles and other lower vertebrates all behavior is driven by the amygdala (Section 4: Chapter 4: The First Emotions - Anger, Fear and Lust). In lower mammals, however, it is the anterior cingulate and not the amygdala that is responsible for their highly instinctive behavior patterns. Only in humans, and possibly the great apes, is the mind sufficiently powerful to have ultimate power in the fashioning of behavior. Thus, in humans, the only significant issue regarding the triad of emotion is which member has the most power over the mind. In this matter, the anterior cingulate gyrus emerges as the dominant partner, for neither the insula nor the amygdala, have strong connections to those parts of the prefrontal cortex that conduct the processes of thought.

While the human anterior cingulate gyrus has the power to solicit the mind in the service of the emotions, it also contains, within its own internal architecture, the bones of a period in our paleontological past when it was solely responsible for driving the behavior of our "mindless" mammalian ancestors. Thus, we find in the scientific literature on rodents, repeated reference to the anterior cingulate in terms of providing motivation, directing attention, making executive decisions in the selection of behavior and extinguishing the warning cries of threat - critical functions that, in humans, can also be initiated by purely mental effort. From these considerations alone the anterior cingulate gyrus emerges as the *executor of emotion* in all species of mammals.

This executive role of the anterior cingulate is also illustrated by its position in the processing of emotionally relevant sensations. In the cortical representation of emotion the insula acts as a *primary sensory receiving area of the cortex*, while, in its executive capacity, the anterior cingulate acts as a *perceptual area of the cortex* specialized for the expression of recognizable domains of emotional experience (Section 2: Chapter 1: The Origins, Mythology and Organization of Consciousness). The insula's connections within the triad of emotion are such that it can send information directly to both the anterior cingulate and the amygdala. By so doing, the insula acts as a cortical sorting station, presumably sending sensory information related to positive emotions to the anterior cingulate and information related to negative emotions to the amygdala, which passes them on through its direct connections to the anterior cingulate. In this vision of emotional processing, the insula is one of the first cortical areas to respond to touch, pain and taste, as well as sensory information from the viscera and the archaic olfactory cortex. The insular cortex can thus be compared to the primary visual, auditory or somatosensory areas of the cortex, except that it is specifically devoted to sensory information that is highly relevant to emotion.

Brain imaging shows that the anterior cingulate is active not only during the classical mammalian emotions of disgust, sadness and joy but also during the experiences fear and anger that are first expressed within the amygdala. Thus, in acting as a perceptual representation of emotion, the anterior cingulate integrates information from the insula and the amygdala into the five archetypal elements of emotional experience, joy, sadness, disgust, fear and anger - fundamental domains of emotion that were identified by the analyses of facial expressions long before the invention of brain scanners (Section 4: Chapter 2: The Communication of Emotion). The anterior cingulate's representation of the five primary emotions provides a focus within human consciousness of the urges that motivate not only all humans, but also all mammalian life. In this way the anterior cingulate enables our empathy with the emotional states of other humans to be extended to all mammals.

Within the healthy social mind the intrapersonal and the interpersonal are united to form the foundations of emotional and ultimately, social intelligence. The anterior cingulate gyrus and the social mind are highly interactive, the cortex of the anterior cingulate gyrus abutting that of the social mind (BA9). The presentation of emotionally charged pictures activates both the social mind and the cortex of the anterior cingulate gyrus. As mentioned previously, people with a highly responsive anterior cingulate gyrus are unusually sensitive to others and, not unexpectedly, have a high level of emotional intelligence. It is, however, crucial to remember that the anterior cingulate and the social mind have very different roles; the anterior cingulate acting as a perceptual center for visceral perturbations while the social mind builds concepts from its socioemotional environment. Thus, when subjects are asked to focus on their raw emotions, brain scans show activation of the anterior cingulate, whereas the social mind only becomes engaged (active) when subjects are told to focus their *attention* to their emotional reactions (*Defining Attention and Imagination*: Chapter 1: Section 7).

Life without Emotion
"The creative faculty in a people as in the child or every creative person, springs from this state of being seized. Man is seized by the revelation of fate. The reality of the natural rhythm of genesis and extinction has seized hold of his consciousness, and this, inevitably and by reflex action, leads him to represent his emotion in an act." Leo Frobenius (1873-1938). German Ethnologist and Archaeologist.

Our emotions are so much part of the undercurrent of our consciousness that we cannot imagine how it would be not to have them. Yet under the banner of logic, many people take pride in claiming to be able to overcome their heart, to be "strong" and to follow the dictates and plans of their trained, focused and, alas, wholly conditioned mind. If we were to accept their claim, then we could say of such a person that their thoughts would take precedence in determining action over any motivational impetus arising from their emotional centers. But are there truly such beings in our midst? For if it really were that their mind always dominated their emotions then surely their organic urges would never find expression in behavior. Their life would be a pitiful existence in which no craving would have the power to solicit actions that might bring about its actualization. Behavior in the service of any instinct or organic need would cease and insulated even from the drive to eat, death by starvation would most surely follow. No matter what people say, the mind is always at the disposal of our emotional centers, always working to placate the demands of instinct. But what if we were deprived of all emotion, would our mind truly have the stature to press ahead and execute plans, hatched entirely within the ether of thought?

In the early 1980s a window of opportunity enabled a comprehension of the place of emotion in the motivation of human beings. At that time there appeared in the clinical literature an account of an extraordinary case involving a woman who suffered a complete though temporary loss of her anterior cingulate cortex, a woman who for a short time was entirely without the organic drives that through the executor of emotion, so effectively call the mind to action. What most concerns us here is the *nature of her experiences* in the weeks following the stroke that transiently shut down the cortex of the anterior cingulate gyrus, effectively removing the executor of emotion from the house of consciousness.

The clinical diagnosis of this rarely reversible condition is *akinetic mutism*. Following her stroke the patient was unable to speak, and though appearing alert, she rarely moved. When she did recover she reported that throughout her ordeal she had been able to hear and comprehend everything that was being said to her. She had, however, not replied because she simply had "nothing to say". She went on to explain that she had nothing to say because, at that time, "nothing mattered". As the only time nothing matters is when we are absolutely emotionally flat, there is again reason to believe that the patient's psychological lethargy also resulted from temporary inactivation of the cortex of the anterior cingulate gyrus. Clinicians had long understood that damage to the cingulate gyrus produced deficits of attention, affect, heart rate, social behavior and (not surprisingly) associative learning, but never before had it been possible to simply ask someone what it was like to be without this part of the cortex. Ever cautious, her neurologists, Antonio Damasio and Gary Van Hoesen (1983) concluded, "It is unquestionable that bilateral damage to the cingulate causes a state of disturbed affect, in which the *expression and experience of emotion are precluded*". Without the executor of emotion it seems that it is impossible to apportion meaning or significance to anything, nor, *ipso facto*, feel the energy of motivation. When the biological drives that support and even spawn life depart from within us, with them goes not only our impetus to act but also that embodiment of instinct that *is* our inner being.

Chapter 4 - The First Emotions - Anger, Fear and Lust

The Dogs of Darjeeling

"We are conscious of an animal in us, which awakens in proportion as our higher nature slumbers. It is reptile and sensual, and perhaps cannot be wholly expelled; like the worms which, even in life and health, occupy our bodies. Possibly we may withdraw from it, but never change its nature. I fear that it may enjoy a certain health of its own; that we may be well, yet not pure." Henry David Thoreau (1817-1862). American Essayist, Poet, Civil Liberties Advocate and Philosopher.

It was in the beautiful Indian town of Darjeeling that I had opportunity to watch the interplay of the emotions orchestrated by the most primitive member of the triad of emotion, the amygdala. The streets of that ridge top town are alive with dogs, the descendents of the manicured pets of the British Raj. Until recently it was the local practice to throw all refuse into the streets. This attracted large numbers of rats that in turn provided food for the marauding canines which were tolerated only because they helped keep down the local rat population.

These street dwellers are often joined by a third species, the monkeys. The monkeys of Darjeeling live in the forest around the temple at the northern end of the ridge. Every so often, they go on foraging expeditions, leaping across the rooftops, looking for mischief and anything that is edible.

It was in this urban zoo that I witnessed the following drama. The monkeys had gathered on the roof of the one story building beneath the parapet of my hotel. By chance a pack of perhaps 10 dogs was assembled in the street below. Looking up and seeing the monkeys peering down, one began to bark. A large monkey bared its teeth in spontaneous reply. Then a snarl, answered by more screeches and grimaces from the rooftop, followed by more snarls and barking from below. In no time the noise had escalated to cacophonic proportions. Minutes passed and bedlam reigned until suddenly, deprived of the opportunity of real battle, the confrontation ceased as quickly as it had begun. Each group sauntered away, the monkeys moving back across the roof, the dogs edging down the road until suddenly both species threw themselves into a flurry of sexual activity.

The emotional center responsible for these bizarre sequences of behavior is the amygdala. In one moment, fired by the fearful faces of the opposition, the amygdala hurls its host into an aggressive display. In the next, deprived of the provocation of combat, the amygdala triggers the urge for rampant sexual gratification. How like the troops of our human armies, whom, as history repeatedly records, experience, in the aftermath of the ferocity of battle, an almost irresistible impetus to rape, pillage and plunder - a repeated testimony to the significant contribution of our reptilian ancestors to the human psyche.

The Origins of War, Oppression and Libido

"Listen to this, and hear the mystery inside:
A snake-catcher went into the mountains to find a snake.
He wanted a friendly pet, and one that would amaze

audiences, but he was looking for a reptile, something
that has no knowledge of friendship….
The snake is your animal-soul.
When you bring it into the hot air of your wanting-energy,
Warmed by that and by the prospect of power and wealth it does massive damage."
Jalāl ad-Din Muhammad Rumi (1207-1273). Persian Sufi Mystic and Poet.

In the Yogic tradition, an obsession with power, money or sex represents blockage of the 3rd or Power Chakra (*Manipura*). The 3rd Chakra is centered on the solar plexus and the adrenal glands. The adrenal glands respond to stress by secreting both cortisol and adrenalin into the blood. When faced with a Herculean task, the 3rd Chakra is considered important for summoning our physiological resources and willpower. For this reason frequent reference is made to the 3rd Chakra within the martial arts where it is seen as being the origin of the masculine "fire energy". It seems we are not unlike the dogs of Darjeeling, except that as icons within the conceptual machinery of the untutored human mind, fear, anger and lust are inevitably woven into power seeking strategies, spiritual and religious doctrines and even the principles of natural medicine.

In animals, fight, flight and sexual display indicate involvement of the amygdala. Similarly, when our amygdala is provoked, we experience fear or anger and, when the source of provocation is removed, the potent desire for sexual reward. The prominent interplay between aggression, fear and sex is a testimony to their relatedness to a single element of the psyche. When we are flooded with thoughts of hatred and mistrust we may assume that the amygdala is working behind the scenes. In its contribution to human paranoia, aggression and the build up of sexual desire the amygdala is central to all political oppression, war, divisive propaganda and a wide range of bizarre and sometimes inhumane, pornographic iconography. Within the human psyche, the amygdala is the generative source of our cognitive desires for power, money and sex - elements that reflect our dominance over others. To help meet the physiological challenges of aggression and fear, the amygdala has the capacity to release *cortisol*, a corticosteroid that helps the body deal with stress. Ultimately, it is the amygdala that, in collusion with the human mind, is directly responsible for the continuing genocide that in the last century alone, saw humanity murder hundreds of millions of their own species.

The 150 million years that spanned the *Age of the Dinosaurs* was the golden age of the amygdala. Indeed, the word *dinosaur* means terrible lizard (Greek; *deinos*, 'terrible' and *suaros*, 'lizard'). It was the amygdala that was responsible for driving the massive *Tyannosaurus rex* to acts of unbridled ferocity and the amygdala that enabled the escape of the relatively defenseless herbivores. The age of the dinosaur was a period when the amygdala held absolute power within the kingdom of animals, a time when it generated all significant behavior. In the human brain it is the amygdala that affords us some insight into the reptilian world. It might even be argued that activation of the more primitive parts of our amygdala enables us to glimpse the highest realm of reptilian awareness. Outrageous as this may seem, it perhaps accounts for the frequent reports of reptilian identity in the vast popular literature on altered states of consciousness. As Jung alluded to, there is every reason to believe that inscribed within the human brain are indelible elements that evolved within, and even before, our distant reptilian past.

Commanding Aggression and Fear

"..in spite of all that has been done by moralists and religious teachers, our emotions are as ferocious as those of any animal, and our intelligence enables us to give them a scope which is denied to even the most savage beast." Bertrand Russell (1872-1970). British Logician, Historian, Philosopher and Nobel Laureate.

In people who are unable to control their aggression, surgical destruction of the amygdala has been successful in reducing the number of aggressive outbursts. However, occasionally a normally peaceful person spontaneously, and without provocation, annihilates another. The "culprit" on such occasions may remember nothing of the event. It therefore seems reasonable to believe that these instances of unpremeditated murder are the result of spontaneous and even epileptic activity in the amygdala.

In primitive vertebrates like the fish, "flight" and "fight" are, like most behavioral routines, the product of hardwired circuits within the nervous system. Command centers within the fish brain determine whether any particular stereotyped behavior is switched on or left switched off. This type of organization is adequate for fish because their life style requires only a very limited number of behavioral repertoires. Clearly such a simplistic control system would be totally unsuitable for higher animals that have behaviorally complex life styles.

Fish have only the beginnings of a cerebral cortex called the pallium (*The Birth of the Cerebral Cortex*: Chapter 3: Section 2). In fish, the amygdala is part of the pallium, a part that is believed to project down to parts of the hypothalamus wherein electrical stimulation causes fish to snap at objects in a manner resembling an aggressive response. In the shark, a parallel of this behavior would be the almost legendary *feeding frenzy*. Anyone who has seen a feeding frenzy in a big shark may be forgiven for assuming they are observing a purposeful act of aggression. It is hard to dispassionately watch a four meter column of pure muscle, fifty centimeters in diameter, armed with row upon row of neatly assembled razor sharp teeth, exploding into an enactment of ravenous consumption. Yet even here aggression is not necessarily an apt word, for when humans speak of aggression they imply anger and intent. From what we know about the brain of the shark, the feeding frenzy is simply a playing out of a stereotyped motor program that achieves the immobilization and consumption of prey. If it were truly a matter of aggressive intent, we might expect that in adversity the shark would desist from such activity but, on the contrary, the feeding frenzy is so powerfully driven that sharks have been observed to keep feeding even though, when injured in the orgy of satiation, they are being set upon and virtually eaten alive by other sharks.

The on-off control of aggression seen in fish could never serve the subtle requirements of animals dependent on a complex social structure. In mammals, for example, the amygdala must retain its role in instigating fight or flight, while also participating in the complex of emotional interactions that are essential to social communication. This accounts for the marked differences between the amygdala in reptiles and mammals. In the reptiles the amygdala is simply a part of the primitive reptilian cortex that elicits aggression, flight or sexual display. In contrast, the amygdala of humans and other higher primates is interconnected with many cortical areas and is composed of at least 13 separate masses of nerve cells (nuclei), many of which are critically involved in a complex array of social interactions. Indeed, a survey of a large variety of primates has shown that the complexity of the social structure of any species is related to the size of those parts of the amygdala that have social significance.

In humans, the amygdala is larger in males than in females, indicating that its overall size may be related to the propensity for aggression. Although it has not been investigated, an enlarged amygdala might explain why 90% of hunter-gather and native tribes are known to engage warfare, 65% waging war at least once every 2 years. Studies of aggression in North America, Australia, New Guinea and particularly South America tribes show that the percentage of men who die from murder is as follows: The Gebusi, 9%; the Huli; 20%, the Namowei, 22%; the Murngin and the Dugum Dani, 30%; the Mae Enga 38%; the Shamatari, 40%; the Jivaro, 57%. In comparison, only 50% chimp males survive, while the number of males murdered in the USA and Europe, is less than 5% even if we include all those murdered in the first and second world wars. Given the contrasts between human populations in their propensity for lethal aggression, it is not surprising that genes versus an individual's social environment are emerging as important factors in the expression of aggressive behavior. The most compelling evidence for this to date being the identification of a so-called "warrior gene" or MAOA gene – a variant of mood altering genes that is expressed in boys who choose to join gangs and who show the greatest inclination towards extreme violence.

Normally, subliminal electrical stimulation of the part of our amygdala involved in fear and aggression evokes negative feelings of foreboding and anxiety, feelings that are associated with visceral responses we regard as unpleasant. It is a characteristic of all control systems is that they must always contain a representation of opposites in order to remain balanced. Thus, electrical stimulation of different parts of the human amygdala evokes pleasant, lustful feelings and a repression of any aggressive inclinations. Similar observations have been made in cats where stimulation of some parts of the amygdala can suppress attack, while stimulating other parts evokes attack.

In recent decades brain imaging has been used to study the response of the human amygdala under a wide range of conditions. Again these studies show that the amygdala contains parts that are responsive to positive stimuli and other parts that are responsive to negative stimuli. For example, our amygdala is highly responsive to unpleasant pictures and to the presentation of anxiety-producing, unsolvable anagrams (word puzzles) such as those used to induce learned helplessness in psychological studies. Conversely, however, our amygdala is also responsive to pleasant tastes, smells and, particularly in men, images of erotic nudes that in a natural setting might elicit lust and even sexual display. Lying on the very boundaries of human consciousness, it is clear that the human amygdala has the power to respond to a wide variety of external challenges and in so doing to register the imminence of events that have great significance for the survival of the individual.

Aggression and fear cannot coexist with pleasant feelings. Thus, when all concern for negative consequences is negated by administration of cocaine, amphetamine or morphine, the amygdala is rendered silent and unresponsive to all normally evocative scenarios. These potent hedonic substances are known to activate ancient reward centers in the core of the brain, centers also targeted by that part of the amygdala that can elicit pleasant feelings while suppressing aggression and fear.

The amygdala sits at the top of a hierarchical system that drives the movements, postures and physiological responses normally associated with both "fight" and "flight". While aggression and fear are clearly antithetical states, they are also part of a theatrical continuum that falls under the single umbrella of *conflict behavior*. In this way the amygdala fulfils an important social role that is critical to all species that are dependent upon a high degree of social interaction. It achieves this in two ways. Firstly, the amygdala has the capacity to influence lower centers that control facial muscles, sweating, dilation of the pupils, the "raising of the hackles" (piloerection), urination, defecation, paralysis (freezing), vigilance, attention, heart and respiratory rate and the release of stress hormones - phenomena common to the states of anxiety, fear and aggression. Secondly, it has the capacity to respond directly to other agents, human or animal, as it receives directly information from specialized areas of cortex that respond to their facial expressions, vocalizations and body language. Thirdly, it receives, largely from the insula, information on the physiological status of the viscera and a registration of the emotionally significant senses of smell taste, touch and pain.

The hierarchical organization of aggression is traceable from the amygdala down through the nervous system. Whereas normally a cat might only attack a real moving mouse, when certain parts of the amygdala are electrically stimulated it will be predisposed to attack any fluffy object of approximately the right size. For example, the cat will pounces upon a ball of wool in the same way we might thump the table when angered by someone who is not even present. In comparison, electrical stimulation at a lower level of the cat's brain (the *lateral hypothalamus*) elicits the complete repertoire of attack behavior without even the need for a suitable target. Further down still, within the ancient core of the brain stem (the *periaquaductal gray matter*), electrical stimulation evokes individual components of the aggression response. Which component is evoked depends on the exact location of the stimulating electrode. Thus, while some areas evoke flushing of the face by transiently increasing its blood supply, others cause the hair of the neck to stand on end or elicit the component movements of hostile facial expressions.

The Social Arm of Fear and Apprehension
"Hoen said: 'The past and future Buddhas, both are his servants. Who is he?' 'If you realize clearly who he is, it is as if you met your own father on a busy street. There is no need to ask anyone whether or not your recognition is true,' replied Mumon." Ekai Kawaguchi (1866-1945). Japanese Buddhist Monk.

Although we are barely aware of it, our emotions are critical in enabling us to distinguish our friends and relatives from strangers. This is demonstrated by a rare clinical condition, known as *Capgras syndrome*, wherein patients believe that close friends or family members are imposters. Pervaded by a resident uncertainty, the same patients typically harbor delusional beliefs about animals, objects and places. Normally when we meet a member of our family or a close friend, we subliminally sense their familiarity by their *vibes*, as well as cognitively recognizing them by their appearance. That is to say we identify them by both our cognitive and emotional responses. In this process of recognition our brain registers their identity (visual and auditory) in specialized parts of the cortex's perceptual systems, the fusiform gyrus (BA37) and the so-called object area (inferior temporal cortex, BA20). Capgras syndrome was first thought to be related to a loss of the ability to see faces or *prospagnosia* – a condition resulting from the malfunction of the facially sensitive part of the object area (BA20). However, Capgras patients can cognitively recognize faces but do not show the normal autonomic (emotional) arousal in response to familiar people.

Capgras syndrome appears to be associated with injury to the posterior part of the right hemisphere – an area containing the fusiform gyrus (BA37). As we have seen, the fusiform gyrus serves the recognition of, and the emotional response to, familiar and unfamiliar people of the same and different race (*The Nature and Nurture of Racism*: Chapter 2; Section 1). It seems that Capgras syndrome results from malfunction of BA37 or the pathways that link this area to the brains emotional centers.

In recognizing someone as familiar friend or potential foe, two fundamental elements of the psyche, mind and emotion, are normally consulted. Of these two elements, the mind has plenipotentiary powers when it comes to instigating speech and behavior. Normally, this is not a problem as the executor of emotion, the anterior cingulate gyrus, automatically informs the mind of its emotion-based assessment of a person as friend or stranger. However, in people with Capgras syndrome information about a person's identity does not reach the anterior cingulate. Whereas normally the mind's rational assessment of familiarity is backed up by information from the emotional center's reading of a person's "vibes", in Capgras patients the emotional centers cannot supply their instinctual confirmation of identity. Without the reinforcing influence of an emotional response, the mind's postulation of a familiar person's identity is basically unconvincing. Faced with this conundrum the Capgras patient comes up with only possible answer - all their friends and relatives must be imposters. The lesson of Capgras syndrome is that even if we have a vast cognitive knowledge of the people around us, without our gut feelings, this is simply not enough to persuade us of either their trustworthiness or their identity.

The anterior cingulate is not the only member of the triad of emotion to receive information about body language and facial expression. Brain pathways exist that supply both the insula and the amygdala with similar biosocial queues. Thus, even though the amygdala is a source of our most primitive, reptilian emotions, it has a profound influence on our typically mammalian, social interactions. In normal people fearful faces powerfully activate the amygdala, which also responds to vocal and bodily expressions of fear in others. When people suffer destruction of their amygdala, they have difficulty identifying fear in facial images, even though they can still learn to visually recognize new faces.

As the amygdala is involved in fear and aggression we might expect that it would respond equally to both fearful and angry faces. This, however, is not the case. For good reason the amygdala is highly responsive to fearful facial expressions and relatively unresponsive to angry expressions that instead preferentially activate a part of the prefrontal cortex that works closely with the amygdala in the prediction of outcomes. By enabling us to empathize with fear in our cohorts without directly encountering the source of that fear, the amygdala has more time to instigate either evasive or defensive action. If instead of fear, the amygdala responded to anger then we would only be aware of a threat when we were directly confronted with the enemy. Clearly the politically expedient concept of bravery is incongruent with the *modus operandi* of the human amygdala. In the covenant of the natural world he who escapes survives while he who stands and fights often dies. In complete accord with this fundamental policy of natural selection, the human amygdala responds incrementally to the level of fear displayed in the faces of others, mimicking within us their presentiments in what is certainly the most ancient form of empathy.

So what do animals and humans do and not do, when they are surgically deprived of their amygdala? As the highest domain of the reptilian psyche, the amygdala is responsible for most of the limited behavior of the reptiles. Without its generative influence, the lizard, snake or turtle simply freezes - a "behavior" commonly seen in intact reptiles when, presumably, the amygdala is quiescent. In the mammal, the amygdala has important social functions beyond the flight and fight paradigms that characterize the reptilian world. When the amygdala is destroyed in a rat, cat, dog or non-human primate, the outcome is an animal that is less fearful, less aggressive, tamer, hypersexual and hyperoral. In the rigid social structure of higher mammals, an appreciation of pecking order is a prerequisite for survival. With the loss of the specter of conflict, the playful, sensual orality of the surviving insula and the anterior cingulate, naturally emerge (*Life and Death at the Crossroads*: Chapter 5: Section 4). However, even the increased frequency of intimate and solicitous advances that result from damage to the amygdala cannot negate the consequences in store for those who disregard the existing social hierarchy. Inevitably the newfound innocence of the "amygdalaless" mammal is far more socially catastrophic than the immobility of the "amygdalaless" reptile.

Because of their rigid social structure the non-human primates are more dependent upon their sense of conflict than any other group of animals, including humans. In the presence of people, monkeys are normally furtive and emotionally reactive. If, however, their amygdala is damaged, instead of trying to escape they settle down to examining one object after another, including any humans or other animals that happen to be present. In this process they show marked orality, indiscriminately putting both food and non-food items into their mouth. Insensitive, to the potential danger of foreign objects, the "amygdalaless" monkey will even break with its strictly herbivorous habits and eat meat. In mammals, *neophobia*, the innate tendency to regard the novel with caution, is critically dependent upon the amygdala.

For the "amygdalaless" monkey the unknown holds no terror. The warning cries, facial expressions and other overt displays that normally signal danger disappear. Although snakes typically evoke intense fear, loss of the amygdala negates any avoidance behavior. At the same time the animal's participation in heterosexual or homosexual behavior increases. Consequently, the "amygdalaless" individual no longer qualifies as a useful member of the group. Less able to judge fear and anger but more playfully inclined, the "amygdalaless" monkey shows a marked insensitivity to social boundaries, randomly challenging stronger individuals and often suffering repeated attacks and even fatal injuries in response to their unbridled precociousness.

Deprived of the cautionary voice of the amygdala, a primate will inevitably suffer social ostracization. Without its amygdala a monkey ceases to either make, or respond to, facial expressions, vocalizations and body language that are a vital part of conflict behavior. All capacity to know when to approach and when to withdraw is replaced by a sensual, exploration of the playful. Learning perhaps from the consequences of being unable to judge friend from foe, the "amygdalaless" monkey soon desists from grooming and in so doing is excluded from participating in an innate activity that is vital to primate bonding. An emotional renegade, the subject inevitably falls from grace. Its social rank plummets and, like the mentally ill within our western societies, it may suffer expulsion from the community and die, prematurely, from the stresses of loneliness or the dangers of isolation.

In humans, the amygdala also has an important influence over how we interact within our social milieu. Electrically stimulating the amygdala in normal people gives the paroxysmal feelings of somebody being nearby. In social phobics, people who suffer extreme anxiety when surrounded by others, the amygdala is so hyper-responsive that it is activated even by emotionally neutral faces. At the other extreme, people who have lost their amygdala have difficulty recognizing facial expressions or matching pictures of similar facial expressions, even though they can identify pictures of familiar faces as well as remember new faces. On the positive side, they also show reduced emotional reactivity and consequently are unusually resistant to both anxiety and irritation.

The amygdala is vital to determining the way we assess the trustworthiness of others. Most people naturally regard strangers as less trustworthy than those they know well. The more we see our leaders on television the more we are inclined to trust them. Asked to judge the trustworthiness of strangers from facial photographs, patients with amygdala lesions were far less discriminatory than normal people. They were, however, still able to correctly judge trustworthiness from verbal descriptions of people.

As we shall see later, the higher non-human primates operate primarily on emotional intelligence. Their existence is thus almost completely social and survival of the individual is critically reliant upon its ability to tune-in to the nuances of monkey or ape society, an impossible task for an animal deprived of its amygdala. It is therefore surprising that in humans, destruction of the amygdala has relatively little influence on survival. However, "amygdalaless" humans do cease to respond emotionally to friends and family, preferring isolation over contact with others. They also demonstrate an exaggerated orality and may indulge frequently in masturbation. That they can cope at all is probably due to the highly cognitive nature of the human being. Unlike the apes and monkeys, human behavior is largely orchestrated in thought. Non-human primates simply lack the means to conjure our cogent philosophies of tolerance. Nevertheless, damage to any of emotional centers, even during adulthood, will compromise the individual's emotional intelligence. Fortunately, however, the human being can still draw upon vast cognitive resources operative within the practical, temporal and abstract domains of mind. Aspergic people, for example, suffer a very low emotional intelligence throughout their entire life yet function adequately within human society by exploiting knowledge gained through the other domains of cognition.

Apes and monkeys are exposed 24 hours a day to a society fashioned almost totally around emotional intelligence. Particularly in western societies the law affords us significant protection from each other. Under our sheltered domestic conditions becoming more sensual, oral and playful and less fearful, anxious and irritable may go largely unnoticed. In contrast, however, loss of the amygdala may be far more catastrophic in highly social, hunter-gatherer societies that operate under the directives of an, albeit, high level of emotional intelligence (*The Mind in the Wild*: Chapter 6: Section 6). Even so, with a powerful and diverse mind the "amygdalaless" human has a possibility of social survival, whereas the inert "amygdalaless" lizard, the sensually submissive "amygdalaless" cat and the socially liberated "amygdalaless" monkey are all conspicuously at risk.

We might ask whether this apparent independence from our inner source of fear and aggression means that we have transcended, just slightly, our animal origins. It is significant that while the conflict orientated amygdala generates fight, flight or sexual display, the anterior cingulate gyrus promotes bonding, audiovocal communication and play (*Origin of our Mammalian Ways*: Chapter 5: Section 4). In this dynamic between the positive and negative emotions, our amygdala ensures that we do not succumb to the fairer passions when the enemy is at the gate. Perhaps of even more importance is that without the amygdala a human being is deprived of part of that "energy field" through which his or her body is subliminally (and empathetically) connected to the presence and negative emotions of other beings. For many westerners who are increasingly immersed in the highly cognitive, isolated and electronically controlled milieu of modern society, such a loss may be barely perceptible.

The Tyranny of Fear in Childhood
"The souls of still born children, fearless because they have not known pain, live in Tenyu Lalu." Remond O'Hanlon, British Author. From: *Into the Heart of Borneo*. Penguin, London, 1985.

Different individuals have a different susceptibility to fear. Consequently, some people thrive on situations most would find threatening, while others are crippled with apprehension over insignificant matters. For people who suffer from high levels of fearfulness just to face day-to-day life can be an act of extreme bravery. Understanding the factors that determine the level of fearfulness of the individual is of great significance to understanding the origins of aggressive and submissive behavior.

In general, four factors contribute to our basal level of fearfulness. The first is our genetic make up. The second is what we are intellectually taught by our parents, teachers, and priests and, increasingly, by the media and our politicians. The third is the level of fearfulness of the people around us. The fourth is the level of abuse we have suffered in childhood.

Let us begin by considering the first contributor - the heritability of our propensity to experience fear. To some extent this is revealed by different responses of individuals to childhood suffering. History tells us that amongst children who have been exposed to the most appalling conditions there are some that grow up to lead relatively normal lives while others subjected to the same treatment, are both physically and mentally destroyed. Indeed, longitudinal studies that attempt to track the level of fearfulness throughout a person's life have shown that, all else being equal, it is highly dependent upon genes and thus inheritance. To some extent the basal level of each of our emotions appears to be set in early infant life. Thus, in relation to fear it has been shown that children who are profoundly shy at the age of 2 are more likely to suffer from anxiety and depression and to manifest inappropriate levels of emotion. Such children have been shown to chronically overproduce cortisol, an important stress hormone.

Cortisol is released from the adrenal glands. It prepares the body for the fight or flight reactions by increasing the rate and strength of heart contraction as well as affecting a wide array of metabolic functions that prepare the body to meet the anticipated challenge. A measure of the level of circulating cortisol is thus a measure of the prevailing level of stress that is directly related to levels of anxiety and fear. Even in the normal infant the experience of intense fear produces a marked increase in cortisol. The link between fear and the level of circulating cortisol results from the power of the conflict-sensitive amygdala to increase the secretion of cortisol into the blood. Thus, when very young monkeys are separated from their mothers, it takes only 20 minutes for their cortisol levels to increase. This response increases dramatically when the monkeys reach an age of 9 to 12 weeks, a time when they first show fear in response to particular target stimuli or situations. The equivalent age in the human infant is 7 to 12 months - a period that immediately follows the maturation of the amygdala.

The greater susceptibility of fearful children and adults to physical illness is, in part, attributable to an overproduction of cortisol. Unfortunately, high levels of cortisol suppress the immune system in order to prevent the overproduction of antibodies in response to injury or infection. Elevated cortisol can also produce gastric ulceration, cardiovascular disease and even disrupt development to that part of the brain (the *hippocampus*) involved in the consolidation of long-term memory. Typically the parents of anxious children also suffer from chronic anxiety and depression and have, in addition, high levels of circulating cortisol. As these children mature, the level of their fearfulness tends to increase as a consequence of their being exposed to parents who also have a genetical predisposition to fear.

The second contributor to our fearfulness is what we are intellectually taught. In recognizing the influences of the intellect on our level of fearfulness we are essentially positing that the mind has the power to conjure particular emotions by activating the appropriate emotional center. The mental evocation of fear simply depends upon the mind's ability to activate the amygdala. However, the amygdala has no direct connections to the human mind. Therefore in influencing the amygdala, the mind is dependent upon the amygdala's powerful interconnections with the anterior cingulate gyrus and the centers of prediction in the orbital cortex (*The Relationship between Mood and Anticipation*: Chapter 3: Section 5).

While the amygdala is responsible for our feelings of fear, it is the mind that determines the subject of our fears. As the social, temporal, material and abstract components of the mind mature progressively over the first 15 years of life, there is a progressive change in the things and issues that evoke fear (Figure 4.2). From birth until the end of the preoperational phase, the things which children most fear change from strange objects, people, odors, loud noises and pain, to largely unseen elements such as the dark, being alone, shadows and fierce animals, to more definite, identifiable psychobiological elements such as monsters, robbers, dreams, ridicule, social ostracization, injury and death.

In order to survive, it is important that the developing primate adopt the fears its parents show towards certain objects or situations. For example, young monkeys have no intrinsic fear of snakes. Only after witnessing their parents display intense fear upon encountering a snake, do they show a fearful response to the same trigger. In the same way human children also learn from their parents by picking up on their fear and associating it with a triggering object or situation. With the progressive disappearance of the natural world, an ever-increasing proportion of western children are taught to fear aspects of nature that would have been accepted with equanimity by their grandparents who had the opportunity of living closer to the earth. On the other hand western parents show little fear towards certain aspects of modern life that can be very dangerous. The result is that their children do not develop a healthy fear of such things. It is, for example, rare that western children develop a fear of cars. Indeed, most western children are obliged to watch their parents performing almost ritualized acts of caring on the family car - acts that often appear to exceed the nurturing extended to family members. The consequence is that the child neither believes nor feels that the car is a potentially dangerous object.

The unique ability of humans to utilize language enables direct access to the child's intellect. Through language it is possible to establish in a child's mind the belief that any chosen person, thing or situation is extremely dangerous. In this process of emotional arousal, the intonations of speech are probably of greater significance than the literary content. Verbal conditioning is most commonly seen in the religious instruction of children, where, for example, they are typically instructed, in dramatic voice, to fear evil deities that are entirely the creation of the imagination of other human beings. In later years, the same fear based manipulation of people is exploited by politicians, the military, the police force and sundry financial interests. To be assured of the magnitude of this phenomenon we need only travel to an alien culture to find ourselves astonished at their superstitions - a response that no doubt would be reciprocated should those people visit and witness the superstitions that are central to our own culture. There can be no doubt that we teach our children what to fear and in so doing create much unnecessary anxiety, stress and even illness while enhancing the potential of the mind to create of angst and hostility.

The third contributor to our fearfulness relates, not to what we are cognitively taught but to the fear we spontaneously pick up from the people around us through the process of automatic empathy (*The Nature of Empathy*: Chapter 2: Section 4). The absence of a mind in lower mammals, and indeed all non-mammalian vertebrates, means that this direct form of emotional transfer is vital to unifying the instinctual reactions of a species to threatening situations. This form of empathy in an inherent property of the human psyche, with the result that the emotional set of the individual is strongly influenced by the emotions of the majority.

The fourth contributor to fearfulness relates to the level of abuse suffered in childhood. Children who are abused are typically more fearful than other children. Apart from permanent psychological damage, they are, as adults, far more likely to suffer from a spectrum of physical conditions that include irritable bowel syndrome, migraine, chronic fatigue syndrome, fibromyalgia and posttraumatic stress disorder.

In the process of caring for their young, many mammals treat their offspring roughly to stop them from repeating a dangerous activity. The delivery of such "punishment" is instantaneous and totally instinctive. In the absence of an operational mind, the learning that occurs within the brain of the young mammal is primarily at the level of emotional memory. The transiently exposure of the young mammal to the instinctive (emotional) reactions of its parents, ensures that its emotional centers are conditioned in a manner that maximizes its potential to survive under the specific circumstances that prevail during its upbringing.

Today in the West, child abuse is regarded as a transgression of the moral code of good parenting. Psychologically, victims of child abuse carry a resident unhappiness for the rest of their lives. Recent evidence indicates that a single episode of abuse can increase the child's levels of cortisol for several weeks. For the developing brain, this is a potentially catastrophic event that may disrupt the growth of those parts of the child's brain that are in the process of maturing at the time of abuse. In this way the tyranny of fear extends beyond the psychological, to produce an individual with aberrant behavior patterns resulting from permanent structural abnormalities within their brain.

Chapter 5 - The Second Emotions - Love, Sadness and Disgust

The Origin of Our Mammalian Ways

"It seems to me that next to *Homo Faber* [man the maker], and perhaps on the same level as *Homo Sapiens* [man the knower], *Homo Ludens*, Man the Player, deserves a place in our nomenclature." John Huizinga (1872-1945). Dutch Cultural Historian.

The first mammals probably evolved as early as 260 mya from a group of long-extinct reptiles called the *therapsids* that in turn evolved around 285 mya. During the transition from the therapsid to the mammalian condition successful mutants became progressively more warm-blooded, developing jaw, skull and body structures so like the mammal that they have been called the *repto-mammals*. The true mammals are, however, identified by the presence of hair, a complex inner ear and mammary glands that enable the nurturing of the young. To enable the complex of nurturing and social behaviors, these bodily characteristics must also have been accompanied by significant additions to the cerebral cortex.

Very few living reptiles play a significant role in enhancing the survival of their young. Indeed, if the opportunity arises, some species will readily cannibalize their offspring. The now-extinct therapsid reptiles may have been an exception to this rule, as some believe that they formed social groups, hunted in packs and even possessed rudimentary mammary glands. In mammals, all nurturing behavior is clearly dependent on the anterior cingulate gyrus. Thus, if the therapsids did suckle their young and show a degree of social organization then it is very likely that their cortex contained at least the beginnings of the cingulate. What is certain is that the presence of the cingulate gyrus in the earliest mammals heralded the appearance of three forms of instinctive behavior. These behaviors are (a) the care and nursing of the young, (b) the audiovocal communication between parents and offspring and (c) play.

The nurturing of young requires an empathetic affiliation between parent and offspring known as *bonding*. Bonding is not a mental process but exploits the mechanisms underlying automatic empathy wherein contact between parent and offspring is sufficient to evoke direct activation of the anterior cingulate gyrus – an area of cortex that is active we experience love or immediately following the injection of powerful opiates (*Sex, State and Orgasm*: Chapter 3: Section 7). Indeed, the Buddhist definition of love as caring and compassion captures the essence of parent-child bonding. Born when still physically and behaviorally immature, a young mammal would rarely survive if its parents were not instinctually motivated to care for their offspring. Indeed, so powerful is the mammalian urge to nurture that history cites several cases where deserted human infants have survived only as a consequence of a wild, non-primate mammal acting as a surrogate parent. That bonding has always been a characteristic of mammalian parenthood is indicated by a now extinct group of mammals, the *multituberculates*, which survived for more than 100 million years even though their young were very small and presumably very immature when born (Figure 6…..).

Along with evolution of parent-infant bonding came a marked improvement in both the auditory and vocalization systems. Many non-mammalian terrestrial vertebrates produce sounds such as the croaks and hisses, but are severely limited in the range of sounds they can produce. With limited vocal abilities these animals have little need for a true inner ear that, in the mammal, enables the perception of a wide range of frequencies. With the evolution of the mammalian auditory and vocalization systems, infant-parent communication could exploit the medium of sound.

Most of the sounds related to infant care are the product of a specialized audiovocal center that again is located in the anterior cingulate gyrus. These mother-infant separation calls are not language but a complex of moans, squeaks and groans of clearly instinctual origin. Nevertheless, aside from human speech and possibly the vocally crude utterances of the great apes, these sounds constitute the highest level of audiovocal communication. So deeply are they entrenched in the mammalian brain that they persist throughout human life, surfacing in all intimate scenarios where words are both inadequate and inappropriate to ongoing proceedings.

The animalistic vocalizations generated by the anterior cingulate are critical to the exclusively mammalian phenomenon of play. Play provides a means for younger animals to interact with their physical surroundings and each other in a low risk setting. In chimp communities, play decreases markedly when the hierarchy is challenged. Only mammals engage in play and the proportion of life spent in play increases as we move towards the human condition. Thus, as a rule of thumb, playfulness lasts for 5% of a dog's life, 10% of a monkey's and 20% of a human's.

At first sight it is curious that the duration of play increases in accord with the evolution of the cognitive centers. The reason for this, however, is that play is a means of training the mind and therefore is found only in those higher mammalian species that have a mind. Essentially play is sustained in accord with the time required for the biological maturation and environmental conditioning of the mind. The longer the postnatal period required for the maturation of the mind, the longer would be the duration over which play is required as a safe, yet cerebrally instructive, process. This may explain why human play survives for so long, tapering off only when, around the 15th year of life, the cortex of the mind is finally mature and ready to embark on the serious business of thought.

Since the postulations of Sigmund Freud, the social mind, in the form of the super ego, has been considered to be repressive of our urges and emotions. However, it is not entirely due to the build up of our mental powers that the anterior cingulate gyrus loses its influence and the child within us begins to fade. The other significant factor at work is the progressive decrease in the level of the neurotransmitter, dopamine. Dopamine is the universal substance of reward. It is released upon the prefrontal cortex in response to all substances of reward, from nicotine to heroin (*The Controllers of State*: Chapter 3: Section 7). Dopamine reduces activity in the cortex of the mind, preventing thought and eliciting, as a corollary, a liberated feeling of internal well being that arises from a concurrent activation of the anterior cingulate. Brain scans show that the anterior cingulate is also activated by opiates, which are also known to exaggerate playfulness and causes dopamine to be released in the prefrontal cortex.

In the stable adult psyche, increased release of dopamine elicits a youthful exuberance and a lessening of skepticism that is fundamental to play. With increasing age all humans suffer a progressive decrease in the level of dopamine in their brains, a corollary of which is the classic age-related decrease in playfulness. It seems that the inclination to play falls with the decreasing neurochemical potential of the brain to render the mind silent while simultaneously activating the anterior cingulate. Throughout adult life, the increasing dominance of the mind, together with the decreasing availability of dopamine, repress our playful, inner child. Only in highly rewarding scenarios, is the mind silenced and the anterior cingulate able to manifest playfulness.

With the evolution of the cingulate, a new benign and sensitive master took control over the behavior of the lower, "mindless" mammals. To do this the cingulate had to have a variety of complex interconnections with other parts of the brain. Thus, alongside its role in representing the primary emotions, the cingulate has the capacity to register body language, produce vocalizations and bodily movements, respond to pain and, by influencing accessibility of information to the perceptual areas of the cortex, direct attention. In addition it participates in decision-making processes related to simple tasks, a function that enables it to provide an executive level of behavioral control in species of mammals that lack the cortex of the mind. Even in the human, where the cingulate expresses its needs through a highly developed mind, the internal organization and connections that enable it to exercise a modicum of executive control, are still evident.

Life and Death at the Crossroads
"Love is not always harsh and deadly sin,
If it be love of loveliness divine,
If it leaves the heart all soft and infantine,
For rays of God's own grace to enter in."
Michelangelo Buonarroti (1475-1564). Italian Renaissance Painter, Sculpture, Poet and Engineer.

The insula is by far the most enigmatic member of the triad of emotion. This is revealed by the symptoms accompanying damage to the insular cortex that range from a disruption of taste, visceral control and motivation, to seemingly bizarre symptoms wherein patients believe that they are not involved in the movement of their body parts. These complexities arise partially because historically the word insula (from the Latin meaning "island") was originally used simply to describe the appearance of a raised "island" of cortex that is only visible when one prizes apart the fissure that separates the temporal lobe from the rest of the brain. In actuality, there was probably never any reason to believe that the cortex forming the insula served only one function. Indeed, subsequent research has confirmed that the insula is subdivided into three regions that serve quite different, though tantalizingly interrelated, roles. These three regions are arranged one in front of the other along the insula. At its anterior end, the insula is devoted to the chemical senses, representing information about both taste and smell. The middle region contains an *organotopic representation* of sensory information from the viscera and exerts a descending control over the body's organs. Finally, the posterior end is activated by touch and pain.

Brain scans show that the insula is active during experiences of pleasant music, tasting, smelling, touching, pain, guessing, singing, rhythm, disgust, guilt, anxiety, morphine, trust, love, sadness, fear, amphetamine, cocaine, facial mimicry, sexual arousal, orgasm, rectal or esophageal stimulation and empathy - a cocktail of experiences perhaps reminiscent to some of an unusually wild night out! The insula is also intimately associated with arrhythmias of the heart. When our beloved appears and our heart misses a beat, it is probably because their appearance and body language activates the insula and, via its descending influences, disrupts of our normal physiological rhythms. For the same reason severe malfunction of the insular cortex due to stroke, epileptic seizures or even emotional stress can cause symptoms of cardiovascular malfunction. Indeed, so powerful is the insula's influence over the heart that electrically stimulating it through implanted electrodes can produce lethal cardiac arrhythmias. Conversely, severe malfunction of the heart is registered by the insula. Via its connections to the amygdala and the anterior cingulate, it is the insula that generates intrinsic feelings of fear and foreboding – feelings that are often misinterpreted as being the consequence of the patient's mental angst over his condition, rather than the direct result of aberrant sensations from the heart.

Within the triad of emotion, the insula acts as a sorting station for emotionally relevant information destined for either the amygdala or the anterior cingulate (*The Triad of Emotion*: Chapter 3: Section 4). This explains why it participates in a wide diversity of experiences and scenarios. In addition, the insula is also connected with much of the orbital cortex – an area that continuously registers the possibility of punishment or reward. It is through its connections with the lateral and medial orbital cortex that the insula has the potential to evoke within us the aura of precarious uncertainty that colors many of the states of awareness in which it participates.

Although the insula's role in cardiac control is of vital importance, the heart is not the only element of our viscera dependent on the insula. For example, electrical stimulation of different sites in the middle part of the insula can elicit salivation, gastric motility, nausea and respiratory arrest. This is possible only because each of our body's organs is allocated exclusive access to a small patch of insular cortex. The result is that there is an orderly representation of the sensory information arising from each organ across the middle part of the insular cortex. Experientially, this organotopic map explains why we can crudely localize sensations arising from certain organs of our viscera. For example, in response to kidney pain we place our hands on the area of our back overlying the kidneys, whereas stomach pain causes us to clutch our abdomen. However, the organotopic organization of the insula is not just to enable us to make some crude judgments about the source of any visceral perturbations. The allocation of a small patch of insular cortex to each organ also provides the structural layout necessary for the insula to exert an independent descending influence over each of the body's organs in accord with the sensory feedback from that organ. Thus, the insula is the highest point in the brain where incoming visceral information is linked to visceral control.

The part played by the insula in human psyche has great significance in the persistence of orality in adult life. Most of our mammalian relatives do not have our clever hands. In this they resemble the newborn child. They are obliged to seek out food and determine each other's sexual receptivity using their mouths and tongues. Only in humans and the higher non-human primates does the use of the mouth in the seeking of food decrease after infanthood. As the cortex of the insula is probably immature for at least the first 6 months of human life, it is unlikely that it can account for the earliest, virtually reflexive, oral phase of infant behavior. However, from early childhood the insula begins to play an important role in monitoring smell, taste and touching of the face, as well as, participating in the evocation of movements of the lips and tongue. In addition, the insula responds to the body language of other people while registering changes in activity of each of our internal organs. The insula is therefore a cortical area where the most primitive, emotionally relevant senses, the status of the viscera and the body language of others are registered and used to generate facial and oral movements critical to the interactions between infant and parent. In adult life the oral disposition of the insula presumably manifests as the acts of kissing and oral sex – activities also commonly seen in the great apes. In the same way as the shadow of our child lives on in the cortex of the cingulate gyrus, the insular cortex continues to voice the oral predisposition of our mammalian ancestors, long after the end of infanthood.

Emotions and the Development of Language

"The lowest savages with the least copious vocabularies [have] the capacity of uttering a variety of distinct articulate sounds and of applying them to an almost infinite amount of modulation and inflection [which] is not in any way inferior to that of the higher [European] races." Alfred Russel Wallace (1823-1913). British Biologist, Explorer, Geographer and Co-founder of the Theory of Evolution by Natural Selection.

Although there are almost 5,500 languages in existence, it is now widely accepted that all are based on a *universal grammar* that appears to be an inherent characteristic of the brains of all humans. All languages can thus be regarded as having an instinctual grammatical core. In the production of speech and synthesis of their first comprehensible sentences, young children do not learn the grammatical rules taught later by their parents or teachers. Instead they express themselves through an inherited grammatical structure that is relatively invariant across cultural boundaries. It is said, therefore, that children learn language in much the same way as they learn how to interact socially - by the exercise of *inductive* rather than *deductive* learning. In this process even the very earliest, monosyllabic vocalizations of the infant are vital to establishing an environment where audiovocal communication between parent and child is in place while the cortex's speech centers are maturing.

The maturation of the emotional centers takes place during the first nine months of life. Only after this period do the auditory centers link up with the articulatory centers

(Broca's and Wernicke's areas) that are ultimately responsible for the interpretation and creation of words. However, even from the moment of birth the infant is capable of vocalizations. These early utterances, including crying, are thought to be produced, almost reflexively, through an archaic brainstem center, the aforementioned periaquaductal gray, that has the power to produce very basic sounds through the oral-laryngeal musculature. Slightly later in development, authority is surrendered to a higher, but still subcortical center, the hypothalamus, which is responsive to states of hunger, thirst and satiation. Later still the amygdala begins to mature and assert its control over the hypothalamus. During this period the infant begins what has been called *early babbling*.

Early babbling is thought to be a vestige of our reptilian ancestors wherein all behavior, including vocalization, was driven by the amygdala. Between 4 and 6 months of age this early babbling (cooing) is replaced by *repetitive* or *late babbling*. The onset of repetitive babbling is thought to be related to the ongoing maturation of the insula and the executor of emotion, the anterior cingulate. Repetitive babbling is formed from strings of syllables that sound increasingly like the melodic and rhythmic elements of true speech called *prosody*. The intonational and melodic quality of repetitive babbling reflects the insula's involvement in rhythm and singing in adults, both phenomena being attributable to the rhythmical activities of body's organs that doubtless find expression in the insula (Section 4: Chapter 3: The Creation of Emotion). In summary, the prosody of speech emerges from the anterior cingulate and the insula as an instinctual element of vocalization long before the articulation of the first words between 9 and 14 months of age.

The exaggerated prosody of repetitive babbling characterizes the vocal interactions between mother and infant that are known as *motherese*. Motherese is so important to speech development that even in 2 month old children, exposure to emotionally flat speech, such as accompanies maternal depression, can retard the development of language. The instinctual origin of babbling is further indicated by both its invariance across different cultures and the observation that even congenitally deaf mothers and their deaf infants use the same prosodic patterns. Furthermore, the level of prosody remains indicative of both the level of emotional awareness and emotional intelligence of the speaker - factors related to the physical size of both the anterior cingulate gyrus and the insula.

It is only a desire for empathy that motivates us to tell others how we are feeling. In the process of doing this we depend not so much upon the definitive meaning of words but upon the prosody of our speech. It is often said that it is not what we say but how we say it. It is the anterior cingulate and the insula that determine "how" we say things. As such it is these areas of cortex that are responsible for those unwanted, and seemingly spontaneous, verbal expressions of our true feelings.

The Ravages of Emotional Memory
"Nothing fixes a thing so intensely in the memory as the wish to forget it." Michel de Montaigne (1533-1592). French Essayist.

In its evolution the anterior cingulate brought to animal life the urge to bond. It is the satiation of this most basic mammalian urge that humans intellectually define as love. Love is universally accepted to be a direct experience of the soul. It follows that the anterior cingulate must be responsible for our sense of our soul. Thus, when two people share love, we see them as soulmates, inured from all darkness and stress simply by their presence in each other's lives. When brain imaging is used to monitor the activity in their cortex, we find activation of both the insula and the anterior cingulate and a concurrent repression of the amygdala.

It is a characteristic of the cortex that not only do its modules elaborate the experience of incoming information but each module also holds a memory of past inputs (*The Micro-organization of Consciousness*: Chapter 2: Section 2). Thus, both the experience of love and the memory of love are elaborated and stored, respectively, in the cortical modules of the anterior cingulate gyrus. The unavoidable danger in this arrangement is that while the anterior cingulate enables us to know love, it is also responsible for the feelings of desperate sadness that accompany memories of lost love. When a loved one departs forever, when the presence of a partner, child or parent is no more, we are literally traumatized by the plaintive call of memories that seem to arise from within the center of our being.

Whereas joy is a direct experience of paradise, sadness is the experience of memories conjured by our anterior cingulate's reminders of paradise lost. While the anterior cingulate enables us to know love, it also archives the scars of love as unrequited emotional memories of this all-pervading oceanic experience. Thus, when a person is haunted by emotional memories of a time when they were bonded *in toto* to another being, we can define a psychologically paralyzing condition that we might call *postlove stress disorder* (PLSD). Fortunately, most normal people do eventually recover from PLSD although recovery, not infrequently, takes several years.

The closing decades of the 19th century marked the beginning of our comprehension of learning within the realm of emotion. The most significant contribution was that of the Russian physiologist and Nobel Laureate (1904) Ivan Petrovich Pavlov (1849-1936). Pavlov showed that dogs could associate a normally meaningless or neutral stimulus, such as ringing of a bell, with the expectation of a food reward (measured by salivation), providing that the ring always preceded the delivery of food. Unfortunately, Pavlov's demonstration that the association of a reward (food) with a previously neutral stimulus (the bell) could elicit a visceral reaction (salivation) soon inspired a swath of studies of the power of punishment (negative reinforcement) in shaping behavior.

In animals and people negative reinforcement can be used to extinguish a behavior and even to induce a prolonged avoidance of the location at which the punishment was administered. When a neutral stimulus such as a bell, always precedes punishment, indicators of anxiety such as sweating and increased heart rate can be used to measure the expectation of punishment. The learning that enables this expectation is known as *fear conditioning*. After Pavlov's work there ensued a grisly period, preserved in the literature of the time, where the western world adopted an *attitude of punishment* and with macabre enthusiasm explored the effectiveness of punishment in the process of child education and criminal reform. The foolish and delinquent ideology behind these efforts was, and is, that threat is sufficient to educate children and to constrain all human behavior within social norms.

The psychological damage resulting from this period must surely have contributed to the perpetration of human atrocities, and particularly child abuse, throughout several subsequent generations. Sadly this strategy, embodied in the awful cliché, "spare the rod and spoil the child," still stands as a viable alternative within the minds of most human beings, who somehow see in punishment and force of arms an effective strategy for the attainment of peace, prosperity and understanding. Today many governments still employ fear conditioning to bring into line those who might otherwise disagree with existing laws or aggressive "defense policies" that are specifically tailored for making profit motivated war on the men, women and children of other countries. When we look within to find what enables these strategies of social and ethnic vandalism, we find the amygdala.

On the positive side, our amygdala is important because it generates the fears and anxiety that propel us away from conflict. Even threatening words can activate the human amygdala, which then has opportunity to elicit escape and thereby avoid potentially injurious hostilities. In prehistoric times when there were so few of us that our greatest challenge was surviving nature, the amygdala served our species well. Unfortunately, however, the amygdala also has the capacity to promote our trespasses against others - a capacity that comes to the fore in situations where overpopulation makes resources a critical factor in survival. In such threatening circumstances the mind soon elaborates paranoid thoughts that enhance fear that may easily turn to anger, aggression and genocide.

In animals, such interactions become stored as emotional memories that serve to directly moderate the expression of their basic urges. In humans, however, things are very different. Not only can the human mind increase the longevity of conflict by holding onto plans for revenge for generations but it can also access detailed records of past conflicts and easily revive perceived injustices. When by force and cruelty we attempt to subjugate others to our will or to seek revenge for past trespasses against us, we are essentially operating at the level of the reptilian amygdala.

It could truthfully be said that modern humans have not learned to live comfortably with their reptilian heritage. For instance, malfunction of the human amygdala underlies a host of anxiety disorders that make up 50% of all health problems in the USA. Anxiety disorders include all phobias, panic attacks, *obsessive-compulsive disorder* (OCD) and *post-traumatic stress disorder* (PTSD). It seems that behind our thoughts the amygdala is continuously conducting its covert operations. When, without obvious cause, we are filled with fear, we may assume that some subliminal trigger has stirred our amygdala. This can happen because the amygdala has the capacity to become active when we encounter a stimulus or circumstance that, in the past, has caused us trauma. Consider, for example, how our nervous system replays the events of a motor accident. Essentially two almost separate processes are involved.

The first enables us to recall the details of the accident, our destination, the names of our passengers, and whether or not it was raining. To everyone else these are stimuli that simply exist at the scene of our accident. For us, however, there is a second process that penetrates deeply into our visceral being. Thus, for no logical reason our breathing increases uncontrollably, our heart pounds and our skin sweats as we find ourselves swept into the panic and fear of uncontrollable catastrophe. Within us, the amygdala has risen to rekindle the experience of abject terror that so consumed us during the carnage of that day.

When the memory of a traumatic event takes up residence within the amygdala, the individual is said to be suffering from PTSD. On the surface a PTSD sufferer may seem like any normal well-adjusted person. It is a simple necessity of life that highly traumatic memories be so repressed that they cannot be accessed and tempered by mental effort. Burdened with indelible emotional memories the PTSD sufferer soon learns to avoid situations that trigger their trauma. Only when by chance they encounter the appropriate trigger do they display and experience the emotional distress precipitated by the actual event.

The human propensity to form emotional memories is a reflection of the importance of instinctual learning to the survival of our less mentally endowed animal ancestors. Indeed, PTSD is only a clinically defined extreme of this wholly natural process which every counselor knows subliminally underwrites the psychosocial nuances of each and every human interaction. While we hardly notice the subtle influences of instinctual or emotional learning, this process may evoke spontaneous flashbacks of seriously traumatizing events. Other symptoms of PTSD include, hyperarousal, such as an exaggerated startle response, a chronic disruption of sleep patterns and a high frequency of nightmares. Until the covert emotional memories are *extinguished*, the life of the traumatized individual continues to be severely disrupted by the emergence of fear and anger at inappropriate moments. In the context of PTSD it is almost impossible to imagine the global magnitude of permanent psychological damage created by the political tyranny of the 20th century that saw the annihilation of some 262,000,000 humans and the physical and mental maiming of many times that number. Such deep psychological damage is inevitably passed on to new generations through maladaptive emotional behavior of both parents and the host society, ensuring that its effects will manifest for several generations. Time and again the altruistic ideals of well meaning people are shattered by the subliminal energies of horrific, emotional memories that guide the moment by moment thoughts and actions of millions upon millions of deeply traumatized individuals.

Tragically, once traumatized, PTSD sufferers are more susceptible to other traumatic situations. With repeated exposures to trauma it becomes increasingly difficult to extinguish the replay of negative emotions. It seems the amygdala is primed by repeated exposure to threat and punishment. Once primed, its capacity for generating negative reactions is greatly enhanced. Such emotional memories may persist throughout the remainder of life with catastrophic effects. The female child repeatedly cornered and beaten by her father and other male members of the family may throughout her entire life react with fear or aggression towards authoritative males. The abusive father is literally "felt" in any dominant male figure, triggering an involuntary reaction that transcends all cognitive comprehension of good intentions, eventually destroying the rapport, trust and stability essential to a normal loving relationship. As always in psychiatric illnesses, the sufferer may offer all manner of cleverly devised explanations to account for their destructive outbursts, but always at the heart of the matter are the errant responses of a hyperactive amygdala.

It is impossible to be in love and fear at exactly the same moment. This is because as the center of conflict and the center of love, the amygdala and the anterior cingulate gyrus reciprocally inhibit one another. When one center is highly active the other is repressed and *vice versa*. This reciprocity between the bad and good emotions becomes conspicuous when brain scans are made of PTSD patients during exposure to imagery scripts specifically designed to activate their traumatic memories. Under these conditions, the amygdala becomes active while the anterior cingulate gyrus is depressed. In experiential terms, their fear and anxiety at such moments far outweigh any positive emotions. Conversely, if the anterior cingulate gyrus is highly active (as when we are blissfully happy) it is possible to show that the amygdala is repressed. In neuroscientific jargon it is said that the executor of emotion, the anterior cingulate gyrus, has the power to exert "top-down inhibition" of the amygdala.

Rewarding substances such as cocaine, amphetamine and morphine alleviate PTSD because they activate the anterior cingulate and inhibit the amygdala. One possible strategy for treating PTSD is therefore to seek ways to enhance activation of the anterior cingulate and so extinguish activity in the amygdala. An example of the successful application of this approach is interwoven with what is surely one of the most tragic yet inspiring stories in human history. In the 1970s, more than a million Cambodians were viciously slaughtered under the ridiculously draconian policies of the revolutionary, psychopathic dictator Pol Pot. Many who survived were brutally tortured both psychologically and physically. Women were forced to watch their pubescent daughters being gang raped and murdered. By ingenious means, many were also made to participate in the death of their own babies. Those that survived were so deeply traumatized, that they were hardly able to move, talk or find the motivation to care for any surviving children. One amongst them, Phaly Nuon, herself a victim of these atrocities, found the strength to set up an orphanage and a center for traumatized women in Phnom Penh. Her therapy was simply to teach her traumatized companions to give each other manicures and pedicures, to tend their own bodies and the bodies of others who had also suffered so much. Slowly her charges began to converse, to begin to see other humans as something more than just another tormentor, to open slowly to trust and eventually make friends. Phaly Nuon achieved this by teaching them to groom, evoking the positive emotions thereby nurturing their shattered psyches by helping them find the tiniest fragments of positive affect. We now know that chimpanzees spent about 20% of their time grooming, an activity that enhances activation of the anterior cingulate and evokes a concurrent repression of amygdala activity. It would, however, be many years before a western world that openly permitted this second holocaust, would understand what this special person intuitively grasped.

If we cannot put our findings into effect, our advanced comprehension of the workings of human psyche means less than nothing. If, as many in power publicly profess, we wish to see a happy and joyful world, we must turn our minds to the service of our positive emotions, individually, collectively and globally. The way of the Buddha is the middle road because thereon the amygdala and the anterior cingulate are never far from balance. It is the way of touching, of caring and compassion and most of all the way of non-violence in both ideology and action. In terms of the human psyche it is a manifestation of the anterior cingulate gyrus wherein are to be found the origins of our mammalian ways.

Chapter 6 - Mind versus Emotion in the Control of Behavior

The Freedom of Will

"What is troubling us is the tendency to believe that the mind is like a little man within." Ludwig Wittgenstein (1889-1951). Austrian/British Philosopher.

Implicit in the term "free will" is the view that humans have the capacity to dispassionately decide what action they will take. Whereas many animals respond in a predictable fashion to particular circumstances, most humans believe that their cognitive abilities avail them of a level of deliberation that transcends their biological drives. This belief is not, however, borne out by either human behavior or by studies of the way the human cortex instigates action. The carefully thought out reasons we give to account for our actions, significant or trivial, are rarely true. We act because we are moved to act, and we rationalize all cognitive contradictions by inventing reasons that sound logical - a process known in psychology as *attribution*.

Our emotions are the essence of our motivation. This fact is intuitively appreciated by all. The manipulation of others through their emotions is a common and normal part of virtually every theater of human interaction. As we have seen, the subtle yet powerful technique of subliminal suggestion specifically targets our emotional centers. The operational principle underlying all political propaganda is not the presentation of facts and logical argument but the emotional arousal of the populace. The arguments of propaganda seek acquiescence from the mind, but whether they are effective in influencing people's behavior depends almost entirely upon whether they arouse their emotions. We are relatively indifferent to the draconian laws and transparent propaganda of a foreign government, even when they transgress the basic rights of other humans. Without any personal involvement, we are inured from the impulses that might otherwise drive us to take action. Similarly, while apparent injustices and the associated rhetoric within our own country can inflame our passions, the foreigner sees little more than trivial, factual detail. It would seem that as our mind is relatively incapable of removing itself from the influence of our emotions that, freedom of will is a common wish but never a reality, of the human condition.

The Origins of Incentive

"Man….enjoys difficulties, seeks trouble, and is challenged by the apparently impossible." Lancelot L. Whyte (1896-1972). Scottish Financier, Industrial Engineer, Intellectual and Author.

All indications are that the mind of the human child is immature at birth and remains so for much of the first year of life. Therefore the simple behavior patterns of the newborn infant - like those of all neonatal mammals - must be driven by neural centers that are configured by genes, entirely for the purpose of satiating the child's immediate biological needs. The emergent behaviors, such as crying and suckling, are composed of stereotyped sequences of movements, recognizable in every child - movements which are orchestrated by subcortical centers within the brainstem (*The Recognition and Subtraction of Consciousness*: Chapter 4: Section 2). In contrast, the details of adult human behavior are concocted in the realm of thought. Slowly between infancy and adulthood the origins of action switch from an entirely instinctual source to a source that contains both cognitive and instinctual elements.

To avoid issues of intention or volition, developmental psychologists use the word *state* to characterize the ever-changing, inner world of the child. At birth the human infant is totally dependent upon its caregivers and its state is entirely determined by perturbations of its viscera. During the first year of life, the interactions between the child's inner world, or state, and its outer world, lead to the establishment of a *neural representation of context*. Over this same period the triad of emotion, Broca's speech area and finally the social mind begin to mature and become operational entities that interact with other parts of the cortex. The context established is consequently specifically tailored to the psychosocial domain of life.

By the end of the first year the "state" of the child is no longer just an urge for satiation. Satiation remains the major objective but now an entirely new cognitive influence emerges enabling the child to recognize, conceptualize and refine the nuances of context in order to more rigorously exploit its circumstances. Whereas attachment in the newborn manifests as an almost reflexive response to touch, smell and taste, by 12 months these stimuli together with vision and audition trigger the more complex anticipatory behavior of the young child. Now as the carer enters the room the sound of the door opening is sufficient to make the child turn its head, focus its gaze, hold up its arms and vocalize an apparent greeting. This ability to respond to the sight and sounds of the caregiver betrays the existence of a rudimentary working model of the child's psychosocial environment wherein its caregivers are the most significant external components.

In the preoperational child, prior to maturation of the material, temporal and abstract mind, the social mind has executive control over behavior. This influence is retained in adulthood in as much as brain scans show the social mind to be important in the *implementation of action*. However, behind the social mind, the source of the motivation to act remains within the cortex's emotional executor, the anterior cingulate gyrus. In this role the anterior cingulate draws upon the state of each member of the triad of emotion in representing the five primary emotions, joy, sadness, disgust, fear and anger. When part of the cingulate gyrus is removed (cingulotomy) as a treatment for chronic depression, anxiety or obsessive compulsive disorder, patients are typically unduly tired in the afternoon, less meticulous in their habits and slower in both their thoughts and actions. More extensive damage to the cingulate produces the motivational paralysis we call akinetic mutism (*Life without Emotion*: Chapter 3: Section 4). Therefore, in both child and adult the executor of our emotions, the anterior cingulate gyrus, is the origin of all motivation and action, retaining thus, the same pivotal role it plays in the lower mammals.

The Endless Cycle of Thought and Emotion
"Animals are instructed by their organs. So remarked the ancients. But likewise, I should add, are human beings, who, however, have the advantage of being able, in return, to instruct their organs." Johann Wolfgang von Goethe (1749-1832). German Poet, Novelist, Playwright, and Natural Philosopher.

Goethe was right. From the lower mammals down to the fish, behavior is wholly given to the instinctual drive towards the satiation of the visceral body. The cortical tissue that enables thought simply does not exist in these beasts. No mind stands in opposition to the id. Only with the evolution of the higher mammals was nature obliged to surrender some of its authority to the processes of thought. However, for reasons of survival, this transference of power could never be complete, for while the mind must be able, temporarily, to repress the demands of the instincts, it must ultimately attend to the urgencies of organic life.

The great danger of the human psyche is that just as our emotions hijack our thoughts, so too can our mind influence those parts of our cortex that elaborate our emotions. The mere promise of eternal love or the threat of deep loss can instantly cause our heart to miss a beat. Through the emotional centers, the human mind can both evoke and subsequently respond to, perturbations of our viscera that are experientially identical to those which seem to arise spontaneously within our body. Thus, the emotional centers and the mind can reciprocally excite each other, in what can become an ever-escalating cycle of emotion and thought - a cycle which in extreme cases can send us cascading towards the paralysis of cardiovascular shock or soaring to the pinnacle of ecstasy. Caught in this cycle of thought and emotion we are apt to inadvertently become indifferent to the laws of nature. It is the power of mind over emotion that distinguishes the human from all animals and explains the turbulence and self-destructiveness that characterizes all of human history.

Only when we need to strive for food, warmth and sex do we return to our biological self. Here is the reason why allowing ourselves to be physically challenged by nature is such a universally centering experience. With all their basic needs met, modern humans normally vacillate between thought and emotion, trying desperately to decipher from these momentary elements of the psyche what their real needs are, as distinct from their imagined ones. Many of our idiosyncratic ways can be understood only when we realize that it is from this precarious position that we are obliged to seek the most advantageous path. Metaphorically, the human mind is, in this context, very much the Devil's playground.

Disgust and the Windows of the Id
"It is only by softening and disguising dead flesh by culinary preparation that it is rendered susceptible of mastication or digestion; and thus the sight of its bloody juices and raw horror does not excite intolerable loathing and disgust." Percy Bysshe Shelley (1792-1822). English Poet.

Disgust is an exclusively mammalian emotion. Reptiles are not given to expressions of joy or disgust as those areas of cortex that enable us to experience these emotions do not exist in the reptilian brain. The huge Komodo dragon (*Varanus komodoensis*) is both a scavenenger and a predator. A voracious hunter, a large Komodo dragon (eg. 2.7 meters, 45kg) will bring down a 150kg stag by breaking a limb before killing it by consuming its intestines, heart and lungs. As a carrion eater the dragon's mouth is well stocked with infectious bacteria. Even if its prey escapes, it usually dies shortly after from systemic infections. Able to smell rotting flesh from up to 8 km away, the dragon need only follow the fetid smell of death to be rewarded by its putrid meal. Like all reptiles, the highest determinant of the Komodo dragon's behavior is the amygdala, a structure that sustains reptilian life by being totally focused on the survival of the individual, a structure that is therefore about more basic matters than the communication of disgust.

Olfaction, taste and touch are the windows through which the first vertebrates sought the sustenance of life. In all terrestrial mammals those sensory fibers which respond to bad food activate areas of the brain that evoke aversion, while those that respond to good food are similarly directed to the areas that evoke exploration and consumption. The genetically specified sensitivities of both smell and taste to various chemicals ensure the rejection of certain potential foods and the acceptance of others. The newborn animal or human will therefore consume or reject offerings in accord with this inherited specification of good and bad - a phenomenon conspicuous in both the olfactory preferences and body odor of different human populations. Clearly, any new mutation that renders an animal or human incapable of detecting the warning smells of disease or danger would guarantee rapid extinction.

Experientially, disgust manifests itself as a turning of the stomach and, in extreme cases, vomiting. In mammals, the communication of disgust has always been important for preventing the eating of food tainted by poison or decay. Like other animals we automatically communicate the experience of disgust by making a universally identifiable facial expression. In disgust, the nose wrinkles, the mouth gapes and the tongue extrudes in response to oral irritation, the upper lip curling back in an expression of revulsion. So universal is this expression that the facial movements of a disgusted human are not so different from those of a disgusted rat. Indeed, some or all of these inherent movements are seen in a wide variety of terrestrial mammals. Only with the evolution of the mind did the "knowing" of disgust become possible. For all the lower, "mindless" mammals, disgust is simply a raw emotion that reflects an innate drive towards aversive behavior.

The Mental and Sensory Origins of Disgust
The vine bears three kinds of grapes: the first of pleasure, the second of intoxication, the third of disgust." Diogenes (412-323 BC). Greek Philosopher.

To understand the origins of disgust we need to appreciate what psychobiologists call *primary* and *secondary reinforcers.* The idea is very simple. The primary reinforcers, taste, smell, touch and pain are those sensory channels that are hardwired to the parts of the cortex that reinforce or extinguish appetitive behavior. Genes determine both their sensitivity and their connections to the still immature brain. It is highly significant that the primary reinforcers have a strong influence over our emotions whereas the distance senses, vision and hearing, constitute the secondary reinforcers.

With respect to olfaction and taste, sensory receptors that respond to chemicals emitted by palatable food will connect to brain areas that facilitate feeding while those that respond to toxins will connect to different brain areas that trigger aversive behavior. In contrast, the access of the distance senses (vision and hearing) to these two brain areas is determined by associative learning. Through associative learning visual images of acceptable food items are given access to brain areas that the facilitate feeding while images of potentially toxic food are given access to brain areas that elicit aversive responses. Auditory signals, though less relevant to disgust, may be similarly associated.

The experience of disgust is associated with activation of the insula in addition to the anterior cingulate. The anterior cingulate represents disgust as one of the five primary emotions while the insula is responsible for representing the visceral perturbations associated with all emotional experience (Section 4: Chapter 5: The Second Emotions - Love, Sadness and Disgust). The cortex at the anterior end of the insula receives information about taste and smell while touch and pain activate the posterior region. The retching that accompanies extreme revulsion arises because just behind the anterior part of the insula is the organotopically organized area that has powerful connections to lower, autonomic centers that, in turn, activate the viscera. In humans, electrical stimulation of this part of the insula evokes abdominal pain, belching, contractions of the stomach, nausea and vomiting - responses that often accompany a particularly disgusting experience.

Facial expressions enable us to express and communicate our emotions but more importantly they enable us to generate empathy by literally eliciting the same emotions in others. In this process only fear is of more significance than disgust. Both fear and disgust give *warning of potential threat*. When an infant is presented with a novel object its response will be largely determined by the facial expression of the child's primary caregiver - a process known as *social referencing* that intensifies as the social mind begins to mature towards the end of the first year of life. If the caregiver responds with a happy expression the infant will approach the object but if the object elicits an expression of disgust or fear it will ignore the object.

As we have seen already, empathizing with the emotion in another's face depends upon our ability to recreate it within ourselves. Disgust is no different. In Huntington's disease the anterior part of the insula that responds to disgusting smells and tastes is malfunctional. Thus, patients with Huntingtons are not only unable to feel disgust but are also unable to detect disgust in facial expressions, non-verbal sounds or the intonations of speech. Consequently, they are isolated from disgust both perceptually and socially.

Many native and hunter-gatherer people habitually smell their food before consumption. This is not true of westerners. The descendents of the Europeans are less adept in the world of olfaction. It seems that the highly cognitive disposition of their psyche has ensured the progressive development of complex strategies to replace the need for a high sensitivity to olfactory indicators of toxicity. With all their basic needs met, the mind of the typical westerner is arguably the primary source of many emotional perturbations. In the pampered western world the mere suggestion of poor hygiene, inappropriate sexual contact or the apparitions of death, mutilation or decay are usually sufficient to elicit facial and bodily expressions of disgust. Indeed, thanks mostly to the advertising industry, some people are so sensitized to the mental imagery of disgust that the slightest suggestion of the odious is enough to induce nausea followed by the appropriate financial outlay to avoid repetition of the experience. At the other extreme the media shield us from the disgusting images of war, ensuring that this emotion does not dissuade us from being party to acts of mass aggression.

The dominance of the mind over the emotions clearly began before the evolution of the hominids, for in the practice of social deception even the apes must repress certain emotions and feign others. In other animals, however, the expression of emotion is a direct, true and transparent indication of their underlying urges. Only humans and, in particular those of European descent, are truly in danger of losing the ability to truthfully communicate their biological needs. In this age the people of European origin are closer than any others to losing contact with their emotions and becoming exclusively, *people of the mind.*

Guilt and the Iconic Representation of Emotion
"Guilt is the source of sorrow, 'tis the fiend, the avenging fiend, that follows us behind, with whips and stings." Nicholas Rowe (1674-1718). English Author and Poet Laureate.

In psychology guilt has been traditionally defined as *self-disgust*. Guilt itself is not a pure emotion but involves our mental concept of ourselves in a social context - part of our self-image known as the social ego (*The Foundation and Composition of the Ego*: Chapter 1: Section 8). To test whether there is a real physiological link between the emotion of disgust and the phenomenon of guilt, subjects were asked to think of something they had done that made them feel deeply guilty while images were made of their brain's activity. These experiments showed that during their experiences of guilt, their mind was active while their insula responded as it did during the experience of disgust. Thus, it is true that the experience of guilt involves thoughts of remorse coupled with feelings of disgust.

When we wield the emotion of disgust against ourselves, we conjure the icon of guilt that thenceforth demands a place within our vocabularies. Guilt assists us in conditioning our children to observe the social loyalties that cement together our families, communities and even our society. Unfortunately, as an icon of the mind, guilt may be associated with whatever issue or circumstance our parents, teachers, priests and politicians choose. The triggers for guilt are entirely a matter of our conditioning. For example, fundamentalist Moslems (mostly male) do not feel guilt about flogging rape victims or excising the clitoris from young girls (a gruesomely painful procedure) while many fundamentalist Christians do not reproach themselves for drinking alcohol and perverting ordinary people's natural inclination towards sex. Guilt may thus be exploited to elicit a wide range of behaviors that do not necessarily benefit us as individuals. It is a matter of historical fact that all forms of subversion, from the marketing of products to the marketing of war and religion, reflect the exploitation of the human propensity for guilt. The mind's influence over the insula and the anterior cingulate enables us to cognitively evoke the feelings and bodily responses of disgust in essentially the same way that we can evoke anger, fear, love and sadness via our mind's influence over our cortex's emotional centers. The link between guilt and disgust is another example of the powerful interaction between mind and emotion that so complicate human life.

Section 4: Recommended Reading

Achterberg, J. *Imagery in Healing: Shamanism and Modern Medicine.* Shambhala Press, Boston, London, 1985.

Appleton, J. P. (Editor). *The Amygdala: A Functional Analysis.* 2nd Edition, Oxford University Press, USA, 2000.

Picard, R. W. *Affective Computing.* 1st Edition, The MIT Press, 2000.

Carter, R. *Mapping the Mind.* Orion Publishing Group, London, 1998.

Darwin, C. *The Expressions of the Emotions in Man and Animals.* Chicago University Press, Chicago, 1965 (first published 1872).

Davidson, R. J. (Editor). *Anxiety, Depression, and Emotion.* Oxford University Press, USA, 2000.

Demause, L. *The Emotional Life of Nations.* Other Press Publishers, New York, 2002.

Damasio, A. R. *The Feeling of What Happens: Body and Emotion in the Making of Consciousness.* Harcourt Inc., New York, 1999.

Damasio, A. R. *Descartes' Error: Emotion, Reason and the Human Brain.* Harper Collins, New York, 2000.

Damasio, A. R. *Looking for Spinoza: Joy, Sorrow and the Feeling Brain.* Harcourt, New York, San Diego, 2003.

Damasio, A. R. and van Hoesen G. W. "Emotional disturbances associated with focal lesions of the limbic frontal lobe." In: K.M. Heilman and P. Satz (Editors), *Neuropsychology of Human Emotion.* Guilford Press, New York, 1983, pp. 85-110.

Ekman, P. and Davidson, R. J. *The Nature of Emotion: Fundamental Questions.* Oxford University Press, Oxford, New York, Toronto, 1994.

James, P. and Thorpe, N. *Ancient Mysteries.* Ballantyne Books, New York, 2001.

Kohl, J. V. and Francoeur, R. T. *The Scent of Eros - Mysteries of Odor in Human Sexuality.* The Continuum Publishers and Co., London, New York, 1995.

LeDoux, J. *The Emotional Brain: The Mysterious Underpinnings of Emotional Life.* Simon and Schulster, New York, 1998.

MacLean, P. D. *The Triune Brain in Evolution, Role in Paleocerebral Functions,* Plenum Press, New York, 1990.

O'Hanlon, R. *Into the Heart of Borneo.* Penguin, London, 1985.

Panksepp, J. *Affective Neuroscience: The Foundations of Human and Animal Emotions* Oxford University Press, New York, 1998.

Rolls, E. T. *The Brain and Emotion.* Oxford University Press, Oxford, 2000.

Schiraldi, G. R. *Post-Traumatic Stress Disorder Source Book.* Lowell House, Illinois, 2000.

Solomon, A. *The Noonday Demon: An Atlas of Depression.* Scribner, New York, 2001.

Section 5

Mood - the Nature of Darkness and Euphoria

"For those who have dwelt in depression's dark wood, and known its inexplicable agony, their return from the abyss is not unlike the ascent of the poet [Dante], trudging upward and upward out of Hell's black depths and at last emerging into what he saw as "the shining world". There, whoever has been restored to health has almost always been restored to the capacity for serenity and joy, and this may be indemnity enough for having endured the despair beyond despair."

"E quindi uscimmo a riveder stelle.
And so we came forth, and once again beheld the stars."

William Styron (1925-2006). American Author.

****

"Desire shot out of the woods like a wolf nipping at my heels. I wanted the skis to dance in the snow. I wanted my poems to be the best. I wanted sex, speed, pleasure."

Judith Maiman, Poet. From: *Illness 1, Poems of a Manic Depressive*. Lone Oak Press Ltd. Rochester, Minnesota, 1992.

Chapter 1 - The Nature, Mythology and Art of Mood

The Character of Mood

"In a strange way, I had fallen in love with my depression. I loved it because I thought it was all I had. I thought depression was the part of my character that made me worthwhile. I thought so little of myself, felt that I had such scant offering to give the world, that the one thing that justified my existence was my agony." Elizabeth Lee Wurtzel, American Journalist, Author and Human Rights Activist. From: *Prozac Nation*. Riverhead, Penguin, USA, 1994.

Like the dark winter skies or the scented breeze of summer, our moods provide the setting for the dance of life. Mood is responsible for the seasons of the psyche, seasons that nurture certain thoughts and extinguish others, seasons that not even the heart can ignore. As our emotions give color to the canvas of human consciousness and our thoughts the designs of its images, our moods determine the brightness and contrast that textures all experience.

While we need to account for at least five primary emotions and four domains of cognition, mood exists as a single primeval force. The direction and magnitude of that force depends upon our position along a continuum that stretches between two extremes, *darkness* and *euphoria*. In the fully blown experience of one extreme, the experience of the other is completely eclipsed. Only from the position of balance can we envisage both.

Originating in the oldest realms of consciousness, mood has a profound influence over our thoughts and emotions, thereby ensuring a degree of correspondence between our psychological and physiological state. By directly influencing our plans and strategies, mood determines how we anticipate the future. In its iconic specification of our innate sense of "good" and "bad", mood can be seen as conjuring that most fundamental of all human distinctions. Experientially, mood is Heaven and Hell, euphoria and darkness and all that lies between.

Mood adjusts our emotions and thoughts to match our hormonal profiles that throughout the process of vertebrate evolution have been tailored to the climatic rhythms of Earth. It is the time scale of mood that most clearly distinguishes it from the other denizens of the psyche. While our thoughts and emotions are transient experiences, our moods usually last for many hours or even days. Indeed, dysfunctional moods may persist for months or even years, pervading every aspect of our life. Nevertheless, emotion, thought and mood are highly interactive. Thus, in good mood we experience positive emotions and positive thoughts while in bad mood, both our emotions and thoughts are negative.

In each and every circumstance of life, mood determines whether we anticipate a punishing or rewarding outcome or to use a popular metaphor, whether we see the glass as either half empty or half full. In the exhilaration of euphoria, success in all things seems inevitable, while in the dark woods of depression, hope is not even a distant memory. In this way mood has great influence over our level of motivation - an element of behavior that, as we have seen is largely determined by the executor of emotion, the anterior cingulate gyrus. When, because of aberrant brain chemistry, mood drifts to extremes, there emerge patterns of behavior that are typically damaging to the individual and the society. In the paralysis of depression we are unable to be proactive, while in the flight of euphoria we are little deterred by the most conspicuous dangers.

The Psychological and Physiological Aspects of Mood

"Power invariably elects to go into the hands of the strong. That strength may be physical or of the heart…. Let it be remembered that physical force is transitory, even as the body is transitory. But the power of the spirit is permanent even as the spirit is everlasting." Mohandas Karamchand Gandhi (Mahatma Gandhi), (1869-1948). Political and Spiritual Leader in India's struggle for independence.

The experience of mood embodies two fundamental and recognizable aspects. The first of these involves our bodily feelings. Both the pervasive anxiety of depression and the zestful agitation of euphoria are felt throughout the body. These extremes of mood are conjured by the anterior cingulate gyrus or the amygdala. Experientially they are therefore prolonged episodes of those normally transient feelings that constitute our emotions. Mood achieves this by commandeering our emotional centers, which themselves have intimate connectional relationships with parts of the brain that register and regulate our physiological state (Figure 5.1). This aspect of mood we will refer to as the *physiological component*.

The second aspect of mood involves our sense of positivity or negativity. This sense determines whether we react to the challenges before us in an optimistic or a pessimistic manner. Clearly some area of the cortex must be responsible for (a) predicting whether a given course of action will lead to reward or punishment and (b) passing this prediction along to the mind where it can influence our thoughts and so affect our behavioral strategy. The area of cortex involved in making these predictions is the *orbital cortex*, so called because it lies on the lower surface of the prefrontal lobes directly above the orbit of the eyes (*The Triad of Emotion*: Chapter 3: Section 4). Because this aspect of mood involves our thoughts, we may refer to it as the *psychological component*. Ultimately, mood is an element of consciousness wherein our memories of the outcomes of past strategies of action are merged with our prevailing physiological status in the synthesis of a recognizable experience from whence we automatically assess the likelihood of success or failure.

The Experience of Mood

"We often saw how even the smallest things could make his spirit soar upwards to God, who even in the smallest things is the Greatest. At the sight of a little plant, a leaf, a flower or a fruit, an insignificant worm or a tiny animal Ignatius could soar above the heavens and reach through into things which lie beyond the senses." Hugo Rahner (1900-1968). German Jesuit and Theologian.

When we ask a friend "How are you today?" we are not asking what she is thinking about. Nor are we inquiring into what emotions she has experienced since getting out of bed. We are inquiring into the prevailing climate of her inner state. We are seeking a direct insight into our companion's mood. The more extreme her mood, the clearer will be the answer we receive. As with all things, the more conspicuous something is within consciousness, the more readily it can be identified, labeled and articulated by the mind. That our friend has no difficulty in understanding our question is evidence enough that mood is a common and easily recognizable part of human experience.

In the space of one minute we may have many thoughts and feelings. Like the familiar strangers we pass in our daily routines, they no sooner have entered our consciousness than they are gone. A flash of bioelectric activity lights up those cortical areas responsible for our thoughts and emotions then disappears purging the attendant experiences from our awareness. Mood, however, is entirely different. Moods are the lodgers of the human psyche and at any time there is only room for one to stay. And stay they do, although how long they stay, varies enormously between individuals and prevailing circumstances.

In normalcy, the extremes of mood are rarely in residence for more than a few weeks, while in severely pathological conditions, they may dominate the psyche for a lifetime. Most moods are agreeable and have minor affects upon our emotions and thoughts. Such moods are like loyal and reliable friends. We refer to quiescent mood as *euthymia*, or *true mood*. A euthymic person is one who is blessed by mood patterns that are sufficiently stable that they do no more than serve the biological rhythms of a healthy life. When euthymia departs, a new lodger immediately takes possession of the psyche. When this lodger is euphoria we anticipate the imminence of our arrival in Heaven. When it is darkness we find ourselves cowering before the gates of Hell. Recognized and symbolized within every religion, no theme is more pervasive in human life than that which emanates from the extremes of mood.

The pathological extremes of mood such as *major depressive disorder* or *prolonged euphoria* (*mania*), represent malfunction of the brain that can only be countered by drugs, or in some extreme cases, neurosurgery. In normal people, however, the manipulation of mood has great relevance to the achievement of happiness and to this end both the East and the West have developed many protocols for improving mood. Ironically, however, these protocols are the antithesis of one another. Thus, in the East it is generally said that our thoughts are largely responsible for our moods, while in the West the prevalent attitude is that our moods are largely a consequence of our circumstances. Both views are true, making it extremely difficult to identify any single causative factor underlying mood. This does not, however, stop our mind from trying, and even mild fluctuations of mood are typically characterized by a high degree of *attribution*, wherein the person blames their depression or euphoria on people and situations that would normally never evoke these states.

Mood and the Origin of the Psyche

"Everything you'll ever need to know is within you; the secrets of the universe are imprinted on the cells of you body." Dan Millman (born: 1946). American Author, Philosopher and Gymnast.

Mood reflects the biological rhythms of life; rhythms that follow the cycles of night and day, the rise and fall of the tides, the waning of the moon and changing seasons - rhythms to which all life is naturally attuned. To appreciate the biological pressures that have led to mood we need to go back more that 1,500 million years to when the first multicellular animals began to appear. Initially, there were only aggregates of free-living, single-celled organisms that benefited from close association with each other. Operating over hundreds of millions of years it was inevitable that the forces of natural selection would result in the component cells becoming increasingly specialized for the more efficient performance of particular tasks. For example, some cells would become specialized for locomotion some would serve sensation and others the taking up and passing on of nutrients. In such a system, communication between the individual cells is an absolute necessity.

At first, intercellular communication was most easily achieved by the production and secretion of special molecules. When released from a cell these special chemical messengers could diffuse throughout the "body" carrying important pieces of information to all receptive cells. Such molecules were the precursors of the hormones that regulate the biological rhythms of all living, multicellular animals. Even though the evolution of the nervous system enabled more rapid communication between different parts of the body, hormones would remain important to the slower regulatory processes of life. With the evolution of the central nervous system, the importance of hormones to physiological condition made it essential that their levels be faithfully represented at the highest echelons of the brain. Only thus could the nervous control of behavior be in harmony with the body's physiological status. For these reasons the areas of cortex supporting mood constitute the first elements of the psyche to evolve.

Mood and the Definition of Good and Bad
"When the Koran or the *hadith* speak of Paradise, Hell or the throne of God, they are not referring to a reality that was in a separate location but to an inner world, hidden beneath the veils of sensible phenomena." Karen Armstrong, British Author and Comparative Theologian. From: *A History of God – The 4000-year Quest of Judaism, Christianity and Islam*. Alfred A. Knopf, New York, 1994.

All humans innately refer to things that are rewarding as good and things that are punishing as bad. But what is it that first tells us what is to be avoided and what is to be approached? Could it be that good and bad have an instinctual origin? Much research has shown that the functional subdivisions of the developing brain are set up by the ingrowths of sensory nerves into the still immature central nervous system. In the newborn human, olfaction, taste, touch and pain are amongst the first sensory inputs to establish connections with the central nervous system. These senses inform the growing brain as to whether a potential food source should be touched and eaten or avoided. If it smells, tastes and feels good it may be eaten but if it smells and tastes bad or produces pain then it must be avoided. Put simply some sensory nerve fibers are genetically specified to respond to "positive" stimuli and evoke appetitive action while others will respond to "negative" stimuli and evoke withdrawal. Thus, the part of the cerebral cortex contacted by the former naturally becomes a representation of "good," while the place contacted by the latter becomes a representation of "bad" (Figure 5.2).

As we have seen, the emotionally relevant senses of taste, olfaction, touch and pain are called the *primary reinforcers* of behavior because ultimately they establish within the brain the basis for assessing alternative actions. Even in the brains of the most primitive vertebrates, the fish, the projections of these primary reinforcers define two separate areas. One of these evokes appetitive action and the other evokes withdrawal. The same principle operates within the human prefrontal cortex where the prediction of reward and punishment arises from the participation of the medial and lateral parts of the orbital cortex, respectively, each of which are specified in early development by the appropriate set of primary reinforcers. In this way, the psychological component of mood becomes a powerful guiding force in the selection of behavior. When we are up, we follow one line of thought but when we are down, we follow another. We would be unable to do this if the system of primary reinforcers, established more than 500 mya in the first vertebrates, had not survived to serve the parts of the human psyche responsible for mood.

The Irresistible Realm of Euphoria
"When I am high I couldn't worry about money if I tried. So I don't. The money will come from somewhere, I am entitled, God will provide." Unknown Psychiatric Patient. Cited in: Goodwin, F. K. and Jamison, K. R. *Manic-Depressive Illness*. Oxford University Press, New York, Oxford, 1990, p. 29.

Euphoria is often defined as an exaggerated state of well being that has no basis in truth or reality. The state of euphoria characterizes the manic phase of manic-depressive illness or, as it is otherwise known, bipolar disease (Section 5: Chapter 5: Diseases of Mood). Except under the influence of certain psychotrophic drugs, it is rare for normal people to experience the totality of euphoria. In euphoria, confidence exudes from every pore. The need for sleep is lessened and goal directed activity increases. The subject feels empowered by divine forces to achieve the absolute and indeed does achieve far more than is possible within normal mood.

To be euphoric is to be possessed by energetic rapture. In the euphoric state we do not see the sunshine - we become it. Nor do we need to pray or pay homage to the Gods, for instead we find ourselves to be one amongst them. Where the panacea of pleasure or bliss is our reward at the end of a successful journey, euphoria is a state wherein each step is primed by an exhilarating expectation of achievement. No barriers are of significance, no sorrows worthy of a moment's reflection, for in euphoria the negative emotions of guilt, sadness and fear are forever banished. In euphoria the amygdala is silenced, fear and trepidation recede, enemies become acquaintances and friends become family. Matters that normally cause us angst seem trivial and easily resolvable. Confidence soars as all social, moral, intellectual and physical barriers dissolve in a rampant celebration of one's unquestionable ability, preeminence and immortality.

While in deep depression we are a drain upon others, in euphoria we are so aggressively independent that we are a danger to ourselves. Because of this, euphoria has attracted much less attention than the motivationally crippling state of depression. When euphoria takes wing within the psyche, empathy, happiness and love become pawns in a brilliantly orchestrated exposé of success. In the pressured speech and hypersexual inclinations of the euphoric state, we are reminded of the "amygdalaless" monkey liberated from the chains of apprehension and unable to envisage the limitations of its social position. Similarly, in humans, the inhibition of, or injury to, the amygdala inevitably inspires the transcendence of normal social etiquette, insensitive behavior and ultimately the breakdown of interpersonal relationships and social ostracization.

Inured from fear and trepidation the euphoric is inclined to radically underestimate danger. For this reason, high doses of drugs such as amphetamine can be very dangerous when mixed with adventurous sports such as base jumping, surfing or skiing. No river is too big to swim, no mountain too high to climb for a strong man who has speed in his body. Money is a divine entitlement and the price of attaining what the heart most desires is but an irrelevant detail beside the exaggerated optimism that all may be conquered. Indeed, history tells us that in the 1960's the use of amphetamines at the presidential level could have easily precipitated global warfare.

Whereas depression paralyses motivation, euphoria is about action. In elucidating the neural basis of darkness we seek a place within the brain where we can divine the anticipation of punishment, the negation of motivation, the evocation of our most negative emotions and the power to suppress all exploratory action. In contrast, in seeking the neural basis of euphoria we seek a part of the brain wherein the anticipation of reward, the repression of darkness, the pleasure of arousal and the machinery for instigating and supporting energetic, exploratory behavior, coalesce into single cohesive, experiential entity.

Compared to darkness, the state of euphoria is difficult to symbolize. Its representations in religion, mythology, art and literature are few. Pleasure and bliss find metaphorical expression in images of Heaven, Nirvana and the Void. Similarly, love is embodied in the most significant deities of each major religion. However, with its self-orientated energy, euphoria is never associated with the attributes of the divine. Euphoria is about earthly action and empowerment. Religious rituals, such as the whirling of the dervishes (a Muslim Sufi sect), are aimed at achieving ecstasy, not euphoria. Their focus is always on calming the mind, rather than energizing it. Within the spectrum of positive states, euphoria is distinctive in its powerful relationship to motivation. In the state of euphoria we are consumed by a cosmic enthusiasm wherein the psyche is held enchanted by an incontestable yet unwarranted *anticipation of bliss* - a preoccupation not easily transcribed into the symbolic. It is exactly this complicated mix of elation, motivation and empowerment that has made euphoria one of the last frontiers of higher consciousness to be mechanistically understood.

The Art of Darkness
"Writing on depression is painful, sad, lonely and stressful." Andrew Solomon, Author. From: *The Noonday Demon: An Atlas of Depression.* Scribner, New York, 2001, p. 13.

Seven hundred years ago, the Italian philosopher-poet Dante Alighieri (1265-1321) laid out for western ears the fundamental characteristics of what today psychiatrists call major depressive disorder. In his Inferno we may join him and the poet Virgil as they descend through the circles of familiar miscreants into the pit of Hell to where Lucifer lies encased in ice at the dead center of the world. On this journey we learn that in Hell, the soul, the very center of love, becomes the substance of such agony that time itself waits for eternity. And it is here, within the bounds of "pain's own residence," that we may also anticipate complete psychological defeat in the form of social degradation and defilement. Within this wholly imaginable realm is the coalescence of physiological and psychological suffering of infinite dimension. Ultimately, Dante brings us face to face with the paralysis of absolute darkness, as above the gates of Hell we are advised of the imminence and inevitability of our defeat in the words, "You that enter here, abandon hope."

We can only imagine that which we have known. That Dante could craft such a story is revealing of a deep personal insight into darkness. That it could attract such universal empathy is evidence of the existence of abject darkness within the psyche of all normal human beings. Nor is Dante alone in his divination of evil, for as we have seen far from medieval Italy, the Tibetans had long since seen in the extremes of visceral pain, the dissolution of the human soul. Darkness is visible in the mythologies and religions of all cultures, manifesting in Zulu legends, in the intricate systems of Hell awaiting the unworthy Buddhist and the demonic abodes that reinforced the monotheistic teachings of the Iranian prophet Zoroaster whose words were to inspire both Christianity and Islam.

In the visual arts, too, darkness is revealed as a conspicuous principle resident within the mind of all humans (Figure 5.3). Thus, in the "black paintings" of Francisco de Goya (1746-1828), pried from the walls of his final resting place, we may see in evil caricature, Saturn devouring his child, manifesting the ultimate travesty of love by employing the very orality that so nurtures infant life to tear apart his offspring. Goya's last paintings echo what is perhaps the most pervasive symbol in the art of the underworld, the *hellmouth*. The hellmouth is the iconic representation of the demonic consumption of the sinful (Figure 5.4). A visual metaphor perversely common in children's literature, the hellmouth appears the artistic renditions of Egyptian, Greek, Roman, Christian, Buddhist and Hindu mythology, as well as many contemporary movies and plays. Three hundred years before Goya, we have Hiëronymus Bosch whose now classical paintings depict, in almost carnival settings, the diabolical intricacies of medieval torment. The victims are humans of both sexes. Starved bodies are sprawled on the ground, physically broken by crucifixion, twisted on elaborate torture machines resembling the instruments so extensively employed by the Catholic Inquisition. Young maidens are stripped naked and publicly defiled. One unfortunate is being devoured head first by a beaked monster while, like the proverbial pie of the children's nursery rhyme, blackbirds escape from his anus. Above, in the same picture, a smaller demon on antiquated ice skates (Bosch was from the Netherlands) searches for new opportunities to inflict torment. Snakes, sharp instruments and whips are everywhere. Every orifice of the body is explored for its potential to evoke suffering as again and again we are confronted with our innate dread of visceral invasion, permanent disfigurement and being eaten alive. Darkness is the lot of Bosch's victims who are psychologically and physically destroyed for our morbid fascination, driving home the unarguable realization that within each of us is the propensity to be transported to an experience of a vibrant living Hell.

Chapter 2 - The Evocation of Heaven and Hell

The Devil's Bread

"The heaviest suffering of the hell realms and the highest happiness of the state of omniscient mind come from your own mind." Lama Zopa Rinpoche, Tibetan Buddhist Lama. From: *Transforming Problems into Happiness*. Wisdom Publications, Boston, 1993.

The wide usage of lysergic acid diethylamide (LSD-25) in the 1960s saw a revival of interest in the paintings of Hiëronymus Bosch. Bosch's paintings captured the dark energies that accompany the experience of a "bad trip". The Swiss chemist, Albert Hoffman (1906-2008), first synthesized LSD-25 in 1938 but it was not until the 16th of April, 1943 that he became the first person to experience its extremely powerful, psychotrophic effects. Prior to this the ingestion of bread made from rye infected with the fungus *Claviceps purpurea* or *ergot* was responsible for the only comparable psychotrophic experience. Among other things ergot contains ergonovine, used in obstetrics to control postpartum hemorrhage and ergotamine, used for treating migraine headaches and the induction of labor. It also contains lysergic acid from which LSD is easily synthesized.

The effect of ingesting the infected rye is known as *ergotism*. Outbreaks of in both humans and farm animals were prevalent in northern Europe during the Middle Ages. In 994 AD it is claimed that such an epidemic killed 40,000 people. In 1722 ergotism is believed to have struck down the cavalry of Czar Peter the Great on the very eve of their invasion of Turkey. The last outbreak of ergotism occurred in southern Russia in 1926-1927, the 1951 report of an outbreak in a small French village being subsequently attributed to mercury used to disinfect seeds. The symptoms of ergotism include convulsions, miscarriages in females and dry gangrene sometimes leading to death. The gangrene results from constriction of peripheral blood vessels that in turn produces a burning pain in the feet, hands, toes and fingers. The psychoactive and hallucinogenic components of ergot combined with the attendant physical suffering produced a state resembling the classical "bad acid trip." To the deeply religious folk of the time, it was quite natural to believe that the pain and bizarre hallucinations of ergotism were of great spiritual significance. Strongly conditioned to the principles of Christian mythology, the love of God and an intense fear of the torments of Hell were central to their daily existence. There can be little doubt that the intense pain and psychic instability of ergotism convinced many that they had experienced a visitation from the Devil or been cast, through some personal misconduct, into the fires of Hell.

Unfortunately, by the time survivors recovered from ergot poisoning the Devil had inevitably slipped away. Humans always need to identify a culprit. When Satan had absconded they turned on the old standby of the times, the witches. Thus, history shows that periods of ergot blight were always correlated with an abnormally high level of witch burning.

To protect themselves the peasants of medieval Europe turned to the church, invoking the powers of St. Anthony whose life was known to have been a continuous struggle against the onslaughts of Satan. Only a saint with experience in resisting the dark arts could possibly have the necessary skills to treat the psychological and physical suffering of the condition. Taunted mercilessly with horrible spectacles, seductive women and flattery, sometimes beaten close to death, St. Anthony was well qualified to be their protector against the scourges of ergot. Had he not resisted Satan's torment many times, redirecting his mind with fervid prayer and penitential acts? Indeed, so exotic were these encounters that the Temptation of St. Anthony has been the subject of several prominent artists amongst whom is the aforementioned, Hiëronymus Bosch. Because of the burning pain and the belief that St. Anthony had the power to heal ergotism, the condition inevitably became known as *St. Anthony's fire*.

LSD and the Bad Trip

"In an instant I was soaked in sweat. I knelt, a naked esophagus poised to strike and inject its vomit into the veins of the living - the vilification of all that was beautiful, the personification of terror - a rotting corpse barely clinging to life as the sole survivor of unspeakable torments. Suddenly nausea overcame everything. Before me lay the covenant of this land where all truth is a hoax, all love, the vehicle of deceit and deception. Only one question reverberated through my mind - the question of whether I would be imprisoned here forever." Unknown Scribe.

The effects of psychotrophic drugs on mood confront us with the astounding realization that our energies, our interpretations, our attitudes and our proximity to bliss and darkness are entirely a reflection of our brain's chemistry. Amid all the wild speculation about expanded consciousness, this was possibly the most significant message gained by the intelligentsia when, in the late 1960's, the recreational use of powerful psychoactive drugs heralded a new chapter in our comprehension of darkness and euphoria. Through its excitatory effects on the brain center controlling vigilance (the *locus coeruleus*), LSD greatly potentiates the amount of information that gains admittance to the cortex (*Drugs and the Alteration of Consciousness*: Chapter 3: Section 7). Both our inner and outer realms of consciousness are affected. The diversity, frequency and intensity of sensations, perceptions, emotions, moods and thoughts are enhanced. Over stimulated, the mind may easily fall into chaos as novel ideas and associations conjure what has never before been conceived. The emotions may easily swing from one extreme to another. One moment we may be the avatar of love, while in the next we may find ourselves spiraling into uncharted depths. Nothing is stable within this exaggerated state of consciousness that is the unique product of what is, in terms of weight-for-effect, still the most powerful psychotrophic drug in existence.

Insights from Recreational Drugs

"With all your science can you tell how it is, and whence it is, that light comes into the soul?" Henry David Thoreau (1817-1862). American Essayist, Poet, Civil Liberties Advocate and Philosopher.

Not surprisingly, the most popular psychotrophic drugs are those that negate experiences of darkness and selectively induce either bliss or euphoria. Such substances are commonly referred to as hedonics. All of them; nicotine, alcohol, cocaine, ecstasy, amphetamine, morphine, heroin and others increase the amount of dopamine in particular parts of our brains, precipitating some degree of bliss (*Drugs and the Alteration of Consciousness*: Chapter 3: Section 7). Some of them, in particular amphetamine and cocaine, also increase the amount of *noradrenalin* (also called *norepinephrine*) in our brains, a factor that sharpens our perceptions and increases our levels of vigilance and motivation. It is because of the energizing effect of cocaine that the Indians of Peru and Bolivia have, for centuries, chewed coca leaves to enable them to keep working under physiologically challenging conditions.

In the same way as the experience of drug-induced bliss or euphoria is a glimpse of Heaven, the experience of a bad drug trip is a journey to Hell. Yet in both cases nothing has changed in the outside world. All that has happened is that a drug has been ingested that has altered the landscape of consciousness by changing the patterns of activity across the entire cerebral cortex. But although a drug can affect cortical activity, it cannot create a realm of consciousness that is not already there. The domains of consciousness available to each and every human are indelibly defined by the relative size and function of each of Brodmann's areas. Even though some drugs can influence one area of cortex more than another, a drug cannot change the domain of experience evoked by any particular area (Section 2: Chapter 2: The Dissection of Consciousness). Put another way, neither our brain's chemistry, nor drugs can create *de novo* what is not already engineered into our cortical architecture. A drug can only exaggerate or attenuate particular preexisting elements of consciousness. However, by selectively influencing systems that control the responsiveness of our cortical neurons, powerful psychotropic drugs facilitate experiences that in normal existence may only rarely, if ever, come our way. In a bad trip we are consumed by the self-generated terror of darkness, while in euphoria we are inspired by the energy of the divine. That mood falls somewhere between two extremes is evidence that within the human psyche, the experiences of euphoria and darkness are the product of at least two separate cortical areas. The relative activity of these two areas not only sets mood but ultimately regulates our thoughts, emotions and behavior.

Pain and the Penetration of the Psyche
"He has seen but half the universe who has not been shown the house of pain." Ralph Waldo Emerson (1803-1882). American Essayist, Philosopher and Poet.

We can divide pain into two types depending on its source within our body. Thus, pain that arises from our skin, joints and muscle is often referred to as *peripheral* or *somatic pain* while pain arising from our body's organs is referred to as *visceral pain*. Pain can also be classified according to the type of experience it evokes within us. Thus, in western medicine, pain is described as having two dimensions. The first is called the *sensory-discriminative dimension* and the second the *affective-motivational dimension*. The sensory-discriminative and the affective-motivational dimensions of the pain experience are somewhat aligned with somatic and visceral pain, respectively.

206

The sensory-discriminative dimension of pain (the "what" and the "where" of pain) refers to our ability to localize the pain in our body and to say whether its source is a burn, a pinprick, an arthritic joint or a injured muscle. It arises from the *somatosensory cortex*, which registers the position and identity of stimuli to the body surface. In contrast, visceral pain is, like all visceral sensations, notoriously difficult to identify and localize. Visceral pain does not influence the somatosensory cortex but instead activates the centers of mood and emotion. Visceral pain is therefore powerfully evocative of the affective-motivational dimension the pain experience. Only when somatic pain is both intense and long lasting does it gain access to these centers, there to have a direct affect upon emotion and mood.

As with mood, intensity is the most significant aspect of the experience of pain. It is intensity, which determines whether an experience of pain will indelibly scar the organic centers of our being. In the art of torture, it is the torturer's intent that the body becomes the vehicle of fear and anguish wherein unavoidable agony paralyzes all conscious action, isolating the victim within a catastrophic experience for which there are no words. The scarring of torture that begins in the body ultimately penetrates the core of the psyche, causing disruption of sleep patterns, an increased frequency of stress related illnesses, post-traumatic stress syndrome and severe depression that frequently leads to suicide. We must face the realization that in every waking moment, literally hundreds of thousands of people bear within themselves the cognitive and emotional memories that are the stuff of our worst nightmares.

The Interaction of Pain and Depression
"But thus do I counsel you, my friends: distrust all in whom the impulse to punish is powerful!" Friedrich Nietzsche (1844-1900). German Philosopher, Cultural Critic and Classical Scholar.

Mood and pain are highly interactive. This is largely because some areas of cortex are involved in both depression and the affective-motivational dimension of the pain experience. Studies show that 80% of people who suffer from intense chronic pain also suffer from depression while 80% of people who suffer from depression report suffering pain that is sometimes without localizable cause. Mood is darkened by a nagging injury and the pain of such an injury is felt more intensely by the depressed. And of euphoria, quite the opposite can be said, for in that state of optimistic urgency, even a serious injury may go unnoticed. Simply looking at pleasant pictures decreases our perception of pain, while looking at unpleasant pictures does the opposite. As in mythology, pain and mood are bedfellows within our everyday lives. When depressed patients begin a course of anti-depressants, they often report that not only are they less depressed but that they feel better within their bodies. And again the opposite is true because exercise has recently been shown to be extremely effective in the elevation of mood. It seems that a common set of generators underlie the experiences of depression and intense pain. Both states constitute the stuff of suffering and both are innately punishing. Both have the capacity to transport the sufferer to an experience of the netherworld, an experience that, as we shall see, becomes almost indelibly etched in the brain's emotional centers.

Intuitively cognizant of the unitary nature of human suffering, it is common for the perpetrators of punishment to combine intense physical pain (torture), psychological torment, social degradation, defilement and condemnation. Victims might be told their loved ones have been raped and murdered and their home or village destroyed. Not only is the creation of darkness central to the art of torture, but it is also a clear objective of all penal systems. In societies where the infliction of physical pain is outlawed, the psychological road to depression is the only way to achieve punishment. When a normal person is incarcerated, isolated from their family and friends and socially disgraced, depression is inevitable (Section 5: Chapter 5: Diseases of Mood). The capacity of the human psyche to anticipate punishment, be it depression or pain, lies at the heart of all strategies for controlling behavior, deemed unacceptable to the host society. We move through life between the goad of darkness and the allure of euphoria. Would that it were otherwise, but, alas, the threat of darkness, no matter how it is achieved seems to be the method of choice for forcibly extinguishing those patterns of human behavior deemed by the majority as undesirable.

Suffering and the Coalescence of the Negative

"Suffering exists in a certain state of consciousness; it is the characteristic feature of that state. Within that state there is no freedom from suffering, because that state itself is the suffering. In it, if you remove one sorrow, another takes its place; this chain continues. You may free yourself from this or that sorrow, but freedom from suffering as such does not happen. The suffering remains, only the causes change." Sri Sri Bhagwan Rajneesh (Osho) (1931-1990), Indian Mystic and Professor of Philosophy and Psychology.

People vary enormously in their propensity to suffer. Some people continue to lead effective lives despite the persistence of agonizing diseases or injuries. Some struggle on from one black dawn to the next, dogged mercilessly by the pervasive canker of clinical depression or chronic pain that would crush less stalwart spirits. Others are crippled by levels of physical discomfort or psychological angst that, to most, seem insignificant. For some people, life just seems to hurt more. Much of this variation may arise from the disparate allocation of cortex to the areas that elaborate pain and mood in different individuals. Culture, general health, genetics, personality, upbringing, exposure to trauma and the attendant stability of mind, mood and emotion all seem to play a part in our propensity to suffer.

In essence, the *state of suffering* owes its existence to discrete elements of human consciousness. Ironically it is only through suffering that we have opportunity to acquaint ourselves with the full potential of the human psyche to elaborate darkness. Our every day pangs of discomfort are, like mild levels of dysphoria, unpleasant yet bearable. Neither truly qualifies as suffering and neither reveals anything of significance regarding the psyche. In contrast, intense chronic pain and deep depression confront us with elements of human consciousness that are difficult for healthy, normal people to imagine. Whether it arises from within our psyche or from our bodily sensations, suffering is by definition the most negative of all human experiences. Suffering wrenches us from our intentions, erodes our will to live and confronts us with the almost macabre interpretations of situations we would normally regard as innocent. Suffering commandeers the soul, invades the visceroemotional centers of our brain and ultimately annihilates our ability to experience or express love. Yet if we do not experience suffering we never have an opportunity to fully comprehend the extremes of human existence. Only by descending like Dante to the depths of Hell can we truly empathize with those who cannot so easily return to the light.

The Grip of Darkness

"A man who is 'of sound mind' is one who keeps the inner madman under lock and key." Paul Valery (1871-1945). French Essayist, Poet and Philosopher.

Eventually a moment comes when within those rarely visited corners of human consciousness, there awakens a sense of incomprehensible dread - a time when we sense the emergence of an entirely alien presence. Before us stands the prophet of doom whose furtive visits remind us of our proximity to death, whose malice mirrors the ugliness of our unworthy ways, whose wrath we risk should we choose to challenge the rigid confines of our societal conditioning. In trepidation we await the half-seen shadow, the unexpected footstep in the empty hallway, the fevered grasp of icy fingers tightening upon our heart, conjuring within us the terror of unimaginable pain, of untimely death and the permanent mutilation of our body. Yet when our panic subsides, and with newfound courage we look into the face of the unknown, there is nothing to see. Satan has gone, slipped away through the cracks of time, there to wait until once again we leave the door of sanity ever so slightly ajar. No more now than a hollow memory, this parasitic worm of the psyche falls into his sleepless trance, content that he has raised within us an awareness of his power to wreak unrelenting havoc upon our soul.

What awakens within us to conjure such forebodings? In darkness we meet fear not as a transient emotion warning of potential threat, but as a cancerous growth that saps our motivation and erodes the very center of our being. Normally our emotions press for the rejuvenation of the body. Not so darkness. Where our emotions demand action and are gone, darkness stays, amplifying our every mistake, crippling the spirit and insidiously seeding every intention with an aura of inevitable failure. Our emotions define our goals, guiding us in each minute, demanding strategic action that will immediately restore our balance with nature. In contrast, darkness has no immediate goal for in its very origin, darkness is about cessation. While euphoria propels us forward to the absolute certainty of stardom, darkness exists to remove us from the stage of life. In darkness we are psychologically, physiologically and physically paralyzed. Darkness renders us frightened, spent and broken.

The Practice of Martyrdom

"The victims of the Catholic inquisition died by means 'which were carefully selected as among the most poignant that man can suffer. They were usually burnt alive. They were burnt alive not infrequently by a slow fire. They were burnt alive after their constancy had been tried by the most excruciating agonies that minds fertile in torture could devise.'" William E. H. Lecky (1838-1903). Irish Historian and Publicist.

In 1489 two Dominican brothers, Jacob Sprenger and Heinrich Kraemer published the first of 19 editions of *Malleus Maleficarum* or *Witch Hammer*. Given the approval of the Pope, the King of Rome and the Faculty of Theology of the University of Cologne this malevolent creation detailed with encyclopedic authority, methods for detecting, examining by torture and sentencing women suspected of demonic possession - serving as the working guide for the Inquisition for 300 years. To their tormentors, the psychological and physical decimation of the unworthy served as an horrific proof of the divine powers of those biblical figures whose spiritual attainment and moral authority were confirmed by their entirely mythological ability to withstand the darkest realms of human experience.

In truth all religions see in the transcendence of darkness an indication of godliness. The whole significance of martyrdom is based upon this principle. Only by overcoming the terrors of martyrdom can one qualify for sainthood in all its guises. The would-be Christian saint must overcome the horrors of Hell just as the devoted Buddhist must face the wrath of demons and the hunter-gatherer must withstand the torment of prolonged and often agonizing initiations. How better to dissuade ordinary people from aspiring to immortality than by establishing an initiation that requires passage through the deepest realms of suffering?

Outside religious mythology, transcendence through martyrdom is exploited by all governments and societies to persuade ordinary people to commit to tasks that will inevitably cause them to suffer. Inspired by the fervor of worthy self-sacrifice, the embattled soldier will fight on despite injuries and horrors that in his everyday life would crush the last vestige of his spirit. In his moment of glory he too will have transcended human suffering. In the tombs and monuments that commemorate our hollow victories over each other, we celebrate this ascendance of millions of our kind, who for a little time stood amongst the ranks of the divine. Politicians, kings and priests alike are well aware that no act so inspires the human heart as the transcendence of darkness.

The Exploration of Darkness
"When you look long into an abyss….the abyss also looks into you." Friedrich Nietzsche (1844-1900). German Philosopher, Cultural Critic and Classical Scholar.

The Golden Gate Bridge in San Francisco is a favorite spot for committing suicide. The fall of 250 feet takes 3 to 4 seconds. Despite hitting the water at around 75 miles per hour, 1% of people survive the fall. Of 7 survivors who were interviewed, all reported peaceful and tranquil feelings during their jumps. None made a second attempt to commit suicide and one man commented on how short life is in relation to how much we have to accomplish. It seems that from being suicidal these individuals emerged from their acceptance of fear and death with a healthy psyche orientated towards survival and accomplishment. Could it be that to walk through the curtain of darkness, there to accept death and yet to go on living, somehow enables the permanent transcendence of psychological torment? Is not the martyrdom of the saints the means through which they have annulled the temptations of Satan and repossessed their psyche in order to perform works of love and virtue?

Such so-called *conversion experiences* are often used in spiritual training with the discrete purpose of liberating the practitioner from the demons that inevitably haunt a conditioned mind. A typical example relates to the training of lamas in Tibetan Buddhism. Tibet has the richest folklore of all cultures. Ghosts and demons are everywhere. In the Land of the Snow it has been suggested that evil spirits generally outnumber the human population. These malevolent beings live in every nook and cranny of the countryside, emerging only to feed upon the vitality of both animals and men. No traveler is safe. So problematic were these emissaries of darkness that it was once the task of official lama magicians to face them and effect their transformation into loyal servants. Transcending fear as a means of transcending psychological darkness has long been part of Tibetan Buddhist practice. In old Tibet this was achieved by the ancient ceremony of *Chod*. On both the physical and psychological front, Chod is a dangerous and threatening undertaking. Its attraction is that it holds promise for permanently inuring the practitioner against fear and paranoia.

In preparation for Chod, a lama selects an ascetic possessing magical powers - an anchorite or apprentice *naljorpa*, who will be given the opportunity of liberating himself. The only condition is that the participant must surrender to events and sensations that awaken a pervasive experience of terror. In the harsh Tibetan terrain, an area is chosen which is known to be haunted by a demon or *Towos*. A Towos may appear in the shape of a ferocious tiger, often depicted in Tibetan art eating the brains of men. The subject is ordered to imagine he is a cow, brought to this place as an offering to the Towos, and is further commanded to emit lowing noises to simulate the plight of the imagined beast. It is anticipated that, consumed by fear, he will enter a trance. Sometimes he is left tethered to a tree for three days and nights during which he must resist the temptation of releasing himself from his bindings. Weariness and starvation combine to produce hallucinations that are pervaded by the feelings of impending doom. So effective is Chod that it is said some go "mad" while others die of shock. However, it is anticipated that the aspirant will eventually witness the role of his mind in creating the objects of his fear, thereby arriving at the *realization* that fear and darkness are not a reality of the world but a product of the imagination. Nevertheless, any premature "incredulity" is deemed to be counterproductive. The subject must emphatically believe that the demons do exist. Only the ideation and experience of abject fear and the subsequent realization of its illusory nature are deemed to be the correct path to incredulity and the detachment from darkness.

To make the exercise more credible, a cemetery or a venue where legend or history records some tragic event, is chosen. A liturgy promotes a sense of doom. The ceremony begins with an exhausting, ritualistic dance. The participant must believe he is preparing himself for demonic consumption - envisaging in detail a series of suggestive commands. Blowing a bone trumpet fashioned from a human femur (*kangling*), he calls upon a familiar feminine deity who, upon arrival, stands before him and cuts off his head with one stroke of her sword. Troops of ravenous ghouls gather, while the goddess severs his limbs, skins him and rips open his belly. The hideous guests spurred on by the rivers of blood that mix with his steaming intestines, fall upon their macabre feast masticating noisily. Yet throughout his imagined agony, the subject must utter words of unreserved surrender, offering his mutilated remains for consumption by the host. Not only must the body be forsaken, but also the spirit too must be surrendered as he delivers up his happiness to the unhappy and his breath to the dying, exhorting his tormentors to consume the remnants of his earthly body.

This first part of the ceremony is called the "red meal". It is followed by the "black meal". In the black meal even the sacred entity of "self" is extinguished. Whereas the red meal involves the torture and decimation of the physical body, the black meal is a descent into the living Hell of psychological darkness. In the process of the black meal the subject must imagine that he is reduced to a small heap of charred bones trapped in a lake of black mud created from human misery, moral defilement and the harmful deeds he has performed in the course of countless lives. He must attain the realization that he is not worthy even as an object of sacrifice, no illusion of identity must remain to distract him from despair beyond despair. The "I" that endured bodily consumption must now itself, sink into the black mud as befits one who has attained utter insignificance. This closes the ceremony of Chod.

The ceremony of Chod is an orchestrated descent into Hell. The purpose of Chod is to experientially expose the psyche's potential for creating fear and darkness. As we will see, the mind's capacity to evoke internal imagery, be it perceptual, conceptual, emotional or thymic (mood related), ensures we are never far from illusion (*maya*). When an anchorite survives Chod he undergoes a realization of the pervasive nature of illusion – a realization that can be applied to all threatening people, situations, objects and ideas. The mind ceases its perverse enchantment with grim superstition, observing both darkness and euphoria with detachment, essentially seeing the contents of thought, emotion and mood as internally generated products of the human psyche. Having passed through darkness the aspirant is freed forever from the tendrils of evil possession. Yet the capacity for the instantaneous evocation of fear in response to real danger remains intact. Chod is essentially a cleverly contrived conversion experience. Those who survive Chod have one thing in common with the survivors of the Golden Gate Bridge, for they too have walked through the curtain of darkness only to find that the psychological aspects of suffering were the creation of their own psyche.

Chapter 3 - The Origin and Purpose of Mood

The Hormonal Vision of Mood

"A woman is sometimes fugitive, irrational, indeterminable, illogical and contradictory. A great deal of forbearance ought to be shown her, and a good deal of prudence exercised with regard to her, for she may bring about innumerable evils without knowing it. Capable of all kinds of devotion, and of all kinds of treason, monster incomprehensible, raised to the second power, she is at once the delight and the terror of man." Henri Frederic Amiel (1821-1881). Swiss Author, Diarist and Philosopher.

Mood profoundly influences whether we anticipate success or failure. To achieve this, mood draws as much upon the condition of our body as it does upon our circumstances. If all other factors are neutral, our physiological status will determine our mood that, in turn, will determine whether our mind generates optimistic or pessimistic thoughts. If our physiological reserves are low we will be inclined to envisage failure, whereas if we are fit we will most likely envisage success. Good mood typically indicates the potential for energetic, goal-orientated activity. As long as our good mood is not drug induced, we may consider that our optimism is in accord with our physical condition. In contrast, when we are ill or in a different part of our hormonal cycle, sensory information from our body's organs will cause us to make excuses for avoiding challenging tasks. By conjuring good mood our body's organs and hormones are giving us the go ahead. Alternatively, if we are in dark mood then either our body is telling us not to proceed, or our psychological state is otherwise compromised (Figure 5.5).

To appreciate better the basic role of mood, it is helpful to try to imagine a person who has only emotions and thoughts. Such a person could certainly take action. Their emotions would still drive their mind to seek the satiation of their bodily urges. However, without an ongoing measure of their physiological condition, the individual might be ill prepared to carry through such action. It is mood that provides the necessary integrated assessment of our internal milieu. Without mood all actions would be dependent upon our immediate needs and urges, irrespective of whether we have the physiological resources to actualize them. The emotions make demands, the mind makes plans, but in the background, mood determines how we anticipate the outcome of our efforts. In the lower, "mindless" mammals, behavior is driven and orchestrated entirely by the anterior cingulate gyrus, the executor of the triad of emotion. However, as mood commandeers the emotional centers, it effectively prevents any large fluctuations of emotion away from its set point. Put simply this means it is extremely difficult to have positive emotions when we are in dark mood and *vice versa*. The factors that ensure the longevity of mood prevent transient fluctuations of the emotions that might otherwise evoke rapid and potentially dangerous changes of behavior. With or without the mind, mood is a potent and persistent regulator of behavior in all mammals.

The Sensory Specification of Mood

"A blind or deaf rat can still survive and mate to stay alive and keep the species going. A rat that cannot smell is much worse off.... It cannot discern the sexual readiness of a mate, or detect the scent of a cat waiting in the bushes." James V. Kohl and Robert T. Francoeur, Neurobiologists. From: *The Scent of Eros - Mysteries of Odor in Human Sexuality*. The Continuum Publishers and Co., London, New York, 1995.

Olfaction is so fundamental to the vertebrate brain that even in adult humans its loss can cause social and sexual dysfunction, while in infants it can result in improper development of the testes, ovaries and the brain's hormonal centers. These insights give us important clues in our search for the origin of mood. Let us go back more than half a billion years to the most primitive fish. The fossilized remains of these animals show that they are almost identical to species that are still alive today. Thus, it seems very likely that they were highly dependent on their sense of smell, and possibly taste, for predicting the consequences of eating various potential foods.

The human infant is also highly dependent on olfaction. The olfactory (or *piriform*) cortex is one of the first cortical areas to mature and one of the first to evolve along the vertebrate lineage. The olfactory cortex is consequently the oldest part of the orbital cortex (*The Psychological and Physiological Aspects of Mood*: Chapter 1: Section 5). With the evolution of the vertebrates the orbital cortex has undergone a tremendous increases in size. This has been achieved not by an anterior expansion of the archaic olfactory cortex, but by the progressive evolution of new, adjoining areas of increasingly complex and advanced forms of cortex in front of the archaic olfactory representation. In this way the primitive olfactory cortex (paleocortex) probably served as the earliest source of what was essentially a primitive form of mood. Through the enormous expansion of the orbital cortex that accompanied the evolution of the vertebrates, this region would eventually become one of the three vital components of the human psyche.

The most fundamental purpose of smell and taste is the discrimination of the edible from the inedible or poisonous. For this reason natural selection has honed the chemical senses such that even in the newborn they are genetically programmed to unequivocally differentiate edible objects from inedible and potentially poisonous objects. Sensory nerve fibers that respond to "good" and "bad" smells connect to different parts of the olfactory cortex that, respectively, mediate, either feeding or aversion. In this process the olfactory cortex relays information about "good" smells to the medial orbital cortex and "bad" smells to the lateral orbital cortex.

The more anterior regions of the orbital cortex also respond to odors such that unpleasant smells activate the lateral part while pleasant odors activate the medial part. They thus follow the lateral versus medial representation of "bad" and "good" odors that originates in the olfactory cortex. In humans, however, the orbital cortex has a complex response to odor that emphasizes its importance to behavior. Whereas the mere wafting of odor into the nose is sufficient to activate the olfactory cortex, activation of the orbital cortex only occurs during sniffing, when we are actively sampling odors. This response is complex in that the orbital cortex of the right hemisphere is activated during sniffing even in the absence of odor, while the orbital cortex of the left hemisphere is activated during sniffing in the presence of an odor. Thus, the right orbital cortex is essentially involved in testing for new odors while the left orbital cortex registers the actual presence of new odors.

Upon reaching the mammalian brain, taste and smell initially activate quite different areas of the cortex; smells being represented in the ancient olfactory cortex while taste is represented in part of the insula (*The Origins of Our Mammalian Ways*: Chapter 5: Section 4). As with olfaction, taste secondarily activates the orbital cortex such that good tastes excite the medial orbital cortex and bad tastes, the lateral orbital cortex. The orbital cortex can therefore be said to support a *hedonic map of smell and taste* that is particularly important to the process of choosing edible versus inedible food. This chemically orientated hedonic map is further reinforced by information about "good" (gentle touch) and "bad" (painful stimuli) sensations from the body that are initially represented in the cortex's somatosensory areas. Thus, even in the relatively huge orbital cortex of humans, good smells and tastes, along with gentle touch, are wired to the medial part the orbital cortex while bad smells and tastes, along with painful stimuli are wired to the lateral part. In this way the lateral orbital cortex represents the potential for negative outcome while the neighboring medial orbital cortex elaborates an awareness of the potential of reward. So it is that in the evolution of the orbital cortex we see the origins of the most significant of all dualistic phenomena - the biogenetical specification within the human psyche of the experiential basis of *good* and *bad*.

The Relationship between Mood and Anticipation
"If pleasures are greatest in anticipation, just remember that this is also true of trouble." Elbert Hubbard (1856-1915). American Editor, Publisher and Writer.

With the advent of brain scanners it seemed that it would be easy to locate the areas of the brain that auger the onset of darkness. However, researchers have been thwarted in their efforts by ethical quandaries. In the extremes of major depressive disorder, the mind is crowded with negative thoughts, the heart is stripped of all motivational energy and the body is pervaded by uneasy, unnerving and even painful sensations. The researcher trying to determine which brain sites are active in depression essentially faces the same problems as the researcher who is trying to locate the areas responsible for experiencing intense pain. It is simply unethical to ask people to suffer. No bribe is high enough to persuade someone being treated for major depressive disorder to stop taking medication and slowly descend into the paralysis of darkness. One might just as well seek volunteers to submit to torture in the interests of furthering our knowledge about chronic pain. Consequently, most studies of depression are on patients who are receiving, or have recently received, medication. While in all such studies there is little doubt that the subjects were dysphoric, it is often questionable whether any were deeply depressed in the classical, catatonic sense. Thus, while brain scan studies have supplied pieces of the puzzle, pointing to the participation of the orbital cortex and the cortex's emotional centers, a complete appreciation of the origins of the depressive experience requires the integration of observations derived from a variety of approaches.

When an area of the cortex becomes highly active of its own accord it is said to be epileptic. Epilepsy may be confined to a small area, as in *petit mal* epilepsy, or cover a wide area of cortex, as in *grand mal* epilepsy. As petit mal epilepsy is confined to a small area of cortex, the symptoms of a seizure can give clues as to the normal function of that particular area of cortex and its contribution to human experience. For example, when a petit mal seizure is focused on the orbital cortex, patients appear to be psychologically terrified and physically afflicted with intense visceral pain. Similar effects are predicted by electrically stimulating the orbital cortex through implanted electrodes, a procedure that induces vomiting, sweating, changes in skin temperature, increases in stress hormones and depression of blood pressure and respiration - responses that are typical of those accompanying intense chronic pain such as occurs clinically and during torture. It seems that activation of the orbital cortex has the capacity to evoke both the psychological (mental) and physiological constituents of human suffering.

In contrast to the negative aspects of orbital activation, a few studies have shown that electrical stimulation of certain parts of the orbital cortex can sometimes produce a positive experience. For instance, when animals are given the opportunity to press a lever and stimulate themselves through an electrode implanted in their orbital cortex they may, in certain cases, repeatedly choose to do so. These apparently contradictory results arise because passing pulses of electrical current into an intricate network of cortical neurons is a notoriously capricious means of localizing function. The technique does, however, reveal the presence of pathways leading away from the stimulated area. The effects of stimulating the orbital cortex therefore showed that some parts of it connect to brain areas that produce negative emotions while other parts connect to areas responsible for positive emotions. Put another way, one part of the orbital cortex conjures feelings of reward while the other conjures feelings of punishment.

Both the medial and lateral parts of the orbital cortex are powerfully inter-connected to the mind. These enable them to influence our thoughts by conveying to the mind their ongoing predictions of outcome. When the medial orbital cortex signals that a given strategy or circumstance is likely to hold reward, then behavior must be orchestrated accordingly. In contrast, when the lateral orbital cortex generates apprehension in order to signal the high possibility of failure or punishment then any goal-orientated behavior must be inhibited. In order to achieve these opposite effects, the medial and lateral parts of the orbital cortex have very different connections to the brain's emotional centers. Thus, the lateral part is strongly interconnected to the source of negative emotions, the amygdala, while the medial part is close to, and strongly interconnected with, the anterior cingulate gyrus that is active during experiences of bliss (*Sex, State and Orgasm*: Chapter 3: Section 7). However, the difference between the medial and lateral orbital regions is not confined to their interactions with the emotional centers. Other connections ensure that the medial and lateral parts of the orbital cortex assist in fulfilling the very different physiological requirements of appetitive versus refractory behavior, respectively. To enable it to participate in the generation of withdrawal or immobility, the lateral part of the orbital cortex receives and evaluates a wide diversity of sensory information. In complete contrast, the medial orbital cortex's participation in goal-orientated action is enabled by its powerful connections to visceromotor (autonomic) centers and an important reward center (*ventral tegmental area*). It is relevant to this that the medial orbital cortex becomes active when people are shown images that they personally judge as beautiful. It seems that the lateral orbital cortex is better able to detect and inform the mind of the potential for negative outcome while the medial orbital cortex has the power to influence the body's physiological control systems in preparation for the energetic pursuit of a perceived reward. In this way the orbital cortex ensures that the states of euphoria and darkness are accompanied by radically different behavior patterns and radically different physiological states.

An excellent illustration of the judgmental role of the orbital cortex can be gained by using brain imaging to see how this area responds when something is at first rewarding and then becomes punishing. This is a very common phenomenon that probably accounts for the cessation of most highly pleasurable activities. One such experiment involved offering subjects chocolate while their brains were being scanned. After eating more than their fill of chocolate, the subject's desire for more naturally became satiated, finally reaching a point where even the mere appearance of the chocolate was repellent rather than inviting. Brain imaging throughout this process shows that, in the desirous phase, eating chocolate increased activity in their medial orbital cortex. Only when subjects became sickened by the thought of eating more chocolate did neural activity move away from the medial to the lateral part of the orbital cortex. The level of activity in the lateral and medial regions essentially mirrored the subject's sense of punishment or reward, respectively. In experiential terms, the craving for chocolate was associated with activity in the medial orbital cortex, whereas an avoidance of chocolate was associated with activity in the lateral orbital cortex. The role of these areas in mood is underscored by recent findings that the medial orbital cortex is one third smaller in depressed individuals. Consistent with this is the characteristic of depressed people to manifest avoidance where others would pursue a potentially rewarding goal.

Humans do everything they can to make their lives predictable, yet they are inevitably confronted by situations where the outcome is uncertain. Is there enough gasoline in the car to get to town, or will we run out and face a long walk? We may not have enough information to make the correct choice. We must gamble and take a chance that our best guess will bring the reward of safe arrival. It is in this situation, when we have insufficient information to determine a course of action, that the orbital cortex raises its voice. The predictive role of the orbital cortex is a general phenomenon. It does not matter whether the subject of our deliberations is chocolate, money, playing cards, people or gasoline. Through the orbital cortex we experience what we may call a *feeling of rightness* - a feeling that, in essence, promotes optimistic action and approach. The orbital cortex is also responsible for the *feeling of wrongness* that extinguishes optimism and demands that the mind seek strategies of avoidance. In its very nature, anticipation is a dichotomous experience that manifests within us a seemingly inherent sense of good and bad. Thus, it is from the orbital cortex that arises the most fundamental of dualistic principles, reward and punishment, or simply good and bad - a principle that is as critical to the guidance of the most complex aspects of our social behavior – our ability to participate in *moral reasoning*. In humans, the orbital cortex is the great regulator of strategy, emerging as an unmanageable entity only when mood is drawn to its pathological extremes.

As the primary reinforcers of behavior, taste, smell, touch and pain specify the two most fundamental antithetical experiences of human existence, good and bad (Section 4: Chapter 5: The Second Emotions - Love, Sadness and Disgust). It is these extremes of expectancy that are embodied in the universal religious concepts; Heaven and Hell. It is the diametrically opposed responses of the primary reinforcers that determine what the human infant will accept or withdraw from and that, during development of its brain, ultimately define the two divisions of the orbital cortex.

More than any other organism humans are availed of the extraordinary capacity to make what are essentially educated guesses about the future. The ability to respond rapidly and effectively to changes in circumstance is a distinctive feature of all higher mammals and this capacity also reaches its zenith in the human being. To survive, it is vitally important that we are able to use reason to reassess our guesses and rapidly reprogram our anticipatory centers from whence they come. What suggests a profit on one day might, on another, indicate loss. To understand how this can happen requires an appreciation of the adult human's high level of dependence upon sight and hearing.

Throughout childhood, the two parts of the orbital cortex become selectively responsive to visual and auditory information in such a way that sights and sounds indicating potentially rewarding versus potentially punishing scenarios are relayed to the medial and lateral orbital cortex, respectively. While the primary reinforcers maintain a consistent influence over these orbital areas, the "learning process" by which the sights and sounds are associated with "good" or "bad" outcomes remains highly malleable throughout adult life, the orbital cortex instantly adjusting to the changing relationships that link the things around us to the prediction of either reward or punishment. In neuropsychological terms the change in behavior accompanying this phenomenon is called *response reversal*. As necessary as response reversal is to human survival, we will see that in abnormal circumstances it may be responsible for psychiatric dysfunction (*Obsessions, Compulsions and Personality*: Chapter 5: Section 5).

As adults, our orbital cortex is availed of a multisensory assessment of our surroundings, the scripts of past outcomes, an outline of our cognitive intentions and strategies, a "knowledge" of our current physiological resources, the facility to interact with our emotional centers and direct access to our autonomic control centers. With the constant tuning and retuning of the anticipatory relevance of visual and auditory information, the adult human is able to continuously adapt to the changing scenarios of everyday life. Only thus can a positive expectation be rapidly converted into a negative one. In this way the orbital cortex acts as a *barometer of circumstance*, making available to the machinations of the mind a continuous reassessment of outcome and in so doing providing a critical guide to the fashioning of our behavior.

When such a system malfunctions we experience the inappropriate and exaggerated expectations of either failure or success that characterize the psychological aspect of all mood disorders.

Chapter 4 - The Psychopathology of Choice

The Alignment of Thought
"Make your choice adventurous stranger,
strike the bell and hide the danger,
or wonder till it drives you mad,
what would have followed if you had."
Charles S. Lewis (1898-1963). Scholar and Author Childrens Stories, Science Fiction and Christianity.

Within the normal bounds of mood, the orbital cortex helps us glimpse the feelings evoked by reward or punishment that may be the outcome of a particular challenge. Its predictive capacity tunes our thoughts towards the most beneficial course of action. Responsible for our feelings of rightness, the medial orbital cortex is powerfully interconnected to the nearby anterior cingulate gyrus, the executor of our raw emotions that is responsible for our positive emotions and is intimately interconnected with the mind. In contrast, the lateral orbital cortex is responsible for our feelings of wrongness and is strongly interconnected with our center of fear and anxiety, the amygdala. Through its influence on the lateral orbital cortex, the amygdala can influence the mind by evoking foreboding thoughts. It is in this way that the human psyche can achieve what psychologists call *mood congruency* - essentially the alignment of our thoughts with our moods (Figure 5.6).

The opposite is also true, for the valence of our thoughts and particularly our autobiographical memories can also powerfully influence the valence of our moods. Thus, when normal subjects were asked to recall autobiographical events they rated as "happy", the medial orbital cortex became active while, conversely, when they recalled events they rated as "sad" the lateral orbital cortex was activated. We remember most vividly events that are in one way or the other of great emotional significance. In returning to us, each memory utilizes the medial and lateral domains of the orbital cortex to resurrect within our psyche the prevailing mood that accompanied the original event. Not only is the orbital cortex the registrar of valence but it also acts as the librarian of the psyche, weighing our deeds and plans on the scales of natural selection before filing them in the brain's center for long-term memory (the hippocampus).

Life without Guidance
"The soul is dyed the color of its thoughts. Think only on those things that are in line with your principles and can bear the light of day. The content of your character is your choice. Day by day, what you do is who you become. Your integrity is your destiny - it is the light that guides your way." Heraclitus (c. 540 - c. 480 BC). Greek Philosopher and Cosmologist.

In lower mammals, damage to the orbital cortex produces a condition known as *neglect* in which the animal appears to ignore injury to its body. In humans much the same thing is observed. Patients with orbital damage appear to be indifferent to mutilation and disease, even though they are cognitively aware of their condition.

Orbital lesions may also cause *euphoric syndrome*, a condition characterized by an abnormally high level of drive and initiative in the unregulated pursuit of reward. Such patients are highly distractible, hypersexual, lacking any concern for moral constraints or even elementary ethical principles. Some of these symptoms resemble those caused by damage to the amygdala, which, as we have seen, is strongly interconnected with the lateral orbital cortex. Indeed, damage to the lateral orbital cortex, like damage to the amygdala, has profound, though slightly different, effects on social behavior.

In the guessing game of life the orbital cortex is critical to the acquisition of appropriate social behavior. So what happens when a very young, preoperational child is deprived of the ability to predict outcome? Alternatively, what happens in the life of an adult human when he or she is similarly deprived?

By virtue of the orbital cortex each child is guided by a prevailing emotional and cognitive premonition of reward and punishment. From the preoperational phase of early childhood, the conceptual representations of the social mind begin to establish the foundation of the psychological, social and moral principles of its host society. These foundations become deeply and probably structurally entrenched in the social mind, exerting their influence throughout the entire life of the individual. Our psychosocial conditioning and our attendant moral reasoning depend very much on the predictive capacities of the orbital cortex. Consequently, when children younger than 16 months suffer damage to the orbital cortex the effect on their social development is dramatic. Even at a young age their behavior is characterized by an indifference to punishment, a high level of aggressive and antisocial behavior, the absence of feelings of guilt and a lack of empathy for others. As adults they engage in moral reasoning only at a very simplistic level typical of that attained by a normal 10 year old. Without the guiding influence of anticipatory feelings, the social mind is only weakly driven towards the establishment of moral principles. Biologically and cognitively indifferent to others, the emergent individual operates on rudimentary social strategies that are strongly orientated towards self-gratification. In this they resemble true psychopaths.

Things are very different when a normal adult is permanently deprived of feelings of rightness and wrongness. By adulthood, the human mind has been engaged for many years in moral reasoning and is therefore already highly conditioned to the mores of its host society. The adult human harbors all manner of beliefs that enable him or her to operate effectively within their society. These mores exist as deep-seated mental constructs within the mind of the individual. They are therefore unaffected by any subsequent damage to the orbital cortex. The adult who suffers orbital damage retains his social conditioning and his powers of moral reasoning. The most significant change is that now he is no longer able to intuitively sense which course of action is right and which is wrong. The inability of the patient to recognize angry faces is only part of this phenomenon. In general, with the loss of the orbital cortex, the substrate for forming associative memories of threatening or inviting circumstances is lost. There remain only the transient experiences of pleasure and pain and the emotional and cognitive machinery that will orientate behavior towards reward. Driven to seek reward, the emergent individual is shallow, impulsive, indifferent and irresponsible. Yet his comprehension of morality is untouched, his cognitive constructs of right and wrong still preserved within his social mind. This curious condition has been aptly named *acquired psychopathy*.

When the orbital cortex is removed, our thought processes are largely dissociated from the anticipation of emotional states that normally guides the formation of our behavioral strategies. Yet the mind remains strongly interconnected with the anterior cingulate gyrus, the source of both motivation and our primary emotions. In the absence of the orbital cortex, the emotional centers have an unfettered influence over the mind and so, at a strategic level, behavior. Without the regulatory influences of anticipation, the orbital patient remains insensitive to threats of social ostracization and even physical punishment, typically displaying a wanton, undivided self-interest.

The Loss of Wrongness

"Good men and bad men differ from each other in their natures. Bad men do not recognize a sinful act as sinful; if its sinfulness is brought to their attention, they do not cease doing it and do not like to have anyone inform them of their sinful acts. Wise men [good men?] are sensitive to right and wrong; they cease anything as soon as they see that it is wrong; they are grateful to anyone who calls their attention to such wrongful acts." From: Society for the Promotion of Buddhism. "The Teachings of Buddha: The Way of Purification." Chapter 1: The Way of Practice, Section II: *The Good Way of Behavior*. Kosaido Printing Co., Ltd., Tokyo, Japan, 1996.

Flattering, impulsive, irresponsible, manipulative, shallow, promiscuous and charming, the true psychopath lacks empathy, compassion and caring. Flat of mood (athymia), the psychopath searches out the bizarre, trapped in a never-ending quest for emotional arousal and reward. They take more risks than others, show no mercy to the opposition and, when intelligent, are careful to appear beyond reproach in their public dealings. Many are attracted to drugs, their intake exceeding that of normal drug users.

Estimates of the frequency of psychopathy vary from 1 to 4% of the general population. There is general agreement that a higher proportion of males than females are psychopaths. The disproportionate number of male psychopaths may have some relationship to the "warrior gene", MAOA that appears to be related to abnormal levels of aggression in males (*Commanding Aggression and Fear*: Chapter 4: Section 4). Because they are typically free from depression and rarely suicidal, psychopaths seldom seek professional help, many remaining *incognito* for their entire life. As a consequence of their self-serving orientation, they are often found amongst the most successful groups; a recent survey in the United Kingdom revealed that almost 1 in 6 managers (17%) fulfilled the criteria of psychopathy.

True psychopathy often manifests in early childhood, indicating that it reflects a possibly inherent malfunction in areas of the brain that serve mood, emotion and the social mind. Psychopathic children have difficulty in recognizing sad and fearful expressions but are able to identify expressions of happiness, disgust, surprise and anger. They are also impaired in identifying sad, but not fearful, vocal tones. In psychopaths, facial expressions that indicate emotional distress fail either to activate the amygdala or to produce the angst we would expect in a normal individual. Normally our brain verifies the identity of familiar people by conjuring up our feelings towards their image. As part of the process of empathy our brain attempts to recreate within us the feelings of the other, by appropriately activating our emotional centers. Both the psychopathic child and the psychopathic adult are unable to do this. Consequently, empathy for the despair and fear being experienced by others is completely missing.

The psychopath has always been a favorite character in the theatre and stories. The unusual mindset of the psychopath adds greatly to intrigue. Their irrepressible need for excessive stimulation guarantees that they will arouse an audience. Indeed, the psychopath often indulges in public behavior that would embarrass most ordinary people. Normal people also occasionally need the excitement of transgressing social boundaries. However, without indulgence in the bizarre, and at times the macabre, the life of a psychopath is a somewhat monotonous confinement to the realms of thought. Asked how she felt about losing access rights to her young child, a young female psychopath could only answer, without a trace of maternal distress, that she was angry. There is little doubt that in the absence of the confusing, yet evocative influence of mood, the psychopath can maintain focus on logical objectives more easily than can the ordinary person, whose thoughts are always subject to the turbulences of emotion and mood.

To know personally, psychopaths are, at first, wonderfully refreshing. They seem attentive and understanding and they may linger in one's entourage for many years. More than anything they are masters and mistresses of flattery. He who is easily charmed, she who has a thirst for compliments is easy prey for the psychopath. The psychopath worms his way into the depths of the victim's personal or business life, nonchalantly transgressing all social mores, therein to take whatever is the object of his desire. As one weary victim of a psychopath wrote; "we traveled together and we traveled first class". The psychopath adheres to that fundamental strategy of good business practice, that the victor does not destroy the enemy's empire but instead waits until the time is right to usurp it for his own use.

Psychopaths are ardent seekers of sexual partners. Devoted to the augmentation of pleasure, they are typically experienced and provocative lovers. Insensitive to darkness, the psychopath can see in the loss of love only the potentially exciting toil of having to replace the object that facilitated his or her access to reward.

The behavioral strategies of psychopaths reflect a conditioned mind that is relatively unfettered by moral principles. Compared to ordinary people, psychopaths are insensitive to social reprimand or physical punishment, a characteristic which ensures that they are also always indifferent to the future consequences of their actions. If the incentive is there they may learn rules about specific situations. For example, they may cognitively learn not to try to seduce the wife of a particular friend but be unable to apply this learning to other couples. Without an intrinsic feeling of wrongness, the mind of the psychopath is not motivated to generalize about social mores. Each antisocial behavior must be approached as a separate, independent and essentially cognitive issue.

In normal people punishment can reinforce their feeling of wrongness. Punishment can to some degree sensitize the lateral orbital cortex. Not so in the psychopath. Supplied with a set of buttons, some of which deliver an unpleasant electric shock, normal volunteers rapidly learn not to press those buttons that evoke pain. Placed in the same situation, the psychopath does not learn to avoid the punishing buttons. For the psychopath, pain seems to be a transient if unpleasant sensation that, lacking anticipatory significance, is without relevance to the future. To the psychopath, punishment is largely ephemeral.

Although the psychopath lacks the feeling of wrongness associated with the lateral orbital cortex, his ability to predict reward, associated with the medial orbital cortex remains intact. When the medial orbital cortex is damaged, patients manifest apathy, irritability, indecisiveness, low emotional expressiveness, poor judgment and planning, lack of initiation, persistence and insight and socially inappropriate behavior. These symptoms are quite different from those seen in psychopathy. For instance, damage to the medial orbital cortex does not significantly decrease a person's ability to empathize with others. Their behavior is actually the antithesis of the high levels of drive, initiative, decisiveness and the reduction of irritability that characterize both euphoria and the psychopathic state. It seems that the medial orbital cortex generates the feeling of rightness that is critical to motivating reward-orientated behavior (Figure 5.7).

In the arena of psychiatric research great effort is being made to discover a cure for debilitating psychiatric conditions like schizophrenia and depression. New drugs that may push the aberrant psyche towards normalcy are constantly being sought. Not so for the psychiatric condition of psychopathy. Psychopaths rarely complain about their condition, seeking psychiatric help only when they recognize that their behavior has repeatedly been the cause of their persecution. However, there has been little interest in developing drugs to alter their psyche towards that of normal humans. Even if effective drugs were developed it is unlikely that the successful, non-violent psychopath could be persuaded to take them in order for he or she to take their rightful place next to the normal rank and file. Even if a "cure" were developed, the true psychopath, newly able to sense the feeling of wrongness, would still have to learn the moral codes that previously were without emotional significance. Diagnosis and treatment in very young children whose psychosocial conditioning is still incomplete perhaps holds the only hope. If treated when very young, the would-be psychopath might be moved to learn the moral codes that are so conspicuously absent from the mind of the typical psychopathic adult.

The Evolution of Inhumanity
"Human beings are like parts of a body, created from the same essence. When one part is hurt and in pain the others cannot remain in peace and be quiet. If the misery of others leaves you indifferent and with no feelings of sorrow, you cannot be called a human being." Abū Muslih bin Abdallāh Shīrāzī (1184-1283/1291). Persian Poet and Mystic.

Anthropologists have proposed that humans are best suited to communities of around 150 people. Beyond this number the social constraints on the behavior of individuals become increasingly weakened. The Yanomamo Indians of Brazil and Venezuela live in villages of 100 to 300 individuals. If the population increases above that level, the village divides into smaller groups. Likewise the Indians of British Columbia and California lived in communities of 30 to 400 people while the North Koreans formed villages of around 100 people. The social constraints that limit behavior within small communities are not sufficiently pervasive to regulate behavior in communities of 500 or more, without the emergence of authoritarian officials. Much the same picture is seen in some chimp communities that attack and take over neighboring communities until the number of individuals exceeds the network of social constraints and the community fragments.

It is likely that all human communities in prehistoric times were small in size. Within such communities the psychopathic personality may have had an important role to play in defense and leadership. It is easy to see how - fearless, remorseless, clear thinking and ever orientated towards reward and arousal - the male psychopath could easily attain power within a small community. Devoid of altruistic concerns, the psychopathic leader might take more than his share of women, food and possessions, yet still be of overall benefit to the community. If we settle on the lowest estimate that of the general population, only 1% are psychopaths, then a community of 200 people would contain only 2 psychopaths. While their indifference to the consequences of their actions might precipitate early death, their sexual promiscuity would greatly increase the survival of their genes and so the preservation of antisocial behavior within the host society. As they are in many ways the antithesis of the depressed individual, the preservation of genes that maximize the feeling of rightness over the feeling of wrongness might be advantageous in reducing the number of people suffering from unipolar depression. So what if in the process of aggressive leadership the psychopath rides roughshod over his own people? What leader takes only his equal share? What rich man can say that he has not left 100 men a little poorer? Many world leaders past and present are known for their callousness, cruelty and a lack of remorse and empathy – characteristics that perfectly fit that *virtual individual*, the wholly profit-motivated, modern multinational corporation. Where there is the thrill of power and opportunity for boundless reward, there too can be found the reassuring words of the psychopath.

In the modern world psychopaths must play a very different role. With a population around 308 million, one can estimate that the USA must contains around 3 million psychopaths. In such a vast complexly interwoven, controlled and regulated society, there are few ways that the psychopathic mind can be of service. Deprived of the aggressive outlets of pillaging other tribes and hunting, the modern psychopath can only satiate his need for arousal and reward by perpetrating his antisocial acts upon his fellows. With a fully functional mind, focused on the service of self, freed from all feelings of wrongness, the modern psychopath is unquestionably the most dangerous creature on Earth.

The Origins of Evil

"This official told me all these details were matters of nightly discussion at the headquarters of the [Turkish] Union and Progress Committee. Each new method of inflicting pain was hailed as a splendid discovery, and the regular attendants were constantly ransacking their brains in the effort to devise some new torment. He told me that they delved into the records of the Spanish Inquisition and other historic institutions of torture and adopted all the suggestions found there. He did not tell me who carried off the prize in this gruesome competition, but common reputation throughout Armenia gave pre-eminence infamy to Djevdet Bey…who had invented what was perhaps the masterpiece of all – that of nailing horseshoes to the feet of his Armenian victims." Henry Morgenthau, Sr. (1856-1946). Businessman and US Ambassador to Ottoman Empire.

The Russian Nobel Laureate, Alexander Solzhenitsyn (1918-2008) called his account of the first level of Russian detention camps, The First Circle. For Solzhenitsyn this was the first ring of Dante's Hell, the first step towards the soviet Gulag, a realm of death and torment that in the name of political ideology enabled a psychopathic dictator to slowly terminate an estimated sixty two million Russian lives. In artistic expression, the link between social, psychological and physical paths to darkness has not gone unnoticed. Yet in Hiëronymus Bosch's pictures it is not people who are doing the butchering. In his imagination the tormentors are not humans but demons. His inference is clearly that humans do not do such things, that evil is not the natural way of humankind. In Bosch's paintings darkness is a human experience not a human action. His perpetrators of darkness are not of this Earth, they are elements of his imagination, things that lurk in the shadows of the normal psyche. They are our fear of the bottomless cliff, of the shadowy movements in the murky ocean depths, of being eaten alive by animals. In their anonymity, Bosch's demons are the very essence of our dread and as such the ever-present denizens of our own psyche. It is, however, human beings, and not imaginary demons, that torture, maim and kill other human beings. As reflected in our mythologies, our brief history and our art for all to see, it is a simple fact that many of us participate in the ruthless maiming and killing our own kind.

As the original psychology and the oldest source of myth, religions are obliged to provide at least a metaphorical construct of the human psyche. Because of this, most religions associate the experience of darkness either with a hostile physical place or the diabolical nature of an invented deity or evil spirit. However, in the absence of a real cause, evil always becomes synonymous with evildoers who are, through the neural processes that govern empathy, always defined as those who are different. In one sense it matters not whether we choose to symbolize our knowing of darkness as an imaginary land, an evil demon, or all those people who practice religions other than our own. What is really important for every human to understand is that the thoughts that fill their darkest moments are conjured by their own psyche. Such experiences may be precipitated by the action of others, but they are created, within us. In Tolkien's great fantasy *The Lord of the Rings*, the forces of good clash with the forces of darkness. Yet we would never think of praying to Tolkien's heroes to protect us from the ravages of the trolls and goblins that serve the dark lord, Sauron. Religious and mythological symbolism is meant to help us understand our own nature, not the nature of others. Indeed, this is the only wisdom they offer. Where is a God, a Yahweh, an Allah, a Jesus, a Krishna, a Buddha or any other diety that can protect you from yourself? We are our own joy as we are our own despair. To indiscriminately kill, maim and incarcerate others because we imagine them to be responsible for our darker moments is to turn away from life's journey towards self-awareness wherein we take personal responsibility for our moods, emotions and, most importantly, our beliefs. Symbolizing the elements of the human psyche, religion and mythology help us to understand life. In our journey of human existence, no responsibility leans more heavily upon each of us than the comprehension and management of our own psyche.

In Germany during the holocaust, Jews were publicly humiliated by being paraded through the streets wearing crude signs around their necks. In the death camps millions were mercilessly slaughtered. The relatively small concentration camp, Dachau, is only 10 miles from the city of Munich, yet it was the venue for the torture, human experimentation and extermination of an estimated 230,000 people. Certainly the people of Germany could not have been ignorant of what was happening within their country. The holocaust began as a macabre politically-motivated, theatre production with the express objective of utilizing societal denouncement, social degradation and the destruction of love in the perpetration of human suffering and death. Yet this very recent chapter of human history does not mean that prewar Germany had more than its share of psychopaths. The reason that a generation of Germans participated in the practice of genocide has nothing to do with the condition of psychopathy. What happened in Germany is no different to what has since happened in Cambodia, Tibet, Vietnam, Indonesia, Rwanda, Sudan, Congo, Ethiopia, Nigeria, Angola, Mozambique, Algiers, Korea, East Pakistan, Guatemala, Yugoslavia, East Timor, China, Afghanistan, Russia, Chechnya, Iran and Iraq or what has happened throughout history. Every nation of significant size, past and present, has had no difficulty in finding large number of citizens willing to participate in the most horrific crimes against humanity.

Odds are that, during the time of the Holocaust, the proportion of Germans who were psychopaths was no different from the proportion in any other country in either war or peace. The German people were simply prepared for such spectacles by the distribution of films and other propaganda purporting to show how the Jews lived in degrading circumstances, sharing their abodes with rats and other vermin. The understanding of thc holocaust and indeed all major crimes against humanity lies in appreciating the nature of the human mind. The same reason accounts for why Chinese people of today permit their government to murder, enslave, forcibly sterilize and torture the peaceful and reclusive Tibetan people while the powerful "civilized" western nations simply watch the ongoing atrocities. It is the same reason that the American people allowed its government, in the name of political ideology, to drop high explosives, carcinogenic defoliants and burning Napalm on defenseless Vietnamese villagers. It is the same reason that the British who first settled Australia hunted down the aboriginals. It is the same reason that caused them to take away the aboriginal children from their families to inflict upon them such a bewildering range of cruelties under the still touted guise of bringing them the so-called virtues of western civilization. The examples of such crimes against humanity are legion. All stem from the vulnerability of the human mind to governmental, societal, religious and parental conditioning.

To appreciate the power of conditioning, one need only imagine that as a young person, one was repeatedly told that all members of an identifiable group are no better than vermin. Imagine that each day your mentors, family and friends reinforce the idea that these people will sap the wealth of your country and seek to undermine all the values and laws that enable your prosperity and the survival of your children. Imagine that all the books to the contrary are burned and that all voices raised in protest are ruthlessly silenced. History tells us that the odds are 1,000 to 1 that unless you have learned the great lessons of existence, unless you understand the nature of the human mind, you will be easily led to play your part in the slaughter of this dangerous minority. Animal liberationists do not work in the abattoirs. Their conditioning is unsuitable for this job. Yet those that do are as completely human as are they. Nazism was not the vehicle of psychopathy but the result of the clever conditioning of the minds of the German people. In that age, there evolved in Germany a national cult that held genocide as an important and necessary agenda. A brilliant communicator with a high level of emotional intelligence, Hitler understood well that the mind is most at peace when it is presented with extremes. Extremes are easy to comprehend. A passionate man in his own right, he was well aware of the power of obsessional belief in directing human behavior. Hitler raised propaganda to a new level, setting an example of the power of societal conditioning which would become a model for the politically ambitious throughout the western world. No one now in power hesitates to use the proceeds of taxation to manipulate, through an increasingly obedient media, the beliefs and opinions of their people. Culprits are always required. It does not matter whether they are Communists, Jews, Christians, Muslims, Hindus, the unemployed, the politically rebellious, the conspicuously criminal or the users of drugs. The minds of the righteous are always available to be indoctrinated with the belief that there is an enemy scheming against the unquestionable ways of the present establishment.

For many people morality, rather than self-knowledge, always remains the great vehicle of life. All governments, societies and religions fear cults, because like cults, governments, societies and, alas, religions utilize their resources to condition the minds of their members, exhorting them to anticipate reward by taking action against those whom they are told may do them harm. It is unfortunate for humankind that, in combination with fear, the processes of education, logic and debate are such effective tools for turning the human mind against members of its own species. Where we might have anticipated freedom and generosity of spirit, the coercive activities of a selfish yet misguided minority have created throughout the entire world attitudes, policies and laws that have little relevance to the human condition.

Adventure is, within any realm of behavior, something that stirs our moods. In the sterility of modern civilization, within our rule bound, repressed, economically enslaved, urban societies, the mind waits to be filled with whatever arrives at its door. Many innocent activities that once provided an exciting and healthy outlet for our cerebral energies are now illegal. Small wonder that stymied at every turn by aggressive, money hungry bureaucracies, young people are drawn to vandalism, violent computer games, drugs, gang violence and suicide. Small wonder that we elect leaders who have never in their lives known thrills that lie beyond political graft, wealth, power and coercion. Our theatres, books, music and computer games are filled with images of aggression, cruelty and death and yet are, as often as not, marketed under the guise of being adult fairytales. The truth is that engaging in such nonsense is a modern person's way of getting the kicks that just staying alive once provided. Most people are prisoners of their work and their social enclave, their idle minds lying like loaded weapons waiting to be discharged in the service of whatever beliefs come their way, seeking always an opportunity to oppose and conquer an imaginary opposition. Modern education pays little heed to the importance of experiencing the arousal of mood. Yet arousal breathes life into the human spirit. In the words of the blind and deaf American author, Helen Keller (1957), "Life is either a daring adventure, or nothing." Tragically, our moods and the attendant feelings of rightness and wrongness that evolved to guide our thoughts have become the products of our thoughts. It is a scenario, in which bad things are simply bound to happen.

Chapter 5 - Diseases of Mood

Major Depressive Disorder - Life as a Lost Cause

"Three passions, simple but overwhelmingly strong, have governed my life: the longing for love, the search for knowledge, and the unbearable pity for the suffering of mankind." Bertrand Russell (1872-1970). British Logician, Historian, Philosopher and Nobel Laureate.

Aristotle is the first person on record to draw attention to the frequency of melancholia in artists, poets, statesmen and philosophers, giving the examples of Plato, Socrates and Empedocles. Today we know that at some time in their life, almost all humans suffer at least one episode of depression. In the USA alone 9 million people (3%) are chronically depressed. More than 2 million of these are children. Depression is one of the leading causes of disability throughout the world, yet even in western countries only half of those suffering from depression will seek help. Depending on whether one includes those suffering from milder forms of depression, 2 to 15% of depressed people commit suicide - a figure that is all the more frightening when one considers the old adage that many depressives are simply too demotivated and disorientated to organize the means of extinguishing themselves.

When we witness depression in another person, we see only the outside manifestation of their condition. From without, it is difficult for normal people to share the consistently negative thoughts that pervade the mind of the depressive or to empathize with the angst that wracks their body. At the level of both the mind and the body, depression effectively destroys any possibility of motivation. These symptoms are the moment-by-moment, hour-by-hour and day-by-day experience of the depressed. Particularly in the logically orientated West, few people see beyond the overt expression of depression and into the inner being where anxiety first takes hold. Yet the chronically depressed never doubt that the restless demons that plague each waking moment, eroding their self-esteem and shattering their relationships with workmates, family and friends, are an immutable part of their being. Where there was once an inner sanctum offering comfort and restoration, now there is only a darkness that traps all effort, negates every hope and instantly aborts those flights of fancy that so often lead to discovery and personal growth. In our outward life, we can move away from a threatening or painful situation or treat and care for a physical injury. It is, however, impossible to escape from that which is within. The deeply depressed are essentially anchored to a purgatory that is the creation of their own brain. The constitution of their world is no less than a covenant with doom.

Until the development of modern antidepressants, the lives of the chronically depressed must have been an unrelenting torment. In the past this state was given various names but today clinicians call it *major depressive disorder* or *unipolar depression*. Depression is a persistent state that can begin even in the preoperational phase of childhood. Unlike the depressed adult, the depressed preoperational child is less likely to attribute their state to the practical or abstract aspects of life and more likely to see its origins to be within the psychosocial domain, as is so often portrayed in the darker aspects of children's stories. Tragically even very young children appear to have a rudimentary awareness that the monster lives, not in the outside world, but in the ether of experience - one troubled 4 year old confiding to his mother, that "today is going to be a black day."

Depression afflicts people in a quantitatively graded manner. In some people, depression is a tolerable aura of gloom, manifesting as a persistent pessimism that casts a shadow across every idea and circumstance. To others depression is a lifelong sentence to the netherworld. For them the mere thought of arising from bed may precipitate feelings of nausea, demanding the absolute commitment of a mind that knows only defeat. There is no escape, no light on the horizon and no hope that action could possibly bring a better tomorrow. Indeed, the mind of the depressive is often so crowded with pessimism and doubt that even imagining joy is impossible. Deep depression is a state wherein the only faith is in the absolute certainty of failure.

The depressed person is pervaded by the sense of being an ineffectual recipient of life. Unassertive and timid, there evolves a taciturn bitterness that can easily flare into an unsustainable aggressiveness. However, alongside these traits, depressives are well equipped to empathize with the negative feelings of others. Thus, they are often kind, patient and understanding, believing, quite incorrectly, that for others, life is also a process of unrelenting psychic toil. Sadly they receive little reward for their efforts, as generally these transient acts of compassion and caring are negated because of the depressive's inability to empathize with the positive and so share in the joyous and unfettered companionship that characterize the relationships between normal individuals. To empathasize with the deeply depressed is to share in their doom and despair.

In past times, the deeply depressed languished within their family homes or were locked away to die prematurely in the obscurity of physical and mental isolation. Now, as a direct result of scientific research, many new varieties of antidepressants are being developed. The pharmacologist, the clinician and the chemist now know exactly what brain systems to target in designing drugs that are useful in the fight against darkness. In this endeavor, the first clue was that the cortex of depressed individuals who had committed suicide contained abnormally low levels of a neurotransmitter called serotonin (also called 5HT for 5-hydroxytryptamine). Serotonin comes from nerve cells located in the ancient core of the brain (the brainstem). These neurons, send their processes to, and secrete serotonin over, all parts of the cortex. Although serotonin is a single substance, it can affect neurons in many different ways. While its role in sleep, movement and bodily sensation is understood, the exact way serotonin influences mood is still unknown. What is known is that increasing its levels in the brain by prolonging its presence relieves depression in many sufferers. The drugs that do this are called *selective serotonin reuptake inhibitors* or *SSRIs*. Today 10% of people in the USA (30 million people) are on SSRIs. Many of the SSRIs are notorious for repression of libido, an affect that seems to stem from an associated decrease in the sensitivity of the skin, particularly that of the genitals. So pronounced is this effect that some experience a general decrease in the desire for bodily contact. It is of the greatest concern that some SSRIs, while alleviating depression, ultimately negate our desire to physically embrace and thereby bond with our fellow human beings.

Depression runs in families and its genetical origin carries an ominous message for human society. While it is arguable that seeking ways to annul the tyranny of depression is amongst the most humanitarian of goals, this process has the deleterious effect of radically increasing the probability of depressives forming stable relationships and producing children. Only one hundred years ago the deeply depressed were often isolated in institutions. Today, our newfound ability to pharmacologically treat depression has (as with several other psychiatric conditions) inevitably increased the likelihood of the genes responsible for this condition being passed on to the next generation. Ironically this will lead to an increased future demand for antidepressants, thereby ensuring an ever-expanding market for pharmaceutical manufacturers.

It is extraordinary that while 30 million Americans use SSRIs, only 9 million are on record as being chronically depressed. That 21 million Americans who do not qualify as chronically depressed, are on antidepressants, perhaps underscores a natural desire to be insulated even from the suffering that is a normal part of existence. This perspective raises two issues relating to the treatment of depression. Firstly, it must be asked whether antidepressants should be used to desensitize people to personal tragedy. Even in the knowledge that depression decreases motivation, it is arguable that negating bad feelings might usurp the impetus of a person to attempt to change their circumstances. Secondly, depression is the universal form of punishment utilized by all societies. The intimate relationship between mental and physical suffering essentially means that both incarceration and corporal punishment effectively create psychological darkness. This is the unspoken intention of the perpetrators who, in their grisly task, represent the host society. Darkness is darkness. Ultimately, there can be no other source of punishment. Between 1978 and 2003, one thousand and twelve male prisoners in English and Welsh prisons committed suicide - approximately 5 times the rate within the general male population. The whole issue of psychiatric illness in the prison setting is a massive quandary. At huge cost, all societies feel compelled to incarcerate a significant percentage of their members, only a few of whom are so dangerous that they need to be isolated from society. The creation of depression and fear is the unspoken goal. Indeed, it is this very state that drives inmates to procure, against all odds, illegal hedonic drugs that for a short while release them from the mental anguish of a completely unnatural, harsh and often cruel existence. Yet just as depression can be annulled pharmacologically, so too can create it be created. The massive psychological and societal damage resulting from incarceration has never been addressed. When it is, then, callous though it may sound, one might imagine a time when prisons are abolished and would-be prisoners maintained in a physically free but depressed state by regular treatment with appropriate doses of depressive agents. Ironically depression is the only psychiatric condition that lends itself to what many see as a means of dealing with those whose actions and ideas contravene the beliefs and personal objectives of the ruling sectors of society.

Not all chronic depressives respond to SSRIs and substantial efforts have been made to target other regulatory neurotransmitter systems that are also conspicuously involved in mood. The most prominent of these are *dopamine* and *noradrenalin* (*norepinephrine*). Amphetamine and cocaine have long been known to enhance mood and both increase the levels of these neurotransmitters. Unfortunately both are highly addictive and in higher doses psychologically damaging. Dopamine is released over the entire prefrontal cortex following activation of a potent reward center, the *ventral tegmental area*, while noradrenalin is released throughout the nervous system, including the entire cortex, following activation of a center that controls our level of vigilance, the *locus coeruleus*. Dopamine levels decrease with age and it has been said that if we all lived long enough we would die eventually from Parkinson's disease - a condition resulting from the chronic loss of dopamine. The rate of decrease in dopamine with age varies between individuals in relation to our individual, genetic constitution. As our levels of dopamine decrease we progressively lose our playfulness as well as our ability to be peacefully happy. With the loss of noradrenalin, as with aging, we become lethargic and unvigilant. Antidepressants that increase the amount of noradrenalin and dopamine are thus proving to be particularly effective in treating depression in the aged. While there can be no doubt that use of antidepressants helps preserve deleterious genes, at the personal level the opportunity to evoke joy where once there was only suffering, remains an irresistible temptation to both the altruistically and the economically ambitious.

Bipolar Disease - Life on the Extremities
"Men ought to know that from nothing else but the brain come joys, delights, laughter and sports, and sorrows, griefs, despondency, and lamentations.... And by the same organ we become mad."   Hippocrates of Kos (c. 460 BC - c. 370 BC), Greek Physician.

Bipolar disorder or *manic-depressive illness* produces distortions of mood and chronic disruption of the capacity for rational thought - symptoms that not infrequently lead to behavior that is unacceptable to both the society and the afflicted. While the manic phase of bipolar disorder is the only psychiatric condition to confer advantage and pleasure, the condition inevitably brings unendurable suffering that frequently erodes the will to live. Like many highly creative people, the life of the composer Schumann was punctuated by years of extraordinary creativity interspaced between years of severe depression and suicide attempts before he died of self-starvation in an asylum.

Bipolar disorder is characterized by episodes of mania, depression and a mixed state. Depressive and mixed episodes are more common in women than men. In the mixed state, depressed mood coexists with aspects of mania. Thus, the patient manifests the loss of appetite, agitation and inability to sleep characteristic of mania and yet is consumed by suicidal thoughts characteristic of depression. In addition, between the periods of disturbed moods there are often periods of stable mood (euthymia). Even for people of stable mood, negotiating life is often a challenging enterprise. The manic-depressive must meet the same challenges of human existence but in doing so is obliged to operate from a center that can rapidly switch between two radically different states.

In the USA 2.3 million people (0.8%) suffer from bipolar disorder or manic-depressive illness. The condition is equally common in men and women and, having a strong genetical basis, tends to run in families. Nearly 20 percent of cases of bipolar disorder lead to suicide, making it the second leading killer of young women and the third of young men. For those that survive, the condition often chronically disrupts work, education, family and social life.

Bipolar disorder typically appears in early and mid-life. One author, commented that as an elementary school child she could not understand why she was sometimes the life of the party and yet, on other days, avoided speaking to anyone, instead spending her lunch hours standing against a cold brick wall. When the illness begins before or early in adolescence, it manifests with symptoms typical of either *attentional deficit hyperactivity disorder* (ADHD) or *conduct disorder*. However, when it begins in late adolescence or adulthood, the first signs are usually a classic manic episode that recurs between periods of normal mood.

For many, manic-depression is a totally debilitating condition. As we have seen, mood operates through the emotional centers that, in turn, have a powerful influence over our thought processes. This sequence ensures that both thought and behavior are appropriate as long as mood is confined within normal limits. Only when the highs are too high and the lows are too low does it become impossible to sustain normal thought patterns. Consequently, the manic and depressive phases of bipolar disorder are associated with grandiose thoughts and the ideation of total worthlessness, respectively. These irrational and obsessive thought patterns often become associated with hallucinations (seeing, hearing or otherwise sensing things that are not there) and delusions (defects in the thought process that lead to deficits in judgment, insight and reality testing) indicative of psychosis.

The critical criterion for diagnosing bipolar disorder is the occurrence of periods of mania and depression coexisting with periods of normal mood. However, although the term bipolar implies switching between high and low mood, certain forms of bipolar disorder show powerful biases towards either mania or depression. Thus, some patients suffer oscillations of mood that range between euthymia and deep depression while in others mood cycles between euthymia and full-blown mania. The frequency of mood swings also varies enormously, the time between episodes ranging from 48 hours to many years. Generally, however, the cycle length varies more between different patients than it does within a single individual.

While mild mood swings are generally manageable, the psychotic symptoms of patients with severe mood swings are often accompanied by feelings of being out of control. Severe mood swings are considered symptomatic of *bipolar I disorder* whereas less severe but abnormally large mood swings, are defined as *bipolar II disorder*. Whilst the unmanageable highs of bipolar I disorder constitute mania, the more manageable highs of bipolar II disorder are referred to as *hypomania*. No equivalent distinction is made between the lows of bipolar I and bipolar II disorder, although case histories indicate that the depth of depression associated with the former consistently exceeds that associated with the latter.

Hypomania manifests as increased energy, mild euphoria, optimism, a decreased need for sleep, racing thoughts, pressured speech, irritability, intrusiveness, increased social and sexual activity, grandiose thinking and enhanced religiosity. It is never associated with the hallucinations so indicative of schizophrenia or the delusions psychosis. Indeed, in a curious way, hypomanics are blessed. Ever alert and active the hypomanic feels more and sees more than ordinary people. While the range of their mood exceeds the normal range, this does not prevent them from living within society. On the contrary, hypomanics often profit economically and socially from their exaggerated optimism, drive and intensity even though their highly exploratory nature drives them to cross normal social boundaries and risk being shunned by the more conservative members of family and society.

As high achievers, many hypomanics have found a place in history to which they have contributed both color and genius. So it is that amongst the famous and the fascinating, as amongst the rich and powerful, are many who fulfill the criteria for hypomania. Winston Churchill, Theodore Roosevelt and Benito Mussolini are commonly cited in psychology texts as high achievers driven by the vagaries of mood. Wherever one finds amongst the successful and famous evidence of charisma and astounding energy interspersed with periods of flatness or despair, one may suspect the presence of hypomania.

The danger of hypomania is that the flights of fancy it generates can inspire exploration beyond the limits of ordinary people. Thus, the domestic lives of many hypomanics are filled with bizarre twists that can ostracize family, friends and society, leaving a legacy of many skeletons in as many closets. Energetic, volatile, lovable, irritable and unpredictable, the hypomanic can offend and yet enchant us with a vigor, stamina and purpose not found in the mundane world of mortal beings.

When such oscillations occur with a periodicity of several days, a person is said to have a *cyclothymic personality*. Although, in this condition, mood swings are not as severe as in bipolar I disorder, their relatively high frequency brings its own set of problems. In the period of a few hours or less the cyclothymic personality can move from abnormally positive mood to abnormally negative mood. For no apparent reason the individual is suddenly thrown into disillusionment and anxiety - a circumstance that usually induces them to vent their new found angst on friends and family and to see conspiracy and threat in the most innocent circumstances. Because of their anger, cyclothymics can be physically dangerous and, on occasion, this has led to them being mistakenly diagnosed as psychopaths. However, the cyclothymic person is not in the least psychopathic. Unlike the psychopath, the cyclothymic clearly suffers and consequently is able to empathize with the suffering in others. Furthermore, unlike the psychopath, the cyclothymic is generally responsive to, social mores. Nevertheless to their family, friends and workmates, the unmedicated cyclothymic presents an insurmountable challenge. No more than a careless word can cause the curtailment of a long-planned venture or the instant resignation from a previously coveted position. Nothing is more heart rending than to watch a loved one moved to such angst and anger that all that is sacred in their life becomes threatened. The spirited, positive person suddenly evaporates into thin air to be replaced by an uncompromising tyrant.

One story tells of a car salesman, who revealed his condition by breaking all sales records during his positive days, while on his bad days he dismissed the customers as troublesome fools. Without medication the cyclothymic's life is a litany of interpersonal disasters studded with euphoric times of great intensity and above average achievement.

For years, researchers had little success in developing a treatment of bipolar disorders. This situation changed with the discovery that a simple salt, *lithium sulfate*, markedly stabilized mood. Unfortunately, high doses of lithium induce lethargy and obesity. Careful and regular measurement of the level of lithium in the patient's blood helps minimize these problems and enables many to lead relatively normal lives. Increasingly, the newer antidepressants are also being used in combination with mood stabilizers such as lithium. A curious and potentially instructive observation is that 75% of unusually creative bipolar patients continued to be productive following stabilization of their mood fluctuations with lithium.

Unfortunately people suffering from bipolar disease are notorious for self-medicating and approximately 60% indulge in illegal recreational drugs amongst which only cannabis has potentially beneficial effects. They are also prone to modifying their own dosage of lithium, sometimes with disastrous results. Despite the curtailment of darkness, the flights of mood experienced by normal people must seem, to the controlled bipolar, a poor substitute for the liberation of mania. "I like my highs" is a not uncommon utterance.

Where clinical intervention is necessary, the earliest treatment of a psychiatric condition is always preferable. Everyone becomes addicted to their behavioral routines irrespective of whether these have good or bad outcomes. Once we have learned a musical instrument or mastered a sport, the sequences of movements are ours for life. In just the same way the mind becomes programmed to accommodate behavioral idiosyncrasies that reflect the predisposition of our moods and emotions. If the mood fluctuations of the bipolar patient are left untreated until late in life, there will remain within the mind all the behavioral subroutines that have helped that person justify, cover and survive the personal, social and physical ravages of unstable mood. The adult mind is, alas, powerfully resistant to reprogramming. For this reason, counseling can play a critical role alongside the pharmacological treatment of a persistent mood disorder.

Attempts to understand the anatomical and physiological causes of mood instability have revealed abnormalities within the emotional centers and the orbital cortex. For example, the size of the anterior cingulate gyrus is reduced in bipolar patients, while in the manic phase of bipolar disorder, the lateral orbital cortex that normally signals the need for restraint, is inactive. In normalcy, fluctuations of mood appear to be determined by the mutual inhibitory interactions between the anterior cingulate and the amygdala. Systems that inhibit one another are intrinsically inclined to oscillate. However, in systems as complex as the amygdala and the anterior cingulate such oscillations may not be strictly cyclical. Instead this system may, in some instances, produce crude oscillations, while in others simply elicit the very occasional switching between one thymic pole and the other - an outcome that essentially describes the highly variable mood profile seen in bipolar disorder. While in normalcy the oscillations of mood are contained, a reduction in the power of one arm of the system might produce sufficient imbalance to ensure the irregular, if not cyclical, switching of mood. The anatomically smaller anterior cingulate in bipolar patients could provide just such an imbalance in the mutual inhibitory coupling between the anterior cingulate and the amygdala that normally ensures stable mood.

Obsessions, Compulsions and Personality
"Habit and routine have an unbelievable power to destroy." Henri de Lubac (1896-1991). French Jesuit Priest.

Bipolar disorder and major depressive disorder are classical mood disorders in that they arise directly from malfunction of neural systems that elaborate mood. There are, however, several serious behavioral anomalies that are not conspicuously associated with aberrant mood but are nevertheless the result of imperfections in the emotional centers and the orbital cortex. The two most significant of these are *obsessive-compulsive disorder* (OCD) and *dissociative identity disorder* (DID) or as it is also called *multiple personality disorder* (MPD). So far, attempts to use brain imaging to reveal the origins of these conditions have been only marginally successful. This is primarily because they are not restricted to thymic or emotional centers, but involve, in addition, the participation of the mind. Thus, OCD involves obsessions in the form of disturbing thoughts and the compulsive performance of rituals believed to be essential for survival. Similarly, although DID is thought to be the product of emotional trauma in childhood, it too manifests through the mind as two or more distinct cognitive constructs of self-identity.

Although little is known about these conditions, it does seem that they arise largely because of the predictive influence of the orbital cortex over our thought processes. For example, patients with OCD are driven by a persistent fear of negative outcomes. Consequently, some are obsessed with germs or dirt to the extent that they need to repeatedly wash. Others feel an irrepressible need to repeatedly check or count things, or live in trepidation that they have harmed someone close to them. While in normalcy ordinary people find achieving a goal to be a rewarding experience, OCD patients simply refocus their angst on another problem. The OCD patient is obliged to live with a nagging, paranoid concern that, while evocative of thought, is itself resistant to all reason. It is easy to appreciate how such symptoms could result from hyperactivity of the lateral orbital cortex or malfunction of the balance between the amygdala and the anterior cingulate - brain systems that often function abnormally in OCD patients.

In 1973 a hugely successful, made-for-television movie called *Sybil* portrayed the life of a shy female graduate student who was diagnosed with MPD. At that time, less than 50 cases of MPD associated with child abuse had been reported. By 1994 this number had risen to an astonishing 40,000 cases made up of 97% females and 97% Caucasian. In 2004 subsequent research showed that MPD, or DID, is rarely if ever caused by childhood trauma but that it is best understood as a culturally-bound and often *iatrogenic* (Greek; *iatros*, 'healer or physician' and *gennan*, 'a product of') condition. Today, it is increasingly appreciated that the origin of the traumatic memories experienced by at least some DID patients are the result of suggestions made by their therapist whom they may have initially consulted about minor problems such as anxiety or stress. It seems that the guided-imagery and reenactments used to recover would-be repressed memory traces actually create *de novo* catastrophic emotional memories. Driven by a strongly conditioned mind these "memories" take up occupancy in the emotional centers and the previously normal patient begins to suffer from post-traumatic stress disorder (PSTD) related to events that never actually took place (*The Ravages of Emotional Memory*: Chapter 5: Section 4).

When it does appear, DID does not manifest as a thymic or emotional deficit but is instead revealed by the emergence of one or more personas that are fundamentally different from the normally prevailing personality of the individual. In a great majority of cases, the triggering factor is childhood sexual abuse or, as we must now posit, the iatrogenic consolidation of the belief that childhood sexual abuse occurred. An understanding of the neurological origins of DID can result from an appreciation of the response of the orbital cortex to turmoil in the psychosocial world of the developing child. As the social mind develops, its most critical task is to create an effective model of ongoing interpersonal relationships. It is therefore critical that the adults with whom the child bonds do not exploit the trust implicit in normal parent-child relations. When instead the person who normally provides warmth, food and shelter becomes the source of physical pain and psychological abuse, there is complete disruption of the conditioning of the social mind. In the loving scenario, the appearance of the parent naturally activates the *medial* orbital cortex that, in turn, elicits a *cognitive premonition of reward*. In total contrast, the appearance of the parent in the role of sexual abuser activates the *lateral* orbital cortex that, in turn, elicits a *cognitive premonition of pain and punishment*. Unfortunately the same parent usually plays the role of both loving carer and sexual abuser. Under these circumstances, it is simply impossible for the child's mind to create an internally consistent construct of parental identity. The result is that, in some sexually abused children, the cortex of the mind becomes divided into two or more operationally (and probably spatially) separate blocks or sets of modules, each of which has the capacity to sustain a different persona and each of which creates and retains exclusive access to two or more separate and distinctive sets of episodic memories (Figure 5.8). If only one additional persona is formed, it will be an essentially rudimentary representation of the persona adopted by the tormented child. Normally the main persona will continue to develop the complexities of a complete personality, often without any knowledge of the existence of the other. What is intended by nature to enable mood to influence behavior, in the face of parental sexual abuse, becomes the source of intense and lasting trauma.

Section 5: Recommended Reading

Blair, R., Mitchell, D. and Blair, K. *The Psychopath: Emotion and the Brain.* Wiley-Blackwell, Malden, Massachusetts, 2005.

Blessing W. *The Lower Brainstem and Bodily Homeostasis.* Oxford University Press, USA, 1997.

Casey, N. *Unholy Ghost: Writers on Depression.* Harper Perennial, New York, 2002.

Cleckley, H. M. *The Mask of Sanity: An Attempt to Clarify Some Issues About the So Called Psychopathic Personality.* 5th edition, Publisher Emily S. Cleckley, 1988.

Sargent, W. *Battle for the Mind.* Heinemann, London, 1957.

David-Neel, A. *Magic and Mystery in Tibet.* Book Tree, Escondido, 2000.

Davison, G. C. and Neale, J. M. *Abnormal Psychology: An Experimental Clinical Approach.* John Wiley and Son Inc, New York, 1982.

Damasio, A. R. *The Feeling of What Happens: Body and Emotion in the Making of Consciousness.* Harcourt Inc., New York, 1999.

Damasio, A. R. *Descartes' Error: Emotion, Reason and the Human Brain.* Harper Collins, New York, 2000.

Damasio, A. R. *Looking for Spinoza: Joy, Sorrow and the Feeling Brain.* Harcourt, New York, San Diego, 2003.

James, A. and Raine, J. *The New Politics of Criminal Justice.* Longman, Harlow, 1998.

Jamison, K. R. *An Unquiet Mind: A Memoir of Mood and Madness.* Vintage, New York, 1997.

Keller, H. *The Open Door.* Doubleday and Co, Garden City, 1957

LeDoux, J. *The Emotional Brain: The Mysterious Underpinnings of Emotional Life.* Simon and Schulster, New York, 1998.

Maiman, J. Poet. *Illness 1, Poems of a Manic Depressive.* Lone Oak Press Ltd. Rochester, Minnesota, 1992.

Melzack, R. and Wall, P. D. *The Challenge of Pain.* 1st Edition, Penguin Global, London, 2004.

Morris, D. B. *The Culture of Pain.* University of California Press, Los Angeles, Oxford, 1991.

Goodwin, F. K. and Jamison, K. R. *Manic-Depressive Illness.* Oxford University Press, New York, Oxford, 1990.

Hare, R. D. *Without Conscience: The Disturbing World of the Psychopaths Among Us.* 1st Edition, Guilford Press, New York, 1999.

Raine, A. *The Psychopathology of Crime: Criminal Behavior as a Clinical Disorder.* Academic Press, London, 1997.

Spira, J. L. *Treating Dissociative Identity Disorder.* Jossey-Bass, San Francisco, 1996.

Styron, W. *Darkness Visible.* Vintage Paperback, New York, 1992.

Society for the Promotion of Buddhism. "The Teachings of Buddha: The Way of Purification." Chapter 1: The Way of Practice, Section II: *The Good Way of Behavior.* Kosaido Printing Co., Ltd., Tokyo, Japan, 1996.

Solomon, A. *The Noonday Demon: An Atlas of Depression.* Scribner, New York, 2001.

Sims, A. *Symptoms of the Mind: As Introduction to Descriptive Psychopathology.* 2nd Edition, W.B. Saunders and Co., Ltd., 1995.

Wurtzel, L. E. *Prozac Nation.* Riverhead, Penguin, USA, 1994.

Zopa, Lama Rinpoche, Tibetian Buddhist Lama. From: *Transforming Problems into Happiness.* Wisdom Publications, Boston, 1993.

Section 6

The Origins of Thought and the Diversification of Culture

"God, at the beginning of time, created Heaven and Earth. Earth was still an empty waste, and darkness hung over the deep.... Then God said, Let there be light..... God said too, Let a solid vault arise amid the waters....a vault by which God would separate the waters which were beneath it from the waters above it.... This vault God called the Sky.... God said, Let the waters below the vault collect in the one place to make dry land appear....the dry land God called Earth, and the water, where it had collected, He called the Sea.... Let the Earth, He said, yield grasses that grow and seed.... God said, Let the waters produce moving things and winged things that fly above the Earth under the sky's vault.... And God said, Let us make man, wearing our own image and likeness; let us put him in command of the fishes in the sea, and all that flies through the air, and the creeping things that move on Earth. So God made man in His own image, made him in the image of God. Man and woman both, He created them...."

Book of Genesis, The Bible

Chapter 1 - The Beginnings of Knowledge

The Origins of Gentleness

"It has always been the business of the great seers to ..[recognize].. through the veil of nature ….. the radiance, terrible yet gentle, of the dark, unspeakable light beyond, and through their words and images, to reveal the sense of the vast silence that is the ground of us all and of all beings." Joseph Campbell (1904-1987). American Mythologist.

There was a time, a time even before the dreaming began, when reptiles dominated the Earth and plundered the sea where the fish had once ruled supreme - a time when the *Amphibia* found a precarious haven in the netherworld between land and water, a time, when the skies lay empty, waiting for the mutations that would give life wings and one day fill the world with the colored plumage of thousands of birds whose songs would greet the dawn and serenade the coming of night. Not even the flowering plants had evolved to beckon the *Insecta* with the flashing brilliance of their flowers and lure them with pungent odors to become the agents of their pollination. Massive dinosaurs lumbered through the cycad forests, rigid in their gait, like gigantic fighting machines preprogrammed to a mindless quest for visceral satiation. Beneath the rocks and ferns the smaller reptiles waited, frozen, alert and ready to strike or scurry to shelter from the tread of the passing giants. All behavior - terrestrial, amphibious and aquatic - was of the moment. All movement was stereotyped, conspicuous in purpose and revealing of a mechanistic core wherein neither compassion nor deliberation, were in the least evident.

Into this near robotic world emerged the first reptilian mutants to carry the traits of the as yet unborn mammal. With the mammalian condition, nature was experimenting with a new design wherein complex behavior rather than brawn, would be increasingly critical to survival. With the evolution of two new emotional centers (cingulate gyrus and insula), parental motivation to care for the young, would replace an outrageous level of fecundity, as the critical strategy for survival. However, more than just motivation would be required to achieve this goal of nurture. In addition to lacking the motivation to nurture their young, reptiles also lacked the mechanical finesse required to care for the delicate, struggling neonate. History records several instances of mammals successfully maintaining the basic needs of human infants. It is, however, hard to imagine a human child benefiting from the attentions of a dinosaur, a giant turtle or an anaconda. In the service of bonding and ultimately, the creation of the mammal, the archaic reptilian motor system required extensive modification commensurate with significant changes to the body and the brain. So it was that the slow but progressive evolution of the mammalian condition brought a new subtlety to animal motion wherein an almost infinite variety of smooth, constantly monitored actions replaced the rigid, centrally programmed repertoires of the reptiles. With the evolution of the mammals, the realm of animal movement gained a new grace. Gentleness had emerged as a significant aspect of life on Earth. Ultimately, fine motor control would serve many aspects of mammalian life, reaching its zenith in the unprecedented manipulative skills of the human being, skills that would enable expression of the vast creative potential of the human mind.

The Energy of Love

"To be surrounded by beautiful, curious, breathing, laughing flesh is enough…
I do not ask any more delight, I swim in it as a sea,
There is something in staying close to men and women and looking on them,
And in the contact and odor of them, that pleases the soul well,
All things please the soul, but these please the soul well."
Walt Whitman (1819-1892). American Essayist, Journalist and Poet.

As a product of the amygdala, the behavior of reptiles is largely confined to fleeing or freezing to avoid predators, attacking as a means of procuring nourishment and occasional bouts of sexual display (Figure 6.1). Consequently, most reptiles are solitary creatures. Some female lizards are even able to store sperm to enable them to repeatedly fertilize themselves without the need to meet again with an eligible male. The role of the amygdala in the generation of attack and escape behavior also manifests in relations between parents and their offspring, some adult reptiles being given to cannibalizing their own young, while their offspring are given to escaping, as best they can, the voracious attentions of their parents.

The mammal is radically different (Figure 6.2 and 6.3). In mammals, bonding and parental care are so important that aggregation is the rule, some species even forming a lifelong "relationship" with a single mate. In lower mammals (eg. rodents), bonding manifests in their propensity to form family groups while, in higher mammals (eg. dogs and primates), one may easily detect allegiances that encompass the family into a pack or community and testify to a complex of relationships suggestive of an operational social intelligence.

Without a cingulate gyrus or an insula, the reptiles, together with the fish and amphibians, have no opportunity to be driven by the positive emotions that so conspicuously motivate the mammal to nurture. To the reptile the peace of visceral quiescence is a reward in itself. In the creation of the mammal, however, natural selection favored a brain wherein a state of exultation transcended the panacea of satiation. In the mammal the installation of positive emotions alongside the baser forces of the reptilian psyche, greatly increased the sources of motivation. The mind could not have evolved in a premammalian age, for the simple reason that the unipolar energies of the amygdala that satisfactorily drive the reptilian instincts, are too confined in purpose to provide a useful source of motivation to the process of thought. With the evolution of the mind in higher mammals, the positive emotions enabled the generation of explorative thoughts while the negative emotions evoked thoughts of a protective, repressive and paranoid nature. Under the guise of mood, the positive and negative poles of emotion provide the motivational extremes that facilitate the mental prediction of success or failure with respect to any plan or intended strategy.

It is often said that it is better, or at least as good, to give than to receive. In the living mammals many behaviors such as grooming, licking or suckling testify to the rewarding nature of tending another individual. As a natural outcome of the processes of empathy, the areas of cortex that give a mammal good feelings are also activated when that individual does things that cause good feelings in other individuals. Indeed, the processes of empathy are so pervasive that they can even operate across the vast behavioral boundaries that separate different species. The facial expressions and body posture of the dog can easily be seen to manifest good or bad feelings in accordance with its master's emotional condition and the opposite is obvious to anyone who has observed the owner of an ailing animal. Mammals, however, will rarely interact with reptiles, whose presence, in keeping with biblical mythology, seems universally to inspire trepidation. The behavioral differences that most conspicuously delineate the reptiles, amphibians and fish from the mammals are, in neuropsychological terms, contingent entirely upon the capacity to share the positive domains of emotion.

In humans, empathy, be it in relation to fear, anger, disgust, joy or sadness, is a potent force within all societies. To have one's amygdala activated by the anger or fear of others is the first step towards being swept into the conflicts of others that may ultimately lead to one's participation in war. To have one's anterior cingulate activated by sharing the sorrows or joys of another is to become part of *Atman*, the all-pervading self wherein, at the dawn of the age of mammals, love itself was born.

The Transcendence of Instinct
"For thought is a bird of space that in a cage of words may indeed unfold its wings but cannot fly." Kahlil Gibran (1883-1931). Lebanese American Poet, Author and Mystic.

There must have been a time when beneath the skull of some long extinct beast the first thought happened. A time when at the highest level of that mutant's brain, at the most critical interface which sees the translation of perception into action, evolution inserted a neural circuit capable of weaving the inner and outer realms of experience into single representation of existence. The first thought, floating amidst perceptual realities, must have been a unique element of experience. Yet on many occasions it may have been followed by pleasant feelings, for the mind of today's thinking mammals projects to the brain's ancient reward centers and its production of a successful solution or strategy is reinforced in much the same way as are those successful sequences of movements, which become the habitual elements of our behavior because they bring reward.

Imagine then that you are the moon, circling the Earth since the beginning of time, able to watch the evolution of the plants and animals and the formation of the continents and the Earth, as we know it today. Able to watch the struggle for survival, as again and again, the polar ice drives all life towards the warmer equatorial zones, there to battle for a niche that might enable survival into future epochs of geological time. So powerful is your celestial telescope that you can observe how even the early mammals depend upon stereotyped patterns of behavior to penetrate every available niche and yet how, at the same time, the fixedness of their ways renders impossible their adaptation to rapid changes in their physical and biological environment. Then eventually there appears an entirely new species, a mammal that stands out from all previous animals because, unlike them, its behavior contains complexities that transcend the easily recognizable subroutines of instinct. Suddenly a new force is apparent. Within this creature an invisible agent is at work. Now at last there emerges a contemplative influence that represses instinctive reactions and systematically directs all action towards the attainment of a hidden, internally defined goal. This agent is thought and, within the cortex of this mammalian mutant, its habitat is a discrete and newly evolved neural complex called the mind.

The Size of the Mind

The mind, once expanded to the dimensions of larger ideas, never returns to its original size. Oliver Wendell Holmes (1809-1894). American Humorist Poet, Physician and Professor of Anatomy and Physiology.

All the areas of Brodmann that support thought in humans (BAs 9, 10, 46 and 47) are present in the prefrontal cortex of the apes and more advanced monkeys, such as the macaques. Why then are they not able, like humans, to imagine and solve complex problems? Why are they unable to invent nuclear weapons, develop vaccines or compose elaborate rituals around an imaginary deity? Compared to the apes, monkeys have small brains. Focused on mechanistic definitions of mentation, cognitive neuropsychologists have suggested that, in the monkey, BA9 (the social mind) monitors performance while BA46 (the abstract mind) implements adjustments in performance. While in the human these terms fall far short of covering the diverse functions of thought, it may be that in monkeys, where these areas are, comparatively, very small, their contribution to behavior can best be framed in a limited operational manner. If this is so for monkeys, then we must look to the larger-brained apes for a more powerful expression of cognition.

Even in advanced monkeys such as the macaque, the cortex is only 1/10 the area of the human cortex. It follows that the mind of the macaque (BAs 9, 10, 47 and 46) must be somewhat less than 1/10 of the spatial size of the human mind. As the surface area of the cortical module does not vary significantly between species, it follows that, on average, the human mind must contain more than 10 times the number of modules that are contained within the mind of the macaque monkey. Moreover, the cortex of the macaque is about 20 to 30% thinner that the human cortex indicating that even at the level of the single module the circuitry of the macaque cortex is again simpler than that of the human. In terms of size, the minds of the great apes (the bonobos, chimps, orangutans and gorillas) and lesser apes (gibbons and siamangs) lie somewhere between the monkey and the human. As there can be little doubt that the processes of thought utilize combinations of modules, then increasing the absolute number of modules is likely to produce an exponential increase in the computing power of the mind (*The Construction of Mind*: Chapter 3: Section 8). Such arguments suggest that with a physically small mind, the thought processes of monkeys may be so subtle that it is difficult to unequivocally demonstrate that they use thought to solve problems. If monkeys can indeed think, then their anatomically small mind may only be able to address problems which, compared to those addressed by humans, are both simple and intimately linked to processes that have relevance only to the most basic, and largely social, nuances of monkey life.

While a small mind might enable certain basic functions, there is reason to believe that its problem solving abilities would be severely limited. To appreciate the limitations that the size of the mind places upon the host's ideational ability, consider the challenge of programming a small and a large computer to do the same complex task. If the programmer is naïve to the task he will naturally adopt the simplest strategy. Usually this will involve a larger number of unnecessarily cumbersome steps that will require the full capacity of the large computer. By clever refining of the program, the simple yet cumbersome steps will be absorbed into more ingenious manipulations until a point is reached where the program can be run easily on the small computer. The smaller computer can now solve the problems for which the program was written even though it could never have served as a platform for inventing the appropriate procedures. We might say that the process of transferring the final software package from the large to the small computer is analogous to the small computer "learning" how to solve this complex problem from the large computer. However, what is most significant is that the inventiveness and creativity required to find the solution to this problem, has only been possible by using the large computer.

The mind is thus and it has long been known that education can increase the score achieved on most tests for intelligence. Consider the case of a typical psychologist with a high emotional intelligence counseling a client with a low emotional intelligence on the resolution of a personal dilemma. With a large area of cortex devoted to the social mind, the psychologists will be adept at finding creative solutions to problems within the psychosocial domain. Upon reaching these solutions, the psychologist will be able to convey the relevant questions or issues, along with the essentials of the resolving strategy, to the physically smaller social mind of the client. The client will then be able to resolve such issues even though he could never have worked them out using his own limited emotional intelligence. The social mind of the client has effectively been educated. A novel set of connections (the software of our smaller computer) has been established within the social mind of our client that will manifest as a significant advance in the overall emotional intelligence of that individual. As we will see, the genetical determination of mental ability and the mind's innate capacity to improve its performance by learning, lie at the heart of all arguments concerning the diversity of human cognitive abilities, as well as, issues of racial or cultural integration.

Chapter 2 - The Origins of Social Learning

Tuning-In to Others

"Learning would be exceedingly laborious, not to mention hazardous, if people had to rely solely on the effects of their own actions to inform them what to do. Fortunately, most human behavior is learned observationally through modeling: from observing others one forms an idea of how new behaviors are performed, and on later occasions this coded information serves as a guide for action." Albert Bandura, Canadian Psychologist and Social Learning Theorist. From: *Social Learning Theory*. Englewood Cliffs, Prentice-Hall, New Jersey, 1977, p. 22.

Part of being highly social animals is that we are critically dependent upon one another. This dependency is not learned but is indelibly written in our genetic make up. The human child is more dependent upon parental care than the young of any other species. Its need communicate is extreme and its attempts to do so begin at birth. Emerging from the womb the newborn's environment changes from a warm, dark, fluid-filled, cavity to a world where touch, sound, vision and satiation fall immediately into spatiotemporal patterns of sensation to which its movements rapidly become entrained. Almost immediately the world outside begins to establish its identifying characteristics at every level of the infant's growing central nervous system. Genes and the environment begin to interact and slowly there emerges the manifestations of that miracle of biological engineering - the operational human brain.

It is easy to discern that the vast majority of parents emphatically believe that their newly arrived baby has a sense of self, the capacity to reason and is making a conscious cognitive effort to communicate. In truth, none of these things are true. Recall that, with little more than a brainstem and not even the primordia of a cortex, the anencephalic child was capable of all the basic behaviors seen in normal newborn infants (*The Recognition and Subtraction of Consciousness*: Chapter 4: Section 2). What we are seeing in the normal newborn, is a masquerade fashioned by the actions of natural selection of those parts of the brainstem that generate infant behavior – a masquerade that in time will fall under the control of the infants slowly maturing mind. In its earliest stages, however, infancy is an essentially "blind" seeking of warmth and nutrition and the selective establishment of those motor repertoires that consistently elicit nurturing from attendant caregivers.

With the emergence of body language, communication begins in earnest. So important is this axis of communication that it is said to convey nine times more information than speech. Only as preoperational infants, when the language areas are already working, do we begin to construct the first inner representation of our social milieu. Only then, as the barely mature gray matter of the social mind begins establishing our emotional intelligence, do our interactions with others begin to manifest as thoughts. Only then, is there at last the beginnings of a mind to give content to all subsequent attempts at speech and a concurrent contemplative deliberateness to behavior. Yet well before the onset of speech the infant is already interacting with carers, drawing them into communication with the irrepressible spontaneity of instinct, driven by its emotional centers to manifest its vast precognitive potential for non-verbal communication. Long before the thinker has arrived the dancer is already upon the stage and there are few amongst us who are not drawn to take his hand.

It is in the nature of mammals that members of a species live together in families, packs, communities, herds or pods. In order for this to work, the behavior of each individual needs to be tuned to that of the group. This is achieved by *social learning*, a term which also embraces the tuning of the human newborn to its social environment. However, in different species social learning often depends upon widely different brain processes. For example, although both dolphins and humans are dependent on social cohesiveness, the brain mechanisms through which they achieve this are almost certainly quite different. Each individual is inherently primed to respond most vigorously to the society of his or her parents. That most of the world's people spontaneously choose to associate with those of similar genetic makeup is a testimony to the subtle and omnipotent influences of genes in the structuring of our social behavior (*The Nature and Nurture of Racism*: Chapter 2: Section 1).

Social learning essentially normalizes the behavior of all individuals, facilitating their interactions and so creating social cohesiveness and an emergent sense of both individual and collective or tribal identity. Animals that are unsuccessful in passing through this process are ostracized or even killed. In human societies the mentally ill and any minorities of foreign race, creed, habit or belief are typically the butt of seemingly unrelenting discrimination which not infrequently flares into outright genocide. We pride ourselves on being above the animals in our ways but history tells us that society after society has indulged in purges which almost always begin with the eradication of those whose behavior does not align closely with that of the majority.

In both animal and human societies the eradication of individuals with abnormal behavior patterns naturally selects strongly for brain circuitry that drives conformity. Consequently, it has been discovered that certain parts of the cortex important in generating specific emotions, sensations and sequences of movement become active when these experiences and behaviors are observed in other individuals. The neurons responsible for this activity are called mirror neurons. In the areas of the cortex concerned with movement these neurons provide an explanation why naïve observers of a sport perform better than naïve individuals who have never watched others participating. More generally it is easy to see how mirror neurons might facilitate the learning of speech as well as enabling us to imagine the perceptions and emotions (empathy) of those around us.

The mechanisms of social learning are so diverse that progress has required the establishment of interdisciplinary forums drawing upon fields as diverse as psychology, psychiatry, ethology, neurobiology, artificial intelligence and robotics. The result has been the definition of three different processes by which the behavior of an animal or human might attune to the behaviors of the living agents by which it is surrounded. These processes are *mimicry, imitation* and *emulation*.

To understand these processes it is easiest to imagine a naïve agent watching another agent demonstrate a set of actions such as the manipulation of an object or even a conversation. In this situation, mimicry (also called *action-level* or *indiscriminate imitation*) is defined as a process by which the naïve agent simply copies the actions of the demonstrator, without giving any indication of understanding the goal. The copied actions do not necessarily achieve anything other than the performance of an essentially hijacked behavior pattern. In contrast, *imitation* is the process wherein an agent copies the actions of another agent but does so with an understanding of the goal of those actions. It is the *comprehension of purpose* that distinguishes imitation from mimicry. The third process is *emulation* (also called *task-level imitation*), defined as the reproduction of the goal without the replication of the actions that enabled the demonstrator to achieve that goal. Emulation therefore involves an understanding of the goal and an understanding that there are alternative means of achieving it.

Mimicry, Movement Primitives and the Mind

"I hear and I forget, I see and I remember, I do and I understand." Confucius (551 BC-479 BC). Chinese Philosopher and Political Theorist.

In humans the urge to copy the actions of another is so strong that when normal people are instructed to "point to your nose" while, at the same instant, the instructor points to a lamp, the subjects usually copy the instructor's action rather than doing what they are told. Humans prefer digital human avatars that imitate their movements even when they cannot detect the imitating. In the dolphin, much social learning is achieved largely through mimicry. Dolphins are very good at mimicking sound and use sound extensively for echolocation, communication and emotional expression. In captivity a dolphin has been observed mimicking the scraping sounds of a diver cleaning the pool's observation window. This animal also replicated the sound of the SCUBA demand valve while simultaneously releasing a stream of bubbles through its blowhole. Dolphins have also been seen mimicking the swimming mode, sleeping posture and grooming actions of a sea lion, even though these movements are not within the normal repertoire of the dolphin. However, the most intriguing account of mimicry occurred when a human observer blew a cloud of cigarette smoke while watching a young dolphin through the aquarium window. The infant swam to her mother, returned and released a mouthful of milk that formed a cloud in the water much like the cigarette smoke. It is difficult to see how these copied behaviors have any functional significance to the dolphin. The sheer diversity of completely foreign behaviors mimicked by the dolphin, strongly suggests the presence of an as yet unknown neural system that is inherently tailored for satiating what seems to be the innate drive within dolphins, to mimic.

Where then do the component movements of mimicry come from? One idea is that they arise from simply switching on selected sets of what are called *movement* or *motor primitives* – actions that form the core of the behavior of many and perhaps all vertebrates. The term is much abused, some suggesting the completely contradictory idea that movement primitives can be learned. The essence of true movement primitives is that they are relatively simple, inherited and can be strung together to compose complex yet archetypal activities such as suckling, making facial expressions and even copulation. True movement primitives are composed of preprogrammed component actions such as moving the hand to the mouth. Such movements are designated primitive because they appear in primordial form at many levels of vertebrate life.

The act of mimicry seems to require a link between a visual representation of body language and the brain's motor centers. Only then can what is seen be accurately translated into what is done. The technical term for this process is *kinesthetic-visual modeling* - a process which lends itself to the idea of motor primitives. For instance, movement primitives might underlie the dolphin's ability to use their front flippers to mimic the arm movements of its trainer while movements of the tail and caudal end of the trunk are used to mimic human leg movements. Not only does this task require that the dolphin somehow represents or overlays the human form upon its brain's representation of its own body, but it also suggests that this crude imitation of our limb movements arises because the neural circuits driving the forearm in humans and the flippers in dolphins share some fundamental similarities.

The more complex and plastic a movement, the more it might be thought of as learned versus inherited. However, it must be remembered that we do not yet know exactly which movements are simply hardwired into our nervous system by genes and which are the result of our adapting to our local environment. The likelihood is that through the tens of millions of years of primate evolution, certain postures and movements have been of such overwhelming importance to survival that genes promoting their presence have been selected for over genes that provide the capacity to make a large variety of alternative movements. To take this one step further even the genetic specification of our skeletal structure can limit or promote certain movements or body postures. The very movements we take for granted as our own, may well have been inherited as a genetically specified sets of actions that were first expressed long, long ago in the antics of a distant vertebrate ancestor.

An example of what could be considered complex movement primitives is revealed when minute areas of the motor (BA4) and premotor (BA6) cortex of awake monkeys are stimulated with tiny electrical pulses. The premotor cortex is rich in mirror neurons (*Tuning-In to Others*: Chapter 2: Section 6). When a single site is stimulated for half a second, the monkeys adopt a particular posture that involves coordinated contraction and relaxation of various muscles and the corresponding movements at many joints. For example, stimulating one site caused the monkey's mouth to open and its hand to shape into a grip posture before moving to its mouth in what appeared to be a stereotyped component of feeding behavior. Stimulating at this site always evoked movement into this posture irrespective of the posture of the monkey just prior to stimulation. Different sites produced different postures but did so in an orderly manner, such that a line of sites across the premotor cortex produced a variety of arm movements that essentially placed the hand in different positions around the body. This system enables the hand to be positioned in the workspace around the monkey, a feature that is so critical to the behavior of all primates that it is almost certainly of genetical origin. Such complex movement primitives appear throughout significant parts of the animal kingdom, essentially ensuring that within each of us there exist perceptible, archetypal motor patterns - patterns to which those perceptual centers registering biological form and motion are inherently tuned to enable us to interact with the biological world far beyond the precincts of humanity.

The mythology of dolphin intelligence owes much to their ability to mimic. Dolphin mimicry is so detailed that it inspires in their trainers a sense of empathy that even transcends the vast gap between the aquatic and terrestrial environments. Dolphins do not have arms or legs. When the dolphin mimics the posture of a human trainer, it would seem that the within the dolphin's brain the visual image of the trainer's body form is effectively transposed upon the form of its own body in order that the appropriate motor primitives (arm movement to fin movement and not tail movement) are accessed. What ensues is the best possible copy a dolphin can make of its trainer's posture.

Like other cetaceans, dolphins have a small prefrontal cortex and so it seems unlikely that their antics reflect cognitive processes such as have been identified in humans and the great apes. In both their natural environment and in captivity, dolphins frequently engage in synchronous leaping and diving. In the dolphin, it seems that mimicry results from brain circuitry that automatically taps an inherited store of movement primitives and so tunes the behavior of the individual to the behavior of other dolphins, or under unusual circumstances, other the antics of other species.

In humans, mimicry plays a distinctive role in the bonding of parent and newborn child. For example, infants less than one hour old have been shown to mimic facial expressions. With much of the cortex still immature, the newborn relies heavily on an inherited set of movement primitives, in particular those that are the seeds of interpersonal communication and emotional intelligence. In earliest form of mimicry, the infant simply activates parts of the face that correspond to those used by an adult demonstrator. If the infant attempts to mimic the protrusion of the tongue, then its attempts begin with simply movements around the mouth. Just the presentation of a face with the tongue protruded is a sufficient trigger to arouse those parts of the infant's motor centers that evoke tongue movements.

When adult humans are asked to imagine a set of actions, an area of the cortex called the *inferior parietal lobule* is activated. When they *imagine the actions of others* the inferior parietal lobule of their *right* hemisphere is activated. However, when they *imagine their own actions* the inferior parietal lobule of the *left* hemisphere in called upon. The cortex of the inferior parietal lobule abuts the area of cortex (superior temporal gyrus and sulcus) used to represent socially meaningful gestures (*The Art of* Children: Chapter 2: Section 3). Damage to the inferior parietal lobule of the *left* hemisphere results in a person, who is unable to mimic - a condition known as *ideomotor apraxia*. In contrast, damage to the prefrontal cortex results in a condition wherein the patient is unable to stop imitating. The deeply autistic child readily mimics the sounds of other people (echolalia). Chronically compromised in the arena of social cognition, there is perhaps insufficient cognitive impetus to repress the socially inappropriate yet innate urge to mimic. The motor centers controlling vocalization are simply stimulated by the vocalizations of others and the child responds in kind. In humans and apes, the cortex of the inferior parietal lobule drives mimicry while the prefrontal cortex exerts a selective inhibition of mimicry. Such an arrangement ensures that mimicry is enabled only when it is deemed, by the mind, to be appropriate.

In early infant life the immaturity of the social mind perhaps accounts for the facility with which babies mimic. With the maturation of the emotional centers (amygdala and anterior cingulate gyrus) and the language areas (Broca's and Wernicke's areas), audiovocal mimicry is established as a part of early language learning. Only around the twelfth month does a volitional imitative element emerge from the newly established cognitive representation of the infant's prevailing psychosocial circumstances (*Emotions and the Development of Language*: Chapter 5: Section 4). The newly preoperational child is able to acquire "a knowledge" regarding the outcome of a set of actions performed by itself or another person, knowledge that enables it to activate the appropriate set of motor primitives, not in an act of mimicry but, for the first time, as an act of imitation.

Imitation

"In ontogeny, infant imitation is the seed and adult theory of mind is the fruit." Meltzoff, A. N. and Decety, J. American Neurobiologists. From: "What imitation tells us about social cognition: a rapprochement between developmental psychology and cognitive neuroscience." In: Frith, C. and Wolpert, D. (Editors) *The Neuroscience of Social Interaction - Decoding, imitating and influencing the actions of others*. The Royal Society, Oxford University Press, Oxford, 2004. p. 110.

Imitation and mimicry both entail copying the actions of another agent but only imitation involves, *a knowledge of purpose*. There is not reason for the brain centers that drive mimicry to be remotely concerned with either the past or the future. Unlike imitation, mimicry is of the moment. In contrast, imitation requires either a mental representation that looks into the future and predicts that replicating the demonstrator's actions will bring the outcome, or a memory of the past wherein performance and outcome are linked.

The transition from mimicry to imitation covers a distinct period of early infancy wherein infants are essentially experimenting with social interaction. Once established, imitation becomes an increasingly important element of social learning. By 14 months, infants pay more attention to adults mimicking them than they do to other adults. The number of gestures they copy also increases. This process continues with older infants occasionally producing mismatching expressions as if to see whether these will be adopted by the attending adult. Older infants are so focused on imitating that they will participate in imitating games for 20 minutes or more, expressing more glee than when watching themselves in a mirror. This period ends around 18 months when, with the structural maturation of the social mind, the infant first becomes able to recognize itself in a mirror and comprehend the basic intentions of others. Equipped with a primordial representation of its psychosocial world, a set of behaviors already tuned to its carers, a sense of self and a newly matured social mind, the human infant has the basic requirements for the establishment of a broadly based emotional intelligence.

Given the importance of imitation in the establishment of human social behavior, what might be its role in animals? The living apes are confined to Africa and Indonesia while monkeys are widespread throughout much of the old and new world. Apes are also large and sometimes difficult to manage, whereas monkeys are small and less threatening. In the West monkeys became important members of the circus or provided street entertainment, collecting money and dancing to the tunes of wandering organ grinders. Even in the ancient Hindu myths of the Upanishads, the monkey was given God-like status as Hanuman the Lord Krishna's monkey General, while the sub-primate animals were represented as "vehicles" upon which the Gods rode.

So human-like were the antics of monkeys that there emerged the lay saying, "monkey see, monkey do". Appearances, however, can be deceptive and after half a century of research it seems that while monkeys do appear to be unnervingly like ourselves, with the exception of a handful of isolated cases, they do not appear to either mimic or imitate the actions of others. Some have suggested that the cortex of the inferior parietal lobule that drives mimicry in humans and presumably apes, is absent from the monkey cortex, or exists only in primordial form. If this is so then the specialization and enlargement of this part of the cortex must have been the product of the advantageous mutations that gave rise to an ancestral ape from which all the living and extinct apes and all humans have descended.

Mirror Self Recognition, understanding of the intentions of others and "imitation" have all been described in the great apes. Gorillas copy bodily, facial and manual actions of humans on the first trial. Chimps model human behavior rather specifically, copying a series of actions even though they do not achieve a goal. The orangutan, Chantek, has been taught to reproduce sounds and copy a variety of actions, including patting the top of the head, touching its tongue with a finger, jumping and blinking. Unable to blink Chantek pushed his eyelid with a finger while unable to jump he attempted to replicate the action by pulling himself off the ground with his arms. Clearly, the impetus to replicate an action is not limited to actions that are within the ape's normal repertoire. The facility with which apes mimic or imitate humans is related to the degree to which they have been enculturated to humanity. Chimps raised by humans, engage more readily in gestural communication, gaze following, language acquisition and distinguishing accidental actions from intentional ones, ultimately achieving the level of a 2.5 year old child.

Whether we call these acts mimicry or imitation depends upon whether the apes discern their purpose. This is very difficult to ascertain. When an ape copies a human gesture such as touching the tongue with a finger, it cannot possibly have any idea of the purpose of the action because a purpose does not exist outside of the human experimenter's protocol. It may well be that all these activities are acts of mimicry and their presence in the apes and humans reflect the expansion of the cortex of the inferior parietal lobule. As we have seen, the human is primed to mimic but this impulse is held in check by the mind. Perhaps the correlation between the abilities of the apes to mimic simple actions and their obvious mental aptitudes is related to the regulatory influence of their mind over the inferior parietal lobule. In apes and humans the emergence of either mimicry or imitation might thus represent periods of mental laxity rather than focused cognitive intent.

The nervous system of all animals is hierarchically organized. In the higher primates the mind is at the top and the motor system at the bottom, while in the lower, "mindless" mammals, the emotional centers hold the executive position so that most if their behavior is dominated by instinct. In higher primates the transference of a behavioral sequence from one being to another can occur at any level. While mimicry involves the motor replication of another's actions, imitation similarly instructs the motor system in association with an appreciation of the purpose of the actions. As the product of both technique and purpose, imitation implies that the overall strategy of goal attainment has been transferred along with the details of the component movements. To highlight this possibility some primatologists have defined two levels of imitation: *action level imitation* and *program-level imitation*. Action-level imitation does not differ from imitation as defined above. If, to achieve a goal, it is only necessary to copy a set of actions, then only action-level imitation will be required. However, if the strategy behind the actions must also be adopted, then program-level imitation is required. In program-level imitation, the demonstrator's instruction is not "do as I do" but "think as I think".

It is important to emphasize that program-level imitation involves education but not inventiveness. In human societies, the vast majority of challenges will have been met by hundreds of preceding generations and their solutions passed on to their descendants. True creativity is an exceedingly rare process. Given that in children, program-level imitation is apparent as early as 16 months, there can be little doubt that it is responsible for the generational transfer of many human behaviors and attendant strategies. Moreover, the vitality with which program-level imitation exists within the great apes is a reminder of its potential in the transfer of ideas between humans and, particularly, between different human cultures.

In program-level imitation, the precise details of a set of actions are less important than achieving a specific number of sub-goals into which the whole procedure may be subdivided. A classical example of program-level imitation is the *modus operandi* used by mountain gorillas to prepare the leaves of large stinging nettles for eating. The task requires the leaves to be removed from the stem, cleaned, folded and put into the mouth. It is of sufficient complexity that, even after many days of watching their mothers, young gorillas must still practice and perfect the technique. Their success depends on their achieving four critical stages of preparation, each involving a particular set of actions. Other parts of the processing procedure can vary but the actions related to each of the four critical stages must be performed precisely. It seems that exact mimicry of the mother's actions by young gorillas is so important to the motor learning required for this task that even individuals whose hands have been mutilated by poachers seem driven to achieve each stage by struggling to replicate the "correct" actions rather than developing, *de novo*, a method more suited to their disability. While mimicry and the existence of mirror neurons can account for the motor learning implicit in this task, the young gorillas appear to cognitively define the four critical steps, registering each as part of a practical plan in much the same way as a builder cognitively registers the critical steps in a plan to build a house.

In animals capable of complex behavior it is not always easy to elucidate the involvement of program-level imitation. The ability and inclination of apes to copy circumscribed human activities provides the best example of this dilemma. For instance, orangutans living in rehabilitation centers have been seen to apply stolen insect repellent, brush their teeth, hold a burning cigarette in their lips, copy an attendant who was chopping weeds from the edge of a path, try to siphon liquid using a hose, attempt (unsuccessfully) to tie a hammock between two trees, copy the procedure for lighting a campfire, even blowing on the smoldering sticks before dipping them in paraffin and use a hammer to attempt (unsuccessfully) to drive nails into wood. Of course, it could be argued that an orangutan watching the camp cook light the fire could not possibly associate the actions with the goal of producing heat and/or cooking food. These behaviors may therefore constitute mimicry rather than imitation, simply because it is very unlikely that the ape appreciates the goal of these classical human tasks (*The Methodology of Mimicry*: Chapter 5: Section 6). However, the truth is we cannot know their cognitive aspirations. Nor can we grasp how fleetingly such activities remain within the ape mind or if indeed, they have any mental origin. Certainly we cannot completely dismiss the possibility that apes enculturated to humans may have sufficient mental competence to entertain the general policy that replicating the complex behaviors of these omnipotent humans might yield unknown rewards. Do these acts indicate that the ape anticipated a specific, cognitively conceived outcome? Alternatively, do they represent simply serial replication of a sequence of human actions? Has the ape mentally conceptualized the attendant goals and strategies or do its actions simply represent the recruitment of those neural circuits that enable the brain to generate mimicry?

Emulation
"There is more than one way to skin a cat." English Proverb, c. 1678.

Emulation is very difficult to show in animals and is probably confined to the higher primates. Like imitation and mimicry, the propensity of an animal to emulate human activities is increased by a prolonged enculturation to humanity. To emulate, an animal must watch another agent achieve a desirable goal and then itself achieve that goal *without* copying the actions of the other. As a process, there is no reason that emulation could not occur within the practical, social or, at least in humans, the abstract domain of intelligence. For example, in the academic world, finding a different means of deducing the solution to an abstract problem is often the principal focus of mental energy. What is significant about the process of emulation is that it identifies the presence of an appreciative knowledge of alternative ways of achieving a demonstrated goal, be it social, practical or theoretical. In all cases, such knowledge indicates the presence of a reasonably accurate, operational model of the social, physical or, in the case of humans, the phenomenological world.

The mechanism of emulation is radically different from that underlying mimicry or imitation, for in emulation, there is no transference of technique. In mimicry, the inferior parietal lobule is prevented from generating indiscriminate replication of action by the inhibitory influences of the mind. This enables the mind to replicate the actions of another agent simply by relaxing its inhibition of the inferior parietal lobule. In contrast, emulation is a direct product of the mind and thus it indicates the unequivocal presence of a significant level of intelligence.

In practice, the term emulation is usually used in relation to practical goals such as the cracking of a nutshell in order to obtain the nut. The process of emulation is therefore said to require *knowledge of the physical environment* and to result in a change in an animal's physical environment. For a long time our astonishing ability to alter our physical environment was believed to be a definitive characteristic of humanity - a process which began in earnest with the tool making activities of our hominid ancestors. In humans, emulation is developmentally linked to a particular level of cognitive development. Thus, children only develop the ability to emulate within the practical domain, when they reach the age of 5 - an age when the child is on the threshold of the concrete operations phase of cognitive development during which the structural, informational and conceptual substrates of practical intelligence are being established (*The Origins of Practicality – The Temporal Mind*: Chapter 3: Section 3). It is now clear that practical emulation begins in early childhood and that its evolutionary origins lie deep within our hominid ancestry, where extinct creatures had creative abilities ranging from that of the great apes of modern times to a level almost equivalent to our own.

Both imitation and emulation require the presence of an operational mind. How then do the lower mammals that essentially lack a mind, exploit mimicry in the process of becoming part of a cohesive social or family group? With only the driving forces of instinct, one must presume that in the process of socialization they are heavily reliant on emotional memories. In adult humans, two extreme examples of emotional memories are trauma (as in post-traumatic stress disorder, PTSD) and that cognitively enigmatic aspect of bonding, called love (*The Ravages of Emotional Memory*: Chapter 5: Section 4). Thus, despite the complexity of human society, emotional memories continue to play a role in establishing and regulating social interactions. The lower mammals differ from humans in that a relatively short time is required for them to reach sexual maturity and the complexity of social interaction, is far less. In the absence of a mind, it seems that emotional memories are sufficient for the developing lower mammal to become attuned to the society of its conspecifics. In the higher mammals, and particular in humans, these same instinctually driven social interactions of early life, provide a vital experientially-based substrate of emotional memories upon which the cognitive frameworks of the social mind are ultimately built.

Chapter 3 - The Evolution of Emotional Intelligence

The Conceptualization of Feelings

"It is very important to understand that emotional intelligence is not the opposite of intelligence, it is not the triumph of heart over head – it is the unique intersection of both." David Caruso, American Professor of Psychology. www.emotinoaliq.org/EI.htm.

The primitive, premammalian emotions of anger and fear do not promote social cohesiveness. Only with the evolution of mammals and the cortex of the cingulate gyrus and the insula was the sharing of positive emotions possible. From that point onwards the scene was set for the evolution of the social mind. However, it would be more than 100 million years before, somewhere in the ascendancy of the mammals, the first pieces of cortex devoted to psychosocial conceptualization evolved. Where instinct once determined action, now its motivational energy would have to be integrated within an acquired psychosocial framework housed within the neuronal labyrinths of the primordial social mind. Whereas in the lower mammals nurture and aggression were emotively inspired, now they were subject to, and even dependent upon, the process of deliberation. No longer could action be confidently predicted from prevailing circumstances as behavior became seeded with *premeditated acts of both kindness and cruelty*. Thought had come to stay and to the observer watching the ways of life on Earth, a new and often enigmatic influence seemed to underlie the behavior of all higher mammals. Now strategies lurked behind their actions - strategies that to the observer were increasingly enigmatic as with further mutations the cortex devoted to thought expanded and diversified.

Prior to the evolution of the mind, nature had saturated all niches that could be penetrated by instinct alone. The only niches left were those favoring mutations that created new areas of the prefrontal cortex wherein the algorithms of reason could be established. Mutants with a mind survived and in that instant of geological time, destiny foresaw the creation of humanity. Quite naturally the first niches to invite the process of thought related to nurturing the individual and servicing the biological needs of the community. The critical duties governing the synthesis of the social mind were the restoration and maintenance of visceral and social harmony (emotional quiescence and peace) and, alas, the divisive seeking of pleasure. The neural connections that enabled the generation of strategies for achieving these objectives inevitably became the foundations of emotional intelligence.

All significant steps in the evolution of the vertebrates are mirrored in the developmental stages (ontogeny) of the human being. It follows that the first form of intelligence to evolve must have been that which first appears in the preoperational stage of cognitive development of the human. We may therefore deduce that the first thoughts, the thoughts of the first mammals endowed with a mind, were fundamental to the psychosocial domain of existence. The first element of the mind to evolve must therefore have been the social mind. With the evolution of the social mind, the immediacy of instinctual action that characterizes the behavior of the lower vertebrates was replaced by strategies derived from an integrated picture of animal life and a specific set of cognitively elaborated, sociobiological rules. As these rules would have to be learned by each generation, a high level of emotional intelligence would, from that point on, confer a distinct advantage upon any new species by enabling the formation of a more cohesive web of social interactions.

Nevertheless, it is very difficult to define a point on the evolutionary tree of animals when the first elements of mind evolved. Even with living mammals, unequivocally demonstrating the existence of intelligence of any kind is extremely difficult. In extinct species, known only as fossils, not only is it impossible to carry out behavioral experiments, but it is also impossible to examine their brains in search of those cortical areas that in humans support cognition. However, from the standpoint of brain structure, the evolution of a rudimentary mind - a piece of cortex devoted to the conceptualization of some critical domain of life - most likely stretches back at least 82 million years to the projected origin of the primates.

This is not to say that only primates are endowed with the capacity of thought. There exists evidence of a rudimentary form of cognition in aquatic mammals and some species of birds. Certainly, people who have lived and worked with dogs have no hesitation in stating that dogs have the ability to think, at least within the social realm. In a two-way food choice dogs will read the body language of human attendants, responding appropriately to their gaze, eye movement or head turning - indicators commonly used by psychologists to infer cognition in human infants. The lay literature also makes clear, if anecdotal, reference to dogs possessing emotional intelligence. Dogs have been shown to be able to learn gestures coding actions but not those coding objects, indicating a social rather than practical orientation of their learning abilities. Against this, however, some animal behaviorists express doubt that dogs possess a true understanding of intentions, suggesting that their behavior is fashioned by conditioning below the level of mentation. In their view the modern domestic dog does not cognitively anticipate dinner but simply moves to the feeding area where it was last rewarded and salivates when it hears the sound of a tin being opened.

Theoretically the mind is an organ specifically designed for the strategic control of behavior. However, to enable adaptation to different environments the mind must be highly sensitive to conditioning. Humans brought up in different environments develop very different sets of ideas, facts and principles that affect their behavior at the strategic level. The social mind becomes tuned-in, or conditioned to, the prevailing social environment. Identical twins brought up in different cultures still spontaneously choose the same clothes and work in similar jobs. However, although they think in the same way, what they think about, and so the conclusions they come to, may be radically different. The result is that while superficially they may do very different things, their approach to doing them will be identical. Similarly, a dog's social environment will not profoundly alter its "personality" but will have profound effects on the manner in which it is expressed. Consider, for example, the following comparison between stray dogs and dogs domiciled with humans. Even though stray dogs may be recently descended from domestic stock they approach each other, humans and other animals in a manner that is entirely different to dogs domiciled with humans. The latter operate on the rules of the home while the former operate on the rules of the street. The strategies behind the behavior of these two dog populations are quite different. Their social minds have been differently conditioned. Thus, in the minute-by-minute formation of their behavior, in the directing of their attention and in the analysis of the global circumstances pertaining in the living world, these two bands of canines are astonishingly and often intractably different. In the same way the social behavior of a man who has lived close to the earth is radically different from the social behavior of one of identical biological heritage who has never left the city. The social mind of each is tuned to a different passage of people, a different level of privacy, social pace and competition. Ultimately, as primates did not evolve from birds, dogs or cetaceans these examples do not resolve the origins of human thought. They do, however, indicate that cognition and the cortical tissues underlying its elaboration may have evolved in several different parts of the animal kingdom, underscoring the critical *importance of strategy* in the struggle for survival.

The definition of the cortical areas involved in human thought may enable the anatomical identification of similar (homologous) regions in the cortex in non-primate mammals. In this way it might be possible to unequivocally determine which animals have the cerebral potential for thought. Recent advances in gene mapping mean that it will make it possible to seek out the seeds of the mind within the genome of any mammal or providing sufficient DNA can be obtained, from extinct hominids such as the Neanderthals. With respect to dogs all that can presently be said is that their prefrontal lobes are conspicuously larger than those of the cats and that the "additional" prefrontal cortex seems to occupy a position similar to that occupied by the social mind (BA9) in primates. Perhaps this accounts for their capacity to express and elicit empathy to a degree that has earned them the title of "man's best friend".

Facial Expressions and Emotional Intelligence
"The Buddha was never melancholy or gloomy. He was described by his contemporaries as 'ever-smiling' (*mihitapubbamgama*). In Buddhist painting and sculpture the Buddha is always represented with a countenance happy, serene, contented and compassionate. Never a trace of suffering or agony or pain." Walpola Sri Rahula Maha Thera (1907-1997). Sri Lankan, Buddhist Monk, Author and Professor of History and Religion.

The sophistication and very existence of emotional intelligence is directly related to the aptitude of a species for emotional communication. Recall that our raw emotions arc simply experiential reflections of our viscerally derived instinctual drives. Therefore anything that enhances the expression of the raw emotions aids and abets the primary task of the social mind – the integration of the emotional state of the individual with their reading of the emotional (or instinctual) state of other beings, be they animal or human.

Recognizing the central importance of facial expressions to communication, Charles Darwin concluded that the complexity of the facial musculature of a terrestrial mammal is a powerful indicator of the level of complexity of its social behavior. In humans, facial expressions are by far the most potent vehicle for broadcasting our raw emotions, some experts claiming that humans are capable of several thousand recognizable facial expressions. The social mind is heavily reliant upon the face as an indicator of the emotions of others and integrating these readings with the emotional state of the individual to generate that conspicuously cognitive element, intent.

Throughout the mammals, and particularly the primates, the complexity of facial musculature increases in relation to social complexity. In the rodents and the cats we can easily observe the expressions of fear or aggression and even disgust. However, it is not until we get to the dogs and primates that the musculature of the face is sufficiently complex to enable the communicative processes so essential to complex social interactions. Even in primates (orangutans accepted), both group size and the level of social interaction are related to mobility of the facial muscles – a property that reflects not only the complexity of the facial musculature but that of the neural network responsible for facial expressions. The highest component of this network is the social mind, its size and complexity naturally determining the individual's potential for emotional intelligence. The emergent generality is that emotional intelligence, complexity of facial expressions and the level of social interaction are, in the majority of primate species, highly interactive and interdependent. It would seem that many of the behavioral and cultural traits peculiar to the facially expressive, hunter-gatherers of sub-Saharan Africa, New Guinea and Australia are clearly generated within this cycle, while many of the behavioral and cultural traits peculiar to the facially impassive Far East Asians are probably generated by elements outside this cycle.

Animals with little facial musculature are limited in their ability to use facial movements for the comprehensive communication of emotions that is the essence of effective social integration. At the lowest end of the spectrum are the premammalian vertebrates, the fish, amphibians and reptiles. These animals have little facial musculature and what they do have (the very primitive, jawless fish, the *Agnatha*, excepted) is devoted to jaw movements that are part of threat display, aggression and feeding, instinctual actions related directly to that archaic emotional center, the amygdala (*Commanding Aggression and Fear*: Chapter 4: Section 4). In keeping with the rule that any species of animal is insensitive to communicative cues it cannot itself generate, these pre-mammalian forms are insensitive to much of the body language and all the facial expressions of higher mammals. There is little to be gained by smiling when transfixed by the slightly swaying gaze of a King Cobra.

Health and the Social Mind
"One might say that the Medicine Wheel of western civilization has looked to the North far too long now, having much knowledge but little feeling." Jeanne Achterberg, American Professor of Psychology. From: *Imagery in Healing: Shamanism and Modern Medicine*. Shambhala, Boston, London, 1985, p.12.

Traditional medicine has long recognized the powerful link between emotions and health. Such relationship is the basis of *shamanism*, which seeks to manipulate the emotions for the purposes of either terminating the life of a wrongdoer or enemy or, as is more usually the case, helping to cure illness. In recent decades neuroscientific research confirming that our emotions are reflections of our visceral life, has driven western medicine to a higher awareness of the relationship between psychological and physical well being.

Before the development of civilization the nature of an illness was largely defined by experience. Within the individual the introspective assessment of feelings was of paramount importance. Diagnosing illnesses and rendering help were similarly dependent upon the ability to empathize and so actually experience the feelings of the afflicted. Today we have evidence from brain scans that empathy does indeed depend upon the activation of our emotional centers (*The Nature of Empathy*: Chapter 2: Section 4). Such feelings may be either good or bad depending on the state of the subject of our empathy. It follows that across the spectrum of human personalities, those who are most sensitive to their own feelings will be those most able to contemplate and diagnose the feelings of others. Such feeling people are indubitably those with a high level of emotional intelligence. Their abilities naturally incline them towards the caring professions where their intimate, though completely intuitive, connection with nature, manifests as an uncanny advantage over those dominated by deductive logic. This link between emotional intelligence and gaining insight into our health must certainly have been a selective factor that influenced the progressive evolution of an enlarged social mind.

Many hunter-gatherer and native peoples have a profound knowledge of natural medicine. In addition, they also used complex reasoning to deduce a logical understanding of illness. One example, is the Incas of Peru, who in the 15th century performed reparative brain surgery and blood transfusions, their success at the latter doubtless reflecting the fact that most South American natives have Group O blood. For reasons unknown, the Incas were unique among the South American Indians in their outstanding practical abilities manifested in the technical precision used in the construction of Machu Pichu. In contrast, however, healthcare amongst most other native peoples seems to have depended upon an innate ability to appreciate and read biology that in turn reflects the prominence of the social mind in the orchestration of their behavior.

Until quite recently humans believed themselves to be the only beings that sought practical cures for illness. The Chinese pride themselves in having published the first known compendium of over 300 natural remedies. However, in recent years many researchers have reported observing the use of medicinal plants by non-human primates. Even bears have been known to pack a rotting tooth with the bark of a tree that contains the active ingredient of Asprin. The mountain gorillas of Uganda eat the bark of the dombeya tree which is laced with antibiotics. The orangutans of Borneo sometimes select certain species of flowers that cure headaches in humans. Both chimps and members of the WaTongwe people seek out the bitter pith from the tree *Veronica amygdalina* because of its toxicity to microorganisms that cause malaria, dysentery, and schistosomiasis. Finally, it has been claimed that chimps can recognize hundreds of different plants many of which may be of medicinal value. It is therefore likely that the ancestors we share with the living apes possessed sufficient mental aptitude to experiment within the realm of natural medicine.

Manouvering in Society

"Society is an interweaving and interworking of mental selves. I imagine your mind, and especially what your mind thinks about my mind, and what your mind thinks about what my mind thinks about your mind. I dress my mind before yours and expect that you will dress yours before mine. Whoever cannot or will not perform these feats is not properly in the game." Charles Horton Cooley (1864-1929), American Sociologist. From: *Life and the Student*. Knopf, New York, 1927, pp. 200-201.

It is generally agreed that in rule learning, the linking of knowledge and the ability to generalize out of the existing context, animals fall into a hierarchy. Thus, apes, the larger Old World (Eurasian) monkeys, the New World (South American) monkeys, the lower (strepsirrhine) primates and non-primate mammals can all learn rules but with an ability that decreases in that order. Of these, only the apes have satisfied the rigorous criteria used by animal behaviorists to test for the existence of thought process. However, some researchers have suggested that the complex social interactions of some monkeys strongly indicate a socially defined intelligence. Much the same story has emerged in relation to personality in non-human primates, primatologists being traditionally uneasy with its definition in monkeys and yet pronouncing, in less formal settings, upon the personality of their pet dog. The following paragraphs outline some intellectually challenging, social activities of monkeys and apes.

When challenged with a technically difficult problem, apes enculturated to human society will often solicit assistance of a human. In so doing they reveal their inclination to solve even practical problems by manipulating others. It is therefore not surprising to find that within wild primate communities, social maneuvering is a common means of enhancing survival of the individual. Brawn may win many battles but the politics of emotion ultimately has the potential of empowering every individual. For instance, in one community only those chimps that had the help of a big brother consistently triumphed over other chimps in contests to become the dominant or alpha, male. For both apes and humans, obtaining food, satiation of mating urges and advancement up the pecking order are very much a case of whom one knows and to whom one is related.

Social deception is another important way of using emotional intelligence to powerfully affect the outcome of many different sorts of challenge. In children the art of social deception develops by 4 years of age and marks the maturation of social mind. Deception essentially indicates that the child's emotional intelligence has developed sufficiently to enable it to comprehend and manipulate others (Theory of Mind). Amongst the apes, deception is a common strategy that enables the individual to survive and reproduce, in a tightly organized, hierarchical society. A young ape may feign play with his sibling in order to get close enough to its feeding mother to steal some of her food. In the baboons (lesser apes) where the alpha male is assured of at least 50% of all matings, two male baboons have been observed to work as a team, one challenging the alpha male while the other surreptitiously obtained a mating from a female.

Deception is also employed by captive apes to outsmart their human carers. For instance, bonobos being trained in symbolic language frequently attempt to deceive their trainers in order to achieve specific goals. These tricks may involve asking their trainer to fetch something, when actually they have noticed that the door has been left unlocked and there is opportunity to escape.

In contrast to the apes, monkeys lack the ability to imitate, to entertain a Theory of Mind or to recognize themselves in a mirror. Although BA9 exists in their prefrontal cortex, superficially they appear to have little emotional intelligence. There are, however, many examples of monkey behavior that might more loosely reflect intelligence in the psychosocial domain. For instance, the brown capuchin monkey (*Cebus apella*) has been shown to have the ability to evaluate a complex social dynamic that is directly related to the expectation of reward. These monkeys had to perform a task where they were rewarded by cucumber or a grape, the grape being the preferred reward. Female monkeys were used because, much like human females, they were more discerning than the males. The monkeys could observe one another performing the task and so monitor the rewards given to each other. The results showed that monkeys refused to participate in the task if they witnessed another monkey receiving an inequitable number of grapes – a response indicating that they have a concept of fairness that can only reflect a modicum of emotional intelligence.

Economists have argued that the cognitive attentions of humans are guided by their social emotions, which they have labeled "passions". Clearly the sharing or not sharing of crucial food resources is an emotionally charged arena of behavior. In the wild, capuchin monkeys readily share their food with each other. In the above scenario it might well have been that the monkeys were so emotionally traumatized by inequity that they desisted from the task even at the expense of foregoing any further reward. How this comes about is the question. It may be, for instance that capuchins are genetically programmed to respond in this way to inequity, that activation of their emotional centers simply triggers an instinctual withdrawal from such a scenario. Alternatively their emotional centers may activate their small social mind, wherein rules of sharing and the best response to inequity might exist as a conceptual construct of early social conditioning.

In a similar experiment chimps responded to unequal treatment in a more complex manner than do the capuchin monkeys. Thus, in a trial where the chimps were rewarded unequally (cucumber or grape) for handing an object to their trainer, individuals only protested if they did not have a very long social relationship with the favored chimp. In this they behave much like humans who do not mind their close friends or family receiving unwarranted rewards but express resentment if strangers are similarly favored. Also like humans, the apes determine resource sharing by adherence to a hierarchical pecking order although chimp mothers do share with their offspring. Chimps and bonobos will announce finding sharable food with loud calls. However, an individual will not attract the attention of others if the food is rare or of a preferred type. Studies of one alpha male chimp showed that it shared meat from its kills only with middle rank males and certain old socially influential males. It did not share with young males rising in dominance or with the beta male. Finally when

265

chimps are presented with an abundance of ordinary food, the priorities of rank were typically suspended. In such instances animals that did not share were refused when they requested sharing.

These scenarios are too complex to be easily explained away as genetically programmed behaviors. When it comes to sharing, apes do appear to have mentally-founded policies that enhance their sensitivity to the nuances of their social circumstances – policies that are presumably established by the early conditioning of their social mind. We are confronted again with the most significant question in the study of behavior; what are the relative contributions of the software of the mind versus the influence of inherited, and thus instinctual, behavioral responses? The high incidence of aberrant human behavior following either intense trauma (PTSD) or the loss of love (PLSD) indicate that a significant part of our learning takes place within our brain's emotional centers that, in turn, have significant control over our bodily functions (*The Ravages of Emotional Memory*: Chapter 5: Section 4). It is obvious that in humans and probably all other mammals capable of mentation, these emotional memories have great influence over the mind, and so, behavioral strategy. In all other vertebrate animals, however, the fundamentals of behavior are packaged as inherited repertoire of instincts upon which powerful and persistent "emotional" memories will assert the necessary authority of the environment.

Emotional Intelligence and Social Structure
"The chimpanzee resolves sexual issues with power; the bonobo resolves power issues with sex…" Frans de Waal, Dutch Primatologist and Frans Lanting, Dutch Photographer. From: *The Forgotten Ape*. University of California Press, Berkley, Los Angeles, London, 1997, p. 32.

In human societies the adoption of a monetary system has been a critical step in the substitution of cognitive strategies in matters that might otherwise have been resolved by purely instinctive action. For instance, the mating success of our male hominid relatives was probably largely dependent on brawn whereas the success of the modern human male is much dependent on his possession of that most desirable resource, money. As we have seen, monkeys and apes are able to appreciate that desirable food stuffs have a societal, as well as a personal, value that enable them to be traded for work or given as gifts to family members. Having established that non-human primates see food rewards as a negotiable currency researchers set about to establish what reward value male macaque monkeys would place on seeing emotively inspiring pictures. The images tested were a gray square (neutral image), low-ranking monkeys, high-ranking monkeys and female hindquarters. Results showed that monkeys would forgo considerable juice reward in order to see pictures of high-ranking monkeys or female hindquarters. However, more juice had to be given (paid) to induce them to view low ranking monkeys. The parallel with humans, who willingly pay large amounts of money to see famous or important people or to view pornography, is obvious. What is, however, most significant is that in setting a price on each image these monkeys were clearly utilizing decision-making processes based on a conceptual construct of their community's social structure and the market value of a rewarding substance. It is almost impossible to see how the instinctual urges or the emotional memories that generate the behavior of lower mammals could enable this level of abstraction. On the other hand, it is very easy to imagine how, with an inner blueprint of its social milieu, a monkey could understand the nuances of exchanging a viscerally rewarding experience for a cerebrally mediated one.

The structure of any society is much determined by the cognitive structure of its members. If practical intelligence dominates the intellect of its members then practicality will be emphasized, if emotional intelligence dominates then psychosocial understanding in the form of a pronounced biological intuition will dominate. The chimps and the bonobos, provide an excellent example of a dichotomy of social structure indicative of a radical difference in the dominant form of cognition. The chimps and the bonobos are regarded as the most intelligent non-human primates. However, their general behavior and their abilities at a battery of cognitive challenges reveal striking differences in both their "personality" and social organization. The social behavior of chimps has been extensively studied both in wild and captive communities. In comparison, difficulties in observing wild bonobos have forced most investigators to confine their studies to captive communities. Although, there are some differences between the behavior of bonobos in wild communities and those in captive communities, these do not significantly negate the marked behavioral differences between chimps and bonobos either wild or captive communities. Moreover, as we are primarily interested in making distinctions and comparisons between the mental apparatus driving the behavior of each species, it is valid to simply compare their behavior within captive communities.

Bonobos are a matriarchal society while chimps are a patriarchal society. Bonobos are very empathetic and strongly resist being separated from members of their group. For a bonobo, the social domain is the focus of life. In contrast, chimps are relatively independent, less socially aware and appear to rate social order and physical prowess above empathy. Captive bonobos have a rampant predisposition to sex. Adults tongue kiss and males express what must surely be an abiding trust, by grasping each other's penis in what has become known as a genital handshake. Although a single intromission typically lasts only 14 seconds, the short duration of pleasure is more than compensated for by the frequency of intercourse - bonobos in captivity, indulging roughly once every hour and a half, compared with once in seven hours in captive chimps. Bonobos also sexually stimulate their young and, in captivity, both genders frequently engage in other homosexual acts although there are no reports of anal penetration. Males do tend to show preferential care for the young of their sexual partners but as a result of their promiscuity "family" boundaries are always obscure. Unlike certain chimp communities and humans, there is as yet no evidence that bonobos practice infanticide or form deadly war parties to attack neighboring groups. There is, however, some evidence that they may attack and eat other mammals. In comparison, chimps eat at least 35 species of vertebrates, including human infants and the young of their own species. Adult male chimps typically have 4 times the strength of a young man and have been known to kill or badly maim adult humans. This is not to say that chimps are less concerned about each other or that they do not form bonds with humans. Mothers will attend a dead infant for days and members of a community will embrace, groom one another and even tend each other's wounds. The problem lies primarily with the males whose aggression is such that although males and females are born in equal numbers, any community typically has almost twice as many females as males. Many, of the 50% of males who do not reach maturity presumably die of murder – a cause that also underlies similar attrition of males in a number of native and hunter-gatherer tribes (*Commanding Aggression and Fear*: Chapter 4: Section 4).

Clearly the differences between chimp and bonobo society are the product of inherently different, cognitively generated agendas. In captivity, bonobos are very good at languages invented for them by human trainers, rapidly learning to communicate through the use of symbols that stand for nouns, adjectives and verbs. Bonobos love watching TV and have been reported to be so receptive to human language that one individual can respond to a limited range of spoken instructions delivered through earphones. In contrast chimps are better at puzzles and solving mazes. When a female bonobo and a female chimp were raised together, the chimp's acquisition of symbolic language lagged behind the bonobo by about 6 months. While the chimp tended to use language in a more restricted fashion, on tasks such as puzzle construction, tool use and maze solving, the reverse was true, the chimp being always ahead of the bonobo.

The bonobo community is the epitome of an emotionally intelligent society, while the chimps appear to be more influenced by practical intelligence, perhaps backed up by a modicum of abstract intelligence. If this is indeed the case then cytoarchitectural studies of the prefrontal cortex of these two species should reveal that relatively speaking, the social mind (BA9) is larger in bonobos than in the chimps, while the material mind (BA47), and possible the abstract mind (BA46), are larger in chimps. Since their evolution from a common ancestor 2.5 mya, natural selection for specific behavioral strategies has had different consequences for the mental aptitudes of the chimps and bonobos, causing them to form societies based on quite different cognitive strategies. One explanation may be that, like today, the bonobos always inhabited a rich environment that facilitates communal cooperation and reduces inter-individual and inter-community hostility, while the chimps inhabited a less forgiving environment that forced the individual and community into often violent competition – an argument that has often been used to account for the marked differences in geographically disparate human societies (*The Diversity of Intelligence*: Chapter 2: Section 8).

Chapter 4 - The Evolution of Temporal Intelligence

The Cross-Cultural Significance of Time

"In Aboriginal Australia, there is a shorter distance between historical time and infinity. As a consequence, infinity is more readily graspable as part of the present." Howard Morphy, Australian Professor of Anthropology and Advocate for Australian Aboriginals. From: "Australian Aboriginal Concepts of Time." In: Kristen Lippincott (Editor). *The Story of Time.* Merrell Holberton in Association with the Maritime Museum, London, 1999, p. 267.

The word time is from the Latin, *tempos* that in turn is derived from the Greek *tempo* or "to cut off". Peoples of European descent (theoretical physicists excepted) envisage time as intimately linked with seeing an end point in an activity - a vision indicative of mental processes that are dominated by a concern for planning and a concept of the future. A perusal of any philosophical text reveals a long list of European scholars who have attempted rational definitions of time. There are, however, few comparable attempts from the sages of India and the Far East or the shamans and witchdoctors of the world's native and hunter-gatherer cultures. To these peoples time in the order of seconds, minutes and hours is of little significance. Even India, renowned for its highly intellectual contributions to philosophy, religion, literature and the theoretical sciences harbors a conspicuous indifference to chronological time that never fails to leave incredulous the visitor of European heritage.

Estimates of when the first modern humans arrived in Australia vary between 42,000 and 60,000 years. When they came the sea level was hundreds of feet lower than today, much of the water being trapped in the polar ice caps. Sumatra and Borneo were fused as a single land mass called Sunda. Mainland Australia, Tasmania and New Guinea were also part of a single continent, Sahul. Only 100 km of sea separated Sunda from Sahul and this was dotted with visible islands that formed a gateway to the great southern land for the first wave of immigrants whose origins lay in distant Africa.

Estimates of the number of Aboriginals inhabiting pre-European Australia ranged from 300,000 to as many as 750,000 individuals, who were divided into many continuously warring tribes. When the British invaded Australia the colonial government encouraged male white settlers to have sexual relations with aboriginal women with the express purpose of "breeding the black out of them". The result is that today many people of Aboriginal heritage also carry genes of European origin. It is therefore necessary to appreciate that all comments about the inherited traits of Aboriginals, and all other native and hunter-gatherers referred to herein, are relevant only to *individuals who have no European ancestors.*

Before the Europeans arrived, food was plentiful and, even in the harshest regions the Australian Aboriginals must have found survival relatively easy. With time the oceans rose and eventually the island state of Tasmania separated from the Australian mainland establishing a significant geographical barrier that eventually blocked further access to Tasmania. There followed very long periods of habitation during which one must presume that, the continuous intertribal conflicts aside, life followed a very regular and simple pattern that indeed flowed like a familiar dream from generation to generation. Even today the Australian Aboriginals speak of the *dreamtime*, a time long before the arrival of the Europeans, when the spirit beings were present in greater numbers. Like ordinary dreams, the dreamtime has no measure in chronological or calendric time. It is likely that the relative stability of their life and their success as hunter-gatherers negated any survival advantage that might otherwise accompany the evolution of cognitive systems powerfully predisposed to planning and concepts of future. Like their surviving African relatives of today, chronological time was never a dominant aspect in the mental processes of these hunter-gatherers who consequently had little impetus to introduce time as a significant element in either their mythologies or their daily life. Even the full-blooded Aboriginals of modern times see no purpose in the western obsession with the passage of time. Like their long line of forefathers, their purpose lies only in the dreaming wherein time is both infinite and of the moment.

The hunter-gatherers of Australia and Africa are not the only preliterate peoples who show a conspicuous disinterest in time. For example, the Pirahã, a small and dwindling, indigenous Amazonian tribe, do not have words that relate to either the past or the future. In addition, their language lacks words for either numbers or colors, their lack of concern for numbers reflecting the indifference to numerals greater than three that has been reported in the Australian aboriginals. The Pirahã's indifference to time is reflected in their spiritual beliefs, wherein the world is inhabited by spirits that influence present events and yet have no relationship to the origins either of people or the world. This coexistence of an indifference to time with an indifference to numbers suggests that, in general, the ability to cognate about time may be critical to the ability to count and the establishment of a numerical vocabulary. Thus, the ability to use numbers may well be bound to the evolution of high levels of temporal intelligence.

While for Europeans time is of great cognitive significance, time is also a pervasive phenomenon that has much significance to the organic aspects of human life. However, chronological time is still of little concern to the social mind. The social mind lives instead in what has been called *psychological time*, the passage of which is almost entirely dependent on our internal state and our social milieu. Psychological time is the norm for the world's hunter-gatherers and those native peoples still living close to nature, while chronological time dominates all societies of European heritage and all other urban environments that have been forced into the European mold of civilization.

Through our pheromones and various less savory and subtle olfactory messengers, we unwittingly broadcast the passage of time as part of the daily, weekly and monthly cycles of our organic centers. As the oldest of our senses, olfaction exerts its subtle and ancient influences as a primary reinforcer in regulating our emotions and moods and thus our behavior. Only rarely, however, do we see time measured in a manner that may have some significance to the emotional and thymic realms of existence. For instance, in bygone days the Chinese and Japanese scored the passing of the hours by the burning of graduated incense, registering the seasons and zodiacal signs by a succession of carefully ordered scents and so linking the passage of calendric time to olfaction. Perhaps using odor to signal the passage of time enabled the entrainment of mood to the seasons and the location of the stars. Ultimately, all things organic and inorganic are affected by time and in this very broad sense all things living and non-living mark its passing. At one level we have the pronouncement of an unknown scribe that, "A second is defined as 1/31556925.9747th of a tropical year", while at the other we might countenance the words of St.Augustine, "What is time? If no one asks me, I know. If I try to explain it to someone asking me, I don't know".

While many cultures are traditionally disinterested in the passage of minutes and hours, there is an abundance of evidence of their taking pains to record time over days, weeks, months and years. There are several reasons for this preference. The first is simply ease of measurement. The temporal precision required to accurately monitor the passage of seconds and minutes is a different matter that was, until recent centuries, beyond even the technologically advanced Europeans. In contrast it is a simple matter to accurately record the passage of days, months and years. One need only, like Defoe's mythical Robinson Crusoe, make notches on a tree.

The second reason for the early development of calendars is cosmology - the science of the universe. In the evolution of human consciousness, the seeds of cosmology are apparent in the animistic beliefs of the hunter-gatherers of Africa, the Andaman Islands, New Guinea, Australia and elsewhere. Disinterested in quantifying the movements of heavenly bodies, these people gave the sun, moon and constellations animate and even personal identities in the myths that formed the core of their ongoing spiritual practices. In so doing they bound calendric time into stories and songs, emphasizing again their spontaneous inclination to interpret the world around them in a wholly sociobiological paradigm. In the written history of the rest of humanity, records of cosmological theories far predate mainstream Greek philosophers such as Plato whose interests in time were consistently more esoteric. The regular movements of the Earth, Sun, Moon and the Stars betrayed the importance of cycles that in prehistoric ages had profound influence on the survival of many widely distributed populations. Thus, cosmology thrived in the ancient cultures of the Native Indians of North America, Aztecs, Mayans, Incas, Chinese, Egyptians, Indians and the Sumerians of Mesopotamia. To these we may add the Europeans of the Middle Ages and the efforts of the Greek scholar Heraclites (540-480 BC) whose calculations predicted a cycle of existence with a finite and definable periodicity.

The third reason is the innate ability of certain human populations in mathematics, geometry and architecture. Plato believed that the heavens had taught us numbers, arguing that mathematics began when people started reckoning the phases of the Moon. However, today we know that the mathematical, geometrical and architectural abilities that have enabled humans to design and build calendars are the product of genetically specified areas of the cortex posterior to those which serve cognition. It is therefore likely that the impetus to categorize time by monitoring the cycles of the cosmos is indicative of an innate ability at both mathematics and spatiotemporal perception and comprehension. Certainly, such abilities enabled the most gifted people of a number of ancient cultures to independently invent and construct devices for monitoring the movement of celestial bodies. From that point there existed the calendric apparatus for investigating time that would inevitably lead to important insights into its passage and our place in the universe.

The fourth reason is the fact that nature follows lengthy cycles that are extremely important to hunting and agriculture. This association of time with biology is apparent in many early calendric systems. Thus, the Aztecs and the Mayans named eighteen of the days making up their twenty-day months, after animals, plants, basic elements (eg.water) or climatic conditions (eg.rain). The remaining two days were given the name of two basic human artifacts - a flint knife and a house. Similarly, the thirteen moon months from the Inuit calendar are named after regular biological or climatic events, each corresponding to an environmental marker. For example, the month of Tirigluit (bearded seal pup) is related to hunting basking seals and moving from igloos to tents, while the next month, Nurrait (caribou calves) is related to the arrival of migratory birds and caribou calving and so on.

The ancients of Europe never doubted the relevance of time to agriculture; Hesiod, in the eighth century BC, writing in a poetical farmer's almanac that, "When Orion and Sirius are come into mid-heaven, and Arturus rises at dawn, then cut off all the grape clusters and bring them home." Time has implications for the biological, psychological, physiological, practical and ideational aspects of life. However, the significance of a high level of temporal intelligence is that it furnishes us with the inclination, and ultimately, the ability, to make extremely well defined plans within the social, practical and abstract domains of existence. The downside is that the thoughts of those so endowed are rarely in the present.

The Beginning of the Future
"Man is the only being that knows death; all others become old, but with a consciousness wholly limited to the moment, which must seem to them eternal. They see death, not knowing anything about it." Oswald Spengler (1880-1936). Philosopher and Social Theorist.

The importance one attaches to measuring time is directly related to one's ability to conceive the existence of the future - a faculty that is completely destroyed by prefrontal lobotomy. Just as humans vary in the values they place on chronology, so too they are divided on the matter of the future. In some populations, the future is regarded as of paramount importance while in others it is of little concern. This line of division is not a result of different belief systems or the conditioning of children to the ways of particular cultures. Instead it is a direct reflection of genetically determined, cognitive processes that naturally vary between populations of humans that have adapted to local conditions during long periods of relative isolation from the outside world. Within such populations natural selection simply operated in accord with the relevance of planning to survival. As in all aspects of human life, concern for the future and a focus in the present are simply two extremes of that part of the genome that determines the power of the temporal mind in fashioning the *modus operandi* of each and every individual. What is clear is that irrespective of its origin, the part of the world that joyfully indulges their preoccupation with planning considers the other part as either lacking in motivation, or suffering from is popularly known as the *manyana* (tomorrow) *syndrome*. And of course, those who can easily make time to watch the sunset regard the temporally inspired as little more than frenetic idiots who need to be humored and, if possible, seduced into the bliss of the now. In truth either cognitive style is a mixed blessing. Without the impetus to plan, much worry can be dropped and life can be, as the mystics recommend, more easily focused on the now. Alternatively, when a person possesses an innate drive to plan, seemingly great things can be accomplished.

The earliest evidence that *Homo sapiens* had developed an acute awareness of the future came from the discovery of a 28,000 year old calendar discovered at Blanchard, France. This discovery essentially pinpoints the first known participation of the temporal mind in a highly creative activity. The artifact shows the phases of the moon carved meticulously on a piece of bone. It is presumed to be a product of the same Paleolithic people whose dynamic, 3-dimensional paintings survive in the caves of southern Europe (*The Bloom of Abstract Creativity*: Chapter 6: Section 6) and whose lineage gave rise to the majority of people inhabiting modern Europe. Although Africa, Asia, India, Australia and New Guinea were populated when this calendar was made, no comparable device of such antiquity has been discovered in these countries. It would seem that the ability and impetus to accurately mark the passage of time and so to make long-term plans must have arisen first in Europe where it would, in due course, play a crucial role in transforming the world.

The Lineage of Planning

"Life can only be understood backwards, but it must be lived forwards." Søren Aabye Kierkegaard (1813-1855). Danish Philospher and Theologian.

To a greater or lesser degree all humans, from the Stone Age hunter-gatherers to the most urban Europeans, have some capacity to plan. The ability to plan appears in early childhood indicating that the temporal mind, like the social mind, must have an early evolutionary origin. In accord with this the cortex of temporal mind (BA10) is identifiable in the prefrontal lobes of both monkeys and apes. In humans, however, seven times more cortex is devoted to BA10 compared with the amount allocated in the apes. It seems that the human aptitude for planning can be attributed to the vast expansion of temporal mind over the 7 million years of hominid evolution that separates us from our common ancestors with the apes. Clearly the genes that increased the allocation of cortex to BA10 have been strongly selected for throughout the evolutionary progression from the australopithecines to modern humans. During the 200,000 years of human existence, selection for mutations that alter the allocation of cortex to BA10 must have created marked and environmentally related differences in the propensity to plan - differences that are still conspicuous across the populations of humans that inhabit the modern world.

Although some degree of planning is of fundamental importance to the life of all humans, it is clear that the propensity to plan varies even between closely related individuals. Indeed, the concern for time and planning is a critical dipole in the well tried and tested Jungian definition of personality. One's predisposition to planning is an inherent aspect of one's mindset and thus of one's psyche. Across the world, different populations also vary in their propensity to plan, each occupying a small part of a broad envelope that represents the total spectrum of planning aptitudes across all humanity.

In order to consider the evolution of planning it is important to understand that not all plans are identical. Planning may relate to any of the other three domains of cognition - social, practical or abstract. All forms are seen to manifest sequentially in the developing human, the child moving from plans of a psychosocial nature in early childhood, to plans of a practical nature in mid-childhood, to plans related to hypothetical issues in the preadolescent years. Plans within the social domain are easily observed in non-human primates and often involve an interpretation of the intentions of other individuals in an attempt to achieve a specific goal by the process of deception. An example of this would be the recorded efforts of an adolescent female gorilla to get close to the infant of a dominant female by making a series of nests that are positioned closer and closer to the mother and infant. Other natural behaviors are indicative of planning related to practical intelligence. For example, chimps will carry hammer stones for long distances in the hope of finding nuts and orangutans will make substantial detours to see whether or not the fruit of particular tree is ripe.

It is very difficult to show that animals are capable of planning within the realm of theories, ideologies or principles. Such planning clearly involves the abstract domain of thought. In the creative process a human inventor might, for example, synthesize a plan using a number of abstract theories, even though those theories are no more than ideas that appear valid because they describe phenomena in the real world. In is, however, very difficult to design methods to test whether an ape is capable of using concepts that describe their social or physical environment to synthesize a higher order concept upon which a plan might be based. There are, however, two possible exceptions in the behavior of chimpanzees. The first relates to the formation of war parties in chimp communities of Gombe, Africa. These war parties are extremely dangerous. Each phase of the maneuver reflects what appears to be a higher- or second-order strategy, in that the goal has complex implications for both the practical and social domain of agressors's lives. Little is left to chance. With all stealth, the chimps advance upon their neighbors reacting to any unnecessary sound with silent threat, whether its perpetrator is a comrade or an accompanying human observer. Success usually involves killing the males and possible older females of the vanquished community. The infants are also killed, bringing the remaining females into estrus and so precipitating their mating with the conquerors.

The second account concerns the observation of a group of male chimps, killing a leopard cub. While the whole chimp community participated in this feat, the critical part of the task was achieved when one male actually entered the birth cave and stole the cub from its mother. This accomplished, the other males participated in its murder. The extreme danger of forming war parties or stealing leopard cubs suggests that such plans must be motivated by strong and persistent beliefs. Although generation after generation of humans have marched off to almost certain death and mutilation in innumerable wars, one cannot help wondering whether, if the perpetrators of the Gombe battles had been humans and not chimps, we would have assumed a high degree of ideological premeditation behind their decision to participate in either activity. Certainly any belief that benefit will accrue from attacking a neighboring community or ridding the locality of a potential predator is suggestive of the participation of abstract thought and reminiscent of higher-order concepts that history shows underlie complex strategies in humans. These observations do suggest that in our closest relatives, as in us, the instinctual drives for sex and power are attained through plans that involve the higher- or second-order integration of social, practical and temporal cues – a synthesis that could only be achieved within the abstract mind (*The Origins of Culture*: Chapter 2: Section 8).

Looking back through the lineage of our hominid ancestors, planning probably followed a slow evolution from some unknown common primate ancestor to modern humans. Throughout hominid evolution the amount of cortex serving each domain of cognition must have progressively increased with the accompanying expansion of the social, temporal, practical and abstract mind, probably in that order. What this means is that the ability and impetus to plan increased throughout hominid evolution in association with other cognitive domains that determine the subject matter of would-be plans. Ultimately the selection of genes that increase the allocation of cortex to the temporal mind (BA10) would have been a vital step in cognitive evolution enabling an ever-increasing sophistication of planned responses to new and even postulated environmental challenges. Sadly, to their eternal detriment and the detriment of the planet, modern humans typically plan far beyond their needs. Such plans may last or even exceed an entire lifetime and have the unfortunate aspect that they are often focused upon achieving a specific goal without concern for the long-term environmental consequences. As a response of the biological world to environmental factors, evolution does not follow any predetermined plan. In concert with other domains of human cognition the evolution of planning is an example of how instead of promoting life, evolution could bring about the eradication of all life. The unique human capacity to make long-term plans endows us with the potential to easily out-strategize the immediate forces that govern nature. Ultimately an enlarged temporal mind is a potent threat to the natural world.

Chapter 5 - The Evolution of Practical Intelligence

The Invention of New Things

"The level of abstraction at which generalization can occur may….be an interesting component of intelligence." Richard Byrne, British Ethologist and Professor of Psychology. From: *The Thinking Ape - Evolutionary Origins of Intelligence.* Oxford University Press, Oxford, Tokyo, New York, 1995. p.153.

The essence of practical intelligence is (a) the ability to learn or recall a pre-existing methodology and (b) the ability to solve a new practical problem. If it exists at all, the *de novo* creation of a methodology is rare and indicative of a very high level of practical intelligence. In contrast, the ability to learn a preexisting protocol is a common part of everyday life and far less challenging to the material mind. Despite these caveats it is generally assumed, perhaps quite incorrectly, that there must have been a point in the evolution of practicality where the comprehension of the physical world became sufficiently detailed to allow the invention of new objects or technical processes. If such was the case, then these inventions must have reflected an unusually high level of practical intelligence. Inventions, be they theories or things, are the product of a long lineage of geniuses. For this reason, the oft-touted ideas of some educationalists, that students learn by attempting to reinvent the wheel or derive even the simplest mathematical algorithm, are quite simply foolish.

Given a selection of objects, all adult humans can improvise a crude tool or a shelter. But it is often said that nothing is new under the sun. Once upon a time perhaps some being did make the first tool or the first shelter, but the odds are that since that time subsequent beings have learned by watching others who in turn have learned from their forbearers. This thesis is supported by the extraordinary ability of humans to learn and pass on new technologies. There have even been examples of apes passing on newly acquired procedures to their conspecifics. The cerebral machinery that enables the transmission of technology is clearly fundamental to the primate mind. Nevertheless, the often, extraordinary accounts of human survival remind us that when faced with imminent death even the most technically inept, uneducated mind will achieve some success in the domain of improvisation if not invention. When it comes to survival, necessity, if not the mother of invention, has, at the very least, been an impelling factor in the evolution of intelligence.

Some people are very clever at technical improvisation. Driven by a powerful material mind, wherein is represented the functionality of a large number of familiar objects, they are capable of a high level of improvisation within the realm of real things. Such people are not easily distracted from their purpose by theories. Such ideas can wait while they take care of the business in hand. However, most things we make are not even the products of this base level of creativity. We are taught technology. Even those of us who are technically inept can be found controlling complex machinery that they could no sooner repair or invent than fly to the moon. Even maintenance workers act in accordance with learned factual information. Indeed, few airline passengers would be comfortable with the knowledge that their plane was serviced by an inventive aircraft technician.

Consider the arrival of the desktop computer and the World Wide Web. Here is an example of a highly complex system that operates upon rules and principles that 20 years ago were completely foreign to most people. Now this new technology has spread throughout the entire world. Sadly it will soon be possible to stagger off a Himalayan peak and into a smoky tea house to find the local shepherd making himself discontented by checking the price of a yak hair jacket in New York. He has educated his practical mind to accept the simple properties of a new set of objects. He does not need to know anything about operating systems or digital information transfer. The only improvisation he will need to do is to keep the smoke away from the silicon. Most of us are no different to this man. The user friendliness that underscores manufacturing and marketing success ensures that we rarely need to challenge our powers of improvisation and invention. Increasingly the facilities of modern tertiary education are diverted to the service of industry, imparting to young people technical procedures that will qualify them to repeatedly perform some complex but routine tasks to fill the coffers of a few. Ironically this is achieved at the expense of teaching them the art of productive wonderment and the principles of rational inquiry that invariably feed invention. The Renaissance man or woman, always a rarity, has become an icon from the distant past, not because of the complexity of modern technology but because of an insatiable greed for immediate monetary profit demands that each individual be devoted to the repetitious performance of a routine technology. Time and again our societies harness the human mind to repetitive tasks, essentially preventing our thoughts from traveling beyond the world of things to seek true revelation in the realms of possibility. Perhaps this is why in a world of 6.5 billion people true creativity is such a rare phenomenon.

Practical intelligence is about *how* to best do things in the material world. In the middle ages it may have been easy to envisage a horseless carriage as an abstract concept but it would have been a far greater challenge to establish the detailed methodologies necessary for the construction of a motorcar. Time and again in human history we see abstract thought driving practical observation and observation driving abstract thought as these two great avenues of human mentation interact. We pay homage to the process of reification, the process of converting a concept into a real thing. But we must also admit that our practical intelligence provides a stable substrate for inspiring our investigations of phenomena. No sooner have our practical creations been completed, than we begin to realize the full spectrum of their possible uses and so again there begins an endless cycle of ideation, manufacture and ideation that has spawned modern life. Within any population, the frequency of significant invention is indelibly bound to the rate of this alternating cycle of abstract and practical thought.

The Origin of Practicality
"It has often been said that no animal uses any tool: but the chimpanzee in a state of nature cracks a native fruit, somewhat like a walnut, with a stone." Charles Darwin (1809-1882). Biologist, Author of *Origins of the Species* and Co-founder of the Theory of Evolution.

The apparently unique ability of our species to farm, construct and use tools, weapons, houses and transport systems is commonly seen as an indicator of an level of intelligence that unequivocally divides humanity from the animals. Darwin referred to our upright posture as being a significant evolutionary step that freed the hands and enabled the making and use of tools. He also suggested that the canine teeth became reduced in size as handheld weapons supplanted their use in fighting and display. Practical ability was thus established as a cardinal gift of humanity. It was against this background that in 1964 the anthropologist Louis Leakey reported simple stone tools associated with the archaic remains of the oldest known member of the *Homo* genus, *Homo habilis*. To the Leakeys, and to many others, the tools of *H. habilis* were indicators of the dawn of creativity. While we may question the degree to which these findings reflect creativity, there is no doubt that the utilization of tools and the maintenance of a tool technology are critical indicators of an operative source of practical intelligence.

The tools were given the name *oldowan*, after the Olduvai Gorge, Tanzania, East Africa. The oldowan tools are made from selected stones that have a number of large flakes split often from only one end. They are so simple in construction that it has been estimated they would have taken no more than 7 minutes to create - an attention span which is in keeping with the small brain and prefrontal lobes of *H. habilis*. It is often difficult to ascribe a specific function to these creations with the result that they have been given names that simply described their geometrical form. Nevertheless they reflect the conspicuous presence of practical intelligence 2.3 million years before the appearance of our own species.

Despite Darwin's passing reference to nut cracking, the view that only humans used tools was to prevail until the 1970s when, working alone in Gombe, Africa, Jane Goodall made the first observations of chimps "fishing" for termites. Termite fishing involves the use of specially prepared sticks to insert into the holes of termite mounds and pull out the termites. Since then wild chimps have been described using a variety of tools such as leaf sponges and "spears" they construct by sharpening one end of a carefully selected stick. Even their use of rocks to crack a nut is no simple matter, but one that is associated with the construction and maintenance of so-called stone tool kits to break open the very hard Panda nuts. As only certain chimp communities use stones to crack nuts this "methodology" is considered to be an indicator of culture (*The Origins of Culture*: Chapter 2: Section 8).

The only other ape to use tools in the wild is the orangutan. As the living orangutans bear a close anatomical resemblance to the long extinct, *Sivapithecus*, that lived more than 12 mya, it is possible that tool use may extend back some 25 to 30 mya to the common ancestor of all apes. There is also evidence that the australopithecines used thin pieces of bone to "fish" for termites and rocks to break animal bones - crude implements that testify to the australopithecines having a material mind. It seems that conspicuous manifestations of practical intelligence and the beginnings of a material mind may have first evolved in the pre-hominid apes and to have already been present in the first australopithecines. There is little doubt that behind the gentle, inquisitive eyes of the orangutan and the chimp, is the cerebral potential to manipulate the physical world in ways that may even exceed the limitations of their physical abilities.

Searching for Solutions

"We think in generalities, but we live in detail" Alfred North Whitehead (1861-1947). English Mathematician and Philosopher.

Jane Goodall's work did much to open the question of whether non-human primates use tools in the wild. However, half a century before, laboratory studies had produced strong evidence that chimps had the capacity for tool use. In 1925 Wolfgang Kolher reported the landmark observations of the so-called *aha response* of the captive chimp, Sultan. Sultan was provided with a number of sticks all of which were too short to rake in a food reward placed well outside of his cage. After many attempts to get the food Sultan gave up and began playing with the sticks eventually joining two together. At this point Sultan seemed to realize the potential of this new construction and jumping up, used it to retrieve the food.

For many years Kolher's observations were considered to be an important demonstration of cognition and intelligence in apes. However, the case for Sultan's cerebral abilities was weakened when other chimps were observed joining sticks while simply playing. Nevertheless, it is still quite possible that by playing with the sticks Sultan was, perhaps instinctually, creating a *perceptual scaffolding* for thoughts relating to how they might be used to obtain the food. But if Sultan was thinking about a solution, then were his thoughts only within the practical-mechanical sphere or were they drawn towards the hypothetical in search of a novel idea?

As both the abstract mind (BA46) and the material mind (BA47) can be structurally identified in the prefrontal lobes of apes, then surely Sultan was capable of both forms of thought. So in the moments before he acted, were Sultan's thoughts bordering upon an intuitive understanding of the physical world that is formalized in the laws of Newtonian physics, or were they centered on the physical parameters of a set of familiar objects (sticks) and a cursory experientially acquired knowledge of their usefulness in everyday life? Was Sultan's thinking largely hypothetical like that of the pubescent adolescent entering Piaget's final stage of cognitive development? Or, alternatively, was it entirely practical like that which first develops in 7 to 11 year old children during Piaget's concrete operational phase of cognitive development?

Because of difficulties in communication it is very difficult to test the abstract abilities of an ape. However, the fact that many populations of humans have difficulty with tests related to abstract thinking indicates that apes are probably most adroit at practical rather than hypothetical thinking. The likelihood is that by playing with sticks in the past, Sultan was familiar of their properties and therefore capable of at least recognizing their potential for obtaining the food. Such an ability is indicative of a modicum of practical intelligence and the presence of an operational material mind.

Monkeys will focus their attention on a human imitating their object related actions. As directed attention in primates is largely driven by the mind (*The Exploration of Attention and Mental Imagery*: Chapter 1: Section 7), this observation indicates what we might call "interest" in the practical domain. Laboratory tests for practical intelligent in monkeys have been based upon assessing their ability, not just to attend to the manipulation of the material world, but to actually invent a solution to novel practical problems. Testing their use of reflective surfaces has, for example, revealed what appears to be practical intelligence. Monkeys are unable to comprehend the intentions of other monkeys or to recognize themselves in a mirror - characteristics generally considered indicative of cognitive ability within the psychosocial domain. Originally it was suggested that the absence of Mirror Self Recognition in monkeys was a result of their simply not being able to comprehend the practical meaning of a reflection. After all when presented with a mirror, the highland tribes of New Guinea, still living as a Stone Age culture, at first found its properties incomprehensible and frightening. However, it was soon discovered that monkeys could use mirrors to reach out of their cage and put pegs in the holes of a hidden surface of a board. In the wild they presumably can use natural reflections perhaps to explore the underside of a riverbank. These observations indicate that monkeys do understand the practical significance of reflections, even though they lack sufficient emotional intelligence to see an application for them with regard to their own image.

Simply learning to do a practical task is not considered sufficient evidence of a high level of practical intelligence. However, a major caveat in demonstrating practical intelligence in an animal is that any manifestation of practicality must be attuned to its normal patterns of behavior. There could, for example, be a vast difference in how a vigorous, energetic species and a more sedentary species, solve practical problems. In one experiment on capuchin monkeys, a nut was placed in a rigid horizontal transparent tube. The nut could only be moved using a stick. To obtain the nut it had to be pushed to the middle of the tube where it could fall out of a hole. Sticks of different length were supplied and the monkey allow to experiment. There were two possible strategies: (a) to try all the sticks quickly and (b) to select one stick after assessing the distance from the end of the tube to the hole at the center.

If we imagine giving this task to a different people, then we would surely expect some to adopt approach (a) and others to select approach (b). Watching these volunteers we would probably consider selection of one stick by some as indicative of practical intelligence and the trial and error strategy employed by others, as indicative of technical frustration. Moreover, we would not be in the least surprised to find that these two groups of people have different personalities that cause them to employ quite different cognitive strategies.

Capuchins are highly energetic animals that live in the South American forests. They feed by what is known as *destructive foraging*. This involves a troop smashing its way through the forest grabbing birds, insects and anything else that comes its way. In retrieving the nut from the tube the laboratory capuchins essentially applied the same strategy of high activity and were able to solve the problem in a few minutes. In World War II the Americans applied the same strategy, firing an estimated 100,000 rounds of ammunition for every enemy soldier killed. If you fire enough shots you have to kill someone and if you stuff enough sticks in the glass tube you are bound to get the nut. However, the method used by the capuchins was even more chaotic.

Instead of trying each stick in turn, their frenetic activity caused them to try sticks at random without even eliminating the ones that didn't work. The result was they often used the same stick several times even though it did not work the first time.

On the basis that the intelligent tool user must notice and remember what makes a tool successful and relate this to the corresponding properties of tools that fail, then it could be said that the capuchin's behavior did not reveal practical intelligence. However, it is also true that the capuchins might have "thought" it best to simply unleash the inherent behavior patterns that so aptly serve them in the wild - a conclusion that would have been quite correct given the rapidity with which they obtained the nut. Alternatively it may be that they are instinctually incapable of anything but an energetic frenzy when food is in the offing. Perhaps in their thoughts capuchins cannot even countenance any other procedure than haste. What is an intelligent strategy for a human is not necessarily so for an animal or for that matter even humans of different cultural origin. We all know people who are demonstrably backward at learning a practical task but we would never consider that they have absolutely no practical intelligence. All people possess practical intelligence but some simply have a smaller material mind than others. The capuchins remind us that, in its most basic form, thought might well have little, if any, observable manifestation.

The Practical Ape

"I went up to a chimpanzee on one occasion when I had ran a splinter into one of my fingers and pointed it out to him. Immediately his mien and expression assumed the eager intensity proper to "skin treatment"; he examined the wound, seized my hand and forced out the splinter by two very skillful, but somewhat painful, squeezes with his finger-nails; he then examined my hand again, very closely, and let it fall, satisfied with his work." Wolfgang Koehler (1887-1967), Phenomenologist and Psychologist. From: *The Mentality of Apes*. Trans. E. Winter. New York, Harcourt, Brace and Co., 1927, p. 308.

Practicality in a primate manifests primarily through the hand. Thus, as we ascend the evolutionary tree towards humans we find that the thumb increases in length so that, in humans, it can easily make contact with the forefinger. If this were not possible we would be like the apes and lack the mechanical finesse required for the creative manipulation of objects. A similar progression is apparent in the brain's motor systems. Thus, in primates the parts of the motor (BA4) and premotor (BA6) cortex that initiate and piece together the components of our movements send their axonal processes down into the spinal cord where they directly activate those motoneurons that innervate the muscles of the hand and fingers. It is the maturation of this descending motor pathway (the corticospinal tract) 18 months after birth that enables fine manual control in the human infant.

We have already seen how apes in constant contact with humans copy complex sequences of behavior such as fire lighting, using a comb or weeding a path. As these behaviors do not lead to a useful outcome it is difficult to be sure why the apes engage in them. Perhaps they believe that if they copy the activities of humans then some benefit will ensue. If so the form of thought driving their behavior is one related to hypothesis and possibility and not practicality.

Other isolated observations are more indicative of practical intelligence in apes. The San Diego zoo has a bonobo colony that is surrounded by a moat. The zoo keepers regularly drain the moat for cleaning. On one such occasion the keepers completed the cleaning and went to the kitchen to open the water valve and refill the moat. Kakowet, an old bonobo, immediately started screaming and waving his arms. It turned out that he had noticed that several young bonobos had entered the moat and were unable to get out. The keepers provided a chain and all climbed out, save the smallest which had to be pulled our by Kakowet.

One of the seminal examples of practicality in apes is the use by certain chimp communities of selected stones to crack Panda nuts. The basic kit consists of two components, a stone anvil and a hammer stone. These are not modified in any way but are sought out for their shape and size. Indeed, if the stones and nuts are located in different places chimps will carry selected stones for long distances. Today the few undisturbed hunter-gatherer cultures still live as Europeans did in the Stone Age. In particular the stone tool kits of the now extinct Tasmanian aboriginals have been compared to those used by the chimps. It would seem that despite having a brain approximately three times the volume of the chimp brain they made little advance in this aspect of technology. There are, however, several possibilities that might account for this quandary. Firstly, the use of stones as tools might have been of little importance to the Tasmanians. Secondly, it is possible that over the tens of thousands of years since their arrival, natural selection may have favored other domains of intelligence (eg. emotional) over practicality such that there was a reduction in of the amount of cortex allocated to the material mind. Thirdly, it is important to remember that the ability to learn the new methodology is most indicative of practical intelligence. In this matter of learning one might envisage extremely large differences between these two cultures even though they essentially share a particular technology. For instance, chimps mature at 16 but take from 7 to 14 years to learn how to use a hammer stone to crack nuts. Given the descriptions of the interactions of the early settlers and explorers with the Tasmanians, it is very difficult to believe that the latter's children could not learn this simple task as quickly as other human populations.

Most indicative of practical intelligence in chimps are the attempts mothers make to train their offspring to crack nuts using *scaffolding*. Psychologists define this as a process whereby a mother may set up things in a manner that will maximize the child's chance of success. That female chimps practice scaffolding indicates very strongly that they have a sufficiently detailed appreciation of the practical steps involved in a process to be able to facilitate the efforts of their young.

Although bonobos do not use tools in the wild, in captivity they show considerable aptitude for learning practical techniques from humans. Moreover, unlike the replication of novel activities by the orangutans and gorillas, the bonobos's feats of practicality have a clear purpose. Kanzi, a bonobo being used for studies of language learning, was confronted with a problem that required a sharp tool. Kanzi was presented with a box containing a food reward. The box was tied shut with string so that all he had to do was find a way to cut the string. Kanzi was not given a knife but allowed access to stone flakes struck off with a hammer by a human observer. Kanzi quickly realized that these could be used to cut the string to obtain the food. In time he became discriminating, testing the sharpness of each stone by placing it to his lips. He also tried using a hammer to strike off flakes of stone without much success. Then one day he invented a new method. He threw a rock on the hard floor causing it to shatter into flakes that he then selected for cutting the string. To be sure Kanzi was acting with intention, his trainers put carpet on the floor, only to find that Kanzi pulled up the carpet and smashed the rock on the exposed floor. Eventually he did master a form of the *percussion flaking* technique, not by using a hammer but by hitting two rocks together, to produce tools that, although crude by oldowan standards, served for the problem in hand.

Given that nobody has yet observed wild bonobos using tools, the efforts of Kanzi in first realizing the potential of sharp stones as cutters and subsequently trying to fashion them, are surprising. Again we have an example of an ape manifesting more sophisticated behaviors as a result of its association with humans. In sport it is frequently said that if you want to improve you should play with someone who is better. However, the most important message from studies of practical intelligence in the apes is that the ape mind appears to have potential beyond that expressed in their every day behavior. As we will see this idea is rarely expressed, yet lies at the heart of so much misunderstanding regarding intelligence, aptitude and the cognitive diversity of humanity.

The Practical Hominids
"It is a somewhat curious fact, that when all modern writers admit the great antiquity of man, most of them maintain the very recent development of intellect, and will hardly contemplate the possibility of men, equal in mental capacity to ourselves, having existed in prehistoric times." Alfred Russel Wallace (1823-1913). British Biologist, Explorer, Geographer and Co-founder of the Theory of Evolution by Natural Selection.

Humans are devoted to the classification of objects. To the Europeans in their conquest of the world, the priority of classifying the fauna, flora and geology was second only to plunder. With great forethought they realized the importance of knowing exactly how to best exploit the countries they conquered. The process of categorization is also apparent in less globally aggressive peoples. For example, the Pygmies of Africa can recognize hundreds of trees and animals that western biologists have since verified as distinctly different species. Also chimps, those living representatives of our archaic origins, can distinguish hundreds of leaves and fruits and have even been observed teaching their young to do the same.

That the non-human primates get into the act indicates that the propensity to classify is indeed a cerebral inclination inherited from our ancestors. In humans, however, the inherent inclination to classify is critical to both the need in language to group like entities and to constructive practicality. As we have seen, these faculties, language and practical thought, are further interrelated within the brain - both BA47 and BA45 (the anterior part of Broca's area) participating in the process of practical thought as well as the production of language (*The Origins of Practicality – The Material Mind*: Chapter 3: Section 3).

Without classification it is difficult to see how it would be possible to either imagine or physically create tools. Chimps, for example, have to have a cursory knowledge of different kinds of rocks in order to pick the ones useful for breaking nuts. The same need holds for the sticks and bones selected by chimps and australopithecines, respectively, to "fish" for termites. Even these simple tools reveal a cerebral system of classification that cannot be accounted for by instinctual drives existent within the brain's emotional centers. We can say this almost emphatically as in the brain of higher primates only the mind is supplied with information pertaining to the physical parameters of objects while what visual and auditory information is sent to the emotional centers is almost entirely of relevance to instinct.

The simplicity of the oldowan tools of *H. habilis* caused skeptics to suggest that they were not really the creation of a cognitive process but the fumblings of a creature with a very high level of visuospatial ability - an argument somewhat weakened by the fact that the arboreal agility of chimps, bonobos and particularly the orangutans would require a high visuospatial ability. Such views, however, could not account for the next highest level of stone tool production - the *achuelean* stone tool culture of *H. erectus*. The name achuelean is derived from the French dig at St. Acheul. However, achuelean tools have also been found buried above the layers containing the oldowan tools of *H. habilis* at the Olduvai Gorge, Africa. They consisted of bifaced, chipped handaxes, cleavers, blades and points the earliest being dated at 1.6 mya - around the time *H. habilis* became extinct but about 300,000 years *after* the oldest remains of *H. erectus* 1.9 mya. Compared to the roughly hewn rocks of *H. habilis*, tool construction was "suddenly" elevated to a level that, without instructional training, most modern humans have difficulty matching. In their constructional complexity, the achuelean tools certainly represented a quantum leap in practical creativity that ensured their continued use with little modification until only 200 kya when anatomically modern humans first appeared.

Given the relationship between brain size and general intelligence amongst modern humans, one might expect that the creation of achuelean tools might be accompanied by a quantum leap in brain size. However, the largest brain size reported for *H. habilis* (around 800cc) is not substantially different from that of the oldest specimens of *H. erectus*. This possibly accounts for the 300,000 year delay between the evolution of *H. erectus* and the appearance of achuelean tools. Certainly by 0.7 mya the brain of *H. erectus* markedly enlarged, reaching 1060 to 1300 cc – a size that overlaps that of modern humans. It is hard to imagine that in the evolution of a larger brain, natural selection would not have favored mutations that markedly increased the percentage of cortex allocated the material mind.

In its epic journeys across Eurasia, *H. erectus* spread achuelean tools from Europe to what are now the islands of Indonesia. To scientists and anthropologists devoted, by their very nature, to theoretical issues, the proliferation of these tools was an unequivocal indication of practical creativity. The literature is filled with statements to the effect that the achuelean tools were "unquestionably products of a mental template that existed in the minds of the makers" or that they reflected a *de novo* ability to "mentally visualize shapes in advance of construction". While there is no doubt that an increase in the size of the material mind would enhance one's comprehension of the material world and the associated mental imagery, it is very unlikely that each and every *H. erectus* had to imagine anew the achuelean tools and to develop a means of constructing them. Consider how many modern humans mentally comprehend even the simplest devices they are obliged to use everyday of their lives. Cast into the wilderness, how many New Yorkers would be able to invent an achuelean tool in order to survive? The truth is that while invention is rare, methodological learning is common. Indeed, many inventions may be the result of aberrations of the mind. Already we have seen how autism occasionally produces savants with extraordinary gifts within the asocial domains of cognition. There is no reason to believe that autism did not occur in our otherwise, emotionally intelligent hominid ancestors. Given the small numbers of *H. erectus*, it is theoretically possible that all the basic techniques used to produce achuelean tools were invented by a single individual carrying a mutation that produced an abnormally large material mind and a correspondingly high practical intelligence. It is further conceivable that this individual's lineage was extinguished before it could contribute more to invention, such that in *H. erectus* history his or her presence was not unlike the visitations of culture bringers in our own ancient mythologies.

Once invented, the methodology of creating achuelean tools, could, like any other methodology, be passed on. There being little choice in technique there was little likelihood that the feat of stone tool creation could be achieved by a different method (emulation). It is more likely that in the same way as young gorillas learn to prepare nettles for eating; the young *H. erectus* would naturally employ program-level imitation in learning to arrive at the significant steps in the tool making procedure.

The next step in practical intelligence heralded the arrival of a new methodology of making stone tools called the *Levallois technique*, after Levellois-Perrt, a suburb of Paris where flint tools were discoveredin the 19th century. This method required more skill and concentration than is necessary to make the achuelean tools. Even modern humans require training and practice to master this technique. It involved shaping a core by removing flakes before striking one critical flake that would become the tool itself. Believed to have evolved in Africa around 300 kya, the Levallois technique had spread to Europe by 200 kya where it was used, in pre-human times, by the Neanderthals to make points and side-scrapers. It is also possible that the first *Homo sapiens*, the so-called anatomical modern humans of Ethiopia, may have also used this technique. The production of these tools became known as the *mousterian industry*. It disappeared from Europe around 40 kya when the Neanderthals were in decline. By 45 kya modern humans were in Europe where they were to produce the large variety of very fine stone tools and 3-dimensional cave paintings that distinguished their culture from those of all other *H. sapiens*.

Tools and art objects were not the only thing indicating the practicality of the Neanderthals. Three wooden spears, found in Germany in layers dated at 400,000 years old, are also indicative of a previously unmatched level of practical intelligence. Not only are these spears carefully crafted but they are properly balanced in the same way as a modern javelin, indicating again the existence of an intermediate level of practicality, more advanced than that of any of the hominids that preceded the Neanderthals.

In the course of its evolution, practical intelligence has passed through a series of steps from the simple adaptations of objects by the chimps and the australopithecines, to crudely hewn stones of the oldowan culture, the bifaces of the achuelean culture, the coring technique of the mousterian industry and the wooden weaponry of the Neanderthals, reaching its zenith in the refined artifacts of the Paleolithic ancestors of modern Europeans. From the primordial practicality of the apes, the progressive expansion of the material mind has driven an exponential increase in technological ability culminating in a modern world where the machine is at last king.

The Methodology of Mimicry
"I do not understand my own actions." Saint Paul (c. 10 AD – c. 67 AD). Leading Apostle of Christianity.

In October 2004, a team of Indonesian and Australian scientists, led by anthropologist Mike Morwood announced the astounding discovery of a new species of hominid in Liang Bua cave on the Indonesian Island of Flores. Nine individuals were identified, dating procedures indicating that their habitation of the area fell between 12,000 and 74 kya. The most complete specimen was the skeleton of a 30-year-old woman nicknamed Ebu. Ebu died 18 kya. With a height of only one meter and a skull the size of a grapefruit, Ebu was thought to be a member of an *endemically dwarfed* hominid species, subsequently called *Homo floresiensis*. The origin of these tiny hominids is controversial. Their skull has some anatomical similarities to the skull of the australopithecines. However, as yet the most likely hypothesis is that they are the dwarfed descendents of a population of *Homo erectus* that are considered to have arrived in the area 840 kya.

Endemic dwarfism is an evolutionary process whereby the size of large animals confined to a circumscribed, resource-limited environment, progressively decreases. Throughout the vertebrates, a smaller body, in general, requires a smaller brain. Yet, despite having a brain of only 417 cc - less than that of the australopithecines and roughly equivalent to the chimp - Ebu's remains were found in association with fire usage and crude stone tools approaching in complexity the achuelean type made by *H. erectus*.

There is reason to be skeptical as to whether a hominid with a brain the size of a chimp could make achuelean tools or use fire. In the annals of ape behavior, one individual is reported to have devised a means of making sharp-edged stones in order to cut the string that was preventing it getting a food reward. This animal eventually did learn from an instructor how to use percussion flaking to make a cutting edge (*The Practical Ape*: Chapter 5: Section 6). The products of this exceptionally gifted individual were, however, far less complex than the tools found with the remains of *H. floresiensis*.

It is possible that *H. floresiensis* stole the tools from other prehumans or from modern humans or, alternatively, that it learned to make tools by simply watching them. These theories have been contested because, (a) as yet, no remains of *H. erectus* less than 50,000 years old have been found in that part of Indonesia and (b) there is no evidence that modern humans were present on Flores more than 10 kya. Against this, however, it needs to be said that Flores is less than 1,000 km away from excavations sites in Java that have proven to be rich in the remains of the wandering *H. erectus*. As some of these remains have been dated at less than 30,000 years old, it seems very possible that *H. floresiensis* may have had company over the tens of thousands of years that it inhabited the island of Flores. If this was so, then, outside theories of theft, we are presented with the possibility that this small-brained hominid actually did make achuelean tools – a possibility that is as challenging to conventional neurology as it is to the, now well-established, relationship between hominid intelligence and brain size (*Brain Size and Intelligence*: Chapter 2: Section 1 and *The Measurement of Intelligence*: Chapter 2: Section 8).

There is one neurological theory that goes some way to explaining this quandary. The clues were revealed when scans of the inside of Ebu's skull enabled scientists to visualize the shape of its brain and, more importantly, to assess the relative size of the prefrontal, temporal, parietal and occipital lobes. These measurements showed that if a reduction in brain volume accompanied the evolution of *H. floresiensis*, then it was focused on the posterior and central sensory-motor areas of the cortex – areas that in accord with endemic dwarfism could be reduced in size because of the ever-decreasing sensory-motor burden that accompanies an increasingly diminutive body. In comparison, the prefrontal lobes (including the cognitive areas, the orbital cortex and the anterior cingulate gyrus), the parietal and temporal cortex, were proportionally less reduced. Clearly, any selective pressures governing the evolution of endemic dwarfism in *H. floresiensis* must have also resulted in a disproportionate retention of parietal, temporal and prefrontal cortex.

The prefrontal cortex fulfils a compendium of vital functions, including intelligence (the mind), prediction (the orbital cortex) and bonding (the anterior cingulate gyrus). Preservation of the prefrontal cortex would have been crucial to the tribal existence of *H. floresiensis*. Likewise, preservation of the temporal lobe would have been critical to the maintenance of auditory acuity, object recognition, reading facial expressions and body language, episodic memory, spatial awareness and the reptilian emotions of fear and anger – elements critical to the navigating of day-to-day life.

Neurobiologists have referred to the prefrontal cortex as the organ of creativity. For this reason the retention of a disproportionate amount of prefrontal cortex in *H.*

floresiensis has been used as a possible explanation for its ability to make tools. Against this, however, is the fact that the brain of *H. floresiensis* is so small that, even with disproportionately large prefrontal lobes, the area of its prefrontal cortex could not greatly exceed that of a chimp. With a total brain volume ranging from 830 to 1,300 cc, the brain of *H. erectus* was two to three times bigger than the brain of *H. floresiensis*. It follows that if the same proportion of cortex was allocated to the prefrontal lobes in each species then the prefrontal lobes of *H. floresiensis* would have been only 32 to 50% those of *H. erectus*. We have to double the allocation of cortex to the prefrontal lobes of *H. floresiensis* just to attain a volume that is roughly equivalent to the prefrontal lobes of the smallest-brained *H. erectus* but that is still only 65% of the largest-brained *H. erectus* (*Brain Size in Human Evoltuion*: Chapter 2: Section 1). Put this another way, we can only match the size of *H. floresiensis's* prefrontal lobes to those of the smallest-brained *H. erectus* if we are willing to assume that two thirds of the *H. floresiensis's* cerebral hemispheres were allocated to the prefrontal lobes.

Crude as they are, these calculations they leave little doubt that the prefrontal lobes of *H. floresiensis* would have been considerably smaller than the prefrontal lobes of any variety of *H erectus*. Armed with a similar sized prefrontal lobes one exceptionally intelligent bonobo (Kanzi) did eventually learn to sharpen stones - a feat that is still considerably less demanding than creating achuelean tools. Consequently, it seems very unlikely that what appear to be the highest "creative" abilities of *H. erectus*, tool making and fire usage, would survive as such if there were a marked reduction in the size of its prefrontal lobes. It seems that if *H. floresiensis* did make achuelean tools then they did so using parts of the brain that are not directly involved with intelligently generated creativity.

The key to this riddle may lie in disproportionate preservation of the parietal cortex. In humans and apes, the parietal cortex is partially composed of cortex that forms the *inferior parietal lobule*, a cortical area that is known to be essential for mimicry and imitation and for imaging the one's own actions (left hemisphere) and the actions of others (right hemisphere). The monkey brain lacks an inferior parietal lobule and unlike humans and apes, monkeys neither mimic nor imitate (*Mimicry, Movement Primitives and the Mind* and *Imitation*: Chapter 2: Section 6). Clearly all species of prehumans, from the first australopithecines to *H. erectus*, would have been adept at mimicry and imitation, simple because, as descendants of the apes and the ancestors of humans, their cortices must have contained well-developed, selectively-advantageous, inferior parietal lobules. Even with its limited mental powers, *H. floresiensis* may have been able to exploit its disproportionately larger inferior parietal lobule to enable it to simply copy the actions of other agents

While mimicry enables the transference of simple "Simon-says" actions, complex sequences of behavior as well as the underlying strategies can be transferred through program-level imitation (*Imitation*: Chapter 2 : Section 6). Mimicry and imitation must have been critical to the tool making activities of all prehumans, including, with its reduced brain, *H. floresiensis*. Even the act of empathizing so crucial to maintaining social cohesiveness, involves what has been called *inner mimicry* - a process wherein specialized parts of our visual cortex informs us of the facial expressions and body language of the other person and enables the recreation within us of the emotional responses of the that person (*The Nature of Empathy*: Chapter 2: Section 4).

Neuroscientific research is showing that both mimicry and imitation play an increasingly significant part in the development and maintenance of a host of behaviors that cross all domains of human endeavor. Even as small-brained infants we are capable of mimicking simple movements. By our second year we are typically "imitating" complex sequences of behavior associated with specific tasks, such serving a meal – tasks about which the infant can only the most rudimentary understanding. There is no doubt that our typical 2 year old would be trying ("pretending") to make stone tools if, instead of watching its parents serve meals, it spent hours each day watching them manufacturing simple implements. Nor does it seem that such transference is limited only to between members of the same species. Apes acculturated to humans "imitate" all sorts of behaviors including some that involve a number of complicated maneuvers such as lighting a fire, trying to use a hammer to drive in nails or using a boat to collect food for an infant (*Imitation*: Chapter 2: Section 6). In theory, a small-brained hominid equipped with mirror neurons and sufficient parietal cortex, may well be able to acquire the behavioral sequences needed to make and find uses for, stone tools - possibly without entertaining any *apriori* purpose.

It is highly likely that, rather than intellect, much of what has been attributed to learning and intelligence in our hominid ancestors might have been the product of brain systems that almost automatically reproduce complex behavioral sequences without any initial need for a cognitively appreciated objective. Although imitation has been defined as copying the actions of another *with* an awareness of their purpose, we have already seen that there is good reason to believe that, at least in non-human primates, the transference of behavior through an essentially "imitative process" often occurs without any *apriori* "knowledge of purpose" (*Imitation*: Chapter 2: Section 6). In terms of reinforcing a behavior, all that is important is that even in the absence of a perceived purpose, performing the behavioral will lead to the attainment of a reward. When this is the case, the *principles of operant conditioning* prevail and the individual has incentive to adopt the copied behavior even though the underlying strategies were concocted within the mind of another agent; an agent that may even be the member of an entirely different species.

In thc West, the importance of mimicry and imitation to human education and societal structure has been sorely underrated. The "discover-it-for-yourself" principles of many contemporary educationists are particularly indicative of a pervasive ignorance regarding the true nature of human learning. To humanity, inheriting an inferior parietal lobule has been critical to stabilizing behavior across generational gaps, potentially enabling the direct transference of body language, practical techniques and even theories and ideologies. Whereas the cognitively-composed elements of each individual's behavior come and go with each passing century, the brain processes underlying mimicry, imitation and program-level imitation have the potential to enable the unadulterated, generational transference of a set of useful actions and principles, virtually forever.

Chapter 6 - The Evolution of Abstract Intelligence

Before the Coming of Yahweh
"The king is the sun, his kingship the image of the sun's course. All his life the king plays 'sun' and in the end he suffers the fate of the sun: he must be killed in ritual forms by his own people." John Huizinga (1872-1945). Dutch Cultural Historian, commenting on the writings of Leo Frobenius.

While climbing in Switzerland early in the 20th century a father and son stumbled on the Drachenloch Grotto (or Dragon's Cave), discovering what many believed to be the oldest evidence of spiritual practice. Inside they found a number of cave bear skulls "arranged" in a "stone cabinet" which occupied more than half the grotto. These remains were said to be 80,000 years old. Only the altitude of the Drachenloch Grotto saved its contents from being crushed by the movements the massive glaciers that throughout several long ice ages scoured all trace of life from the valleys far below. One of these skulls was arranged on two leg bones and held at an upwardly inclined angle by a thigh bone (tibia) inserted through the zygomatic arch or cheek bone. Anthropologists argued that inserting the bulbous head of the tibia through the zygomatic arch, requires an axial twisting motion that could only be achieved by a manually dexterous hominid. As modern humans only arrived in Europe around 45 kya, these objects were thought to be indicators of a *cave bear cult* invented by the Neanderthals. As such they would be the first indicators of symbolism that might be representative of a very basic, animistic religion.

Over the years the case for the ritualistic arrangement of bones in Drachenloch grotto has been considerably weakened. Careful analysis revealed that the cave contained the remains of tens of thousands of bears, indicating its repeated use by these animals over a long period. Despite this, evidence has accrued of ritualistic behavior amongst the Neanderthals, in the form of Neanderthal remains adorned with jewelry and gravesites decorated with what appear to be symbolic markings. Skeptics have claimed these findings represent the activity of *Homo sapiens*, who coexisted with the Neanderthals from as late as 35 kya in Europe and as early as 130 kya in the Middle East, archaic forms being dated as early as 190 kya. The finding, in Europe, of a mammoth tooth, with adhering red pigment, dated at between 78,000 and 116,000 years of age, is good evidence that the Neanderthals did fashion art objects well before the arrival of modern humans in Europe. The discovery of what appears to be a ritualized dismemberment of Neanderthal bodies is further evidence that, unlike any of the hominids that preceded them, the Neanderthals entertained an essentially ethereal concept of death. The motivation and cerebral ability to compose and perform rituals with the dead and to worship spirits of any kind, testify to the existence, in the Neanderthals, of a domain of contemplation that lies squarely within the hypothetical.

It has always been a curiosity that the Neanderthals had a brain that was slightly larger than that of modern humans. While much of this expansion may have been related to expansion of the sensory-motor areas required to cope with their larger body, it might also have been accompanied by an increase in the size of their prefrontal cortex and in particular BA46. The result of such an increase in the size of the abstract mind might have been sufficient to enable it to elaborate the ideas underlying ritualistic behavior. Only thus would the Neanderthals have been cerebrally moved to link abstract concepts such as the "spirits" of cave bears and the "spirits" of their own dead to a second abstract concept, that of the "after life". As the DNA of the Neanderthals is presently being sequenced, we may in time be able to read within it the dimensions of the cortical areas that constituted their mind. Then perhaps we will be able to better guess whether they may have generated complex hypotheses, such as there exists a God, or Gods to whom all things and feelings beyond comprehension, can be attributed.

Size and Performance in the Hypothetical

"Is man merely a mistake of God's? Or is God merely a mistake of man's? Friedrich Nietzsche (1844-1900). German Philosopher, Cultural Critic and Classical Scholar.

Given that monkeys have some cortex devoted to BA46 it would be most surprising if the brains of *all* our hominid ancestors did not also have a considerable amount of cortex allocated to their abstract mind. Furthermore, unless the connectivity of their brains was radically different to that of humans and all other living higher primates, then BA46 must have had an operational role more or less identical to the abstract mind in humans. Again the issue of whether the pre-Neanderthal hominids were motivated by abstract thought probably relates specifically to the size of their abstract mind.

At present the only evidence that apes and the higher monkeys can envisage theoretical problems and hypothesize solutions is that their prefrontal lobes do contain the region (BA46) that is structurally similar to the cortex that forms the abstract mind in humans. In contrast, we know that humans contemplate the hypothetical because we can watch ourselves doing just that and hear from others that they are similarly employed. We can also see in human history that certain individuals have made astounding discoveries from insights gained entirely through the process of making hypotheses about the phenomenological world. These discoveries form a unique domain of creativity that is totally dependent on abstract thought of the form that develops in the formal operations phase of childhood. Significant ability in such endeavors presumably marks those few individuals who are endowed with a very large BA46 (Figure 6.4).

Compared to humans, the size of BA46 in apes and monkeys is very small. The tiny marmoset monkey with a brain not much bigger than that of a rat, has within its substantial prefrontal lobes, a few square millimeters of cortex identifiable as BA46. When an area of the mind is physically small it is reasonable to presume that it can only be utilized for a very limited number of functions. Nevertheless, as long as it receives the same types of connections from the rest of the brain then its operational brief for performing those functions may still be same as in creatures in which that area is of larger size. In humans with a large abstract mind, hypothetical thought plays a constant and obvious role in the fashioning of behavior. Indeed, the abstract mind of humans appears to have plenipotentiary powers over the synthesis of much behavioral strategy. This was probably not the case in our pre-Neanderthal ancestors and nor is it likely in today's living, higher, non-human primates. In all these creatures we might imagine abstract thought playing only a formative role in behavior, interacting with the other domains of cognition but rarely if ever gaining the energy required to produce prolonged behavioral repertoires on the basis of its formative inputs - time and space.

Apes show no sign of engaging in any form of spiritual practice. The only hint of abstract intelligence comes from the abilities of captive chimps at tasks such as puzzle and maze solving - tests that are simple versions of those used to define abstract intelligence in humans. In the wild, however, indications of their ability to think in the abstract are either meager or inconspicuous. Once again it seems that when in contact with humans, or when challenged in controlled laboratory situations, apes express cerebrally motivated behavior that is more sophisticated than has been detected in the wild. As we will see this is also true of humans, where contact between long isolated, hunter-gatherer cultures and Europeans has often resulted in the former developing cognitively based skills such as the production of 3-dimensional art that eluded them for the tens of thousands of years that preceded European contact.

What can explain this difference between the primates in the wild and primates in contact with beings capable of advanced thought? One reason is that we might expect the mind of any higher primate to have an absolute capacity that is beyond that required to meet the daily demands of its natural lifestyle. To put it another way, each domain of the mind may well have a built-in safety factor that ensures that its size, and thus its computing capacity, is over and above that necessary in meeting day-to-day challenges. Such a safety factor will enable the host animal to cope with unusually complex, life-threatening problems or respond opportunistically to unexpected sources of education. A simple biological reason for this is that the cortex receives a very large quota of the brain's blood supply and that the high levels of cortical activity required during periods of intense thought are very energy costly. Natural selection would certainly favor a cognitive machine able to perform on a day-to-day basis without evoking the stress of extreme demands on energy. We might therefore expect that any mammal with a mind, including humans, will have a *modus operandi* that is easily attainable given the computing power of their mental apparatus.

The Mind in the Wild

"It was noticed by Muldrow that members of this tribe [the Me'en, a remote Ethiopian tribe], when given a page from a children's coloring book, would smell it, examine its texture, listen to it while flexing it, even attempt to taste it, but entirely ignore the picture." Jan Deregowski, Art Psychologist From: "Illusion and culture." In: *Illusion in Art and Nature*. Eds. Gregory, R.L. and Gombrich, E. H., Duckworth, London, 1973, p. 167.

Where the mind is concerned there has always been great debate as to whether a given population learnt its cultural ways or whether these arose as a consequence of their inheriting unique mental, emotional and thymic characteristics. Largely because of the European obsession with complex reason and abstract creativity, this debate has essentially focused upon the products of abstract thought. In general terms, the issue is to what degree does cultural change depend on the process of learning and to what degree is it dependent on the introduction of new mutations that increase or otherwise alter cognitive ability? The picture is eternally confusing. The learning school is fond of pointing out that language is a learnt behavior. However, language is best learnt in a critical period of development that begins even before the maturation of the social mind. Those who support the view that genes have considerable influence over the cognitive style of a culture, point to many examples showing that, like physical attributes, cerebral gifts and their attendant behavioral preferences, run in families. Clearly the mind has great potential to expand its powers through learning, yet its absolute potential in any individual seems to be defined by the genetic specification of cortical architecture. Just as there exists a vast diversity of physical and physiological characteristics between different races or populations, so too there must surely be an equivalent diversity in the allocation of cortex to the four domains of the mind – a phenomenon that translates directly into a diversity of cognitive styles, a clear geography of thought and potentially, culture (The *Diversity of Intelligence*: Chapter 2: Section 8).

Since the first humans left Africa somewhere between 70 and 100 kya, modern humans have migrated across the entire world. Nevertheless, we need only go back a few centuries to find a world with less than a half a billion people where discrete populations lived for many millennia in relative isolation. What little we know about their cultures tells us that they fell into geographical patterns that, like language itself, are distributed along the migratory route of early humans across a hitherto uncharted world. For example, most of the hunter-gatherers cultures are contained in an arc across the Indian Ocean that passes through the tip of India, the Andaman and Nicobar Islands, the New Guinea Highlands to Australia. Anthropologists of the early 20th century referred to these people as the Australoids and frequently commented on the very basic differences between their cultures and those of Europe, Asia and the Americas. The key to understanding these differences is that the hunter-gatherer seems to be entirely dominated by the social mind such that their ways are largely the product of their emotional rather than abstract intelligence. Their rites, languages and social mores as well as their interpretations of the unknown were entirely related to psychological, biological and essentially animistic concepts. In line with this cerebral inclination their art was traditionally focused on painting their own bodies. In the realm of practicality they were satisfied for tens of thousands of years with relatively simple devices mostly constituting weaponry and shelter. In comparison, the descendants of the Paleolithic Europeans employed the systematic use of hypothesis and experimentation to elucidate the basic principles underlying the physical, biological and psychological worlds before applying these insights and knowledge in a systematic manner to invent complex machinery, establish modern medicine and build huge cities. Having achieved these goals, they then set off to explore and pillage a world that was essentially defenseless against the allure of their offerings, the power of their sophisticated weaponry, the metaphorical complexities of their ornate religions and their totally divisive way of life.

Intent upon exploitation of essentially defenseless cultures, the Europeans touted the politically correct argument that their presence would enable those countries to develop a technologically advanced lifestyle for themselves. History shows that as far as the native and hunter-gatherer societies go this was a totally naïve and spurious ideology of entirely divisive purpose. With the exception of some Asian countries which already showed signs of considerable technological and philosophical complexity, nothing short of slavery and annihilation awaited the native and hunter-gatherer peoples. In reality, the European invasions did little more than provide a grisly theater for studying the, often catastrophic, interactions that repeatedly occur when peoples of radically different mind sets and racial backgrounds are forced, by greed or foolish ideologies, to be members of a single society.

Art and architecture are perhaps most revealing of the inherent differences in cognitive style. With regard to architectural principles, the European invasions soon revealed that hunter-gatherers such as the Zulus and the San or Bushmen, and many native populations have little inherent concern for what is known as *carpenteredness*. This is essentially the mental motivation to design and build in accordance with angles and straight lines. Even long before the formalization of Euclidian geometry, carpenteredness was a vital component of the constructions of the early Europeans. In contrast, the simple dwellings and irregular land boundaries of the hunter-gatherer and many native societies, illustrate a marked indifference to corners and angles. Analysis of their spatial perception soon showed that indeed many hunter-gatherers had difficulty either seeing perspective or, more to the point, giving it priority in assessing a scene. Instead they seemed to spontaneously contemplate the world in a 2-dimensional framework centered very much upon themes derived from the biological and social realms - themes characteristic of a dominant emotional intelligence.

The natural inclination for the hunter-gatherers to meet the challenges of survival with emotional intelligence is not restricted to perception, architecture or construction. Whereas agrarian societies favor games of strategy, the hunter-gatherers like games that require physical skill or that depend upon chance – elements that reflect a mindset perfectly adapted to the hunter's need for physical prowess and the gatherer's acceptance of the rules of chance. Indeed, in 1883 anthropologist Edward Man (1846-1929) recorded that the Andaman Islanders regarded agricultural labor as "a degrading occupation and fit only for such as have forfeited their freedom." To many hunter-gatherer societies the European obsession with interfering with nature in an attempt to increase her abundance, seemed absurd.

In the same way as art is a definitive key to the cognitive performance of children, it also provides the most fascinating example of both inherent cultural differences and the propensity of the mind to surpass its normal limits of performance (Figure 6.5). Generally speaking the pre-invasion pictures of all hunter-gatherers are very simple in form. Dating back more than 40,000 years the oldest Australian rock paintings are possibly the work of the descendants of the earliest emigrants from Africa. These pictures typically show groups of figures either performing a ritual or engaged in hunting. Even recently, the ancient rock paintings of the Australian aboriginals and those that survive in Africa have been described as stick figures that lack the proportions and perspective necessary to impart depth, as well as, the fluidity of form needed to create a sense of dynamic reality.

Body art is probably the earliest form of art and the discovery of ochres aged at more than 300,000 years indicate that it may have originated amongst the Neanderthals. Just as the social mind evolved before the abstract mind, it seems that the performance of body art preceded illustrative art. Thus, in their natural state many hunter-gatherers felt no inclination towards illustrative art and yet frequently painted and otherwise decorated their bodies. To these emotionally intelligent people, the idea of decoration of the body was clearly of more significance than the idea of using art to permanently record the position and form of the things and phenomena that surrounded them. Observations made at the time of their first contact with Europeans are particularly germane to these principles. For instance, when first contacted by the Europeans, the Tallensi of Northern Ghana were found to be completely devoid of representational graphic art. Asked to draw something both adults and children produced very crude stick figures of animals and humans often filling in the surrounds with zig-zag lines of the type still used in modern Africa to decorate house walls or leatherwork. Asked to draw their village they produced a diagram with a scattering of very crude stick figures representing animals and people. Orientation in space seemed less important for the non-human elements in a drawing. Thus, in the drawings of the Bushmen, animals were represented at all angles including upside down, while people were mostly drawn in an upright position. Typically, however, an animal drawn on the ground was considered asleep while if it was drawn on a wall it was awake. Also reported in these early studies were the difficulties many native Africans had with relating the size of objects in pictures to their distance from the observer and with detecting visual illusions that depend on diagonal lines to provide an index of depth and size.

The American Indians or the *Clovis people* reached the Americas by crossing the land bridge that once ran across what are now the Bering Straits. Before leaving North Eurasia, they split from these "Siberians", some of whom would migrate southwest into Europe to become the first Europeans (*The Bloom of Abstract Creativity*: Chapter 6: Section 6). Traditionally, the American Indians produce graphic art and sculpture with a highly symbolic content that emphasizes animal powers and the internal skeletal structure of animals – the latter appearing in the art of European children in the concrete operational phase of cognitive development and that of the Australian Aboriginals. Again like the art of the hunter-gatherers, the traditional creations of the American Indians tend to lack a convincing representation of either the third dimension or the fluidity of movement. It seems that prior to European contact, their art was primarily driven by forms of intelligence emanating from the practical and emotional domains of cognition.

The accurate representation of the third dimension is seen in the drawings of the majority of European children when they move from the concrete operations phase (7 to 11 years) into the formal operations phase (11 to 15 years). This shift is accompanied by the maturation of the abstract mind and the *de novo* ability to generate hypotheses about intangible phenomena. A cognitive processing of space and time are clearly essential to a comprehension and subsequent artistic rendition of both perspective and movement. Prior to the formal operations phase, the drawings of all children (other than autistic savants) tend to be simplistic 2-dimensional representations of the world. This relationship between artistic expression and the dominant aspect of mind is borne out by several studies which show that the switch into the formal operations stage of cognitive development is far less prominent in hunter-gatherers whose behavior and art continues to be primarily organized around emotional rather than abstract intelligence. What is astounding is that under the influence of the Europeans, the children of both, Native Americans and African hunter-gatherers, rapidly learned to produce art with the scaled perspective essential for portraying the third dimension.

To explain these observations it is necessary to assume that in their natural habitat every individual has a mental capacity that enables him or her to easily meet the basic demands of existence and yet, with tutoring and practice, may develop skills that do not emerge naturally as part of the inherent composition of their mind. To put it another way, like apes acculturated to the complexities of human behavior, humans can also get more out of their mind than is required for their survival in their natural environment (*Imitation*: Chapter 2: Section 6).

For a long time, we have known that the neural interconnections within the cortex of a rat raised with many toys far exceeds that of a littermate which has been confined to an empty box. This result has relevance to the human mind simply because the connectional plasticity of one piece of cortex is much like another. The aptitude of any human for tasks requiring abstract, practical, emotional or temporal intelligence can thus be improved with the relevant teaching and practice, which presumably increases the connectivity and processing power of elements of the mind serving that particular domain of cognition. Whenever any population has been obliged to live in daily contact with the cognitive doctrines of an alien culture, the innate tendency for conflict is also accompanied by some cross-cultural transference of, hitherto unrealized, skills and ideologies.

The games, architecture and prehistoric art of the hunter-gatherers and the native people of the world tell us that they are not, like the early Europeans and their descendants, dominated by the cognitive processes of the abstract mind. Instead these activities reveal cultures founded primarily on the practical and emotional domains of human cognition. This conclusion is further supported by careful surveys showing that African Americans do poorly on those questions in the western IQ test that target abstract intelligence. The mental faculties of the world's hunter-gatherers and the native peoples are adapted to generate behavior that enabled them to survive for tens of thousands of years without irreversibly destroying the natural world. To these people the ways of modern western society offer only stress, discontent and great potential for failure.

The Bloom of Abstract Creativity
"Pre-historians, who have traditionally interpreted the evolution of prehistoric art as a steady progression from simple to more complex representations, may have to

reconsider existing theories of the origins of art." Valladas, H., Clottes, J., Geneste, J. M., Garcia, M. A., Arnold, M., Cachier, H. and Tisnerat-Laborde, N. (2001). Palaeolithic paintings. Evolution of prehistoric cave art. *Nature* 413, 479.

Sooner or later every human population has to struggle to survive. Under rigorous climatic conditions, such as those in Europe between 40 and 10 kya, food and shelter may only have been attainable through a process of making and testing hypotheses – the business of the abstract mind. All humans are so dependent on cognition that when nature changes the rules, necessity becomes the mother of cognitive evolution and ultimately, an increased inventive ability.

It has been shown that 80% of modern European men are related to Paleolithic ancestors who arrived in southern Europe approximately 45 kya. The other 20% are related to Neolithic farmers who originated from the *fertile crescent* between the Tigris and Euphrates rivers of Mesopotamia. Approximately 10 kya these Neolithic farmers began spreading westward through Europe taking with them their seemingly innate, predisposition to farming and establishing successive bands of agriculture across western Europe.

The first Europeans were the *Aurignacians*. By 35 kya, the Aurignacian culture of southern Europe was at its peak, creating sophisticated rock art and finely crafted tools of antler, bone and ivory. Around 40 kya the temperature began to drop in the build up of the last glacial maximum, which began 24 kya and ended approximately 8,000 years later (16 kya). These changes threatened the survival of the Aurignacians, who by 25 kya were confined to a few pockets scattered across southern Europe.

The next wave of migration began 33 kya. The invading people were called the *Gravettians*. The Gravettians are thought to be from central Asia but it has also been suggested that their unique characteristics evolved while they were living on the plains of Poland, Northern Germany and further east. The most important of these characteristics was an enhanced mental ability to invent improved weaponry, fishing nets and warm clothing, including sewn furs and woven textiles. It was also the Gravettians who made the voluptuous Venus figurines – the oldest known sculptures.

The extreme cold between 24 and 16 kya would have been a powerful selective pressure for the evolution of an increasingly dominant abstract mind in both the Aurignacians and the Gravettians. However, although many modern Europeans carry Aurignacian genes, the Aurignacians were already reduced to small enclaves even before the onset of the glacial maximum, 24 kya. Those that did survive took refuge in the Iberian Peninsula and the Ukraine, while the more cognitively sophisticated Gravettians retreated to the Balkans. Whereas previously, practical, psychosocial and a modicum of abstract thought could have adequately served humanity's needs, the extreme cold would increasingly require inventiveness based, like the scientific method, on hypothesis and experimentation – a vehicle of invention that would be enhanced by the selection of any genes that might increase the amount of cortex allocated to the abstract mind, BA46.

Although survival is critical, it is always those activities that are simply an expression of freedom that best represent the forms of thought dominant within the individual. Examples of such activities are art, architecture and games – activities chosen by people in moments when they are free from the demands of day-to-day survival. Of all such activities art probably provides the greatest freedoms and so is most highly indicative of the underlying forces of creativity. The Aurignacians were the first artists in human history to successfully capture the third dimension, enabling them to convincingly portray both form and movement - abilities characteristic of the logical operations phase of cognitive development in European children. The oldest European cave paintings so far discovered are located in the Lascaux Grotto. These were painted 38 kya, a few thousand years after the habitation of southern Europe by the Aurignacians. Beyond the rigid, patterned figures of the hunter-gatherer tribes of Africa and Australia and the stylized icons of the American Indians, the cave paintings of Europe catch the dynamic flow of movement, form and space that only those dominated by abstract thought could have envisaged (*Defining Attention and Imagination*: Chapter 1: Section 7). Somewhere between 30 and 45 kya, when the Aurignacians and Gravettians were en route to southern Europe, there evolved a people who had an entirely new mentality. Its arrival signified the evolution of a dominant abstract mind from which would emerge all the Indo-European civilizations that, like H. G. Well's Martians, "were to bring so much calamity to Earth".

Section 6: Recommended Reading

Bandura, A. *Social Learning Theory*. Englewood Cliffs, Prentice-Hall, New Jersey, 1977.

Byrne, R. *The Thinking Ape: Evolutionary Origins of Intelligence*. Oxford University Press, Oxford, Tokyo, New York, 1995.

Dautenhahn, K. and Nehaniv, C. L. (Editors). *Imitation in Animals and Artifacts*. A Bradford Book, MIT Press, Cambridge Massachusetts, London, 2002.

Deregowski, J. B. "Illusion and culture." In: *Illusion in Art and Nature*. Eds. Gregory, R.L. and Gombrich, E. H., Duckworth, London, 1973, pp. 160-191.

Deregowski, J. B. *Distortion in Art: The Eye and the Mind*. Routeledge and Kegan Paul Books Ltd., London, 1984.

Deregowski, J. B. *Illusions, Patterns and Pictures: A Cross-Cultural Perspective*. Academic Press, London, 1980.

De Waal, F. and Lanting, F. *Bonobo: The Forgotten Ape*. University of California Press, Berkley, Los Angeles, London, 1997.

Frith, C. and Wolpert, D. (Editors). *The Neuroscience of Social Interaction: Decoding, Imitating and Influencing the Actions of Others*. The Royal Society. Oxford University Press, Oxford, 2004.

Cavalli-Sforza, L. L, Menozzi, P. and Piazza, A. *The History and Geography of Human Genes*. Princeton University Press, Princeton, 1993.

Cavalli-Sforza, L. L. *Genes, People and Languages*. North Point Press, New York, 2000.

Cooley, C. H. *Life and the Student*. Knopf, New York, 1927.

Goleman, D. *Social Intelligence: The New Science of Human Relationships*. Hutchinson, London, 1998.

Gregory, R. L. and Gombrich, E. H. (Editors). *Illusion in Art and Nature*. Duckworth, London, 1973

Rajkowska, G. and Goldman-Rakic, P. S. (1995). Cytoarchitectonic definition of prefrontal areas in the normal human cortex: II. Variability in locations of areas 9 and 46. *Cerebral Cortex* **5**, 323-337.

Horton, D. *The Encyclopaedia of Aboriginal Australia: Aboriginal and Torres Strait Islander History, Society and Culture*. Aboriginal Studies Press for the Australian Institute of Aboriginal and Torres Strait Islander Studies, 1994.

Humphrey, N. *The Inner Eye: Social Intelligence in Evolution*. Oxford University Press, USA, 2003.

Huizinga, J. (1955, first published in German in 1944). *Homo Ludens - a Study of the Play Element in Culture*. Beacon Pree, Boston, 1955.

Jobling, M. A., Hurles, M. E. and Tyler-Smith, C. *Human Evolutionary Genetics: Origins, Peoples and Disease*. Garland Publishing, New York, 2004.

Keeley, L. H. *War before Civilization*. Oxford University Press, New York, Oxford, 1996.

Koehler, W. *The Mentality of Apes*. Trans. E. Winter. New York, Harcourt, Brace and Co., 1927.

McDonald-Pavelka, M., *Monkeys in the Mesquite: The Social Life of the South Texas Snow Monkey*. Kendall/Hunt Publishing Co., 1993.

Meltzoff, A. N. and Decety, J. (2004). "What imitation tells us about social cognition: a rapprochement between developmental psychology and cognitive neuroscience." In: Frith, C. and Wolpert, D. (Editors). *The Neuroscience of Social Interaction - Decoding, imitating and influencing the actions of others*. The Royal Society, Oxford University Press, Oxford, 2004. pp. 109-130.

Morphy, H. "Australian Aboriginal Concepts of Time." In: Kristen Lippincott (Editor). *The Story of Time*. Merrell Holberton in Association with the Maritime Museum, London, 1999, pp. 264-267.

Morwood, M. and Van Oosterzee, P. *The Discovery of the Hobbit: The Scientific Breakthrough that Changes the Face of Human History*. Random House Australia, Sydney, London, 2007.

Nisbett, R. E. *The Geography of Thought: How Asians and Westerners Think Differently....and Why*. Nicholas Brealey Publications. London, Yaramouth, Maine, 2003.

de Waal, F. B. M. *Our Inner Ape: The Best and Worst of Human Nature*. Granta Books, London, 2006.

Pinker, S. *The Language Instinct: How the Mind Creates Language*. Harper, Perennial Modern Classics, New York, 2007.

Ruspoli, M. *The Cave of Lascaux*. Harry N. Abrams Inc., New York, 1987.

Squire, L. R. *Memory and the Brain*. 1st Edition, Oxford University Press, 1987.

Sykes, B. *The Seven Daughters of Eve*. Corgi Books, London, 2001.

Valladas, H., Clottes, J., Geneste, J. M., Garcia, M. A., Arnold, M., Cachier, H. and Tisnerat-Laborde, N. (2001). Palaeolithic paintings. Evolution of prehistoric cave art. *Nature* **413,** 479.

Tobias, P. V. and Biesele, M. *The Bushmen : San hunters and herders of Southern Africa*. Human & Rousseau, Cape Town, 1978.

Section 7

Reality and the Control of Consciousness

"Once upon a time, I, Chuang-Tzu, dreamt I was a butterfly, fluttering hither and thither, to all intents and purposes a butterfly.......suddenly, I awoke.........now I do not know whether I was then a man dreaming I was a butterfly, or whether I am now a butterfly dreaming that I am a man."

Chuang-Tzu (c. 4th Century BC). Chinese Philosopher.

Chapter 1 – Attention and Imagination

The Subjectivity of Mental Imagery

"…awareness of the obvious involves suppression of fantasy, minimization of conceptual activity, and the elimination of anticipation or reminiscences." Claudio Naranjo, Chilean Psychologist and Author, and Robert E. Ornstein, American Psychologist and Author. From: *On the Psychology of Meditation.* Penguin Books, USA, 1972, p.88.

It is evening. You are lounging on some rocks overlooking the sea, savoring the beauty of each passing wave, sculpting from its raging tumult the terrified eyes, the frothing mouths of Ocean's cavalry as they charge hell-bent towards the beach, there to be annihilated by the steadfast garrisons of *Terra Firma*. Watching until, at last, the watcher and the watched have become one. Watching when without warning something barely perceptible stirs and there comes the inevitable moment of change. Instantly, the battle recedes, its armies dispersed, fleeing, as it were, the fields of consciousness to be replaced by the warm, scented immediacy of a familiar presence. Your lover has crept up from behind you and although you cannot see her you feel the softness of her touch. And in your mind, where only seconds before the legions of Earth and Ocean rode to certain death, there are now only wishful longings for the timeless intimacy of that first embrace. While on the edges of your awareness the war continues unabated, no longer are your thoughs drawn only to visions of cataclysm. Now the once hostile mind willfully surrenders to the tender yet carnal apparations of love, mercilessly driven by an unshakable belief in a Utopian tomorrow, when intoxicated with bliss, time itself will at last have reason to stop. The transformation is complete. Where only an instant ago there was the carnage of war, now there is only your lover - your lover, the rocks and the restless sea.

The existence in all humans of the process of imagination, underscores the powerful interactions between the seat of thought and the rest of the cortex from whence, be they from our visceral or somatic body, all our perceptions arise. By reaching out across the cortex the mind literally commandeers those areas of the cortex responsible for perception, creating, in the process, "images" that reflect, aid and abet its immediate designs. Look into the face of your beloved. Here is someone who within you is everywhere, someone who is part of your every thought, whose soul seems indistinguishable from your soul and whose presence pervades the entirety of your life. Without effort your mind automatically focuses attention upon those higher visual areas that enable you to see her countenance, appreciate her form and savor her every movement. Yet this mind is no *tabula rasa* there simply to obscure one's partner. It is, on the contrary, a mind increasingly driven by instinctual cravings, a mind that strives to reach back to the neural foundations of those desirable perceptions with the explicit purpose of using the processes of imagination to embellish those images that consistently herald pleasure. Such moments, however precious, are often accompanied by a conspicuous transcendence of reality. Gone are the warts and wrinkles. The crone has become a Goddess, the aging despot a God. In the process of envisaging your beloved, reality is simply impossibility. Beauty is not in the eye of the beholder but in the mind of the beholder. And it is well that it is so, for physical perfection is short-lived. Although there can be no doubt that the genetic specification of the size and power of all relevant areas of our cerebral cortex have a fundamental effect on our perception of beauty and ugliness, the influence of the mind on perceived imagery ensures that we only ever "see" the world through our parental, societal and religious conditioning.

Defining Attention and Imagination

"Everyone knows what attention is. It is the taking possession of the mind, in clear and vivid form, of one out of what seem several simultaneously possible objects or trains of thought. Focalization, concentration of consciousness are of its essence. It implies withdrawal from some things in order to deal effectively with others, and is a condition which has a real opposite in the confused, dazed, scatter-brain state." William James (1842-1910). American Psychologist and Philosopher.

While imagination is a wholly creative phenomenon wherein our mind conjures images of novel objects, people and even complex situations, directed attention is a process whereby we can focus on particular things that have already entered our awareness. The term *mental imagery* does not refer only to internally generated, visual images, but includes auditory phenomena like internal dialogue (the common practice of conducting conversations in our head), as well as the imagining of somatic, olfactory, gustatory sensations, those visceroemotional experiences we call feelings and even future activities. In each case, mental imagery involves the *de novo* activation of the relevant perceptual or episodic representations (Figure 7.1). Directed attention does not involve the creation of mental imagery but operates by placing the relevant cortical representations under a physiological microscope, essentially amplifying, to discernable levels, their otherwise subliminal responses to the sight, touch, sound, smell, taste, feeling or episode that is of interest to the mind. Directed attention facilitates the expression of information in selected domains of consciousness while imagination activates otherwise silent areas of cortex to conjure images of an entirely internal origin. So it is that the simple vision of passing waves becomes first the object of our attention and then the subject of the creative embellishments of our imagination.

The mind and only the mind, has the capacity to construct mental imagery while directed attention is driven by both the mind and, in its role as the executor of emotion, the anterior cingulate gyrus (Figure 7.2). Consequently, directed attention is a faculty accessible to both the processes of thought and the instinctual urges that motivate the behavioral patterns of the lower, "mindless" mammals. In lower mammals such as rodents, the anterior cingulate gyrus substitutes for the mind (Figure 7.3). Indeed, its very conservative executive role in the human cortex probably reflects the primitive mammalian condition in which, the areas of cortex (BAs 9, 10, 46 and 47) that elaborate thoughts, are completely absent. The role of the anterior cingulate gyrus in focusing our attention in accord with our instinctual drives must certainly provide a critical support to the cognitively immature human infant. In adult humans, however, the most commonly observed manifestation of this process is probably our involuntarily, innate and often clandestine attraction to erotic imagery. As the name suggests, we owe our capacity for mental imagery to the mind, whereas our ability to direct our attention, though largely mental in origin, is also under the control of our instinctual drives.

In the presence of a powerful mind, reality is possible only for the most insignificant of things. When people's gaze is monitored while they look, for the first time, at a complex picture, it can be shown that they focus only upon very specific parts of the picture and inadvertently treat all else as irrelevant background. The human mind's capacity to focus our attention and to create internal imagery is so subtly pervasive that only when all thought stops and the mind is silent can we begin to really see our surroundings and observe what is actually happening. Normally the mind has its own agenda and, in the process of directing attention, searches each scene for things it considers to be relevant. In this sense, the mind spontaneously acts as a highly selective, yet capriciously creative, observer. Indeed, every person falls prey to the subtle and seductive energies of the mind while only a few awaken to the shocking realization of the, often gross, distortions of reality that arise as a consequence of beliefs and attitudes contrived within the wholly unnatural medium of thought. Only when the mind is silent, only then when we are detached from the trance of our conditioning and the confines of our mental heritage, do the processes of our attention and imagination rest. Only then do we truly witness what is before our eyes and what is truly within us.

The untrained human mind, ripe with intention, simply cannot be restrained from applying its wholly acquired beliefs to the processes of attention and imagination. For the untrained mind every scenario becomes the focus of its deductive processes and every event a consequence of its innate obsession with cause and effect, so much so that eventually its inevitable miscalculations caste a foreboding shadow across the gates of truth. As a consequence of the human mind's capacity to create internal imagery and direct attention, the human operates, like no other organism, almost entirely within the realm of cerebral fantasy. All humans are inadvertently aware of the illusory qualities of the mind, for be it in sex, war or religious ceremony, the essential purpose of all fantasy is to bring our, otherwise renegade, thoughts into line with the prevailing energies of our id.

The Exploration of Attention and Mental Imagery
"The eye sees only what the mind is prepared to comprehend". Henri Bergson (1859-1941). French Philosopher.

In the early 1980s the Swedish neuroscientist Per Roland was the first neuroscientist to use a brain scanner to reveal the origin of attention and imagination. While scanning their brain, Roland first asked his subjects to simply watch an object moving on a screen. He then asked them to close their eyes and try to visualize the object moving in the same manner. When, the subjects were actually watching the moving object, the areas of cortex that registering visually detectable movement (BA39) and the form of objects (BA20) as well as the primary visual receiving areas and the mind, all became active. In contrast, when the subjects closed their eyes and attempted to imagine the moving object, there was no activity in the primary visual receiving areas even though the mind and the perceptual areas registering movement and form were activated.

Though imagination is clearly inspired by our observations, it is, in practice, an entirely internal construct. Because Roland's stimulus was a moving object, the mind and the higher visual areas involving movement (BA39) and object perception (BA20) were always activated when his subjects attended to the object. In his *attention task* his subjects had their eyes open, with the result that activity in the perceptual representations (BA20 and BA39) was always accompanied by activity in the cortex's primary visual receiving areas. However, when his subjects were performing the *visual imagination task* things were very different. With their eyes closed, the cortex naturally received no visual input. Consequently, the primary visual receiving areas were silent and yet the mind and the appropriate visual perceptual areas were still active. These results show very clearly that the experience of mental imagery is the summed experience of one's thoughts driving the cortex's perceptual areas to create imagery. The same phenomenon also prevails for all other domains of sensation, be they somatic, auditory, olfactory, gustatory or visceroemotional in origin. More recent work shows that the mind can also evoke activity in the hippocampus – an area of cortex instrumental in storing and recreating episodic memories. Roland's discoveries resolved forever the source of mental imagery. His pioneering work would prompt future investigations into the realistic, involuntary and pathological hallucinations of the schizophrenic (*The Freewheeling Mind of Schizophrenia;* Section 3; Chapter 4) as well as providing a firm basis for understanding the differences between the intentional generation of mental imagery and the ethereal imagery of dreams (*The Cortex in Sleep and Dreams*: Chapter 2: Section 7).

The mind is first and foremost the *organ of intention*. When the mind is challenged with developing ideas and strategies it often relies upon the cortex's perceptual representations for creating the images and scenarios that constitute a quasi-reality upon which the processes of imagination. By expressing in imagery its ongoing thoughts, the mind has opportunity to internally test its own deliberations. Without this possibility the mind could only ever test our would-be solutions by manifesting them in the real world, a process that would clearly have disastrous consequences.

The Manipulation of Mental Imagery
"We request that every hen lay 130 to 140 eggs a year. The increase can not be achieved by the bastard hens (non-Aryan) which now populate German Farm yards. Slaughter these undesirables and replace them." Nazi Party News Agency, April 3rd 1937.

The cortex's perceptual areas are not only the windows of the mind but also serve as "image" banks loaded with perceptual templates that are accessible to our mental processes. It is the sorting of raw sensory information into the cortex's perceptual areas that enables color, shape, motion, weight, texture, size, sound, smell, taste and each emotion to find meaningful expression in human consciousness. It is only because we possess some very specialized perceptual areas that represent complex

307

elements of experience such as, body language and facial expressions, that these things can be the focus of our attention or the subject of our imagination.

The difference between imagery of sensory origin and intrinsically generated imagery, is that only the former is dependent on information from, and activation of, the cortex's primary sensory receiving area. This difference presumably explains why mentally created imagery virtually always has an ethereal quality that distinguishes it from imagery of sensory origin. This link with reality, conferred by the cortex's sensory receiving areas, is illustrated by observations of patients who have suffered damage to parts of their cortex involved in bodily sensation. As well as representing sensory information arising from the skin, these *somatosensory* areas also collect information from sense organs that measure the movements of our joints and the degree of stretching of our muscles. It is this sensory monitoring of muscle length that is the first step in providing us with a perceptual awareness of the positioning of our body and limbs. Occasionally a stroke or traumatic injury will cause irreparable damage to those perceptual areas of the cortex responsible for monitoring the body's form. If this damage also extends into the sensory receiving areas then, when his eyes are shut, the patient is rendered incapable of knowing his body's posture or the position of his limbs. What is most significant, however, is that such patients are not spontaneously aware there is anything wrong. That is to say, they have no reason to believe that any domain of experience is missing. A totally different picture emerges in a similar group of patients who have suffered damage that is totally confined to the perceptual areas. Like the former group, these individuals lack an awareness of the position of their body. However, unlike the former group, they *are* continuously aware that there is something wrong. Within these patients, the intact sensory receiving areas appear to create the ghost of a familiar but absent experience – an experience that without the appropriate perceptual areas cannot be converted into an identifiable perception (*The Gift of Awareness*: Chapter 1: Section 2). As we have seen, only in schizophrenia does the mind appear to have the capacity to activate the primary sensory areas, imparting to the auditory hallucinations of schizophrenics a profound, though flawed sense of reality (*The Freewheeling Mind of Schizophrenia*: Chapter 4: Section 3).

It is very difficult to imagine things we have not seen. This is because mental imagery exploits our cortex's perceptual areas and draws upon our episodic memories stored in the hippocampus. All such areas have been tuned by incoming information about things and events in the outside world. It is because of this that our ability to imagine and manipulate our mental images of objects, reflects our ability to examine and manipulate real objects. For example, the time employed to scan a visual scene is matched by the time employed to mentally imagine the scene. Similarly, if we are asked to imagine the form of a familiar object after it has been rotated, the time it takes is linearly related to the degree of rotation. Clearly the perceptual centers involved are tied to the physical dynamics of the real world wherein the turning of objects is progressive rather than instantaneous – a feature that may well change as the perceptual systems of generation after generation are increasingly exposed to the instantaneous changes of imagery made possible by computers.

Exactly what can be created in mental imagery by any particular individual is strongly influenced by the environment in which they were raised. This is so because the cortex organizes itself around the information it receives. For example, when kittens are reared in a visual environment of vertical bars their visual cortex becomes relatively unresponsive to horizontal bars. The same thing may well be true of human populations who spend their life in flat treeless plains, or alternatively, forests of tall trees. In the human, however, the presence of a powerful mind means that people raised in desert environments will not only have a diminished ability to see verticals but will also be diminished in their ability to employ vertical constructs in their mental imagery. As a consequence of the absence of verticals during brain development, both the perception and the mentally elaborated concept of the vertical dimension will be compromised.

As we have seen, mental imagery plays an important part in the production of art. Nevertheless, most people believe that when asked to draw something, they carefully sketch the subject of their vision. They do not believe that their mind plays a critical role in envisaging the object while they believe they are accurately reproducing its form. Yet even very young autistic savants, when asked to reproduce a complex scene, glance at the picture for only a few seconds before, in keeping with the nature of their surviving mental processes, reproducing it in profound, yet exclusively mechanistic, detail (*The Mechanistic World of Autism*: Chapter 4: Section 3). In the reproduction of scenes, ordinary people also rely very strongly upon their ability to conceptualize objects and translate these concepts into tangible mental images. Only when asked to reproduce *unreal figures*, does the contribution of mentalization to internal imagery, become obvious. Unreal figures are objects drawn in a manner that is simply impossible in reality. In a typical unreal figure the edges of a box move out of their normal plane and join with other edges in a manner that can be witnessed in the drawing but cannot be integrated with the way things are seen in the real world. Escher's *Relativity* is an example of art that exploits our eerie fascination with the conspicuously normal when it is presented in a geometrically impossible format.

If we are asked to draw a familiar object, we do not have to copy each detail but instead we can work from our mentally evoked image of the object. This construct, which begins as a concept, is transformed into visual imagery by the mind's influence over the perceptual center that is responsible for representing the form of objects. This task is far more daunting to people who have lost the ability to see objects as a consequence of malfunction of the so-called object area (BA20), a condition known as *visual agnosia*. When asked to draw a common object such as a cup, these patients cannot see the whole object but are only able to detect and replicate the lines that form the edges of the cup, simply because this information, and only this information, is still available within the intact primary sensory area of their cortex's visual system. Whereas it takes most people a few seconds to draw a cup, the visual agnosic patient is obliged to slowly reconstruct the cup by drawing the lines that form the boundaries and edges of the image. Deprived of a perception of the whole object, the visual agnostic is unable to use his mental concept of a cup to generate and maintain a mental image. The thought or concept is in his mind but there is no longer a cerebral screen on which to create the appropriate imagery. The conundrum he faces is therefore much like the normal person challenged with the task of drawing an *unreal figure* (eg. the impossible triangle) for which no conceptual framework can exist in a mind exclusively conditioned to the geometrical realities of the real world. The visual agnostic lacks the perceptual substrate necessary for him to create an internal image of objects, while the normal person cannot generate the mental concept required for him to create an internal image of an unreal figure. As a consequence, the time taken by the visual agnosic to sketch a familiar object is similar to the time it takes normal people to draw an unreal figure. For different reasons both individuals are obliged to focus on, and to progressively reproduce, small details in their attempts to reproduce the whole.

A plethora of visual illusions demonstrate that the rendition of reality elaborated by the cortex's perceptual representations is not necessarily accurate. Perceptually speaking, the straw sitting in the glass of water is definitely bent at the point where it passes through the surface. If it were not for our mind's ability to recall that straws are usually straight and to note that the apparent bend occurs exactly at the air-water interface, we might, like a small child, accept this illusion as reality. However, the educated adult mind is not so easily fooled and even if it does not already have the knowledge to explain the origin of a potential illusion, it will soon generate the simple procedures necessary to test whether the straw is straight or bent.

It has been suggested that blind people are more commonly musically gifted because some of their unused visual areas are responsive to sound. An alternative view is that without any visual input, the blind are acutely focused on sound, if for no other reason that to gather information about their surroundings. In normal people, musical ability has been related to the amount of cortex contained within the *planum temporale of the right hemisphere*. The planum temporale (part of BA42) is one level removed from the cortex's primary auditory receiving area (BA41) and therefore serves the perception, rather than the raw sensation, of sound. The planum temporale essentially acts as the perceptual substrate for auditory mental imagery involving both musical and non-musical sounds – tasks on which the musically gifted out perform ordinary people. It again seems that our perceptual abilities and our ability to create mental imagery are linked in that both are determined by the amount of cortex allocated to the relevant perceptual areas.

One of the most significant areas of mental imagery relates to the mind's influence over the cortex's motor areas. For a long time it has been known that watching other people perform a complex set of movements, such as a sporting maneuver, actually improves the first time performance of naïve participants. Even the heart rate and respiration rate increases when subjects mentally rehearse physical exercise, some researchers claiming a concurrent increase in muscle strength comparable to that achieved through real exercise.

Motor imagination typically involves the subthreshold activation of those parts of the cortex's motor areas that have the capacity to generate the movements associated with what is being imagined. In this process movement of the eyes is quite naturally very prominent. When subjects listen to someone reading, their eyes involuntarily move left and right or up and down as the story makes reference to these dimensions. This is not surprising considering that a coordinated response to sound and sight is critical to the way humans explore their surroundings.

Many challenges to imagination do not monopolize any particular motor or perceptual domain. When a group of adults were asked to use mental imagery in relation to their craving for food, 40% created visual images, 30% gustatory and 16% olfactory. Clearly people vary in their ability to produce mental images within any particular domain of perception. This phenomenon must be strongly influenced by inheritance because, when it comes to smell, only some people are capable of forming very vivid, yet mentally evoked, renditions of particular smells – a process which is always accompanied by sniffing. When asked to imagine a good smell these individuals involuntarily generate a large sniff, while only a small sniff accompanies their efforts to imagine a bad smell. The process of imagining a particular perception (eg. a smell) is intimately linked to that part of the motor system driving the related movements (sniffing).

The content of mental imagery is highly dependent upon whether the social, material, temporal or abstract domains of cognition are seeking expression through the process of imagination. When subjects attempt to imagine moving 3-dimensional images, activity is found within the abstract mind (BA46) and those perceptual representations that enable us to experience the position and movement of objects. In contrast, the social mind (BA9) only participates in imagination when there is a need to generate the mental imagery of social interactions by activating those perceptual areas that are responsible for our awareness of the body language and biodynamic movements of other agents and our own emotional responses. Thus, listening to stories that require a comprehension of the intentions of the characters, not only activates the social mind but via the process of imagination, also activates the perceptual area that normally represents body language - an activation that is particularly strong when the subject is asked to imagine themselves participating in the story.

The same organizational principles underlie our imaginings of future scenarios. This process begins in the temporal mind (BA10), which draws upon the cortex's store of episodic memories by activating the hippocampus. In addition to spatial memory, the hippocampus is responsible for consolidating and archiving episodic memories (*Dreams and the Transfer of Emotional Memories*: Chapter 2: Section 7). Considered as just another piece of cortex, the hippocampus behaves like the perceptual areas of the cortex, in that it can be activated by the mind for the purposes of elaborating whole episodes of our past. To imagine the future, or to create a fictitious story, the mind is obliged to solicit the aid of the hippocampus to draw upon an ensemble of relevant past events - an ability that is lost if the hippocampus is damaged. Rather than coherent scenes, patients with hippocampal damage can only imagine fragmented collections of sensory images, such as smells and sounds – elements of experience that are stored in the cortex's perceptual areas. In the process of imagination, the hippocampus serves as a neural platform specifically designed to enable the mental elaboration of episodic memories – a function fundamental to the creation of fictional stories.

When we are guilty of showing a lack of empathy we are commonly told to imagine the feelings of another person (*The Nature of Empathy*: Chapter 2: Section 4). Implicit in this is the understanding that we are all able to use our mentally-inspired, imaginative processes to activate our emotional centers in a manner that will generate within us the feelings of that other person. Clearly, this process is heavily dependent upon the beliefs we hold about their state. As we have seen, however, empathy does not always require the mind. Automatic empathy can occur from the direct and sometimes subliminal effects of facial expressions on our emotional centers (*The Face of Emotion*: Chapter 2: Section 4). Alongside this, it is vital to remember that, more than any other species, humans have the capacity to employ controlled empathy and so to create within themselves what they *believe to be* the feelings of an independent agent, be it a person or an animal.

In one such study volunteers were given painful stimuli while their brains were being scanned. Among other areas the painful stimuli activated the insula and the anterior cingulate, both of which participate in the affective-motivational dimension of the pain experience (*Pain and the Penetration of the Psyche*: Chapter 2: Section 4). In second part of the experiment volunteers were told that, upon a given signal, a loved one attending the sessions was also going to be given the same painful stimulus. Simultaneous brain scans of these volunteers showed activation of the same parts of insula and anterior cingulate as were activated when they actually received the painful stimuli but, as in controlled empathy, this activity in the emotional centers was accompanied by activation of the mind.

This form of imagination accounts for the hitherto mysterious action of *placebos*. A placebo is an inactive substance such as saline that is given to someone experiencing pain under the guise of it being a "pain killer" or analgesic. Even though the placebo itself has no direct effect on the nervous system it does, in many cases, produce relief from pain. The effects of this belief-mediated deception are nevertheless real, so real that they can be reversed by a drug, called naloxone that very selectively blocks the actions of our endogenous opiates, thereby negating our brain's natural ability to produce analgesia (*Drugs and the Alteration of Consciousness*: Chapter 3: Section 7). To study the effects of a placebo on the brain's pain centers, subjects were given painful stimuli with and without a placebo while having their brains scanned. The results showed that the placebo produced a clear decrease of the pain-induced activity in the anterior cingulate gyrus and the insula. What was, however, equally significant was that along with the emotional centers, the cortex of the mind and the orbital cortex were also highly active during the period when the painful stimulus was being anticipated. Upon administration of the placebo, this anticipatory activity in the mind and the orbital cortex decreased along with pain related activity in the emotional centers.

These experiments illustrate two examples of the power of imagination and the mind over our emotional centers, firstly, in relation to activating them in the generation of controlled empathy and secondly, in inhibiting them as a simple consequence of the belief that a substance is a painkiller (*The Nature of Empathy*: Chapter 2: Section 4). Both experiments thus emphasize the power of the mind, our mental conditioning and our beliefs in determining the moment-by-moment details of our reality.

The Cultural Exploitation of Mental Imagery
"What a piece of bread looks like depends on whether you are hungry or not." Jaläl ad-Din Muhammad Rumi (1207-1273). Persian Sufi Mystic and Poet.

Mental imagery has a facile quality in that it reflects the contents and focus of the mind. Art begins when the first parts of the child's mind begin to mature (*The Art of Children;* Section 3; Chapter 2). It is surely because of this link between the power of thought and its capacity to evoke imagery that ensures that humans are the only organisms that are driven to practice art. Religious iconography is universally enchanting because it inevitably contains the mindset of its creators whose thoughts were doubtless focused on glories of spiritual ecstasy or the transcendental qualities of whatever deities or religious symbols they were imagining. However, it is the role of all artistic endeavors to mentally transport us from the humdrum concerns of the day and to deliver to us a sublime revelation concerning our collective and individual psychic identity. First in story and finally in art, there emerge images intentionally designed to transport the viewer to ideational visions that, whether good or bad, are deemed significant by the artist the content of whose mind inevitably reflects the fundamentals of their life within a small window of human history. Imagination could not work without mental imagery, be it visual, auditory, tactile, kinesthetic, emotional or even thymic. Certainly without our capacity for mental imagery, art would, very simply, not exist.

The power of imagination and its relationship to the mind infiltrates all religions but, as we have seen earlier in relationship to the ceremony of Chod (*The Exploration of Darkness*: Chapter 2: Section 5), this phenomenon is particularly prominent in Buddhism. The Buddha's somewhat clandestine revelation of the Tantric path to enlightenment arose out of the realization that the bliss of sexual union is no different from the bliss of spiritually evoked transcendence. The Perfect One's insight is much supported by modern studies of how the human brain creates reward. Indeed, science and spiritual introspection are in total agreement that there is no duality to the experience of bliss or that bliss is a singular, if graded experience created within the brain by the activation of a single identifiable network. Buddha's realization was exploited in ancient Tantric practices that still survive in occupied Tibet. In practice, the mind is slowly focused upon one of the 84 masters of Mahāmudrā. Mahāmudrā is a name for the highest tantric path of Buddhahood. These masters were called Mahāsiddhas or Great Attainers. They lived in India between the 8th and 12th centuries. Each Māhasiddhas has a different appearance, a different life history and a different personality. Some have been criminals. There is no exclusion for earthly deeds. Most are male but some are female.

In the preorgasmic bliss of sexual union, the image of one's partner is pervasive. The essence of Tibetan Tantric practice is to replace the image of one's beloved with the selected Māhasiddha. Ultimately it is hoped that the aspirant will only have to successfully envisage the Māhasiddha to be transported to a state of bliss. In this Tantra is like all religions in that images created by humans are deliberately given such transporting powers that even imagining them, silences thought and evokes ecstasy. In Tibetan Tantra, the fixation on a Māhasiddha as a deity inspiring the oceanic feeling of love, ultimately gives the power of transcendence back to the imaginative powers of the practitioner. In the imagining of a divine lover, there flowers the realization that ecstasy is part of our inherent nature that can exist and flourish independently of the world of people or things. It is said that in old Tibet, many Tibetan couples became actualized through the practice of Tantra. Its long history is testimony to humanity's pre-scientific awareness of the power of mental imagery.

Chapter 2 – The Origins and Purpose of Dreams

The Prophetic Nature of Dreams

"What if you slept
And what if
In your sleep
You dreamed
And what if
In your dream
You went to heaven
And there plucked a strange and beautiful flower
And what if
When you awoke
You had that flower in you hand
Ah, what then?"
Samuel Taylor Coleridge (1772-1834). Romantic Literary Critic, Poet and
Philosopher.

Plato, Aristotle and Cicero argued that dreams were not prophetic. Plato was, however, somewhat inconsistent on this point, sometimes stating that dreams enable divine intervention in the lives of humans but elsewhere maintaining that they reflected the animalistic elements of the psyche. More down to earth than his mentor, Aristotle believed that dreams arose from our surroundings and our cognitive preoccupations during wakefulness, an aspect of dreams that Freud would later refer to as merely the *day residue*. However, not all Greek scholars were so dismissive of the idea that dreams might have significance to the life and destiny of the individual. The Greek soothsayer Artemidorus Daldianus (c. 2nd Century AD) is attributed with writing of the most famous book on dream interpretation, the *Oneirocritica* (Greek *oneiros*, 'a dream'). Even today, the art of interpreting the symbolism in dreams is called *Oneirocriticism*, an endeavor that hard line Jungian psychotherapists once believed required many years of studying comparative mythology.

The 19th century English poet, Samuel Talyor Coleridge is best known for his poem about the Mongol conquer, *Kubla Khan*. This poem was said to have come to him while he was in a dream state elicited by the influence of opium. Less well known is the fact that Coleridge was obsessed with dreams and devoted much energy to analyzing and defining their nature. Throughout his notebooks three general themes emerge for the origin of dreams; (a) that dreams are caused by the Gods intervening in the lives of men, (b) that they are elaborated as responses to the physiological state of the body and, (c) that they result from the action of malignant spirits.

The issue of whether dreams are divine prophecies is mentioned throughout the Old Testament. For example, in the first book of Kings, chapter 28, verse 6: "And he consulted the Lord, and he answered him not, neither by dreams, nor by priests, nor by prophets." Even the Islamic prophet Mohammed (or Muhammad, c. 570-632 AD) is cited as saying, "He, who does not believe in the true dream, does not believe in Allah or in the Day of Reckoning". Later, however, Mohammed is said to have forbidden dream divination because it had so heavily influenced daily life among pre-Islamic peoples. Mystics it seems have always had to tread a fine line between espousing the significance of the unexplainable while, at the same time, emphasizing the tried and tested value of practicality.

Faced with the same challenge, Homer, in his *Odyssey*, sought a middle road wherein dreams may be true or false, their veracity depending upon which of two dreaming gates they emerge from. Thus, in her dream Penelope tells Odysseus, "Those dreams that pass through the gate of sawn ivory deceive men, bringing words that find no fulfillment. But those that come forth through the gate of polished horn bring true issues to pass, when any mortal sees them."

Knowing what we now know about the origin of dreams it is easy to see that the issue of their prophetic significance will never be resolved. In other forms of prophecy such as the Tarot cards, we are presented with broad metaphorical stories from which we inadvertently seek out our personal destiny in accord with our personality preferences. In such matters, we are, in truth, seeking a reflection of our personal identity hoping all the time that we are being shown actual truths about our future. Yet because our dreams are fashioned by our brain they are already tailored to our individual nature. The indistinct, ethereal elements of our dreams have a familiar aura that seems to bear a distinct, yet indefinable, relationship to our destiny. However, as indicated by the frequency of nightmares in psychologically damaged individuals, the nature of our dreams is clearly sensitive to our life experiences.

Like all other states of consciousness, dreaming exploits the cerebral cortex as the only available substrate for creating experiences. Just as both the environment and the inherent structure of our cortex participate in determining the waking experiences of each individual, then so too must each play a part in sculpting the experiences of dream. As our dreams are composed by the activation of different cortical areas, the dreams of any individual will therefore be influenced by the amount of cortex allocated to each domain of consciousness (*The Allocation of Consciousness*: Chapter 2: Section 2). Just as the relative size of Brodmann's areas determines our abilities while we are awake, so too must the allocation of cortex to or the damage of, Brodmann's areas influence the content of our dreams. Thus, patients who as a result of cortical damage have lost the ability to see faces (*prosopagnosia*), have dreams that are inhabited only by faceless people. Joseph Campbell's quote that "Dreams are private myths; myths are shared dreams" can be best understood in this context. As our dreams, like our wakeful experiences, are inseparably reliant upon the detailed architecture of our cerebral cortex, they may indeed be regarded as private myths. However, as the same domains of consciousness are represented in the cortex of all normal humans, it must also be true that humanity's dreams will always be composed around fundamental elements that naturally find expression in myth.

The Cortex in Sleep and Dreams
"That we come to this Earth to live is untrue: We come but to sleep, to dream." Aztec Poem, Anonymous.

Virtually all humans spend one quarter to one third of their life asleep. In terms of the daily requirement the norm is 7.5 to 8 hours/night while the range extends from 4 to 10 hours/night. During sleep the whole cortex is switched into a less reactive state wherein its responsiveness to incoming sensory information is markedly reduced. Until the invention of brain scanners, brainwaves recorded from the surface of the skull, provided the only objective measurement of the different states of consciousness that underlie sleep and wakefulness. Brainwaves are oscillating electrical fields that are generated by the massed action of the billions of nerve cells that make up the cerebral cortex. As such they can be used to study the different operational states through which each piece of cortex passes every 24 hours.

Although the movement from wakefulness to sleep seems like a gradual process, it is underwritten by relatively abrupt changes in brainwave frequency. Brainwaves have been divided into five categories: *gamma* (40 cycles/second), *beta* (12-30 cycles/second), *alpha* (8-12 cycles/second), *theta* (4-8 cycles/second) and *delta* (0.5-4 cycles/second). The primary justification for creating these categories is that each of these ranges, or bandwidths, reflects both a different operational state of the cortex and different states of human awareness. During alert and active exploration our brainwaves oscillate in the gamma range (*Constructing the Gestalt*: Chapter 4: Section 2). In predators like the cat, gamma waves are present during hunting, while in prey species, like the rabbit, they accompany times when extreme caution is required. Conversely, gamma waves never appear during vegetative behaviors such as feeding or sex, times when, to our occasional embarrassment, we are typically less than vigilant. In the normal awake state, our brainwaves oscillate within the beta range. The onset of drowsiness is heralded by the appearance of theta waves that characterize what is called Stage 1 sleep. The progression from Stage 1 to Stage 2 sleep is marked by the appearance of short (eg. 1 second) bursts of higher frequency alpha oscillations superimposed on top of the theta waves. These alpha bursts are called *sleep spindles* and with the appearance of each sleep spindle subjects often seem to momentarily fall asleep. The onset of sleep is correlated with a further decrease in frequency to the delta range of 0.5 to 4 cycles per second. The delta range of frequencies is divided into two stages of sleep, Stage 3 and Stage 4. Stage 3 is characterized by delta waves of 2 to 4 cycles/second and the continued occurrence of alpha sleep spindles. In comparison, Stage 4 sleep is associated with a disappearance of sleep spindles and lower frequency delta waves in the range of 0.5 to 2 cycles/second.

At the very point where we are dropping off to sleep, it is not uncommon to experience what are called *hypnogogic hallucinations*. Often given magical connotations, this state is characterized by vivid, usually visual imagery and thoughts containing fragmented minidramas. The hypnogogic stage is followed by 90 minutes of deep or slow wave sleep, so called because the cortex generates large amplitude, low frequency, delta waves. There follows a 10 minute period of what is known as *paradoxical* or *rapid eye movement* (REM) sleep. In the great majority of people, REM sleep is always accompanied by dreaming. Only sometimes do dreams occur during non-REM sleep. During REM sleep, the cortex generates small amplitude, irregular, *desynchronized* brainwaves. The desynchronized brainwaves contain a high complement of oscillations in the gamma range, which otherwise only appear during periods of alert, exploratory wakefulness. It seems that during dreaming our closed eyes search an "imaginary" scene while our desynchronized brainwaves show that, although our cortex is asleep, it is also in a state of quasi-vigilant exploration.

Rapid eye movements are detectable in the human fetus shortly after conception. For a short period around the 5th month of pregnancy REMs persist for 24 hours a day before tapering off to around 8 hours per day at birth. As even at birth very little of the cortex is mature, it is hard to accept that REMs in these early developmental stages indicate dreaming. At birth sleep occurs in 50 to 60 minute bouts that begin with REM sleep rather than slow wave sleep. By 2 years of age, when the brain's long-term memory system (the hippocampus) first becomes operative, the duration of REM sleep falls to 3 hours per 24 hour period. From that developmental stage onwards, the total amount of REM sleep continues to decrease towards the adult pattern of 2 hours per night composed of 4 separate episodes of REM sleep and dreaming. These episodes get progressively longer such that the fourth period of REM sleep, which just precedes awakening, lasts 20 to 30 minutes. It is from this last period that dreams are most often remembered.

There is an old proverb that says; "sleep is better than medicine". In rodents sleep deprivation can cause death sooner than starvation. Clearly, as all animals sleep it would seem that sleep must be important to health. Prevented from sleeping, rats die within 2 weeks but even if they are only deprived of REM sleep and allowed a normal amount of non-REM sleep, they survive for only 5 to 6 weeks. In children, abnormally low levels of deep sleep can inhibit the secretion of growth hormone leading to a condition known as *psychosocial dwarfism*. This condition is often associated with a chaotic and dysfunctional family life as shown by the restoration of normal growth rates following the establishment of healthy sleeping routines.

The effects of sleep deprivation on adults have been rigorously tested. Results show that humans are very resistant to sleep deprivation. This may explain why westerners of the present generation sleep 20% less than the previous generation. Even when deprived of sleep for 205 hours – a period exceeding 8 days and nights – subjects showed few deficits in their ability to perform tasks. While hallucinations and illusions occurred, they were rare in the first 60 hours of deprivation. Reflexes were also unimpaired although tremors, instability of eye position and reduced pain thresholds indicated that sleep deprivation does have some basic neurological effects. In contrast, vital signs such as heart rate, blood pressure, respiration and temperature, changed little during the first 160 hours of deprivation.

The identification of REM sleep and dreaming as an integral part of sleep opened the doors to the scientific analysis of dreaming. Experiments were soon designed to study the psychological, physiological and neurological affects of selectively depriving subjects of dreaming. The first of these reported that a loss of REM sleep resulted in hallucinations and psychosis (confused thought). Repetition of these studies did not, however, confirm these early results. Instead the subjects of these experiments showed only irritability related to their overall loss of sleep.

Nevertheless, these experiments did reveal a pressing human need to maintain REM sleep at a normal level. By the last night of the 6 to 10 day course of these experiments, subjects had to be awakened between 33 and 50 times, respectively, to prevent them entering REM sleep. Upon cessation of the deprivation period subjects initially spent around 4 hours per night in REM sleep compared with 2 hours per night prior to the experiment. It seems that our brain has an innate requirement for dreaming that would surely not exist if dreaming were simply an epiphenomenon of sleep.

Sleep and Dreams in Animals

"…dogs, cats, horses, and probably all the higher animals, even birds, have vivid dreams…" Charles Darwin (1809-1882). Biologist, Author of *Origins of the Species* and Co-founder of the Theory of Evolution.

Unfortunately, as animals cannot report their experiences it is actually impossible to say whether or not they dream. Only the powerful association between REMs and human dreaming has enabled sleep researchers to see whether the neural mechanisms underlying human sleep and dreaming are present in animals. The brainwave patterns characteristic of non-REM and REM sleep in humans can be recorded from all mammals including the primitive egg laying, echidna. Even birds have REM sleep although this disappears shortly after hatching. The detection of short periods of higher frequency brainwaves during sleep in some reptiles, has led to the identification of so-called *active sleep* – an exclusively reptilian phenomenon that sleep researchers consider to be the evolutionary origin of the neural mechanisms underlying human dreaming.

In the animal world, sleep patterns are tailored to the niche occupied by any given species. Consequently, the time spent sleeping each day varies enormously between species. Animals such as the opossum and the bat sleep 18 to 20 hours per day while the elephant and giraffe sleep 3 to 4 hours per day. This variation is partially related to diet, sleep duration decreasing as one moves from the carnivores to the omnivores to the herbivores. Many animals go through many relatively short sleep-wake cycles in a single day. In general the duration of the sleep cycle is related to the size of the animal's body and brain. For example, the long-tailed shrew has sleep cycles of only 8 minutes in comparison with 1.8 hours in the Asiatic elephant.

When it comes to sleep, the most bizarre departure from the human condition is the phenomenon of *unihemispheric sleep.* Unihemispheric sleep occurs in marine mammals such as manatees, seals and the cetaceans (whales and dolphins) and in several species of birds, including the domestic chicken. During unihemispheric sleep, the brainwaves generated by one hemisphere indicate that it is in a wakeful state while the brainwaves from the opposite hemisphere, indicate that it is in deep sleep. In this condition, the eye on the opposite side from the sleeping hemisphere is closed. In cetaceans, unihemispheric sleep is the rule, the slow waves of deep sleep almost never occurring in both hemispheres simultaneously. The reason advanced for this is that the smaller cetaceans are virtually never immobile and must therefore always maintain one hemisphere awake. That unihemispheric sleep is a phenomenon primarily linked to the aquatic environment is further suggested by the sleep patterns of seals that must survive in both the water and on the land. In the aquatic environment they participate in unihemispheric sleep, not only closing the contralateral eye but also resting the flipper opposite the sleeping hemisphere. Their unihemispheric sleep state is only rarely associated with REM. Upon making the transition to land, the unihemispheric slow waves disappear and are replaced by bilateral brain waves that, in terrestrial mammals, are associated with wakefulness and typical periods of both non-REM and REM sleep. It seems that even more than sleep itself, the processes and consequences of dreaming have such global significance that they must operate simultaneously in both hemispheres.

Dreams and Movement

"In sleep there is a total suspension of our voluntary power, both over the muscles of our bodies, and the ideas of our minds; for we neither walk about nor reason in complete sleep." Erasmus Darwin (1731-1802). Physician, Natural Philosopher, Physiologist, Inventor, Poet and grandfather of Charles Darwin.

Watching the pawing movements of a sleeping dog, Aristotle wrote that it must have been dreaming of the chase. The chances are that he was quite correct. Careful monitoring of eye movements just before waking people from REM sleep reveals that their movements do reflect dream content. For example, if they had been dreaming about ascending and descending stairs, then the eyes move up and down but if their dream was about watching ping pong then their eyes moved in the left-right axis – responses that resemble the eye movements of awake subjects actively listening to stories that prompt gaze to be directed in the horizontal or vertical direction.

Not content with moving the eyes, the dreaming cortex's motor centers also actively attempt to perform the bodily actions of the dream, failing only because, as a corollary of dreaming, the brainstem inhibits all motor outflow to the muscles of the body. Indeed, if this brainstem center is destroyed in a cat, the animal will stalk around the room during REM sleep as if it were hunting a non-existent mouse. Despite the inhibition of bodily movement, human dreamers still report dreaming of bodily movements, indicating that the cortex's motor command centers continue to configure the would-be movements of dreams and in so doing generate kinesthetic feelings even during the effective paralysis of dream.

Although we do not remember them, we all perform movements during sleep. The less we move the better we say we have slept. However, even the soundest sleepers shift position around 8 times each night while the lightest may move more than 30 times. During deep non-REM sleep the level of excitability of the brain's motor centers is too low to evoke movement, while during REM sleep bodily movement is prevented by inhibition of motor outflow. Consequently, bodily movements tend to occur immediately before and after REM periods such that they can roughly indicate the beginning and end of dreaming. When couples begin to share the same bed every night their movements inevitably tend to become crudely synchronized. This in turn results in the synchronization of their non-REM and REM sleep such that there is a greatly enhanced chance of that they will dream at the same times.

In the USA approximately 15% of children have at least one episode of sleepwalking while up to 6% have many episodes. In adults, sleepwalking does not begin during dreaming but in the deep phase of sleep when there are high amplitude delta waves in both hemispheres. Although the causes of sleepwalking are uncertain, it does seem to have a genetical basis, as indicated by the story of a family of sleepwalkers who while asleep congregated at the kitchen table overnight. Sleepwalkers may dress themselves and spend up to 30 minutes before returning to bed. During their escapades they retain the ability to avoid obstacles and precarious edges, indicating that the sleeping brain is still able to provide guidance required to negotiate the external world – an observation which is particularly fascinating in relation to whether there is a need for consciousness in the generation of behavior (*The Recognition and Subtraction of Consiousness*: Chapter 2: Section 2).

A more serious condition than sleep walking is what is referred to as *Rapid Eye Movement Behavioral Disorder* or *RBD*. The prevalence of RBD is far higher in males than females and there is some evidence that it may be precipitated by antidepressants that increase levels of serotonin (*Major Depressive Disorder - Life as a Lost Cause*: Chapter 5: Section 5). The high proportion of people with RBD who develop Parkinson's disease suggests that RBD might enable the early diagnosis and intervention in the progress of this otherwise fatal condition. In RBD, the inhibition of bodily movement is inoperative and the dreamer unwittingly acts out their dreams. In contrast to the activities of sleepwalkers, the activities of RBD patients always seem to have a highly emotive content. Thus, one account tells of a subject who, while dreaming he was playing football, arose from bed and tackled his wardrobe. In other cases, patients with this disorder have been known to injure themselves or their spouses by attacking them while still dreaming. In an even more bizarre instance, a respectable middle-aged woman, in an apparently stable relationship, would leave the house and, while remaining in dream, have sex with strangers. While such aberrant behavior is embarrassing and even dangerous in women, its occurrence in men almost certainly leads to catastrophic legal and social problems. It seems that when we dream our emotional centers are free to express instinctive behaviors that would normally be held in check by our mind's considerations of social mores and prevailing circumstances. In this much at least, Plato's evocation of our animal propensities to explain dreaming is relatively close to the mark.

The Content of Dreams
"….we are affected with a variety of passions in our dreams, as anger, love, joy, yet we never experience surprise…. For surprise is only produced when any external irritations suddenly obtrude themselves, and dissever our passing trains of ideas." Erasmus Darwin (1731-1802). Physician, Natural Philosopher, Physiologist, Inventor, Poet and grandfather of Charles Darwin.

Dreams are a bizarre state of consciousness wherein we may experience seemingly relevant scenarios and enjoy physical and even mental capabilities beyond the biological confinements of the human condition. In dreams we may defy gravity and yet still sense the danger and exhilaration of our newfound weightlessness. In dreams we may fulfill our heart's desires without concern for the consequences of our wanton impulsiveness. In dreams, feelings that have been lingering on the edge of our awareness are given unfettered opportunity to manifest themselves in consciousness as intuitively relevant, thematic escapades. Once converted to patterns of cortical activity, these dream experiences can be registered in the long-term episodic memory banks of the hippocampus (*Dreams and the Transfer of Emotional Memories*: Chapter 2: Section 7). Yet, possibly because the events of the day leave transient memory traces in the modules that make up each cortical area, they too permeate our dreams, there to be mixed with our ongoing emotional tensions that through dreams emerge unimpeded into the shadow world of sleep (*The Micro-organization of Consciousness*: Chapter 2: Section 2).

Like all experiences, dreams play themselves out in cortical space. Consequently, the frequency with which different sensations appear in dreams is roughly indicative of the area of cortex allocated to each. Therefore, since in the archetypal human much of the cortex is devoted to vision, virtually all dreams contain visual content, while 65% contain auditory, 8% vestibular (balance and sense of gravity), 4% thermal and 1% tactile, olfactory or gustatory. In 79% of dreams there is a sense of movement in the lower extremities even though the body remains relatively immobile, held in semi-paralysis to protect us from our emotional tensions and our normally suppressed, innate urges that otherwise assert themselves in the fashioning of dreams.

Our dreams are often populated by other people, 49% of whom are known to us personally, while 35% can be generically identified by their social role or vocation (e.g., protector or policeman) and the remaining 16% are novel. Of the people who appear in dreams, most can be easily identified as having emotional significance to the dreamer. Vivid emotions are reported in 84% of dreams, of which, in normal people, half are positive and half are negative. Of dreams containing emotions, about 14% contain only one emotion while two or more were present in 86%. Joy is the most frequent emotion, appearing in 36% of dreams while anger appeared in 17%, anxiety and fear in 11% and sadness in 10%.

The Composition of Dreams
"The physician Erasmus Darwin established the cause of dreams in the workings of the arterial and glandular systems, and in the internal senses of hunger, thirst and lust. Nightmares were caused by indigestion. All of these physiological systems 'are not only occasionally excited in our sleep, but their irritative motions are succeeded by their usual sensation, and make a part of the farrago of our dreams'." Jennifer Ford, Philosophy/Romantics Scholar. From: *Coleridge on Dreaming, Romanticism, Dreams and the Medical Imagination*. Cambridge University Press, Cambridge, 1998, p. 15.

The writings of Coleridge, Erasmus Darwin, and even his grandson Charles Darwin, reflected a common, though incorrect, belief of the 18th and 19th centuries – specifically that the content of dreams is the product of our imagination (*Defining Attention and Imagination*: Chapter 1: Section 7). Aware of how easy it is to conjure up visual or auditory mental imagery, the European doyens of that era naturally believed that the mind was responsible for the imagery of dreams. They did not, however, see the mind or thought as being the generative source of dreaming. Instead they believed that the impetus to dream emanated from perturbations of the viscera, the specifics of which determined the nature of each dream. In a modern view of their ideology we might say that they saw the mind as producing the imagery demanded by the brain's visceral representations. Consequently, their ideas did have some similarities to those of another European Sigmund Freud, who in the late 19th century proposed that dream content was the direct product of the subconscious workings of the id. In modern vernacular, Freud's subconscious influences are clearly attributable to emotional memories stored within the brain's emotional centers; in particular, the anterior cingulate gyrus, the insula and the amygdala. Today we appreciate that our emotional memories of love, sadness, disgust, fear, anger and even pain are deeply ingrained within the triad of emotion, and particularly, the anterior cingulate gyrus. The modern day Freudian view would thus be one in which the state of dreaming results from the psyche's emotional centers directly activating the cortex's perceptual representations that, in turn, give rise to the imagery of dreams. That the critical elements of our dreams are created by our emotional centers and not the mind, may explain why in dreams there is a lack of logic and a prominence of emotions and why the majority of the people in dreams have emotional or social significance to the dreamer.

Experientially most REM dreams lack any appreciation of time, being pervaded instead by an acute sense of the moment. With the advent of brain scanners it has been possible to simply see which parts of the human psyche participate in composing dreams. These studies show that all REM dreams are associated with activity in the executor of emotion, the anterior cingulate gyrus. What is, however, most astounding is that during REM dreaming the mind and the orbital cortex – the two elements of the human psyche that are exclusively concerned with time and the future - are rendered silent. Put simply, thought and predictive anticipation are basically absent from REM dreams. Thus, although many people spend a great deal of time trying to rationally analyze their dreams, it appears that the content of most REM dreams has little relationship to thought, rationality or cognitively inspired memories. Instead, the essential themes of REM dreams appear to be manifestations of those often subtle and subliminal elements of memory that relate to significant emotional perturbations, past and present, that are archived as emotional memories within the emotional centers. In this context, dreaming emerges as a reflection of the present and past status of our inner milieu. In spiritual terms, the experience of dream is therefore an insight into the all-pervading, inner self (*Atman*) or the Buddha within (*Emotion and Religion*: Chapter 1: Section 3), while in psychological terms it provides a knowledge of the self, referred to as *autonoetic awareness*. It is for these reasons that dreams contain a predominantly first-person perspective and a sense of being continually present.

Unfortunately, all attempts to attribute the phantasmagoria of dreams to cognition have only been indicative of a poor appreciation, both of the highly systematic nature of human thought and the essentially organic relationship of our emotions to our visceral urges that drive all instinctive behavior. Only in emotion do we find the turbulence of phase and form so necessary to the ephemeral lucidity of the dream experience. In REM dreams the dreamer has no voluntary control over attention nor any idea of, or concern for, what will happen next. Facts and reality go unchecked, bizarre events are passively accepted and neither context nor temporal flow, are stable. The content and nature of non-REM dreams is quite different. Unlike REM dreams, non-REM dreams resemble *daydreams* in that they relate to real-life events, contain a narrative and involve, albeit often confused, thoughts. Subjects report feeling as if they were not dreaming at all but were awake and felt that they had some cognitive control over the direction, if not the specific content, of their dream. However, the content of non-REM dreams is generally low, reflecting the reduction in the excitability of the cortex that characterizes deep sleep. The emergent picture of non-REM dreaming is one where, in complete contrast to REM dreaming, the normal balance of power between the mind, mood and emotion is retained within the relatively unresponsive, sleeping cortex.

Superficially, dreaming seems to be a unique state, wherein the influence of emotion together with the absence of the cognitive and predictive elements of the psyche, produce an experience that is entirely momentary in nature. Dreams are not, however, the only time when the quiescence of the mind and the anticipatory centers allow our instinctual urges unimpeded expression in an essentially timeless milieu. The other situation when these conditions are met is that of play. As we have seen, play is itself a product of our emotional centers and, in particular, the anterior cingulate gyrus (*The Origin of Our Mammalian Ways*: Chapter 5: Section 4). While dreams express our emotional tensions in the essentially sleeping cortex, play expresses them in the awake brain during the relative safety of conspecific pantomime. What play achieves in wakefulness, dream achieves in the near paralysis of sleep.

Instinct and the Imagery of Dreams
"As a thinker Descartes considered that the dreams expressed a movement of the organs of the sleeper, that they constituted a language translating a desire." Lancelot L. Whyte (1896-1972). Scottish Financier, Industrial Engineer, Intellectual and Author.

All agree that dreams have an irresistible, metaphorical quality. Dream images are poignantly archetypal and yet enshrined in constructs that loosely reflect those indefinable, pervasive forces that emanate from our most private and inaccessible feelings. The relationship between the dream state and our instinctual drives that conjure our emotions is further underscored by the frequent manifestations of sexual desire during REM dreaming, in the form of erections in men and orgasm in both sexes. At one level our dreams reflect common human themes that arise naturally from the universality of visceral life while at another they represent our personal emotional history by focusing on objects and scenarios that have particular significance to our past and present emotional life. As our viscera are probably much the same as those of our hominid ancestors, the basic themes expressed in their dreams are probably identical to those of modern humans. Many scholars have proposed that for tens of thousands of years dream themes have formed the germ power of the mythologies of all human cultures. In reality, the source of that power is the anterior cingulate gyrus, the executive center of all emotion, the inner self of all spiritual-religious dialogue, the driving force behind instinctive mammalian behavior, the central core of the mammalian psyche and the architect of our dreams (*The Origin of Our Mammalian Ways*: Chapter 5: Section 4).

Like each phase of sleep, dreaming is switched on and off by specific centres in the brainstem. However, once in the dream state, it is our emotional centres that determine the content of our dreams. This capacity of our emotional centres to create the imagery of dreams is a heritage from our most distant mammalian relatives. Before the evolution of the mind in the higher mammals, the anterior cingulate gyrus was the highest center in the mammalian brain. In the absence of a mind, the anterior cingulate gyrus was essentially responsible for integrating visceral, somatic and external sensory information, focusing attention and, through its motor centres, instigating action. As the executor of emotion each of these roles are naturally biased towards the psychosocial realm. Apart from strong emotional memories, even the human anterior cingulate lacks the operational capacity to construct and act upon sophisticated conceptual models of the outside world. In the lower, "mindless" mammals the anterior cingulate simply drove its host towards the instinctual satiation of vital urges, guided by its emotional memories and yet unable to take into consideration the complexities any mitigating circumstances. We need only observe within ourselves the persistent, yet often unwanted demands of powerful emotions, to comprehend how in the lower mammals the anterior cingulate can have plenipotentiary power over behavior.

The anterior cingulate gyrus is part of a network that involves many of the cortex's other perceptual representations. As the executor of human emotion and the driving force behind the behavior of the lower mammals, the anterior cingulate also has the capacity to evoke activity in other areas of the cortex. It is this network that during sleep presumably enables the anterior cingulate to activate wide areas of the cerebral cortex in the elaboration of dreams. Dream is possible only because the anterior cingulate gyrus has this ability to arouse the sleeping cortex. In this the anterior cingulate's *modus operandi* is reminiscent of the way the human mind generates mental images by activating the cortex's perceptual areas (*The Exploration of Attention and Mental Imagery*: Chapter 1: Section 7). However, in the case of the mind, the activation of other cortical areas is part of the process of imagination whereas, in the case of our emotional executor, activation of other cortical areas is a hangover from a point in our distant mammalian past when all behavior was instinctual – an influence which emerges to create the experiences of our dreams, only when our mind is asleep. Just as in the process of imagination the mind fails to activate the cortex's primary sensory representations, so too are the primary representations spared activation by the anterior cingulate during the composition of dreams. The imagery of both imagination and dreams is therefore composed entirely within the cortex's perceptual representations. As a consequence, both the imagery of imagination and imagery of dreams share an abstract, surrealistic and even metaphorical quality that lacks the sensory detail typically present in cortex's representations of objects and scenarios that actually exist in the outside world.

The Dark Side of Sleep

"In vain to scream with quivering lips she tries,
And strains in palsy'd lids her tremulous eyes;
In vain she *wills* to run, fly, swim, walk, creep;
The will presides not in the bower of sleep!"
Erasmus Darwin (1731-1802). Physician, Natural Philosopher, Physiologist, Inventor, Poet and grandfather of Charles Darwin.

To the healthy person, sleep and dreaming offer a panacean retreat far from the maddening crowd. However, to other less fortunate individuals, the bower of sleep is haunted by unimaginable terrors. Just as anxiety, fear and anger are party to the wakeful experience of depression, these emotional states emerge during sleep to become the foundations of both *nightmares* and *night terrors*.

Whereas nightmares are essentially bad dreams, night or sleep terrors resemble non-REM dreams in that they appear in deep sleep, lack the vivid imagery of dreams and seem to involve the mind. Unlike nightmares, night terrors are usually confined to the first 90 minutes of sleep. Their symptoms include screaming, sweating, confused thoughts, increased heart and respiration rate and a sudden awakening. Night terrors typically occur in children between the ages of 3 and 12. Unlike night terrors, nightmares usually occur during REM sleep, involve imagery and are not confined to any age group. Like night terrors, nightmares are associated with increases in heart and respiration rate and increased sweating – responses that, in wakefulness, are characteristic of both fear and intense pain.

Historically, nightmares were often thought to be caused by indigestion. Certainly perturbations of the viscera frequently find expression in dreams. Not only are the emotional centers active during dreaming but one member of the triad of emotion, the insula, acts as a primary receiving areas for visceral information, relaying it to both the amygdala and the anterior cingulate (*The Triad of Emotion*: Chapter 3: Section 4). As a consequence, patients with irritable bowel syndrome and inflammatory bowel disease tend to dream about their bowels or about soiling themselves. In contrast to our visceral senses, the access of touch, smell, taste, vision and hearing to the cortex's primary receiving areas is markedly reduced during sleep. Thus, although indigestion is certainly not the only cause of nightmares, there are good reasons to believe in a strong visceral involvement in the generation of both good and bad dreams.

The subjects of dreams are complex and wide ranging, incorporating self-image, fears, insecurities, strengths, grandiose ideas, sexual orientation, desire, jealousy and love. The subjects of nightmares are also drawn from this compendium. Both ongoing stress and the emotional memories of stressful, past events, can enhance the possibility of nightmares. Ongoing stress may have either a physical or psychological origin. The most common source of psychological stress is relationship breakdown. In a sample of 90 subjects undergoing marital separation, the dreams of 70 (78%) reflected how they were coping. In contrast, the most common physical stress is chronic pain. Although rare in the dreams of healthy individuals, pain appears in 30% of the dreams of burn victims. As we have seen pain contains two components, a sensory-discriminative and an affective-motivational dimension (*Pain and the Penetration of the Psyche*: Chapter 2: Section 5). However, only the more emotionally disruptive, affective-motivational dimension of pain, which typically results from either chronic somatic pain or pain of visceral origin, activates the brain's emotional centers. Only this aspect of pain and the associated emotional memories, play a significant role in the elaboration of nightmares.

If not the most common source of nightmares, past traumas are the most persistent. Sexual abuse victims with post-traumatic stress disorder may have up to 5 nightmares/week for 20 years or more (*The Ravages of Emotional Memory*: Chapter 5: Section 4). Similarly, even years after the event, survivors of torture suffer reduced overall sleep time, an absence of deep, stage 4 sleep, frequent waking during REM sleep and frequent nightmares. Again, the same process that enables our emotional memories to subtly influence many aspects of our behavior also has a powerful influence over our dreams.

The Role of Sleep and Dreams in Learning
"…what could not be repeated at first is readily put together on the following day; and the very time which is generally thought to cause forgetfulness is found to strengthen the memory". Marcus Fabian Quintilian (c. First century AD). Roman Rhetorician.

Historically, the only evidence that sleep enhances memory and learning was that its absence appeared to be deleterious to our cognitive abilities. All manner of observations seemed to indicate that resting of the nervous system enhances learning. For example, cockroaches learn which arm of a Y maze leads to food much better if between training sessions they are prevented from moving by wrapping them in silver paper. This enforced inactivity between training sessions presumably focuses mechanisms of neural plasticity on the single issue of learning the Y maze. In general, it is in the nature of neuronal circuits that their frequent utilization results in the strengthening of their interconnections and a concurrent consolidation of their role. Spurious activity can be considered as disruptive to learning.

Modern studies of gene expression provide categorical evidence of sleep-related changes in brain function. For example, day-night fluctuations have been observed in the reading of 10% of the genes expressed in the nerve cells of the rat's cortex. One particularly important gene (zif-268) which controls the expression of other genes and participates in activity-dependent changes of neural connections, is read only during REM sleep, but then only if the rat has been previously exposed to an enriched, novel environment. On this basis alone dreaming appears to enable the translation of altered circumstances into neural connectivity – a process fundamental to learning.

When we watch a person or an animal change their behavior in response to a novel situation, we correctly assume that learning has taken place. This, however, does not mean that the subject's brain has made any accessible record of the changed circumstances. Only the willful archiving and retrieval of material constitutes what we normally mean by the word memory. However, even changes in the simplest elements of behavior or perception indicate connectional changes in the nervous system that theoretically constitute a memory trace of past events. These virtually subliminal memories are engraved into our nervous system much as past fluctuations of weather are preserved in geological strata or the annular rings of trees.

There is good evidence that motor and perceptual learning are facilitated by sleep and even specific parts of the sleep cycle. In a sequential finger tapping task, subjects showed a 20% improvement after one night's sleep even though no improvement was measured after 12 hours of wakefulness or when sleep was prevented on the night following training. Even a 90 minute, midday nap after training produced considerable (16%) improvement. In a second study subjects were trained to perform a visual discrimination task that required them to distinguish a set of diagonal bars against a background of horizontal bars. Disruption of selected parts of the sleep cycle showed that learning this perceptual task was selectively dependent on the integrity of slow wave sleep in the first quarter of the night and the amount of REM in the last quarter.

As well as playing a role in motor and perceptual learning, evidence exists that sleep and REM dreaming are involved in the highest forms of learning such as the *de novo* generation of new insight. The first example involves the Tower of Hanoi test, a mathematical puzzle that involves both planning and insight and therefore is at least partially dependent upon temporal intelligence (BA10) (*The Origins of the Future – the Temporal Mind*: Chapter 3: Section 3). Normally subjects improve when retested a week after training, however, this improvement is not seen if REM is experimentally reduced the night after training – a finding which is all the more curious because brain scans show the mind to be silent during REM dreaming.

The dependence of the ability to learn new insights upon sleep is even more striking in the second example. In this study subjects were taught a complex algorithm for solving a group of equations. A simpler solution existed but none of the subjects discovered this during training. However, when tested 12 hours later a subset of subjects had discovered the simpler method of performing the task. Moreover, the probability of this was doubled after one night's sleep. Thus, sleep enhanced the gaining of insight from the task even though subjects did not know there was insight to be gained. Again, although the mind participates in non-REM dreaming, its quiescence during REM dreaming suggests that it may continue to analyze problems even when it is active at a level below that required to generate either the experience of thought or a measurable signal using a brain scanner. In summary, it seems that both sleep and dreams are states wherein the very selective changes in neural circuitry that underlie learning are unimpeded by the cacophony of activity that, during wakefulness, monopolizes cortical circuitry for the purpose of generating behavior that is relevant to prevailing circumstances.

Dreams and the Transfer of Emotional Memories

"Everlasting layers of ideas, images, feelings have fallen upon your brain as softly as light. Each succession has seemed to bury all that went before. And yet in reality not one has been extinguished … countless are the mysterious handwritings of grief or joy which have inscribed themselves successively upon the palimpsest of your brain; and, like the annual leaves of aboriginal forests, or the undissolving snows on the

Himalaya, or light falling upon light, the endless strata have covered up each other in forgetfulness. But by the hour of death, but by fever, but by the searchings of opium, all these can revive in strength. They are not dead, but sleeping." Thomas De Quincey (1785-1859). English Author.

Even the most primitive vertebrate animals are dependent upon the ability to establish accurate memories of past events. Indeed, the highest level of the brain of the fish, the pallium – the primordia of the cerebral cortex - is largely composed of two centers that are both devoted to memory, a lateral region, which stores spatial memories and a medial region, which stores emotional memories. Each of these domains of memory is critical to survival, spatial memory being essential for negotiating the outside world and emotional memory for recording an organism's visceroemotional responses to the events or objects it encounters. As an animal cannot operate on the basis of two separate memory traces it is essential that the centers of spatial and emotional memory talk to one another. Without an axis of communication, episodes of visceral satiation or deprivation could never be associated with a particular location. The fish's memory of its visceral response to eating a prawn would therefore never be related to its memory of where it found the prawn. To effectively serve any animal the sources of emotional and locational memory must communicate at least to the point where the memory of place is annotated with the memory of the level of satiation or deprivation associated with that place.

With the evolution of the amphibians and reptiles, what was the lateral and medial divisions of the fish pallium have, respectively, become the cortex of the hippocampus and amygdala. As the only emotional center available in the brains of lower vertebrates, the amygdala is responsible for preserving visceroemotional memories while the hippocampus registers the spatial location of viscerally significant events. With the evolution of the mammals the amygdala was joined by two new areas of cortex, the anterior cingulate and the insula that also participate in the preservation of emotional memories (*The Origin of Our Mammalian Ways*: Chapter 5: Section 4). Also as a corollary of mammalian evolution, the hippocampus gained increasing complexity, maintaining its registry of spatial location but integrating this information with other details of increasingly episodic events that were critical to satiation and survival. Whereas the reptiles have only the amygdala to fashion emotional memories, the mammals have in addition, the anterior cingulate and the insula. Consequently, in the organization of its behavior, the mammal has an even stronger requirement for a mechanism that regularly integrates the diverse store of memories held in the emotional centers with the spatially-related episodic memories stored within the hippocampus – a process which in the lower, "mindless" mammals presumably goes on without any involvement of thought processes.

Throughout more than 500 million years of vertebrate evolution, the communication between centers of spatial and emotional memory has remained vitally important. Even the evolution of the human mind, with its capacity to conceptualize and integrate the emotional and practical domains of existence, has not negated the need for integration of emotional and episodic memory at their source. Human psychology is such that the mind is severely challenged when it is simultaneously bombarded with the independent, fundamentally different and often contradictory voices from the emotional and practical domains of existence. The only reason this situation does not normally occur is that our brain has the capacity to incorporate the nuances of emotional memory into what would otherwise be purely factual episodic memories. Only when the original emotional experiences cannot be interpreted because they are too traumatic, does this process fail, leaving the attendant memories imprisoned within our brain's emotional centers. The key objective of many therapies is to draw forth such memories, thereby enabling patients to witness and integrate them with the factual details of related episodic memories, all within a safe, cognitively controlled, environment.

Normally our emotional experiences are not so intense and bewildering. Nevertheless many of the important nuances of our day-to-day emotional life are simply archived within our emotional centers. Only when our emotional reactions are too strong do we have the opportunity to see that there remains within us indistinct and unresolved emotional issues. From this point, there can be only two solutions to the problem. The first simply involves allowing the passage of time to slowly erode either the emotional or cognitive memory of the episode. The second involves the integration of our emotional memories with the practical details that are already part of our episodic memories. It is this second solution that is addressed by interactions between our emotional centers and our hippocampus – interactions that many believe are achieved through the process of dreaming.

It is well known that even the non-emotional content of long-term memories is selected on the basis of its relationship to emotional perturbations. As the brain's emotional centers are active during REM dreaming, dreaming can essentially be regarded as an emotional experience. In this way dreaming has the potential to emotionally texture the otherwise realistic, episodic memories being held in abeyance by the hippocampus pending either their extinction or their incorporation into the brain's long-term archives of significant events. As we have seen in relation to PTSD, intransigent emotional memories are the source of much experience-induced psychological dysfunction (*The Ravages of Emotional Memory*: Chapter 5: Section 4). It is even possible that the persistence of highly negative emotional memories and the attendant nightmares reflect a diminished hippocampal capacity sometimes associated with PTSD and documented as an outcome of prolonged childhood abuse.

There are two ways that dreaming could provide a means of integrating our emotional and episodic memories. The first involves *thinking* about our dreams so that we incorporate their emotional nuances into our cognitive accessible, hippocampal memory banks. If this ever happens it must be a very inefficient process because unless we are woken up while dreaming, we typically remember less than 5% of our dreams. Only 0.5% of psychologically normal people are unable to ever remember their dreams, even when awoken from REM sleep. The second way bypasses the mind and supposes that the experiences of dream can directly modify our episodic memories by penetrating the hippocampal circuitry during REM sleep. In this model, it does not matter whether or not we remember our dreams. The only issue is whether, by enabling the emergence of subliminal emotional memories into cortical space, dreams facilitate the penetration of these memories into the hippocampus wherein their content may be integrated with the non-emotional, episodic elements in the formation of multifaceted, integrated, episodic memories.

In its evolutionary origin, the hippocampus is a neural system for registering the spatial location of an animal with respect to its surroundings. London taxi drivers who are required to memorize the location of all the streets of London, a feat known as *The Knowledge*, have a larger than normal hippocampus. The hippocampus contains many nerve cells that are known as *place cells* because they become active only when the animal or person is in a certain part of their home territory. When a rat learns a maze, particular sets of these cells begin to fire each time the rat is at a certain point in the maze. When the rat has learnt the maze these same place cells fire just before the rat reaches the place to which they have been tuned. Experientially, the human parallel is the way we are able to anticipate a room in our house before we have even moved into the hallway.

As highly social animals the consolidation of long-term episodic memories is particularly important to human survival. The term *infantile amnesia* refers to the condition in which infants cannot remember anything because of the immaturity of the hippocampus during the first two years of life. In adults, however, experiences are retained for a short time within the mind as part of the process of *working* or *short-term memory*. If an episode is to be committed to long-term memory, it is transferred from the mind to the hippocampus that over the next 3 to 6 months will consolidate it into long-term memory. If the hippocampus in both hemispheres is damaged during this period then not only will all future experiences be denied a place in long-term memory but all experiences that occurred from 3 to 6 months (the time taken for memory consolidation) before the damage will also be permanently lost. To patients who have lost their hippocampus the past must become an increasingly distant experience while the present must always be refreshingly new.

We have, to this point been looking at the hippocampus as a specialized system for consolidating episodic memories. It is thought that it achieves this by synchronously activating the different parts of the cortex that participated in the original experience and so essentially reviving the experience again and again. The long-term effect of this is the slow strengthening of transcortical association neurons such that they bind the relevant parts of cortex together into a memory-specific network (*Constructing the Gestalt*: Chapter 4: Section 2). Through their participation in this network, these cortical areas will tend to be synchronously active such that any significant facet of the original experience (eg. a pervasive color) has opportunity to activate the whole network and elaborate the entire episodic memory. For example, the memory of a scenario in which our pet dog is chasing a cat, might involve a network that joins together modules in the visual, auditory, olfactory, touch, motor and emotional areas of the cortex but not (hopefully) areas involved in taste. As we are dealing with an episode, the hippocampus, the center of episodic memories, will also be activated. When the network is active we experience the holistic memory of our dog chasing a cat. Just hearing our dog's bark might be sufficient to conjure up a holistic image of our dog, but is less likely to recreate the whole scenario. Alternatively, if we are thinking about the episode, then the mind will have opportunity to recreate the whole scenario by activating the hippocampus, which, in turn, will recreate all facets of the episodic memory. If our dog dies, this network will slowly degrade such that some aspects of our dog might fade from our memory, while others will persist.

In the process of committing experiences to long-term memory the hippocampus works with another highly specialized area known as the *entorhinal* cortex (BA28). Historically, both the hippocampus and the entorhinal cortex were classified, along with the emotional centers, as part of the limbic system (*Life on the Edge - The Limbic System* Chapter 3: Section 4). The entorhinal cortex is unique in that it is interconnected with all other areas of the cortex. Consequently, only the entorhinal cortex has the potential to bring things in from all over the cortex and to, in turn, selectively convey information back to any point. It is easy to appreciate how these global interconnections might facilitate the synchronization of activity in two or more cortical areas until such time as they become bound together by the strengthening of the relevant transcortical association neurons. The interconnections between the entorhinal cortex and the cortex's perceptual representations are particularly strong, indicating that information represented in the cortex's primary sensory receiving areas has less significance to our long-term memories, in the same way as it is less relevant to imagination, attention and dreaming. Brain scans show that activity in the hippocampus and entorhinal cortex is increased during REM sleep above the level seen during either non-REM sleep or wakefulness.

The question is how does this system keep a memory alive during the period of its consolidation? By virtue of its global interconnections, the entorhinal cortex can transfer any 2-dimensional mosaic of synchronous cortical activity from the cortex to the hippocampus and back again. As we more readily remember emotional arousing events, the inclusion of the cortex's emotional areas in this mosaic doubtless enhances the penetration of an emotionally charged scenario into long-term memory. Nerve cells in parts of the hippocampal and entorhinal cortex participate in special neuronal circuits that are essentially loops where information concerning an experience can be temporally stored by cycling it around and around. The entorhinal cortex's participation in these loops enables selected pieces of information to be tapped off and sent to relevant cortical areas where it will eventually be stored and permanently associated with other pieces that were simultaneously sent to other areas of the cortex. We might think of these hippocampal-entorhinal loops as literally keeping all perceived elements of a multifaceted scenario alive for 3 to 6 months until selected parts are sustained by their incorporation into a newly established transcortical network. Once established this cortical network binds together the related perceptual representations into a single multifaceted yet cohesive episodic memory of the emotionally, or, we might say, instinctually relevant aspects of the original scenario.

How then can the processes of dreaming interact with the hippocampal-entorhinal system that is busily consolidating patterns of cortical activity into long-term memories? Clearly as long as this system is switched on, there is no reason to believe that it will treat the patterns of cortical activity that underlie dreams any differently to those that underlie normal experiences. As the emotional centers are the only part of the psyche active during dreaming, each and every dream must have at least some emotional content that will be of significance to the interpretation of memories held within the hippocampal-entorhinal system. A vital clue as to how the information in dreams might penetrate the hippocampal-entorhinal system appeared when scientists recorded brainwaves, not from the surface of the skull, but directly from the hippocampal cortex of the rat. These hippocampal brainwaves had the frequency of 6 cycles per second characteristic of the theta wave bandwidth and were present only during alert wakefulness and REM sleep – states that are associated with the presence of desynchronized brainwaves over the rest of the cortex. In the awake rat, the desynchronized brainwaves coexist with the hippocampal theta wave during exploratory behavior. Even the whiskers (the rat's primary exploratory organs) twitch in synchrony with the theta rhythm indicating a clear linkage between search behavior and the rhythmical activity of the brain's system for memory consolidation. Whereas, it is obvious that animals are most likely to have experiences that are important to remember when they are alert and in exploratory mode, it seems that this state also persists during dreaming. The participation of the hippocampal-entorhinal system in dreaming suggests that long-term episodic memories are colored by the entire gamut of emotional memories associated with the original experience. If these insights into the association between dreaming and emotional memory are correct, then we can conclude that REM dreams provide a period of bodily paralysis and mental quiescence that enables the emotional centers to cast their, often pent up, memories into human consciousness – an opportunity that will be exploited by the hippocampal and entorhinal cortex, for purpose of fashioning long-term, cognitively accessible memories (Figure 7.4).

Chapter 3 – State and the Controllers of Consciousness

The State of Consciousness

"One side will make you grow taller, and the other side will make you grow shorter." *Grimm's Fairytales*. Jacob Grimm (1785-1863) and Wilhelm Grimm (1786-1859). The "Brothers Grimm" were German Academics, Linguists and Folk Historians.

In the matter of *state*, we are very different from one another. In everyday slang, state is commonly referred to as the "space" that we are in. You do not sleep as deeply as one person, nor as lightly as another. You are alert while your friend is dreamy and detached. You are depressed and unmotivated but your friend is happy and creative. State isolates us within our individuality, hiding from us the worlds of others.

Like consciousness, state is a global phenomenon. To understand state it helps to envisage the cortex as an imaginary planet. The physical conditions on this planet, the temperature, the atmosphere, the minerals, the winds and rainfall etcetera, define its state, which in turn, determines the sort of life it can sustain. If conditions are very different from those on Earth then we will be obliged to imagine forms of life that are very different to the animals and plants of Earth. Our new planet exists in a state that is quite different from the state on Earth and the life that inhabits it naturally reflects this difference. Unlike a planet, however, our cortex can switch very quickly between many different states. One day it may be like our imaginary planet, and yet on another, like Earth. Just as the state of our imaginary planet determines what sort of organisms it can support, then so too does the state of our cortex determine what patterns of neural activity can inhabit its neuronal circuitry – patterns that determine how we experience existence.

When we refer to our *state of consciousness* we are referring to the physiological condition of our whole cerebral cortex and not the transient patterns of activity that generate individual experiences. Any activity, brain system or drug that globally alters the physiology of the cortex is therefore said to have the capacity to influence our state. Because changing the state of the cortex inevitably enhances the responsiveness of some areas while reducing the responsiveness of others, certain experiences may predominate in one state, while in another, they may be unattainable. While one drug makes us feel happy and warm another might render us fearful and aggressive.

A change in state might involve changes in the excitability of the entire cortex such as we experience when we are hypervigilant or, alternatively, falling into sleep. Our normal cycles of sleep and wakefulness are the most familiar changes of state. However, many other cortical states, or states of consciousness, are common to our day-to-day life. For example, sexual arousal, bliss and depression can be seen as states of consciousness in that they too result from global changes in the physiology of our cortex. Other states exist that are known only to circumscribed groups of individuals that can be identified in every society. These states are those that arise from the recreational use of neuroactive drugs or the introspective meditative practices of the spiritually orientated.

Attaining a common ambience of sensation, mood and thought is fundamental to achieving a greater union between people. Ritual, be it social, religious or sexual, is actually a way of bringing the consciousness of two or more people into a similar state or space. A boring lecturer soon casts his audience into a state of drowsiness, whereas an enlightening address might have evoked a state of vigilance. When humans of like mind gather in religious or other ceremony, it is with the unspoken goal of sharing a common state. Religious fervor is one of the most infectious states. In such times it is said, "we gather together in the presence of God". No matter what his guise, God is the great statesman of the human consciousness.

Every anesthetist owes his position to the fact that each person's brain chemistry is unique. General anesthetics are drugs that shut down consciousness. They do this by effectively inhibiting the neurons of the cerebral cortex thereby, bringing us into the state of unconsciousness. The anesthetist must monitor each patient closely when administering an anesthetic. His primary goal is to obliterate consciousness without shutting down those parts of the brain essential to our vital functions. Some people require more anesthetic, some less. By monitoring our vital signs, the anesthetist manipulates our state of consciousness, turning it down until it just disappears and then allowing it to return only when the surgeon's work is done.

More than any other biological factor, state brings to our lives both great confusion and great mystery. Changes of state have such subtle effects upon consciousness that we can easily miss the fact that we are no longer the same. It is said that relationship is a mirror. It is therefore, not uncommon for people to become aware of their own mood swings only after the reactions of others enable them to see the mood-related changes in their own behavior. Even when the swings are massive, people often remain imperceptive of internal change, attributing their mood to altered social or physical circumstances, even though these may conspicuously lack the potency required to effect a lasting change in state.

The Controllers of State
"Unusual….states include: soporific states, produced by alcohol and opium; excited states, produced by 'loco weed' and nutmeg; and hallucinatory states, produced by LSD, mescaline and ayahuasca. Depending upon the contexts in which these pharmacologically active substances are ingested, they may be used for withdrawal from daily stresses, for meaningful religious experiences, for psychotherapeutic purposes, or for improved functioning in the presence of starvation or oppression." Ari Kiev, Transcultural Psychiatrist and Business Psychologist. From: *Transcultural Psychiatry*. Penguin Books Ltd., Harmondsworth, England, 1972.

The regular cycle of day and night is alone sufficient reason to have built into the nervous system a device for altering its state. At the simplest level such a device might calm the nervous system at night and increase its excitability during the day, or *vice versa* for nocturnal creatures. The central nervous system can also switch into a number of different states outside the day-night cycle. Within the archaic core of the human brain are four major neural systems that are specifically for switching the cortex from one state to another and, as a corollary of this, altering the state of our

335

consciousness. These systems are collectively called the *extra-thalamic projection systems*. To neuroscientists this term carries the message that although these neuronal systems have a global influence over the cortex, they do not deliver specific, analyzable sensory information to the cortex but instead regulate its overall state.

The extra-thalamic projection systems first evolved deep in our vertebrate ancestry. They arise from four groups of neurons (nuclei), located in the brain stem, each of which secretes a different neuroactive chemical from their cortical terminals. The *nucleus raphe* secretes *serotonin* (also called *5-hydroxytryptamine* or *5HT*). The *locus coeruleus* secretes *noradrenalin* (*norepinephrine*). The *basal nucleus of Meynert* secretes *acetylcholine*. The *ventral tegmental area* secretes *dopamine*. The nucleus raphe and the nucleus of Meynert innervate the whole cortex while the tiny locus coeruleus, although containing only 9000 neurons not only influences billions of neurons across the whole cortex but also many neurons within the rest of the central nervous system. In contrast, the ventral tegmental area innervates only the prefrontal cortex and therefore has a selective effect over the state of the psyche but no direct effect on the sensory, motor or perceptual areas of the cortex.

In the lower, "mindless" mammals, such as the rat, these systems are activated or inhibited in relation to the physiological state of the body. For example, when the body signals a state of hunger these systems will alter the state of the cortex to enhance the level of the rat's vigilance, whereas when the body signals fatigue they will participate in the maintenance of sleep and dreaming. With the evolution of the mind in the higher mammals, three of these systems fell under a degree of mental control. Thus, in monkeys, apes and humans, we find that some nerve cells in the cortex of the mind project down to the brainstem and connect to the locus coeruleus, the nucleus of Meynert or the ventral tegmental area. It is these descending connections from our cognitive centers that give us a modicum of mental or voluntary control over the state of our consciousness. Unlike the rat, we can use our mental faculties to will ourselves to be vigilant even though our feelings are those of lethargy. Indeed, it is completely in keeping with the plenipotentiary powers of the human mind that it needs to have an optional control over cortical state in order to manifest its strategies irrespective of how one is feeling or what time of day it is. It is this linkage between the mind and the extra-thalamic projection systems that gives human beings the dubious virtue of being able to partially transcend the physiological dictates of the body. Without the mental control of cortical state, human ambition to achieve gigantean physical feats, such as climbing Everest or spending years in tropical jungles trying to kill all alien humans, could never be put into effect.

The neuroactive chemicals released into the cortex by the extra-thalamic projection systems have very complex effects. There are two reasons for this. Firstly, some of these chemicals (eg. noradrenalin and acetylcholine) work partially as neurotransmitters and partially as *neuromodulators*. As neurotransmitters they are released from synapses onto individual cortical neurons. As neuromodulators, however, they are released into the spaces between the cortical cells and diffuse throughout the cortex, modulating the response of many neurons to activity in pathways that actually do bring new information to the cortex. Secondly, like all neurotransmitters and neuromodulators these chemicals work by binding to special sites in the membrane of cortical nerve cells called *receptors* - a chemical interaction that essentially triggers a bioelectrical and/or a biochemical response in the cortical cell. What complicates matters is that there are many (more than 10, in the case of serotonin) different receptors waiting to bind each of these neuroactive chemicals, each receptor type having the potential to evoke a different response in the host cortical neuron. The effects on any cortical neuron of any one of these neurotransmitters or neuromodulators thus depend on what receptor types are present on the surface of that neuron.

For these reasons the roles of the extra-thalamic projection systems in human behavior are still under intensive examination. There are, however, two relatively clear examples of how these systems contribute to behavior. The first involves the locus coeruleus, noradrenalin and the state of vigilance (Figure 7.5). With its potential to release noradrenalin over most of the nervous system, the locus coeruleus is in an excellent position to control nervous excitability. When the locus coeruleus is activated it reduces any spontaneous activity in cortical neurons but at the same time increases their response to incoming sensory information. The locus coeruleus thus increases the *signal-to-noise ratio* of the cortex, thereby enhancing our awareness of incoming information – a process, which translates into the phenomenon we call vigilance.

The second example of the involvement of the extra-thalamic systems in state focuses on the ventral tegmental area and dopamine (Figure 7.6). Dopamine is released from the cortical terminals of neurons located in the ventral tegmental area. As these neurons only project to the prefrontal cortex, dopamine is confined to that area. We have already seen that dopamine enhances play and is central to the experience of reward. When dopamine is released in the prefrontal cortex it shuts down activity in the mind and the orbital centers of anticipation while enabling activity in those parts of the anterior cingulate gyrus that are responsible for good feelings. The resultant state is one that is fundamental to all blissful experiences.

Like the locus coeruleus and the nucleus of Meynert, the ventral tegmental area receives connections from the mind indicating that it can respond to our cognitive processes. It is probably this pathway that enables us to be rewarded for mentally resolving problems of an entirely intellectual nature. As dopamine from the ventral tegmental area inhibits the mind, the connection between the mind and the ventral tegmental area enables the mind to switch itself off. Through it, particular lines of thought can be curtailed, either when the mind deems them to have been appropriately concluded, or when mitigating circumstances require that the mind be reoriented towards more pressing matters. The newly empty mind is then free to engage its thought processes in the resolution of the new crisis. It is the escalation of this process of terminating thoughts to chaotic levels that is fundamental to the excess dopamine theory of schizophrenia (*The Freewheeling Mind of Schizophrenia*: Chapter 4: Section 3).

Normally, dopamine from the ventral tegmental area essentially generates within us a rewarding experience while a deficiency of dopamine causes us to become anxious and sad. The memory, short or long-term, of a rewarding experience, presumably reinforces the psychological impetus to repeat any successful thought pattern or activity. However, it is dopamine from another brainstem center (the *substantia nigra*) that seems to play a direct role in learning via its reinforcing actions on many aspects of behavior extending from simple movement to cognitive reasoning. These reinforcing actions of dopamine relate to its effects on a sub-cortical brain center called the *basal ganglia*. Different parts of the basal ganglia interact powerfully with different parts of the cortex. Thus, three parts or nuclei - the *caudate, putamen* and *globus pallidus* - are involved with learning a set of movements that are associated with reward. Habitual activities, such as the mannerisms of smoking a cigarette, are typical manifestations of this process. Another part or nucleus of the basal ganglia - the *nucleus accumbens* – is devoted to the cortex of the prefrontal lobe and presumably enables reinforcement, not of patterns of movement, but of specific patterns of thought. The changes in neural circuitry that underlie both forms of learning are believed to be the result of dopamine being released within the basal ganglia upon the successful performance of an activity be it a movement or a thought. The dopamine released in the basal ganglia thus has quite a different effect to, and comes from a different source than, the dopamine released in the prefrontal cortex – the former affecting our motor and cognitive learning but having no effect on our feelings while the later is directly rewarding in that it evokes the good feelings associated with the successful completion of a task or a thought process.

Drugs and the Alteration of Consciousness

"This Soma is a god; he cures
The sharpest ills that man endures.
He heals the sick, the sad he cheers,
He nerves the weak, dispels their fears;
The faint with martial ardour fires,
With lofty thoughts the bard inspires;
The soul from earth: heaven he lifts,
So great and wondrous are his gifts.
Men feel the god within their veins
And cry in loud, exalting strains:
'We've quaffed the Soma bright
And are immortal grown:
We've entered into light,
And all the gods have known.
What mortal now can harm,
Or foeman vex us more?
Through thee, beyond alarm,
Immortal god, we soar'".
From: *The Rigveda*. As quoted in Wilkens, W. J. *Hindu Mythology*. Heritage Publishers, New Delhi, 1982.

All recreational drugs, from nicotine to LSD, alter the state of our consciousness. Most exert their effects via the neurotransmitter and neuromodulatory actions of noradrenalin, acetylcholine, serotonin or dopamine that are released from one or more of the extra-thalamic projection systems. Although all psychoactive drugs have some affect on those parts of the cortex that constitute the psyche, only some are conspicuously hedonic in that they abate anxiety and facilitate a pleasurable state while, in some cases, quieting the mind. Prior to the new wave of *designer drugs*, the most popular hedonic psychoactive drugs were marijuana, amphetamine, cocaine, ecstasy, nicotine, alcohol and the opiates; opium, pethidine, morphine and heroin. As all of these substances produce good feelings, all are likely to leave the user looking forward to the next episode. The strength of this wishing is a measure of the degree of what is called *psychological dependence*. In terms of its potential to induce drug-seeking behavior, this wish is no more or less potent than is the desire for sex in the elicitation of sex-seeking behavior. What is more dangerous in terms of becoming addicted, are the possibilities of *physiological dependence*. Nicotine, alcohol and the opiates are all dangerous in that if taken repeatedly in sufficient quantities they can produce marked physiological dependence.

The tendencies of the individual to become physiologically dependent appear to have a genetical basis. Genetically engineered rats, called Lewis rats, become dependent on heroin after only one exposure. Physiological dependence occurs because the repeated administration of certain drugs that activate nerve cells in the brain's reward centers, cause changes in the sensitivity of those nerve cells to those drugs. This process, in which more and more of the drug is required to give the same effect, is called *tolerance*. If one becomes tolerant to a rewarding drug, cessation of administration will evoke *withdrawal*, a bodily and nervous process, which is essentially a reversal of the drug's positive effects. Recreational drugs vary in their potential to produce physiological dependence. For example, marijuana never produces serious physiological dependence, while at the other extreme repeated heroin usage results in a very rapid build up of tolerance such that the individual is soon driven to seek out the drug in order to avoid the horrible experience of opiate withdrawal.

The potential for physiological dependency is also strongly influenced by the rate of onset of a drug, which depends, in turn, on how it is administered. For example, injecting morphine intravenously is more addictive than administering it intramuscularly or orally because it results in a bolus of the substance almost instantaneously hitting the reward centers. This is unfortunate because drug takers particularly enjoy the *rush* that accompanies the intravenous administration of powerful psychoactive drugs.

Understanding the rewarding effects of recreational drugs is best explained through the actions of two separate brain centers; the ventral tegmental area and the locus coeruleus. Opiates cause activation of the cells in the ventral tegmental area causing them to release dopamine throughout the prefrontal cortex. As well as this cerebral action, opiates also affect many other parts of the nervous system including the enteric division of the nervous system that controls gut motility. Opiates are particularly potent in blocking the ascending pathways that feed the affective-motivational aspect of pain (*Pain and the Penetration of the Psyche*: Chapter 2: Section 5). Through their actions on the brainstem and spinal cord, opiates abolish all bodily discomfort while relaxing the viscera and the skeletal muscles. At a higher level, opiates depress mental activity, quieting both the mind and the anticipatory centers in the orbital cortex, while activating the anterior cingulate gyrus. Thus, the opiate induced pattern of activity within the psyche resembles that seen during dreaming or during experiences of cerebral bliss that accompany love, meditation or orgasm. Indeed, morphine, the first powerful opiate to be prepared from opium, derives its name from the Greek God Morpheus, the God of sleep and dreams - an association intended to convey the dreamlike, playful, discomfort-free and worry-free state of opiate induced relaxation.

The discovery of opiate receptors in the brain meant that either the nervous system had evolved a mechanism to enable humans to savor the opiates, or that there must exist within the brain a naturally occurring, endogenous source of opiates that require a matching set of opiate receptors. Naturally, the latter proved to be the case. A number of small molecules (peptides) that act through the opiate receptors were soon identified as neurotransmitters that are released from the synapses of specialized, opiate-containing, nerve cells. When released, these *endogenous opiates* allay anxiety, inhibit the central nervous system's responses to pain or cause activation of dopamine containing neurons in the brain's reward centers. In the central nervous system the most common endogenous opiate is called *enkephalin* (or *endorphin*).

Whereas opiates induce a state of blissful disinterest, amphetamine, cocaine and ecstasy produce a state of exhilarated activity best described as euphoria (*The Irresistible Realm of Euphoria*: Chapter 1: Section 5). During drug-induced euphoria, the amygdala and the anticipatory centers in the orbital cortex are both inhibited. The experience of euphoria involves a recognizable element of bliss, a high level of vigilance and a hyper-excitable state characterized, in part, by increased locomotory activity – a state that would require both the activation of the dopamine containing nerve cells of the ventral tegmental area and the noradrenalin containing nerve cells of the locus coeruleus. However, neither amphetamine nor cocaine works by activating nerve cells in these brainstem centers. Instead these substances operate on the cortical terminations of these two sets of neurons; amphetamine enhancing the release of dopamine and noradrenalin while cocaine prolongs the presence of both by blocking their reuptake into the synapses that released them. Excessive use of these substances produces the confused patterns of thought that constitute *psychosis*.

In terms of its actions on the brain, the body and behavior, marijuana is by far the most theoretically interesting of all the recreational drugs. Marijuana is a natural product present in different species of the cannabis plant. Cannabis is related to the hops (*Humulus sp.*) and belongs to the family *Cannabaceae*. Over the thousands of years of human usage, many varieties of cannabis have been developed in an attempt to manipulate the concentration of the main psychoactive ingredient, delta-9-tetrahydrocannabinol (THC). Despite this, most experts agree that all varieties stem from three different species, *Cannabis indica*, *Cannabis sativa* and *Cannabis ruderalis*.

Marijuana enhances the pleasure of sex, rewarding images and sounds, eating and thought, characteristics that prior to the wide use of ecstasy gave it the status as the only true *aphrodisiac*. What distinguishes marijuana from all other recreational drugs is its capacity to enhance, rather than simply elicit, reward. While THC does cause some dopamine release, its most powerful action is in increasing the amount of dopamine released by all other rewards, whether or not these are the result of other hedonic drugs or naturally rewarding activities, like eating and sex. All other issues aside, there is very little doubt that if any given society were to legalize the recreational use of THC and simultaneously ban the recreational use of alcohol, then domestic and social violence would be virtually abolished.

As we have seen, the descending connections from the mind to the ventral tegmental areas provide a mechanism through which our thoughts can elicit a reward. By also facilitating this channel of reward, marijuana facilitates the generation of novel ideas and perspectives. However, by increasing the release of dopamine, marijuana also facilitates the termination of thoughts and the mind's capacity for short-term or working memory. The rambling conversation of the "stoned" individual is attributable to these effects of marijuana.

Psychoactive drugs mostly work on the same neural systems that, when dysfunctional, contribute to most psychiatric conditions. Consequently, it is critically important that people with such conditions exercise great care before exposing their brain to any recreational substance. Unfortunately, the mentally ill are highly predisposed to medicating themselves with any prescription drugs or legal or illegal recreational drugs. It would, however, be a falsehood to say that all recreational drugs affect any particular psychiatric condition negatively. There are, for instance, indications that marijuana may actually be helpful in bipolar disorder. However, marijuana is *most definitely contraindicated for use by either schizoid individuals or schizophrenics* (*The Freewheeling Mind of Schizophrenia*: Chapter 4: Section 3). The reason is partially to do with the mild, paranoia-producing properties of marijuana, but is possibly also a result of marijuana-induced increases in the release of dopamine. Already predisposed to chaotic thought, marijuana has the potential to further disrupt the mind of the schizophrenic while simultaneously eliciting paranoia. In schizophrenics, repeated use of marijuana can facilitate the build up of unstoppable, chaotic and paranoid thoughts to a level where suicide can seem the only escape.

The only answer to such dilemmas is the introduction of school education programs that are not exercises in scare mongering but are aimed at providing a firm knowledge base about the physiological and experiential effects of all common recreational substances - irrespective of whether they are legal or illegal. Education is, after all a process wherein we provide students with information and rational frameworks and allow their intelligence to do the rest. When young people first venture into the world at large, it is education and not the attitudes and superstitions of uninformed adults or the domestic propaganda of timid governments or power-orientated demands of ambitious police chiefs that truly helps them set their own guidelines. In a reaction to the futility of wasting billions of dollars on enforcing laws that contravene the personal desires of an appreciable percentage of the population of every country, some more enlightened governments (most recently, Portugal and Mexico) have decriminalized the personal use and possession of, not only of cannabis but also, other recreational drugs.

In a misplaced response to the antiwar activities of the late 1960s, US President Richard Nixon proclaimed his infamous and ill conceived, *war on drugs*. His objective, and that of the monied industrialists he represented, was to find rational, rather than economic or purely cultural, reasons for making those recreational drugs that so inspired the 1960s counterculture, illegal. The emergent policies and propaganda were to have disastrous social effects, polarizing the society and even families. Alongside this, however, the monetary cost to the American people was to become astronomical. In 2003 the US Federal Government would spend 19.2 billion dollars on its war on drugs while the State Governments spent a further 20 billion dollars. In 2003, the Bush administration is recorded as having paid the US media 170 million dollars just commercially promoting its antidrug legislation. Nevertheless, in the late 1960s an army of neruoscientists reorientated their research towards attempting to establish the damaging effects of exposure to marijuana, attracted not by the rational of the government's arguments but simply by the availability of funding.

Contrary to common perceptions, research science does not advance by having mission-orientated expectations but by an open-minded testing of intelligently constructed hypotheses. In terms of Nixon's objectives, the war on drugs was, in every way, an ongoing disaster. In terms of new discoveries, however, it revealed the reward-related participation of many previously hidden and highly significant brain processes. It soon became obvious that just as opium, pethidine, morphine and heroin work because many of our nerve cells have opiate receptors, so too are the effects of cannabis mediated through a set of naturally occurring *cannabinoid receptors*. Further investigations showed that these specialized cannabinoid receptors are located on nerve cells in parts the brain that are clearly involved in the creation of the "stoned" state – a state characterized by an exaggerated perception of pleasure, the transient repression of short-term memory and a loss of awareness of, or concern for, one's location.

Like the relationship between the presence of opiate receptors and the existence of endogenous opiates, the elucidation of cannabinoid receptors was a clear indicator of the presence within our brain of naturally occurring, *endogenous cannabinoids*. This explains why, unlike alcohol, marijuana has quite specific and positive effects on the brain. Indeed, the experiential effects of marijuana indicate that when released, our endogenous cannabinoids are responsible for the *state of peaceful ambience* such as prevails in times of intimate or romantic interlude.

Amongst the first endogenous cannabinoids to be isolated were *anandamide* and *arachnamide*. Subsequent research has shown that a variety of endogenous cannabinoids occur in ordinary somatic cells as well as in nerve cells and that cannabinoid receptors are not restricted to nerve cells but occur on many cell types including certain malignant tumour cells. The result of these studies has been the recognition of an *endocannabinoid system* – a system considered to underlie many of the potential therapeutic advantages of marijuana use, including analgesia, muscle relaxation, immunosuppression, sedation, improvement of mood, stimulation of appetite, suppression of vomiting, lowering of intraocular pressure in glaucoma, reduction of oedema in post-traumatic swelling, inhibition of excitotoxicity (neurons firing to death) after brain injury and the stimulation of mechanisms underlying the process of natural death (*apoptosis*) in cancer cells. It is ironic that although everyone believes in the importance of justifying research endeavours before funding them, Nixon's irrationally inspired war on drugs resulted in such important findings about the potential therapeutic value of the very agents and habits he sought to politically devalue. Since then, the development of synthetic molecules with potencies up to one thousand times that of THC holds great promise for exploitation of the natural actions of the endocannabinoid system.

Alongside the purely hedonic recreational drugs are a family of substances that are highly psychotropic and yet relatively inert in relation to the evocation of pleasure. The most commonly known substances in this class are mescaline from the peyote cactus (*Lophophora williamsii*), psilocybin from the so-called "magic" mushrooms (*Psilocybe sp.*) and, of entirely synthetic origin, LSD-25 (*The Devil's Bread*: Chapter 2: Section 5). Of these, LSD is the most fascinating both in terms of its experiential effect and the fact that the ingestion of as little as 50 millionths of a gram is sufficient to trigger a "trip". Pharmacologically LSD is believed to act through one of the many serotonin receptors. Experientially, however, its effects are most likely the result of activation of the locus coeruleus. Indeed, if one were to search for a site where the tiniest quantity of a neuroactive drug would maximally affect the brain, one would naturally choose the locus coeruleus (*The Controllers of State*: Chapter 3: Section 7). By acting on the locus coeruleus, LSD essentially increases the responsiveness of most of the central nervous systems including the entire cortex – an affect that translates into an augmentation of every aspect of conscious experience, from simple sensations to all domains of perception, emotion and thought.

The purpose of the cortex's perceptual areas is to reassemble information from particular domains of sensation. However, in the presence of LSD two normally discrete sensory pathways such as sound and vision, may interact at the perceptual level such that visual images become responsive to sound and *vice versa*. Interestingly this phenomenon, known as *synaesthesia*, occurs naturally in a small percentage of otherwise normal adults and is also thought to be present in all infants younger than 4 months. Through its action on the locus coeruleus, LSD elicits a state of hyper-vigilance in which the individual's focus can very easily drift between thoughts, sensations, perceptions and emotions. At the same time all the transcortical interactions between the centres of emotion, thought and perception continue to operate. The result is that any bizarre idea concocted by the now highly excitable cortex of the mind can, through the circuitry serving imagination, easily be translated into equally bizarre "images" and emotions conjured within the cortex's perceptual areas. In attempting to create meaningful conceptual frameworks, the mind naturally generates all manner of strange ideas and perspectives, at least some of which are

343

useful and unique insights. The LSD state is not so much one of higher consciousness but one of highly altered consciousness involving combination of cognitive, emotional and perceptual experiences that would never appear in normal states of consciousness.

The lay literature of the 1960s and 1970s is filled with personal accounts of the LSD experience. Even a cursory glance at these publications is sufficient to convince one that the vast majority of novel ideas and perspectives arrived at while under the influence of LSD are essentially without relevance to day-to-day life in the real world. There are, however, very occasional, well-documented claims of LSD providing critical insights on important matters that, in at least one case, appear to have led to Nobel prize-winning discoveries. With its innately fashioned mechanisms for formulating conceptual frameworks of the world, it is easy to see how the mind might respond to limited periods of abnormal and even chaotic consciousness by generating completely novel insights into important matters, be they personal, practical or entirely abstract.

The activation of the locus coeruleus by LSD has a curious parallel in heroin withdrawal. Heroin powerfully inhibits the locus coeruleus, decreasing the levels of vigilance that might otherwise contravene the warm, dreamlike, playful opiate state. Unfortunately, in the same way as nerve cells in the ventral tegmental area become less responsiveness (become tolerant) to successive doses of heroin, the nerve cells in the locus coeruleus become increasingly less inhibited with each exposure. Consequently, when the heroin dependent individual is deprived of the drug, the ventral tegmental area becomes less excitable and the locus coeruleus becomes more excitable. Essentially, the locus coeruleus responds to withdrawal of heroin in much the same way as it might to LSD. The somewhat restless, ever-searching demeanor of the deprived heroin addict is not so much due to them intentionally seeking out the drug or the resources to purchase it, but to an irrepressible manifestation of an abnormally active locus coeruleus. At a more advanced stage of withdrawal the cortex is essentially thrown into an LSD-like state of hyper-receptivity. At the same time the dependent individual is afflicted with chills, nausea and cramping of the stomach and skeletal musculature - bodily events which naturally activate parts of the cortex involved in generating wracking pain, intense anxiety, fear, panic, anger and acute dysphoria. Because of the combination of physical trauma with activation of the locus coeruleus, the experience of heroin withdrawal somewhat resembles ergot poisoning (ergotism or St. Anthony's fire) or a bad LSD trip (*The Devil's Bread* and *LSD and the Bad Trip*: Chapter 2: Section 5). Via their influence over state, psychoactive drugs do indeed have the power to transport us through the doors of perception and into the psyche, wherein we may come to know both Heaven and Hell.

The human brain has the innate potential to swing from darkness to bliss, from somnolence to vigilance or from anger to love – a potential which once realized most naturally becomes a primary focus of the reward-orientated, human intellect. Virtually all humans have, at times, attempted to artificially alter the state of their consciousness such that good feelings replace bad. Indeed, there has never been a period of history when this has not been so and it is safe to say that there will never be such a period. All manner of human activities such as meditation, prayer, self-flagellation, exercise, high altitude climbing, and diving, create within the practitioner some relief from the tyranny of thought and worry. While state is a fundamental property of the nervous system of even the most primitive animals, only humans have the intellectual power to take over the controls, wresting consciousness from the hands of nature and striving eternally to reshape it into an ever more satisfactory form.

The Legality of Drugs
'Some men need some killer weed,
And some men need cocaine.
Some men need some cactus juice,
To purify their brain.
Some men need two women,
And some need alcohol.
Everybody needs a little something,
But Lord I need it all.'
Shel Silverstein (1930-1999). American Poet, Singer-songwriter, Muscian, Cartoonist, Screenwriter and Author of Childrens Books.

The reason commonly given for making it illegal to take a drug is that the substance is *believed* to be highly addictive. In its essence, however, addiction is not a drug-related pathology but a natural phenomenon that is an inherent property of the brain and consequently underlies many aspects of behavior. For example, one may be addicted to quite ordinary every day activities such as sex, work or television. What then is the essence of addictive behaviors that distinguish them from other activities that compose our daily routines? The most common answer is that addiction is revealed by (a) an inability to regulate the seeking behavior that actualizes the reward and (b) the continuation of such behavioral sequences despite significant negative consequences. In these terms, addictive behavior is, by definition, a behavior wherein the mind no longer retains any authority over the urges of the body but is essentially enslaved to their satiation. There are two factors at work here. The first is the threat of painful, physiological withdrawal that accompanies discontinuation of some recreational drugs. The second is the conditioning of the mind (psychological addiction) to the attainment of that reward. Both these phenomena play a part in normal behavior. For example, with relation to physiological dependency, athletes often become dependent on exercise and suffer mild withdrawal if it is prevented. Similarly, the process by which the mind is conditioned is essentially the process by which beliefs are established irrespective of whether they relate to the existence of God or the apparent benefits of a rewarding activity. Considered in this manner it seems that addiction is a very common operative in human behavior that has perhaps evolved to hold individuals to particular behavioral routines at both the cognitive and instinctual level. However, what is problematic about addiction is that the object of the addict's urges is not necessarily something, which, like the satiation of sexual desire or hunger, is of significance to survival. Instead addiction may involve the pursuit of an objective that, like a recreational drug, has no relevance to survival or, even worse, results in significant personal catastrophe.

The idea that addiction is not dependent upon the participation of the mind is unequivocally illustrated by the fact that addiction is not confined to humans but can be easily induced in lower mammals, like the rat – a mammal that essentially lacks any appreciable mental capacity. Given the opportunity to use a lever to self-administer heroin, rats will cease all other activities and repeatedly administer the drug. Lacking the cognitive apparatus to question the long-term outcome of continuous lever pressing, the rat simply keeps up the activity until it succumbs to exhaustion or dies of an overdose. The only thing that distinguishes the procurement of sex or food from the satiation obtained by self-administering heroin, is that the latter wastes a lot of energy on an activity that, even if it was not ultimately lethal, does not enhance survival. Indeed, in the West, the highly addictive nature of drinking large quantities of alcohol, smoking cigarettes and taking heroin are of justifiable concern only because they inevitably lead to a shortening of human life and a waste of human energy. Ironically, however, many westerners do not need to expend any energy to survive and so the issue of them wasting time and energy is not, at the level of the individual or their community, of much significance. Again the problem with using addiction as a principle for making things illegal is that the addictive processes in the brain are involved in many aspects of normal behavior that are essential to the life of humans and all other mammals.

Irrespective of whether a person is addicted to a drug, video games or work, their addictive behaviors are always driven by misplaced urges. One might imagine that with a powerful and independent mind, the average educated human could sample a hedonic drug and then simply walk away from the opportunity to repeatedly experience pleasure. This, however, is rarely the case. As a result of its subordination to desire, the human mind is so often a fickle ruler. The fully blown experience of pleasure and the rapid build up of tolerance and dependence quickly persuades many humans to repeatedly indulge in artificial reward. Despite the possession of a powerful mind, when it comes to the need to service the urges that underlie their cerebrally expressed desires, humans are little different from rats. In the West food and shelter are often guaranteed. One can only conjecture that as an increasingly large proportion of people spend an increasingly large portion of their energy exploring the artificial worlds of the digital revolution, the waste of human energy in the equally artificial, pharmacological pursuit of pleasure will have few consequences for either our productivity or survival.

Unlike the hedonics, powerful psychotropic drugs like LSD, mescaline and psilocybin are not sufficiently pleasurable to cause craving. Indeed, only humans can be persuaded to self-administer this class of drugs, courted into their use by the cerebrally fascinating, and often instructive, distortions of our perceptual, emotional and cognitive realms. It seems that only humans have the mental capacity to generate the necessary inquisitiveness to actively pursue new and unusual cerebral states.

Let us consider what is surely the most important issue regarding the legality and illegality of recreational drugs; their effect on the length and quality of human life. The figures are utterly astounding. In the year 2,000, tobacco use was responsible for 4.9 million deaths worldwide, alcohol for 1.8 million deaths. In comparison, heroin, cocaine and amphetamines together accounted for only 223,000 deaths a mere 3% of the 6.7 million people killed each year by alcohol and cigarettes. Thanks to the influence of profit orientated, colonial invaders of the 18th and 19th centuries in encouraging the use of tobacco, today's developing nations are still the hardest hit. Today, the annual death toll from tobacco use alone, far exceeds the annual death toll suffered in wars and the worst cases of genocide. In the USA alone, tobacco kills around 400,000 people or 1.3% of its population every year. On top of this alcohol accounts for another 80,000, while the cocaine and heroin are together, responsible for a mere, 2,500 and 2,000 deaths per annum, respectively. In comparison, 40,000 Americans die each year in road accidents and another 60,000 in workplace accidents. It is a sobering thought that if the use of alcohol and tobacco were abolished 6.7 million people would be saved each year, from a slow and distressing death – a number equivalent to the commonly cited death toll of the holocaust, almost eight times the global road toll (approximately 860,000) and roughly 3 to 6 times the average number killed annually in wars and other human conflicts. It is surely a matter of universal wonderment that when pharmaceutical drugs damage health, courts order drug companies to payout tens of millions of dollars, yet when vigorously marketed, legal, addictive substances, kill and maim millions, no compensation is forthcoming. Perhaps in our overpopulated world, we should recognize that we owe a great debt to those few outrageously wealthy individuals whose livelihood is an annual legacy to the misery, suffering and slow death of millions. It is their political acumen and promotional skills that continue to "persuade" a bevy of timid and essentially ignorant politicians, in *every* country of the world, to allow each successive generation to be incessantly encouraged to indulge in the ultimately lethal, joys of smoking and drinking.

There are no confirmed accounts of a single death resulting from the use of marijuana. It is often incorrectly stated, even by medical doctors, that cannabis smoke has the same cancer producing potential as tobacco smoke. In truth, however, typical tobacco smoker smokes around 10 to 30 cigarettes per day while even regular marijuana smokers rarely exceed 2 or 3 "joints" per day. Even if cannabis smoke was as carcinogenic as tobacco smoke, the relative cancer risk of the two forms of smoking, are obvious. More than anything, it is the illegality of cannabis that greatly increases the health risk associated with its use. Indeed, the same could be said for all illegal drugs. For example, while tobacco addicts can obtain nicotine tablets to avoid the harmful agents in cigarette smoke, no such commercially prepared aid is available for cannabis users. With the usage of cannabinoid-like substances in the treatment of various ailments, researchers have already experimented with different routes of administration, including sublingual application and cannabinoid containing aerosols, both of which use the purified, active ingredient (THC) and are thus relatively safe and controllable. In the same manner that anti-abortion laws drive young girls to risk their lives and future fertility in illicit backyard clinics, the laws against smoking marijuana place the world's estimated 147 million regular users unnecessarily at risk of contracting throat and lung cancer.

At the other extreme from marijuana, the seductive properties and rapid build up of dependence make heroin use a very real danger. The street costs of heroin are so great that the typical addict is obliged to enter crime or become a prostitute to maintain their habit. Only the privileged few who have unlimited financial resources appear to be able to sustain a lifelong heroin habit without the attendant social demise.

Heroin is normally prepared from morphine which can be extracted from the opium poppy. Although clinically available as a pharmaceutical product under the name *diacetyl morphine*, heroin is only available to the public on the black market. The classic pattern of addiction therefore involves an introduction, often by a friend or a pusher, until dependence is achieved, after which time the individual is physiologically obliged to seek out an illegal supply each and every day.

While scientists and psychologists have delved deeply into the nature of addiction, most governments have ignored the essence of their findings and remained fearful, inert and unimaginative in their strategies for dealing with the issue of drug taking. Those who have personally experienced heroin addiction or have been close to addicted people are aware of the extreme difficulties in terminating the habit. Once dependent, many people suffer the societal consequences of having a heroin habit for the remainder of their lives, often dying young from the side effects of a traumatic, antisocial and clandestine lifestyle. As illustrated by the current rapid increase in heroin usage, legislation and the draconian enforcement measures are inept strategies for regulating the use and supply of drugs. The tens of billions of dollars and vast human effort spent each year making war on drug users and drug suppliers, is about as effective as were the attempts of the American police between 1920 and 1933 to enforce the prohibition of alcohol. As it was then, so it is today, the illegality of drugs remaining as the primary generator of all criminal activity associated with drug use. The reality is that illegal recreational drugs are relatively cheap to extract or manufacture. Only the laws and the regular police crackdowns, keep the street price high. From the criminal's point of view, keeping recreational drugs illegal is an absolute guarantee of a large and steady income. Yet so widely have these simple facts been ignored that one cannot but be suspicious of links between government policy makers, the tobacco companies, the breweries, the police and the illegal drug trade.

Laws and corruption are inseparable bedfellows and it follows that unnecessary laws breed unnecessary corruption. People will always, either react against or exploit, repression, no matter what aspect of their freedom it impinges upon. What is particularly destructive is that when substances are pronounced illegal, all opportunity to advise temperance or honestly discuss safety issues relating to their use is completely lost. Instead each generation of young people is sent forth into the world with half-truths or simply lies that are the product of ignorance, fear and, wherever the sale of legal substances are involved, rank commercial opportunism. It is surely very clear that there will be no progress in this ongoing façade until governments comprehend and accept the human propensity to alter consciousness. Only then can they hope to deal with it in an intelligent and honest way that avoids forcing unworkable, moralistic and politically expedient attitudes upon their citizens. Until then, a vast number of people, many of whom are in their youth, will remain unnecessarily exposed to the very real dangers of inhaling carcinogens, drinking excessive alcohol or taking essentially unknown substances prepared in backyard laboratories by unscrupulous members of an ever-present, well-heeled, black market.

Only a few recreational drugs are highly addictive but there is no doubt that this property does pose very real problems for the user. What then are the possible answers to the problem of people taking highly addictive drugs? There are two. The first relies on further neuroscientific research and the second on common sense. In relation to research, we have already seen that neuroscientists have identified the underlying biochemical processes responsible for the build up of tolerance and physiological dependency. The stage is therefore set for the development of new drugs which block tolerance and dependency. Such drugs would not block the pleasurable effects of, for example, heroin but if taken with heroin would prevent only those biochemical changes that lead to tolerance. The result would be that opiates could be used by those so inclined without risk of the physiological dependence and addiction. With the substantial imbalance of male and female births, the regular tolerance-protected use of opiates might provide a useful substitute for the panacea of intimate family relationships that inevitably will be denied to 50 million of the world's male population who will be unable to find an available female and who will most likely channel their loneliness, anxiety and sexual frustration into domestic violence, riots and wars. Staring us in the face is the neurobiological truth that human instincts are such that denying activation of the anterior cingulate, by either sex, bonding or drugs, severely enhances the probability of amygdala activity and the attendant paranoia and overt hostility.

The second strategy has often been openly discussed but rarely employed. Although foolproof, it has been repeatedly buried by the influence of powerful yet profoundly ignorant, conservative factions. It involves registering heroin addicts and, as at commercial prices, heroin is easily affordable, simply allowing them to buy their daily requirement at the local pharmacy. The immediate effect of this strategy would be to abolish the black market, which as we have already seen is, like all other markets, completely dependent on the dynamics of supply and demand. Such a strategy would *not* promote the spread of heroin, for as long as those supplied were verified to be *chronically addicted* they would be most unlikely to share their daily allowance. The possibility of pregnancy in female addicts represents the only serious problem of this approach. The babies of opiate dependent mothers are born with this dependence and have to be nursed through physiological withdrawal. The solution is again imperfect but when one considers that almost 2 infants (1.9) in every 1,000 are born permanently disabled by fetal alcohol syndrome and that smoking causes a substantial number of prenatal deaths (6%), premature deliveries (7-10%) and low birth weights (17-26%), the issue of neonatal heroin withdrawal seems a more tolerable evil.

Ultimately, it is very likely most humans will always be drawn to changing the state of their consciousness. Recently the effects of injecting antibodies to nicotine as a means of preventing the reward of smoking, has been tested. These antibodies mop up the nicotine molecules after they are absorbed into the blood from the lungs and thus prevent them binding to those brain sites that give the reward, or good feeling, of smoking. Nobody yet knows the long-term effects of this treatment but it is clearly a method that could be applied to many reward substances, including those that like our endogenous opiates are manufactured by the brain itself. The potential of permanently affecting the brain's reward systems certainly suggests that extreme caution should be exercised. Certainly, one would hope that treatment could only be given to consenting adults and never as a consequence of parental, religious or state authority.

It is by a multidisciplinary understanding of the social, neurobiological and political dynamics of the human need to temporarily alter consciousness that we may anticipate, not a solution to this seemingly insoluble dilemma, but a strategy that optimizes humanitarian outcomes. With the age of the computer, drug design and production has become increasingly easy. In the prevailing climate of social and legal prohibition there will always be great rewards for the development and marketing of new recreational drugs. Each time the supply of relatively safe recreational drugs like marijuana is curtailed by police crackdowns there is new opportunity on the street for pushers to introduce new and often dangerous, substitutes. A contemporary example of this process in action is the worldwide epidemic of methamphetamine (ice), a substance that releases large quantities of dopamine but in the process permanently destroys the nerve cells that produce dopamine as well as those that produce serotonin, resulting in symptoms resembling the severe movement disorder and the intractable depression of Parkinson's disease.

Despite the readily available information on the neurotoxic properties of substances like alcohol and methamphetamine, the pathological usage of legal and illegal drugs continues to increase. Most western governments continue to display a rank insensitivity to this complex issue, choosing always to serve the vested interests of a privileged minority rather than championing the health and freedom of the common people. In US prisons, for example, 20% of inmates have been incarcerated for non-violent drug offences. Many others are guilty of crimes, committed solely to get money to obtain illegal drugs on the black market. In 2002, approximately 700,000 Americans (0.23% of its citizens) were incarcerated in US jails for possession of cannabis, 90% (630,000) of whom were convicted simply for possession. In Australia (population 21 million), things are equally absurd, with approximately 75,000 people (0.4% of its citizens) being charged with possession of illegal drugs within a single year. In truth, all these people are no different to the multitude of legal drug users in that they are ordinary citizens who are simply responding to the irrepressible obsession of human beings with altering the *state* of their consciousness. It is surely a matter of wonderment to all intelligent beings that the decision processes that have caused the illegalization of some substances and not of others are so clearly flawed and so utterly devoid of social, medical or humanitarian concerns.

Just as only humans seek a spiritual center and emerge with ideas about Gods and Spirits, so too are humans alone in their propensity to chemically explore the psyche. The human obsession with using drugs is perhaps a reflection of their desire to transcend many of the physical limitations of the brain and body. Yet the usage of legal or illegal drugs is an extremely complex issue. Prior to new legislation introduced over the last century in many western countries, drug issues were primarily social and medical. In the West, the prominence of the story of Moses delivering the Ten Commandments from God perhaps accounts for the fact that westerners often confuse laws and legality with morality. Nevertheless, the illegalization of many recreational drugs in the latter half of the 20th century has persuaded the ever fearful arch-conservatives of western world to (a) adopt deeply entrenched attitudes to others who continued to indulge and (b) to harbor a host of incorrect beliefs relating to the effects of those drugs on the brain, the body and the persona – beliefs typically seeded by the police and other governmental agencies through controlled media outlets. Listening to the daily spin and rhetoric one could be excused from feeling that these excercises in social propaganda are so vehemently expressed that they contravene the defining characteristics of democracy. Today, the matter of illegality clouds the real issues surrounding drug use, creating a tangle of attitudes, twisted educational policies, false beliefs, inhumane laws and bad parenting. Perhaps more than any other area of human dysfunction our contemporary attitudes to recreational drugs cry out for what the Buddha would have called the middle road. The middle road does not seek for the non-existent perfect answer but embraces both the vagaries of the human spirit and the serendipity of individual destiny in the seeking of an optimal path along which the majority of people may negotiate life in safety, comfort and the joy of self-discovery.

Sex, State and Orgasm

"Man lies in a woman's womb only to gather strength ..,.. The woman ….. is fulfilled, each act of love a taking of man within her, an act of birth and rebirth, of child-bearing and man-bearing. Man lies in her womb and is reborn each time anew with a desire to act, to *be*. But for woman, the climax is not in the birth, but in the moment the man rests inside of her." Anais Nin (1903-1977). Cuban/Spanish/French Author and Diarist.

With the discovery of the endogenous opiates it was generally assumed that sexual pleasure and particularly orgasm resulted from the secretion, into the blood stream, of the endogenous opiate, enkephalin. Certainly, only the intravenous injection of powerful opiates like morphine matches the instantaneous bliss of orgasm. Both morphine and orgasm were known to powerfully inhibit the affective-motivational aspect of the pain experience. For example, the vocalization of rats to repetitive painful stimuli is suppressed during orgasm just as it is by the intravenous administration of morphine. This suppression is so clear that it has been possible to literally calibrate the pain suppressing effects of orgasm against a known dose of morphine. When this was done, the result suggests that in the rat, orgasm is equivalent to receiving a dose of morphine so large that it would approach lethal levels in a human. More than any other, this single experiment underscores the extremely powerful effect of orgasm in totally and instantaneously changing the state of our consciousness from a highly active, cognitively aware mode to a hyper-relaxed, dreamlike trance of virtually total immobility.

Despite the power of morphine in mimicking the experience of orgasm, researchers were unable to detect more than a very slight increase in the concentration of circulating enkephalin before, during or following orgasm. Instead of enkephalin, the systemic concentration of a hormone called *oxytocin* increased slightly during sexual arousal and markedly upon orgasm. Oxytocin is found in both males and females. It is released from the pituitary gland, a very important endocrine gland located on the undersurface of the brain. The release of oxytocin prior to birth stimulates contraction of the uterus while its release in response to suckling, stimulates the secretion of milk. Oxytocin is also responsible for the slow, precoital build-up of pleasure and the ultimate crescendo of orgasm. In male animals injecting oxytocin into certain areas of the brain evokes penile erection while intravenous administration shortens the ejaculatory latency and the post-ejaculatory interval. In men it facilitates bonding by reducing aggression and increasing sociability; factors that have lead to it being used to modify the socially ostracizing behavior of people suffering from Asperger's syndrome and autism.

The answer as to how a hormone so intimately related to the processes of birth, can also create sexual bliss, was provided by experiments on the effects of the opiate antagonist *naloxone*. Naloxone is a neuroactive drug that very selectively blocks the actions of opiates but does not directly affect the actions of oxytocin. Indeed, the specificity of naloxone has enabled it to be used to demonstrate that the abolition of pain by both placebos and acupuncture is mediated by the release within our central nervous system, of our endogenous opiates. When administered prior to sexual encounter, naloxone essentially blocks the pleasure of foreplay, intercourse and orgasm. As these rewarding experiences have been related to increased systemic levels of oxytocin, the pleasure annulling effects of naloxone indicate unequivocally that the role of oxytocin in sexual gratification is to stimulate the release our endogenous opiates at all relevant sites within our central nervous system.

Sexual encounter normally begins with gentle touching and the warmth of bodily contact, stimuli that are both pleasurable and known to release oxytocin. The link between secretion of oxytocin and socially positive stimuli is seen as part of the hormonal basis for reducing stress, enhancing sexual opportunity and regulating the nurturing behavior so critical to the mammalian propensity for maternal bonding (*The Origins of Our Mammalian Ways*: Chapter 5: Section 4). The increased secretion of oxytocin during intercourse makes touch increasingly provocative of pleasure while simultaneously quieting the mind. These effects are identical to those of morphine that, unlike oxytocin, does not release the endogenous opiates but simply mimics their actions on the brain. In the presence of oxytocin, the sensations carried by the nerves that run from our skin are no longer of mere practical significance. Now they penetrate the psyche, affecting our emotions and so pressing us to generate copulatory repertoires that themselves increasingly heighten our pleasurable sensations. No longer plagued by everyday wants and wishes, this loop between action and pleasure inevitably ushers us into a world where touches, smells, form and here and there a vision as from a dream, transport us with ever-increasing momentum to a shared experience of Nirvana. Movement, volume, size and colors pass unnoticed, as sightless eyes bear witness to an ever-changing cadence of mental images in which, as lovers we are inseparable, indistinguishable and yet so perfectly described. No longer enslaved to the ego, bodies flow together like fluids poured into a common vessel, cradled in an opiate heaven by virtue of our mammalian benefactor, oxytocin.

The essential element of sex is the penetration of the body of one partner by the penis or some mechanical substitute, brandished by the other. Heterosexual or homosexual union, it makes no difference. Already the breathing has increased and the heart races. Is not the very essence of sexual intercourse, no less than an opportunity to communicate with another at an essentially visceral level? Is this not why more than any other activity sexual union has the potential for bringing about the fusion of souls, a potential which when fully actualized, we spontaneously refer to as love? Is it not this relationship of sex to the ultimate intimacy of love that makes rape such a detestable act?

Like pain, ecstasy is one of those enigmatic aspects of human experience that is not confined to any particular perceptual, emotional or cognitive domain. Such experiences are among the most complex to understand as they are inevitably composed of component experiences conjured at several different levels of the cerebral cortex. Only the advent of brain scanners has enabled the comprehension of the experiential components that compose the essence of all ecstatic experiences be they orgasm, love, highly rewarding substances or meditation. As these states clearly involve quite different overt behaviors, each will be associated with activation of different combinations of the sensory, perceptual and motor representations of the cerebral cortex. However, unification of such states is not related to the patterns of activity in the sensory, perceptual and motor areas but to the archetypal patterns of activity within the parts of brain that compose the psyche – the orbital cortex, the anterior cingulate gyrus, the insula, the amygdala and the mind (Figure 7.7). It is in these areas that brain scanners repeatedly reveal the psyche's formula for bliss wherein the concerns of the mind, the predictions of the anticipatory centers in the orbital cortex and the warnings of the amygdala are silenced, enabling the authority of love to at last prevail.

Section 7: Recommended Reading

van den Boogert, K. and Davidoff, N. *Heroin Crisis. Key Commentators Discuss the Issues and Debate Solutions of Heroin Abuse in Australia*. Bookman Press, Melbourne, 1999.

Campbell, J. *The Mythic Image*. Bollingen Series, Princeton University Press, Princeton, Oxford, 1974.

Darwin, E. *Zoonomia, or the Laws of Organic Life*, 2nd Edition, 4 Vols, London, 1794-6.

De Quincey, T. *Confessions of an English Opium Eater and Other Writings*. Grevel Lindop (Editor), Oxford University Press, Oxford, 1989 (first published 1821).

Farah, M. J. *Visual Agnosia: Disorders of Object Recognition and What They Tell Us about Normal Vision*. Bradford Books, Masschusetts, London, 1990.

Ford, J. *Coleridge on Dreaming, Romanticism, Dreams and the Medical Imagination*. Cambridge University Press, Cambridge, 1998.

Greenspan, S. I. and Shanker, S. *The First Idea: How Symbols, Language, and Intelligence Evolved from our Primate Ancestors to Modern Humans*. Da Capo Press, Cambridge, Masschusetts, 2006.

Hobson, J. A. *Dreaming: An Introduction to the Science of Sleep*. Oxford University Press, USA, 2004.

Jouvet, M. (translated by Laurence Garey). *The Paradox of Sleep: The Story of Dreaming*. MIT Press, Masschusetts, 1999.

Kiev, A. *Transcultural Psychiatry*. Penguin Books Ltd., Harmondsworth, England, 1972.

Langston, J. W. and Palfreman, J. *The Case of the Frozen Addicts*. Pantheon Books, New York, 1995.

Naranjo, C. and Ornstein, R.E. *On the Psychology of Meditation*. Penguin Books, USA, 1972.

McCarley, R. W. *Brainstem Control of Wakefulness and Sleep*. Plenum Press, New York, London, 1990.

Ordway, G. A., Schwartz, M. A. and Frazer, A. *Brain Norepinephrine: Neurobiology and Therapeutics*. Cambridge University Press, Cambridge, 2007.

Roland, P. E. *Brain Activation*. Wiley-Liss, New York, 1997.

Sacks, O. *Awakenings*. Picador, London, 1982.

Sacks, O. *The Man Who Mistook His Wife for a Hat*. Picador, London, 1985.

Schlosser, E., *Reefer Madness: Sex, Drugs and Cheap Labor in the American Black Market*. Mariner Books, Boston, 2004.

Squire, L. R. *Memory and the Brain*. 1st Edition, Oxford University Press, 1987.

Stafford, P. *Psychedelics Encyclopedia*. J. P. Tarcher, Inc., Los Angeles, 1982.

Taberner, P. V. *Aphrodisiacs - The Science and the Myth,* University of Pennsylvania Press, Philadelphia, 1985.

Wilkens, W. J. *Hindu Mythology*. Heritage Publishers, New Delhi, 1982.

Section 8

The Nature, Intellect and Future of Humanity

"....ever since men began to think introspectively about themselves, they have made guesses, and sometimes had profound intuitions, about those parts of their own nature which seemed to be predestined. It is possible that within a generation some of these guesses will have been tested against exact knowledge. No one can predict what such an intellectual revolution will mean: but I believe that one of the consequences will be to make us feel not less but more responsible towards our brother men."

Charles Percy Snow (1905-1980). English Physicist, Author and Government Advisor.

Reflections and Introduction

"Man will become better only when you will make him see what he is like." Anton Chekhov (1860-1904). Russian Playwright.

Without a clear understanding of the human psyche it is impossible to sensibly address the issues that are central to our survival, issues like the ecology of the planet, the economy and the maintenance of peace and health. Until now, belief in the divine origins of man and the Earth has overridden the great revelations of science, mysticism and philosophy and placed total responsibility for our future in the hands of wholly imagined deities. Consequently, humans have been either unable or unwilling to rationally and objectively address the behavior patterns that have created the impending catastrophe of present circumstances.

As always, belief and the emergent faiths are the true villains. It seems that from its beginnings, the human mind has sought to resolve its inner conflicts by creating believable concepts that act as newfound elements of "knowledge" and "understanding". Without any real truths about life and our universe, the human mind of past generations was quite simply driven to invent a substitute for human responsibility. This was achieved by creating ideas about divine intervention and its place in our individual and collective destiny. Westerners have for centuries enjoyed ridiculing native cultures that may, for example, believe that the island they live on is actually the back of a giant turtle moving slowly across the ocean floor, much like a mythological tectonic plate. Nevertheless, when it comes to matters of life and death, the degree to which intelligent, highly educated humans are willing to adopt antiquated mythological explanations of things, is truly astounding. Although the USA is one of the most scientifically advanced cultures on Earth, a survey conducted in 1991 revealed that 100 million (33%) Americans still believed that God created man in his own image at some time during the past 10,000 years. Nor is there any sign of a new enlightenment: a recent survey indicating that 76% of Americans believe in the biblical account of creation, 79% believe that the miracles described in the bible actually took place and 76% believe that angels and the devil exist as physical beings. Nor can this be a due to a lack of intelligence, as, by definition, only 50% of the population have an IQ of less than 100, so that there must be at least 26% of people with above average IQs who also believe in creationism and the reality of angels, the devil and any other biblical agents. Even today, certain religious leaders frequently negate all documented human knowledge to the contrary and attempt to instill, in their congregations, the belief that Hell and Heaven are real physical places and that the Devil and God are actual beings. While the extension of the metaphor into reality might seem a harmless liberty, its instantaneous effect is to disempower the individual and, in so doing, alleviate him or her from any long-term responsibility for humanity, the planet or themselves.

More than ever, there is a crucial need for all people to comprehend the real truths about human nature that will enable them to become newly aware of what is driving our individual and collective behavior. The key to this modern comprehension of the ways of humanity are to be found in the many new insights arising from neuroscience, neurology, psychiatry, psychology, biology, ethology, anthropology, ethnology, archeology, primatology, mysticism, meditation, altered states of consciousness, history and spirituality. Perhaps we might realistically anticipate that, in the future, a new breed of intelligent, highly educated and informed religious leaders will take heed of these sources of insight and understanding when concocting their list of the "shoulds" and "shouldn'ts" of human life.

So far on our journey, we have seen how it is in the nature of mind to be harnessed to our animal centers and yet how it nevertheless retains its capacity to transcend feelings in its search for a logically consistent strategy. It is the mind that emerges as an organ that is powerfully drawn to extremes, perhaps because of the inherent simplicity of black and white answers when compared with the high energy burden of seeking always a reasoned middle road. Beyond the realms of thought we have seen how our raw emotions are organized into two camps, the exclusively mammalian camp (the anterior cingulate and the insula cortex) and, lingering still on the very edge of consciousness, the archaic reptilian camp (the amygdala). We have watched as these emotional centers engage the mind in an endless struggle for dominance over behavior. Yet in the matter of dominance, we have seen that only the tenacity of mood presents any real challenge to the human mind - a challenge mounted equally by both the physiological and psychological realms. It is from these simple building blocks of mind, emotion and mood that something so versatile, capricious, ingenious and dangerous, as the human being, emerges.

In our progression from birth to adulthood, the neonatal psyche is the seed from which our inherited genetical programs and the vagaries of experience create the individual. It is said that relationship is a mirror in which we have opportunity to see reflections of ourselves. As such, we may seek in our relationships, both with each other and with the natural world, a true and unbiased reflection of our individual and collective nature. Newly armed with our knowledge of the human psyche, we can, at last, cast off the multitude of superstitions that have so dominated the thoughts and actions of humans. Perhaps, for the first time, we have the opportunity to envisage our true identity and so come to understand why it is that we pose such a threat to each other and to our ailing planet. From this understanding, there is at least a chance that we may, by intelligent intervention in what appears to be our inherently pathological behavior patterns, avert cataclysm and the attendant massive human suffering. Despite the enormous odds against us, perhaps there is still a chance that we may rise from the ashes of human destructiveness and, putting aside our indefensible beliefs, begin at last to use intelligence to enhance, rather than threaten, our survival and the survival of all other forms of life.

In this final section, we will seek a realistic view of human nature by exploring how the interactions between each part of the human psyche contribute to our beliefs and our behavior. The first chapter will explore the contribution of the psyche to a number of well-known human concepts that have little to do with intelligence. The second chapter will examine the diversity of human intelligence and its contribution to creativity and culture. The third and final chapter will outline how the developing mind gives rise to intelligence and the means through which we might create and utilize superhuman intelligences to help us avoid what is surely our impending extinction.

Chapter 1 - Ghosts of the Human Psyche

The Foundation and Composition of the Ego

"Mirror, mirror on the wall, who is the fairest of them all". *Snow White and the Seven Dwarves. Grimm's Fairytales*. Jacob Grimm (1785-1863) and Wilhelm Grimm (1786-1859). The "Brothers Grimm" were German Academics, Linguists and Folk Historians.

The word *ego* is Latin for "I". In Sigmund Freud's terms the ego consisted of the executive functions of personality. As such the ego's task is to orchestrate behavior in such a manner that the urges of the *id* are satiated within the constraints of societal mores that are embodied in what Freud called the *superego*. In modern terms, Freud's ego is composed of all thought processes that are focused on the individual, while the super ego is specifically the product of those thought processes that relate to the individual in the society – processes of our social conditioning that are established within the developing social mind of every preoperational child. It is within the human psyche that the opposing forces of the id and the ego must find a precarious balance.

Brain scans reveal that the mind is activated when people are shown their picture or instructed to contemplate statements such as "I am a good friend" or "I forget important things" – responses that indicate the existence of concepts centered around the ego. Both the evolution of the ego and its maturation within the individual human are related to two significant, behavioral landmarks. The first is the ability to understand the intentions of others, or to exercise a Theory of Mind - a process that is clearly contingent upon having a mental capacity large enough to organize behavior and at the same time, harbor a concept of self versus a concept of others. The second is the ability to recognize that one's reflection in a mirror is an image of oneself; a process known as Mirror Self Recognition that again requires a concept of self. In children both these abilities appear around 18 months of age while, in evolution, their expression corresponds to the evolutionary boundary between the monkeys and the apes. Apes have both abilities but monkeys have neither.

By the 18th month only the social mind is operative. Self-recognition and Theory of Mind abilities in young children are therefore indicative of cognitive processes that lie exclusively within the psychosocial domain. Consequently, in its earliest form, the ego is defined only within the context of the child's emotional responses to its social environment. As the child moves through the remaining Piagetian stages of cognition, this ability to conceptualize the self naturally extends to the material and abstract domains of thought, thereby giving rise to different dimensions of the ego.

If Mirror Self Recognition and Theory of Mind abilities are products of the mind, then it would seem that both must be established within the individual by simple experimentation showing that (a) the image in the mirror is of one's self and (b) other people's thoughts can be successfully imagined. Neither of these phenomena could arise from instinct because to have a realization of one's physical identity requires a platform within consciousness that is independent of our instinctual drives, while to imagine the thoughts of others is simply an aspect of the broader process of imagination that, in turn, is entirely dependent upon cognition (*Defining Attention and Imagination*: Chapter 1: Section 7). Instinct gives rise to instantaneous reactions but cognition always requires a period of deliberation. When hunter-gatherers living in an essentially Stone Age culture, in the New Guinea highlands were given a mirror, they failed to recognize their image becoming highly distressed. Only after a period of deliberation were they able to accept that the reflection was their own image. In enabling us to look at ourselves, mirrors clearly reinforce the ego by providing more information to the mind about our facial expressions, body language and general appearance. The power of reflections in reinforcing the ego has led to mirrors being banned in certain monasteries, because countenancing one's own image reinforces the ego, thereby drawing awareness away from the inner self and into the mind where energy is so easily squandered in the illusory world of thought. It is ironic that the major goal of spiritual practice is to reverse this cardinal step in human evolution wherein the expansion of our cognitive abilities has enabled a preoccupation with our self-image that often approaches narcissistic levels.

The great experiment of meditation enables us to appreciate the eastern vision that the ego is no more than the representation of the self within the ephemeral ether of thought. Essentially the same view was taken by William James whose insights caused him to partition the ego into three separate parts. Writing in the late 19th century, James, a deeply introspective philosopher, proposed that the ego of an adult is composed of a "social me", a "material me", and a "spiritual me". As products of the mind, our beliefs have a powerful influence over how we define ourselves. A staunch Christian, James was naturally inclined towards the term, "spiritual me" to describe the way we identify ourselves within abstract thought. In the light of modern frameworks of thought, it seems more appropriate and less confining to call this element of the ego the "abstract me". It is a tribute to James that his tripartite subdivision of the ego reflects so precisely the social, material and abstract domains of conceptual consciousness that we now know emerge from structurally distinct areas of the prefrontal cortex (BAs 9, 47 and 46).

The identification of different parts of the ego with sequentially maturing, anatomically discrete areas of the human mind, carries with it the implication that, like thought itself, the different elements of the ego also arise sequentially throughout childhood. This has great clinical relevance, for if a child is exposed to a period of abuse, the ensuing damage to the ego will be strongly related to the part of the mind that is developing at the time of insult.

The first glimmerings of a concept of self arise from the infant's involuntary expression of its visceroemotional needs and its registration of the responses of its carers. It is undoubtedly this exchange that lays the foundations of the social ego. It could be said that the primordia of the social ego and of emotional intelligence are one and the same. Both mark the start of the preoperational phase of childhood that constitutes the beginning of thought.

In ideal circumstances, a cohesive social ego emerges along with a social identity that is finely tuned to a physically and psychologically healthy environment. In an emotionally dysfunctional environment, there is less chance of this happening. In such circumstances the conditioning of the maturing social mind will necessarily contain compensatory algorithms (or networks) that lead to maladaptive social strategies, which, in turn, lead to conflict, stress and ultimately a loss of physical fitness. The catastrophic effects of compromising the development of the social ego can be understood by considering the challenge of social interaction to the deeply autistic person (Section 3: Chapter 4: Aberrations of the Mind). Deprived, for neurological reasons, of a functionally operational social mind, the social ego of the autistic person is chronically diminished or even non-existent. In less altruistic societies, this lack of a "social me", would certainly have critically threatened survival. Indeed, though spared this extreme, many victims of early child abuse have, nevertheless, a distorted concept of their social identity that almost inevitably plays havoc with their personal relationships, and often their physical health, for the remainder of their lives.

As far as the material mind is concerned people, animals and the self are simply physically and functionally identifiable, living objects. Within the material mind, the representation of objects and people is in accord with their practical usefulness. It is through the ruminations of the material mind that we may press for the physical, kinesthetic and vocational skills of people to be formally indicated by their uniform. In the realm of practicality, the uniform is an easy way of identifying the functionality of a specific group of people, just as we might attend to a selection of objects because they share a functional commonality. The material mind's guiding principle of usefulness is as central to the material ego as it is to practicality. Yet the "material me" also embodies concepts of status and responsibility, along with the attendant rules and laws that exist in all man-made hierarchies. Just as the material mind of the left and right hemispheres, respectively represent the parametric and symbolic qualities of objects, so too does it respond to both the practical and symbolic significance of the uniform. This manifestation of the material ego reaches it zenith in autism, where, in the absence of an operational social mind, some autistic children automatically conceptualize themselves as physical devices that have to be plugged in and switched on prior to performing the routine tasks of daily life.

The maturation of the material ego parallels the maturation and programming of the material mind throughout middle childhood. Abuse in this stage will necessarily affect the establishment of a healthy concept of the material self, resulting in a sense of societal worthlessness, a diminished perception of practical ability and a sense of failure to conform to rules and laws. Normally, however, adult life sees the material ego undergoing a conspicuous and adaptive transition, forsaking the quest for socioemotional harmony for the symbolic manifestations of vocational achievement and status that often attracts affirmations and honors from the host society.

Within the domain of his "spiritual me", William James recognized that we "think of ourselves as thinkers", thereby expressing his contention that our abstract mind is able to reflect upon the nature of our own thoughts. Known as *metacognition*, this process is a highly significant component of the abstract ego. With the maturation of the abstract mind, the potential to entertain possibilities and to gain self-understanding, take on an entirely new dimension. Provided with an opportunity to entertain possibilities and no longer bounded by the reality of the physical or social worlds, the ego-related, abstract fantasies of the pubescent teenager are almost limitless. Only with maturity, do the plenipotentiary powers of the abstract mind over the other domains of cognition, enable it to elaborate an all-encompassing expression of the ego alongside an often subtle appreciation of the individual's personality – cognitively inspired entities that have great significance to both the identity and destiny of the individual.

In the teenager, this new hypothetical focus upon the self can easily bring desperate feelings of existential isolation. In an existential sense, who we are and who we may become, inevitably lead to *teenage egocentrism*. In the words of William James, "The art of being wise is the art of knowing what to overlook". Certainly the art of living with an abstract mind is most definitely the art of weaving a sensible hypothesis by the intelligent choice and integration of thematically relevant concepts. The typical pubescent adolescent has yet to gain such wisdom and hence is at risk of the divisive, yet entirely hypothetical propositions of politicians, religious leaders, advertising agencies and their parents. Should the adolescent be traumatized while the abstract mind is maturing, then the establishment of a set of maladaptive beliefs and related behavior patterns, is inevitable.

Love, Sex and the Soul

"The need for love characterizes every human being that is born. No psychological health is possible unless the 'inner nature' of the person is fundamentally accepted, loved and respected by others." Abraham H. Maslow (1908-1970). American Psychologist, Philosopher and Originator of Self-actulaization Theory of Psychology.

Love comes as if from nowhere and departs to whence we cannot say. Love defies all boundaries, caring nothing for our hallowed social mores, ridiculing openly the litany of ideas and reasons around which we struggle to compose our life. For love, humans will cross all political, religious and social boundaries. For love, humans will kill other humans or allow themselves to be killed. So universal is the need for love that only the deeply cynical and the fearful can turn from its invitation. Love is the dove of peace, the flowering of the rose in the morning sun and all else that is perfect in nature. Yet love may come on many a wing, borne perhaps by our child, whose laughing eyes and joyous innocence awake anew our wonderment at life. Even in the act of war we are haunted by love, as in that transcendent moment when, before the onslaught of battle, all the world is stilled and there passes through the ranks of the damned the gentle touch of something long forgotten in the foolish pursuit of death. Nothing more or less than this moment, so lost in time, is love.

The path of love is a journey from our naturally egocentric mind to our soul - a journey that is the essence of all spiritual practice and, behind the façade of dogma, all religions. Even the word love is generally considered as virtually synonymous with the word God. God is nothing if he is not love, for not only must he accommodate our soul but he must stand against the denizens of Hell who, as champions of the dark side of the psyche, would commit us to an eternity of fear, anger, hatred and anxiety. So it is that the Christian scriptures tell us, "Beloved, let us Love one another, for God is Love". Likewise the Hindus say, "One can best worship the Lord through Love". To the Buddhist, love is "caring and compassion" and they are appropriately instructed to "cultivate in the world a heart of Love". The Muslims recognize the supremacy of love and God over the individual ego, in the saying, "Love is this, that thou art little and God is great". Judaism emphasizes societal bonding in the command that "Thou shalt Love the Lord thy God with all thy heart and thy neighbor as thyself", while Taoism speaks of love as a vital necessity stating that "Heaven arms with Love those it would keep alive". Confucius states that "To Love all men is the greatest benevolence" and Sikhism beseeches us to love with the promise that "God will regenerate those in whose hearts is Love". To the business orientated Jains, love and its absence are seen in terms of profit and loss; "The days are of most profit to him who acts in Love". It is surely the singular and, ultimately, only significant task of each and every religion to bring us back to love and in so doing to ensure the triumph of our mammalian sentiments over our more hostile reptilian urges.

Love is universally accepted as a virtual principle of human existence. Yet although love may have many origins, for most people it first becomes recognizable when they begin to form romantic attachments. All people begin life with the capacity for love, simply because the emotional centers we have inherited from our mammalian ancestors mature in early infancy and drive us to bond with our carers. As infants and children we continually experience the sharing of love that constitutes normal parental-child bonding. Romantic love, however, only flourishes following the attainment of sexual maturation - a time that corresponds to the period when the abstract mind has become operational. This coincidence between an adolescent's ability to cognitively process the phenomenological world and its drive to emotionally bond with another person, ensures that love becomes a central theme within its ideational model of the world. Like space and time, love is experienced and yet cannot be directly observed. Thus, although love may be part of many conceptual frameworks within the temporal, practical and, especially the social, mind, as an intangible phenomenon, it can only be conceptually represented within the abstract mind. As well as intangible phenomena, the abstract mind represents, as higher-order concepts, the many beliefs we hold that are essentially hypotheses. In any society, such beliefs may range from scientific revelations that, for example, matter is made of atoms, to theological propositions that an invisible, divine presence determines our destiny. So it is that in the newly mature abstract mind of the pubescent teenager, the higher-order conceptual representation of the phenomenon of love has opportunity to interact with higher-order concepts representing beliefs that have been embedded in the mind entirely by the conditioning of his or her host society. As we have seen, the integration of the concepts love and God, along with those of darkness and the Devil, are the defining matrices of virtually all religions – matrices composed of the extremes of emotional or thymic experience and the entirely illusory products of imagination (*The Art of Darkness*: Chapter 1: Section 5 and *Defining Attention and Imagination*: Chapter 1: Section 7).

It is through romantic love that we can most easily know the essence of paradise, both in the sense of ecstatic pleasure and a pervasive sense of well being and belonging. While romantic love begins with tender nuances, it inevitably leads to sexual consummation. Words cease to be of significance as communication moves from touch and form and then, with penetration, to the viscera and the very origins of emotion. Tongues entwine as the senses are flooded with supple images of rampant sexuality and the energies of the mind are consumed by erotic fantasy. Only with the onset of orgasm, when all thought stops and the ego dissolves into nothingness, are we pervaded by a consuming sense of oneness, as with the release of oxytocin, we are transported to a mindless state of bliss wherein all internal feelings are rendered harmonious and pleasant. "I love you," we whisper to each other, but in the reality of that moment, there is no "I" or "you", there is only love.

The ancients recognized that love has a multiplicity of forms. Thus, the word love relates to the Latin terms *amor* and *caritas* while in Greek we find the terms *philia*, *eros*, and *agape*. Philia is the kind of love involved in friendship that is commonly expressed as fondness. In contrast, amor and eros refer to love based on sexual desire, and caritas and agape the sense of a higher or selfless love. With brain imaging it is possible to trace the origins of each of these forms of love. For instance, when people who are deeply in love are shown a picture of a friend, the anterior cingulate and the insula, are activated along with the mind. A similar result is obtained if they are shown pictures of themselves. However, when subjects were shown pictures of their beloved, only the anterior cingulate and the insula participated in the response while the mind remained silent (Figure 8.1). This response of the psyche to the presentation of an image of one's beloved resembles that of automatic empathy, wherein one's emotional centers automatically respond in isolation from other elements of the psyche. In contrast, seeing an image of oneself or a friend activates the psyche in much the same manner as that seen in controlled empathy, wherein both the mind and the emotional centers participate. In terms of the Latin and Greek perceptions of love, it would seem that philia involves the mind activating the emotional centers while caritas or agape refer to the independent and direct response of the emotional centers to the image of a loved one – a phenomenon basic to parent-infant bonding. Finally, a number of studies have confirmed the involvement of the anterior cingulate and the insula in masturbation, foreplay and orgasm, aspects of relationships that involve sexual desire and eroticism and so constitute the essence of both amor and eros.

As the cortex of the anterior cingulate and the insula evolved to motivate mammals to bond with and thereby care for their young, it is not surprising to find that activation of these centers is critical to the experiences of love, sexual arousal or orgasm. However, activation of the anterior cingulate and insula does not entirely describe the origin of these states for they are also contingent upon the suppression of activity in the amygdala and the orbital cortex. In this way, fear, anger, hatred and anxiety are not permitted to disrupt our intimacy and the anticipatory actions of the orbital cortex are prevented from interfering with our psyche's immediate imperative to bond. More than any other theater of human interaction, it is in the bonding between infant and parents that we most surely see manifested the metaphorical triumph of Heaven over Hell

Within the psyche, the pattern of activity associated with the experience of love is virtually identical to the pattern induced by the administration of powerful opiates like morphine or heroin. Administration of these drugs causes an almost immediate activation of the anterior cingulate and the insula coupled with inhibition of activity in the mind, the orbital cortex and the amygdala. The resultant experience is therefore one wherein the passage of time, the generation of anxiety, fear or aggression and readiness of the mind to generate worry, are all repressed. Thus, in its essence, the administration of opiates mimics the all-pervading, oceanic feeling of love. The bliss induced by strong opiates is so intense that repeated use negates the individual's need to seek human affection or even human company. So compellingly pleasant is the opiate state that addicts typically show a complete indifference to the pleasantness or otherwise of the surroundings in which they take the drug. Like love, opiates sustain the individual and negate the angst and loneliness that wait in the shadows of daily life.

Where truth is the realization that arises from entering our visceral being, love is the direct experience of our biological essence. Thus, love is all pervading, for though each person may have different thoughts and beliefs, at the visceral level we are very similar to each other and even to vertebrate animals that long preceded our presence upon Earth. All humans have the same organs doing the same things each day and night. Within us our breathing, blood flow, heart rate, gastric contractions, hormonal secretions and all other functions are monitored and their fluctuations expressed in the responses of the emotional domains of consciousness. Fueled by the viscera, the all-pervading self, inner self or soul of each human being emerges from a core that is relatively invariant across all humanity. This does not, however, mean that all humans experience their emotions in an identical manner. We must allow that individuals do vary in the intensity with which they experience different emotions. Again such differences probably reflect differences in the allocation of cortical space to the representation of each organ or class of organ. In a gross sense, variation in the expression of good versus bad emotions probably stems from gene-dependent variations in the size of the anterior cingulate gyrus or the amygdala between different individuals within any given population and particularly between individuals of geographically isolated populations.

Much is written about attaining bliss through prayer or meditation. The scriptures of a wide variety of religions and spiritual practices are adamant that finding romantic love, indulging in sex or administrating of opiates are not the only means of evoking bliss. What these activities do have in common is the propensity to inhibit thought - a condition that when accompanied by a healthy, replete viscera is critical to the experience of bliss. The Buddha himself frequently enunciated the importance of meditative practice to limiting the machinations of the mind and to ultimately achieving the "no mind" state. Indeed, one might say that, when all their biological urges have been met, those mammals that lack the cortex of the mind are simply delivered to a state of bliss. Unfortunately, humans cannot so easily avoid the tyranny of thought. Left to its own devices, the human mind pays little heed to periods of visceral homeostasis but instead embroils us in a quest for one mentally created objective after another. The Buddha recognized that, as an instrument of extremes, the human mind runs contrary to the middle way that more often follows the path of least resistance. It is for such reasons that developing the ability to quiet the mind is central to all techniques of meditation and ultimately all paths to realization.

How can silencing our thoughts facilitate our experience of bliss? The answer is that when the executor of consciousness is out of the office, then other domains of the psyche are allowed to take part more freely in the creation of experience. Without the mind and the anticipatory centers of the orbital cortex, our experience of the inner realms is necessarily confined to our emotional centers. In this process the *status quo* of our bodily functions plus the level of any ongoing physical pain and any inherent predisposition to depression, become the determinants of our psychological disposition. If we are deeply depressed or suffering intense pain, quelling the mind will not help us to experience bliss. To conjure bliss both the visceral and somatic body must be healthy and relaxed. When these conditions are fulfilled, then the attainment of "no mind" enables the individual to occupy a domain of consciousness that is concerned only with the basic rhythms of our visceral centers - rhythms that have their origins in the physical and organic forces that regulate all animal life.

This link between transcendental experience and the viscera need not be envisaged as being in any way sacrilegious. In recognizing the relationship between the human soul or inner self and our visceral nature, we also give recognition to the archaic relationship between the viscera and the rhythms and cycles of nature - elements that have become encoded within the visceroemotional centers over more than 500 million years of vertebrate evolution. The soul or inner self is a reflection of the forces of nature from whence the identity of God most certainly emerges. When humans destroy or permanently disrupt nature, they are essentially vandalizing the very substance of God.

The Tibetans recognize that the self is not an immutable source of bliss but is essentially lost when the body is wracked with pain or we are cast into darkness by the vagaries of mood. When, in such times we say that we "have lost our self", we do not mean that our ego has been damaged. Instead we mean that we cannot find inside us the retreat that we have known since our earliest childhood memories. In the pain of disease or the angst of depression, the inner self is no longer the residence of bliss. Where once the anterior cingulate and the insula conjured feelings of love and bonding, now a hyperactive amygdala brings only anxiety and darkness. It is not surprising that in such times people turn to religion in search of the inner sanctum of the soul that was previously their daily bread.

The Nature of Enlightenment and Realization

"It is not besides the point, particularly in the case of beginners, to teach them to look into themselves and to direct their minds inward by means of breathing....until, with God's help, advancing to a greater perfection, [they] make their minds impermeable and impervious to all that surrounds them.... [This enables] the standing still of the mind and of the world, forgetfulness of what is below, initiation into secret knowledge of what is above, the putting aside of thoughts for what is better than they." Saint

Gregory Palamas (1296-1359). Monk of Mount Athos, Greece, later Archbishop of Thessaloniki.

In modern vernacular, enlightenment refers to the state of being enlightened, which in turn is defined as attaining spiritual insight and so freeing a person from the endless cycle of birth, death and rebirth. Enlightenment offers the possibility of rising above the suffering of life and of realizing the futility of thought in the face of the predominantly serendipitous nature of existence. Enlightenment does not alter personality. After enlightenment we may well continue gathering wood and fetching water or repairing motorcars in exactly the same way as we did previously. Nevertheless, enlightenment does evoke a change in one's priorities largely as a consequence of the accompanying realizations about the fundamental nature of human existence. The enlightened state involves many realizations, such that an enlightened person is often said to be *realized*. For instance, it would be unlikely that a realized person would agree to work in a factory manufacturing weapons that bring death and injury to others. Freed from the cacophony of thought, the enlightened being is naturally closer to his or her instincts and, in particular, those emotional centers which conjure empathy, bonding and love.

The lay literature abounds with reports of often spontaneous, *transcendental experiences* after which the individuals involved claimed to be rendered permanently enlightened. The events that trigger these experiences include near drowning, surviving suicide, climbing high mountains, space travel, being confronted with radically different cultures, comprehending the nature of a complex problem, taking psychotrophic drugs, tantric sex, sensory deprivation, social isolation, out-of-body and near-death experiences and prolonged prayer or meditation. It is important to recognize that such experiences are never the result of mental effort or cognitively orientated teaching. Unfortunately, the accounts tell us little about the nature of transcendence, other than that, like *conversion experiences*, they mark a surrendering of our motivational energies to our emotional centers wherein are represented the ultimate truths about human nature. What is clear is that from this enlightened or realized state, one may witness the transitory, capricious and illusory nature of thought, alongside the veracity of mood and emotion.

Historically the word enlightenment has been used in both eastern and western cultures to mean quite different things. In Europe during the 18th and late 17th century, *The Enlightenment* referred to an intellectual movement that celebrated the power of reason and individualism above the long established, draconian traditions that effectively bound the majority of people to the service of a ruling aristocracy. Ideologically, The Enlightenment fostered the understanding of the universe and so was critical, not only to improving the lot of the individual but also to fulfilling the universally important goals of knowledge, freedom and happiness.

Only in emphasizing the importance of happiness and freedom did the European vision of enlightenment bear any resemblance to the eastern vision. While the European Enlightenment was associated with social revolution, enlightenment in the East represented a revolution within the consciousness of the individual. Whereas the

European emphasis was on the power and potential of thought, the eastern vision of enlightenment was centered on acceptance and the realization of our instinctual, organic essence. Enlightenment in the East constituted a reorganization of the natural hierarchy of the human psyche wherein the mind was trained to be less divisive in the fashioning of behavior, thereby rendering the individual more sensitive to his or her emotions and perceived emotional indicators (eg. body language and facial expressions) of other people. It might therefore be said of the enlightened or realized individual that they are permanently more in touch with the fundamental nature of people - a condition that bears close resemblance to the concept of *sophrosyne*, invented by the ancient Greeks to mean the bringing together of all elements of wisdom within a single individual.

In reality, the eastern concern with the danger of thought is not directed at the use of the mind in the every day affairs of living. It is, however, directed at the mind's propensity to go beyond the satiation of our immediate day-to-day needs and to adopt, without hesitation, ideologies and attitudes that have severe consequences for other humans and the natural world. For many millennia the East has realized that the human mind is a distinct organ of the brain endowed with virtually plenipotentiary powers over behavior. Consequently, if the other elements of the psyche are to be allowed expression then steps must be taken to control the mind. In terms of self-identity, this battle between instinct and thought is a battle between the expression of our inner self or soul and our mentally elaborated self-portrait that constitutes the ego. By enabling us to watch the play of our thoughts rather than being part of them, prolonged and regular meditation inevitably makes the cortex of the mind less excitable and less likely to draw us unnecessarily into the illusory world of cognition. The result is an individual who is less likely to experience the self-imposed stresses that naturally result from the mental elaboration of complex schemes and a firmly established ego. While this transformation neither increases or decreases intelligence, it rids the mind of the unnecessary thoughts, thereby enabling one's mental processes to be willfully applied to problems of immediate and real significance. It is this awareness of the present, a concurrent ability to focus the mind and an emergent calmness that distinguishes the realized person from the ordinary person. Indeed, it could be effectively argued that the realized person has the ability, or at least the opportunity, to apply the appropriate domain of the mind to each and every circumstance, rather than simply react from whatever cognitive domain normally dominates their psyche. In this alone, a realized person has opportunity to albeit transiently transcend the limits of their personality.

The Nature of Wisdom
"By definition wisdom is the understanding of life and how to live it; and for as long as men have sought wisdom it has been apparent that wisdom is correlated to our capacity to *perceive more* and *understand more.*" James L. Christian, Philosopher. From: *An Introduction to the Art of Wondering*. 3rd Edition, Holt, Rinehart and Winston, New York, London, Sydney, 1977, p. 64.

It is often said that out of the mouths of babes comes great wisdom. We say this and yet we do not trust the running of our affairs to children. This is particularly so in highly technical western cultures. When westerners journey in technologically simpler cultures, they are astounded at the responsibility placed upon young children. Never could they imagine someone in the West allowing children such independence of action in worldly affairs. So rarely do we entrust western children to carry through the essential tasks of survival that we have even made laws forbidding children to participate in most serious matters. Many westerners take a moral stance on the employment of children often extending their attitudes to foreign cultures of which they have little understanding. In western education much is made of our special schools where children are expected to take some responsibility for their day-to-day actions. Yet in most non-European societies, young children carry out vitally significant tasks, contributing to the survival of their families for much of each and every day. If we westerners are so often witness to the wisdom in the words of our children, why is it that we do not give them a significant voice in our affairs? Why is it that as part of their education we do not allow them to work at least some of the time alongside us? Why do we not seek their opinion on matters of significance?

The answers to these questions lie in understanding the difference between knowledge and wisdom. Knowledge is acquired throughout both childhood and adult life. Whether it is concerned with the physical world (technology), people (psychology) or theories (science and philosophy), knowledge is always factual. Knowledge can be conveyed using descriptive language while wisdom can often be expressed only through art, myth and metaphor. Yet although facts alone do not constitute wisdom, wisdom cannot arise from factual ignorance. Wisdom is the understanding of life. Wisdom arises from the successful integration of the world around us and the world within us. It is this relationship between the inner and outer realms that is critical to our attaining profound insights into our individual and collective identity – insights that are arguably the most important key to the gaining of wisdom. An individual might well attain a deep understanding of the psychosocial, practical or abstract issues of life but only when each real life situation automatically taps the appropriate dimension of the mind, do we have evidence for the attainment of wisdom. In western psychology, such a person is said to be *actualized.*

The journey through childhood sees a slow change from a preoccupation with the psychosocial, to an obsession with the factual and the hypothetical. Our systems of employment-orientated education attempt to exploit this drive for the acquisition of worldly knowledge. Thus, as the child suicide rates in highly technological cultures indicate, the progression through childhood is rarely accompanied by significant efforts to aid the child's comprehension of the psychosocial dimension of life. Repeatedly conditioned to the importance of facts, the typical western child can easily miss arriving at significant realizations about both themselves and the nature of humanity. "My young men shall never work. Men who work cannot dream, and wisdom comes in dreams." These words of the American Indian prophet Smohalla leave no doubt that not all human cultures are dominated by an obsession with the practical. The confusion and loneliness experienced by the western teenager, the fragmentation of the family and ultimately the disintegration of societal mores in deference to the dictates of modern economics, have spawned a cavalier indifference towards assisting our offspring understand themselves in either the context of their inherent personality structure or their psychosocial environment.

When the ancient Greek scholar Empedocles remarked that it is impossible to find a wise man, the poet Xenophanes is said to have replied, "Naturally, for it takes a wise man to recognize a wise man." A clever answer indeed but who are the mystics who bring only grace to our short history? What distinguishes the consciousness of a Jesus, a Buddha or a Krishna from that of an ordinary person? It is easy to find story after story of the childlike nature of the enlightened ones. The following words of Swami Abhayadatta (1866-1939) make it clear that the mystics are to a man or woman, rascals, radicals, non-conformists, law breakers and undeniably charming in the pristine clarity with which they envisage human life. "For the uninitiated Indian the word siddha evokes magical power above all; if a yogin can walk through walls, fly in the sky, heal the sick, turn water into wine, or even levitate and read minds, he deserves the title siddha. If that same yogin has a crazy glint in his eye, smears himself with ashes, moves himself or others to tears with his song, calms street mongrels by his presence, tears a faithful woman from her family, wears a *vajra* - a symbol of immutability - in his yard-long hair-knot, eats from a skull-bowl, talks with the birds, sleeps with lepers, upbraids demagogues for moral laxity, or performs with conviction any act contrary to convention while demonstrating a 'higher' reality, then he is doubly a siddha. Common people impressed by appearances have no conception of the siddha's esoteric aim - *Mahãmudrã* - and cannot know that a siddha may also be an inconspicuous peasant, an office worker, a king, a monk, a servant or a tramp." The mystic may or may not be formally knowledgeable. In terms of factual information he or she may be wealthy or poor. But each and every realized one has in common with each and every normal child, a clarity concerning the biological essence of being human. It is this mental realization and measured expression of the innate that constitutes the first glimmerings of wisdom.

Yet in the West, what flowers in the awareness of the little child, what elaborates all that it says or does, is simply lost in the process of producing a sophisticated and knowledgeable adult. The truth is that western adults have been forced to place aside what comes out of the mouths of babes. We pay it lip service only. We exclaim that it touches something within us, but in truth we have forgotten what this is. The divine within is asleep. So always we place aside the utterances of babes, as we devote ourselves to achieving an endless list of social, materialistic or idealistic goals. In this way we die as human beings and in this way too we inadvertently ensure that our children's glimpses of wisdom are short lived. When we have achieved, and achieved again and again, without the promised relief from struggle or when, deprived of food or shelter or love, we are forcibly drawn into our visceroemotional centers, only then do we hear what the child within us is saying. Only then do we seek out the wise man or woman, the mystic, the guru, the lama, the shaman or the priest and beseech them to help us from the endless wheel of life. Only then do we beg them to destroy the labyrinth of schemes and desires that have replaced our being.

"In the middle of the journey of our life, I came to myself within a dark wood, where the straight way was lost." These opening lines of the first canto of Dante's

Inferno refer to the mid-life descent of everyday western man into darkness - the beginning of what we call the *male mid-life crisis*. Existence has a way of reaching out to us and tapping us with its Zen stick, reminding us that we have lost sight of the true essence of life. Wisdom is something that we began to know as children. Wisdom flowers naturally within the growing child. Ironically, it is the attitudes and obsessions of our parents, teachers and priests, along with a merciless, corrupt and political malleable economic system, that banish wisdom.

In the matter of wisdom, even theory-orientated western psychology has begun to embrace the virtues of a golden childhood. As mystics say, why raise a child when you can raise a God? Yet today, as ever, the adult of a golden childhood is a rarity. When we do encounter an adult with a healthy, normal, untraumatized and altruistically conditioned psyche, we cannot help but be touched by the lighthearted clarity of their every action. Always they seem to so easily find the truest way. Like children and like the mystics, they may not be materially successful, nor filled with either factual knowledge or the clever ideas of the intelligentsia. Unfortunately, they are never chosen as our leaders. Nevertheless, their presence amongst us is a reminder of that which lies at the kernel of each human being and of what all societies are created to nurture. Within them, the divine is not only awake but is entwined in the intricate dance between the psyche and everyday existence.

When westerners return from less technically orientated cultures, they often claim to have discovered a long forgotten wisdom. Something that was always inside has awakened to question the significance of all acquired knowledge and draw them, often for the first time, into the realm of the mystical. And so it is also when the inhabitants of the less divisive lands make their way to the vast industry-based societies of the western world. Soon forgotten are their rites and rituals that for generations uncounted transported their predecessors to the timelessness of bliss. Now they must adapt to the tyranny of economic ownership. Now they are confronted with the great illusion of western democracy wherein the Gods are banished and each ordinary citizen is said to be able to control his or her destiny. Greeted by severe information overload and the long-established principles of rank over-productivity, their old world recedes, taking with it not only the acceptance of suffering but also the peace of acceptance.

The typical western adult loses wisdom as a consequence of a socially imposed estrangement from the magic of childhood. It is the gift of personalizing everything makes a child ever open to the metaphorical. The child can easily appreciate the significance behind a fantasy like Alice in Wonderland. It does not care that caterpillars talk to little girls about kings and queens who are drawn from a pack of playing cards. Operating on the principles of inductive rather than deductive learning, the child's comprehension of "story" is instantaneous. All is meaningful, as indeed it was intended to be. The little child is absolutely certain that we can talk to and be understood by, inanimate objects. For the child, the whole world is a vibrant myth. If the father's car breaks down, the child may speak to it by name, reprimanding it for being lazy or demanding that it stop causing so much trouble. The longer the child remains in ignorance about the true nature of the car and the physical and mechanical principles that make it work, the longer it will go on talking to cars. We all know adults who give names to their cars and various other useful objects. While such habits can be charmingly innocent, they are universally misleading. We simply cannot allow our children to live only within the myths of early childhood. The winter will come and the crops must be gathered and stored. We must take care of the business of life and inevitably train our children to meet the cognitively complex challenges of survival in the modern world. Too much emphasis on the material or the ideological and you destroy the Buddha within, too little and you have spawned an idiot.

Chapter 2 - The Significance of the Mind

The Nature of Human Intelligence

"The Empires of the future are the Empires of the mind." Winston Churchill (1874-1965). English Politician, British Prime Minister and Nobel Laureate.

Only in the last century has it become clear that intelligence began to evolve in animals that lived prior to the appearance of either modern humans or even our earliest hominid ancestors. It is possible to say this, firstly because behavioral experiments show that apes are capable of thought, and secondly, because brain imaging has shown that our thoughts are conducted within identified areas of our cortex that are homologous to similar areas in the cortex of both monkeys and apes. This strongly supports the thesis that apes and at least the higher monkeys have the capacity for thought. It is, therefore very likely that intelligence expanded along the ancestral line of the apes and monkeys. It is, however, also possible that future research will identify a form of social or emotional intelligence in behaviorally advanced non-primate mammals, such as the dogs and their close relatives, the seals and the bears. Just as the fundamentals of language are inherited, thought, as the product of the nervous tissue of the mind, must also be a heritable property. Just as we now recognize that the ability to speak is the product of what has been called a *language instinct*, we may also speak of a *thought instinct* - an instinct that is largely responsible for the diversity of behavior in humans and to a lesser degree, their nearest living representatives the apes.

The dictionary definition of intelligence is the ability to acquire and apply knowledge and skills. In elucidating the stages of cognitive development in children, Piaget provided a basis for the idea that human intelligence has multiple origins. His theories were to gain notoriety some 60 years later when educators subdivided intelligence into eight independent forms; musical, linguistic, bodily-kinesthetic, interpersonal, intrapersonal, naturalistic, spatial and logical-mathematical intelligence. Operationally, however, intelligence reflects our ability to acquire, assimilate and otherwise manipulate concepts within the media of thought. As such it is difficult to see how sporting or musical ability or even language acquisition are highly dependent upon intelligence. Firstly, there are cases of people who virtually lack prefrontal lobes and the tissues of the mind and yet are capable of grammatically perfect language that lacks significant content. Secondly, musical, sporting and linguistic ability usually emerge in children long before the maturation of the mind is complete. Young people who seem to instinctually excel in one of these areas, rarely if ever have cognitive insight into the origins of their talent. Gifted guitarists, for example, often begin playing purely by instinct and only later in their careers gain a conceptual appreciation of the formal rules of music. We commonly refer to people with such gifts as "naturals" primarily to underscore our feeling that their abilities are not solely a product of learning and practice but of their inherited genetic makeup.

In contrast to the acquisition of skills, the conceptual manipulation of the interpersonal, intrapersonal, naturalistic, spatial and logical-mathematical processes is definitely the work of the mind and so can be truly defined as intelligence. Each of these categories arises from the volitional focusing of emotional, temporal, practical or abstract intelligence, or a combination thereof. Thus, interpersonal, intrapersonal and naturalistic intelligence all fall within the emotional, social and biological domain that is served by the social mind and its product, emotional intelligence. Similarly, the comprehension of spatial and logical-mathematical processes is the business of the temporal, material and abstract components of the mind. The only thing that skills like music, sport and linguistics have in common with our cognitively based skills is that they arise form part of the cortex. The only difference is that the cortex serving insight is confined to BAs 9, 10, 46 and 47 of the prefrontal lobes, while that serving musical, sporting and basic linguistic skills is confined to the cortex's sensory, perceptual, motor and language areas.

Many studies have shown that the connectivity of the cortex responds to training. However, there is no evidence that training alters the size of Brodmann's areas. Improvement, either at the level of skill or insight, must therefore involve changes of neural connections within circumscribed areas of cortex. The only difference between the process of gaining a new insight and that of developing a new skill is that the former involves changes that relate specifically to the cortex of the mind while the latter involves changes within the cortex's sensory, perceptual and motor representations. This difference between the volitional integration of concepts in the resolution of a problem and the learning of methodological information and technical skill highlights the oft-forgotten difference between true education and technical training. True education teaches people to think effectively, providing numerous concepts and insights to stimulate their thoughts. Education therefore targets the cortex of the mind, while technical training more frequently targets cortex behind the prefrontal areas.

Finally, although thought is the highest function of the human brain, there is no global consensus about its place in human existence. Thus, while in the East, thought has been regarded as a process that draws the seeker away from the inner self or soul, the prevalent western view has been that thought and, particularly creative thought, is evidence of humanity's proximity to God. To the western world, Godliness is about thought, intelligence and the mystery of creation, while to the eastern world the actual experience of Godliness is achieved through the quieting of thought and the consequent emergence into consciousness of the inner self or soul. In one view, the path to God is through the mind and a cognitive understanding of the world. In the other view, the path to God is through an introspective journey to the heart of our emotions and the very essence of our instinctual urges. Clearly, there exists a global dichotomy in what people believe is the purpose of intelligence, one view claiming that the intellect and education will ensure the longevity of our species and the other claiming that intelligence is useful only in addressing the day-to-day matters of survival and that to use it otherwise is to invite man-made catastrophe. As we will see, these alternative attitudes are not so much the product of cultural conditioning as they are the differences in the composition of the western and eastern mind.

The Measurement of Intelligence

"Conceptions of intelligence(s) and methods to measure them continue to evolve, but there is agreement on many key points; for example, that intelligence is not fixed, and that test bias does not explain group differences in test scores. Intelligence research is more advanced and less controversial than is widely realized, and permits some definite conclusions about the biological bases of intelligence to be drawn." Gray, J. R. and Thompson, P. M. (2004). Neurobiology of Intelligence: Science and Ethics. *Nature Neuroscience Reviews* 5, 471-482.

If you ask a top sportsperson whether they believe their outstanding ability is a result of intensive training, they will always say that while they have worked very hard, they had, from the beginning, an innate ability. If you ask a conspicuously intelligent person whether they believe that their intelligence is a result of their education, they will likewise say that although their education helped them develop their mind, it was their above average mental abilities that in the first place enabled them to enjoy the process of becoming well educated. Oddly, some of these same intelligent people often argue vehemently against the politically incorrect stance that the dominant form and level of our intelligence is largely inherited. It seems that to be politically correct it has become necessary not only to misconstrue factual truths about the nature of humans but also to contravene our personal truths. Unfortunately, reality is not always as humans might wish it to be and one need only look at the lineages of certain families to see that like any other gift, cognitive aptitude, or a lack thereof, appears to be passed on from parents to children as simply another trait emanating from our genes.

Early in the 20th century Charles Spearman presented data indicating that the same people tend to perform well in a diverse range of cognitive tests. To account for this he put forward the hypothesis that *general intelligence* was dependent upon a single element that he called the *g factor*. Spearman's g factor was said to be a measure of overall intellectual performance. According to Spearman, intelligent people are good at a wide variety of things, whereas people of low intelligence are not very good at any. An alternative view might be that high intelligence manifests exclusively in those tasks that demand a high level of cognition and is unrelated to other less cerebral activities, such as hunting, gardening and cooking. In terms of Brodmann's areas, this view would hold that intelligence is dependent only upon the amount of cortex allocated to the mind for division between BAs 9, 10, 47 and 46. Thus, not only would a highly intelligent person be adept at meeting cognitive challenges but they would naturally excel within the domain of cognition served by whichever of these four areas is largest.

That intelligence is almost exclusively a biological property is revealed by the increasingly conspicuous relationship between high intelligence and head size, brain size, the amount of grey and white matter in the cortex, the size of the prefrontal cortex, and finally, the amount of cortex in the mind - defined crudely as the cortex of the dorsolateral surface of the prefrontal lobes. This, however, is not the whole story. Other data show that the size of a variety of cortical areas outside the mind is also positively correlated to intelligence. These areas include a number of the perceptual and even primary sensory receiving areas of the cortex. It seems that in people of high intelligence, not only the mind, but also many other areas of the cortex, are simply larger. This makes good sense, when we consider that although neither sensation nor perception is necessarily related to intelligence, they are the only windows through which our mind can assess, and so cognate about, the outer and inner worlds. In addition, the size of our perceptual areas will naturally affect our abilities to use imagination as part of problem solving because imagination depends upon our mind commandeering the perceptual areas of our cortex as a screen for representing our ideas as internal "images" (*The Exploration of Attention and Mental Imagery*: Chapter 1: section 7). Even though enlarging one's mind would substantially increase one's ideational powers, without a concurrent enlargement of the cortex's sensory and perceptual areas, one's enhanced cognitive abilities might not have opportunity to contribute significantly to external manifestations of one's intelligence.

Brain imaging allows us to see what areas of the cortex are active when people perform tasks that powerfully challenge the mind (high g tasks), as against other tasks (low g tasks), that do not. When this is done the abstract mind, BA46, emerges as the single area of cortex that is consistently associated with Spearman's g factor, while the social, temporal and material mind (BAs 9, 10 and 47) contribute only on some occasions. At the highest level the abstract mind (BA46) must concoct an integrated picture of all four domains of cognition. For this reason the abstract mind participates in the resolution of complex problems more than any of the other domains of cognition.

When we talk loosely of a person's intelligence being related to the amount of gray matter they possess, we are referring exclusively to the gray matter within their cerebral cortex. Using brain scanners, it has been possible to make precise measurements of the amount of grey matter in the cortex of identical (monozygotic) twins. When this is done the results show that the volume of their brains is, like their IQ, close to identical. Even the volume of grey matter in the prefrontal cortex of identical twins is similar, while the volume of grey matter in the sensory, motor and perceptual areas of the cortex is more variable. Even in identical twins, those areas of cortex most exposed to the outside world are subject to different influences on their development while those areas forming the psyche or the inner realms of consciousness are influenced by genes. These studies therefore support others that unequivocally demonstrate that both the size of the brain and the size of the prefrontal cortex are controlled by genes and that both these parameters are also powerfully correlated to general intelligence.

The relative power of each domain of human thought is critical to determining both the person's cognitive aptitude and their personality. It is therefore very revealing of human nature that there is an enormous variation in the amount of cortex allocated to the social mind (BA9) and the abstract mind (BA46) of different individuals. Alongside this there is little evidence that the environment can significantly change the size of Brodmann's areas. Genes do, it seems, determine the size of each area of Brodmann within any individual and so, potentially, within any human population. At least some of these genes must be the product of the series of mutations that accompanied the evolutionary progression from the first primates to have a physically tiny abstract "mind" to the modern human being (*The Size of the Mind*: Chapter 1: Section 6).

Virtually all anthropological reasoning about the aptitudes of our hominid ancestors is based on the relationship between brains size and intelligence. Nevertheless when applied to modern humans, this simple fact instantly becomes a political issue. Yet there is absolutely no doubt that both the mean brain size and the mean level of general intelligence do vary between existing human populations or races. With respect to brain size, careful studies have revealed a global progression wherein the East Asians have the largest mean brain size, followed by those people of European origin and finally the world's hunter-gather tribes - the Akka pygmies of the Congo having the smallest brains of all humans. As we have seen IQ is primarily related to the functionality of the abstract mind (BA46). Attempts to measure general intelligence across different societies, reveal that the mean IQ of East Asians is 105 while those of European descent who today inhabit a wide diversity of cultures, is, by definition, set at 100. In contrast, American Indians and Hispanics have a mean IQ of 90 compared to 85 for African Americans and 70 for the natives of sub-Saharan Africa that includes areas occupied by the Akka and other pygmy tribes. This should not surprise anyone for the cultures of the world's hunter gatherer populations are indicative of a powerful influence from the social mind and its product, emotional intelligence. Again we see that in all its forms, intelligence is highly determined by genes and influenced by natural selection in the same manner as all other characteristics. For example, the Ashkenazim Jews have a mean IQ of 115 presumably as a consequence of generations of selective interbreeding between individuals of above average intelligence. Given that, like the body, the development of the brain is under genetical control, it would be extremely surprising if intelligence were immune from the influences of natural selection.

Over the last 30 years it has become politically fashionable to say that attempts to measure IQ of non-Europeans lack controls for cross-cultural differences. Those who feel obliged to take this view, therefore claim that there is no objective evidence that human populations differ from one another in the form, mean level or range of intelligence. Nevertheless, many studies have made serious attempts to design tests that take this into account. What is certainly true is that brain size and IQ vary significantly within all populations and that therefore the national or racial origin of any individual cannot be used to provide more than a statistically qualified guess of either parameter. Biology does not follow the rules of fairytales. The biological realm is a battlefield wherein genes ensure that any drift towards equality or similarity are dissolved into that critical resource, of natural selection, diversity. Like equality, similarity is little more than a foolish wish. When it comes to accepting and assisting our fellow beings, then such ideas are utterly worthless. Humans are vitally dependent on their thought processes. Consequently, it would be extremely surprising if all humans shared the same form or level of mentality. If we really wish to understand people of different race, we need to assess the nature of their intelligence. When we speak of IQ we are primarily looking at functioning of the abstract mind; a cognitive system that is specialized for the comprehension of intangible phenomena. As tests are developed to specifically target emotional, practical and temporal intelligence, they may well caste a totally different light upon the global diversity of human intelligence. It is arguable that, for a species so dependent upon intellect, the attainment of self-knowledge is vital to its peaceful survival.

One of the most curious aspects of intelligence is the repeated observation that scores on virtually every type of intelligence test are increasing with each successive generation. This phenomenon was discovered in the 1980's by a New Zealand political scientist, James Flynn and was subsequently dubbed the *Flynn Effect*. Increases are in the order of 3 to 6 IQ points per decade depending on the country being studied. For example, over a period of 30 years, IQs in Belgium, Holland and Israel increased by around 20 points while in Denmark and Sweden they increased only 10 points. Initially the poorer performance of old people on IQ tests was thought to be an indication of a degenerating mentality. However, it is now thought to represent a real increase in the mean intelligence of the younger generations. In terms of the form of intelligence, these increases are not related to the accumulation of factual knowledge but instead to abilities in the realm of the abstract, which typically underlies our conceptual understanding of both life and the physical world.

The question the Flynn Effect raises is, how could our intelligence possibly be changing at a rate far beyond that of brain evolution? Although, there is no consensus on the origins of the Flynn Effect, the improvements in cognitive performance are measured with the conventional IQ test and so fall largely within the province of the abstract mind (*The Origin of Hypothesis - The Abstract Mind*: Chapter 3: Section 3). As we must presume that the average size of the abstract mind is unlikely to be increasing with each successive generation, we are forced to seek a cause within the fabric of abstract intelligence. In accord with its plenipotentiary powers, the abstract mind is the only element of the mind that entertains concepts of concepts, weaving into strategy first-order concepts forwarded from each of the other three elements of cognition. Ultimately, it is within the domain of abstract thought that are evolved the deep insights into our physical and social environment and our selves – insights that have spawned the multitude of theories and inventions that are the unmistakable mark of a new, emergent humanity. The last few centuries constitute a period of human creativity where within a single generation many a complex mystery became a simplistically constructed entity that could now be neatly filed as a significant yet single higher-order concept. One early example is the term "market" which emerged around 1776. Other examples of terms embodying complex higher order concepts are natural selection (1859), percentage (1860), random sample (1877), charisma effect (1922) and placebo (1938). Today even the mystery of life can be learned from a textbook in a few hours and each day brings us closer to truly witnessing cogent theories which embody the nature of our collective identity. To a university student studying in the late 1800's even the word "brain" would have had a radically different meaning than it would to a modern day student. Yet all that truly differentiates these two students is that one has the benefit of conceptual knowledge acquired over one hundred years of neuroscientific research that, in turn, has been condensed into millions of research papers and thousands of books. With each successive generation, the educated peoples of the world have opportunity to envisage life and the world through a circumscribed set of tried and tested higher-order concepts – a process that pushes up our deductive powers and with them, our IQ.

The hostility that the issue of intelligence fuels between intellectually disparate groups reflects a subliminal appreciation of its importance to individual success. Within human society, high intelligence is correlated with economic and other forms of achievement. At the global level too, the mean level of intelligence in a country is correlated with its gross national product. However, while the economic benefits of intelligence are conspicuous, its moral value is pure fantasy. Moral principles are not inherited but are conjured in thought as part of our societal conditioning. For instance, in the time of the inquisition the Catholic Church believed it was moral to torture people to death in the name of God. There is even less evidence that a high level of intelligence is related to happiness. Intelligence may bring wealth but to paraphrase the King of Bhutan, the gross national happiness is surely more important that the gross national product.

Assessing the intellectual aptitude of an individual is critical to their finding a fulfilling role within society. In the not too distant future brain scanners may enable us to measure the size of those areas of Brodmann that constitute four divisions of the mind enabling us to compare this anatomical measure of cognitive aptitude of an individual with their actual competency in each of the four domains of the mind. This should enable the relative contributions of emotional, practical, temporal and abstract mind to an individual's intellect to be assessed while measurements of the overall size of the prefrontal lobes could provide an objective measure of their *overall cognitive potential*. Now that we have reached the brink of global catastrophe, now that we no longer instinctively "know" what to do, we must in this twilight time of nature, strive for a rational comprehension of human intelligence and use this knowledge as never before.

The Natural Selection of Intelligence

"If our stay in port could have been extended we would have had a real opportunity of obtaining a very interesting insight on the lifestyle of human beings so close to nature, whose candor and kindness contrast so much with the vices of civilization." Joseph-Antoine Raymond de Bruni d'Entrecasteaux (1739-1793), French Admiral and Explorer; commenting on his meeting with the Tasmanian aboriginals upon landing at Cockle Creek, Tasmania in 1792. .

The physical vulnerability of humans is such that they could never have survived, far less become the dominant form of life, if they had not possessed intellectual abilities that were unprecedented even amongst their hominid ancestors. However, as with all traits, determining just what selective pressures have led to the existing geographic diversity of intelligence is far more tenuous. It is possible to demonstrate natural selection in action by manipulating the environment of captive populations of rapidly reproducing organisms like fruit flies or bacteria. Removing an essential nutrient, for example, results in the death of most individuals but the few that survive then reproduce to form a new population that is no longer dependent on that nutrient. We cannot, unfortunately, put a large number of humans in a jar and cull all those who do not demonstrate enough practical intelligence to reinvent the wheel or who are too emotionally unintelligent to form a protective social group. The closest we can come to this experiment is to examine the geographic distribution of particular human cultures and to seek past environmental factors that may have influenced the natural selection of particular realms of cognition.

Why then were the Paleolithic Europeans and their descendants, dominated by a high level of abstract and temporal intelligence while the hunter-gatherers remained dominated by a high level of emotional intelligence? The most persuasive and commonly offered answer is related to the relative abundance of tropical latitudes as against the rigors of polar latitudes. This relationship is known as *Rapaport' rule* and it states that, compared with equatorial regions, polar regions offer less biodiversity. Not only is it more difficult for plants and animals to find a niche in polar regions but it is also more difficult for humans to find plants and animals for food. This explains why cultural diversity also tends to be maximal in equatorial regions and to decrease markedly at northern latitudes (*The Origins of Culture*: Chapter 2; Section 8). To the environmental rigors of the northern latitudes, we can add the effects of the ice ages, the last of which ended 11 kya. The intense cold of the ice ages must have reduced biodiversity to an absolute minimum and posed a constant threat to human life. While emotional intelligence might enhance tribal unity, it is difficulty to see how it could directly facilitate survival in conditions of low biodiversity and extreme cold. The only way humans could have survived such conditions is by being highly inventive. During the migration of the Paleolithic people into southern Europe 45-50 kya, extreme cold must have eliminated all but the most resourceful individuals. In time the passing of the ice ages would leave a people whose cognitive style was honed by natural selection to the processes of ideation, hypothesis and invention - abilities that would characterize their descendants and give them a distinct competitive advantage over other human populations, as well as a unique ability to transcend the forces of nature.

The Diversity of Intelligence
"The denial of genetic difference among human beings with respect to intellectual and character traits is based on fallacy. This ideology is particularly pernicious when applied to education." Ernst Mayr (1904-2005). German-born American Geneticist and Evolutionary Biologist.

Human society resembles that of the bees in that it is composed of groups of individuals who have aptitude for the specific tasks necessary for the survival of the whole population. However, while the behavior of the different castes of bees is the result of genetically determined differences in the neuronal circuitry of their nervous systems, the behavior of different human personalities is largely the result of genetical differences in the allocation of cortex to each domain of the mind. This diversity of cognitive style or personality ensures the existence of individuals who are inherently suited to the archetypal roles that exist in all human societies. The hunter, the gatherer, the medicine man, the fieldmarshall, the priest, the actor, the scientist, the engineer and the politician represent a selection of the archetypal mindsets found in all human populations. Just as each domain of the mind is essential to each individual, so too must each human population have access to the insights of each personality type.

While the rapidity, accuracy and complexity of human thought can be related to intelligence, it is the nature of our thoughts that determine what strategies we will spontaneously employ to solve problems. Just which *modus operandi* is chosen by an individual, is a reflection of the relative power of the four different components of their mind - a formula that largely determines their personality. Each personality type will favor a particular approach, whether or not that approach is the most appropriate. A person with a large material mind (BA47), will automatically be drawn to consider the practicalities while a person with a large social mind (BA9) will drawn to consider the personal and social issues. Even though the best solution may lie within the practical domain, the emotionally intelligent individual, dominated by a powerful social mind, will initially see only a psychosocial answer. In the satiation of their desires, people with different personalities typically adopt completely different strategies. While the builder builds in order to procure the essentials of food and sex, the actor acts to achieve the same end. The individual differences in the amount of prefrontal cortex allocated to BAs 9, 10, 46 and 47 ensures that different people have different personalities and that they are spontaneously drawn to entirely different, yet archetypal, strategies of survival contingent upon the inherent structuring of their mind.

Owing to its genetic origin, personality does not change during a human lifetime. Tests of personality utilize questions that have no relevance to survival or commonly held belief, such as "do you rush to answer the phone?" What is important is that the questions are sufficiently personal that the subject feels they have complete freedom of choice. Questions such as, "do you go to work on Monday morning?", are not helpful because this is usually an economic necessity in which there is no option for personal preference. The human mind clearly has the capacity to entertain conceptual frameworks, such as the fundamental importance of work, even if they are alien to the natural biases of its dominant cognitive domain. Like the apes and the more advanced monkeys, humans can be motivated by reward to temporarily adopt the persona of another individual or even transiently or superficially adopt the ideologies of an alien culture.

So it is that despite the inherent stability of human personality, the human mind has the capacity to deviate from its inherent preferences in order to meet challenges in a different domain of existence. However, in the same way as the behavior of psychopaths can be altered only with respect to a particular scenario, the normal individual can only be mentally conditioned to produce out-of-character behavior in response to very specific circumstances. When the demands of a job conflict with an individual's personality preferences on too many fronts, the inevitable outcome is unhappiness, inefficiency and stress.

The cardinal importance of behavioral strategy to human survival assures us that, in the evolution of humans, the components of the mind and the genes that determine their relative influences, must have been, and still are, under extremely strong selective pressures. If, in a particular environment, empathetic social cohesiveness is critical to survival, selection will push towards increasing the size and computational power of the social mind. If, on the other hand, practicality is critical, then selection will modify a population towards one in which many members have a large and dominant material mind. This does not mean that any of the four domains of cognition will be lost. As conditions like Williams syndrome and Autism illustrate, all domains of thought are necessary components of the healthy psyche. What it does mean is that natural selection must certainly have tuned the mental composition of any relatively isolated population to the nuances of their environment. As a result of this process, the spectrum of personality types within any population can act as an, albeit crude, descriptor of the whole population.

Before the huge population increases and mass migrations of the last 5 centuries, it must have been stunningly obvious to any celestial observer that the thoughts of each circumscribed population were fashioned around a unique set of environmentally appropriate templates. Even today, the radical differences in the societal structure and rituals of different human populations provide constant fascination to the inveterate traveler. Each population or nation appears to have a recognizable "personality" - a phenomenon that social psychologists have called *modal personality*. Modal personality refers to the most common personality type in any population and leaves the less common varieties of personality, unrepresented. Consequently, modal personality should not be used to elucidate the personality of the individual. Modal personality does, however, mean that there exists, a *geography of thought* that reflects a parallel geographic variation in the genetically determined composition of the human mind that, in turn, must have strongly influenced the pre-modern cultural map of humanity (Figure 8.2).

For the purposes of discussion, let us consider three major groups of people; (a) the Caucasians who inhabit Europe, Britain, the Middle East, much of supra-Saharan Africa and India; (b) the Far East Asians of Japan, Korea and China; (c) the hunter-gatherer tribes of the Andaman Islands, New Guinea, Australia and sub-Saharan Africa. Of these three groups, the Caucasians are unique in that they have flourished largely because of their astounding inventive abilities. In his, *A Short History of the 20th Century*, Australian historian Geoffery Blainey states, "In the early industrial revolution, the age of steam, the notable inventor was usually a Scot or an Englishman. In the second inventive era, running from about 1850 to the First World War, he was more likely to be an American". Even long before modern times, European inventiveness had resulted in (a) the complex abstractions embedded in the major Caucasian religions, Hinduism, Islam, Christianity and Judaism, (b) the invention of writing, mathematics, science, agriculture, geometry, art, philosophy and complex architecture and (c) the construction of four of the five earliest civilizations. In particular, the three-dimensional cave paintings of Paleolithic Europe indicate that as early as 38 kya Europeans were availed of a level of abstract and temporal intelligence, and the attendant forms of creativity, that exceeded any preexisting human population.

Research into the cognitive origins of European inventiveness has focused on comparisons of how people of European origin and Far East Asians see themselves with respect to the world around them. To further reduce the effects of environment, some studies have compared people of Far East Asian parentage who were born and raised in America, people we will refer to as *Far East Americans*, with Americans of European heritage. Although a host of tests have been applied, the most common is simply the response of the subjects to questions designed to reveal the manner in which they conceptualize their day-to-day life and themselves.

When this is done the Far East Asians emerge as being far less concerned with their individual aspirations and far more concerned with their identity as it relates to other people and societal norms. Even though they were born and raised in America, Far East Americans have difficulty describing themselves without reference to a particular situation, using phrases such as "I am fun-loving with my friends" or "I am serious at work". In contrast, Americans of European heritage find it hard to see themselves in a situational context, typically answer, "I am what I am". Whereas the European Americans are highly individualistic, the Far East American sees himself as a functional entity within human affairs and more broadly, the cosmos. In what is often mistaken for the traditional ways of the Far East, the mind of archetypal Far East American is easily conditioned to believe that; (a) it is critical that to strive to better fulfill one's designated role and (b) it is wrong to radically contest prevailing circumstance. To the Far East Asian, avoiding being disgraced, dishonored and ostracized is a fundamental reflection of an essentially non-European mindset. Indeed, so great is their admiration for the *status quo* that those of Far East Asian descent are typically apologetic about their shortcomings, often expressing a real desire to better fulfilling their social obligations. A story is told of a young Canadian psychologist who, after working for several years in Japan, began applying for jobs at North American universities. His advisor (presumably an American) was horrified when he discovered that, rather than promoting himself, the young man began with a list of apologetic acknowledgments of his unworthiness for each position. In the words of an unknown eastern scribe, "the peg that stands out is pounded down". Individualism, so valued in the West, is an anathema to the modal personality of the Far East.

There are numerous other differences that distinguish the Far East Asian mind from its European counterpart. Traditionally, Chinese music was monophonic with all singers and instruments following the same melody, while in western music each instrument has a distinct part. Westerners are inclined to say, "thank you", when people complete routine tasks that, in the East, are simply regarded as someone's duty. Choice is less valued in the East than in the West. Thus, Chinese, Koreans and Japanese cannot easily comprehend why Americans need so many different breakfast cereals or why Italian supermarkets have at least five aisles devoted to pasta.

The propensity of the Far East Asian mind to identify its host in societal terms is often mistakenly interpreted as a cognitively-expressed desire for emotional bonding indicating a high level of emotional intelligence. Alas, however, this is not the case. East Asians are usually prohibitively uncomfortable in interactive, group counseling, sessions, which present little threat to emotionally intelligent people. History and current events also give a strong indication that the collective *modus operandi* of the Chinese, Koreans and Japanese is little influenced by emotional intelligence. The societal doctrines that unite their people are not founded upon the formation of emotional bonds. Even at the family level social interactions in eastern societies are rigidly defined. Their *modus operandi* can be contrasted, with that of hunter-gatherers like the !Kung, an African pygmy tribe, whose modal personality is, like other hunter-gather tribes, clearly dominated by emotional intelligence. While Far Asians return from a highly structured workplace to adopt a tightly defined family role, the men of the !Kung sit around a collective fire and with great emotional vigor boast of their personal conquests that reflect their ability to surmount fear in the face of danger. Even the American Black Nationalist Leader, Malcolm X must have been intuitively aware of the power of genetics in the determination of human mentality when he stated that "Deep within the subconscious of the black man in this country, he is still more African than he is American".

In their relative independence from emotional intelligence the Far East Asians resemble modern day Europeans, particularly those from Britain and northern continental Europe and Russia. However, a paucity of emotional intelligence is not characteristic of all Caucasian populations. For example, the national identity of India is characterized by a high level of abstract intelligence, typical of the other European nations, coupled with a profound level of emotional intelligence that imparts an endearing, empathetic quality to India's modal personality. Although it is certain that amongst the 1.2 billion Indians are many who possess a very high practical and/or temporal intelligence neither practicality nor temporal concerns are the forte of India's modal personality. Indeed, India's magnificent contributions to philosophy, mathematics, theoretical physics, literature, theater and spirituality and their emergent talents at computer programming are all indicative of a tantalizing combination of the abstract and psychosocial domains of thought that are unencumbered by the constraints of either time or physical reality.

Psychology and counseling are professions that attract emotionally intelligent people. However, it would be quite incorrect to consider that because emotional intelligence is vital to controlled empathy it is always associated with altruistic, humanitarian behavior. Like many successful political orators and social leaders, Hitler was a man of high emotional intelligence. Emotional intelligence can be a two edged sword. On one hand it enhances the ability to empathize with the sorrows of others but on the other, it enables the mind to generate the reptilian emotions, fear and anger that quickly expunge all possibility of caring and compassion. Indeed, emotional intelligence plays a prominent role in defining the nature of human aggression. Women are typically more emotionally intelligent than men and yet it is said, "Hell hath no fury like a woman scorned". While the abstract and practical domains of thought seek to injure and kill aliens in a cold, systematic and practical manner, the psychosocial domain of thought liberates from the amygdala, a viciousness matched only by the untamed beast.

There is no better example of the diverse roles of the intellect in the perpetration of war than a comparison of the deeds of the English and the Indians during the Indian

Mutiny of 1857. Although the British regarded the Indians as inferior, they were curiously drawn to their intellect and natural affability. It is therefore all the more shocking to find that upon receiving news of mutiny spreading across the subcontinent, a number of British commanders ordered their sepoys to stow their weapons and assemble on the parade ground, whereupon they had them all shot. In another grisly episode, the Indians captured Cawnpore and after slaughtering the men, locked an estimated 200 women and children in a house that was to become known throughout India as the *House of the Ladies*. In the ensuing days about 25 died of cholera and dysentery before it was decided to kill the remainder. Five individuals were selected. Armed with swords, they entered the house and, over many hours, hacked the occupants to death - emerging only if they needed to replace a broken sword. By nightfall the task was achieved, the screams had stopped and the doors were closed despite the groans of a few whose end would come when in the morning, the dead and the dying would be thrown down a nearby well. One could make a similar comparison between the carefully planned methods used by the Germans for systematically exterminating 6 million Jews, with the impulsive butchery of close to one million Tutsis and Hutus in Rwanda. While to the abstract or practical mind, murder and mass murder are matters of careful planning, to the social mind they are achieved by the mere liberation of unbridled savagery. Only humans have the mental capacity to wreak death and suffering with such variety.

Religion is another area that illustrates the fundamental differences between the Far East Asian and the European mindset. Consider, for example, the edicts of Confucianism compared to those the major Caucasian religions, Christianity, Islam, Judaism and Hinduism. More of an ethical philosopher than a religious zealot, Confucius (551 to 479 BC) struck a definite chord with the ancient Chinese psyche. So revered was he that almost 80 generations of his descendants are said to be buried in the *Forest of the Exulted Sage*. Confucius's philosophy outlined the morally correct way to conduct oneself within the family, community and society wherein virtue, self-discipline and duty were inseparable qualities. In contrast, three of the four major Caucasian religions, Christianity, Islam and Judaism, emphasized the entirely abstract ideas that we are each under divine scrutiny and that the human soul is on a journey towards an eternal afterlife in either Heaven or Hell. While it is true that each of these religions addresses practical issues by giving detailed guidance as to how to lead life, they also assert that one's earthly efforts to uphold the faith are the surest way of earning a place in Heaven. Whether one engages in cooperative and productive interactions with one's fellow humans is of secondary importance. Hinduism is even less focused on practicality, emphasizing instead the natural progression of life by defining four stages or *Ashramas*, the last of which, that of becoming a *Sannysin*, provides opportunity for seeking enlightenment. Bad and good behavior is less defined and certainly the riotous, egocentric behavior of the Hindu Gods is the very antithesis of the Confucian way. In Hinduism, bad behavior is held in check simply by the threat of being reincarnated as a cockroach instead of a prince.

The Chinese followed a progression through three major religions, Taoism, Confucianism and more recently Mahayana Buddhism, which provided a relief from the strictures of Confucianism. Taoism probably began in the 8th century BC, coming to fruition in the 3rd century BC with the completion of Lao-Tzu's classic text, the *Tao-te Ching* (Chinese for the *Classic of the Way of Power*). In its original form, Taoism was a religion of wonder and magic, linking the universe with human affairs and particularly, health. The Taoist sees existence and destiny as determined by the opposing forces of the universe amongst which the most conspicuous are those of Yin, the feminine, dark and passive, and Yang, the masculine, light and active. In Japan its parallel was Shintoism, from Shinto meaning the way of the mystical or the divine. Shintoism worshiped an omnipotent divine spirit, *Kami* that embodied good and evil and empowered all things natural, whether they are animate or inanimate. In imparting reverence to the opposing forces and cycles that pervade the natural world, both Taoism and Shintoism, like the animistic religions of the hunter-gatherers, were giving symbolic recognition to the valence and biological origins of emotion and mood. Just as Taoism became more practically orientated under the influence of Confucianism, so too Shintoism moved away from its animistic beginnings to become more centered on the value systems of the Japanese people.

The Caucasians have been responsible for concocting many philosophies such as Plato's Republic, Marxism, communism, democracy, McCarthyism, fascism, the Six Philosophies which lie at the center of Hinduism, and many other "isms' too numerous to mention. By comparison, the philosophical journey of the Chinese from Taoism to Confucianism and Buddhism is, theoretically, simplistic. Even modern Chinese philosophers are more interested in the application of factual knowledge than in abstract theories. European engineers who have worked in China often compliment their Chinese counterparts on their technical and organizational efficiency but are quick to add that they are less able when an imaginative solution is required.

Ten thousand years ago, when human populations were relatively small and very much at the mercy of natural phenomena, their spiritual practices paid homage to the sun, the moon and many other entities of the natural world. With the beginnings of organized civilizations, humans became increasingly dependent upon their inventions and the emergent technologies. Only the hunter-gatherers and to a lesser extent, the Islanders of Pacific and natives of the Americas remained highly dependent upon, and in awe of, the natural world. With the creation of civilization the Caucasians and the Far East Asians became increasingly insulated from environmental factors. It was probably this new independence from nature that encouraged them to cease worshiping natural phenomena and to transfer their reverence to deities, symbolic objects and ideologies that were entirely the product of their minds and their imagination. Dominated by the abstract mind and driven by similarly abstractly composed egos (the "spiritual me" of William James), the Caucasians were naturally drawn to the creation of ideationally complex religions to account, not only for their existence, but for the mystery surrounding their own success in producing the testable theories about phenomena that are the essence of all significant inventions. The Far East Asians, dominated by a practical mind and driven by a practically orientated ego (the material me" of James), increasingly developed a reverence for a socially pervasive practicality that further reinforced their natural inclination towards efficient material productivity. In China this mental bias found full expression in Confucianism, while in Japan it was marked by the drift of Shintoism from its animistic origins to a materialistically oriented, moral code that covered family, social and vocational relationships.

The Thoughts of the Ancients

"Man prefers to believe what he prefers to be true." Francis Bacon (1561-1626). English Philosopher, Statesman, Author, Lawyer, Essayist and Lord Chancellor of England.

Since ancient times humanity has passed through a mechanical revolution and, in the last 100 years, an electronic revolution. Nevertheless, the differences in *modus operandi* that distinguish Far East Asians from Caucasians of European origin are merely a reflection of differences that existed for 5 kya between the Chinese and Greeks of the ancient world. This is not so surprising given that 80% of modern Europeans can be traced back to ancestors who lived in Paleolithic Europe. If the data were available, it is a reasonable bet that essentially the same differences would be seen between the Paleolithic Europeans and the human populations that first settled in China, tens of thousands of years ago.

When social psychologists make retrospective comparisons between ancient Greece and ancient China, the emergent differences are as fundamental as those that divide individuals of radically different personality. The matter of cause and effect provides a good example. To the ancient Greeks causality arose from phenomena that described the properties of objects in space and time, while to the ancient Chinese, causality was determined by the uncontrollable, unpredictable and often antagonistic forces of nature. While the Greeks believed it was possible to understand cause and effect, the Chinese believed that the relationships between cause and effect were unfathomable, magic or even non-existent. As it is the human mind that directs our attention and conjures our imaginings, the different mindsets the ancient Greeks and Chinese naturally caused them to attend to different aspects of their environment and so to exercise their imagination in quite different spheres of endeavor. Thus, while the practical Chinese developed arithmetic, they failed to develop geometry or deductive Algebra. When compared to Caucasian territories that include the Middle East, Northern Africa, Britain, Europe and India, there is relative little evidence of significant mathematical research within ancient China.

Prediction is another realm of difference, the ancient Greeks taking the typical western view that prediction can be achieved by analyzing the past and the present, while the ancient Chinese, like their modern counterparts, consider it to be a matter of magic or *meaningful coincidence*. It is one of the limitations of a dominant practical intelligence that, when the links between cause and effect or past, present and future, are not obvious, superstition provides a ready solution. The conclusion that the Gods were angry with us and caused the volcano to erupt is not reflective of someone who contemplates the phenomenological world with any depth. The ghosts that haunt the newly practical 8 year-old, concrete-operational child, either disappear or become comprehensible, hypothetical, and often religious, entities, when the maturation of its abstract mind enables rationally deduced possibilities to replace culturally preserved superstitions. In the presence of a powerful abstract mind, mysterious phenomena are soon embodied into hypotheses that may either be tested scientifically or regarded as the sacrosanct beliefs of complicated religions. The persistence of biologically orientated superstitions amongst the hunter-gatherer and native populations reflects modal personalities that are powerfully influenced by emotional intelligence and largely independent of the influences of the abstract mind. Clearly the relationship between cause and effect is heavily influenced in accord with the domain of cognition that countenances the matter. Where the ancient Greeks saw the hypothetical significance of objects and situations, the ancient Chinese saw only their static functionality and the ever-capricious furor of the cosmos.

Education was also radically different between these cultures. The word "school" comes from the Greek, *skholē* meaning leisure, philosophy or lecture place. In ancient Greece, school served as a place where the sons of the rich could indulge their curiosity and learn the art of debate. Debate is also a tradition within India where, for millennia, it provided a forum for mystics to compete with one another, the winner taking the loser's disciples. In contrast, neither wonder nor debate, were encouraged within ancient China as both these activities could lead to radical, and thus antisocial, conclusions – an attitude that persists in modern China.

Even the analyses and elucidation of the different cognitive domains, so critical to the process of education, can be traced back to the ancient Greeks. Roughly one hundred years after Confucius pronounced upon the importance of practicality in both material and social realms, Plato and Aristotle were attempting to define the domains of human thought in a manner that, more than 2,000 years later would be substantiated by experiments using modern brain scanners. In modern terminology, Plato's *techne* is practical intelligence while his *episteme* was, according to Aristotle, equivalent to abstract intelligence. As we have seen, it was Aristotle who clarified his mentor's insights, by embodying the independence of abstract and practical thought in the terms, *intellectus practicus* and *intellectus speculativeus*. No equivalent insights into the human psyche were forthcoming from ancient China or any other non-Caucasian population.

Around 3000 BC the Chinese created the only civilization outside of the Caucasian enclave that included Crete, Egypt, Mesopotamia and the Indus valley. Recently revealed archeological discoveries suggest that even the first Chinese civilization might have been partially the product of early immigrants who essentially carried their genes for a high abstract intelligence, along the ancient Silk Road. Elsewhere in the world, another 2000 years would pass before the Olmec people formed first Mesoamerican civilization in southern Mexico.

In the matter of invention as with the creation of cities, only the Chinese have seriously challenged the Caucasians. However, when it comes down to specific inventions of the Chinese, such as irrigation systems, ink, porcelain, the magnetic compass, stirrups and the wheelbarrow, all lie within the practical domain. The Chinese did not reveal the mysteries of electricity, magnetism, X-rays, molecular and cellular structure, evolution, heredity or the human psyche. Scientific progress is highly dependent upon the analysis of phenomena - a subject that was scrupulously avoided by the great Chinese thinkers. The genius of the ancient Chinese, like that of modern Far East Asians, lay in their practical and organizational abilities. Efficient manufacturing receives natural priority over research and invention. Their high level of material productivity is indicative of a modal personality dominated by temporal and practical intelligence. True science demands an independence of thought that has been shunned by the collective psyche of the Far eastern nations. For these reasons, the Far East Asians have, compared to the Caucasians, contributed little to the progress of science. In Far East society, a person thinking and acting independently in accord with entirely abstract ideas is typically regarded as an antisocial radical and a threat to the *status quo*.

The Origin of Alien Philosophers

"Although Aristotle and Confucius had enormous impact on the intellectual, social, and political histories of the peoples who followed, they were less the progenitors or their respective cultures than the products." Nisbett, R. E. *The Geography of Thought - How Asians and Westerners Think Differently....and Why*. Nicholas Brealey Publications. London, Yaramouth, Maine, 2003, p. 29.

Philosophies and philosophers are said to reflect their parent society. One explanation is that the newborn would-be philosopher is mentally conditioned by the culture into which he is born. Another is that, as a consequence of the influence of genes over the structuring of his mind, the philosophical individual is simply born with a personality that predisposes him to a particular philosophical stance that reflects the modal personality of his society. Both statements are true. Philosophy is about argument and logic and so is an exclusively mental pursuit. As such, the importance to an individual of philosophizing and to some degree their philosophical stance, must surely be powerfully influenced by the relative power of the four different domains of cognition that compose the mind.

Studies of identical twins have revealed an astounding level of similarity on traits that can only be attributed to higher mental functions - functions related to the *modus operandi*, philosophical stance and personality of an individual. Thus, identical twins share traits such as shyness, political conservatism, dedication to work, orderliness and intimacy and to a lesser degree extraversion or introversion, conformity, creativity, optimism and cautiousness. Even if separated since birth, identical twins will tend to choose identical clothes or pictures with a level of accuracy and attention to detail that far exceeds the similarities of choice between unrelated people even when they share the same personality.

While the cortical structure that typifies any population must have a profound affect on its culture, there is also an abundance of evidence showing that mental conditioning also has a profound affect. Consider for example, the case of the identical twins that were raised separately, one as a Nazi and one as a Jew. When they met they were wearing very similar clothes and shared all manner of similarities typically found in identical twins. However, although they admitted to feeling drawn to each other, they had great difficulty finding commonality in all matters that related to their very different conditioning. Such examples suggest that a useful theoretical paradigm is to consider that many thoughts either powerfully reflect the inherent structuring of the mind or powerfully reflect the conditioning of the mind - all other thoughts being the product of the interaction of these two constraints.

Irrespective of their cultural origins, all people have a mind made up of the same four components. Someone who in one culture is in an extreme minority, might in another culture find a modal personality identical to their own. Societies have ways of honing their identity. Although the individual with a rare personality type is a valuable resource, they often suffer persecution and death because, as a minority, their cognitive style frequently opposes that of the *status quo*. It is amongst such individuals that we find the alien philosopher. One example, from ancient Greece is Heraclitus (c.540-c.480 BC), who championed cosmology and the energy of fire in a manner in keeping with the importance of natural phenomena in the animistic leanings of Taoism and Shintoism and the spiritual practices of the Inuit, North American Indians, Aztecs, Mayans, Incas, Egyptians, continental Indians and the Sumerians of Mesopotamia. Another, this time from ancient China, is Mo-tzu (470-331 BC) who emphasized methodology and standards alongside universal love, harmonizing with the philosophical themes being espoused by mainstream philosophers in ancient Greece. The existence of alien philosophers shows clearly that the cultural conditioning of the mind is not universally successful in establishing a person's natural philosophical stance.

Creativity, Modal Personality and the Mind
"It is the function of creative man to perceive the relations between thoughts, or things, or forms of expression that may seem utterly different, and to be able to combine them into some new forms – the power to connect the seemingly unconnected." William Plomer, (1903-1973). South African born, British author.

The principal gift of the Caucasians is invention and, in particular, the forms of phenomenological imagination that inspire pure ideational creativity. As this form of creativity requires the setting up of ideas or hypotheses, it betrays the presence of a large and dominant abstract mind (BA46); BA46 of the left hemisphere being responsible for erecting ideas that are then evaluated by BA46 of the right hemisphere. In contrast, the principal gift of the Far Asians is practicality. The essence of practicality is a detailed comprehension of the nature of real things. Practicality is related to the power of the material mind that, in turn, reflects the size and computing power of BA47. However, the representation of the material world is not entirely devoid of a subjective component. Thus, while BA47 of the left hemisphere is concerned with the parametric properties and functional identity of objects and people, BA47 of the right hemisphere is concerned with their symbolic potential. Because of its role in the functional and symbolic categorization of animate and inanimate things, BA47 works closely with Broca's motor speech area (BA45 and 44) in the production of language - a fact that may explain why the writing of practically orientated peoples, like the Chinese, is highly symbolic and yet lacks the biological imagery so prominent in hieroglyphics.

Even though the Chinese are appear to be less emotionally reactive than many other nationalities, the gift of practicality comes with an important subjective component. This is revealed during lie detection tests when the material mind is activated in concert with those emotional centers that generate anxiety. This, seemingly enigmatic, link between practicality and visceral arousal clearly reflects the *imperative of truth* within the practical realm of existence. Theories are only ideas and emotions are only transient feelings. When it comes to the world of theories and emotions there are no benchmarks for discerning the truth. In contrast, the presence of an object or a person is an undeniable truth. Creativity within the practical realm does not involve flights of mental fancy but instead is highly dependent on the physical properties of people and objects and their functional interrelationships. Only within the practical realm of cognition is the lie conspicuous misleading. A lie within the practical realm blatantly contravenes the operational principles that are the very substance of practical creativity, causing the material mind to respond by activating autonomic control centers that in turn create visceroemotional disharmony. To the practically minded person the difference between truth and lies is as distinct as black and white – a distinction that is fundamental to both the Taoistic and Shintoistic visions of the universe being defined by the opposing forces of good and evil.

The dominance of the practical mind in the archetypal Far East Asian manifests in what is called their *field dependency*. Field dependency refers to the degree to which the perception of an object is influenced by its background. One test for field dependency, called the Rod and Frame Test, involves viewing a rod through a long square tube. Subjects are asked to say whether the angle of the rod is altered when the tube is rotated. The results showed that, even when born and raised in America, Far East Asians are far more likely than Caucasians to be to unable to judge the angle of the rod in isolation from the axial orientation of the tube. The practical mind seeks the interrelationships of objects, while the abstract mind focuses on the hypothetical, wherein the rod and the box may well have completely independent properties that may fully explain their nature. As a consequence of being innately field dependent, the inventive capacity of the archetypal Far East Asian is limited to that interrelationship between objects - a paradigm that is the very essence of practical invention and the antithesis of the phenomenological focus of Caucasian thought. Far East Asians typically believe they are less able to control things and events and so must resort to fine adjustments to achieve a desired outcome. In complete contrast, Caucasians have faith that control will emerge from a deeper understanding of phenomena associated with things and events.

The differences between the modal personality of the countries Far East and the Europeans are somewhat parallel to the differences between the *sensate* versus *intuitive* personality as defined by Carl Jung. The sensate person attends to the factual and structural details of the world, being highly dependent on their senses as the source of practical inspiration. The intuitive person attends to the ideational world and is highly dependent on analyses and their comprehension of theories. The sensate person is technically orientated and practically creative. The intuitive person is orientated towards theories and is ideationally creative. In the realm of insightful invention, it is indicative of the abilities of each group that only a very small percentage of sensate people have won the Nobel Prize for science.

With its capacity to entertain possibilities, the abstract mind can evaluate ideas originating in practical, psychosocial or temporal domains of cognition and, if necessary, assert its power of veto over their would-be influence on behavioral strategy. In this internal battle of the minds, the powerful material mind of the archetypal Far East Asian will have the more dominant voice, even though the other domains of cognition will continue to contribute to the ongoing formation of strategy. Similarly, the archetypal Caucasian psyche, though dominated by the abstract mind, will still employ the other domains of cognition. For example, although the theory of relativity appears to be spawned entirely within the abstract mind, Einstein acknowledged that he used the clock tower in Bern, Switzerland as a physical prop that enabled him to imagine a practical experiment through which he was able to reach his revolutionary insights into time. In this process he was clearly usurping the energies of the material mind to bring it to bear upon an issue that could only be properly addressed within the abstract mind.

Although the Far East Asians have the highest IQs of any population and are highly creative within the realm of practicality, history shows that when it comes to unearthing the secrets of nature and human existence they are no match for the Caucasians. Why is it that the Caucasians have been responsible for most significant inventions? Although creativity seems to be correlated with an IQ of 120 or above, a high IQ is not indicative of what has been called a high *Creativity Quotient* (CQ). The insights required for creative genius seems to correlate with a number of unusual personality traits such as mental and emotional immaturity. Creativity is often said to involve *lateral* or *divergent thinking*, the ability to switch from one perspective to another and an inclination to make novel associations - attributes that naturally lead to ideational fluency. Einstein and the Bern clock tower is a typical example. In terms of the structure of the human mind, a high CQ appears to be the product of a powerful interaction between the different realms of cognition, for example, the gaining of new insights into phenomena concerning particle physics by the application of principles germane to the social world.

The interaction of cognitive domains in the creative process also explains why creative people are able to combine playfulness with discipline, responsibility with irresponsibility, extraversion with introversion, pride with humility, rebelliousness with conservatism and passion with practicality. Creative women are frequently more dominant than other females, while creative men are often more sensitive and less aggressive than other males. The increasing recognition that psychoactive drugs occasionally reveal vitally important insights probably reflects just such an aberration of normal process wherein quandaries are serendipitously addressed by a normally inappropriate domain of cognition. Whereas one's IQ must be broadly related to the computing power of each component of the mind and particularly that of the abstract mind, it seems that one's CQ is contingent upon a high level of traffic between the normally separate domains of the mind.

Another source of multi-cognitive insights may be the existence within the mind of a newly discovered area that structurally, at least, appears to be a combination of BA46 and BA9 and thus may have the capacity to integrate the functions of the abstract mind and social mind (*The Origins of Understanding - The Third Eye;* Chapter 3: Section 3). Alternatively, the creativity of an individual might simply reflect the strength of interconnections between the social, temporal, material and abstract domains of cognition rather than IQ that must surely reflect the absolute size and computing power of BAs 9, 10, 47 and, particularly, 46.

When social psychologists look at the origin of major theories, they find that those developed by American born intellectuals of European origin are not as broad as those invented by resident Europeans. The most likely reason for this is that the breadth and depth of education go hand in hand with the level of creative achievement. America certainly has some first class educational institutions. Yet its primary and high school curricula are no match for the depth of a traditional European education, where while still at school, students often study subjects covering the entire gambit of education. Over the last fifteen years Australia has dismantled its inherited European system of education and substituted an unwieldy collection of narrow, technically orientated, marketable courses in its place. While prior to this change its small intellectual community had produced some theories of fundamental significance, its already paltry government research budgets now largely fund technical work that is often of only local or political significance. In a world faced with increasingly urgent and complex problems such flagrant wastage of intellectual potential is a formula for disaster. Only a broad, in-depth education can provide the diversity of knowledge, conceptual understanding and insight so critical to lateral thinking and the intellectually creative act.

The Origins of Culture

"The destinies of a people are shaped by their modes of thought, and their real history is therefore the history of their culture." Donald A. Mackenzie (1873-1936). Scottish Journalist, Author, Archeologist, Anthropologist and Mythologist.

Humans are masters of cultural diversity. We hunt, fish, forage, cultivate and raise a host of edible domestic animals. We collectively indulge in all sorts of relationships including polygamy, polygyny, polyandry and monogamy, construct all manner of dwellings, speak or have spoken, 7,000 different languages and eat a vast variety of foods. Finally, humans entertain an almost limitless range of beliefs, customs and associated rituals, many of which have little if any relationship to the forces of either nature or the instinctual elements of the human psyche. Yet, the dictates of each society's customs are slavishly adhered to each day, week, month or year so much so that in an oblique reference to instinct, we refer to their performance as "second nature". For the newly arrived alien, there is a great incentive to imitate local customs and thereby lessen the likelihood of being placed in an out-group (*The Nature and Nurture of Racism*: Chapter 2: Section 1). When in Rome it is best to do what the Romans do or one might end up as the entertainment at the Coliseum. Irrespective of their racial origin any human adopted into, and raised in, a foreign society will, automatically and with little effort, adopt the customs of their host society.

Culture is one of those words that everyone understands until they are pressed for a watertight definition. By 1952 there were at least 164 published definitions of culture ranging from "learned behavior" to an "abstraction of behavior". For most people, however, the nineteenth century British anthropologist Edward Burnett Tylor (1832-1917) provided what became the classical definition of culture: "Culture….is that complex whole which includes knowledge, belief, art, morals, law, custom, and any other capabilities and habits acquired by man as a member of society." This definition implies that, (a) culture is restricted to the human species and (b) culture is not inherited but learned under the influence of the host society. Unfortunately subsequent research has thrown both assertions into question.

In relation to the view that culture is restricted to the human species, novel behavioral repertoires that are clearly learned by each generation have been described in several different colonies of non-human primates. Before grooming another individual, the bonobos at San Diego Zoo slap their chest, clap their feet or clap their hands in front of the other's face. This "custom" has not been seen in other colonies of bonobos and so is clearly independent of genes. In humans, similar behavioral routines are often referred to as cultural characteristics that are unique to particular societies. It is significant that, compared to humans, cultural activities are far harder to identify in the apes. Only the possession of a powerful yet functionally and structurally diverse mind, divides humans from animals as effectively as does the manifestation of complex cultures. The important question is; exactly how are the elements of culture passed from one generation to the next?

Although it is clear that mimicry, imitation and learning must each be important to the maintenance of "customs", research continues to show that genes have a powerful, deterministic influence on many aspects of behavior that, several decades ago, would have been attributed entirely, to societal conditioning. Most importantly, genes control the amount of cortex allocated to each area of Brodmann. Consider two hypothetical populations between which the frequencies of those genes that influence the size and computational power of each domain of the mind are significantly different. By definition, any two such populations would manifest different modal personalities that would be reflected in marked cultural differences. Almost as important would be the frequency of genes that regulate the size of those areas of Brodmann that serve primary sensory, perceptual (including our visceral perceptions or emotions) and motor functions. As individuals, the acuity of each of our senses, the accuracy of our perceptions and the strength of each of our primary emotions, significantly influence our cultural compatibility. If we imagine a group of individuals who share a common bias in each of these cerebral entities, then we begin to appreciate the indisputable influence of genes in what has been called culture.

Genes have cardinal affects over our anatomy, our biochemistry, the regulation of our hormones, our responses to stress, our vulnerability to pathogens and our congenital predisposition to a host of illnesses. All such things can radically influence the culture of a population. Even more compelling is the long and ever-increasing list of culturally significant aspects of behavior that linked to specific genotypes. To cite a few examples, genes have been shown to influence our attentional abilities, our predisposition to addiction, aggression, promiscuity, gambling, many subtle aspects of language and even the involvement of men in the nurturing of children. From an entirely different angle, the often bizarre similarities of choice made by identical twins are compelling evidence of the definitive role of genes in determining even the most minute, behavioral preferences. What is critical to realize is that these genetical influences are not confined to circumscribed components of behavior but extend their influence over broad and significant areas of human existence; areas that are commonly regarded as indicative of cultural differences.

In 1959 the American anthropologist Leslie A. White (1900-1975) provided a more useful definition of culture that avoided reference to either learning or the abstraction of behavior. In an essay entitled, *The Concept of Culture*, he proposed that when events and things are considered in relation to humans (or presumably apes), they constitute behavior but when they are considered in relation to one another they become culture. We may, for instance, use our knife and fork in a certain way and in so doing are merely behaving. If, however, we consider the manner in which knives and forks are used in relation to which meal is being served, we are contemplating elements of culture and not the component behaviors. As only the mind can conjure an independent relationship between things and events of extraneous origin then, according to White's definition, culture must be entirely the product of mental conditioning. It would *ipso facto,* be quite incorrect to apply the term culture to events and things that are only related through the instinctively driven behaviors because these behaviors are always inextricably bound to biological urges that are the driving force in all mammals.

In 1976, Richard Dawkins put forward the name *meme* for a unit of mentally transmittable, cultural information. He envisaged memes moving from one mind to another in the same manner as genes move from one generation to the next. Examples of memes are catch phrases, beliefs, attitudes, fashions or techniques. Just as higher-order concepts can help us communicate a set of interrelated ideas (*The Construction of Mind*: Chapter 3: Section 8), interrelated sets of memes could be transferred to another person in a cooperative group called *memeplexes* or *meme complexes*. In theory, memes that are conspicuously deleterious to the success of a generation will not be taken up by the next but will become "extinct" in preference to new memes that are of more adaptive value.

The coinage of the term meme gives explicit definition to the cognitively-mediated transference of behavior that is independent of genes. The term itself does not, however, help us delineate the contribution of genes to human behavior from the contribution of learning, mimicry and imitation. Memes do, however, provide a means of differentiating between two cultures. Consider the marked attitudinal differences towards the fostering of creativity and achievement, that distinguishes the people of European ancestry who inhabit the USA from those who inhabit Australia. Both societies are very wealthy and both have been in existence for only 2 or 3 centuries (8 to 12 generations). Yet these societies have radically different attitudes towards the fostering of creativity and achievement. Firstly, Americans generally look upon their countrymen as capable of great achievements whereas, aside from sport, Australians have little confidence in the abilities of their countrymen and often denigrate or simply ignore individuals who show great potential or aptitude – a deep-seated attitude, long known as the *tall poppy syndrome*. Secondly, rich Americans donate hundreds of billions of dollars to institutions, charities and the arts and sciences in their country, while, on a *per capita* basis, wealthy Australians contribute less than 25% of their American counterparts. Thirdly, as the archetypal *meritocracy*, America makes every effort to attract talented people, consults and backs its experts, shows respect for their efforts and values leadership. In contrast, aside from sport, Australians are so indifferent to the achievements and abilities of their countrymen that many tens of thousands of the most talented and intelligent individuals opt to live and work overseas in the service of more encouraging, forward-looking, go-ahead and less apologetic societies. Despite its wealth and its sophisticated intellectual heritage, Australia, with its blundering, faction-serving, political system and deeply embedded, inferiority complexes, is at risk of becoming the archetypal *mediocracy*.

The question is, do these differences reflect differences in the genetical constitution of these two groups or are they indicative of settlement by groups of humans conditioned with radically different memeplexes? The Europeans who pioneered North America were freemen, while the first Australian colonies were established by convicts who worked as slaves under the authority of what weer mostly cruel and despotic rejects from the British establishment. Thus, there is good reason to believe that the people who founded these two societies were subject to very different conditioning – one fostering memes related to proactive effort and the other memes related to forced labor and punishment. Of the Europeans who settled North America and Australia, the former were composed of many individuals from continental Europe while the latter were mostly from Britain. A very high percentage of modern Europeans carry genes that characterize the locality inhabited by their ancestors. Thus, there is also reason to suspect that differences in both the attitudes and behavior of people from different parts of Europe might, at least partially, reflect genetical differences that influence the expression of things like, empathy, language, intelligence, attention, mood, aggression, fear, gambling, nurturing and a predisposition to addiction or promiscuity. Ultimately, what so conspicuously distinguishes the Caucasian cultures of the USA and Australia are the distinctive differences in the history of their thoughts, differences to which both nature or nurture may contribute.

What does raise all manner of quandaries regarding the determination of culture is the prominence of mimicry and imitation in fashioning the behavior of both apes and humans. We have already seen how these phenomena may play an unprecedented part in the transmission of complex behavioral patterns in prehumans (*The Methodology of Mimicry*: Chapter 5: Section 6). It is blatantly obvious that mimicry, imitation and particularly, program-level imitation, must each play a vital part in the generational transmission of stereotyped, behavioral and attitudinal patterns. Even what we presently know regarding the origins of each aspect of human behavior is sufficient to seriously challenge the plenipotentiary role of mentation in the construction and maintenance of what we call a culture.

Just as the adopted child gravitates towards the *modus operandi* of its natural parents, the culturally displaced child will be inadvertently drawn towards the culture of its natural parents. All societies contain radicals who, like the alien philosopher, operate preferentially on an assemblage of memes that are conspicuously different from those that govern the thoughts and actions of the majority of their countrymen. It seems that at least some of the conceptual frameworks on which memes are based, do have a genetically conferred stability that can inure them even from the incessant pressures of societal conditioning. History records many instances of one culture invading and dominating another. Yet even when the memes of the dominant culture have been enforced through draconian laws, this alone has *never*, in recorded history, enabled the complete transference of a culture prior to extensive interbreeding and the consequent mixing of genes. Examples are legion but perhaps none is better than the continuing cultural rifts, that even today, separate African Americans from their Caucasian counterparts. Despite having elected a black president of mixed racial heritage, America remains a deeply racist society. For the individual in a foreign environment, memes and customs can be easily copied but this rarely, if ever, masks his or her inherently preferred *modus operandi* that, in their country of origin, would typically be highly compatible with the prevailing culture. The effective integration of diverse cultures will only be achieved after prolonged interbreeding and not, ill considered, idealistic theories or forced policies of multiculturalism. Sadly, when this has finally happened, the vast diversity of humaity that so enriches our world will be gone forever.

The abstract mind provides a mental platform that is exclusively devoted to establishing second-order concepts from first-order concepts that have themselves been conjured by the three other division of the mind (Figure 8.3). These second-order concepts are essentially identical to memeplexes. It is this human ability to *metacognate* that is the true origin of culture. It follows that the complexity of a culture must be directly related to the mean power (size) of the abstract mind within any population. This explains why the emotionally intelligent hunter-gatherers only created relatively simplistic, animistic religions that are strongly linked to the realities of the natural world, while the Caucasians created Islam, Christianity, Judaism, Hinduism and Buddhism – religions that are so conceptually complex and highly metaphorical that they could only be the product of societies that are dominated by the abstract mind. Ultimately, the culture of a population constitutes a set of second- or higher-order concepts, concepts that, by their entirely ideological nature, can only be composed in the ether of abstract thought.

Finally, to appreciate how the human cortex creates culture, it is helpful to reconsider how *our comprehension of existence moves from sensation to perception to conception* (*Brain Size and Intelligence*: Chapter 2: Section 1). Typically, a single module in one of the cortex's perceptual areas will represent information derived from a network of modules each located in one or more of the cortex's primary sensory receiving areas. In the same way, each module in the cortex of the social, material or temporal mind will represent, as first-order concepts, the products of discrete networks of modules in the perceptual areas. Let us consider, for example, how our abstract mind (BA46) conceptualizes a stranger who is a dominant authority figure – a cultural entity found in many but not all societies. Presented with a threatening male, our social mind (BA9) might allocate a single module to integrate our perceptions of his gestural and body language with the response (fear) of our emotional centers. In the same instant, our material mind (BA47) may allocate a single module to represent the concept of an authority figure by drawing on perceptual areas that reveal the identity and rank of the person. In this manner our unfamiliar, unpredictable, authoritarian male is first represented as first-order concepts within both our social and material mind. If it is sufficiently important to survival, these first-order concepts will be sent to the abstract mind where they will be integrated into a *single* second-order concept of, for example, impersonal, enforcer of the law – a second-order concept that could be easily archived within a single module of the abstract mind. Through the networking of modules within the abstract mind, each second-order concept could be integrated and interrelated with other second-order concepts to create higher-order conceptual frameworks such as, in the above case, anarchy, the policed state or the protection of the weak. These second- and higher-order concepts, and the frameworks in which they participate, are the stuff of metacognition, the origin of all hypotheses, beliefs, ideologies and faiths as well as that most enigmatic entity of human existence that we call culture.

Chapter 3 - The Future

The Creation of Mind

"A hen is only an egg's way of making another egg." Samuel Butler (1835-1902). English Satirist, Critic and Author.

The mind begins as billions of living neurons waiting to be tuned to a particular form of information. Like all complex biological systems, this system is limited by the general need to conserve metabolic energy. Not only does neuronal activity have a high energy cost but at roughly 60,000 neurons per cubic millimeter, the cortex of the mind contains the highest density of neurons found in the biological world. During growth of the human nervous system, and particularly the cerebral cortex, there is an over production of neurons. As normal development progresses many neurons are eliminated. This attrition of neurons and their spurious connections is thought to represent the tuning of the brain's neural circuitry. Neurons that form "incorrect" connections are purged, while those that form "correct" connections are maintained. From a strictly behavioral standpoint we may therefore say that the human being is only the vehicle through which a human mind has opportunity to create another mind.

Let us imagine ten billion cortical neurons within the infant's maturing social mind regularly receiving information about two temporally related events, the mother's smile and the baby's satiation. By this stage genes have already spelled out the areal size of BA9 and the modular architecture of its internal circuitry. Within BA9 some neurons will respond to one input, some to another and some to both. Just as the bean counters in our economic system sack any employees who they believe are not productively occupied, the brain will try to minimize the expenditure of metabolic energy by eliminating unnecessary or unused neurons. We might imagine that those neurons that are retained will be those which, as a consequence of being activated by two sources instead of one, are simply used more often. Inevitably the survivors will be part of a complex neuronal circuit dedicated to the interactive nuances of the mother's smile and the infant's satiation. What remains within the infants developing mind is an essentially iconic representation of this archetypal relationship between mother and child – an icon that, across all humanity, symbolizes bonding. From that moment onwards, this icon becomes an experientially accessible, conceptual entity within higher consciousness, preserved forever within either a single or a discrete set of modules within the social mind (BA9) as the basic conceptual framework of nurture.

It is easy to see how essentially the same process is repeated with respect to the other realms of cognition. At puberty when the neuronal circuits of the abstract mind become physiologically mature, they are sent information about space and time from the cortex's perceptual areas the *dorsal stream*. Just as the circuits of the social mind organize themselves in response to information about the body language of others and the host's emotions, so the circuits of the abstract mind organize themselves around the intangible phenomena of space and time. However, unlike emotion and body language, space and time cannot be directly perceived or independently conceptualized. Like other intangible phenomena, space and time can only be represented as higher-order concepts that are dependent upon the integration of first-order concepts elaborated primarily within the social, material or temporal mind.

The material mind differs from the abstract mind in that its purpose is to create first-order concepts from perceptual information about the physical world, thereby establishing a conceptual basis for practicality. Perceptual information about the functional and symbolic identity of real things, including both objects and people, is delivered to the newly mature BA47 via the *ventral stream*. Slowly throughout mid-childhood the neural circuits of the material mind establish a format wherein objects and people are organized into functionally discrete groups that serve both practicality and language. As in all divisions of the mind (and probably all parts of the developing nervous system), the most powerful constraint over the developmental process will be the *minimization of energy expenditure* in terms of both the numbers of surviving nerve cells and, through what we might call the *paradigm of silence*, their activity.

The Construction of Mind

"Kasparov....claims to see into opponents' minds during play, intuiting and exploiting their plans, insights, and oversights. In ordinary chess computers, he reports a mechanical predictability, stemming from their undiscriminating but limited look ahead and absence of long-term strategy. In Deep Blue, to his consternation, he saw instead an 'alien intelligence'.... In these cases, the evidence for an intelligent mind lies in the machine's performance, not its makeup." Hans Moravec, American Research Professor in Robotics, in reference to the comments of Russian Grand Chess Master, Gary Kasparov, about playing the supercomputer Big Blue. From: *Robot, Mere Machine to Transcendent Mind*. Oxford Univ. Press 1999.

There are those who are convinced that the failure of artificial intelligence research to create a cognitively-able machine is because thought requires consciousness. As an element of human experience thought is indeed an element of human consciousness. It is, however, eminently possible that consciousness itself is an epiphenomenon. Indeed there is some evidence that our awareness of what our cortex is doing actually lags behind its actions by up to half a second (*The Experience of Mechanism*: Chapter 4: Section 2). If this is so then the experience we know as thought is actually a posthumous rendition of integrative mental processes that have already happened. It follows that our belief that because we have an awareness of our thoughts, the decisions they come to are under our influence, may be quite spurious. Just because we experience our thoughts, emotions, moods, perceptions and sensations does not mean we can control them anymore than the schizophrenic can intentionally prevent the mental chaos. The direct consequence of this separation of the experience of thought from its underlying mechanistic processes, is that there is no reason to believe that a thinking machine needs to be "aware" anymore than a sophisticated robot needs to be "aware" of its vast array of sensors or its central processors. We do not need to recreate consciousness in order to make a thinking machine. A bionic mind is a real possibility, though its creation will, like the atom bomb, the silicon microchip and genetic engineering, inevitably have the consequences of, once again, opening Pandora's Box.

Our new insights into the neurobiology of the mind mean that we are on the threshold of being able to create a *bionic mind* in hardware, software or mathematical algorithms. Contemporary robots can sense various physical and even social cues in the environment, integrate these with a large memory store of information, and respond by activating one or more of a number of preset behavior patterns to achieve one or more preset goals. In contrast, a robot with a bionic mind could have an independence of decision based on an ever-growing library of concepts that embody all significant aspects of its social, practical and even ideational environment. Such a robot could carry out the general objectives of its human controllers without need for specific instruction in the multitude of small decisions that are involved in actualizing any significant plan. If it is one of a fleet of similar robots, it may enlist the assistance of other robots, instructing them at the conceptual level as to their overall part in procedures. This transference of information at the conceptual level resembles the so-called program-level imitation by which young mountain gorillas learn from their mothers how to prepare stinging nettles by adopting the strategy of the procedure rather than precisely copying the actions of their mother (*Imitation*: Chapter 2: Section 6).

The cortex of the mind is, like all other cortex, composed from modules. In a human the amount of cortex allocated to each component of the mind (BAs 9, 10, 47 and 46) is quite limited in the number of modules it can accommodate within its boundaries. Indeed if we look at the relative size of the social mind (BA9) and the abstract mind (BA46) we find enormous variation, such that in some individuals one area may be twice as large and contain twice as many modules as the same area in another individual. Oddly there has, as yet been little quantification of the variation in the areal size of BA46 or BA9 in humans. However, a crude estimate of the area of cortex allocated to abstract mind (BA46) taken from published illustrations of 5 human brains would suggest that BA46 ranges from 100 to 400 mm^2. If we use a figure of 0.25 mm^2 for the area of a single module (*The Micro-organization of Consciousness*: Chapter 2: Section: 2) then we can estimate that the abstract mind can contain between 400 and 1,600 modules.

How can the seemingly vast complexity and diversity of our perceptual and cognitive experiences be generated by relatively small numbers of modules? The answer must be that individual modules participate in unique networks of modules that evoke an equally unique perceptual or cognitive experience. For the sake of argument, let us consider that only 2.5 mm^2 of cortex is allocated to the material mind (BA47) for conceptualizing the physical world and that this small patch of cortex can accommodate only 10 modules (*The Allocation of Consciousness*: Chapter 2: Section 2). Despite this small number of modules, the number of ways of combining these modules is 10! or 10x9x8x7x6x5x4x3x2x1. Even within this tiny area there are 3,628,800 different, though not wholly independent, networks available for representing concepts relating to either the parametric (BA47, left hemisphere) or symbolic (BA47, right hemisphere) properties of objects and people. What is, however, revealing of the inherent power of the cortex's organization, is that if we were to add an eleventh module to this system, the number of combinations of modules increases by a factor of 11 from 3, 628,800 to 11! or 39,916,800. To generalize, the addition of a single module to any cortical area will increase the number of combinations of modules within that area by a factor equal to the new total number of modules.

In reality each of the four cortical areas that compose the human mind are probably always at least 10 times 2.5 mm^2 in area, and therefore contain at least 100 modules that could be interconnected in an astronomically large number (100!) of ways. The addition of a single module would increase the number of available combinations by a factor of 101. These observations, along with the enormous variation in the size of BAs 9, 10, 46 and 47 between different individuals, underscore the vast differences in cognitive ability that must exist between different individuals – differences that determine both the relative computational power of each division of their mind and the magnitude of their general intelligence.

An entirely different approach to constructing a mind emerges from our ever-increasing knowledge about the functions of particular human genes coupled with our growing aptitude at genetic engineering. Already scientists have successfully used genetic engineering to create mice with a brain twice the normal size and to manipulate the size of particular areas in the cortex of the mouse. In less that a decade we will know the details of the genetical control of the size of Brodmann's areas in the human cortex. As we have seen, altering the size of the emotional centers should enable some modification of the balance between the urge to nurture and the urge to fight. Similarly, by altering the size of the perceptual and/or motor areas it will be possible to create people with augmented skills covering music, sport and a host of vocationally significant technical aptitudes. However, most important is the very real possibility of adjusting the size of BAs 9, 10, 46 or 47 in order to manipulate the absolute and relative power of each domain of thought. The doubling in size of any of these areas will not only double the number of cortical modules but vastly increase the number of combinations of modules that might be used to represent individual concepts. The result will be an individual with exceptional aptitude in that particular cognitive domain. It is likely that autistic savants with almost incomprehensible abilities at temporal calculations, 3-dimensional art and remembering the words, if not the grammar, of many languages, represent rare cases wherein some of the cortex normally allocated to the social mind has presumably been taken over by another domain of cognition.

Through genetic engineering it should be possible to markedly increase one domain of intelligence without compromising the amount of cortex allocated to the other domains. Our present knowledge of personality reveals that people's behavior reflects their dominant domain of cognition. Thus, we can presume that when one domain of the mind is enlarged over all the others, the individual will spontaneously use their great cognitive advantage whenever possible. When that domain of intelligence is relevant to the problem in hand we might expect a rapid and novel solution that may never have been "discovered" by ordinary mortals. The only sobering thought is that, if they are fertile, these genetically engineered geniuses could spawn a new breed of humans who would be far more intelligent than ordinary humans yet still driven by their biological urges to compete with others in the eternal struggle for dominance and survival.

The Evolution of Politics and Economics
"Great minds discuss ideas,
Ordinary minds discuss events [& facts],
Small minds discuss people."
Eleanor Roosevelt (1884-1962). First Lady USA, 1933-1945.

The hierarchical organization of power is seen throughout the world of mammals. Hierarchical organization is particularly obvious in packs of wolves or dogs and colonies of monkeys, where the winner of physical contests is regarded as the leader and the losers compete for their own place in the peck order. Hierarchy is good for a species as it ensures that the strongest or most intelligent individuals get more matings and so have an increased opportunity to pass on their advantageous genes. Both chimps and bonobos form hierarchically organized societies that are ruled by a dominant or alpha male. Both species also recognize an alpha female whose emergence from the ranks is rarely associated with serious aggression. In the chimps, the position of alpha male is fiercely contested in battles with the strongest individuals. In vivid contrast, aggression surrounding the appointment of an alpha male in bonobos is minimized by a presumably innate social mechanism whereby the son of the alpha female typically assumes the alpha male status. This makes a lot of sense in terms of natural selection, for in a society where monogamy is never observed, the only obvious genetical relationship is that between mother and child. The appointment of the alpha female's son to the dominant position of alpha male ensures the passage her genes to the next generation.

Some degree of hierarchical organization seems to be innate within most mammalian species. Nevertheless, when it comes to the governing of human populations, hierarchy is not always a conspicuous element. The Navajo Indians, the Hottentots, Mbuti Pygmies, Kung San and the Inuit are all said to be societies in which distinctions of wealth, power and status are minimized. Instead of violence, antisocial behaviors often attract ridicule and ultimately social ostracization that, in a hostile environment, can be tantamount to death. Peaceful cooperation and cohesiveness in the face of danger are critical factors. It seems that within each individual, the powerful social dictates of emotional intelligence and its byproduct, politics, do not promote the instinctive drive towards individual power and status but are instead directed at a communal resolution of conflict. Like the social constructs of captive bonobo societies, the atypical social organization of these human societies is most likely generated by inherent characteristics within the makeup of their psyche. Unfortunately, the majority of human populations are quite different, in that they readily form definite hierarchies, typically ruled by, a domineering and ruthless, if not psychopathic, leader (*The Evolution of Inhumanity*: Chapter 4: Section 5).

The great message of primatology, anthropology and neuroscience is that intelligence is not the exclusive province of humans and that some basic level of cognition probably existed for tens of millions of years before we evolved. Thought is a process that provides an organism with the opportunity to respond to, modify or override what would otherwise be automatically expressed as relatively stereotyped, instinctual, behavior patterns. In contrast, instinct is, by definition, the compendium of innate drives that generate those recognizable patterns of behavior that are entirely triggered by the immediate circumstances. In the presence of a mind, the emotional centers that house the cortical substrates of instinct are rarely allowed to influence behavior without first being integrated with a previously established, mentally elaborated, set of rules and principles. In this process, instinctual drives serve as the generative, motivational force underlying the otherwise cognitive creation of behavioral strategy. These observations enable us a clearer insight into the origin of our obsession with politics and our fascination with politicians. In particular, it has been shown that much of the social behavior of apes is conspicuously cognitive in origin and so is not limited to the instinctual behavior patterns characteristic of lower mammals. Instead, the behavior of apes follows distinct lines of socially orientated logic – lines that, to our eternal amusement, are easily recognizable as familiar constructs that form the core of emotional intelligence in all humans. Nevertheless, we can find little within the behavior of apes that prompts us to imagine them doing tasks that require a high level of practicality or planning. For apes, in general, the primary source of cognition and the architect of the strategic elements of their behavior is emotional intelligence. It is as a direct consequence of this that their forte is politics. Politics has the potential to achieve hierarchical order without serious injury or the loss of life. When social maneuvering reaches a stalemate, the bonobos are, like humans, more likely to oil the wheels of politics with sex, whereas the chimps, again like humans, more often resort to physical violence.

Unfortunately, this seemingly neat correlation between acquired behavior and the mind versus innate behavior and our instinctual drives, requires one very important caveat, namely that the existence of emotional memories shows that much learning takes place within those centers which drive those otherwise stereotyped, innate elements of behavior. Furthermore, the boundaries between the innate and the acquired also become less distinct when we consider that, in thinking organisms genes powerfully influence the progressive maturation and, ultimately the structural composition of the mind. Essentially, the smaller, less powerful mind of the chimps and bonobos forms the intermediate tier of our psyche, essentially constituting the generative core of human cognition. As an archaic element of the human mind, this entity is responsible for those cognitive strategies that are fundamental elements of our social behavior – primordial strategies that would have been as conspicuous in the behavior of our earliest hominid ancestors as they are to the behavior of the living apes.

It follows, that within the human psyche, we may identify a tripartite hierarchy of labor. At the lowest tier are our emotional centers that are responsible for the elaboration of the instinctual elements of our behavior, thereby binding us indelibly to the animal world. Above this, on the second tier, sits our social mind that generates our emotional and social intelligence, a modicum of which so conspicuously drives the humanistic aspects of ape social behavior and enables the empathy most people feel with apes, monkeys and even dogs. On the third highest tier is a conglomerate of our practical, temporal and abstract domains of intelligence that so conspicuously distinguish humanity from all other lifeforms. Yet even here we need to observe that our separation is not complete, for the apes and monkeys have in their cortices each of the areas of Brodmann that, in the much larger human cortex, engage the practical, temporal and hypothetical realms.

The role of mentality in monkey behavior is still to be elucidated. It is, however, clear that the behavior of apes contains many of the components of the cognitively driven behavior of preoperational children (1 to 6 yo) that is dependent upon the integrity of the social mind (BA9) and is almost entirely devoted to the interpretation and development of social behavior. Like the preoperational child, apes are skilled at deception, social manipulation and divining the intentions of others. The *modus operandi* of a child in the early parts of the preoperational phase is the product of the middle tier of our psyche that constitutes the core elements of our emotional and social intelligence, which we share with the apes. It is from this very basic level of human cognition that emerges the politician and the cerebral energy that drives the irrational, emotive business of politics.

Where then does humanity err? The answer to this critical question does not lie in philosophy or religion or science alone but in a broader, all-encompassing comprehension of human nature. Like our primate ancestors, we are highly social. However, as a consequence of our penchant for the practical, we have to deal with the world on two fronts; one involving our relationships with others and one involving our performance in the physical world. Like social animals, humans overcome the inevitable power struggles involved in coordinating large numbers of individuals, by establishing a leader. Like the apes we seem inexplicably drawn to the appointment of an alpha human, usually a male, who we hope will take responsibility for our individual and collective well being.

Historically humans have chosen their leaders on the basis of their physical strength, their relationship to the previous leader or the wishes of the majority of the people. These different procedures reflect three quite different ideologies. The first, argues that a leader must be physically strong and sufficiently intelligent to take charge in the hunt or the battle. The second emphasizes the importance of inheritance, implying, often incorrectly, that the sons and daughters of a ruler will inherit his or her leadership qualities. The third, posits that, because someone has the ability to sway the hearts and minds of a majority of the populace, they must actually have the aptitude to lead. Of these three alternatives, only the first holds any promise of success and then only because a person who is willing to lead in battle can at least be said to have the courage and commitment to lay down their own life in the defense of their subjects and, of course, their privileged position. The second alternative is obviously based on a misunderstanding of the inheritance of personality. History is filled with examples showing that leadership qualities are not necessarily passed on to the children of an incumbent leader. Moreover, DNA comparisons reveal what we might call the *bonobo factor* – that one in five children is unrelated to their assumed father. Finally, the third alternative, rule by an elected member of the public, is quite simply, absurd, even though it is a principle upon which all modern democracies are based. What may, in its inception, have seemed an egalitarian way of establishing leadership, soon became corrupted by the sheer power and influence of monied interests over both, the appointment of, and decisions made by, democratically elected politicians. Even the most cursory glance at the nature of personality shows very clearly that he or she who can court others is someone who enjoys being courted by others and consequently lacks the independence of thought so critical to the role of leader.

Democracy fails because most humans address the choosing of a leader through completely illogical, personal value judgments, elaborated primarily within their social mind. Yet when we reflect on the sort of person we would like as a leader, we naturally think of someone who has a singular commitment to doing the best he or she can for our country. More than anything we are seeking an independent mind that will not be swayed by financial contributions or bribes, courted by flattery or biased by moral attitudes or deep-seated religious beliefs. So often we hear the term benevolent dictatorship, in reference to a hypothetical country run by a powerful, honest and humanitarian individual. Unfortunately, the political path to power and influence is not one that selects for a candidate's capacity to make the unbiased, logical decisions one might expect from a sensible, rational, intelligent and honest leader. Instead, people choose the candidate they feel comfortable with, someone who gives seemingly personal, reassurances of our longevity, wealth and safety. A clear example of this principle concerns what is known as the *timbre of the voice*. The timbre is composed of deep, barely perceptible sounds with frequencies below 500 cycles per second. When all higher frequencies are filtered out of speech, all words are lost and there remains only a low hum. The frequency of this hum varies between people. In the course of a conversation the timbre of different participants tend to converge in a manner indicative of rank or status. Thus, the timbre of a low ranking or less confidence individual will move towards the timbre of a high ranking, dominant individual. Only if the dominant individual is focused on making the less dominant person feel comfortable, does the former's timbre move towards the timbre of the latter. Successful candidates for the US presidency tend to have a dominant timbre, one exception being George W. Bush whose voice contained a slightly subordinate pattern, reflective perhaps of the marginal and possibly non-existent majority that saw him elected to the presidency. Normally the timbre of a candidate's voice is, like body language, an important determinant of electoral success, yet neither has any significance when it comes to making the important decisions associated with leadership. When we put aside our ideologies and look objectively at what emerges from our democratic systems, we find only the politician.

The Oxford dictionary defines a politician as "a person who acts in a manipulative and devious way, typically to gain advancement", while it defines politics as the activity of seeking power and status. Similarly, the Macquarie Concise Dictionary defines a politician as "a seeker or holder of public office who is more concerned to win favor or to retain power than to maintain principles". Clearly, these definitions could just as easily apply to the behavior of both preoperational children and apes. This is not a coincidence but a reflection of the importance of emotional and social intelligence to the business of politics – a reflection that is surely an indictment of the means through which we establish leadership.

Politicians welcome change. Change provides opportunity for movement and manipulation. Changes enable politicians to impress the populace with new "initiatives" that display, and often reinforce, their power over others. Primatologists have observed similar behaviors amongst our closest relatives. One example is the report of an alpha male chimp that would dislodge huge boulders and send them thundering down a dry riverbed. He would then sit down and wait while his subjects moved slowly towards him, bobbing, grunting and groveling to express their respect. Human leaders also instigate rituals that reinforce their subordinate's vision of them as all-powerful. The most bizarre example of this is a ritual devised by Saddam Hussein, the recently executed tyrant of Iraq, who required male subordinates to greet him with a kiss under his armpit – an area known to secrete pheromones that sexually attract females. Like dictators, politicians are also given to asserting their power over the populace by displays of military strength and even by making war on other countries, while condoning open discrimination against minority groups within their own country. In this process they typically use emotive language to arouse our inherent xenophobic feelings and to establish in the minds of the populace, out-groups that become the scapegoats of all societal ills (*The Nature and Nurture of Racism*: Chapter 2: Section 1). On a great many issues, modern politicians choose only to defend those moral issues that they believe will bring them the most votes. Cognizant of another of Napoleon's insights, that "a soldier will fight long and hard for a bit of colored ribbon", politicians, like dictators and kings before them, establish rituals that embroil a hierarchically organized populace in ceremonies that emphasize and celebrate their high office. While in power, they typically orchestrate scenarios where they, or those that support them, are edified, while those that oppose them are publicly humiliated, imprisoned, tortured or killed. Citations from the Turkish parliament of show how the countries leaders and politicians devised the protocol for murdering of 2.1 million Armenian men, women and children. What began as the egalitarian and even altruistic policies of democracy has, in the hands of politicians, become little more than a smoke screen, behind which the rich consistently become richer and the ever increasing numbers of poor are obliged to fight over what little is left.

History provides an abundance of evidence that, as leaders, elected politicians are no better, and arguably worse, than the kings, czars, emperors, military dictators or even warlords. While royalty has the independence of wealthy and powerful origins, the politician usually has to rise from the ranks by honing his or her manipulative skills to the business of gaining the power, wealth and status, which most people incorrectly believe to be indicative of leadership abilities. The warlords of modern Africa, like those of medieval China and Mongolia, slaughter and brutalize large numbers of innocent people. Their contribution to human misery is, however, miniscule where compared to the 76 million murdered in the Peoples Republic of China and 62 million murdered in the Soviet Gulag.

Bereft of any real qualification for leadership, the politician is obliged to solicit and accept the financial backing of the rich and powerful, often compromising or even surrendering any serious convictions he or she might have that conflict with self-orientated interests of such people. Politicians, who attempt to achieve high office by adhering to sensible, egalitarian principles either fail or are assassinated by parties unknown. In contrast, politicians who befriend industrialists, tolerate large-scale organized crime and, by the politically and bureaucratically sanctioned bribery of media moguls, seek to control the dissemination of information, are likely to achieve and retain high office. Once appointed, their whole effort is to manipulate the media, the laws, the interpretation of the laws, moral attitudes and even electoral boundaries, all with the singular objective of getting re-elected with an even more powerful mandate at their disposal. Nowhere are the powers of mimicry and imitation more evident. It is said that, just as the young criminal mind is educated by seasoned criminals within our prisons, it is only possible to learn to be a successful politician by serving an apprenticeship in politics. In only a few centuries, politics has become a profession in its own right, a profession so bizarre that our leaders are often little more than amateur actors who are physically groomed to appeal to the majority of the public and who are told what to say and how to say it by public relations experts. But perhaps the most damning aspect of politics is that, almost by definition, it involves interpersonal competition. Most people would agree that the job of running an entire state or country is highly demanding. It is therefore surely a matter of concern that even after their successful election, career politicians in many countries are still driven to compete with the opposition far more than they are driven to become knowledgeable or even aware of the critical issues facing modern governments. This phenomenon surely reaches its zenith in the Australian parliament where during any sitting one can hear professional politicians literally spending hours and untold quantities of taxpayer's money, sniping at one another in a manner not unlike that of a classroom of undisciplined, preschool children. Beside the irresistible opportunity to engage in one-upmanship, real issues pale into insignificance if not obscurity. These activities are motivated by the singular consideration of how many votes can be accrued by successfully putting down members of the opposing party – a wholly destructive objective that has nothing to do with sensible decision making or the process of effective and efficient leadership. This is not surprising because, particularly outside Europe, it is not hard to find intellectually bankrupt presidents and prime ministers who (a) have no knowledge, training or talent at running a country, (b) are conspicuously biased towards the demands of big business and (c) are, with regard to maintaining their power and position, ultimately ruthless.

How could this have come about from the well-intentioned proposals of democracy? The answer to this can be seen looming out of our primate heritage. As we have seen, male monkeys will forgo a food reward for a glimpse of a picture of a high ranking male or the hindquarters of a female monkey. Similarly, chimps show a clear awareness of social organization, when they preferentially share food with their "friends" and selectively exclude sharing with individuals who have failed to share on previous occasions. Though orchestrated by the mind, such behaviors clearly reflect the instinctual drive for power, status and sex.

Humans, and particularly male humans, are likewise irrepressibly drawn to imagery of "important" people or provocative images of females. Humans also do favors for their friends and relatives. When George W. Bush became president of the United States he immediately appointed his friends and relatives to variously highly paid, important positions, setting an example of nepotism that was subsequently followed by some of his highly influential underlings. The unification of power, sex and money in the 3rd or Power Chakra (*Manipura*) gives metaphorical expression to the commonality of these rewards in all humans (*The Origins of War, Oppression and Libido*: Chapter 4: Section 5). Given the ability of politicians to manipulate others and their consistent orientation towards these essentially reptilian emotions, it is difficult to find rational reasons that explain why ordinary citizens are so willing to trust them to deal honestly or effectively the running of their communities, states or countries. All we can be sure of is that, given the personality types most likely to succeed in the game of politics, our democratically elected leaders of the future will continue to be drawn from a pool of people who have little of the knowledge, training or ethical commitment required to lead and to maintain domestic and global peace in the face of rapidly shrinking world resources.

It is ironic that while human behavior is so heavily dependent on the mind, we choose our leaders with little concern for their overall knowledge, training or intellectual abilities. Listening to election rhetoric one gets an impression that humans are seeking a savior, who rather than having abilities to deal with real problems, is, like the kings and queens of old or the heroes of our religious mythologies, simply empowered by a "divine connection". This is, of course, complete rubbish. There are no supermen, no superwomen and, as history shows, no saviors. People who seek high political office usually do so because they see opportunity to use their abilities to manipulate the emotions of others in order to attain wealth, power and status. It is extraordinary that, at election time, most humans happily surrender their power to whichever candidate's rhetoric makes them feel the most secure, whether he or she be an actor or a failed businessperson. In the West, we require people to be professionally trained to do the simplest jobs, yet we nonchalantly put our nations in the hands of people who typically have no deep comprehension of history, geography, philosophy, psychology, economics, science, technology, education, the arts or health or the multitude of other disciplines which have critical relevance to running a country, relating to its people and dealing with the ever-compounding issues of the modern world.

Instead of seeking to serve the people, politicians typically contrive all manner of schemes that give advantage to their wealthy, powerful supporters. Some even foster global conflicts to maintain the sales of munitions manufacturers who have supported their political ambitions. The system is so entrenched in the governmental and bureaucratic fabric of nations that it is impossible to see how it can be peaceably dismantled. Each time it is brought into question, promises of revisions are no sooner made than they are forgotten as a consequence of politicians using their power over the media to create, new, completely artificial crises that can be used to justify maintaining the *status quo*. Life goes on, one war following another, the attendant butchery, torture and abject poverty hidden behind a façade of propaganda, composed and broadcast by an essentially enslaved media – propaganda not aimed at an alien aggressor, but carefully composed to convince an ever more poorly educated populace that they should continue surrendering their individual power to their democratically-elected leaders.

If we address the issue of leadership from the position of competency, then it is relatively easy to envisage a better way of running countries. As the human mind is singularly responsible for circumstances in the modern world, it is to the human mind and human intelligence that we must look for solutions. The key to the human mind is education. While the mind is the physical substrate of intelligence, education is the universal language of the intellect. Yet, when it comes to the most important jobs, a perusal of the qualifications of the world's leaders would suggest that we do not really believe education and training to be relevant to their work.

Let us imagine an alternative system where to run for parliament, or congress, or to stand for prime minister or president requires attaining a high level of education in the appropriate disciplines. In this new system the aspiring leader must enter university, spend four years completing a special undergraduate program involving subjects specifically selected to give them insight into the many disciplines that are critically relevant to the running of countries and participating in international relations. If they do outstandingly well and still wish to enter government they must enroll in a doctoral program and conduct research in one broad area of fundamental importance to national or international affairs. Only upon successful completion of their doctorate can they stand for office. By the time they are ready for this, most will be in their late 20s, highly educated and have a deep commitment to both the truth and rational decision that will make it less likely that they will be as easily corrupted as their present-day counterparts.

Along with the politician, the economic system represents another self-defeating element of human culture that emerges from our evolutionary past. As humans became increasingly independent of nature and increasingly dependent upon technology and science, it was to be expected that the trading of natural resources and labor would be replaced by a generalized value system such as money. Both monkeys and apes are able to conceptualize reward as something more than a transient pleasurable experience. Not only do male monkeys forego food rewards in order to see pictures of dominant individuals or sexual imagery but trained female monkeys will cease work if they see other individuals given a greater reward than they are receiving. In both cases it is clear that, at some higher level, a food reward becomes a negotiable unit of currency that can buy a circumscribed amount of effort or the thrill of seeing a dominant individual or a provocative image. When we get to the apes, the game is raised to encompass their intimate social and family relationships. With a larger social mind, chimps are able to moderate their protests over inequities in food rewards such that they object only when a greater reward is given to a stranger but not when it is bestowed upon individuals with whom they have had a long, close relationship (*Maneuvering in Society*: Chapter 3: Section 6).

No matter how we interpret these findings it is clear that here, amongst the living non-human primates, is the beginning of what we call the *economic system* - the manipulation of wealth in accord with a cognitively contrived set of principles. In human society, economics has become so pervasive that virtually everything is negotiable at the right price. Trapped in the economic system most individuals are obliged to expend their life's energies largely for the benefit of the rich and powerful and a generalized material reward called *money*. The food rewards of the chimps and monkeys are to them as money is to us - both may be traded for sex and glimpses of power and both are voluntarily surrendered to close friends and relatives. What is different is that food holds its value while the value of money is manipulated by economists who serve the rich and powerful. It is food and not money that is an integral part of the web of life, just as it is food and not money that is the governing factor in the most critical of all equations – that which embodies the balance of nature and contains the unalterable rules that guarantee the preservation of life.

The great problem with the economic system is that not only does it generalize reward but it also generalizes resources. To the economist sitting in his New York office money is the substance that makes the world go round. Superficially it does not seem to matter where it comes from, particularly because most of today's humanity appears to hold the entirely incorrect, cavalier belief that monetary schemes are of themselves and have no impact on the real world. This of course is a convenient western illusion. Humans live upon the Earth and so will inevitably be obliged to look to its natural resources for their sustenance. To the economist the resource, be it a forest, the skins of a rare animal or an oil rich coral reef, is also just money. Through the economic system decisions are completely isolated from the strictures of the natural world. It is estimated that by the year 2040 our economic interests will have destroyed all the natural habitats that support our closest relatives, the apes. Environmentalists predict that within the next two years what remains of the massive rainforests of Borneo – the last stronghold of the orangutan – will have been totally destroyed under the supervision, no less, of the Indonesian Government. Having equated all rewards and resources with a quantity of money, economists have moved on to create banks, trusts, superannuation policies, a vast variety of taxes and tax loop holes that virtually obscure the fundamental relationship between basic resources and the natural world. The common person has absolutely no possibility of understanding this system, far less having any effect upon it. He or she is simply a pawn in the game of money. More than any other man-made system, economics is the enemy of nature.

The Mental Limitations of Humanity
"Intelligence is what we use when we don't know what to do." Jean Piaget (1896-1980). Swiss Child Psychologist, who showed that children go through preset stages of cognitive development.

The mind is an instrument of extremes. This follows naturally because the purpose of the mind is to compare and contrast alternative interpretations and strategies and, in so doing, to swing from one extreme to the other. It is rare to meet people, and particularly young people, who do not take a definite side on every issue. To be moderate in view, to seek a balance and ultimately to manifest wisdom, are anathemas to the opportunistic values of modern society, which consistently and incorrectly interprets decisiveness as intelligence. Yet nowhere is the Buddha's insistence of the middle road more important than in our attitudes, ideas and beliefs. The practice of meditation has the singular purpose of stilling the mind – a state often referred to as "no mind". The operative principle here is that when one has trained one's mind to remain without thought for even ten minutes, then one is far less likely to be drawn to the extremes of thought that are the substance of bias. Steeped in our belief-orientated religions the middle way hardly seems to be an option. Yet not only is this a possible path for each person, but it is mandatory if one wishes to annul the anxiety and stress of championing the extremes of opinion.

The middle way is the way of trained mind. Many physiological studies have shown the physical and mental benefits of regular, lifelong meditation. Although meditation through prayer is part of Christianity, Judaism and Islam, the direct experience of "no mind" it is rarely sought, and even more rarely achieved, by the individuals within these religions. Unfortunately, the emphasis on good and evil, faith in ancient scriptures and a necessarily hypothetical God is incongruous with the concept of the middle road. Few people appreciate that the quest to empty the mind is an endeavor to annul its trivial pursuits and plumb its vast potential for intelligently, metered action. Whereas we might hope that, irrespective of our race, creed or class, religion might encourage us to extend caring and compassion to each other, its major influence instills in its practitioners fundamental attitudes that are repeatedly used to justify racial and religious intolerance, the mutilation, exploitation and rape of innocent men, women and children, the destruction of alien cultures, mass murder and torture, on an utterly astounding scale. The human mind, the most complex and fascinating piece of living tissue ever to evolve, has yet to be harnessed to the well being of humanity.

The recent history of humanity is one of incredible feats of intellectual achievement. This so-called *ascent of man* has reflected the evolution of the human mind not only throughout a long succession of our, increasingly intelligent, hominid ancestors but also since the appearance of our own species 200 kya. Until the evolution of the more advanced primates, our celestial observer studying the ways of animals could never have envisaged that a phenomenon called cognition would transform the Earth. Like each and every one of our hominid ancestors the first modern humans were obliged to lead a hunter-gatherer existence. Nevertheless, in less than 200,000 years, or 10,000, 20-year generations, certain geographically circumscribed, human populations have created an almost totally urban life wherein the natural world is barely visible. So great is this transition that even the food stuffs and building materials of modern civilizations bear little resemblance to the natural products that still sustain today's hunter-gatherers.

Unfortunately, alongside their discoveries and technical achievements, humanity has maintained an unparalleled appetite for inflicting pain and death upon its own kind. In the revisions of his classic text, Death by Government (1994), the great historian of genocide, Rudolph Joseph Rummel gives us the horrendous details of wars, revolutions, genocide, tyranny and man-made famines that in the 20th century alone caused the death of an estimated 262,000,000 men, women and children, only one seventh of whom, were military personnel. This figure is roughly equal to the total number of humans in existence only 2 kya. To this crucible of darkness we can add the suffering of at least another billion people who have been so mutilated and psychologically damaged that they are no longer functional members of human society. Given our hostile, self-orientated ideologies, ruthless behaviors, burgeoning population, ever-shrinking resources and the political tomfoolery of modern times, there is every reason to predict that we will continue to trespass against each other until we enter a period of unparalleled self-destructiveness.

When put into the broad perspective of biological fitness, the propensity of *Homo sapiens* to use their intelligence to annul the regulatory forces of nature and to make war on each other can only be regarded as grossly dysfunctional. If our rank exploitation of nature continues for another century and we are unable to arrest the man-made escalation of temperature, there is the extreme likelihood that the lack of land, food and fresh water will, one way or another, cause the eradication of several billion people. These ills, like the unique virtues of humanity, are attributable to a single element - the human mind. In comparison, the mind of the apes is a relatively simple organ that gives them a modicum of ideational ability but is almost entirely usurped in the satiation of their instinctual needs. Endowed with a mind that is much larger than the mind of the apes, the first modern humans embarked on an essentially cognitive journey. Outside the possibilities of genetic engineering, no other species has ever been, or ever will be, so dependent on cognition. Sadly, however, the same intelligence that has enabled us to successfully exploit the Earth has not been of sufficient magnitude to enable us to avoid the pathological ramifications of our unbridled personal and collective greed.

While it is accepted that the cognitive styles and overall IQ of individuals vary, modern educational theory has purposely concealed the true diversity of human intelligence. The operational meaning of a high versus a low, IQ has been lost as a whole generation has been subjected to lies that are necessary to maintain many politically correct attitudes. Even apes vary in intelligence such that some individuals can perform Theory of Mind and Mirror Self Recognition tests, while other individuals repeatedly fail. With respect to humanity, intelligence determines a vast range of abilities, people with extremely low IQs being severely limited in most aspects of life, while people with high IQs can easily master a wide range of challenges. Perhaps the introgression of genes from our less intelligent hominid ancestors has permanently enhanced the diversity of human intelligence, despite the selective advantages of intellect to the individual. In both apes and humans, the propensity to bond with and care for family members, may have repeatedly lead to the survival and subsequent reproduction of less intelligent individuals and the consequent preservation of their genes. In the face of ever-changing environments, diversity is often the key to survival of any species. It is even possible that just as human populations benefit from a diversity of cognitive styles or personalities, the apes also benefit from an inherent intellectual diversity.

Collectively, humans are intelligent enough to invent ways of destroying each other in large numbers and irreparably damaging nature. They are not, however, intelligent enough to work out and agree upon ways of living peacefully with each other and serving their basic needs while also remaining in harmony with nature. Nor are the claims that such wisdom existed amongst the hunter-gatherers and native peoples in anyway accurate. Rousseau's myth of the "noble savage" has long since died. Two anecdotal stories come to mind. The first tells of two New Guinea hill tribe chiefs who prior to being taken on a flight in a small plane asked if they could load up some rocks and leave the plane door open, explaining that they wished to drop the rocks on the neighboring villages. The second concerns an African tribe, the Dowayos, who berated a resident anthropologist for not bringing a machine gun so that they could shoot all the antelope in the neighboring lands. It is easy to see that the respect for nature, so often attributed to the native and hunter-gatherer tribes, was simply the result of them being unable to invent the weaponry and machines with which to vent their insatiable urge to hunt and kill – an urge that since South African independence has seen the wholesale slaughter of large numbers of animals that previously enjoyed the protection of well managed game parks.

A major source of the escalating human problem is that, given the complexities of their existence, even modern humans have a relatively short intellectual lifespan. The human intellect does not become whole until the maturation and conditioning of the abstract mind during puberty and the immediately post-pubescent years. Even if education is given priority over all other things, it would probably still take until the late 20s for even the most intelligent individuals to have accumulated sufficient information, personal insight and life experiences to even begin to countenance all the nuances and details contributing to truly global problems. By this stage the strictures of an all-pervading, economic system will have ensured that they will be preoccupied for many years with accumulating money and possessions necessary to survive and raise a family in the modern industrialized world. When they finally attain financial security they are usually so deeply conditioned that they are unable to think outside the morass of political corruption, obtuse ideologies, religious dogmas and purposely incomprehensible, economic policies. Little energy is left to seek an understanding of human life, to contemplate ways to enhance the altruistic behavior of humanity or to help care for the Earth. Instead most westerners live as individuals, blindly competing with each other for greater power and wealth, ever indifferent to the rank exploitation of nature that feeds their self orientated lifestyles.

Although only humans have an appreciable level of intelligence, their intelligence is only sufficient to exploit and ultimately drain the resources of nature. The human being is like other mammals in that it is driven by the life preserving forces of instinct. It is unlike any other mammal, in that its instinctual drives become the substance of complex plans created entirely within the ether of thought – plans that typically extend far beyond the biological needs that they were composed to satiate. Even though the higher echelons of human intelligence have carried us far beyond instinct, they still cannot guarantee the longevity of our species. Should humans fail to come to grips with their dysfunctional behavior patterns their rapid extinction is an absolute certainty. Unfortunately, before this happens, human exploitation will ensure that hundreds of thousands of species of animals and plants will also be forced into extinction. Part of addressing our imminent demise is to realize that, when it comes to intelligence, we are completely alone. There is no evidence for unseen beings whose benevolence ensures our survival. There are no culture bringers to provide solutions, nor any saviors with a portfolio of miracles. There are only billions of human minds scanning the inner and outer horizons, talking to their emotional centers that are speaking back to them of things they can only imagine. The gap between our thoughts and our emotions is as significant as the gap between verbal language and body language - how we feel and what we say, are often entirely different. Psychologically speaking, the psyche of even the most stable individuals is a battleground for the perennial conflicts between thought and emotion. It is this internal battle that in the unstable individual easily escapes into the outside world where it repeatedly fuels the horrendous conflicts that punctuate every century of human history.

Humans are simply not intelligent enough to resolve their dilemmas rationally. Almost without exception their actions reflect a chaotic mix of emotion and thought (Figure 8.4). Even though our essentially animal instincts are compatible with nature, outside the practice of meditation, humanity cannot hope to annul the destructive powers of the human mind. Our only hope is to become more rational, more logical and, in all ways, more intelligent, either by manipulating our genes or by constructing a bionic mind that far exceeds the computational power of our biological template. Even if a vast mind were to become a reality, it will still fall upon ordinary humans to firstly condition it to best serve humanity and secondly to act upon what it can tell us. If we fail at this, as we have in most collective tasks, all our outstanding gifts, our abilities to see and create beauty, to overcome disease, to both know and transcend instinct and to understand the universe, will come to nothing. So it will be that in future eons our imaginary celestial observer will see the brief period of human habitation as just another cataclysmic chapter in the story of life on Earth.

"Uno itinere non potest perveniri ad tam grande secretum."

"The heart of so great a mystery can never be reached by following only one road."

Quintus Aurelius Memmius Symmachus (d. 524 AD)

Section 8: Recommended Reading

Abhayadatta, Swami (translated by K. Dowman). *Masters of Mahãmudrã: Songs and Histories of the Eighty-four Buddhist Siddhas*. State University of New York Press, New York, 1986.

Blainey, G. *A Short History of the 20th Century*. Viking, Australia, 2005.

Christian, J. L. *An Introduction to the Art of Wondering*. 3rd Edition, Holt, Rinehart and Winston, New York, London, Sydney, 1977.

Darwin C. *Descent of Man*. Penguin Classics, London, 2004.

Dawkins, R. *The Selfish Gene*. Oxford University Press, Oxford, 1976.

Flynn, J. R. *What is Intelligence: Beyond the Flynn Effect*. Cambridge University Press, Cambridge, 2007.

Fromm, E. *The Art of Loving*. Thorsons, London, 1995.

Gardener, H., *Frames of Mind: The Theory of Multiple Intelligences*. Basic Books Inc., New York, 1983.

Gray, J. R. and Thompson, P. M. (2004). Neurobiology of Intelligence: Science and Ethics. *Nature Neuroscience Reviews* **5,** 471-482.

Greene, R. *The 48 Laws of Power*. Viva Books Private Ltd, New Delhi, 2000.

Hall, C. S. and Lindzey, G. *Theories of Personality*. 3rd Edition, John Wiley and Sons, New York, 1978.

Hartmann, T. *The Last Hours of Ancient Sunlight: Waking Up to Personal and Global Transformations*. Mythical Books, Northfield, Vermont, 1998.

James, W. *Psychology: The Briefer Course*. Henry Holt and Co., 1892.

Jobling, M. A., Hurles, M. E. and Tyler-Smith, C. *Human Evolutionary Genetics: Origins, Peoples and Disease*. Garland Publishing, New York, 2004.

Keeley, L. H. *War before Civilization*. Oxford University Press, Oxford, New York, 1996.

Matsumoto, D. and Juang, L. *Culture and Psychology*. 4th Edition, Wadsworth Publishing, London, 2007.

McDonald-Pavelka, M., *Monkeys in the Mesquite: The Social Life of the South Texas Snow Monkey*. Kendall/Hunt Publishing Co., 1993.

McGrew, W. C. *Chimpanzee Material Culture: Implications for Human Evolution.*. Cambridge University Press, Cambridge, 1992.

McGrew, W. C. *The Cultured Chimpanzee: Reflections on Cultural Primatology*. Cambridge University Press, Cambridge, 2004.

McGreal, I. P. (Editor). *Great Thinkers of the Eastern World*. Harper Collins Publishers, New York, 1995.

Mitchell, D. *Cultural Geography: A Critical Introduction*. Blackwell, Oxford, 2000.

Moravec, H. *Robot, Mere Machine to Transcendent Mind*. Oxford University Press, Oxford, 1999.

Nisbett, R. E. *The Geography of Thought: How Asians and Westerners Think Differently....and Why*. Nicholas Brealey Publications. London,Yaramouth, Maine, 2003.

Nyberg, H. (Editor). *The Scientific Study of General Intelligence: Tribute to Arthur R. Jensen*. Pergamon, New York, 2003.

Otterbein, K. F. *How War Began.* Texas A & M University Press, 2004.

Reese, W. L. *Dictionary of Philosophy and Religion, Eastern and Western Thought.* Humanities Press Inc., New Jersey, 1980.

Rummel, R. J. *Death by Government.* Transaction Publishers, New Brunswick, New Jersey, 1994.

Sternberg, R. J. (Editor). *Wisdom: Its Nature, Origins, and Development.* Cambridge University Press, Cambridge, 1990.

Wilson, C. *The Criminal History of Mankind.* 2nd Edition, Mercury Books, London, 2005

de Waal, F. B. M. *Chimpanzee Politics: Power and Sex Among Apes.* 25th Edition, The John Hopkins University Press, Baltimore, 2007.

Wright, R. *The Moral Animal.* Abacus Press, London, 2004.

Palast, G. *The Best Democracy Money Can Buy.* Constable and Robinson. London, 2002.

Sternberg, R. J. (Editor). *Handbook of Intelligence.* Cambridge University Press, Cambridge, 2000.

Figure 1.1 Illustration showing the two experientially distinct realms of human consciousness; the Outer World which is comprised of our sensations and perceptions of the world around us and the Inner World which is comprised of our thoughts, emotions and moods and which also constitutes the human psyche.

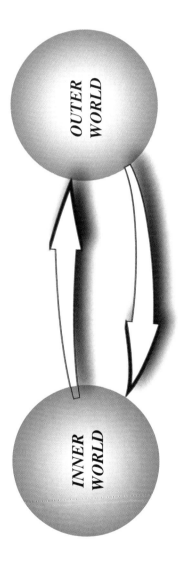

Duality of Consciousness

OUTER WORLD

INNER WORLD

INNER WORLD = THE PSYCHE

Figure 1.1

Figure 1.2 Illustration showing the increasing proportion of the entire cortex allocated to the prefrontal cortex (blackened area) of, in order, the cat, dog, monkey, ape and human. The brains in this series are not shown to scale. In life the size of the brain along this series increases many times over. Consequently, along this series there is a huge increase in the amount of cortex allocated to the prefrontal functions. Note that although humans evolved from apes and apes from monkeys, the diagram is not meant to imply that monkeys evolved from dogs or that dogs evolved from cats.

The Expansion of the Inner Realms of Consciousness (in Mammals)

THE ASCENT OF CONSCIOUSNESS

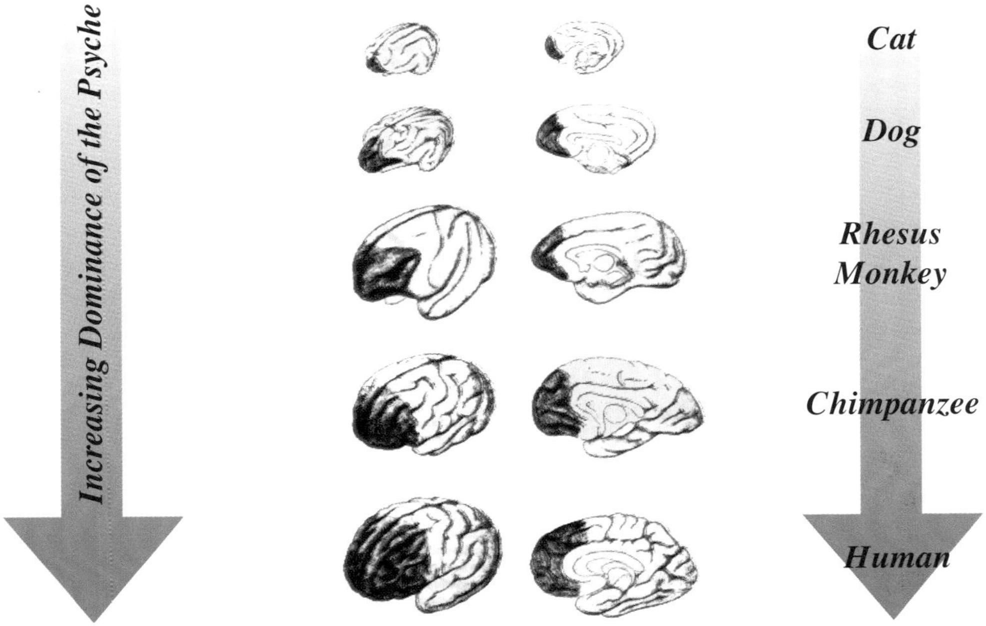

Cat

Dog

Rhesus Monkey

Chimpanzee

Human

(Brain sizes not shown to scale)

Increasing Dominance of the Psyche

Figure 1.2

425

Figure 1.3 Graph showing the progressive increases in the population of modern humans, Homo sapiens, since their evolution approximately 200,000 years ago. The arrow indicates the approximate point when Homo sapiens first migrated into Europe and produced the first 3-dimensional, dynamic art. Behind the graph is shown the distribution of electrical lighting across the entire globe that approximately correlates with the colonization of the Earth by modern Europeans over the 18th, 19th and 20th centuries. The table on the right shows the progressive increases in human population, past and predicted (*), alongside the life span of a single human born in 1974 when there were only 4 billion people in the world and the predicted population at 10 year intervals up to 2050.

Population Growth of Humanity, *Homo sapiens.*

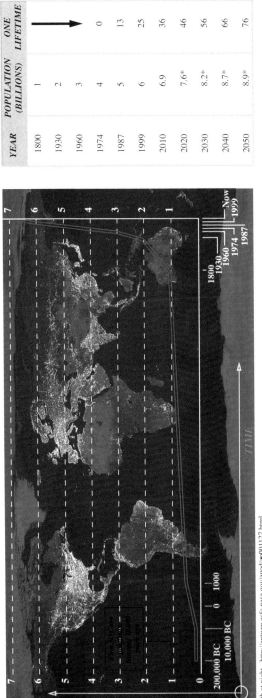

Earth at night - http://antwrp.gsfc.nasa.gov/apod/ap001127.html

YEAR	POPULATION (BILLIONS)	ONE LIFETIME
1800	1	→
1930	2	0
1960	3	13
1974	4	25
1987	5	36
1999	6	46
2010	6.9	56
2020	7.6*	66
2030	8.2*	76
2040	8.7*	
2050	8.9*	

Figure 1.3

Figure 1.4 Left is shown the, so-called, Freeman icepick method which in the mid-20th century was used extensively to sever the prefrontal lobes from the many thousands of mentally disturbed patients, including a number of difficult children. On the right, is a diagram showing the plane of section in relation to the different areas of the human cortex. Note that the plane of this cut essentially severs or chronically damages the areas involved in thought (BA9, 10, 46 & 47), mood and emotion (areas not visible from this perspective; see Figure 1.5) and probably also the most anterior part of the Broca's speech area (BA45/44). The lobotomized individual may retain the capacity for simplistic speech but has chronically diminished powers of reason, planning, and motivation. Adapted from Snow, P. J. (2003) J. Consciousness Studies 10, 3-17.

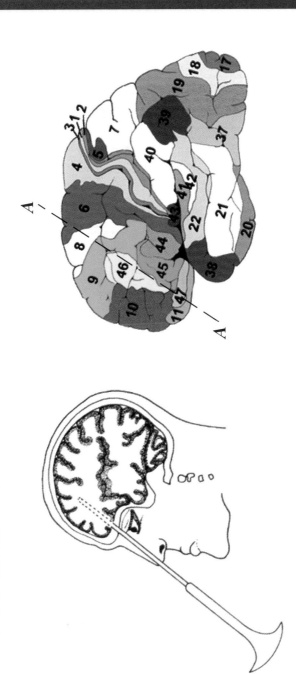

Figure 1.4

Figure 1.5 Illustration showing the evolutionary sequence of development of the prefrontal cortex. The first region to evolve was the cortex of the orbital surface. In primitive vertebrates this began as an olfactory area, slowly increasing in size until, in primates, it contained a number of structurally distinct areas (Brodmann's areas 11, 13 and 14 shown) and fulfilled the complex psychological function of mood that modulates our predictions of the outcome of any scenario. The second region to evolve was the medial surface (Brodmann's areas 24, 25 and 32); the source of our primary emotions, motivation and bonding that appeared within the brain of the earliest mammals, 260 million years ago. The third region to evolve contained the cognitive areas (the mind) and formed the dorsal and dorsolateral surface of the prefrontal cortex. The first of these cognitive areas (Brodmann's area 9) serves social and emotional intelligence and probably evolved in the higher non-primate mammals. Next to evolve was the area serving practical intelligence and language (Brodmann's area 47) followed by the area which serves abstract intelligence (Brodmann's area 46). The area serving planning or temporal intelligence (Brodmann's area 10, not shown) occupies the frontal pole of the cortex and probably evolved in concert with Brodmann's area 47 and its product, practical intelligence. This evolutionary progression reflects precisely the sequence of maturation of these areas in the human child and the sequence of cognitive stages of childhood development, defined in European children, by Piaget. See text for further discussion.

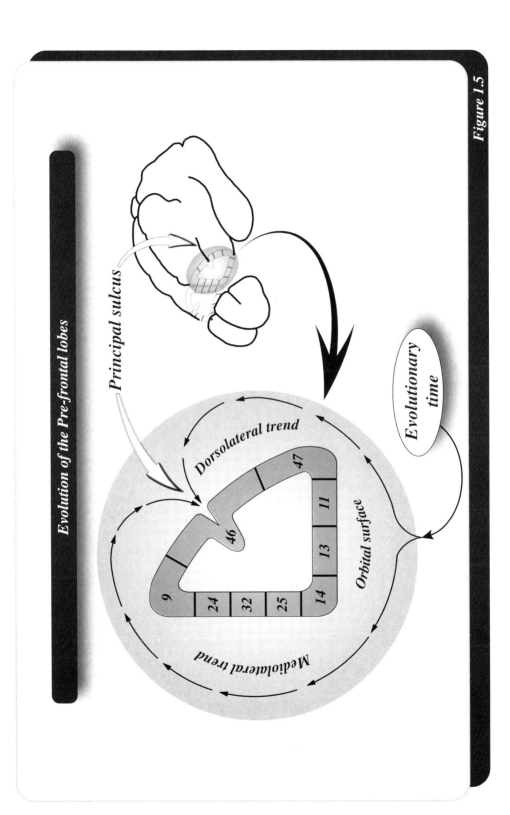

Evolution of the Pre-frontal lobes

Principal sulcus

Dorsolateral trend

Orbital surface

Mediolateral trend

Evolutionary time

46

47

11

13

9

24

32

25

14

Figure 1.5

431

Figure 1.6 Illustration showing the experiential nature and function of the three elements of the human psyche; mind, emotion and mood.

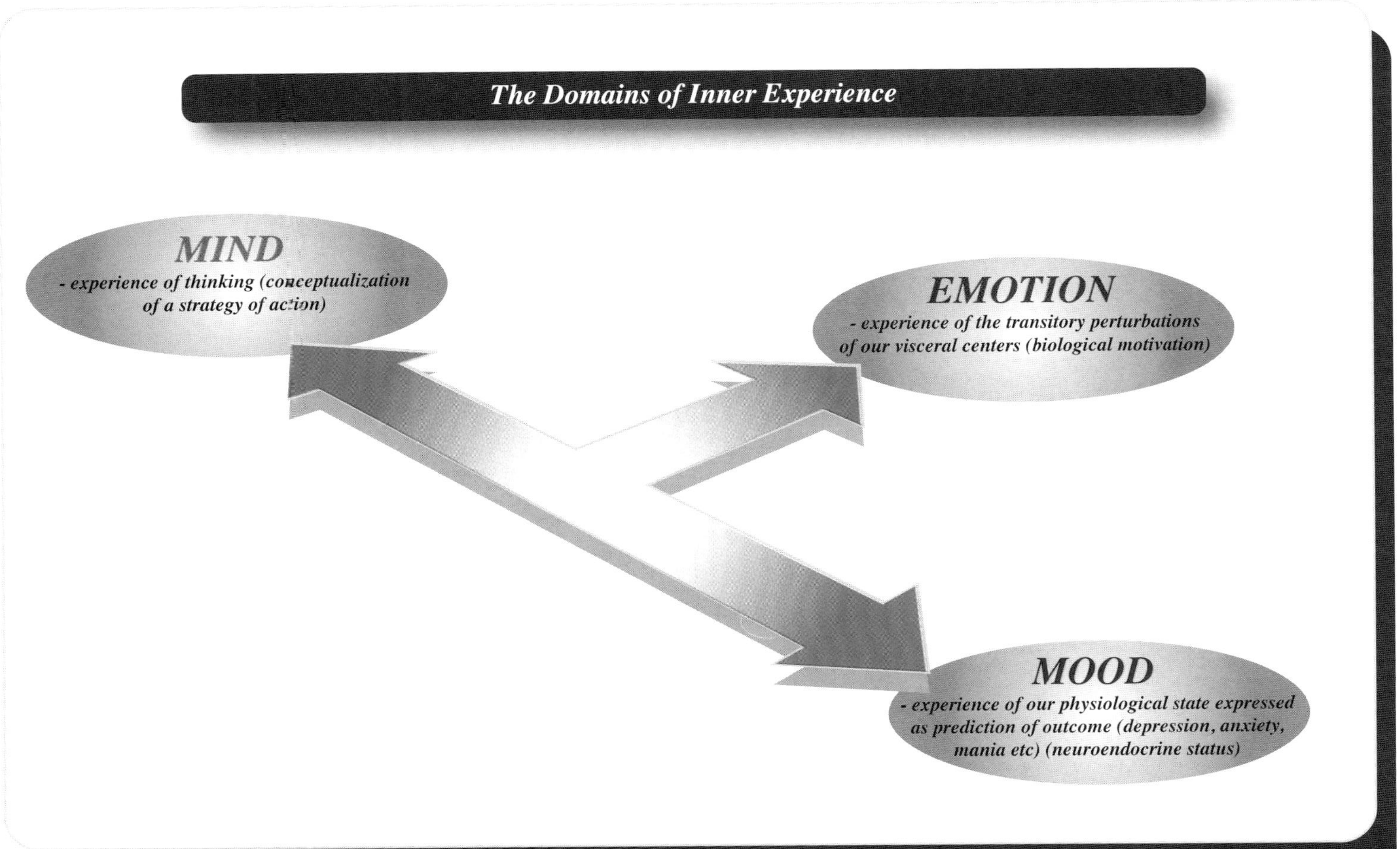

The Domains of Inner Experience

EMOTION
- experience of the transitory perturbations of our visceral centers (biological motivation)

MOOD
- experience of our physiological state expressed as prediction of outcome (depression, anxiety, mania etc) (neuroendocrine status)

MIND
- experience of thinking (conceptualization of a strategy of action)

Figure 1.6

433

Figure 1.7 Components of the psyche shown in relation to their inputs and outputs and their purpose in the minute-by-minute, hour-by-hour and day-by-day dynamic of both human consciousness and human life.

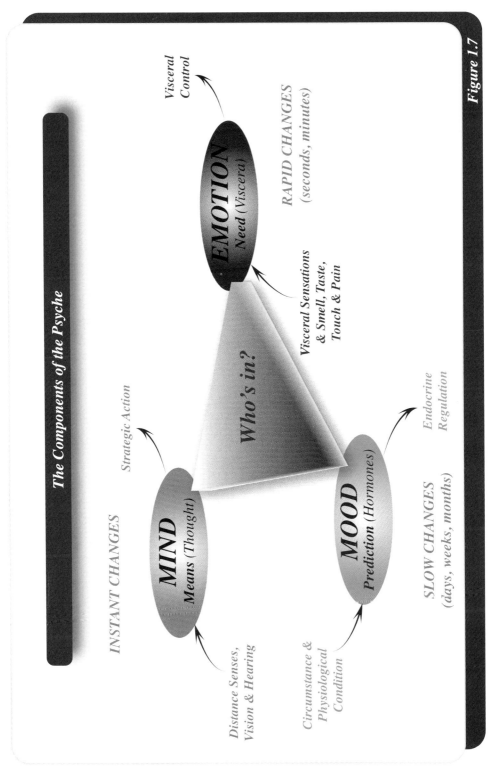

The Components of the Psyche

Visceral Control

EMOTION
Need (Viscera)

*RAPID CHANGES
(seconds, minutes)*

*Visceral Sensations
& Smell, Taste,
Touch & Pain*

Who's in?

Strategic Action

MIND
Means (Thought)

MOOD
Prediction (Hormones)

*Endocrine
Regulation*

INSTANT CHANGES

*SLOW CHANGES
(days, weeks, months)*

*Distance Senses,
Vision & Hearing*

*Circumstance &
Physiological
Condition*

Figure 1.7

Figure 2.1 Traditional methods of resolving problems in the West (left) and the East (right). In the East, the sitting Buddha symbolizes the paradigm of "no mind". Regular meditation brings a persistent calm to the mind enabling the practitioner to intensely focus his or her thoughts upon matters of immediate significance. In the West, Rodin's Thinker symbolizes the European penchant for the using reason to comprehend the world and resolve problems – a process that ignores the errant, mischievous and highly dangerous nature of human thought and its inadvertent products, faith, hope and belief. The Sitting Buddha is reprinted with permission of Princeton University Press, from Joseph Campbell's The Mythic Image © 1974 Princeton University Press, 2002 renewed PUP.

The Resolution of Problems: East vs West

Figure 2.1

EASTERN WAY

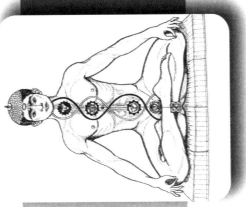

**NO MIND
(Quiescent Mind)**

versus

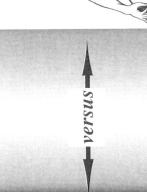

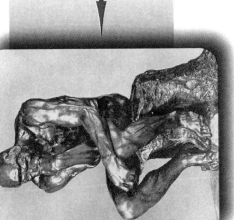

**THOUGHT
(Active Mind)**

WESTERN WAY

Figure 2.2 Illustration showing Brodmann's subdivisions of the human cerebral cortex and, at a microscopic level, the modular organization that extends across the whole the cortex. Each area of Brodmann serves distinct domains of human experience and each interacts with different parts of the nervous system and thereby plays distinctive roles in our perception and behavior. The size of individual areas varies between different people and is largely determined by inheritance – a fundamental fact that explains why talents of all kinds so often recur in successive generations of the same family. The estimate of the total number of modules in one hemisphere provides a maximum figure. It is based on the assumption that, across the entire cortex, single modules are the same size as the one illustrated. Modules in different parts of the cortex are different shapes but the calculation nevertheless illustrates the principles at play in the creation of human consciousness. See text for specific references to individual areas.

438

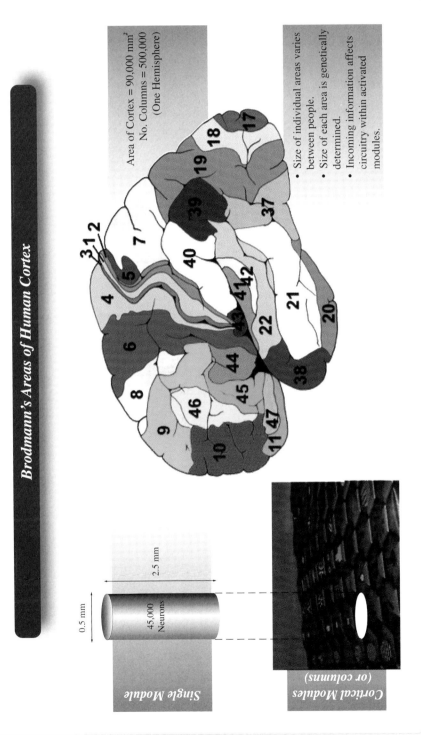

Brodmann's Areas of Human Cortex

Area of Cortex = 90,000 mm²
No. Columns = 500,000
(One Hemisphere)

- Size of individual areas varies between people.
- Size of each area is genetically determined.
- Incoming information affects circuitry within activated modules.

0.5 mm

2.5 mm

45,000 Neurons

Single Module

Cortical Modules (or columns)

Figure 2.2

439

Figure 2.3 Lord Shiva (Siva), the most powerful God of the Hindu trilogy, is said to represent unmanifest consciousness. In modern terms, this would translate into the very substance of the quiescent cerebral cortex, the part of the brain capable of elaborating that completely intangible phenomenon we call consciousness. It is said that when Shiva dances he takes on the form of Nataraja, the cosmic dancer, whose archetypal form is symbolized in the Om (Aum) sign that, in turn, represents the "no mind" consciousness of the sitting Buddha. When Shiva dances, our previously quiescent cortex is activated and, within us, as with the coming of day, we awaken and in Hindu vernacular, "the universe sings".

Nataraja

Aum or Om

Lord Shiva

Lord Shiva

Figure 2.3

Figure 3.1 Illustration representing the relationship between Piaget's stages of cognitive development in children and the sequential maturation of the different divisions of the mind – a process that is reversed when old age brings mental deterioration (black stars). The three figurine inserts give an example of the art typical of the normal child in the preoperational, concrete operational and formal operations stages of cognitive development. See text for further discussion and information.

Development Sequences of the Human Mind

Planning
(Begins at
3 to 6 years)

Senescent
Phase
(60-100 years)

Preoperational
(1-7 years)

Formal
Operational
(11-15 years)

Sensorimotor
(0-1 year)

Concrete
Operational
(7-11 years)

Figure 3.1

443

Figure 3.2 Illustration showing the organization and interactions between the areas of Brodmann that compose the human mind (BA9, 10, 46 & 47). Also shown are how the mind interacts with the emotional centers (anterior cingulate gyrus; BA24, 25 & 32) and the areas underlying the predictive (psychological) aspect of mood (orbital cortex). The social mind (BA9) receives information from areas of the cortex that enables us to perceive facial expressions, gaze and body language. The dorsal stream delivers information to the abstract mind (BA46) from cortical areas which enable us to judge, and so experience, space and time – intangible phenomena in that although they are known to us, they cannot be sensed directly. In contrast, the ventral stream delivers information to the material mind (BA47) and the anterior part of Broca's area (BA45) from cortical areas that enable us to perceive the identity of objects and people. The temporal mind (BA10) is involved in the cognitive process of planning, whether the plans are to do with the practical, socioemotional or abstract domains of cognition. Wernicke's area is involved in the deciphering of speech and passing this information on the Broca's motor speech area (BA45 and BA44). Wernicke's area also receives information about writing and body form, the latter providing a possible reason as to why the invention of hieroglyphics preceded the invention of writing. Adapted from: Snow, P. J. (2003) J. Consciousness Studies 10, 3-17.

The Structural and Operational Basis of Human Thought

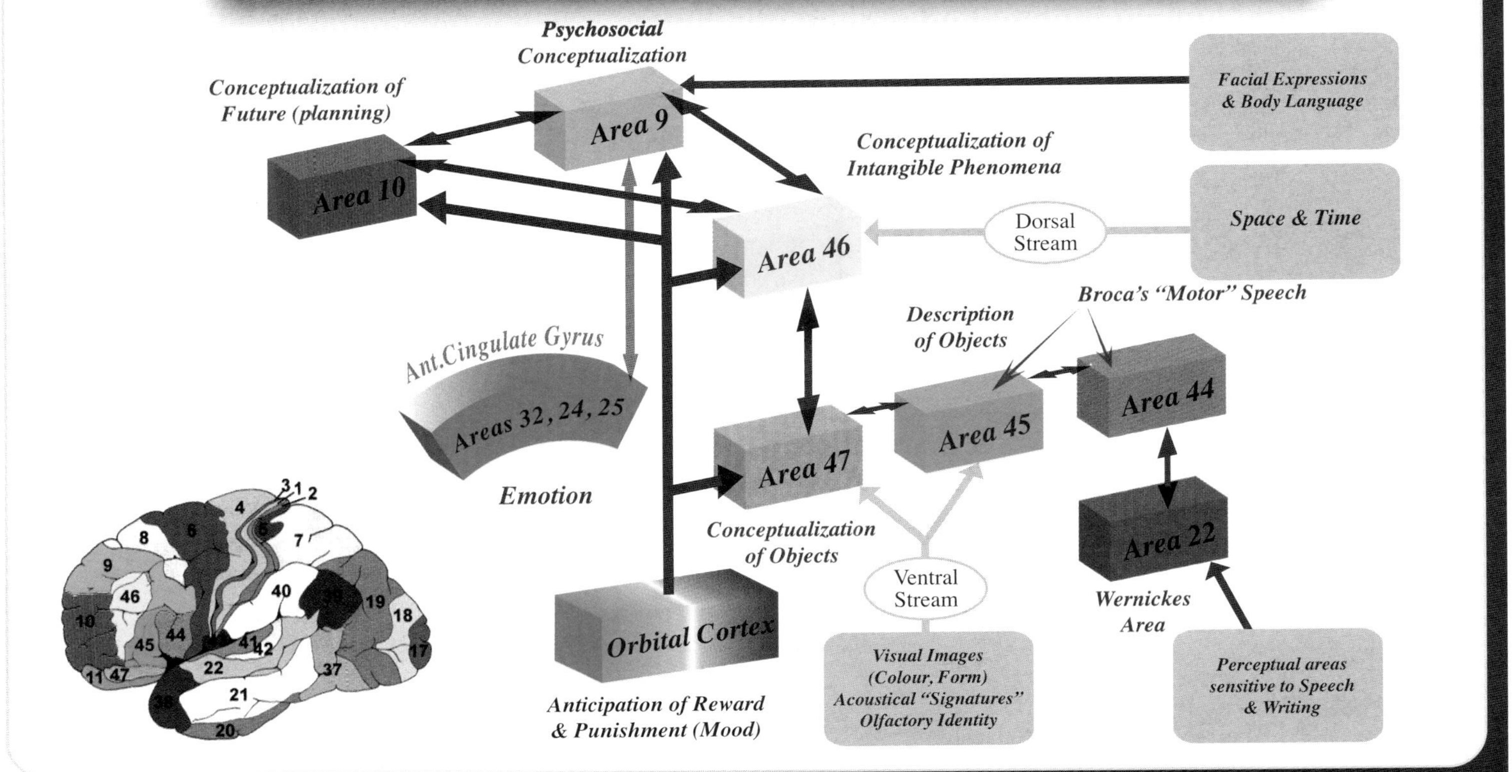
Psychosocial Conceptualization
Conceptualization of Future (planning)
Area 9
Area 10
Conceptualization of Intangible Phenomena
Facial Expressions & Body Language
Space & Time
Dorsal Stream
Area 46
Ant.Cingulate Gyrus
Areas 32, 24, 25
Emotion
Description of Objects
Broca's "Motor" Speech
Area 44
Area 45
Area 47
Area 22
Conceptualization of Objects
Ventral Stream
Wernickes Area
Orbital Cortex
Anticipation of Reward & Punishment (Mood)
Visual Images (Colour, Form) Acoustical "Signatures" Olfactory Identity
Perceptual areas sensitive to Speech & Writing
3 1 2
4
6
8
7
9
46
10
45
44
40
39
19
18
17
41
42
22
37
21
38
20
11
47

Figure 3.2

Figure 4.1 Illustration showing the interconnections (red arrows) between the three members of the Triad of Emotion*; the anterior cingulate gyrus, amygdala and insula. Also shown are the connections (blue arrows) that link each emotional center to the orbital cortex and interconnect the mind to the orbital cortex and, as executor of emotion, the anterior cingulate gyrus. The orbital cortex is a region which participates in mood by providing a prediction of the positive versus negative outcome of any particular endeavor. The anterior cingulate interconnects specifically with the medial orbital cortex (green) and while the amygdala interconnects specifically with the lateral orbital cortex (red). The anterior cingulate mediates positive affect and in positive mood works with the medial orbital cortex to generate optimism. The amygdala mediates negative affect and works with the lateral orbital cortex to generate pessimism. Both divisions of the orbital cortex influence the mind, to create strategies that are in keeping with either optimism or pessimism, depending on whether the medial or lateral orbital cortex, respectively, is active. See text for further explanation.

446

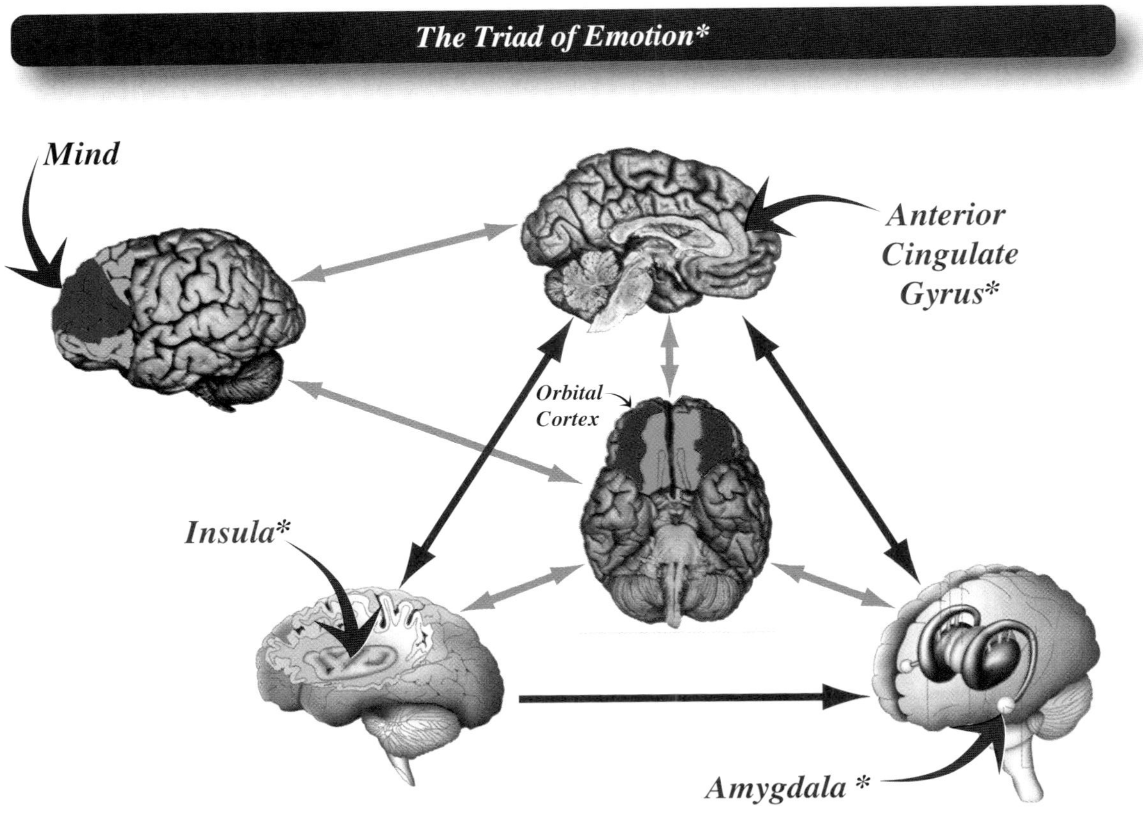

The Triad of Emotion*

Anterior Cingulate Gyrus*

Amygdala*

Orbital Cortex

Insula*

Mind

Figure 4.1

447

Figure 4.2 Illustration showing the progressive changes in the sources of fear that accompany the maturation of the four anatomically discrete parts (*) of the human mind (BA 9, 10, 46 and 47) and Piaget's stages of cognitive development in children. Note that the source of fear changes, from biological entities, to social scenarios, to concrete elements of life and finally to hypothetical elements, as emotional, temporal, practical and finally abstract intelligence become operational – a series of changes that are accompanied by the establishment of the relevant components of the ego as defined long ago, by William James.

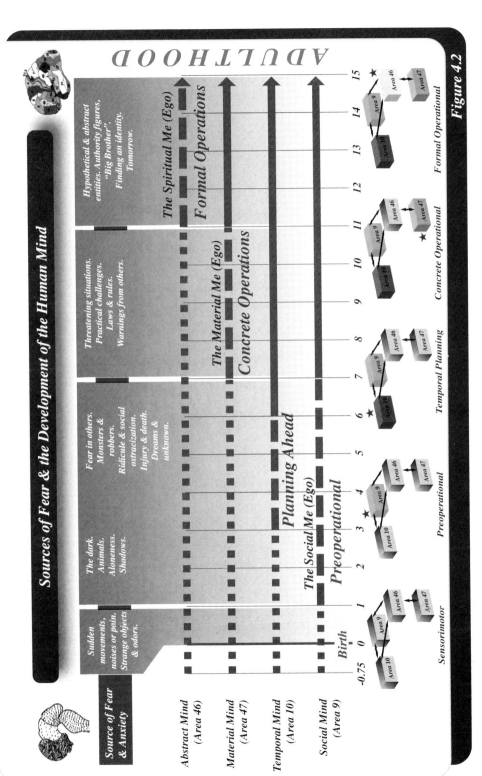

Sources of Fear & the Development of the Human Mind

Figure 4.2

Figure 5.1 Illustration showing the interconnections (red arrows) of the components of the psyche which participate in the generation of mood; the orbital cortex* and the members of the Triad of Emotion*; the anterior cingulate gyrus, amygdala and the insula. Also shown are the connections (blue arrows) that link the mind to the orbital cortex and, as executor of emotion, the anterior cingulate gyrus. The orbital cortex is a region which participates in mood by providing a prediction of the positive versus negative outcome of any particular endeavor. The anterior cingulate interconnects specifically with the medial orbital cortex (green) and while the amygdala interconnects specifically with the lateral orbital cortex (red). The anterior cingulate mediates positive affect and in positive mood works with the medial orbital cortex to generate optimism. The amygdala mediates negative affect and works with the lateral orbital cortex to generate pessimism. Both divisions of the orbital cortex influence the mind, to create strategies that are in keeping with either optimism or pessimism, depending on whether the medial or lateral orbital cortices, respectively, is active. See text for further explanation.

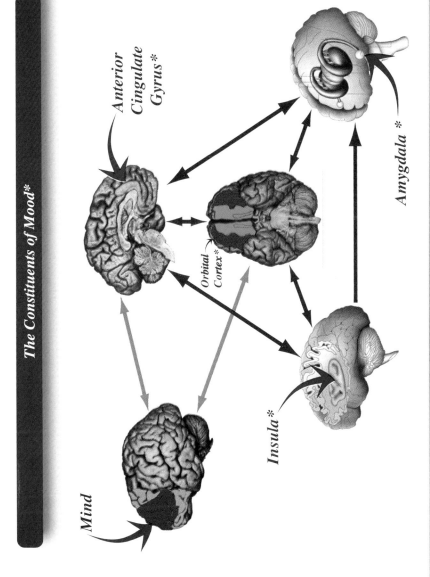

The Constituents of Mood*

*Anterior Cingulate Gyrus***

*Orbital Cortex***

*Amygdala***

*Insula***

Mind

Figure 5.1

451

Figure 5.2 Illustration showing how bodily pain (left), unpleasant tastes and bad odors (center and right) coalesce in the lateral orbital cortex (red), there to generate a cautionary bias that the mind will interpret as indicative of a potentially dangerous situation (pessimism). In contrast, gentle touch, pleasant tastes and good odors coalesce in the medial orbital cortex (green), there to generate a permissive bias that the mind will interpret as indicative of the potential for success (optimism). It is because of this role in providing a very early (possibly even prenatal), sensory definition of "bad" and "good" that odor, taste, touch and pain are called the primary reinforcers. See text for further explanation.

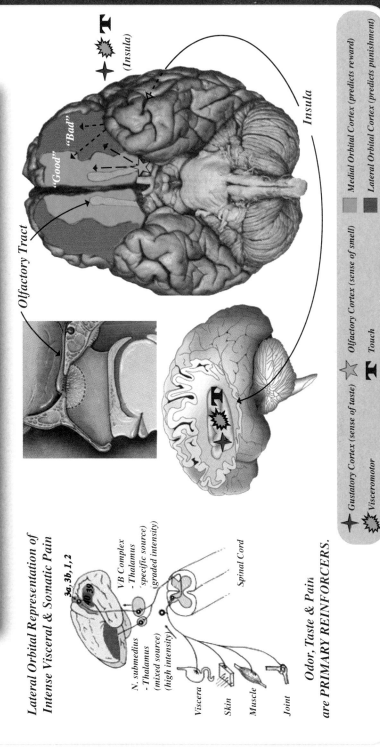

The Establishment of "Good" & "Bad" in Human Consciousness

Olfactory Tract

"Bad"

"Good"

(Insula)

Insula

*Lateral Orbital Representation of
Intense Visceral & Somatic Pain*

3a, 3b, 1, 2

40 39

V-B Complex
- Thalamus
(specific source)
(graded intensity)

N. submedius
- Thalamus
(mixed source)
(high intensity)

Spinal Cord

Viscera

Skin

Muscle

Joint

*Odor, Taste & Pain
are PRIMARY REINFORCERS.*

Gustatory Cortex (sense of taste)   Olfactory Cortex (sense of smell)

Viseromotor   Touch

Medial Orbital Cortex (predicts reward)

Lateral Orbital Cortex (predicts punishment)

Figure 5.2

453

Figure 5.3 The art of darkness. (a) Hiëronymous Bosch' painting of the torment of humanity shows the torture and degradation of humanity by demons that are conspicuously not human. The implication is that evil is not of our making but the product of an independent demonic force emanating from Hell. (b) Francisco de Goya's image of Saturn devouring one of his children – a common practice amongst reptiles. (c) The torture and temptation of St. Anthony and his transcendence of suffering – a hypothetical association of pain with the Devil and its negation by God. (d) The Rings of Hell through which Dante, descended. Each successive ring represents an increasingly serious moral misdemeanor and an increasingly horrendous level of suffering, symbolizing the use of invented religious mythology to enforce particular societal mores. Images by Bosch and de Goya are reproduced with the permission of Muses Nacional del Prado. Image of the Temptation of St. Anthony reproduced with the permission of Art Resources, New York.

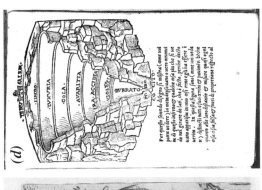

Figure 5.3

455

Figure 5.4 Christian art showing Luther presiding over the symbolic balance between Heaven and Hell. As icons Heaven and Hell represent the human psyche's innate capacity to generate the extremes of mood seen in manic euphoria and deep depression. On the left Heaven is portrayed as the innocent sacrificial lamb, the crucified Jesus and the legions of the pious. On the right Hell is portrayed as a hellmouth consuming sinners, amongst whom the high clergy and the aristocracy are, as ever, well represented. Reproduced with the permission of Art Resources, New York.

Figure 5.4

364. Luther Preaching the Word. Lucas Cranach the Younger. A.D. 16th century

Figure 5.5 Illustration of the human psyche in a normal, well balanced individual. Note that the instinctual responses (grey boxes) are generated by two members of the Triad of Emotion; the anterior cingulate (left) and the amygdala (right). Compare with figures 5.6.and 5.7. See text for further explanation.

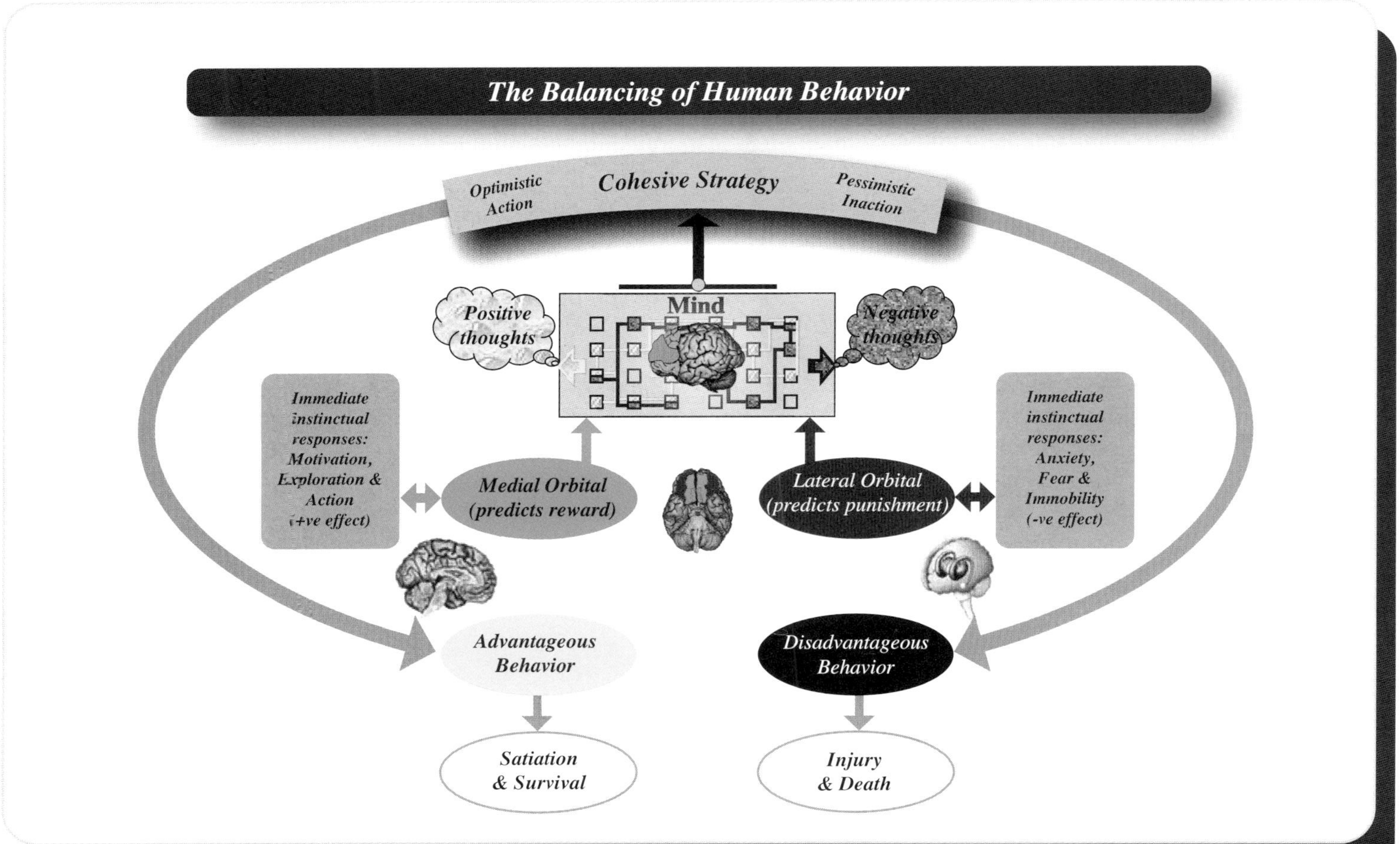
The Balancing of Human Behavior
Optimistic Action
Cohesive Strategy
Pessimistic Inaction
Mind
Positive thoughts
Negative thoughts
Immediate instinctual responses: Motivation, Exploration & Action (+ve effect)
Medial Orbital (predicts reward)
Lateral Orbital (predicts punishment)
Immediate instinctual responses: Anxiety, Fear & Immobility (-ve effect)
Advantageous Behavior
Disadvantageous Behavior
Satiation & Survival
Injury & Death

Figure 5.5

Figure 5.6 Illustration showing how the human psyche shifts from the balanced state (see: Figure 5.5) to one that generates depression; a state wherein the lateral orbital cortex is active so that the mind becomes involuntarily preoccupied with failure. At the same time, the amygdala, which is strongly interconnected with the lateral orbital cortex, actively generates the instinctual responses of fear, anxiety and behavioral paralysis (immobility) while holding positive emotions in check by reducing activation of the anterior cingulate gyrus. In this condition, the state of the psyche is the opposite to that seen in psychopathy (compare with Figure 5.7). See text for further explanation.

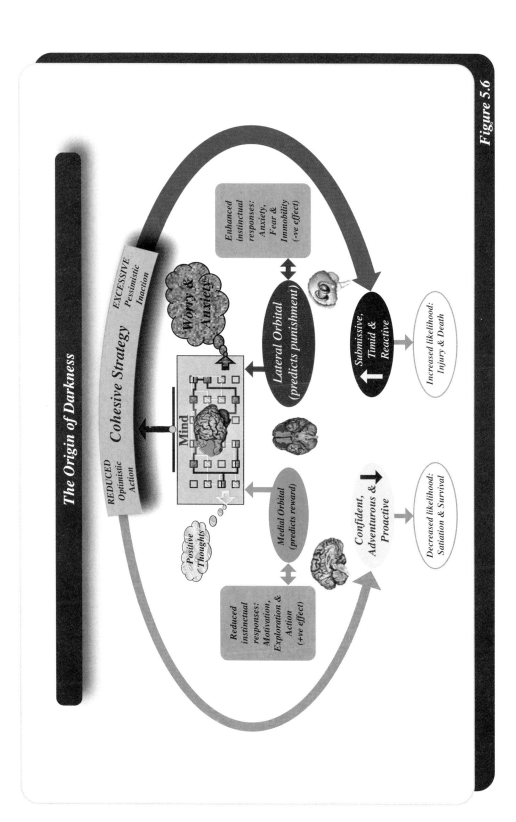

The Origin of Darkness

Figure 5.6

Figure 5.7 Illustration showing how the human psyche shifts from the balanced state (see: Figure 5.5) to one that generates psychopathy; a state wherein the lateral orbital cortex is deactivated or damaged so that the medial orbital cortex becomes dominant over the mind which, as a consequence, becomes involuntarily preoccupied with success and disinterested in caution. At the same time, the anterior cingulate, which is strongly interconnected with the medial orbital cortex, actively generates the instinctual responses in the form of exaggerated motivation and increased explorative action. Enhanced activity in the anterior cingulate gyrus also holds the instinctual responses of fear, anxiety and behavioral paralysis (freezing) in check by reducing activation of the amygdala. In this condition, the state of the psyche is the opposite to that seen in depression (compare with Figure 5.6). See text for further explanation.

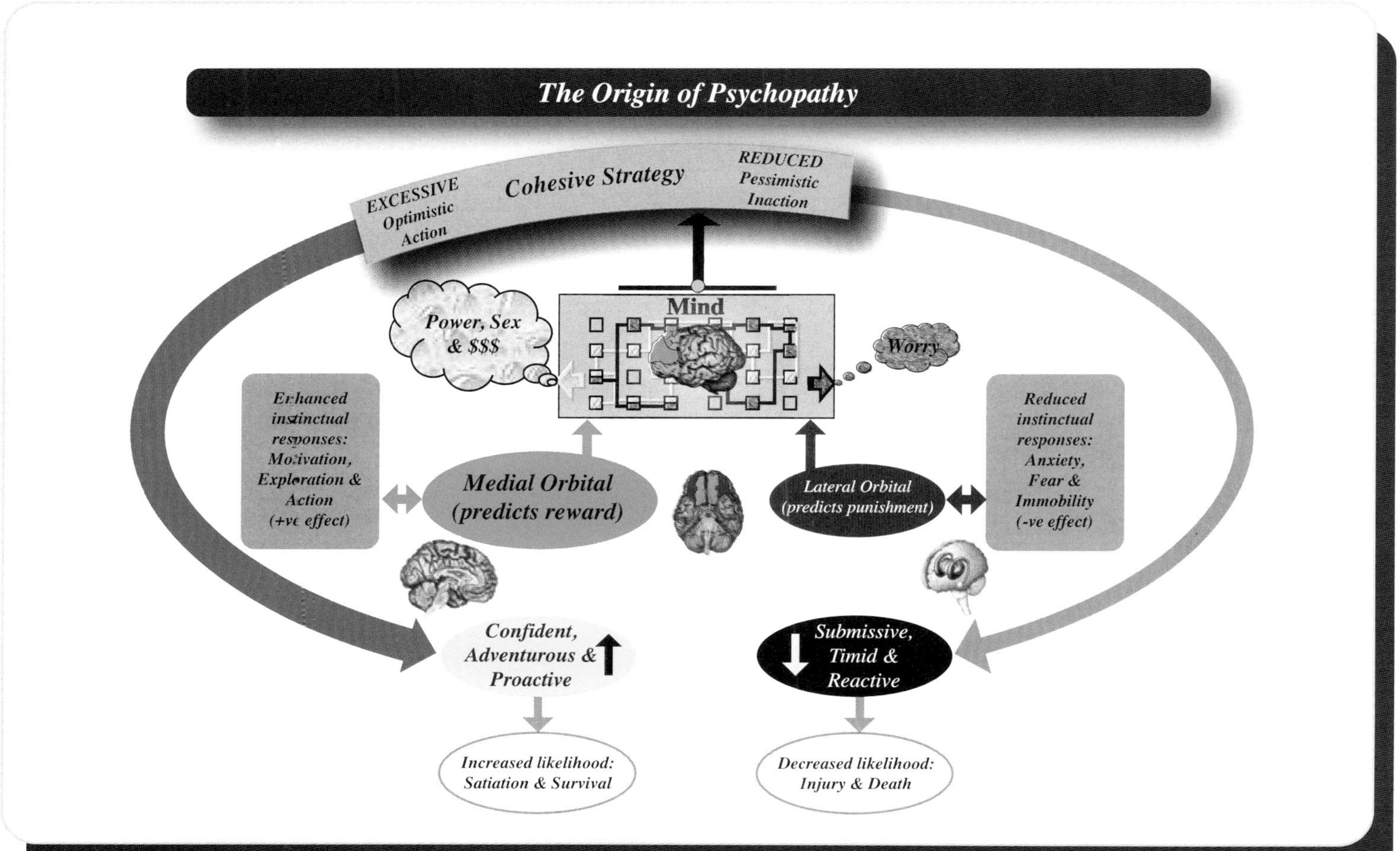
The Origin of Psychopathy
Cohesive Strategy
EXCESSIVE Optimistic Action
REDUCED Pessimistic Inaction
Mind
Power, Sex & $$$
Worry
Enhanced instinctual responses: Motivation, Exploration & Action (+ve effect)
Medial Orbital (predicts reward)
Lateral Orbital (predicts punishment)
Reduced instinctual responses: Anxiety, Fear & Immobility (-ve effect)
Confident, Adventurous & Proactive
Submissive, Timid & Reactive
Increased likelihood: Satiation & Survival
Decreased likelihood: Injury & Death
Figure 5.7

Figure 5.8 Illustration showing how highly contradictory emotional scenarios, such as parental sexual abuse, can cause the splitting of the mind into what are virtually two (or more) different cognitive constructs which function as the distinctly separate minds and consequently generates two quite different personalities. In such a condition one persona is dominant, typically complex and commonly present, while the other persona is subordinate, typically shallow and more rarely observable.

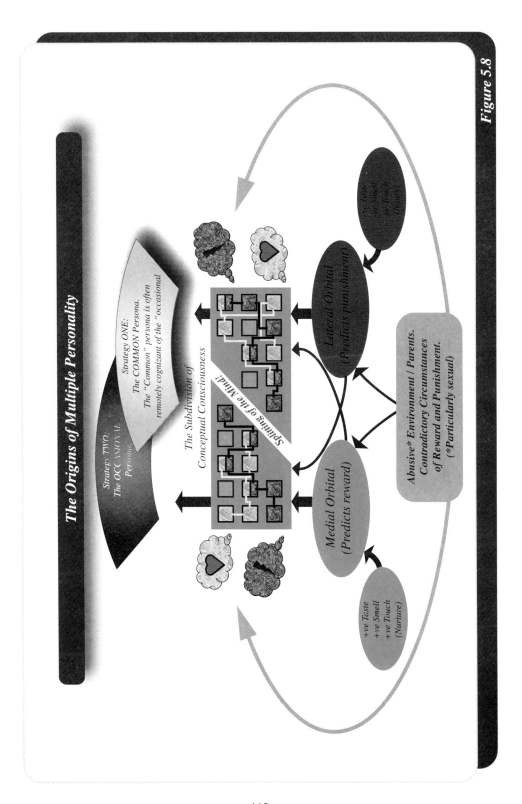

The Origins of Multiple Personality

Strategy ONE:
The COMMON Persona.
The "Common" persona is often remotely cognizant of the "occasional

Strategy TWO:
The OCCASIONAL Persona.

The Subdivision of Conceptual Consciousness

Splitting of the Mind!

Lateral Orbital
(Predicts punishment)

Medial Orbital
(Predicts reward)

-ve Taste
-ve Smell
-ve Touch
(Injury)

+ve Taste
+ve Smell
+ve Touch
(Nurture)

Abusive* Environment / Parents.
Contradictory Circumstances
of Reward and Punishment.
(*Particularly sexual)

Figure 5.8

465

Figure 6.1 Illustration showing the origins of behavior in fish, amphibians and reptiles. The behavior of these animals is driven by the amygdala acting through a motor command center capable only of generating of a set of stereotyped fixed action patterns, the most complex being fight, flight and sexual display. The amygdala integrates incoming sensory information that is biased towards the primitive senses of smell, taste and touch (the primary reinforcers). The distance senses, vision and hearing, are present but are relatively unsophisticated. The olfactory cortex serves a function crudely analogous to the orbital cortex of mammals, in that smell (and probably taste, touch and pain) is used to interpret the environment and to predict the likelihood of reward or punishment. Thus, olfaction and the other primary reinforcers compose what is, operationally speaking, an archaic form of mood. The place where the mind would be in the higher mammals is shown by the dashed lines.

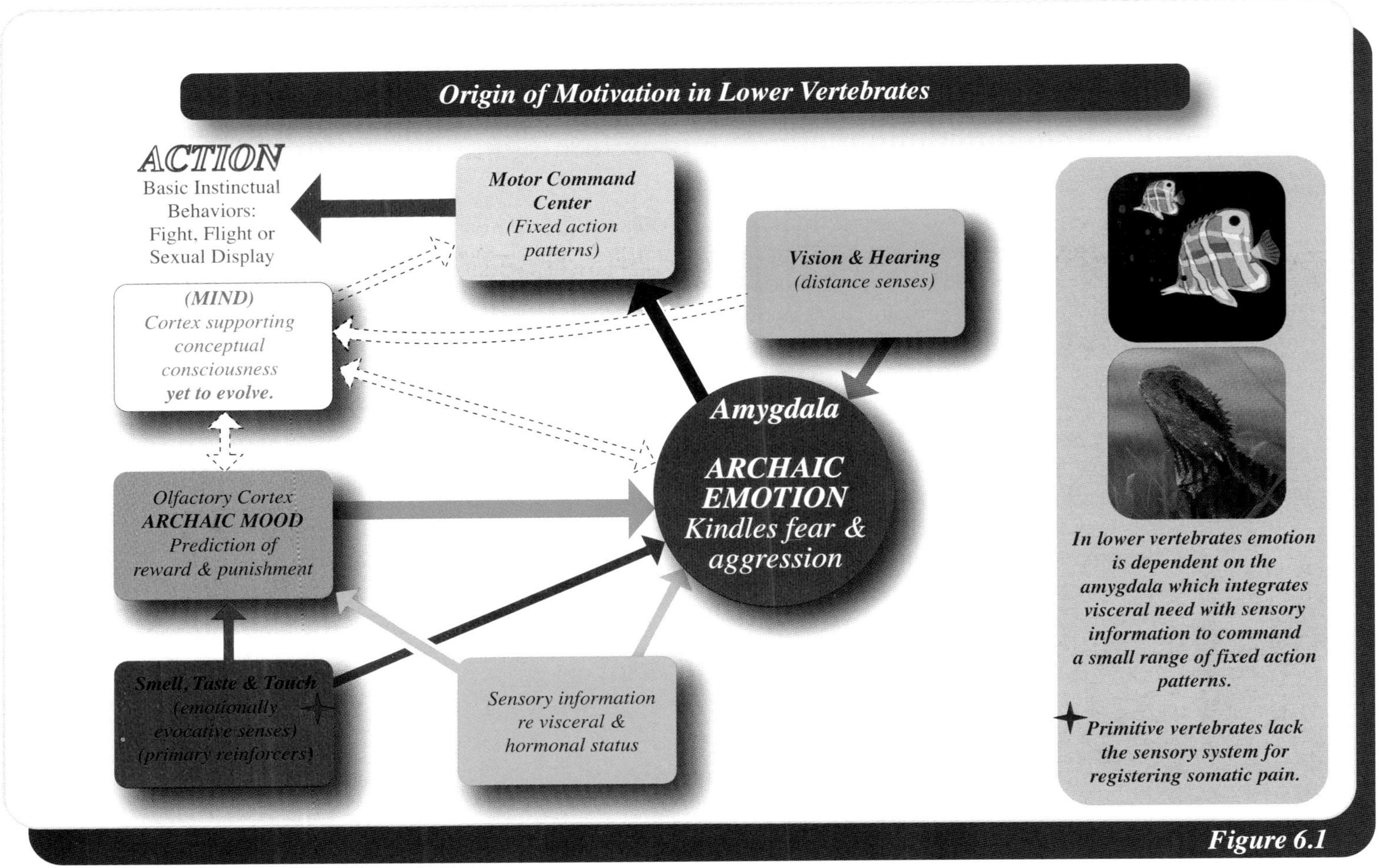

Origin of Motivation in Lower Vertebrates

Vision & Hearing (distance senses)

Amygdala
ARCHAIC EMOTION
Kindles fear & aggression

Motor Command Center (Fixed action patterns)

Sensory information re visceral & hormonal status

ACTION
Basic Instinctual Behaviors: Fight, Flight or Sexual Display

(MIND)
Cortex supporting conceptual consciousness yet to evolve.

Olfactory Cortex
ARCHAIC MOOD
Prediction of reward & punishment

Smell, Taste & Touch (emotionally evocative senses) (primary reinforcers)

In lower vertebrates emotion is dependent on the amygdala which integrates visceral need with sensory information to command a small range of fixed action patterns.

Primitive vertebrates lack the sensory system for registering somatic pain.

Figure 6.1

Figure 6.2 Illustration showing the origins of behavior in the primitive mammal condition wherein the part of the cortex that engages in thought (the mind) has not yet evolved. In the mindless mammals all complex behavior is driven by the brain's executor of emotion, the anterior cingulate gyrus. The repertoire of essentially instinctive behavioral acts is generated by what, compared with the lower vertebrates (see: Figure 6.1), is a relatively sophisticated, cortical, motor command center. The distances senses (vision & hearing) convey biologically relevant perceptions to the anterior cingulate gyrus and the orbital cortex. The orbital cortex participates in mood by enabling the prediction of success or failure in any endeavor – a role it fulfils by weighing up information from the primitive senses (smell, taste, touch & pain), biological information from the sophisticated distance senses (vision & hearing) and the animal's prevailing emotional and physiological condition. The living mindless mammals probably include all non-primates, except perhaps dogs and possibly their closest relatives, the seals and bears. The place where the mind would be in the higher mammals is shown by the dashed lines.

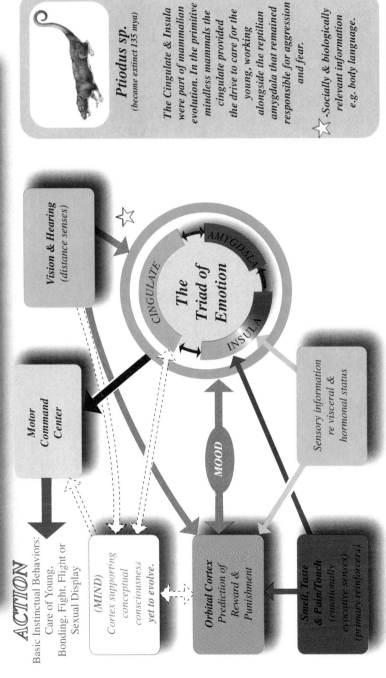

Origin of Motivation in Primitive Mammals

Piodus sp.
(became extinct 135 mya)

The Cingulate & Insula were part of mammalian evolution. In the primitive mindless mammals the cingulate provided the drive to care for the young, working alongside the reptilian amygdala that remained responsible for aggression and fear.

☆ -*Socially & biologically relevant information e.g. body language.*

Vision & Hearing *(distance senses)*

☆

CINGULATE

AMYGDALA

The Triad of Emotion

INSULA

Motor Command Center

MOOD

Sensory information re visceral & hormonal status

ACTION
Basic Instinctual Behaviors: Care of Young, Bonding, Fight, Flight or Sexual Display

(MIND) Cortex supporting conceptual consciousness yet to evolve.

Orbital Cortex Prediction of Reward & Punishment

Smell, Taste & Pain/Touch (emotionally evocative senses) (primary reinforcers)

Figure 6.2

469

Figure 6.3 Illustration showing the origins of behavior in the humans, primates and possibly higher, non-primate mammals, like the dog. In these species, the part of the cortex that engages in thought (the mind) has evolved to do the bidding of the brain's executor of emotion, the anterior cingulate gyrus, which continues to be the primary source of motivation (see: Figure 1.6). The emergent behavior is therefore a mix of the instinctive behaviors seen in the lower vertebrates (see: Figure 6.1), those additional instinctive behaviors that are exclusively mammalian (compare Figure 6.2 with 6.1) and those cognitively generated elements of behavior that reflect the presence of an intelligence. These changes in the neural control systems underlying behavior are paralleled by changes in the body's motor systems that reach their zenith in humans and provide for us the fine manipulative abilities necessary to create, in the real world, the objects of our ideations.

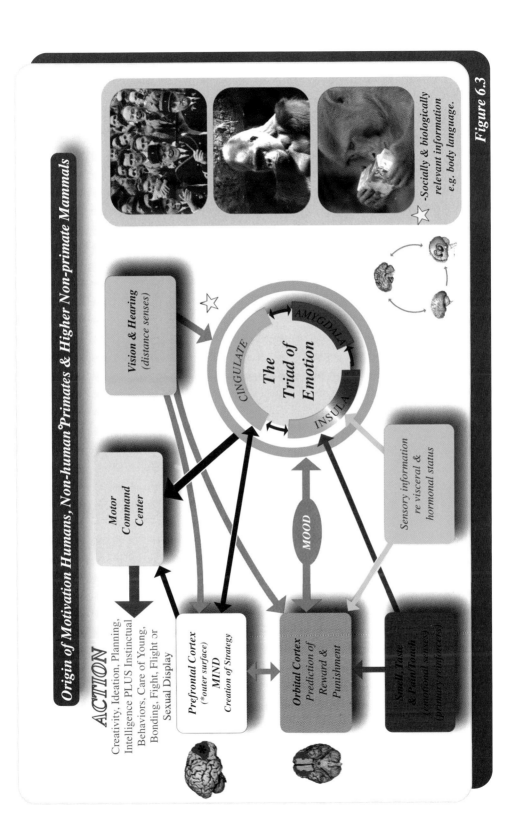

Origin of Motivation Humans, Non-human Primates & Higher Non-primate Mammals

ACTION
Creativity, Ideation, Planning,
Intelligence PLUS Instinctual
Behaviors, Care of Young,
Bonding, Fight, Flight or
Sexual Display

Vision & Hearing
(distance senses)

Motor Command Center

Prefrontal Cortex
*(*outer surface)*
MIND
Creation of Strategy

The Triad of Emotion

CINGULATE
AMYGDALA
INSULA

MOOD

Sensory information re visceral & hormonal status

Orbital Cortex
Prediction of Reward & Punishment

Smell, Taste & Pain/Touch
(emotional senses)
(primary reinforcers)

-Socially & biologically relevant information e.g. body language.

Figure 6.3

471

Figure 6.4 Illustration showing the variation in the area of prefrontal cortex allocated to the social mind (BA9, colored blue) and the abstract mind (BA46, colored green) in five different adult humans. Note the vast differences in the amount of cortex allocated to each of these cognitive centers in different individuals. Because of the modular organization of the cortex, even small increases in the area of cortex composing any particular area of Brodmann, greatly increases that area's computing power. It is therefore possible to postulate that the individual with the largest area 9 (e) will have the highest emotional intelligence, while the individual with the largest area 46 (a) will have the highest abstract intelligence. As the size of each of Brodmann's areas is determined by genes and not the environment, we might logically expect that the relative size of these two divisions of the mind vary significantly between people of radically different personality or ethnic origin. Adapted from: Rajkowska G. & Goldman-Rakic P. S. (1995). Cerebral Cortex 5, 323-337.

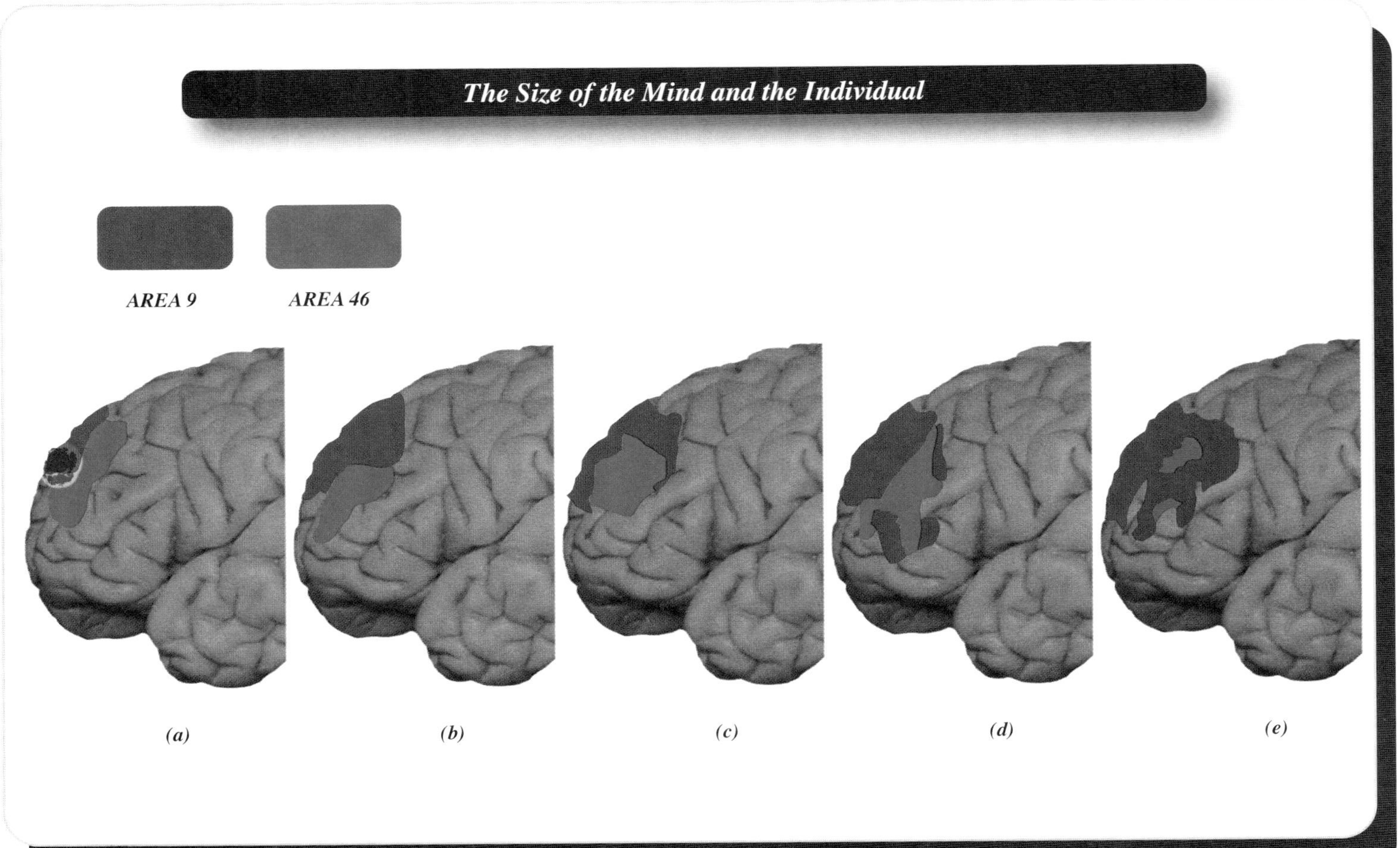

The Size of the Mind and the Individual

AREA 9

AREA 46

(a)   (b)   (c)   (d)   (e)

Figure 6.4

Figure 6.5 Art, artifacts and the cognitive abilities of different cultures. (a) Paleolithic calendar, 28,000 years old, attributed to early Europeans and indicating that they were cognitively preoccupied with time and planning, indicating an evolutionary increase in the size of their temporal mind (BA10). (b) Paleolithic cave paintings of the early Europeans, made between 30,000-38,000 years ago and indicating their ability to cognate about time and space and the product, movement, indicating the evolution of an enlarged abstract mind (BA46). (c) Chinese art dated at only 3000BC (probably post-European contact) showing cognitive appreciation of dynamic, 3-dimensional movement. (d) American Indian art of 1850's showing essentially 2-dimensional style that characterizes their artistic abilities prior to the European invasions. (e) American Indian art of 1950's showing an underlying cognitive appreciation of dynamic, 3-dimensional movement. (f) Titled as the Earliest art these crisscross patterns* from the Blombos Cave, Africa are typical of decorative style used still used in African villages; 70,000yo. Reproduced with permission of the AAAS Copyright Clearance Center's RightsLink. (g) Drawings of African tribe, the Tallensi prior to them having any contact with Europeans. See text for further discussion.

474

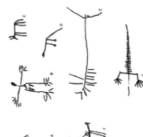

Art and Artifacts of Different Cultures

Figure 6.5

Figure 7.1 Diagram illustrating the mind's capacity to elaborate internal imagery by actually activating, de novo the cortex's perceptual areas. Many of these areas are related to perceptions of the outside world, however, the mind also has the capacity to excite the executor of emotion, the anterior cingulate, and so elicit, directly, specific primary emotions in a process known as controlled empathy (*). This influence of the mind over our perceptual areas is the basis of all imagination, whether it is of objects, the appearance of people or, as in the case of empathy, emotions.

The Mind, Imagination & Controlled Empathy

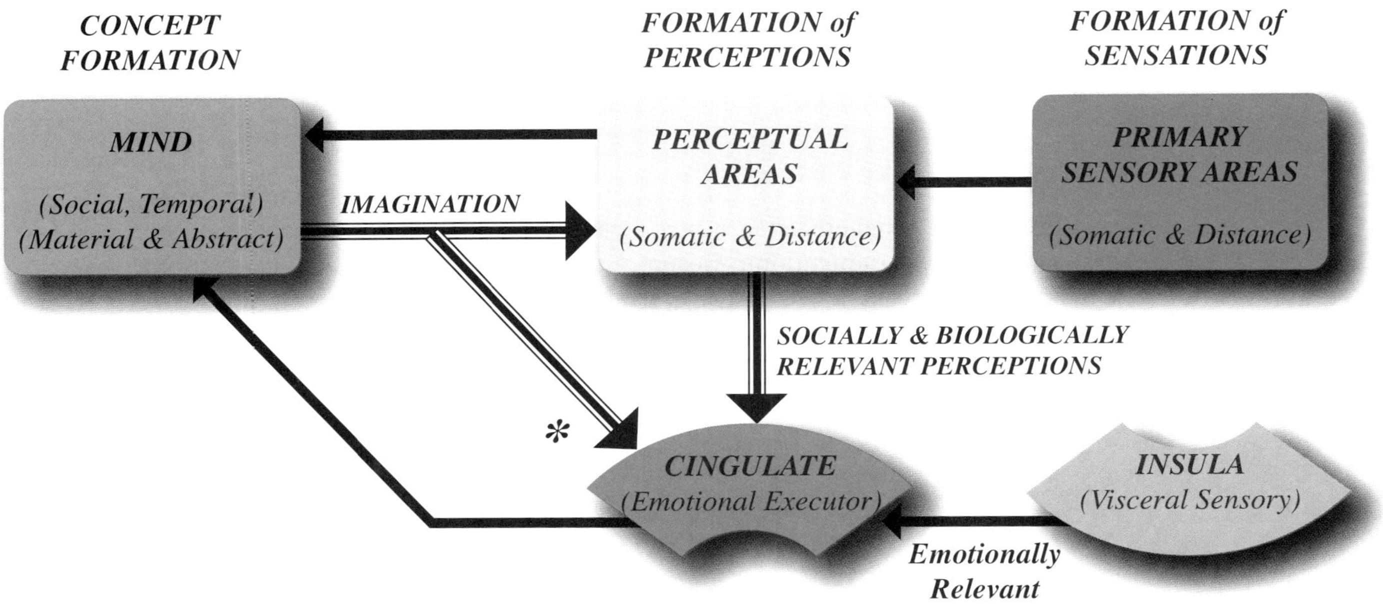

CONCEPT
FORMATION

FORMATION of
PERCEPTIONS

FORMATION of
SENSATIONS

PRIMARY
SENSORY AREAS
(Somatic & Distance)

PERCEPTUAL
AREAS
(Somatic & Distance)

SOCIALLY & BIOLOGICALLY
RELEVANT PERCEPTIONS

INSULA
(Visceral Sensory)

CINGULATE
(Emotional Executor)

Emotionally
Relevant

IMAGINATION

MIND
(Social, Temporal)
(Material & Abstract)

*

* Controlled Empathy - imagining emotions.

Figure 7.1

477

Figure 7.2 Diagram showing how the mind and the executor of emotion, the anterior cingulate gyrus, are able to direct attention. Both the mind (#) and the anterior cingulate (*) independently have the capacity to subliminally increase the excitability of the cortex's perceptual representations causing these areas to become more sensitive to incoming sensory information. The result is that incoming sensory information has a stronger excitatory affect on the particular perceptual area(s) and a concomitantly greater prominence in consciousness.

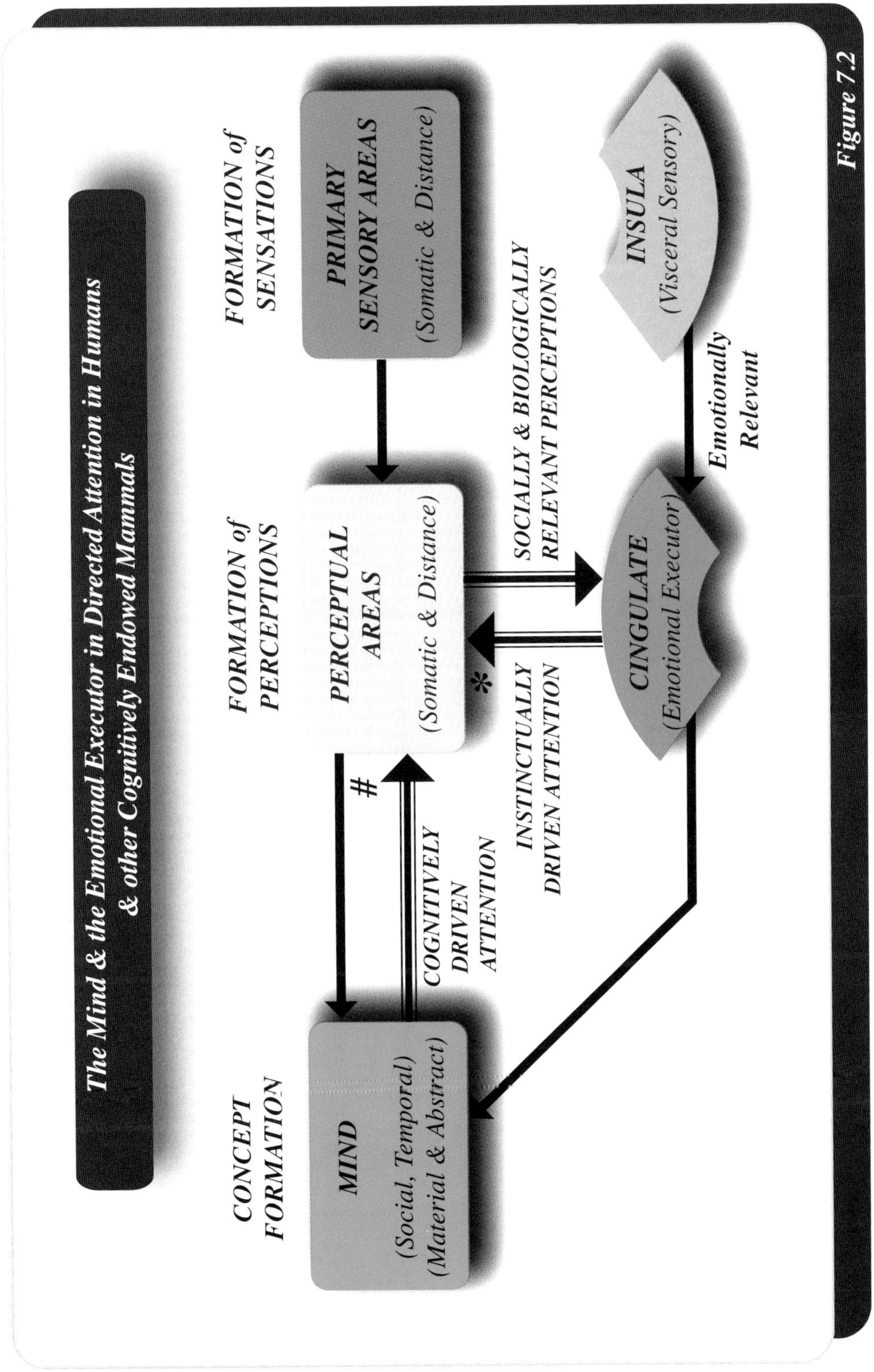

The Mind & the Emotional Executor in Directed Attention in Humans & other Cognitively Endowed Mammals

FORMATION of SENSATIONS

PRIMARY SENSORY AREAS
(Somatic & Distance)

INSULA
(Visceral Sensory)

SOCIALLY & BIOLOGICALLY RELEVANT PERCEPTIONS

Emotionally Relevant

FORMATION of PERCEPTIONS

PERCEPTUAL AREAS
(Somatic & Distance)

*

CINGULATE
(Emotional Executor)

INSTINCTUALLY DRIVEN ATTENTION

#

COGNITIVELY DRIVEN ATTENTION

CONCEPT FORMATION

MIND
(Social, Temporal)
(Material & Abstract)

Figure 7.2

479

Figure 7.3 Diagram showing how, in those lower mammals that lack any cognitive centers, the brain's executor of emotion, the anterior cingulate gyrus, has the capacity to subliminally increase the excitability of the cortex's perceptual representations (*) to incoming sensory information. The result is that incoming sensory information has a stronger excitatory affect on the particular perceptual area(s) and a concomitantly greater prominence in consciousness. The place where the mind would be in higher mammals is shown by the dashed lines.

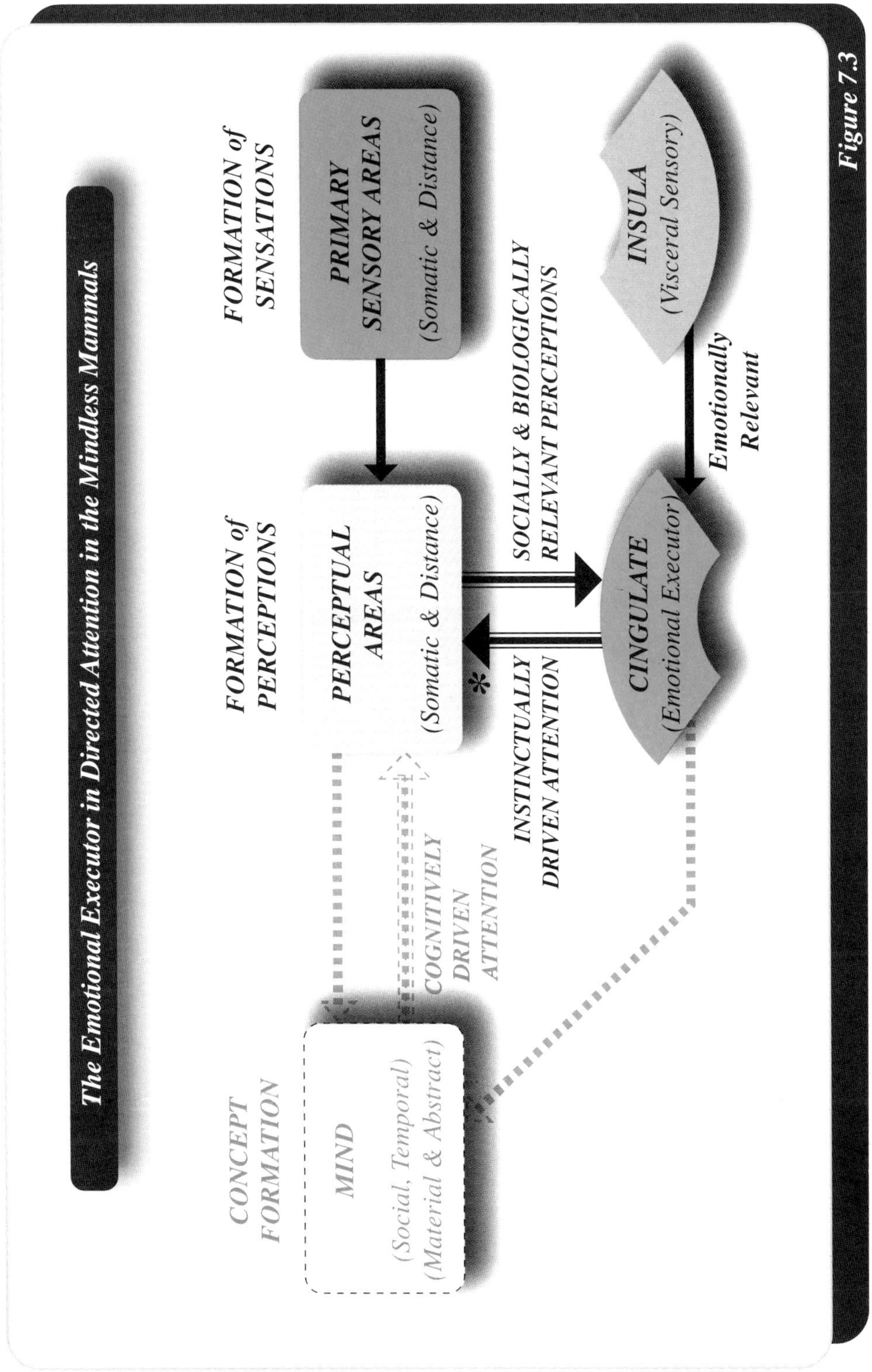

The Emotional Executor in Directed Attention in the Mindless Mammals

FORMATION of SENSATIONS

PRIMARY SENSORY AREAS (Somatic & Distance)

INSULA (Visceral Sensory)

SOCIALLY & BIOLOGICALLY RELEVANT PERCEPTIONS

Emotionally Relevant

FORMATION of PERCEPTIONS

PERCEPTUAL AREAS (Somatic & Distance)

CINGULATE (Emotional Executor)

INSTINCTUALLY DRIVEN ATTENTION

COGNITIVELY DRIVEN ATTENTION

CONCEPT FORMATION

MIND (Social, Temporal) (Material & Abstract)

Figure 7.3

481

Figure 7.4 Theoretical construct of the brain processes involved in the generation of dreams generation and the relationship of these processes to the cognitive assimilation of emotional memories afforded by the process of dreaming. The elemental perceptual experiences of our dreams are elaborated as internal images by activation of the cortex's perceptual areas. Dreams appear to be driven by the brain's executor of emotion, the anterior cingulate gyrus, often in accord with both shallow and deep seated emotional memories. In keeping with the "nowness" or "timelessness" of dreams, both the mind (strategy) and the orbital cortex (prediction) are silent. During dreaming, the entorhinal cortex (**) is thought to process the responses of the entire cortex and encode these into the long-term memory banks in another part of the cortex called the hippocampus (*). In the case of nightmares, the drive to dream originates from negative emotional memories that are probably stored in the amygdala (not shown) before being relayed to the anterior cingulate gyrus which then activates the cortex's perceptual representations to create the cognitively accessible, highly negative imagery of nightmares, from within the cortex's perceptual areas. See text for further explanation.

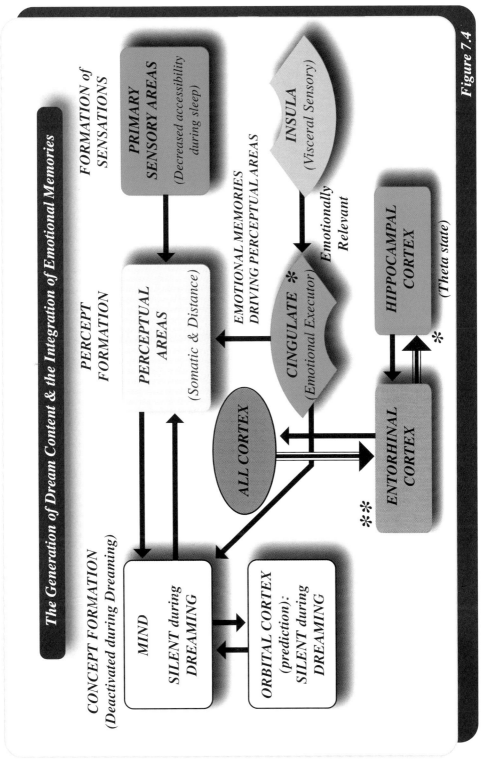

The Generation of Dream Content & the Integration of Emotional Memories

FORMATION of SENSATIONS

PRIMARY SENSORY AREAS
(Decreased accessibility during sleep)

INSULA
(Visceral Sensory)

EMOTIONAL MEMORIES DRIVING PERCEPTUAL AREAS

Emotionally Relevant

PERCEPT FORMATION

PERCEPTUAL AREAS
(Somatic & Distance)

CINGULATE *
(Emotional Executor)

HIPPOCAMPAL CORTEX
(Theta state)

*

ALL CORTEX

ENTORHINAL CORTEX

**

CONCEPT FORMATION
(Deactivated during Dreaming)

MIND
SILENT during DREAMING

ORBITAL CORTEX
(prediction):
SILENT during DREAMING

Figure 7.4

Figure 7.5 Illustration showing how the mind controls vigilance by activating a small neural center caller the locus coeruleus (LC). Although a very small in size, the locus coeruleus projects to virtually every part of the brain and releases noradrenalin (or norepinephrine) that, in turn, increases the excitability of many parts of the nervous system including the cortex. Increasing the excitability of the cortex's sensory and perceptual areas, results in an enhanced sensitization to incoming sensory information – a condition that is critical to achieving a state of vigilance. The locus coeruleus is considered to be the critical site of action of LSD.

Vigilance and the Human Mind

PATHWAYS DELIVERING NORADRENALIN TO THE ENTIRE CORTEX.

DESCENDING INHIBITORY PATHWAYS FROM THE MIND TO THE LOCUS COERULEUS (LC).

Figure 7.5

Figure 7.6 Illustration showing how the mind can evoke reward by directly activating the brain's reward centers, in this case the ventral tegmental area (VTA). When activated, for example by circulating opiates, the dopaminergic neurons in the VTA release dopamine across much of the prefrontal cortex. Dopamine inhibits most prefrontal cortical neurons and therefore has the potential to silence the mind. When the mind successfully concludes a thought, one can imagine that it might directly activate the VTA (via its descending connections with that nucleus) which, in turn, will release dopamine that will restore peace by quieting the mind and making it ready to address the next issue. Intense though requires an enormous amount of metabolic energy. Quieting the mind is for this reason a desirable state that has both physical and emotional benefits. Quieting the mind is the ultimate goal of all spiritual practice.

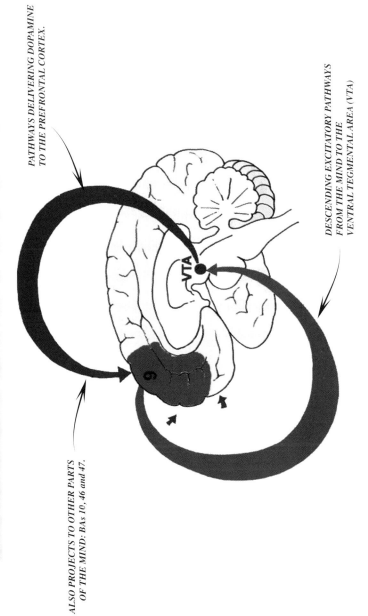

PATHWAYS DELIVERING DOPAMINE
TO THE PREFRONTAL CORTEX.

DESCENDING EXCITATORY PATHWAYS
FROM THE MIND TO THE
VENTRAL TEGMENTAL AREA (VTA)

ALSO PROJECTS TO OTHER PARTS
OF THE MIND: BAs 10, 46 and 47.

Figure 7.6

487

Figure 7.7 Diagram illustrating how the psyche registers reward, irrespective of the source or circumstance of the reward. The critical conditions for the elaboration of all bliss states are (a) a suppression of neural centers mediating negative emotions (the amygdala), thought (the mind) and all predictive inclinations (the orbital cortex) and (b) a concurrent activation of the anterior cingulate gyrus. This brain state is at least partially the result of activation of a reward center (the ventral tegmental area, see Figure 7.6) which releases dopamine on the prefrontal cortex.

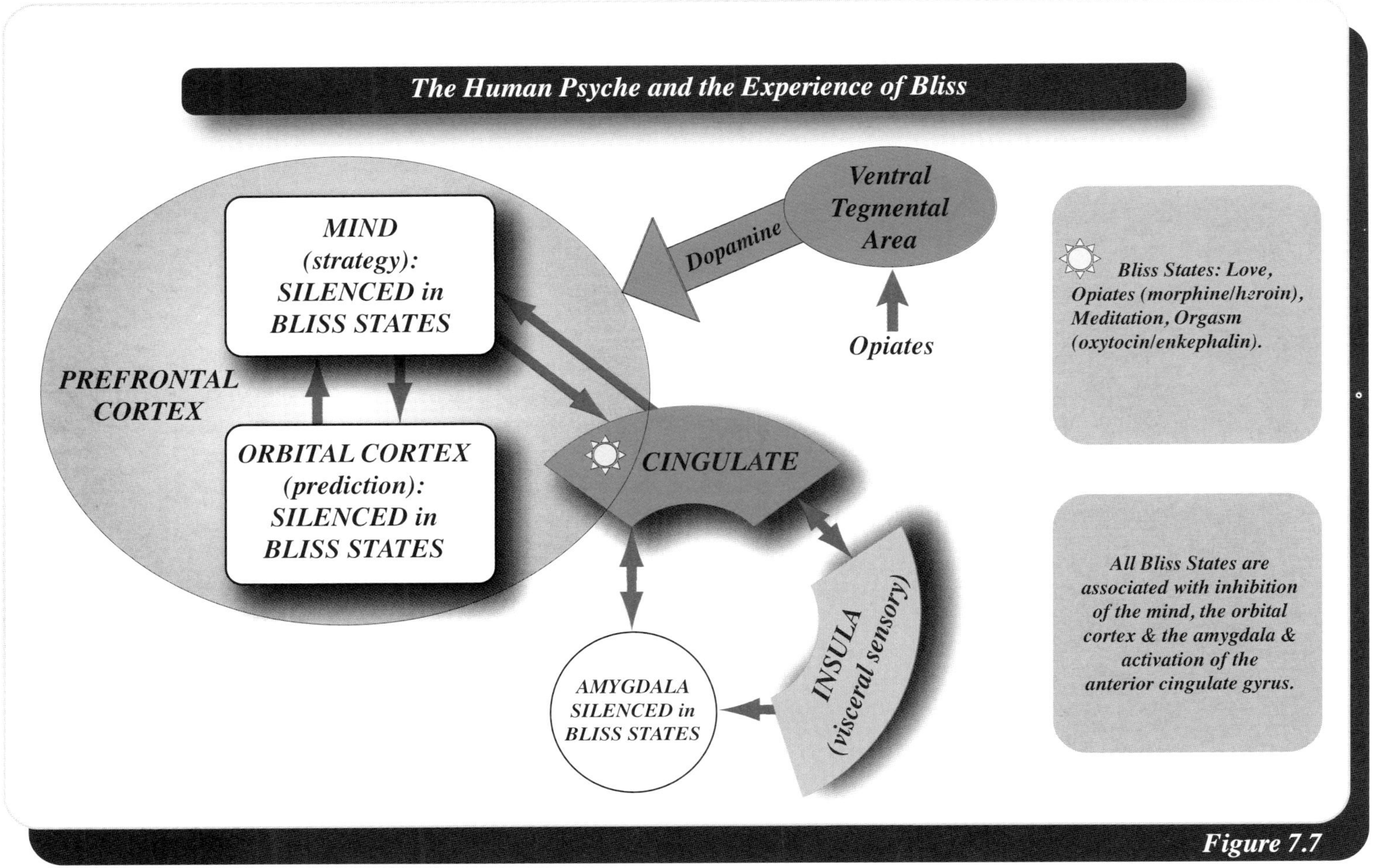

The Human Psyche and the Experience of Bliss

Bliss States: Love, Opiates (morphine/heroin), Meditation, Orgasm (oxytocin/enkephalin).

All Bliss States are associated with inhibition of the mind, the orbital cortex & the amygdala & activation of the anterior cingulate gyrus.

Ventral Tegmental Area

Opiates

Dopamine

CINGULATE

INSULA (visceral sensory)

AMYGDALA SILENCED in BLISS STATES

PREFRONTAL CORTEX

MIND (strategy): SILENCED IN BLISS STATES

ORBITAL CORTEX (prediction): SILENCED in BLISS STATES

Figure 7.7

Figure 8.1 Illustration showing cortical activity when subjects are presented with the picture of someone they love. Note that the insula and anterior cingulate gyrus are both activated but the mind and the orbital cortex (not visible) are silenced. It is instructive to note that this pattern of brain activity resembles the "no mind" state of meditation where the participant is pervaded with an acute "sense" of oneness and of existing only in the moment. A similar pattern of activity is seen during the experiences of orgasm and following the administration of opiates (eg. morphine).

"No Mind" and the Experience of Love

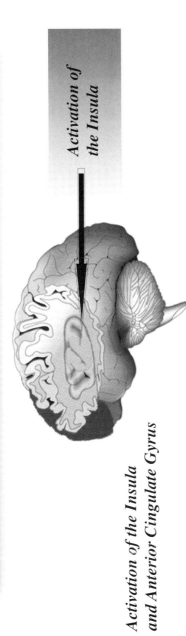

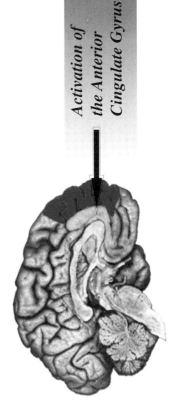

Activation of the Insula

Activation of the Anterior Cingulate Gyrus

Activation of the Insula and Anterior Cingulate Gyrus

Inhibition (silencing) of the Mind.

Orbital Cortex Inhibited

Figure 8.1

Figure 8.2 (a) to (d) Illustration showing the aptitudes of a series of hypothetical individuals, whose thoughts are dominated by one of the four domains of cognition as a result of one cognitive area being much larger than the other three. When BA9 is dominant, the individual's most prominent form of intelligence is emotional intelligence (a). A similar relationship exists between the size of the other three parts of the mind (BA10, 46 & 47) and the forms of intelligence they support (temporal, abstract and practical) (b), (c) and (d). (e) to (h) Illustration of the outcome of enlarging the source of two domains of cognition such that they conjointly dominate the behavior of the individual As the size of Brodmann's areas is determined by genes, it follows that, in any relatively isolated human population, selection will have operated to bring forth the forms of intelligence that best serve survival. The result of this process is the natural selection of a modal personality (see text) that will be a potent determiner of the culture of that population. Adapted from: Snow, P. J. (2003) J. Consciousness Studies 10, 3-17.

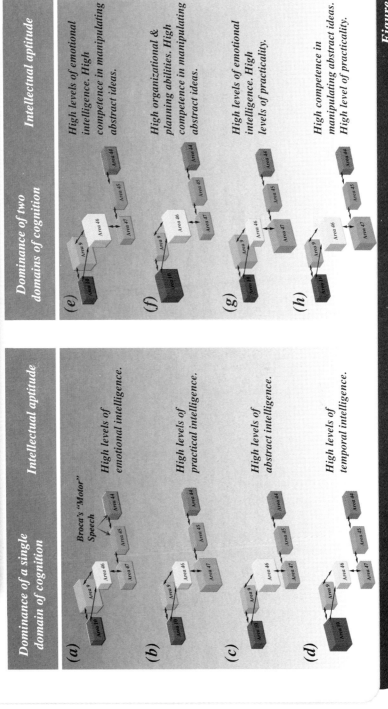

The Relationship between the Structure of the Mind, Intellectual Aptitude and Culture.

Dominance of a single domain of cognition

Intellectual aptitude

(a) Broca's "Motor" Speech — High levels of emotional intelligence.

(b) High levels of practical intelligence.

(c) High levels of abstract intelligence.

(d) High levels of temporal intelligence.

Dominance of two domains of cognition

Intellectual aptitude

(e) High levels of emotional intelligence. High competence in manipulating abstract ideas.

(f) High organizational & planning abilities. High competence in manipulating abstract ideas.

(g) High levels of emotional intelligence. High levels of practicality.

(h) High competence in manipulating abstract ideas. High level of practicality.

Figure 8.2

493

Figure 8.3 Construction of abstract intelligence and the origins of metacognition. Illustration showing how the social, temporal and material domains of cognition (BA9, 10 and 47) are form first-order concepts (see: SocC1-4, Pract C1-4 or TempC1-4) from our perceptions of the world around us. These concepts are first-order because they are derived from realities in the socioemotional and physical realms of existence (lower ellipses). These first-order concepts are essentially pure in that they are confined to only one realm of cognition and one realm of existence. These first-order concepts constitute the major informational input to the abstract mind (BA46). With its circuitry that has been conditioned to "process" the intangible phenomena, the abstract mind creates second-order concepts (or concepts-of-concepts; CC1, CC2, CC3) from a synthesis of the conceptual products of the social, temporal and material domains of thought. In this way the abstract mind essentially thinks about our other thoughts thereby creating the almost exclusively human faculty of metacognition.

494

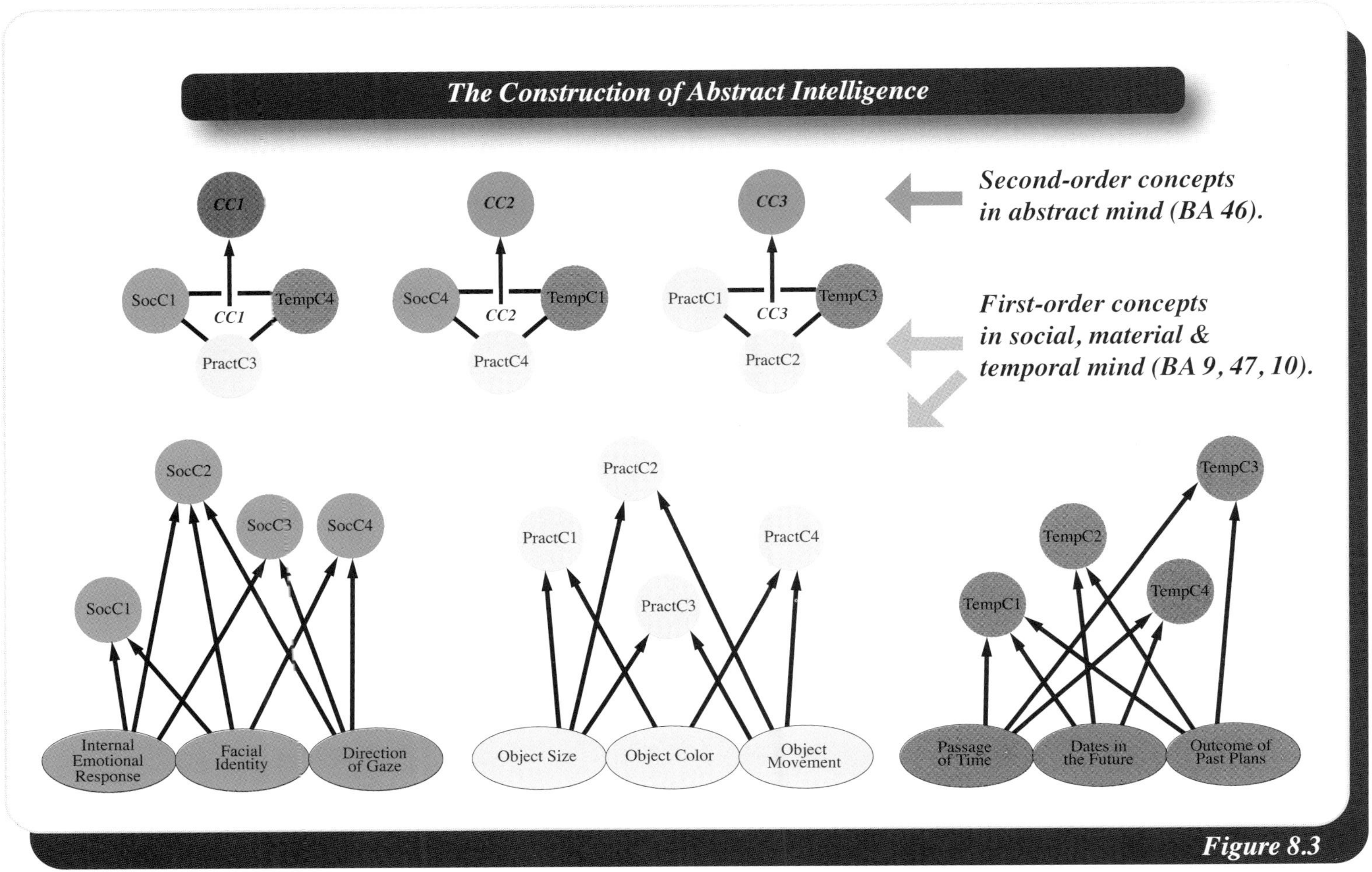
The Construction of Abstract Intelligence
Second-order concepts
in abstract mind (BA 46).
First-order concepts
in social, material &
temporal mind (BA 9, 47, 10).
CC1
SocC1
TempC4
PractC3
CC2
SocC4
TempC1
PractC4
CC3
PractC1
TempC3
PractC2
SocC1
SocC2
SocC3
SocC4
Internal Emotional Response
Facial Identity
Direction of Gaze
PractC1
PractC2
PractC3
PractC4
Object Size
Object Color
Object Movement
TempC1
TempC2
TempC3
TempC4
Passage of Time
Dates in the Future
Outcome of Past Plans
Figure 8.3

Figure 8.4 Illustration showing the organization of the human psyche and how it manifests different levels of behavior depending on the individual's mood, emotions and mental predisposition.

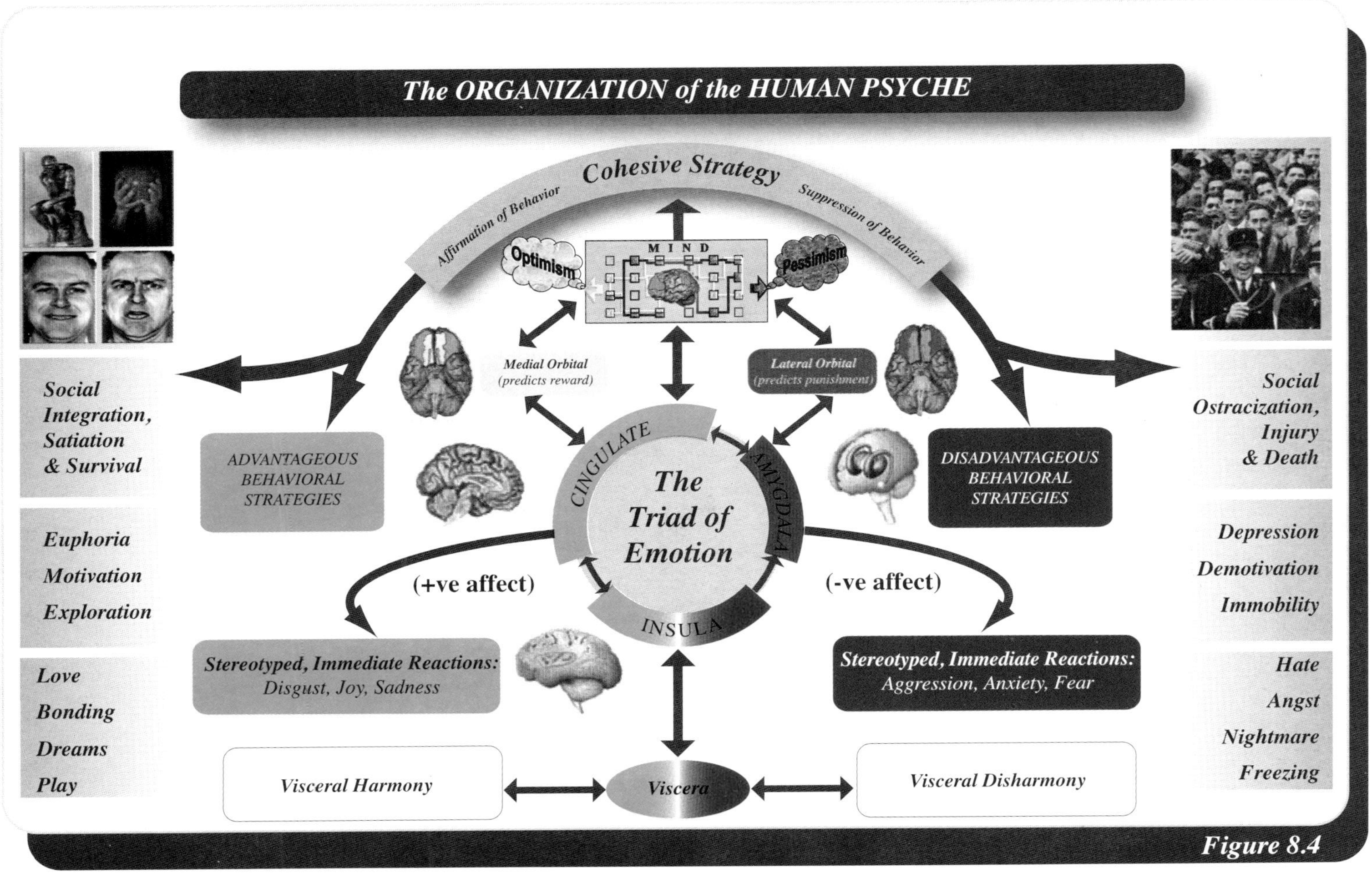
The ORGANIZATION of the HUMAN PSYCHE
Cohesive Strategy
Affirmation of Behavior
Suppression of Behavior
Optimism
MIND
Pessimism
Medial Orbital
(predicts reward)
Lateral Orbital
(predicts punishment)
Social
Integration,
Satiation
& Survival
ADVANTAGEOUS
BEHAVIORAL
STRATEGIES
CINGULATE
AMYGDALA
The
Triad of
Emotion
INSULA
DISADVANTAGEOUS
BEHAVIORAL
STRATEGIES
Social
Ostracization,
Injury
& Death
Euphoria
Motivation
Exploration
(+ve affect)
(-ve affect)
Depression
Demotivation
Immobility
Love
Bonding
Dreams
Play
Stereotyped, Immediate Reactions:
Disgust, Joy, Sadness
Stereotyped, Immediate Reactions:
Aggression, Anxiety, Fear
Hate
Angst
Nightmare
Freezing
Visceral Harmony
Viscera
Visceral Disharmony
Figure 8.4